STRATEGIC MANAGEMENT AND BUSINESS POLICY

McGraw-Hill Series in Management

Fred Luthans and Keith Davis, *Consulting Editors*

Allen: The Management Profession
Arnold and Feldman: Organizational Behavior
Benton: Supervision and Management
Buchele: The Management of Business and Public Organizations
Cascio: Managing Human Resources: Productivity, Quality of Work Life, Profits.
Cleland and King: Management: A Systems Approach
Cleland and King: Systems Analysis and Project Management
Dale: Management: Theory and Practice
Davis and Newstrom: Human Behavior at Work: Organizational Behavior
Davis and Newstrom: Organizational Behavior: Readings and Exercises
Del Mar: Operations and Industrial Management: Designing and Managing for Productivity
Dobler, Lee, and Burt: Purchasing and Materials Management: Text and Cases
Dunn and Rachel: Wage and Salary Administration: Total Compensation Systems
Feldman and Arnold: Managing Individual and Group Behavior in Organizations
Finch, Jones, and Litterer: Managing for Organizational Effectiveness: An Experiential Approach
Flippo: Personnel Management

Sartain and Baker: The Supervisor and the Job

Sayles: Leadership: What Effective Managers Really Do . . . and How They Do It

Schlesinger, Eccles, and Gabarro: Managing Behavior in Organizations: Text, Cases, Readings

Schroeder: Operations Management: Decision Making in the Operations Function

Sharplin: Strategic Management

Shore: Operations Management

Steers and Porter: Motivation and Work Behavior

Steinhoff and Burgess: Small Business Management Fundamentals

Sutermeister: People and Productivity

Vance: Corporate Leadership: Boards, Directors, and Strategy

Walker: Human Resource Planning

Weihrich: Management Excellence: Productivity through MBO

Werther and Davis: Personnel Management and Human Resources

Wofford, Gerloff, and Cummins: Organizational Communications: The Keystone to Managerial Effectiveness

STRATEGIC MANAGEMENT AND BUSINESS POLICY

THIRD EDITION

Lawrence R. Jauch
Northeast Louisiana University

William F. Glueck
Late of the University of Georgia

McGraw-Hill Publishing Company

New York   St. Louis   San Francisco   Auckland   Bogotá   Caracas
Hamburg   Lisbon   London   Madrid   Mexico   Milan
Montreal   New Delhi   Oklahoma City   Paris   San Juan
São Paulo   Singapore   Sydney   Tokyo   Toronto

This book was set in Times Roman by the College Composition Unit
in cooperation with Waldman Graphics, Inc.
The editor was Kathleen L. Loy;
the cover was designed by Caliber Design Planning, Inc.;
the production supervisor was Leroy A. Young.
New drawings were done by Fine Line Illustrations, Inc.
Project supervision was done by The Total Book.
R. R. Donnelley & Sons Company was printer and binder.

STRATEGIC MANAGEMENT AND BUSINESS POLICY

3 4 5 6 7 8 9 0   DOCDOC   9 2 1 0

ISBN   0-07-032339-9

Library of Congress Cataloging-in-Publication Data

Jauch, Lawrence R.
  Strategic management and business policy.

  (McGraw-Hill series in management)
  Glueck's name appears first on the earlier edition.
  Includes bibliographies and index.
  1. Corporate planning. 2. Management. I. Glueck,
William F. II. Title. III. Series.
  HD30.28.J38   1988   658.4'012   87-7191
  ISBN 0-07-032339-9

ABOUT THE AUTHORS

LAWRENCE R. JAUCH is the Biedenharn Professor in Management at Northeast Louisiana University. He has taught at Kansas State University and Southern Illinois University at Carbondale. He completed his dissertation with Dr. Glueck while they were both at the University of Missouri. Professor Jauch is the coauthor of 14 texts and supplements, and has published over 50 papers, monographs, and cases. He has consulted with planning executives in several countries. Dr. Jauch is currently on the editorial review boards of *The Academy of Management Review* and *The Journal of Management Case Studies*. He chaired the Business Policy and Planning Division of the Academy of Management in 1983–84.

WILLIAM F. GLUECK was Distinguished Professor of Management at the University of Georgia at the time of his death in 1980. He was a Fellow and President of the Academy of Management. Professor Glueck authored over 20 books (including *Strategic Management and Business Policy* and *Readings in Business Policy from Business Week*, both published by McGraw-Hill) and over 150 articles, monographs, and cases. He was a Fulbright scholar and spent many years as a food industry executive. He served on the editorial review boards of *Long Range Planning, Journal of Business Strategy,* and *Academy of Management Journal.*

To Bill

CONTENTS

PREFACE

The third edition of this book, like its predecessors, is designed to meet the needs of students of business policy and strategic management. The following additions and changes have been made in the text of the third edition.

1 The text has been rewritten and updated, especially to reflect the major structural changes in the U.S. and world economies which impact strategic thinking.

2 The discussion and the model have been altered to stress a greater integration of topic areas.

3 Chapter 2 has been expanded to include a discussion of the roles of the general manager.

4 The discussion of the environment has been expanded to two chapters. Discussions of the industry environment and the international environment have been included.

5 International strategy material has been incorporated in other chapters as well, especially 7, 8, and 10.

6 The chapter on strategy alternatives has been expanded to two chapters (6 and 7). This helps students better grasp the concept of types of strategies and their variations.

7 The majority of exhibit vignettes describing applied concepts have been updated to provide meaningful illustrations of key points and topics as they are applied by various organizations.

8 Much of the elaboration of research studies and theories which were in supplementary modules in the previous edition have been deleted. Thus the readability of the basic text has been improved, but the integrity of previous editions has been maintained as explained below.

A key strength of previous editions of this book was the attempt to summarize the state of the art of business policy and strategic management. This included a blending of both prescriptive and descriptive ideas of theorists, practitioners, and researchers in the field. The body of work on the process and content of strategic management has been expanding rapidly. If an attempt had been made to incorporate all this material in the basic text of this latest edition, the result would have been confusion for the reader. The basic material still rests on a firm foundation of up-to-date research, theory, and practice. Extensive references are also available to the reader. But many of the details of some research and various additional techniques, theories, and viewpoints formerly part of the supplementary modules have been condensed or eliminated. The key conclusions and findings from this supplementary material are highlighted and summarized in the chapter itself. Those interested in exploring particular subtopics in greater depth might refer to the instructor's manual where extensive references are provided beyond those cited in the book. These were reduced to provide room for new text.

As we prepare to face the challenges of the 1990s, it is increasingly evident that managers are planning the strategies of their enterprises for their own survival and that of our civilizations. We hope that this book will contribute something to that mission.

This book is the product of many people. First and foremost is the foundation laid down in the first edition by the coauthor, William F. Glueck. His untimely death in 1980 was a blow to many of us. His inspiration and guidance are sorely missed. I continue to dedicate this edition to his memory and have made every attempt to continue the tradition of excellence he exhibited in all his endeavors.

I would also like to thank those who reviewed the book at various stages in its development. They include Helen Deresky, State University of New York at Plattsburgh; Bahman Ebrahimi, North Texas State University; R. Duane Ireland, Baylor University; Aaron Kelly, University of Louisville; Mary Frances Lewis, Illinois State University; Michael W. Pitts, Virginia Commonwealth University; Michael C. Shaner, St. Louis University and Gerald L. Speth, University of Indianapolis.

I should also mention the influence of many colleagues in the Academy of Management. I have been fortunate to have had the opportunity to receive and review the work of a large number of scholars active in advancing the field of strategic management. They are too numerous to mention here, but the references attest to their significant influence on my thinking and the development of this edition.

My appreciation also goes to Audrey Preston, Donna Reynolds, and Tammy Nack, who assisted in the preparation and typing of the manuscript, and to the Management Department at Southern Illinois University at Carbondale and Northeast Louisiana University for providing work environments conducive to productive efforts. My editor, Kathleen L. Loy, provided additional motivation to complete the task in a timely fashion, for which I am grateful. Last but not least, my family has had to bear my petulance for far too long; I trust their indulgence and tolerance have not been stretched beyond the limits.

As is customary, I will accept blame for errors of commission and omission. I hope that any errors that are discovered will be brought to my attention so that they may be corrected in future editions.

Lawrence R. Jauch

STRATEGIC MANAGEMENT AND BUSINESS POLICY

CHAPTER OUTLINE

CHAPTER 1

AN INVITATION TO STRATEGIC MANAGEMENT

OBJECTIVES

- To learn what the strategic management process is
- To understand why strategic management takes place
- To learn how strategic management takes place in modern businesses
- To learn about strategic decision-making processes
- To understand how strategic management is practiced in the not-for-profit and public sectors

INTRODUCTION

This book is about decision making and actions which determine whether an enterprise excels, survives, or dies.[1] This process is called "strategic management." The job of strategic managers is to make the best use of a firm's resources in a changing environment.

If you looked at a list of the largest and most successful firms in 1908, 1938, or 1968 and compared it with a list of those in 1988, you'd be amazed! Few of the leaders then are leaders now despite their economic power then. That's what happens when strategic management is inadequately done.

Let's look at this situation in a different way. Most of us have a work life of about 42 years. Put yourself in the shoes of a person who retired in 1985. Exhibit 1.1 gives

---

[1]We use the terms "enterprise," "organization," "company," and "firm" interchangeably. Some are profit-seeking, others not-for-profit; but all can utilize a strategic management process. Similarly, terms such as "manager," "strategist," or "executive" are substitutes for variety.

1

EXHIBIT 1.1   TEN COMPANIES' EXPERIENCES DURING ONE BUSINESS EXECUTIVE'S WORK LIFE

Company	1943	1985
American Can	Manufacturer of tin cans, packages and containers	Financial, specialty retailing and packaging company with almost half its operating income deriving from financial services
Coleman	Small manufacturer of lamps, stoves, heaters, and accessory items	Leading manufacturer of outdoor recreational equipment including camping gear, trailers, sailboats, and target guns
Genentech	Did not exist	Genetic research corporation in an emerging industry
W.T. Grant	One of the larger variety-store retailers	Out of business
Honeywell	Leading manufacturer of various types of temperature-controlling and heat-regulating devices	Major producer of information processing and control systems for environmental, industrial, and aerospace applications
IBM	Engaged mainly in manufacturing, selling, and leasing various kinds of tabulating, accounting, and payroll machines, typewriters, and related supplies	World's largest manufacturer of computers and information-processing equipment and systems, ranging from microcomputers to large-scale mainframes
Parker Pen	Major producer of fountain pens and patented pencils with network of approximately 40,000 retailers	Leading manufacturer of pens and other writing instruments but derived more than 80 percent of its revenues from temporary help services
Pitney Bowes	Small manufacturer of postage meter machines and related equipment	World's largest manufacturer of postage meters and mailing equipment, and manufacturer of dictation systems, copiers, facsimile machines and retail labeling equipment
Raytheon	Small producer of cathoderay tubes and other electronic equipment	Leading factor in air defense missile systems and other government electronics products
Wheeling Steel	Large profitable steel producer and principal manufacturer of finished steel and fabricated steel products	Now known as Wheeling-Pittsburgh Steel; the nation's seventh largest integrated steel producer filed for protection under Chapter 11 of the Federal Bankruptcy Code

a brief summary of what 10 firms were like when the retiree began work and what they were like at that person's retirement.

A close examination will show examples of success and failure and stability and complete change, as well as many stages in between. Some of these changes occurred because of pressures from the outside—from government, competitors, and consumers. Others developed because the employees and management made decisions to change the nature of the business. The exhibit also tells of firms that haven't changed their businesses—they just approached them differently.

Just as this executive experienced these changes in a lifetime, so will you. You may experience even more changes than these in your career.

Because this book focuses on top-level decisions, you may have a problem with the relevance of the subject matter for your short-term career interests. But several reasons can be given for why the knowledge you can gain in the study of strategic management is practical and useful for your early career stages:

1 You are likely to perform better in your function, regardless of your level in the organization, if you know the direction in which the organization is going. As the manager of a subunit, you would like to know how what you do fits into the broader picture. If you know how your function contributes, you should be able to do a better job of helping the organization reach its objectives. If your unit is successful and higher-level managers realize how you contributed to this success, this will reflect positively on you. Furthermore, lower-level units often interpret strategies and policies set at higher levels. If you understand why those were established, you can implement them more effectively. Finally, if you understand how your job relates to others in the organization, you will be in a better position to effectively work with peers when cooperation is called for and compete for resources when the time comes.

2 In your study of the strategic management process you will begin to identify factors which may lead to significant changes in the organization. Some of these strategic changes could be positive or negative to you personally. For instance, a major divestiture could eliminate your unit! Or a new market thrust or product development could make your unit more critical for organizational performance. If you understand what factors may be pushing the organization in certain directions and how your job fits in, you might decide to change or keep your job. Foresight about critical organization changes can be a real asset to your career.

3 If you are aware of the strategies, values, and objectives of higher-level managers, you are in a better position to assess the likelihood of acceptance of proposals you might make. For instance, you might be in a position to suggest better ways to meet competition, improve the production or R&D effort, increase personnel skills, and so on. Or if you are auditing the financial statements, you might discover a way to improve the treatment of accounts. As you consider offering your suggestions, tying the reasons to your assessment of the interests of higher-level managers is likely to enhance their acceptance and your visibility.

Thus we believe that an understanding of how and why strategic decisions are made can be helpful to you in terms of securing resources beneficial to your subunit, improving your job performance, and enhancing your career development. This book's purpose is to help you make sense of the strategic management process while you are a first-line manager and a middle manager. It is also designed to help prepare you to become a successful top manager. Its goal is to show you that if you understand the business policy and strategic management process before you get to the top, you'll be a more effective manager. And you are more likely to reach the top once you understand this process [1].[2]

The book also is designed to fulfill a teaching function in schools of business, management, and administration. The material is designed to help you integrate the functional tools you have learned. These include the analytical tools of production-operations management, marketing management, financial management, accounting, physical distribution and logistics, and personnel and labor relations. All these provide help in analyzing business problems. This book and the materials in it provide you with an opportunity to learn *when* to use which tools and how to deal with trade-offs when you cannot maximize the results or preferences of all the functional areas simultaneously.

The task of understanding a company's strategy and judging its effectiveness is not an easy one. It requires that you look at how the company has come to grips with the challenges and opportunities facing it. It requires that you make judgments about whether the business or other organization is well run and how to improve its operations and results. This is a challenging job, the job of top managers of divisions or companies. It will provide you with a new understanding of how companies succeed or fail.

WHAT IS STRATEGIC MANAGEMENT AND BUSINESS POLICY? [2]

''Strategic management'' is the term currently used to describe the process on which the book focuses. It will be defined shortly. But first let's review previously used terms for this process so that they will not be unfamiliar to you if you come across them. ''Business policy'' is a term traditionally associated with the course in business schools devoted to integrating the educational program of these schools and understanding what today is called strategic management. In most businesses in earlier times (and in many smaller firms today), the focus of the manager's job was on today's decisions for today's world in today's business. That may have been satisfactory then. However, the changes illustrated in Exhibit 1.1 and similar ones taking place all around led to a different approach to management.

---

[2]Reference footnotes are not used in this text. Instead, end-of-chapter references are grouped into numbered sections. These sections are referred to in the text by bracketed numbers, and labels in the references indicate general topical areas. The references provided are those which we specifically cite or make direct use of in the text. Your instructor may wish to provide additional research references on selected topics which provide more depth on given subjects and which provide the basis for many of our statements and summaries of research.

Instead of focusing all their time on today, managers began to see the value of trying to anticipate the future and to prepare for it. They did this in several ways.

• They prepared systems and procedures manuals for decisions that must be made repeatedly. This allowed time for more important decisions and ensured more or less consistent decisions.

• They prepared budgets. They tried to anticipate future sales and flows of funds. In sum, they created a planning and control system.

Budgeting and control systems helped, but they tended to be based on the status quo—the present business and conditions—and did not by themselves deal well with change. These systems did provide better financial controls and are still in use. Later variations included capital budgeting and management-by-objectives systems.

Because of the lack of emphasis on the future in budgeting, long-range planning appeared. This movement focused on forecasting the future by using economic and technological tools. Long-range planning tended to be performed primarily by corporate staff groups, whose reports were forwarded to top management. Sometimes their reports and advice were heeded (when they were understood and were credible); otherwise, they were ignored. Since the corporate planners were not the decision makers, long-range planning had some impact, but not as much as would be expected if top management were involved. Then, too, they were producing first-generation plans.

''First-generation planning'' means that the firm chooses the most probable appraisal and diagnosis of the future environment and of its own strengths and weaknesses. From this, it evolves the best strategy for a match of the environment and the firm—a single plan for the most likely future.

Today's approach is called ''strategic planning'' or, more frequently, ''strategic management.'' As will be seen in Chapter 2, the board of directors and corporate planners have parts to play in strategic management. But the starring roles are for the general managers of the corporation and its major operating divisions. Strategic management focuses on ''second-generation planning,'' that is, analysis of the business and the preparation of several scenarios for the future. Contingency strategies are then prepared for each of these likely future scenarios. We return to this topic at the end of the chapter.

But these are our distinctions, and the terms ''long-range planning,'' ''strategic planning,'' and ''strategic management'' have as many definitions as there are experts. The terms ''strategic management,'' ''strategy,'' and ''policy'' will be used often in this book. So let's define our terms.

Strategic management is a stream of decisions and actions which leads to the development of an effective strategy or strategies to help achieve corporate objectives. The strategic management process is the way in which strategists determine objectives and make strategic decisions.

> *Strategic decisions are means to achieve ends. These decisions encompass the definition of the business, products and markets to be served, functions to be performed, and major policies needed for the organization to execute these decisions to achieve objectives.*

> *Plans and policies are guides to action. They indicate how resources are to be allocated and how tasks assigned to the organization might be accomplished so that functional-level managers execute the strategy properly.*

> *A strategic business unit (SBU) is an operating division of a firm which serves a distinct product-market segment or a well-defined set of customers or a geographic area. The SBU is given the authority to make its own strategic decisions within corporate guidelines as long as it meets corporate objectives.*

The strategic management process for a business which has organized itself with only a single SBU is given in Exhibit 1.2. Each of the strategic management elements and decisions in the strategic management process is explained in more detail in Chapters 2 through 11, as indicated in Exhibit 1.2. This model is used throughout the book to relate the material to that covered previously and that which will come later. The phases of the model in Exhibit 1.2 are as follows:

• *Strategic management elements:* The general managers who are involved in the process of determining strategy to accomplish objectives are first described in Chapter 2. Then we discuss the mission, business definition, and objectives of the enterprise. We also describe a gap analysis in some detail here.

• *Analysis and diagnosis:* Determining environmental problems and opportunities and internal strengths and weaknesses. This involves recognizing problems and/or opportunities and assessing information needs to solve the problems and heuristics for evaluating the information.

Chapter 3 presents factors in the general environment, such as economic, technological, and government conditions, which create threats and opportunities for the firm. Chapter 4 discusses analysis of the industry and international environments and presents a tool to help summarize the diagnosis of the environment: ETOP. Chapter 5 covers the analysis of internal conditions which provide strengths the strategist can use and weaknesses that prevent strategies or need correcting. This chapter also suggests a tool to focus the diagnosis of internal factors: SAP.

• *Choice:* Generating alternative solutions to the problem, assessing them, and choosing the best ones.

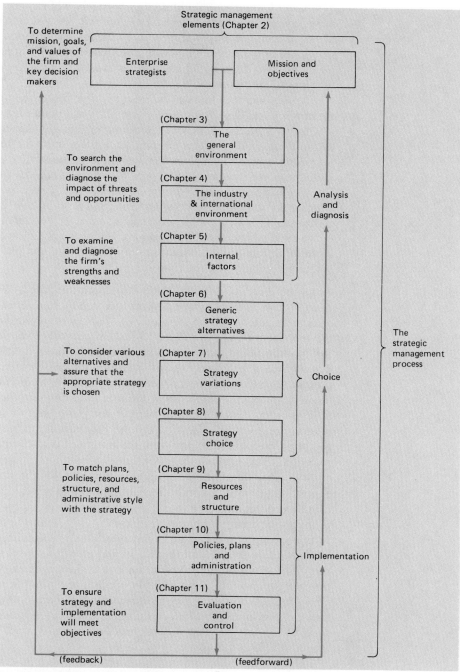

EXHIBIT 1.2   A model of strategic management.

Chapter 6 maps out generic strategy alternatives of expansion, stability or retrenchment, and combinations. Chapter 7 extends this discussion to describe different ways in which such generic strategies can be carried out. Chapter 8 describes the factors that affect how managers might choose from among the strategy alternatives. It explains the use of the ETOP and SAP as applied to closing gaps in objectives, while recognizing the impact of the strategists.

 • *Implementation:* Making the strategy work by building the structure to support the strategy and developing appropriate plans and policies.

Chapter 9 describes resource allocation, organization structure, and planning processes. Chapter 10 explores policies to be developed for functional areas and the leadership aspects of implementation. These administrative processes must be integrated with the strategy to close gaps in order to attain desired objectives.

 • *Evaluation:* Through review of results and future possibilities, determining whether the strategy is working and taking steps to make it work.

Chapter 11 is a part of implementation in that the evaluation, feedback, and control of the strategy under way is important. But evaluation also includes feed forward to serve as an input to determine whether the strategy and plans as decided will work before proceeding with the choice.

As the diagram suggests, these phases are integrated. While it is convenient to discuss them as if they were a sequential step-by-step series of activities, in reality each phase affects all the other phases. Thus as strategists are performing analyses, the implementation of past strategies and choices will be considered. The choice phase for new strategic directions requires a consideration of the ability to implement. For the most part, however, we will discuss each phase of the strategic management process separately, because it is extremely difficult to discuss all the parts simultaneously. In fact, strategic management is a *continuous* process. To say that it is a process rather than a series of steps is not just a shift of words. The parts of the process are interacting. Analytically we can separate them; in reality we can't. As cases and businesses are analyzed, the integrated whole requires comprehensive explorations. This process, then, is a guide to improving strategic thinking.

Note, too, that Exhibit 1.2 is also drawn up for the firm which is using first-generation planning, the most frequent approach at present. More advanced firms are using second-generation or contingency planning. In this system, the choice and implementation decisions appear as in Exhibit 1.3. Note that in this case the firm chooses several scenarios of the future environment (analysis and diagnosis) and strengths and weaknesses given different futures. It then prepares several strategies and plans and short- and medium-range implementations of the strategies. When the future arrives, the firm puts into effect that strategy which it is capable of implementing and which comes closest to meeting the environmental conditions outlined in each scenario and strategy. For simplicity's sake, Exhibit 1.2 will be used throughout the book. But you should keep in mind that if contingency planning is used, the modification of the model in Exhibit 1.3 applies.

Exhibit 1.2 is also drawn for a single-business-unit firm. For a firm that is a multiple-strategy business unit, the model must be modified.

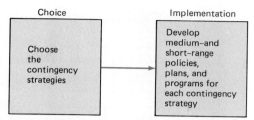

Choice   Implementation

Choose the contingency strategies

Develop medium–and short–range policies, plans, and programs for each contingency strategy

EXHIBIT 1.3   **Strategic management model for second-generation planning (modifies Exhibit 1.2).**

STRATEGIC MANAGEMENT IN MULTIPLE-SBU BUSINESSES [3]

In small businesses or in businesses which focus on one product or service line, the "corporate-level" strategy serves the whole business. This strategy is implemented at the next lower level by functional plans and policies. This implementation process will be discussed in Chapters 9 and 10. This relationship is illustrated in Exhibit 1.4.

In conglomerates and multiple-industry firms, the business often inserts a level of management between the corporate and functional levels. In some firms, these units are called "operating divisions" or, more commonly, strategic business units (SBUs). In these firms, the strategies of these units are guided by the corporate strategies, but they may differ from one another. This situation operates as shown in Exhibit 1.5.

Each SBU sets its own business strategies to make the best use of its resources (its strategic advantages) given the environment it faces. The overall corporate strategy sets the long-term objectives of the firm and the broad constraints and resources within which the SBU operates. The corporate level will help the SBU define its scope of operations. It also limits or enhances the SBU's operations by means of the resources it assigns to the SBU. Thus at the corporate level in multiple-SBU firms, the strategy focuses on the "portfolio" of SBUs the firm wishes to put together to accomplish its objectives.

For example, Mobil Corporation hired a new chief executive with the charge of revitalizing Montgomery Ward, one of its poor-performing SBUs. The SBU is being pared down and turned into a specialty retailer since it has not been able to compete well as a general merchandiser. Corporate-level management set goals and has its own strategy (that of divesting Ward if it doesn't perform); but the SBU has determined its own strategy for how to redefine its business and compete effectively.

EXHIBIT 1.4   **Relationship of corporate strategy and functional plans and policies at single-SBU firms.**

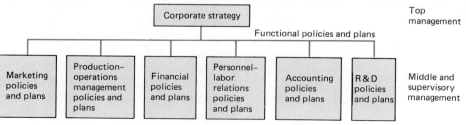

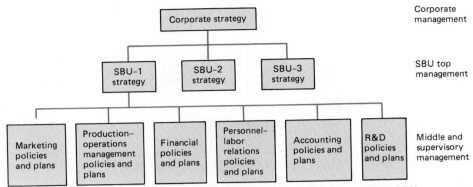

EXHIBIT 1.5   **Relationship among strategies and policies and plans in firms with multiple SBUs.**

Some writers make distinctions between corporate strategy, business strategy, and functional-level strategy, maintaining that corporate strategy focuses on the mission of the firm, the businesses that it enters or exits, and the mix of SBUs and resource allocations. Business strategy, then, focuses on how to compete in an industry or strategic subgroup, and how to achieve competitive advantage. At the functional level, plans and policies to be carried out (by marketing, manufacturing, personnel, and so on) are designed to implement corporate and business strategy to make the firm competitive. We discuss all these issues at various places in the book. Mission and business definition are discussed in Chapter 2; Chapters 6 to 8 describe entry, exit, and SBU mix; and Chapter 9 describes resource allocation. Chapter 4 describes the international and industry competition; and Chapters 4, 10, and 11 discuss how to compete and use and develop competitive advantages. But we agree with Boswell that the distinction between business and corporate strategy is partly artificial. They are interrelated. And, as Roger Smith, chairman of GM, has stated, ''Unless we want to play a perpetual game of catch-up, we . . . have to do more than just meet our competition on a day-to-day basis. We have to beat them in long-term strategy.'' Choices about *how to compete* should be considered in the decision about *whether* to exit or enter a business, as our earlier example about Montgomery Ward illustrated. And the implementation of a strategy will determine how effectively the choice will be carried out. Hence, we believe that the process described here can assist in the reader's thinking about business *and* competitive strategy.

As mentioned before, the model in Exhibit 1.2 is for a single-SBU firm. For a multiple-SBU firm the model is adjusted so that the process is conducted at corporate *and* SBU levels. The results of these processes feed into one another. However, at both levels, the process involves appraisal, choice, implementation, and evaluation.

Strategic decision making in multiple-SBU firms involves interrelationships between corporate-level and business-level planning. As can be seen in Exhibit 1.6 the corporate-level executives first determine the overall corporate strategy. They do this after examining the level of achievement of objectives relative to their SBUs and other businesses they could enter. Next they assess how the SBUs are doing relative to each

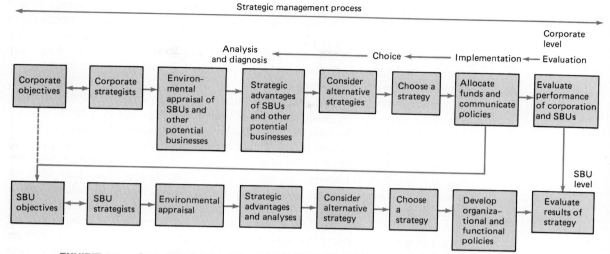

EXHIBIT 1.6   **A model of the strategic management process for a firm with multiple SBUs using first-generation planning.**

other and potential SBUs. Then they allocate funds to the SBUs and establish policies and objectives with them.

At this point the SBUs analyze, within the guidelines set by the corporate level, how they can create the most effective strategy to achieve their objectives.

This model is, of course, a simplified representation. Depending on various organization designs, the interrelationships among units and planning processes can be quite complex in a series of iterative interactions across levels and subunits. Moreover, conflicts between the corporate level and the SBU level can create problems for both. SBU managers usually seek greater resource allocations in an attempt to expand their units. Corporate level, however, may wish to stabilize a unit or use cash flows from one unit to support another SBU. For example, while the head of the tobacco unit at Philip Morris in the early 1980s wanted growth in cigarette volume and new-product development, funds were being used to promote sales of the Miller Brewing acquisition. Discussions between SBUs and corporate level must consider overall goals and resource needs.

WHAT IS A STRATEGY? [4]

> *A strategy is a unified, comprehensive, and integrated plan that relates the strategic advantages of the firm to the challenges of the environment. It is designed to ensure that the basic objectives of the enterprise are achieved through proper execution by the organization.*

A strategy is the means used to achieve the ends (objectives). A strategy is not just any plan, however. A strategy is a plan that is *unified:* it ties all the parts of the enterprise together. A strategy is *comprehensive:* it covers all major aspects of the enterprise. A strategy is *integrated:* all the parts of the plan are compatible with each other and fit together well. These are prescriptions; we will return to some descriptions of strategy after clarifying some terms.

A strategy begins with a concept of how to use the resources of the firm most effectively in a changing environment. It is similar to the concept in sports of a game plan. Before a team goes onto the field, effective coaches examine a competitor's past plans and strengths and weaknesses. Then they look at their own team's strengths and weaknesses. The objective is to win the game with a minimum of injuries. Coaches may also not wish to humiliate an opponent with a 100-0 score. They may wish not to use all their best plays but to save some for future opponents. So coaches devise a plan to win the game.

A game plan is not exactly a strategy, however. A game plan is oriented toward only one game. A strategy for a firm is a long-run plan. A game plan is oriented against one competitor only, and is only for one game, not a whole season. A firm deals with a number of competitors simultaneously and with the government, suppliers, owners, labor unions, and others. A strategy is oriented toward basic issues such as these: What is our business? What should it be? What are our products, functions, and markets?[3] What can our firm do to accomplish objectives? The Dallas Cowboys' coach doesn't ask questions such as these. Still, it may help you understand the concept of strategy as a plan which is the result of analyzing strengths and weaknesses and determining what the environment has to offer so that the firm can achieve its objectives.

Exhibit 1.7 suggests the original strategy of Federal Express and various alternative strategies the firm considered to expand the business. Note that the firm could expand products, markets, or functions, or all three. These are only one set of strategies that firms consider based on their configuration of goals, external conditions, and internal factors. Chapter 6 describes strategies in more detail.

Strategies, as suggested, must also be implemented effectively. Players can drop the ball or miss their blocking assignments. The coach may have an excellent game plan, but the game is played on the field. For successful performance, then, the unified, comprehensive, integrated plan includes operational concerns. Most of you are probably more familiar with operational management and plans. Exhibit 1.8 highlights some of the differences.

The strategic plan, then, must be integrated with operational concerns. This will be discussed later in the book. But recognize here the importance of both. Exhibit 1.9 points out one example of how strategy and implementation must be combined for success. In other words, the probability of success is enhanced with the combination of good strategic planning *and* good strategic implementation. Good strategy with poor implementation or poor strategy with good implementation is likely to lead to problems.

---

[3]Note: When we refer to products, mentally add the word ''service'' if appropriate for the kind of organization you are analyzing.

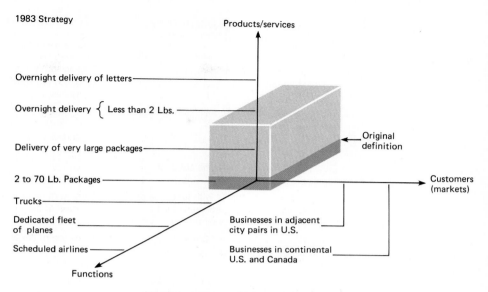

1983 Strategy

Products/services

Overnight delivery of letters

Overnight delivery { Less than 2 Lbs.

Delivery of very large packages

Original definition

2 to 70 Lb. Packages

Trucks

Dedicated fleet of planes

Scheduled airlines

Functions

Businesses in adjacent city pairs in U.S.

Businesses in continental U.S. and Canada

Customers (markets)

(A) Original strategy with initial expansion

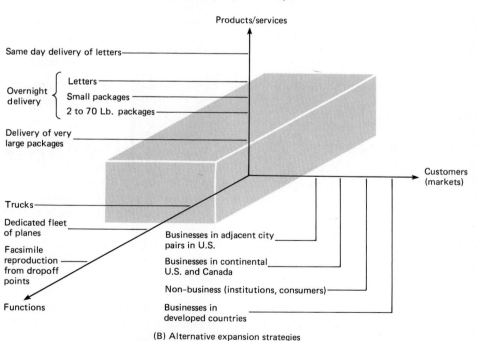

Products/services

Same day delivery of letters

Overnight delivery { Letters, Small packages, 2 to 70 Lb. packages

Delivery of very large packages

Trucks

Dedicated fleet of planes

Facsimile reproduction from dropoff points

Functions

Businesses in adjacent city pairs in U.S.

Businesses in continental U.S. and Canada

Non-business (institutions, consumers)

Businesses in developed countries

Customers (markets)

(B) Alternative expansion strategies

EXHIBIT 1.7   Strategy alternatives to expand Federal Express.
Adapted from George S. Day, Strategic Market Planning *(St. Paul, Minn.: West, 1984.)*

EXHIBIT 1.8 DIFFERENCES BETWEEN OPERATIONAL MANAGEMENT AND STRATEGIC PLANNING

Operational management	Strategic planning
1 Concerned with goals derived from established objectives.	1 Concerned with the identification and evaluation of new objectives and strategies.
2 Goals usually have been validated through extensive past experience.	2 New objectives and strategies can be highly debatable; experience within the organization or in other companies may be minimal.
3 Goals are reduced to specific subgoals for functional units.	3 Objectives usually are evaluated primarily for corporate significance.
4 Managers tend to identify with functions or professions and to be preoccupied with means.	4 Managers need a corporate point of view oriented to the environment.
5 Managers obtain evidence of their performance against goals relatively promptly.	5 Evidence of the merit of new objectives or strategies is often available only after several years.
6 Incentives, formal and social, are tied to operating goals.	6 Incentives are at best only loosely associated with planning.
7 The "rules of the game" become well understood. Experienced individuals feel competent and secure.	7 New fields of endeavor may be considered. Past experience may not provide competence in a "new game."
8 The issues are immediate, concrete, and familiar.	8 Issues are abstract and deferrable (to some extent) and may be unfamiliar.

Source: Robert Mainer, "The Impact of Strategic Planning on Executive Behavior," a special commentary (Boston: Boston Consulting Group, 1968), pp. 4–5.

IS STRATEGIC MANAGEMENT USED? [5]

You might be wondering if the concepts in this book are applied in practice. Do organizations really go to all this trouble? A number of studies support the idea that *strategic management is now widely practiced in industry.* For years, strategic management was advocated but received little attention. Now it seems to be practiced by most large- and medium-sized firms and by the more sophisticated smaller firms. And in 1977, *Business Week* initiated a weekly section called "Corporate Strategies" describing strategic management in various enterprises. Each week this section is one of the longest in the magazine, and it is a source for many of the exhibits in this book. We think that those who practice strategic management have a higher probability of success, which we will discuss shortly. Before we do so, you might be interested in some sketches of firms which have tried strategic management approaches (Exhibit 1.10).

Note that the exhibit contains both successes and failures. Just because a firm practices strategic management doesn't guarantee success. Their plans can be good as well as bad. Several of the plans that didn't work may have been based on faulty assumptions or unforeseen changes in the environment, or may have been the result of diversification away from areas that managers knew something about. Moreover,

EXHIBIT 1.9   STRATEGY MINUS IMPLEMENTATION = PROBLEMS

When F. Ross Johnson moved in to head Standard Brands in 1976, he faced a firm with a 10-year history of emphasis on short-term earnings, low marketing budgets, and increased prices, all of which had resulted in one of the food processing industry's slowest-growing companies. The firm had failed to develop new products and had become more dependent on the cyclical corn syrup refining business. Johnson mapped out a bold new strategy and recruited a new planning staff to map out the details. Unfortunately, over the next 4 years Johnson learned a bitter lesson: "A good strategy—unaccompanied by equally good execution—is not the answer to any company's problems."

The firm's efforts in the next 2 years resulted in "some of the most celebrated failures in the food industry." The first new product developed internally was a marketing disaster when it failed the consumer taste test. A line of snack foods going head-on against industry leader Frito-Lay also failed. Of course, unexpected price increases didn't help either. But the major problems resulted from poor implementation.

For one thing, the new planning team failed to make needed changes in an antiquated marketing structure. Second, the corporate planners were making centralized operating decisions which they were ill-prepared to handle. Third, too many outsiders unfamiliar with the business were placed in leadership positions. Finally, the legacy of previous resource allocations made a turnaround more difficult.

In 1978, Johnson changed his approach, concluding that "proper implementation requires the experience of operating specialists—not the heavy-handed rule of the half-dozen corporate planners who were hired to develop the strategy." A commitment was made to allocate greater resources for promotion and new-product development; sales and distribution functions were reorganized; the reins of control were passed to operations specialists, many of whom were already within the company's executive ranks; and a program was started that began to promote and transfer operating executives within the company so that they could develop broader experience. As can be seen, implementation and strategy must go hand in hand for a firm to be successful.

Source: Adapted from "When a New Product Strategy Wasn't Enough," *Business Week,* Feb. 18, 1980, pp. 142–146.

many firms may have relegated planning to a formal planning staff and not involved the line managers who were charged with implementing plans. Moreover, even good plans might not be successful because of poor implementation.

Our next section will discuss the reasons why strategic management should be practiced; and Chapter 2 will discuss the role of the planning staff and the line in this process. The entire book deals with ways in which strategic management can be executed more successfully to improve the probability of success.

Many firms in the United States apparently use these approaches. What about firms in other countries? This book has been written from the perspective of authors who have lived most of their lives in the United States. We have consulted or traveled in Canada, Latin America, Europe, Asia, Africa, and Australia. But our knowledge of these areas is based mostly on reading, so most of this book is based on practices in North America. However, the ideas in this text are used to varying degrees by firms in other countries. And as Chapter 4 will explain, the international environment must be carefully examined as a basic source of opportunity and threat. Be assured that international firms are thinking strategy. These ideas are also applied by many nonprofit enterprises and the public sector. The Appendix indicates the extent to which those concepts have been applied in these organizations and different areas of the world.

EXHIBIT 1.10   A SAMPLING OF STRATEGIC PLANNING'S TRACK RECORD

Plans That Didn't Work . . .			. . . and Plans That Did		
Company	Strategy	BW assessment	Company	Strategy	BW assessment
Adolph Coors	Regain lost market share and become a national force in the beer industry	Largely unsuccessful because of weak marketing clout	Abbott Laboratories	Become less vulnerable to cost-containment pressures in traditional hospital products	Won a leading share of the diagnostic-products market through acquisitions and internal development and built a highly profitable dietary supplements business
American Natural Resources	Offset sagging natural gas sales by diversifying into trucking, coal mining, oil/gas exploration, and coal gasification	Ran into trouble because anticipated gas shortages and higher prices failed to materialize	Bausch & Lomb	Regain dominance in soft contact lenses through intensive marketing and aggressive pricing; become a major force in lens solutions	Boosted share of daily-wear lens market to 60 percent
Exxon	Diversify into electrical equipment and office automation, offset shrinking U.S. oil reserves by investing in shale oil and synfuels	Failed because of poor acquisitions, management problems in office automation, and falling oil prices	Bekins	Return to profitability by selling real estate, building market share in basic moving business, and remedying poor diversification moves	Increased moving's market share through improved marketing; divested bad businesses
General Motors	Gain market share by outspending U.S. competitors in the race to offer more fuel-efficient, downsized cars	Failed as import market share grew; modified strategy to pursue diversification	Borg-Warner	Offset the cyclicality of manufacturing-related businesses	Expanded into financial and protective services through acquisitions and internal development; services now account for a third of earnings
International Multifoods	Diversify away from flour milling by developing niche products in consumer foods and expanding restaurant business	Largely unsuccessful because of management timidity, problems overseas, and the recession	Dayton Hudson	Maintain impressive sales and earnings growth by diversifying retail operations	Jumped to number 5 in retailing by dramatically expanding Target, Mervyn's promotional apparel, and B. Dalton Booksellers chains

EXHIBIT 1.10   (*Continued*)

	Plans That Didn't Work ...			...and Plans That Did	
Company	Strategy	BW assessment	Company	Strategy	BW assessment
Napco Industries	Become the dominant distributor of nonfood items to grocery stores	Ran into trouble through bad acquisitions, logistical and management problems, and the recession	Gould	Move from an industrial and electrical manufacturer into an electronics company via divestitures and acquisitions	Built electronics to 100 percent of earnings by buying nine high-tech companies and divesting old-line operations
Oak Industries	Diversify into subscription TV and cable TV equipment	Failed because cable TV competition was underestimated; also did not keep abreast of TV equipment technology	National Intergroup	Improve efficiency of and reduce dependence on steel operations	Became an efficient steelmaker by modernizing; diversified into financial services, sold a steel plant to workers, and sold a 50 percent share of steel operations to Nippon Kokan
Shaklee	Streamline product lines and become the leading nutritional products company	Ran into trouble because of the recession and sales-force turnover	New England Electric System	Reduce dependence on oil by switching to coal, developing other fuel sources, and promoting conservation	Switch to coal saved over $200 million, cut oil consumption 58 percent
Toro	Capitalize on brand recognition and reputation for quality in mowers and snowblowers by expanding into other home-care products	Failed because of snowless winters and distribution mistakes; new management changed strategies	Ralston Purina	Refocus on basic grocery products and feed business	Shed mushroom and European pet food divisions, revitalized core business through product development and improved marketing
Trailways	Survive in the bus business by striking alliances with independent carriers and persuading regulators to hold Greyhound to 67 percent of intercity bus traffic	Failed because of deregulation and Greyhound's market-share war	Uniroyal	Revive ailing tire business and abandon lackluster businesses	Shut two U.S. tire plants, shed many foreign and U.S. operations, and is expanding in specialty chemicals

Source: Companies were selected from those whose strategies were described by *Business Week* in 1979 and 1980 and reassessed by *Business Week*, September 17, 1984, pp. 62–68.

WHY STRATEGIC MANAGEMENT? [6]

Up to this point in the chapter, you have been introduced to the concepts of strategic management, strategies, SBUs, and similar ideas. You've probably been saying, "That's interesting. And some firms use strategic management. But why should I be interested?" After all we just told you that many of these plans don't work. In the introduction to this chapter we gave you three personal reasons why you should be interested in these topics. This section will give you some other reasons for learning more about strategic management.

A number of reasons are given by authors and executives as to why firms (and other institutions) *should* engage in strategic management. Exhibit 1.11 lists some of the major points and some common reactions from those who question the value of this process.

Our position is as follows:

1 Some of the irony about change is that it makes planning more difficult. However, firms need not just react to change; they can proact or even make changes happen. Much will be said in this book about changes businesses face and how these changes have increased dramatically in the past half century. Strategic management allows a firm's top executives to anticipate change and provides direction and control for the enterprise. It will also allow the firm to innovate in time to take advantage of new opportunities in the environment and reduce the risk because the future was anticipated. In addition, it helps ensure full exploitation of opportunities. While the manager of a utility may not know the price of oil, the demand for electricity, regulations regarding nuclear power, or technological changes to allow the use of solar energy, decisions about investment in a new plant to come on stream 20 years from now cannot wait. Long-term planning is absolutely necessary, with assumptions about these factors in the future. Assumptions may not be right; but decision makers are paralyzed if they wait for complete certainty (which never comes).

In sum, strategic management allows an enterprise to base its decisions on long-

EXHIBIT 1.11   REASONS FOR AND REACTIONS TO THE VALUE OF STRATEGIC MANAGEMENT

Pros	Cons
1 Strategic management allows firms to anticipate changing conditions.	Conditions change so fast, managers can't do any planning, especially long-term planning.
2 Strategic management provides clear objectives and direction for employees.	Objectives must often be vague and general.
3 Research in strategic management is advancing so that the process can help managers.	Managers pay little attention to research, and studies are not well done.
4 Businesses which perform strategic management are more effective.	There are many reasons for success, and many firms are effective without *formal* planning.

range forecasts, not spur-of-the-moment reactions. It allows the firm to take action at an early stage of a new trend and consider the lead time for effective management. "Chance," said Louis Pasteur, "favors the prepared man." The strategic management process stimulates thinking about the future. Plans resulting from the process should be flexible enough to allow for unanticipated change.

2 As we will note in Chapter 2, there are proponents of vague objectives with some interesting reasons for their position. Nonetheless, most people perform better (in terms of quality and quantity) if they know what is expected of them and where the enterprise is going. This can also help reduce conflict. Effective strategic management points the way for the employees to follow. Strategic management provides a strong incentive for employees and management to achieve company objectives. It serves as the basis for management control and evaluation. Strategic management also ensures that the top executives have a unified opinion on strategic issues and actions.

3 While there are methodological problems in research in this area, many good studies are now being done. Just 20 years ago much of what was known about strategic management was based on single case studies or anecdotal evidence. The last few years have seen an explosion of research. We cite some of this evidence in support of the positions taken in the book. The references [7] for this section cite some of the recent summaries of research. In 1977, the Business Policy and Planning Division of the Academy of Management held a conference summarizing the research in the area, and special conferences devoted to research in strategic management are held every year in the United States and Europe. And two new journals devoted entirely to strategic management were launched in 1980 and 1981.

In general, we know more about effective strategic management than we did, and this makes its study more worthwhile. As for whether managers pay attention to this research, all we can suggest is that our earlier section noted that strategic management is now widely practiced. Indeed, much of the research efforts focus on what those practices are.

4 There is no such thing as a definitive study which *proves* that strategic management *causes* better performance. In fact, some studies suggest better performance leads to strategic planning. There are some studies and theorists suggesting that strategic planning makes no difference for performance. But the majority of studies suggest that there is a relationship between better performance and *formal* planning [8]. Our summary statement is that *businesses which perform formal strategic planning have a higher probability of success than those which do not.*

There are many reasons for this proposition. Some of them are as follows:

• Strategic management is one way to systematize the most important of business decisions. Business involves great risk taking, and strategic management attempts to provide data so that reasonable and informed gambles can be made when necessary.

• Strategic management helps educate managers to become better decision makers. It helps managers examine the basic problems of a company.

• Strategic management helps improve corporate communication, the coordination of individual projects, the allocation of resources, and short-range planning such as budgeting.

Because of the studies of strategic management, many businesses make sure it is a part of their management development programs. The American Assembly of Collegiate Schools of Business strongly suggests that accredited schools of business should teach strategic management, believing that persons exposed to strategic management will develop a broad understanding of the general manager. Strategic management focuses on business problems, not just functional problems such as those of a marketing or financial nature. Strategic management helps build a knowledge of management and develops the attitudes necessary for being a successful business generalist and practitioner. It should also help individuals learn how to assess a business so that they can determine whether they wish to be employed by it or purchase its stock.

Successful companies are successful for many reasons: adequate resources, good people, luck, good products and services, and so on. This is *not* to say that strategic management is all you need to make a success of your business career, but it looks as if it is worth learning about.

STRATEGIC DECISION-MAKING PROCESSES

We began this chapter by stating that this book is about a particular set of decisions. So far we have outlined the strategic planning process, defined strategy, and indicated where it's used and why it's important. In this section we will examine decision-making approaches. Since the remainder of the book will come back to these ideas again and again, it's useful to understand the framework underlying the approach we will follow.

Before outlining the framework, we should point out that in any applied field which combines art and science, you are likely to find two approaches—prescriptive (or normative) and descriptive. Prescriptive approaches tell you how things *ought to be done*. Descriptive approaches tell you how things *are done*. A common theme running through this book is that a blending of these two approaches is likely to be more fruitful. Keeping this in mind, let's look at some prescriptive and descriptive explanations of strategic decision making.

How Does a Decision Maker Make a Decision?

Various theories have been suggested about how decisions are made. Let us examine these first. Most writers focus on three approaches: rational-analytical, intuitive-emotional, and behavioral-political.

Rational-Analytical Decision Maker [9]

In this model, the decision maker is a unique actor whose behavior is intelligent and rational. The decision is the choice this actor makes, in full awareness of all available feasible alternatives, to maximize advantages. The decision maker therefore considers all the alternatives as well as the consequences of all the possible choices, orders these consequences in the light of a fixed scale of preferences, and chooses the alternative that procures the maximum gain.

This is the oldest decision theory. It prescribes a rational, conscious, systematic, and analytical approach. It has been criticized because

1 The decision maker is often not a unique actor but part of a multiparty decision situation.

2 Decision makers are not rational enough or informed enough to consider all alternatives or know all the consequences. And information is costly.

3 Decision makers make decisions with more than a maximization of objectives in mind. They tend to "satisfice," that is, make a decision expected to yield a satisfactory, as opposed to an "optimal," outcome. Besides, the objectives may change.

So descriptions of actual decision making question the validity of "rational" processes.

Intuitive-Emotional Decision Maker [10]

The opposite of the rational decision maker is the intuitive decision maker. This decision maker prefers habit or experience, gut feeling, reflective thinking, and instinct, using the unconscious mental processes. Intuitive decision makers consider a number of alternatives and options, simultaneously jumping from one step in analysis or search to another and back again.

Some who prescribe intuition or judgment as the preferred approach point out that in many cases, judgment may lead to "better" decisions than "optimizing" techniques. For example, consider sensitivity analysis on a tool such as the economic order quantity (EOQ). EOQ models suggest that there is an optimal order quantity considering trade-offs of ordering and holding costs. Yet you can stray far from optimal in most cases without a very significant impact on total cost differentials. Here, then, judgment concerning other factors in the decision situation could lead to a better *overall* decision about order quantities, rather than holding fast to deciding what the rational model prescribes. In fact, the timing of when to implement a decision based on the analysis may require an intuitive feel for what the data are telling you. In many cases, judgment such as this might be preferable to relying on the analysis. Recognize, then, that analytical models are tools to *help* the decision maker refine judgment.

Those opposed to this approach argue that

1 It does not effectively use all the tools available to modern decision makers.

2 The rational approach ensures that adequate attention is given to consequences of decisions before big mistakes are made.

Political-Behavioral Decision Making [11]

A third point of view suggests that real decision makers must consider a variety of pressures from other people affected by their decisions. An organization interacts with a variety of stakeholders in a series of interdependent exchange relationships. Unions exchange labor for decent wages and job security. Customers exchange money for products and services. Owners exchange capital for expected returns on investment. Suppliers exchange inputs for money and continued business. Government exchanges protection and economic security for taxes. Even competitors exchange information with one another through trade associations or other contacts. The list of agents and expectations goes on. *A stakeholder is any group or individual who can affect or is affected by the achievement of an organization's purpose.*

Each stakeholder gives the organization something and expects something in return. To the extent an organization has a favorable exchange relationship (gets a bit more than given) compared with other organizations and stakeholders, it has more power. More powerful stakeholders have more influence over decisions because the organization is more dependent on these stakeholders. A majority stockholder can have a greater influence on decisions about reinvestment versus dividend payout than if stock is widely held by many small owners. If the firm is labor-intensive, more attention may be paid to union leaders' demands for better wages than to the desires of stockholders for more profit, because the union might shut the firm down.

Given these realities, decision makers do a juggling act to meet the demands of the various stakeholders. Through political compromise, they attempt to merge competing demands so that a coalition of interests emerges that will support the decision.

This mode of decision making is a descriptive theory suggesting that the organization in which the decision maker works limits the choices available. Decisions are made when the several people involved in the process agree that they have found a solution. They do this by mutual adjustment and negotiation following the rules of the game—the way decisions have been made in the organization in the past. The decision maker must consider whether the decision outcome can be implemented politically.

A Synthesis on Decision Making

The human being is a mix of the rational and the emotional. We also know that the environment is a mixture of the analyzable and of chaotic change and pressures. Strategic management decisions therefore are made in a typically human way: using the rational, conscious analysis and intuitive, unconscious "gut," in light of political realities.

As stated earlier, some prescribe that one component or another *should* be larger. However, because of individual differences and differences in the stability of the environment, the amount of the rational versus the intuitive versus the political varies by the decision maker and the decision situation. In some cases the analytical component is very large; in others, the emotional set may dominate. For example, Bill Ziff, the magnate behind the billion dollar Ziff-Davis Publishing Company, sold off much of his empire because he became "more and more bored." He put TV stations up for sale because, he says, "they were not a turn on." But as Exhibit 1.12 suggests, the interaction of the three approaches (shaded area) defines where we think much decision making probably occurs. We would prefer that the analytical component be larger than the others. In fact, we prescribe an analytical-rational approach, tempered by realities in the situation. Thus when you set about to make decisions, you should apply the tools you learn. But truly rational analysis will also incorporate analysis of

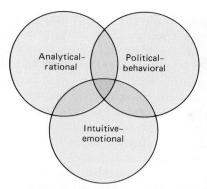

EXHIBIT 1.12 **Components of strategic decision processes.**

the political-behavioral and intuitive dimensions in the decision situation. Indeed various techniques such as dialectic inquiry, devil's advocacy, hierarchical analysis, and influence diagrams have evolved to help managers with these complex and messy problems. These systems allow managers to recognize and rationally structure the judgmental and political factors which will undoubtedly influence them [12].

Thus we suggest that a blending of these prescriptive and descriptive approaches helps you better understand how decision makers operate. And as you assess cases or business problems, attempt to diagnose the political or emotional realities of the situation in addition to using the analytical tools at your disposal. The recommendations you make are likely to be much more meaningful if you do this. Now, let's explain the significance of these ideas for the strategic management model used in this book.

Strategic Management and Strategic Decisions [13]

As you look again at Exhibit 1.2, note that the phases in the model are interrelated. As we examine strategic management elements, we will outline who the decision makers are, what organizational objectives are sought, and how those objectives are arrived at. You will find that the processes involved in making decisions about objectives involve political pressures and value orientations of individuals involved with the organization. As we discuss the analysis and diagnosis of external and internal factors, you will find that there are analytical approaches and that there are also descriptions of how perceptions and political influences affect the assessments made. Our discussion of choosing among alternatives will suggest some analytical techniques to aid in the identification of strategies and prescriptions about why some might be better than others under certain circumstances. But often there are only a few proposals recommended to strategists that will be considered at any given time. In addition to rational analysis, political factors and intuition play a role in the selection of a proposal. For implementation, behavioral-political factors become particularly critical. And as evaluation is done, a rational analysis of criteria is possible; but the interpretation and explanation of results may involve other elements.

Related to this is the issue of whether strategic change is evolutionary or revolutionary. A major line of work in this area is based on the assumption that incremental processes are, and should be, the prime mode used for strategy setting. Such a philosophy is best represented by the work of Quinn and Mintzberg. Quinn describes how 10 large companies actually arrived at their most important strategic changes. He suggests that *formal rational planning* often becomes a substitute for control instead of a process for stimulating innovation and entrepreneurship. He recommends that incremental processes be consciously used to integrate the psychological, political, and informational needs of organizations in setting strategy.

Earlier we provided a prescriptive definition of strategy as a unified, comprehensive, and integrated plan. Mintzberg describes strategy as a pattern in a stream of decisions. The pattern may not be comprehensive, unified, or integrated. This descriptive definition implies that decisions are often made piecemeal, and outcomes may be unintended. In essence, the strategy may be changed in an evolutionary manner without executives even realizing it.

However, there may be hidden costs in incremental changes. In particular, piecemeal approaches to strategy and structure may result in internal disharmonies. Making decisions about individual projects on their own merits, without considering broader strategic implications, can result in an "emerging" strategy which is de facto different from the intended strategy. Thus delays in these changes might better be made until such time that a "quantum," or revolutionary, change is justified by reconfiguring the entire system—its strategy, structure, policies, resource allocations, and so on.

Perhaps the dispute can be explained by noting that prescription and description do not converge. Descriptively, a number of researchers observe incremental evolutionary adjustments to strategy being the norm in practice; prescriptively, in order to achieve internal and external consistency, strategy change is often viewed as necessarily revolutionary. This book attempts to blend these perspectives.

Another way to look at this is to ask, What might encourage a decision maker to begin to think about the need to make a strategic change? We think that a gap analysis is a useful way to explain this. Exhibit 1.13 shows a scheme we will be referring to from time to time. It suggests several important considerations for strategic decision makers to ponder.

As a result of decisions made in the past, the organization has evolved in a particular way with a particular strategy to accomplish a set of desired outcomes. At any given time (t_1), a formal evaluation might be made of how the strategy is working. Perhaps more commonly, a proposal for some new activity or change in the strategy will be

EXHIBIT 1.13   **Strategic gap analysis.**

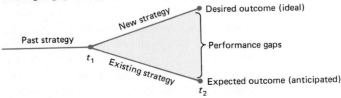

offered for consideration. In the process of contemplating the need for change, the proposal is likely to be considered in relation to the gap between the *expected outcomes* of continuing with the existing strategy and the *desired outcomes* from making a change for the future (t_2) with the proposed new strategy.

As we go through the book, we will discuss a number of conditions which could lead to this gap. For instance, Chapter 2 discusses objectives and decision makers. If these change, then desired outcomes could be altered, leading to a perceived need for change. As external conditions are assessed (Chapters 3 and 4), the expected outcomes could be altered if significant changes are expected (i.e., continuing with the past strategy might not allow the firm to take advantage of an opportunity to reach a more desirable outcome, or its continuation could lead to outcomes which are unsatisfactory). A diagnosis of internal factors (Chapter 5) might reveal that certain areas of the firm are declining in performance and that the expected results of continuing as is will lead to a gap. Similarly, as implementation is considered (Chapters 9 to 11), continuing past policies or procedures may suggest that they will no longer lead to expected outcomes, or better ways might be found to accomplish desired outcomes. Hence, an "incremental" project proposal might trigger a more comprehensive process of strategic thinking which may lead to revolutionary change.

At the choice stage (Chapter 8), several conditions must exist in the nature of this gap before decisions will be made to make a change or accept a proposal.

1 *The gap must be perceived to be significant.* Some theories refer to this as a minimum threshold of perception. The idea is that if you expect to be close to where you want to be, no change is required. If you want a 10 percent market share and expect to get 9½, you may not change anything.

2 *The decision maker must be motivated to reduce the gap.* Given multiple outcomes, the gap, even if significant, must pertain to an important objective. The trade-off required to reduce a gap in one objective at the expense of a larger gap in a more important objective may reduce the motivation to make any alterations.

3 *The decision maker must believe that the gap can be reduced.* If the organization is seen as incapable of reducing the gap, the gap may be ignored. If the gap is a sales decline in corn and the decline is expected to be due to inadequate rainfall, the choice may be to continue to try to grow corn.

If any of the three conditions is *not* present, it is likely that no change will be made or that the desired outcomes will be changed to be consistent with expected outcomes.

If a change is made and the overall process is effective, the desired outcomes will be reached; then the process will start all over with new and probably higher desired outcomes. As a change is implemented, if the desired outcomes prove to be unrealistically high, or if unforeseen changes in the environment occur, or if the implementation is ineffective, the desired outcomes might have to be lowered incrementally, or a contingency plan might have to be put into effect to deal with the new circumstances (Chapter 11). In all these instances, note that the various phases shown in Exhibit 1.2 are linked together. In effect, this gap analysis can occur at any stage in the overall process. For example, an internal analysis might reveal that the firm is not currently capable of reaching the desired outcomes with its current resources. It could try to build additional resources to reduce the gap if management believes it can reduce the gap this way; if not, this resource constraint could be a reason for resolving the gap differential by altering desired outcomes. Thus strategic choice and evaluation are ongoing in all parts of the model outlined in Exhibit 1.2 and can lead to strategic change, goal alterations, or changes in implementation.

If you look carefully at the three conditions which must prevail before the gap will trigger action, you will note that perception, motivation, and belief are involved. As we explained before, intuitive, rational, and political decision factors will converge to influence the managers' thinking regarding the nature of a gap (Exhibit 1.12). Exhibit 1.14 shows how these factors have influenced the assessment of strategic gaps of a large advertising agency.

Before discussing our last topic, we should point out that our primary emphasis in this book is on the strategic management *process* more than the *content* of strategy. That is, we emphasize planning processes for strategic management, decision-making approaches for formulating objectives and strategies, and processes for implementing strategy. Thus we focus on the factors influencing strategy selection and implementation. This does involve examining various types of strategies and ways to implement them. But we do not attempt to prescribe *the strategy* a firm should follow or *the policies and plans* to implement a *particular* strategy in a *particular environment*. There are two major reasons for this:

- While some patterns are evident, firms are unique, and content must often be situation-specific.

EXHIBIT 1.14   THE GAPS AT LEO BURNETT

Leo Burnett is one of the top 10 ad agencies in the United States in total billings. Yet it has the smallest number of clients among that group, with only one new account added in the last year. Its strategy is to land "blue-chip" accounts—"companies that need advertising, increase their ad spending over the years, and pay their bills on time."

Its approach has been to stick with a campaign for a client year after year, such as the "Friendly Skies" slogan of United, the "Good Hands" pitch of Allstate, Star-Kist's Charlie the Tuna, and Kellogg's Tony the Tiger. Many clients are strong backers of what they see as winning campaigns. But some smaller clients—such as Litton Industries, with an account estimated at $5 million—have left for other agencies. And many on Madison Avenue suggest that the agency's creative work has become un-even, pointing to the uninspired introduction of RCA's videodisc.

Such a potential gap is not perceived to be significant to Burnett officials. They are content with their traditional way of doing business, and they have eschewed trying to grow by gaining more clients or diversifying into other service areas as many of their competitors have done. CEO John Kensella states, "We plan to stay an advertising agency. We're willing to plan for the long term and wait for the pieces of business we want. We want to do the best work possible for our clients, make sure our people are well-paid, and see that our stockholders make money. None of that has anything to do with size."

Clearly, the gap (perceived by Burnett executives) between the desired outcomes and expected future outcomes is insufficient to lead them to alter their strategy.

Source: Adapted from "A Blue-Chip Strategy Pays Off," *Business Week*, Nov. 16, 1981. pp. 188ff.

• There is little generalizable research available which supports the generic content statement that "firm A will reach objective B with strategy C in environment D by implementing plan E."

In the analysis of cases, you will have an opportunity to apply the process to arrive at prescriptions for the content of a strategy plan for a given firm. And you will find common approaches and factors which must be considered in the analysis. But it is unlikely that there is *one best way* to successful strategic management.

TIMING AND STRATEGIC MANAGEMENT [14]

Before we summarize, the topic of timing deserves mention, since it will also crop up again. In the gap analysis, we did not specify a time period, yet that could also influence the analysis. If your desired outcome is to double the market share in a 2-year time period, your assessment about gaps between expected and desired outcomes will be different than if that desired outcome were to extend over a 10-year period. Very different interpretations will be given to a diagnosis of internal and external conditions, depending on whether your plan is long-term or short-term.

Descriptively, the terms short-range and long-range have no precise meaning but rather express relative periods of time. In the oil industry, or in the case of electric utilities, it is often necessary to extend plans 20 to 30 years into the future. Forest products companies such as Georgia-Pacific have reforestation plans that extend well into the latter half of the next century. The average lapse of time from the sowing of a fir seedling to its harvest at maturity is 99 years. At the other extreme, long-range plans for the manufacturers of children's toys may extend no more than 6 months to a year. In such industries it is virtually impossible to safely predict how quickly popular fads will come and go. Under such circumstances, examples of short-range plans might include a weekly production meeting and a quarterly budget.

Though no set answer can be given to the question, How long should a long-range plan be?, certain prescriptive criteria can be suggested as guidelines.

1 How far into the future do the firm's *fixed commitments* extend? Such commitments would include long-term indebtedness and contracts. If a firm is obligated to make mortgage or lease payments over 30 years, for instance, it would seem wise to have a financial plan for that period of time.

2 How much *uncertainty* is associated with the future? Without exception, predictive efficiency drops off over time. In some instances, the future may even be unpredictable after only a few years. In such cases it makes little sense to develop complex plans covering extended time horizons. While plans could be based on pure intuition or guesswork, their true value would be limited. On the other hand, the absence of uncertainty can lead to long-term plans which *shouldn't* be made, because they become overly rigid. For years, firms in regulated industries could develop long-term plans without concern that conditions would change radically. These firms, such as Western Union, often became bloated, slow-moving, and poorly positioned to deal with change. When deregulation occurred, they were ill-prepared to deal with the need to plan strategically, or they were locked into long-term fixed commitments which did

not allow them to maneuver readily. Many failed, while others, such as some trucking firms, began to apply strategic thinking. That is, managers began to anticipate the future and devise flexible plans to proactively move their firms in desired directions.

3 What is the *lead time* required to ready a product or service for sale? For example, it typically takes 3 to 5 years for a new series of computers to reach the market following its development. So planning periods are strongly influenced by product development considerations. While the lead time for a new line of women's dresses may be only 6 months, many firms are forced to plan well into the future if their products are ever going to be developed at all.

Given these considerations, it is not uncommon to find that planning is often done on a "rolling" basis. Under this system an organization may develop a 5-year plan of future operations and update it on an annual basis. Thus as the current year of a 5-year plan closes, the plan is extended, or rolled forward, to include a "new" fifth year. Such a procedure allows an organization to revise its plans on the basis of new information and to maintain a degree of flexibility in its commitments. It is at this time that a comprehensive gap analysis of the entire business is desirable. Thus both long-range, or strategic, plans and short-term or operational, plans to implement strategy can be integrated with one another.

Unfortunately, many U.S. executives seem to have abandoned long-term strategic management to concentrate on short-term profitability. There are a number of reasons for this, including pressure from Wall Street, and rewards for short-term results rather than long-term performance.

For example, managers often buy back stock, or pursue other strategies to protect their own position of control or improve the stock price. Short-term investor interest (often large institutional holders who buy and sell large blocks of stocks or bonds) will often force the hand of management. And as we pointed out earlier, some failures in plans are due to faulty strategic planning. Again, there could be other reasons for lack of success. But strategic plans do often rest on premises or assumptions about the future which may be uncertain or unreliable. Instead of abandoning strategic thinking in favor of short-term performance, however, we believe the concept should be expanded to the next generation—contingency management. Here, the firm uses *anticipatory flexibility* by establishing a long-term plan which anticipates a probable future, but incorporates flexibility to maneuver and alter the plan if the assumptions on which it is based are found to be inaccurate. This is slightly different from the notion of "surprise" management. That is, managers can try to anticipate surprises (such as an environmental disaster, death of a president, or a new-product introduction by a competitor) and plan a contingency response which would be ready in such an eventuality. However, the idea behind anticipatory flexibility is not necessarily to provide a specific plan for a surprise. Rather, it is to achieve the ability to alter a strategy in several directions—usually requiring slack in the system. In other words, the plan to begin with recognizes that diversions or variations are likely as time goes on. This does not negate the usefulness of surprise management. Rather, flexibility complements a contingency plan. Our concept of strategic management is also grounded in this concept, which will be referred to again.

Consistent with this is the idea that strategic management requires some risk taking. Exhibit 1.15 serves to tie together our thoughts in this regard. Note that Pepsi incor-

EXHIBIT 1.15   TAKING THE PEPSI CHALLENGE

From within the ranks of the consumer product marketing giants, PepsiCo, Inc., has emerged as this generation's innovator and new product leader. Pepsi has accumulated a wide variety of consumer product successes despite recent slips and tumbles experienced by other industry powerhouses including Phillip Morris, Procter & Gamble, and Coca-Cola. Besides having the nation's best-selling soft drink, Pepsi has helped Taco Bell and Pizza Hut become two of the fastest-growing restaurant chains in the country. Pepsi was hoping to flex its marketing magic once again by purchasing Seven-Up to reverse the falling market shares and profits of the lemon-lime soft drink. But that deal fell through.

The backbone of this confidence is a "fast-moving, risk-oriented management with an exquisite sense of timing." While Pepsi employs analytical research and test-marketing tools similar to those of its rivals, it also realizes the importance of instincts or intuition as decision-making assets. Because the demands of regional, national, and even international markets can change so rapidly, a degree of intuition is essential to flexibility in keeping a step ahead of the competition. Executives at Pepsi value their instincts so much that they have risked millions by being the first out with a 100 percent NutraSweet formula, even before a test market could be performed for fear that Coca-Cola would be tipped off. Pepsi's top management allows its managers to operate with a great deal of autonomy and encourages quick actions in return for expected performance. When opportunities arise, usually the difference between success and failure is not that of failing to recognize the opportunity but instead that of not correctly and quickly acting upon the opportunity before the competition does.

However, does a point exist where even the best intuition or good hunch won't be enough to go on when determining investment allocations? This point does exist in some organizations, while not being present in others, depending upon the risk or comfort level of each individual management team. As in every case, though, for each company not willing to take a chance on a hunch, there is another one ready to take the risk in search of larger market shares and profits. And at this time Pepsi has accepted the challenge!

Source: Adapted from A., Dunkin, "Pepsi's Marketing Magic: Why Nobody Does It Better," *Business Week*, Feb. 10, 1986. pp. 52–57

porates intuitive and rational decision making along with a concern about anticipating the future and taking risks as they make incremental moves toward their long-range strategy and goals.

SUMMARY

This chapter has introduced you to the world of strategy and strategic management. It has shown you how budgeting evolved into long-range planning, which in turn has evolved into strategic planning and strategic management.

The chapter has also defined some key terms.

• Strategic management is a stream of decisions and actions which leads to the development of an effective strategy or strategies to help achieve corporate objectives.

• Strategic decisions are means to achieve ends. These decisions encompass the definition of the business, products to be handled, markets to be served, functions to be performed, and major policies needed for the organization to execute these decisions to achieve objectives.

• A strategic business unit (SBU) is an operating division of a firm which serves a distinct product-market segment or a well-defined set of customers or a geographic area.

• A strategy is a unified, comprehensive, and integrated plan that relates the strategic advantages of the firm to the challenges of the environment. It is designed to ensure that the basic objectives of the enterprise are achieved through proper execution by the organization.

• Policies are guides to action. They indicate how resources are to be allocated and how tasks assigned to the organization might be accomplished so that functional-level managers execute the strategy properly.

The strategic management process was set up and differences in the process between single-SBU and multiple-SBU firms were clarified. Then it was emphasized that for ease of presentation the parts of the strategic management process would be discussed one at a time. But in reality the phases of the strategic management process are interactive; the process is continuous, with several parts occurring simultaneously. Strategies and policies must be formulated and implemented with each other in mind.

Several examples of the use of strategic management were provided, suggesting that this approach is widely used in larger organizations, even though there are successes and failures. The Appendix also indicates that the concepts are used in different parts of the world and in nonprofit enterprises and the public sector.

Why strategic management is instituted was discussed next. The main reasons are as follows:

• Strategic management helps firms anticipate future problems and opportunities.

• Strategic management provides clear objectives and directions for the future of the enterprise.

• Research in strategic management can be helpful to practicing managers, and it seems to suggest that formal planning contributes to success.

This last reason is important enough to summarize in propositional form. This method will be used in the summaries of the chapters throughout the book.

Proposition 1.1

Businesses which develop formal strategic management systems have a higher probability of success than those which do not.

This chapter also introduced you to some basic concepts running through the book. We noted that this text tries to integrate both *descriptive* and *prescriptive* approaches to strategic management. And we indicated that the focus of the book is on the *process* of strategic management. The most basic process discussed is decision making; we outlined three basic modes: rational-analytical, intuitive-emotional, and behavioral-political. Our synthesis suggests that all three modes are used in strategic decision making, and we showed how these ideas relate to our model of the strategic management process.

We also discussed how these concepts relate to gap analysis. Before a decision is made,

- A gap must exist between desired outcomes and the expected outcomes.
- The gap must be perceived to be significant, thus deserving attention.
- The decision maker must be motivated to reduce the gap.
- The decision maker must believe that something can be done about the gap.

Proposition 1.2

Decision making is a multiphase process. Effective decision makers combine rational and intuitive approaches to making complex, unstructured decisions. They also consider the political feasibility of the decisions.

Finally, the chapter pointed out the importance of timing for strategic decisions and strategic planning. We noted that long-term strategic plans versus short-term operational plans are situation-specific. The time frame for strategic planning is probably based on the nature of the time associated with fixed commitments, the degree of uncertainty in the future, and the lead time needed for start-up. In any case, *anticipatory flexibility* is seen as a superior way to account for the need for long-term strategy while allowing for short-term changes as assumptions are proved right or wrong.

The appendix for this chapter describes strategic management in nonbusiness settings and in different parts of the world. In the chapters that follow, we examine in more detail the strategic management process and important issues about strategic management. Chapter 2 discusses the key elements of strategic management: the strategic decision makers and the decision outcomes (objectives). Then the strategic management process is described, beginning with Chapter 3.

We hope that you will find the journey that lies ahead of you both interesting and rewarding. We hope that you will take advantage of the opportunities available to you.

Appendix: Users of Strategic Management [15]

The primary focus of Chapter 1, and of the book in general, is on strategic management in the private sector in North America. But perhaps more than a third of you will spend all or parts of your careers in not-for-profit or public sectors. Further, as our world gets ''smaller,'' you need to be aware of what's going on in other countries. This appendix will introduce you to our ideas about how the concepts of strategic management are applied in these different settings. Chapter 4 elaborates on the international setting.

The public sector includes federal, state, and local government bodies and federal corporations such as Amtrak, Conrail, the U.S. Postal Service, Canadian National Railways, Renault,

British Air, and Rolls-Royce. (With changes in governments, some of these organizations are being moved to the private sector.) Collectively, these are huge employers of managers and specialists. The not-for-profit sector includes nongovernment, nonprivate groups. Examples of these include most community general hospitals, private colleges and universities, independent research institutes such as the Midwest Research Institute, trade unions, political parties, churches and synagogues, charities such as the Red Cross, interest groups like the NAACP or Common Cause, consumer cooperatives, and arts organizations such as symphonies, ballet companies, museums, and repertory theaters. We will classify countries following our description of public and not-for-profit sectors.

Is strategic management useful in the public and not-for-profit sectors? It appears that it is. Many of the enterprises in these sectors are managed like small- and medium-sized businesses, since they have many of the same characteristics.

There are similarities and differences between the private and other sectors. Many enterprises in the nonprivate sector are more complicated to manage because the manager has to face many more constraints (such as active and diverse stockholders) than in the private firm. It appears reasonable to conclude that these institutions will receive benefits similar to what businesses receive if their management groups practice effective strategic management.

Cases that focus on the operations of several nonbusiness sectors have been included in this book. These allow you to apply the tools of strategic management across different sectors.

We are learning more about the strategic management of public and not-for-profit enterprises. Several authors have described the strategic management of these two sectors in general. Others focus on part of the strategic management process for all these enterprises, such as environment forecasting. But most of the information is written about strategic management of specific institutions. Let us review briefly some of the better studies of these institutions.

Strategic Management of Hospitals [16]

In the United States, community hospitals are in the not-for-profit sector, except for the 850 or so proprietary (for profit) hospitals. There are about 3500 not-for-profit hospitals. In other countries, including Canada, all hospitals are in the public sector. The mental hospitals and Veterans Administration and municipal hospitals in the United States are in the public sector and number about 2700. The focus of this section is on the not-for-profit hospitals.

In our opinion, these institutions are the most difficult enterprises to manage. The hospital administrator must deal first with many objectives, and many of these are hard to quantify. The objectives include quality patient care, research, professional training, cost efficiency, growth in size, and community prestige. The administrator is responsible to a board of trustees, which is usually composed of community leaders and physicians. Although the members of the medical staff can use the hospital facilities, usually they are not the hospital employees. The hospital's funds come from patients, donors, and third-party groups such as Blue Cross, Medicare, and insurance companies. The employees vary from highly trained professionals to semiskilled workers.

One study found that even though the law requires hospitals to be involved in strategic management, most hospitals practice it informally (if at all) on a regular basis. Webber and Dula, using concepts similar to those in this book, have outlined how hospitals could improve their strategic management.

Strategic Management of Colleges and Universities [17]

In the United States there are over 3000 colleges and universities, many of which are in the public sector. Typical of these are the state universities such as the University of California and the University of Wisconsin, municipal universities, and local or state-supported colleges such as Dade County Community College. The third-sector (private or independent) colleges and universities vary from wealthy, well-known institutions such as Harvard and Stanford to hundreds of colleges known mostly to their alumni and local communities.

The university presidents and chancellors are faced with a multitude of objectives, many of which are hard to measure. These include effective teaching, the creation and dissemination of research, and service to society, not to mention the unofficial goals such as developing winning sports teams. The president's strategic management also involves a board of regents (often prominent citizens or alumni), faculty with tenure, the professional staff (sometimes unionized), and sometimes a militant student body. Funds come from tuition, research grants, donations, legislatures, and ancillary operations such as dormitories, the food service, the bookstore, bowl games, and television stations.

Universities are faced with serious strategic challenges from time to time. California universities in the public sector faced the challenge of Proposition 13. All universities face the reality of a significant decline in the number of students in the 1980s because of a lower birthrate.

Strategic management offers some sources of help for universities. Several writers have described effective strategic management for colleges and universities not too differently from the approach of this chapter. And there is one case study which indicates that success and failure do result from the strategies chosen. For example, the past successes of Swarthmore, Antioch, and Reed Colleges have been attributed to the strategic management of these institutions. New York University is financially and educationally sounder because of President Sawhill's turnaround strategy in the late 1970s. And Beloit College has survived because of its turnaround strategy. It is possible to identify specific strategies of colleges. For example, the New School for Social Research has flourished because of its approach to adult education.

Outside the United States, most universities, schools, and hospitals are owned and financed by the government. In these cases there is little direct fund raising or ''market''-support activity. But strategic decisions are required there too. Since long-term financial support decisions are based on factors such as population and on performance criteria such as student-staff and patient-staff ratios, strategic plans are also important for their success. And in western Europe, some mergers have taken place among these institutions.

Strategic Management of Churches and Synagogues [18]

Like their less ''holy'' peers, churches and synagogues face environmental challenges and internal problems. There are approximately 300 national church and synagogue bodies and hundreds of thousands of local churches and synagogues.

Priests, ministers, or rabbis are sometimes subject to a hierarchy of bishops or central headquarters. Sometimes they face a church or synagogue board. Their income comes from gifts and endowments. Membership fluctuates as member values, the local community, and the internal organization change. For example, *Fortune* reported on the financial problems of Roman Catholic religious orders. Their membership has declined rapidly, and remaining members tend to be older, while the orders' fixed costs such as those for buildings or pensions are increasing.

Various experts have shown how strategic management can help improve church and synagogue performance. Adair has reported on how the Church of England (Anglican church) has tried strategic management to stem its decline in participation and membership. Hussey has helped outline and implement a strategic management system for a small Methodist church; and Reimnetz, a Lutheran pastor, has shown how a strategic management system helped church educational services.

Strategic Management of Arts Organizations [19]

Most of the arts organizations in the United States are small "businesses," with relatively few employees. Symphonies, opera companies, ballet troupes and other dance companies, theater groups, and museums are the most typical. Many of these enterprises hire people for part-time rather than full-time work.

The managers of these institutions have a difficult time generating financial support from ticket sales, gifts, and grants. Ancillary businesses, such as stores, have been used to supplement revenues. The managers' titles vary from curator to impressario. Most of these institutions survive because of the talent and dedication of their leaders. Success also comes from a dedicated and competent group of volunteers who substitute for paid employees and help raise money.

Relatively little has been written about strategic management of the arts. But a couple of writers have shown how strategic management can help make the arts organization more effective too.

Strategic Management in the Public Sector [20]

The public sector includes all enterprises whose major direct source of funds is a government body. Most often, these enterprises are owned by the government. Sometimes they are quasi-independent corporations such as the U.S. Postal Service, Air Canada, and Conrail.

Public enterprises sometimes pursue objectives different from those of private- and third-sector enterprises. Public managers must be able to deal with more complex internal and external environments than private- and third-sector managers. The hierarchy to which public managers are responsible is usually divided among executive (mayor or city manager, governor, prime minister, president) and legislative (Parliament, Congress, legislature, city council) branches. And out-of-office politicians and the press seek to expose the public managers. (They are called "inefficient bureaucrats" by these two groups.)

Politicians can interfere with the public manager's job. Often, they want the merit system to be bent according to their will. This is a remnant of the spoils system. Voters organize into pressure groups to influence the executive and legislative bodies and thus the public managers. These characteristics of the public manager's job and environment should lead you to conclude that strategic management is much more complex and difficult in the public sector, which is indeed the case.

Despite the difficulty, some analyses provide clues for effective strategic management in the public sector. At the federal level, the Tennessee Valley Authority prospered because of good strategy. And James Webb was an excellent strategist for NASA. Strategic management could be used by the Congress, and it could be improved at the federal level, according to several authors.

Strategic management can be practiced at the state and provincial levels. George Romney used strategic management while he was the governor of Michigan. Michael Howlett, a professional politician, and Muskin, an academic, provide some useful information for initiating and implementing strategic management at this level. Finally, at the local level, strategic management makes sense too. It works in city government, according to some writers.

A special case of strategic management in the public sector involves the military. Probably the first major institutions engaged in strategic management were the military organizations. Earlier works on business strategy used many terms developed by such military theorists as von Clausewitz; these terms have been used recently to describe marketing tactics. It is generally recognized that much of the success of the great generals of history was due to their strategic planning. You would probably not know about generals such as Rommell and MacArthur without the strategic planning done by themselves and their staffs. Of course, the implementation of strategy also affects success in the military setting.

Strategic Management in Other Settings [21]

Little is known about the strategic management of unions, political parties, independent research institutes, charities, and interest groups. Other institutions rise or fall partly because of the effectiveness or weakness of their strategies. There are no more Whig or Federalist political parties. Some unions such as the Knights of Labor and the IWW did not succeed. The literature is just beginning on the strategic management of these groups but is developing well for the strategic management of libraries. Much more work must be done in these settings. However, it appears fruitful to encourage this work to make these enterprises more effective and responsive to societal needs.

This appendix should lead you to conclude that strategic management can contribute to the meeting of objectives in the not-for-profit and public sectors. Those interested in these sectors should gain from this book too.

Strategic Management Around the World [22]

It appears that the factors affecting strategic management in countries other than the United States and Canada include educational, behavioral, legal and political, and economic factors. After reading, traveling, and thinking about this issue, we find it useful to think about effective strategic management by dividing the world into three categories. Chapter 4 will present another scheme to categorize countries according to types of resources they have, since this takes on strategic significance as the international environment is analyzed.

Fully Developed Countries

The fully developed nations' economic, educational, behavioral, and legal and political conditions are most like those in the United States and Canada. Basically these countries include Australia and New Zealand, Israel, South Africa, Japan, and most European countries (United Kingdom, West Germany, France, Austria, U.S.S.R., Belgium, Luxembourg, the Netherla· Switzerland, Italy, Sweden, Norway, Denmark, and Finland).

A quick glance at this list indicates that there are significant political differences (U.S.S.R. versus West Germany), cultural differences (Israel versus Japan), and other differences among this group.

References for this section indicate that the *processes* used by managers in these developed countries are more similar to than different from the processes used in the United States and Canada. However, the content or outcome of strategic choices varies due to the factors just mentioned. Thus more U.S. managers are trying to learn why the Japanese have become more successful in world markets.

Developing Countries

Very little has been written about strategic management practices in developing countries such as Brazil, Mexico, Argentina, Venezuela, Chile, Spain, Portugal, Nigeria, Saudi Arabia, Iran, Libya, Taiwan, India, Greece, Singapore, Korea, China, and most of eastern Europe (especially Yugoslavia, East Germany, Rumania, Czechoslovakia, and Poland). In some of these countries, however, with planned economies, we would expect that long-range planning concepts are in use.

Third-World Countries

We know almost nothing about strategic management in the 90 or so third-world countries such as Egypt, Upper Volta, Bolivia, Burma, Pakistan, and the Philippines. It is suspected that relatively little strategic management goes on in these countries and little in the developing countries. But there are sophisticated firms in countries such as Brazil, Mexico, Venezuela, Saudi Arabia, and Iran.

It appears that the material in this book is directly relevant to developed countries and the more sophisticated firms in the developing and third-world countries. As we move to a more global economy, our expectation is that more firms will begin to use the concepts outlined in this book, tailored to the unique circumstances faced by each. That's why we have added an extended discussion on the international environment in Chapter 4.

REFERENCES

[1] Basic References about Strategic Thinking

Ansoff, H. I.: *Implementing Strategic Management* (Englewood Cliffs, N.J.: Prentice-Hall, 1985).

Abell, D. F.: *Defining the Business: The Starting Point of Strategic Planning* (Englewood Cliffs, N.J.: Prentice-Hall, 1980).

Hofer, C., and D. Schendel: *Strategy Formulation: Analytical Concepts* (St. Paul, Minn.: West, 1978).

[2] The Evolution and Definition of Strategic Management

Ansoff, H. I.: "Strategy Formulation as a Learning Process: An Applied Managerial Theory of Strategic Behavior," *International Studies of Management & Organization,* vol. 7 (Summer 1977), pp. 58–77.

Ginter, P. M., and D. D. White: "A Social Learning Approach to Strategic Management: Toward a Theoretical Foundation," *Academy of Management Review,* vol. 7 (1982), pp. 253–261.

Hall, W. K.: "SBUs: Hot, New Topic in the Management of Diversification," *Business Horizons,* vol. 21 (February 1978), pp. 17–25.

Kudla, R. J.: "Elements of Effective Corporate Planning," *Long Range Planning,* vol. 9, no. 4 (August 1976), pp. 82–93.

[3] Strategic Management for Multiple SBU Firms

Ellis, J. E.: "Ward's Makes a Desperate Move Uptown," *Business Week,* Aug. 26, 1985, pp. 34–35.

Lorange, P.: *Corporate Planning: An Executive Viewpoint* (Englewood Cliffs, N.J.: Prentice-Hall, 1980).

Vancil, R. F.: "Strategy Formulation in Complex Organizations," *Sloan Management Review,* vol. 17 (Winter 1976), pp. 1–18.

[4] Defining Strategy

Boswell, J. S.: *Business Policies in the Making* (London: George, Allen & Unwin, 1983).

Chaffee, E. E.: "Three Models of Strategy," *Academy of Management Review,* vol. 10 (1985), pp. 89–98.

Hobbs, J. M., and D. R. Heany: "Coupling Strategy to Operating Plans," *Harvard Business Review,* vol. 55 (May–June 1977), pp. 119–126.

Porter, M. E.: *Competitive Strategy* (New York: Free Press, 1985).

Shirley, R. C., "Limiting the Scope of Strategy: A Decision Based Approach," *Academy of Management Review,* vol. 7 (1982), pp. 262–268.

Smith, R. B.: "The 21st Century Corporation," speech to the Economics Club of Detroit, Sept. 9, 1985.

[5] The Use of Strategic Management

Barnes, J. H.: "Cognitive Biases and Their Impact on Strategic Planning," *Strategic Management Journal,* vol. 5 (1984), pp. 129–137.

Boulton, W. R., S. G. Franklin, W. M. Lindsay, and L. W. Rue: "How Are Companies Planning Now?—A Survey," *Long Range Planning,* vol. 15 (1982), pp. 82–86.

Capon, N., J. V. Farley, and J. Hulbert: "International Diffusion of Corporate and Strategic Planning Practices," *Columbia Journal of World Business,* vol. 15 (Fall 1980), pp. 5–13.

Curtis, D. A. (ed.): *Strategic Planning for Smaller Business* (Boston: Heath, 1983).

Henry, H. W.: "Then and Now: A Look at Strategic Planning Systems," *Journal of Business Strategy,* vol. 1 (Winter 1981), pp. 64–69.

"Publisher's Memo," *Business Week* (January 9, 1978).

[6] The Value of Strategic Management

Bresser, R. K., and R. C. Bishop: "Dysfunctional Effects of Formal Planning," *Academy of Management Review,* vol. 8 (1984), pp. 588–599.

Camillus, J. A.: "Strategic Planning Systems in the Eighties," paper presented at the Strategic Management Society Conference, 1984.

Miller, D.: "Common Syndromes of Business Failure," *Business Horizons,* vol. 20 (November 1977), pp. 43–53.

Saunders, C. B. and F. D. Tuggle: as answered by David Hussey, "Who Says Planners Don't?" *Long Range Planning* (October 1977), pp. 83–85.

[7] Some Summaries of Strategic Management Research

Anderson, C., and F. Paine: "PIMS: A Reexamination," *Academy of Management Review* (July 1978), pp. 602–612.

Hofer, C.: "Research on Strategic Planning," *Journal of Economics and Business,* vol. 28 (Spring–Summer 1976), pp. 261–286.

Lamb, R. B. (ed.): *Advances in Strategic Management,* vol. 1–3 (Eastchester, N.Y.: JAI Press, 1983, 1985).

Schendel, D. E. and C. W. Hofer: *Strategic Management: A New View of Business Policy and Planning* (Boston: Little, Brown, 1979).

[8] Formal Planning and Organization Success

Armstrong, J. S.: "The Value of Formal Planning for Strategic Decisions," *Strategic Management Journal,* vol. 3 (1982), pp. 197–212.

Baird, I. S.: "Assessing the Effectiveness of Planning Systems," paper presented at the Academy of Management Meetings, 1984.

Donham, W.: "Essential Groundwork for a Broad Executive Theory," *Harvard Business Review,* vol. 1 (October 1922), pp. 1–10.

Frederickson, J. W.: "The Comprehensiveness of Strategic Decision Processes," *Academy of Management Journal,* vol. 27 (1984), pp. 445–466.

Kudla, R. J.: "The Effects of Strategic Planning on Common Stock Returns," *Academy of Management Journal,* vol. 23 (1980), pp. 5–20.

Robinson, R. B., and J. A. Pearce: "The Impact of Formalized Strategic Planning on Financial Performance in Small Organizations," *Strategic Management Journal,* vol. 4 (1983), pp. 197–207.

[9] Rational Decision Models

Beach, L. R., and T. R. Mitchell: "A Contingency Model for the Selection of Decision Strategies," *Academy of Management Review,* vol. 3 (July 1978), pp. 439–449.

Eilon, S.: "More Against Optimization," *Omega,* vol. 5 (1977), pp. 627–633.

Lenz, R. T., and M. A. Lyles: "Paralysis by Analysis: Is Your Planning System Becoming Too Rational?" *Long Range Planning,* vol. 18 (August 1985), pp. 64–72.

——— and ———: "Crippling Effects of 'Hyper-Rational' Planning," working paper 956, College of Commerce, University of Illinois, 1983.

Murray, M.: *Decisions: A Comparative Critique* (Marshfield, Mass.: Pitman, 1986).

Simon, H. A.: *Administrative Behavior* (New York: Free Press, 1957).

[10] Intuitive Decision Making

Isaack, T.: "Intuition: An Ignored Dimension of Management," *Academy of Management Review,* vol. 3 (October 1978), pp. 917–922.

Mintzberg, H.: "Planning on the Left Side and Managing on the Right," *Harvard Business Review,* vol. 54 (July–August 1976), pp. 49–58.

Rowan, R.: "Managerial Hunches and Intuition," *Fortune,* Apr. 23, 1979, pp. 111 + .

———.: *The Intuitive Manager* (Boston: Little, Brown, 1986).

[11] Political Decision Theory

Dill, W. R.: "Strategic Planning in a Kibitzer's World," in Ansoff, Declerk, Hays (eds.). *From Strategic Planning to Strategic Management* (New York: Wiley, 1976), pp. 125–136.

Freeman, R. E.: *Strategic Management: A Stakeholder Approach* (Boston: Pitman, 1984).

Gray, B., and S. S. Ariss: "Politics and Strategic Changes Across Organizational Life Cycles," *Academy of Management Review,* vol. 10 (1985), pp. 707–723.

MacMillan, I. C.: *Strategy Formulation: Political Concepts* (St. Paul, Minn.: West, 1978).

Mitroff, I. I.: *Stakeholders of the Organizational Mind* (San Francisco: Jossey-Bass, 1984).

Narayanan, V. K., and L. Fahey: "The Micro-Politics of Strategy Formulation," *Academy of Management Review,* vol. 7 (1982), pp. 25–34.

Pfeffer, J.: *Power in Organizations* (Marchfield, Mass.: Pitman, 1981).

[12] Techniques to Integrate Decision Modes

Hart, S., M. Boroush, G. Enk, and W. Hornick: "Managing Complexity Through Consensus Mapping," *Academy of Management Review,* vol. 10 (1985) pp. 587–600.

Ramaprasad, A. and E. Poon: "A Computerized Interactive Technique for Mapping Influence Diagrams," *Strategic Management Journal,* vol. 6 (1985), pp. 377–392.

Schweiger, D. M., and P. A. Finger: "The Comparative Effectiveness of Dialectical Inquiry and Devil's Advocacy," *Strategic Management Journal,* vol. 5 (1984), pp. 335–350.

———, W. R. Sandberg, and J. W. Ragan: "Group Approaches for Improving Strategic Decision Making," *Academy of Management Journal,* vol. 29 (1986), pp. 51–71.

Schwenk, C. R.: "Effects of Planning Aids and Presentation Media on Performance and Affective Responses in Strategic Decision Making," *Management Science,* vol. 3 (1984), pp. 263–272.

Welles, C.: "What's Next for the Unpredictable Bill Ziff?" *Business Week,* Apr. 14, 1986, pp. 102–106.

[13] Integrative Decision Making

Burgelman, R. A.: "On the Interplay of Process and Content in Internal Corporate Ventures," *Academy of Management Proceedings* (1984), pp. 2–6.

Carter, E. E.: "Project Evaluations and Firm Decisions," *The Journal of Management Studies* (1971), pp. 253–279.

Cosier, R. A.: "Dialectical Inquiry in Strategic Planning: A Case of Premature Acceptance?" *Academy of Management Review,* vol. 6 (October 1981), pp. 643–648.

Donaldson, G., and J. W. Lorsch: *Decision Making at the Top* (New York: Basic Books, 1983).

Hambrick, D. C., and S. Finkelstein: "Managerial Discretion," in B. Staw and L. L. Cummings (eds.). *Research in Organizational Behavior,* vol. 9 (Eastchester, N.Y.: JAI Press, 1987).

Lindblom, C. E.: *The Policy Making Process* (Englewood Cliffs, N.J.: Prentice-Hall, 1980).

Mason, R. O., and I. I. Mitroff: *Challenging Strategic Planning Assumptions* (New York: Wiley, 1981).

Miller, D. H., and P. H. Friesen: *Organizations: A Quantum View* (Englewood Cliffs, N.J.: Prentice-Hall, 1984).

Mintzberg, H., and J. A. Waters: "Of Strategies, Deliberate and Emergent," *Strategic Management Journal,* vol. 6 (1985), pp. 257–272.

Murray, E. A.: "Strategic Choice as a Negotiated Outcome," *Management Science,* vol. 24 (May 1978), pp. 960–972.

Murray, M.: *Decisions: A Comparative Critique* (Cambridge, Mass.: Ballinger, 1986).

Quinn, J. B.: *Strategies for Change: Logical Incrementalism* (Homewood, Ill.: Irwin, 1980).

[14] Timing in Strategic Management

Ansoff, H. I.: "Managing Strategic Surprise by Response to Weak Signals," *California Management Review,* vol. 18 (Winter 1975), pp. 21–33.

Bedeian, A. G., and W. F. Glueck: *Management* (Elmhurst, Ill.: Dryden, 1983).

Camillus, J. C.: "Reconciling Logical Incrementalism and Synoptic Formalism—An Integrated Approach to Designing Strategic Planning Processes," *Strategic Management Journal,* vol. 3 (1982), pp. 277–283.

Graham, R.: "The Timing of Radical Organizational Change: The Revitalization Process at AT&T," working paper, Wharton School, University of Pennsylvania, 1981.

Leff, N. H.: "What You Don't Know Can Hurt You," *Business Week,* Mar. 14, 1983, p. 12.

Maremont, M.: "How Western Union Went from Bad to Worse," *Business Week,* Jan. 28, 1985, pp. 110–116.

Priest, A. L.: "Why Corporate Stock Buybacks Don't Really Pay Off," *Business Week,* June 25, 1984, pp. 33.

Tushman, M. L., W. H. Newman, and E. Romanelli: "Convergence and Upheaval," working paper S.C. #49, Graduate School of Business, Columbia University, 1985.

"What Deregulation Has Done to the Truckers," *Business Week,* Nov. 9, 1981, pp. 70+.

[15] Users of Strategic Management

Hatten, M. L., "Strategic Management in Not-for-Profit Organizations," *Strategic Management Journal,* vol. 3 (1982), pp. 89–104.

Hay, R. D.: *Strategic Management for Non-Profit Organizations* (Santa Barbara, Calif.: Kinko's, 1986).

Lachman, R.: "Public and Private Sector Differences," *Academy of Management Journal,* vol. 28 (1985), pp. 671–680.

Nutt, P. C.: "A Strategic Planning Network for Nonprofit Organizations," *Strategic Management Journal,* vol. 5 (1984), pp. 57–75.

Ring, P. S. and J. L. Perry: "Strategic Management in Public and Private Organizations," *Academy of Management Review,* vol. 10 (1985), pp. 276–286.

Unterman, I., and R. H. Davis: "The Strategy Gap in Not-for-Profit," *Harvard Business Review,* (May–June, 1982), pp. 30–40.

[16] Hospitals Use Strategic Management

Carper, W. B., and R. J. Litschert: "A Comparative Analysis of Strategic Power Hierarchies in For Profit and Not-For-Profit Hospitals," paper presented at the Academy of Management meeting, 1982.
———— and ————: "Strategic Power Relationships in Contemporary Profit and Nonprofit Hospitals," *Academy of Management Journal,* vol. 26 (1983), pp. 311–320.
Webber, J., and M. Dula: "Effective Planning Committees in Hospitals," *Harvard Business Review* (May–June 1974), pp. 133–142.

[17] Universities Apply Strategic Management

Clark, B., and M. Trow: "The Organizational Context," in T. Newcomb and E. Wilson (eds.), *College Peer Groups* (Chicago: Aldine, 1966).
Doyle, P., and J. Lynch: "Long Range Planning for Universities," *Long Range Planning,* vol. 9 (December 1976), pp. 30–46.
Huff, A. S., and J. M. Ranney: "Assessing the Environment for an Educational Institution," *Long Range Planning,* vol. 14 (1981), pp. 107–115.
Thomas, R.: "Corporate Strategic Planning in a University," *Long Range Planning,* vol. 13 (1980), pp. 70–78.

[18] Religious Groups Use Strategic Management

Adair, J.: "Formulating Strategy for the Church of England," *Journal of Business Policy,* vol. 3 (1973), pp. 3–12.
Hussey, D.: "Corporate Planning for a Church," *Long Range Planning,* vol. 7 (April 1974), pp. 61–64.
Reimnetz, C.: "Testing a Planning and Control Model in Non Profit Organizations," *Academy of Management Journal* (March 1972).
Wasdell, D.: "Long Range Planning and the Church," *Long Range Planning,* vol. 13 (June 1980), pp. 99–108.

[19] Arts Organizations Apply Strategic Management

Margolis, S., and J. Traub: "Business Comes to the Arts," *The MBA* (March 1978), pp. 11–25.
Raymond, T., and S. Greyser: "The Business of Managing the Arts," *Harvard Business Review* (July–August 1978), pp. 123–132.

[20] Strategic Management in the Public Sector

Cartwright, J.: "Corporate Planning in Local Government," *Long Range Planning* (April 1975), pp. 46–50.
East, R. J.: "Comparison of Strategic Planning in Large Corporations and Government," *Long Range Planning,* vol. 5 (1972).
Howlett, M.: "Strategic Planning in State Government," *Managerial Planning* (November–December 1975), pp. 10–16; 24ff.
Muskin, S.: "Policy Analysis in State and Community," *Public Administration Review,* vol. 37 (May–June 1977), pp. 245–253.

[21] Strategic Management in Other Organizations

Keating, B. P., and M. O. Keating: "Goal Setting and Efficiency in Social Service Agencies," *Long Range Planning,* vol. 14 (1981), pp. 40–48.

Kennington, D.: "Long Range Planning for Public Libraries—A Delphi Study," *Long Range Planning,* vol. 10 (April 1977), pp. 73–78.

McGrath, W.: *Development of a Long Range Strategic Plan for a University Library* (Ithaca, N.Y.: Cornell University Libraries, 1976).

[22] Strategic Management in Other Countries

Bazzaz, S. J., and P. H. Grinyer: "Corporate Planning in the U.K.: The State of the Art in the 70s," *Strategic Management Journal,* vol. 2 (April–June, 1981), pp. 155–168.

Gotcher, J. W.: "Strategic Planning in European Multinationals," *Long Range Planning* (October 1977), pp. 7–13.

Hayashi, K.: "Corporate Planning Practices in Japanese Multinationals," *Academy of Management Journal,* vol. 21 (1978), pp. 211–226.

"Progress in Planning: An International Review," Special Issue of *Long Range Planning,* vol. 15 (1982).

"The Stalled Soviet Economy: Bogged Down by Planning," *Business Week,* Oct. 19, 1981, pp. 72–83.

STRATEGIC MANAGEMENT ELEMENTS

CHAPTER OUTLINE

STRATEGIC MANAGEMENT ELEMENTS

OBJECTIVES

- To understand the roles of the general manager
- To learn who the strategists of an enterprise are, how these groups relate to each other, and how the strategists affect the strategic management process
- To understand what mission and objectives are, how they are formed and change, and how they relate to the strategic management process

INTRODUCTION

Our discussion of strategic management begins with an analysis of the strategic management elements: the strategists who are involved in the process and the mission and objectives of the enterprise. We also apply some of the decision-making concepts discussed in Chapter 1 as they relate to the formation of objectives. Exhibit 2.1 presents the model of strategic management, highlighting the chapter's focus. We will elaborate on these elements and integrate them into their place in the strategic management process. We begin by defining the actors in the process of strategic management—those involved with strategic decisions and actions. Then we move to the starting point of the process—mission and objectives.

THE GENERAL MANAGER—MORE THAN JUST A STRATEGIST [1]

General managers are key players in the strategic management process. Before discussing the particular strategic roles they play, we find it useful to determine who the

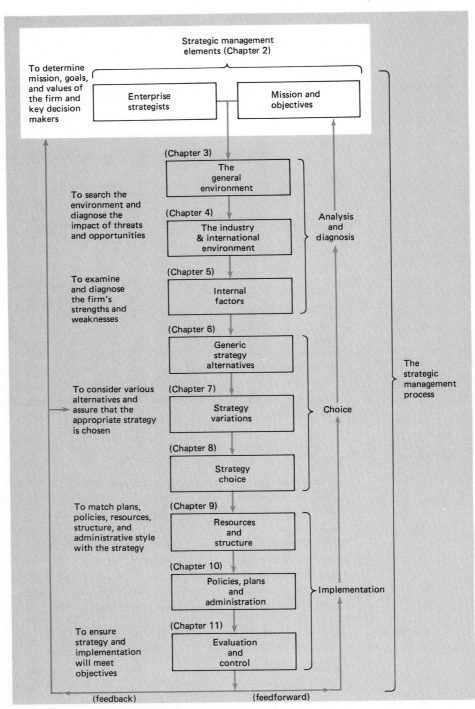

EXHIBIT 2.1 **A model of strategic management.**

general managers are and what they do in organizations, for they are more than just strategists.

The general managers of a firm are executives at the pinnacle of the enterprise or SBUs who are responsible for the survival and success of the corporation. They have titles such as chairman of the board, president, senior vice president, executive vice president, and vice president. If the business is divided into strategic business units or operating divisions, then the persons at the top of these units are also general managers.

But who are these people called general managers (GM), and what do they do? A 1976 study of general managers in the top 500 U.S. corporations revealed the following profile based on the most frequently found characteristics. The typical GM was a male who made over $200,000 a year. He was about 60 years old and probably graduated from college but did not take advanced work. He probably came from a working-class family and worked his way through the marketing part of the organization.

Yet such a profile tells us little. Other backgrounds and ways to the top may depend on economic conditions and strategies of the organization. For instance, in the late 1970s many corporations became more interested in profit margins than in building up their market share or entering new businesses; this led to an increase in the number of GMs promoted from the controllers' ranks.

While a 1982 study found little differences from those of the 1976 study, other conditions are changing the face of corporate elites. A record number of acquisitions, mergers, and proxy battles have squeezed out "redundant" managers. Foreign competition and slower-growing domestic markets have also forced out some managers. Accelerated technological change requires general managers with different skills. And deregulation has created major change for formerly protected companies. Hence, old-line traditional industrial leaders are being displaced by high-tech entrepreneurs (Steven Jobs, formerly of Apple, An Wang of Wang Laboratories), service gurus (Donald Burr of People Express, William McGowan of MCI), corporate rejuvenators (Lee Iacocca of Chrysler, John Welch of General Electric), and asset shufflers (T. Boone Pickens of Mesa Limited Partners). These individuals, and others like them, are having an impact on corporate direction, and are serving as new role models for other chief executives and general managers. They have often founded their own firms, are on the frontiers of deregulated industries, are saving smokestack industries by borrowing skills and values from entrepreneurs, or are shifting assets and consolidating the old economic base. With an economy in transition, new people such as these are emerging as general managers.

Still, the general manager needs a variety of skills and has many roles to play, just as they have always had. Top-level jobs are assumed to require more emphasis on conceptual skills with less need for human relations or administrative skills and low requirements for technical abilities. The jobs of lower-level managers are seen as emphasizing technical requirements without much need for conceptual ability. So the skill mix changes with the demands of the job. Top managers are urged to be generalists rather than specialists. While this approach has some value in helping us understand managers and their jobs, we still must ask, What does the GM do?

WHAT DO GMs DO?

The traditional impression is that the GM is a reflective thinker who maps out strategy, designs an organization to implement the plan, and guides troops through the necessary maneuvers to accomplish objectives using vast experience and insight. The GM is the entrepreneur (sets goals), strategist (plans), organization builder (organizes), leader (directs), and chief implementer (controls). The task is to lead the firm or SBU through uncharted territory in less-than-certain circumstances.

These tasks may not be so neatly compartmentalized as you might suspect. Human, technical, economic, and political circumstances are only partly subject to rational analysis. The general manager must integrate pieces of a puzzle, some of which may be missing, distorted, or not even yet made, and most of which are continuously changing. According to the Harvard Business School, general-management leadership "requires judgment, courage, empathy, the ability to articulate and persuade."

Exhibit 2.2 contrasts what general managers actually do with what theorists say they should do. The studies indicate that the general manager must simultaneously handle several different activities on a schedule which provides little time for contemplation. In the process, intuition and judgment become the preferred decision-making models. Mintzberg's list of roles provides an example of the different types of activities a GM may be asked to perform. Let's use his categories of interpersonal, informational, and decisional roles to guide the discussion.

Interpersonal Roles   As the symbolic *figurehead* of the organization, the GM performs numerous routine ceremonial duties of a legal or social nature. This is often important in legitimizing the firm to outsiders. As a *leader,* the GM has responsibility for staffing the organization and training and motivating subordinates. In the *liaison*

EXHIBIT 2.2   A CONTRAST OF THEORY AND RESEARCH ON THE GENERAL MANAGER (GM)

Areas	The research says that general managers	The theorists say that general managers should
1 Time allocations	Avoid spending great amounts of time on one issue	Spend concentrated time to get results
2 Time horizons	Seek activities that are current, preferring "hot" information	Formulate effective strategies that require consideration of major current and future trends
3 Information sources	Prefer verbal sources and avoid documented information	Formulate effective strategies that require thorough environmental and organizational analysis
4 Planning processes	Discuss strategy in meetings, but such work is fragmented and lacks focus	Formulate effective strategies that require commitment, focus, and concentrated effort
5 Basic purposes	Have work that is fragmented with no concentration of effort or pattern of activities	Have as a basic purpose that of establishing organizational goals and developing the strategies needed to achieve them

Source: Adapted from C. W. Hofer, and C. N. Toftoy, "How CEOs Set Strategic Direction for Their Organizations," paper presented at the Academy of Management Meeting, 1984.

role the manager maintains a network of outside contacts to obtain favors and information. Note that the GM can accomplish liaison tasks while engaged in activities related to the figurehead role.

Informational Roles   In the role of *monitor,* managers read periodicals and reports, make plant tours, or observe meetings to seek information about the organization and its environment. As a *disseminator,* the GM transmits much of the information received to outsiders and insiders. Information about the organization is also transmitted to outsiders through the mail, phone calls, or board meetings as the manager acts as a *spokesperson* for the organization. Once again, note how the liaison, leader, or figurehead role can do double duty for the collection and distribution of information.

Decision Roles   As an *entrepreneur,* the GM performs strategic functions of initiating projects to take advantage of opportunities. Strategy and review meetings are conducted to do this and to correct problems or solve crises when the role shifts to that of *disturbance handler.* As *resource allocators,* managers authorize budgets and approve requests for the allocation of human, monetary, and material resources. Finally, the top manager is responsible for representing the organization as a *negotiator* for contracts with labor unions, major suppliers, or major customers.

In effect, the GM must spend substantial amounts of time in being the organizational leader and personal leader and in communicating with stakeholders outside and inside the organization. This would seem to leave little room for involvement with strategic planning or for service as the ''architect of organization purpose.'' Yet this role seems to encompass all the others.

The formulation of strategy, goals, and plans for implementation is often considered the exclusive realm of the general manager. Yet many different individuals may be involved in the strategic management process. *Boards of directors,* who review the results of the strategies and *chief executive officers,* are the main corporate-level strategists. *Corporate planning staffs* help top managers in planning and implementing the strategies, and *consultants* may be hired to help corporate planners or do the corporate planning work if there is no corporate planning staff. *General managers* of strategic business units and *lower-level participants* are also involved with goal setting and strategy formation and implementation. So our next sections focus on the strategic management role of these participants in the process.

CORPORATE-LEVEL STRATEGISTS

The board of directors and chief executive officers (CEOs) are the primary groups involved with corporate-level strategy making. In the special case of start-ups or family-owned businesses, the entrepreneur is both the general manager and chief strategist. This section describes the role of these groups in the strategic management process.

The Board of Directors and Strategic Management [2]

The ultimate legal authority in businesses is that of the board of directors. In other institutions, equivalent boards (e.g., trustees) have similar authority. Boards are held responsible to the stockholders for the following duties: ensuring the continuity of management (replacing or retiring ineffective managers); protecting the use of stock-holders' resources; ensuring that managers take prudent action regarding corporate objectives; approving major financial and operational decisions of the managers; representing the company with other organizations and bodies in society; maintaining, revising, and enforcing the corporate charter and bylaws.

The board is legally mandated to control the organization and be centrally concerned with maintaining operations and effectiveness. It is often seen as the representative of the owners, so knowledge of the organization's operations, business acumen, and industry perspective are key prerequisites for membership.

Until the 1960s, many boards consisted mainly or exclusively of top-level managers. Obviously, these "inside" boards would simply ratify their own decisions. But more boards have accepted "outside" members, and some boards have a majority of outsiders. Some boards are even taking on leaders of labor unions with which they deal.

Are outside boards any different from inside boards? Maybe. Some outsiders are selected simply because they are friends of top managers or because they represent a minority group. If one assumes that executives don't wish to provide information detrimental to their own policies or proposals, a passive outsider may act much the same as an insider. According to one official of the Securities and Exchange Commission (SEC), "We saw directors treated like mushrooms—something you keep in the dark and heap manure on."

In the past, most boards were not actively involved in the strategic management of firms except in times of crisis, when their major act was to replace the chief executive. Now, outside boards are becoming more active for several reasons. First, shareholder suits have increasingly charged directors with failure to fulfill their responsibilities. (The Penn Central bankruptcy is credited with precipitating these actions.) Second, the New York Stock Exchange has required its members to form audit committees composed of *outside directors,* and most of the largest U.S. corporations now have these committees. Third, the SEC has increased investigations of the negligence and misconduct of directors. Fourth, the 1977 Foreign Corrupt Practices Act requires directors to be alert to political payoffs by corporations.

Membership on boards is increasingly being used as a means to more closely link the corporation to other organizations. For instance, to obtain a large loan the company may "elect" a banker to the board. Even competitors may be on the board, although this is prohibited by the Clayton Act of 1914. And those representing powerful political interests may be seated on the board.

The increase in outsiders has paralleled changes in the structure of many boards. Many boards have created nominating committees for recruiting and selecting new *outside* directors. There has been an increase in audit committees even though management still controls the source of the data. Outside directors are being paid more, and nonbusiness groups are more active in demanding representation. Overall, there has been a subtle but important shift in board membership and management control. Activists are replacing mushrooms.

Nonetheless, the percentage of outside directors on boards of the largest 1000 industrial companies dropped in 1986 to 57 percent from 63 percent in 1985. The cost or unavailability of liability insurance and the increasing time burdens due to a wave of takeovers and divestitures have made the director's job less appealing to many.

Can the Board Actively Pursue Strategy Formulation? [3]

With more active outsiders, more boards are involved with linking strategy with subsequent corporate action. They are beginning to support new strategies, attract resources, and protect the organization from outside threats. For instance, the outside directors at Mead Corporation helped management fight off a takeover attempt. As the board is used to link the company with powerful outsiders, even more outsiders may be selected.

Boards are likely to become more active in evaluating corporate strategy and performance. With more active outside members with managerial experience, boards may become more than rubber stamps in evaluating major strategic changes. And they are likely to evaluate corporate performance on both financial and nonfinancial grounds. The board rarely runs the company. Yet the power of the board in strategic formulation is often apparent when ''strategic decision points'' are reached. That is, the board is important with respect to issues of mission and identity (e.g., approving mergers) or the selection of a new chief executive officer. Indeed, the greatest power most boards (and stockholders) have to influence strategy rests in their ability to remove a CEO and appoint a new one.

To the extent that outside directors continue their recent decline in number and directors act with an eye toward preventing personal liability, active questioning and scrutiny of executives' strategic recommendations may suffer. And efforts to make boards effective guardians of shareholder interests may fail.

Effective strategists discuss their strategies with the board to find out how the board feels about their stewardship. But the primary active role in strategic management remains with the top manager of the firm, and many top managers are members of the board.

The CEO as Strategist [4]

Crucial to the success of strategic management is the role of the corporate-level general manager: the chief executive officer (CEO). The CEO is responsible for defining what business the firm is in and matching the best product-market opportunities with the best use of the enterprise's resources. This person must conceptualize the strategy and then initiate and maintain the strategic management process.

It has been argued that the large number of work interruptions and variety of demands from the roles of the general manager described earlier do not allow the CEO time for reflective thinking or planning on the job. Managers have a great deal to do. Planning is only one of several activities competing for a manager's attention. Planning often involves thinking, paperwork, and time alone. Most managers do not like or have precious little time for these activities. Managers tend to prefer to be doers, not thinkers. Further, managers prefer to act on immediate problems because they generate immediate feedback. If a customer makes a rush order and the manager helps out, the customer's thanks are given *now*. Planning deals with future events, and the rewards (if any) are deferred into the future. Most of us prefer to take our rewards now rather than later. Moreover, the number of roles expected of the manager as supergeneralist may become so difficult that it is beyond the capability of any one person. The formal experience and training of today's CEOs may not have prepared them to cope with their environment. Thus some go so far as to suggest that CEOs spend more time *managing the process* of strategic planning than they do making strategic decisions. Yet we believe that the roles played by the CEO set the tone for strategic formation.

Even though different styles will exist among organizations and CEOs, when managers devote time to specific kinds of activities, the roles overlap. In a negotiating session information may be collected and disseminated to insiders or outsiders, and decisions may be made concerning resource allocation which in effect result in strategic decisions. Thus while Mintzberg found that only 13 percent of the manager's time was devoted to strategy per se, strategic planning is intertwined with other functions. Further, he found that the CEO alone was making major key decisions about programs to solve particular problems or exploit particular opportunities. Thus the CEO is a pivotal figure in strategic formation. Moreover, managerial values (discussed later in this chapter) influence how the CEO may perform these roles (see Exhibit 2.8). Some fear that managers' values have shifted from entrepreneurial risk taking to a greater concern for the short-term bottom line. This may lead to a lack of innovation and new-product development. But the changes noted earlier may be a response to these conditions. Hence, CEO roles and values play a significant part in strategic management.

As various roles are performed, more or less emphasis on particular roles and values will influence the type of planning in the organization. In very large organizations, the emphasis may rest with resource allocation and internal negotiation to ratify decisions made at divisional levels. More time will be devoted by the CEO to figurehead or liaison functions with external groups and boards of directors. In smaller firms the entrepreneur role is likely to be of more critical importance. Let's look a little more closely at this special case.

Entrepreneurs as Strategists [5]

Entrepreneurs are individuals who start a business from scratch. Several hundred entrepreneurs do that each hour in the United States, and the pace seems to be accelerating. Financial incentives and the lure of an opportunity to make a new-product contribution seem to motivate more individuals to strike out on their own. About 95 percent of U.S. businesses are entrepreneurships or family businesses. Family businesses are of two types. *The family-operated firm* is a business whose major ownership influence is a family, and *all* or most of the key executives are family members. *A family-influenced firm* is a business whose major ownership influence is a family, and some of the key executives are family members.

The entrepreneur is the main (and in most cases the only) strategist in the entrepreneurial firm. The strategic management of a family business falls between that of entrepreneurial firms and that of corporate firms. The chief strategist of the family firm must consider the preferences of the family members who are active in the management of the firm and/or lead family members of the ownership group. These family members are part of the coalition which runs a family firm. In this way, the strategists of the family firm are somewhat like the corporate strategists. In some family firms, the chief strategist has the full support of the family, which does not interefere except in a crisis. In such cases, the family business strategist can operate much like an entrepreneur in developing a strategy.

It has been found that there are a few differences between owner-managed and publicly held companies with regard to objectives, strategies, and strategic decision factors. One significant objective that you can find in a family or entrepreneur's business is the desire to remain independent and provide an outlet for family investment and careers for the family. When the chief strategist leaves this position, a difficult transfer-of-power situation arises. Owner-managers also seem to stress sales

EXHIBIT 2.3   A FEW FAMILY BUSINESSES AS OF 1985

- Lester Crown is taking over for his ailing 89-year-old father Henry. The family has controlling interest in General Dynamics, own big blocks of stock in (and hold sway over) another half-dozen public corporations, and operate a vast portfolio of real estate holdings. Net worth is estimated at around $1.5 billion.
- Samuel C. Johnson is the chairman and chief executive of S. C. Johnson & Son, the $2 billion consumer products giant his great-grandfather founded in 1886.
- Forest Mars, Sr., still controls the candy company which makes Snickers, M&Ms, 3 Musketeers, Milky Way, and other candies.
- Sanford "Sandy" McDonnell is the CEO of Mc-Donnell Douglas in St. Louis. James "Mr. Mac" McDonnell (Sandy's uncle) is chairman of the board.
- M. G. "Jerry" O'Neill was chairman of General Tire & Rubber Co. until an outsider was brought in. His family has run the company since 1915.
- Frederick Stratton, Jr., is the chief operating officer of Briggs & Stratton Corp., producer of lawn-mower engines and other products.
- Sam M. Walton built over 817 Wal-Mart Stores,

Inc., from a single five-and dime in Newport, Arkansas. The family's 39 percent stake in Wal-Mart shares is worth about $4.2 billion.

A few other family-influenced firms you may have heard of include:
- Du Pont family: 17.5 percent of E. I. Du Pont worth $3.3 billion
- John Dorrance and family: 57.5 percent of Campbell Soup worth $2.1 billion
- David Packard: 17.2 percent of Hewlett-Packard worth $1.9 billion
- Bancroft family: 54.7 percent of Dow Jones & Co., Inc., worth $1.9 billion
- Bronfman family: 38.5 percent of Seagram Company worth $1.9 billion
- Ford family: 7.7 percent of Ford Motor Company worth $1.1 billion
- August Busch: 13 percent of Anheuser-Busch worth $85.7 million
- Joan Kroc: 8.6 percent of McDonalds worth $710 million

Source: Adapted from "The Crown Family Empire," *Business Week,* March 31, 1986, pp. 50–54; "Sam Walton of Wal-Mart," *Business Week,* Oct. 14, 1985, pp. 142–147; "Trying to Bring Out the Old Shine at Johnson Wax," *Business Week,* Aug. 13, 1984; "General Tire," *Business Week,* Feb. 13, 1984, pp. 76–80; "Where Management Style Sets Strategy," *Business Week,* Oct. 23, 1978; "Briggs and Stratton 39 Year Old Chief Begins to Alter Stodgy Image of Firm," *Wall Street Journal,* Oct. 10, 1978; "Mars," *Business Week,* Aug. 14, 1978; "Super Rich Owners of American Business," *U.S. News and World Report,* July 21, 1986, pp. 36–44.

growth, have greater use of labor than capital, and adopt a policy of charging lower prices than publicly held firms.

There are thousands of examples of entrepreneurial and family strategies and strategists. Two of the more publicized entrepreneurs you might be familiar with are Ted Turner (sports teams and cable broadcasting) and John DeLorean (bankrupt auto manufacturer). Exhibit 2.3 furnishes examples of a few more who are less notable, perhaps. And the number of these types of business leaders appears to be increasing. The business world has rediscovered some satisfaction in creating and building a company. The more humanistic values usually involved in a family business have regained their appeal along with concerns of becoming just another number in the large corporate organization. Plus, more top posts at family businesses are opening up as founders approach retirement age and their baby-boom children are ready to take over.

The control of a family business firm often evolves from the control of the previous family business executive. And the strategic management process often does involve members of the family other than the current chief strategist. While most entrepreneurs are men, increasing numbers of women are starting their own businesses. And while they are not yet a large force, more women are also emerging as venture capitalists (those who are willing to risk investing in chancy enterprises).

When an entrepreneur's organization has been successful and evolves into a large firm, the individual is often faced with a problem. The motivations and skills of starting a firm and building it are often no longer appropriate to the demands of operating the larger firm. Its challenges may call for competent managers who can see beyond the brilliance of the founder's original vision. The entrepreneurs often find that these challenges are not what interest them. At that point (which is difficult to pinpoint) it is time for new strategists to take over.

Strategists and Failure [6]

So far we have examined strategists and entrepreneurs in corporate or family firms which seem to be successful. But not all strategists are successful. What kinds of problems might cause failure?

Several analyses have found how the corporate-level strategist fails by pursuing the following defective strategies:

• *The firm fails when power-hoarding strategists create overambitious, incautious strategies which ignore environmental signals.* These strategists have not developed adequate strategic management systems.

• *The firm fails when power-hoarding strategists refuse to change the past strategy.* This again is true because these strategists do not accept advice from subordinates and don't search the environment themselves.

• *The firm fails when the chief strategists do not create a strategy.* These strategists expect the firm to run itself without a strategy.

• *The firm fails because the strategists create an overambitious strategy given the weakened resource base of the firm.* In this case, the strategists have not adequately analyzed their strategic advantages and disadvantages.

Other analyses found similar problems and suggested that managers were preoccupied with current structural problems or improving personnel skills needed in the future. When this occurs, we usually find that management succession results, or the family business is sold. A later Exhibit (2.9) provides an example of executive succession after the founder of Control Data Corp. experienced difficulties. However, many executives are reluctant to let go. The thrill of having power and the feeling that no one else can do the job quite as well keep some strong-willed corporate leaders (Harry Gray of United Technologies, David Lewis of General Dynamics, Armand Hammer of Occidental Petroleum) at the helm well into their seventies or eighties in a few cases.

BUSINESS-LEVEL STRATEGISTS

We have now discussed how the top manager, sometimes in conjunction with board members, plays the major role in setting corporate-level strategy. Four other groups of individuals are potentially involved in crucial roles in strategic management. These include SBU managers, corporate planners, consultants, and lower-level managers. Let's examine their roles in strategic management.

SBU Executives as Strategists

If a firm is organized into SBUs, the head of the SBU plays the general-manager role at the business level. If corporate strategists encourage it, SBU managers set the strategies for their units or businesses. Essentially, the SBU strategists perform roles similar to those of top managers for their businesses and attempt to get the best results in their business segment given their resources and the corporate objectives. In first-generation planning, they create multiple strategies on a contingency basis.

Earlier we indicated that entrepreneurs are involved with starting their own businesses. But the corporate world has recognized some value in establishing an entrepreneurial climate within some of their SBUs. The word often heard to describe this is "intrapreneurship." In essence, the SBU manager is encouraged to develop new ventures, or the SBU itself may be a new venture established within the existing corporation. For example, the MacIntosh computer was developed by a separate newly created unit within the Apple organization. Apple did not want to stifle the creativity or enthusiasm of this new-product development by housing it within the mainstream. However, creation of internal ventures are ultimately expected to be consolidated into the ongoing organization. As ventures grow and require new levels of investment, corporate involvement increases. Corporate procedures and objectives may conflict with the independent start-up environment of new ventures—more structure and control is introduced. Hence, the SBU manager under these circumstances plays the role of entrepreneur and strategist. As with independent entrepreneurs, SBU managers may have to be replaced when the entrepreneurial functions are completed as the venture becomes more important to corporate level.

Planners and Strategic Management [7]

Some firms, mostly large and complex ones, have provided their chief executives and SBU managers with planning staffs. These planners are staff specialists who are trained in strategic management techniques and who provide staff-support services and recommendations on strategic management decisions. A planning staff can participate in many aspects of the strategic management process, such as identifying new business opportunity, maintaining environmental scanning, reviewing strategic performance, providing analyses of strategy alternatives, and so on.

There is some debate about whether a planning staff should *do* planning or *facilitate* planning done by the line. There is an argument that specialists can take time to closely examine proposals and projects without having the burdens of running existing operations.

Critics of this approach point out the usual problems of acceptance by line managers of staff activities and recommendations. Using a staff to do planning increases the probability that planning will be done but decreases the probability that the plans developed will be used. One writer characterizes this as a ''paralysis of analysis.'' Planners may be seen as having their heads stuck in the clouds, while from the staff point of view the line managers have their feet stuck in the mud. This can lead to the isolation of a separate planning staff. Indeed this appears to have occurred in the late 1970s when strategic planners were allowed to become dominant figures in their companies. As their power grew and the influence of operating managers declined, hostility escalated. The result: few of the strategies were implemented.

This problem occurred at Standard Brands (see Exhibit 1.9). Just as some suggest that the CEO should manage the process of planning, others urge that the planning staff should contribute not by doing but by ''selling'' a planning ''culture'' to the line. Thus the task of the planning staff would be to develop a plan for implementing planning throughout the organization. These authors also argue that a planning staff can play an evaluative role and a consulting role.

Practitioners in the 1980s appear to be doing just that. Some of the leading proponents of strategic management have cut the size of their planning staffs at corporate, group, and divisional levels. General managers, having participated in the process of putting together strategic plans are now more aware of the usefulness of strategic planning. The new generation of CEOs believe that they and their key general managers should be the strategic thinkers.

Thus in practice the role of a planning staff varies with the organization and the power of other participants in strategic planning. The staff members may not play a significant role unless they are represented in the power structure and can influence decisions regarding the implementation of plans. *But most of the evidence indicates that a planning staff rarely, if ever, seriously participates in the strategic choice process.* This is the crucial job of the general manager, and the staff serves as the executive's research and follow-through team.

Throughout the book, the roles which can be performed by corporate planners will be discussed. This is especially true with respect to the chapters on analysis and diagnosis (Chapters 3 and 5), alternative choice preparation (Chapter 6), and implementation (Chapters 9 and 10) and evaluation (Chapter 11). Chapter 9 will describe in more detail the operations of corporate planning staffs.

Strategic Management Consultants [8]

Another influence on the strategist can be a consultant in strategic management. Many consultants offer advice in the area of strategic management. Much of this advice comes in the form of designing and helping to implement a formal strategic management system for an enterprise. Others conduct studies as part of the strategic management process. In this respect, they are serving the role of corporate planning departments when no department exists or when management prefers an outsider's view. Some of these consultants become chief strategists of firms after their interaction with them. Further, some CEOs have also developed advisory boards to give advice on technical matters or to evaluate special projects or trends affecting the business.

Like corporate planning departments and their executives, the consultant serves primarily as an adviser to the chief strategist and performs such strategic management duties as the strategist requests. In the case of small businesses, firms using consultants in this fashion perform better.

Lower-Level Participants [9]

Suffice it to say that when you find yourself in middle-management positions, you will not be intimately involved with strategic choice. But you may be providing data or ideas which can affect future choices at higher levels. And lower levels implement strategy (or prevent its implementation). To the extent that you understand who has power and what their roles and values are, you are in a better position to offer ideas and suggestions which have a higher probability of acceptance and recognition. And you can implement plans and policies consistent with strategic intent. This is one way to increase the visibility and power of your own subunit. Thus we encourage you to consider the roles and values of strategists carefully.

Next we turn to the starting point of the strategic process which these actors influence—mission and objectives.

MISSION AND OBJECTIVES

The two most basic questions faced by corporate-level strategists are, (1) What business are we in? and (2) Why are we in business?

An answer to the first question requires a consideration of the mission definition, or the scope of the business activities the firm pursues. The second question involves establishing objectives to be accomplished. Both questions help define the nature of the business and provide a framework for analysis, choice, implementation, and evaluation processes.

The Mission and Business Definition [10]

For long-term survival (often viewed as the ultimate objective), most organizations must legitimize themselves. This is normally done by performing some function which is valued by society. Of course, some functions are valued more highly than others, and priorities can change over time. In the United States, professional sports teams are valued for their entertainment function, and they have become big business.

Organizations which make a net contribution to society are likely to be called "legitimate." These organizations are likely to be allowed to survive over the long term. Challenges to legitimacy are not frequent, but once made they can damage survival potential or limit the scope of action and increase the cost of doing business. For example, over a dozen of the largest U.S. defense contractors were under investigation in 1985 for cost and labor mischarges, bribery and kickbacks, defective pricing, and so on (e.g., the infamous $400 toilet seats). Congress acted to stop payments on some contracts and made it harder to acquire the more lucrative contracts because the legitimacy of the action of these firms was called into question.

Many organizations define the basic reason for their existence in terms of a mission statement. Such a definition can provide the basic philosophy of what the firm is all about. It usually emanates from the entrepreneur who founded the firm or from major strategists in the firm's development over time. The mission can be seen as a link between performing some social function and more specific targets or objectives of the organization. Thus the mission can be used to legitimize the organization.

When the mission of a business is carefully defined, it provides a statement to insiders and outsiders of what the company stands for—its purpose, image, and character. Exhibit 2.4 indicates how Hallmark defines its mission. When Hallmark considers strategic proposals, it can refer back to its definition with a basic question: Does the proposal fit our mission?

Mission definitions can be so broad as to be meaningless, or they can merely be public pronouncements of ideals which few could ever reach. As you will see later,

---

EXHIBIT 2.4   THE MISSION OF HALLMARK

"When you care enough to send the very best" is one of America's most recognized corporate slogans. What does it stand for? What business is Hallmark in? What is its mission?

Hallmark's strategy has been one of diversification far beyond cards. Its customers are also buying books, candles, party supplies, pewter and crystal items, bath products, fine pens and pencils, and jewelry. How do these all fit? What's the grand vision?

Several key elements are involved. The company has creative talents, processing talents, and marketing skills all focused around an image of quality. And it has to provide its 6000 independent dealers with a number of relatively high priced items to create volume and revenue beyond that created solely by cards. Thus items in its product mix are design-oriented and sold primarily to women. Hallmark's self-defined mission: bring quality to social expression.

When it acquired a costume jewelry manufacturer, industry sources saw it as "a shrewd move . . . to expand . . . the lines sold through its traditional outlets. Women don't know if jewelry is good quality or bad. If you can't trust Hallmark, who can you trust?" With jewelry and related items dealers can round out their inventories with numerous products in Hallmark's mix. The acquisition fit neatly into Hallmark's creative, quality, design-oriented, social-expression philosophy.

Hallmark has consciously and carefully created a clearly defined mission and strategies to implement it. Its mission is an ideological position statement of its image and character and what the company stands for and is trying to achieve. It provides a basis upon which to determine the scope of products, markets, and technologies in its domain.

Sources: Adapted from "Hallmark Now Stands for a Lot More than Cards," *Business Week,* May 29, 1978, pp. 57–58; "Hallmark Tries Out the Jewelry Trade," *Business Week,* Nov. 3, 1975, p. 29.

the specificity and breadth of goal or mission statements are important considerations for strategists. But a good mission statement focuses around customer needs and utilities. For example, AT&T is in communications, not telephones; Tenneco is in energy, not just oil and gas; MGM provides entertainment, not just movies. The customer needs for communication, energy, or entertainment are not product-specific—nor are mission statements. Avon defines itself as being in the beauty business. The mission of most public universities is to provide teaching, research, and public service—but many also provide entertainment (sports teams).

The mission must be clear enough so that it leads to action. Organizations must at some point establish specific targets to shoot for which will be used as guides for evaluating progress. NASA's mission in the 1960s was to begin space exploration and land a man on the moon. Without establishing specific goals to get to along the way, we might be still waiting for that first ''small step.'' So firms also must express their mission and philosophy by establishing statements about the grand design, quality orientation, atmosphere of the enterprise, and the firm's role in society.

After Roger Smith took over as chairman of General Motors, he moved quickly to solve some problems at GM and altered its strategy. As part of the process, he distributed ''culture cards'' to be carried in the pockets of executives to remind them of their new mission. The card reads

> The fundamental purpose of General Motors is to provide products and services of such quality that our customers will receive superior value, our employees and business partners will share in our success, and our stockholders will receive a sustained, superior return on their investment.

Other firms consciously (or subconsciously) develop ''core principles,'' or norms, which guide decision making or behavior. These principles serve as mechanisms for self-control to guide managers at all levels of the organization. Hence, if quick decisions are needed at lower levels of an organization, such core principles serve as guides to making decisions or taking action consistent with the overriding mission and strategy of the business. These are different from policies in that they are frequently part of the culture, or ways of doing things, that emerge in the informal organization.

In practical, everyday decision making, most organizations are not immediately concerned with questions of continued existence. Survival for most is relatively assured within the time frame of thinking of those in charge. And the mission tends to become an ideological position statement which is only occasionally referred to in support of legitimization. So what tends to occupy the minds of the molders of organization purpose are various objectives to improve performance. However, prescriptively, a mission statement and core principles ought to serve as guidelines for strategic decisions rather than as a set of platitudes. Otherwise, short-term thinking can get in the way of the long-term best interests of the organization in society.

Business Definition

Part of the mission statement is the definition of the business itself. By this we mean a description of the products, activities, or functions and markets that the firm presently pursues. Products (or services) are the outputs of value created by the system to be sold to customers. Markets can refer to classes or types of customers or geographic regions where the product and/or service is sold. When we refer to functions, we mean the technologies or processes used to create and add value. For example, in agriculture one might plant and grow seeds, harvest crops, mill grain, process the grain into various food products, and distribute or retail the finished product. Each stage adds value and represents a separate function. Some firms do all the functions while others do a limited number or only one. Consider a full-service airline versus a no-frills carrier. One operates full-service ticket counters in airports and downtown locations; the other may ticket on the plane, offer no interline ticketing, offer few fare options, and so on. The no-frills airline may use first-come–first-serve seating versus ticketing at gates. On board, the no-frills carrier may not serve food or drink or charge extra for the service. The full-line carrier may provide free baggage checking while the no-frill firm charges or provides no interline baggage connection. Each of these options represents a service or function configuration. Functions of ticketing, gate operations, on-board service, and baggage handling can provide options for adding value to services provided.

A good business definition will include a statement of products, markets, and functions. For example, a business definition for Apple might state the following: *We design, develop, produce, market, and service microprocessor-based personal computers in United States and foreign countries.* In contrast, Tandy might be defined as *a U.S. manufacturer and retailer of consumer electronic equipment.* Note that Tandy performs fewer functions than Apple and is a bit more restricted geographically, but it has a wider product definition. *Westinghouse manufactures, sells, and services equipment and components which generate, transmit, distribute, utilize, and control electricity.* Note that this definition includes a very broad line: it specifies a focus around which the products are related but ignores market issues (except for the notion that its markets involve electricity). In its 1985 Annual Report, Schulumberger asks, What are our businesses? The answer:

> First, we are an oilfield services company, bringing technology to the oil industry anywhere, anytime. [We are] also an electronics company. We are ready to expand in the international markets through leadership in electricity, . . . electronic payments, . . . instruments, bringing technology to the utilities, to the aerospace industry, to the banking community . . .

A good statement of the business definition of the firm should meet certain criteria: it should be as precise as possible and indicate major components of strategy (products, markets, and functions). Some go a bit further than this by also indicating how the mission is to be accomplished. Note that Hewlett-Packard (Exhibit 2.5) meets the criteria of defining the mission and business definition and takes the next step of indicating the kind of management desired and policies necessary to attain the mission. Each of these aspects is described in more detail throughout the book.

Defining the mission and business definition is the starting point of strategy analysis. It answers the question, What business are we in? When performing the initial gap analysis described in Chapter 1, we find that such a statement indicates where the firm's current strategy has been going up to this point in time, and what results

EXHIBIT 2.5   THE MISSION AND BUSINESS DEFINITION OF HEWLETT-PACKARD

Hewlett-Packard's business is concentrated on developing high-quality products which make unique technological contributions and are so innovative that customers are willing to pay premium prices. Products are limited to the areas of electronic testing and measurement and to technologically related fields. Customer service, both before and after the sale, is given primary emphasis. The financial policy is to use internally generated funds to finance growth and avoid long-term debt and to resort to short-term debt only when sales growth exceeds the return on net worth. H-P seeks to attract high-caliber and creative employees with the opportunity to share in the success of the company through high wages, profit sharing, and stock-purchase plans. Job security is increased by keeping fluctuations in production schedules to a minimum by avoiding consumer-type products and by not making any products exclusively for the government. The managerial policy is to practice "management by objective" rather than management by directive; corporate objectives provide unity of purpose, and H-P gives employees the freedom to work toward these goals in ways that they determine are best for their own area of responsibility. The company exercises its social responsibility by building plants and offices that are attractive and in harmony with the community, by helping to solve community problems, and by contributing both money and time to community projects.

Source: Adapted from D. Crites and R. Atherton, "Hewlett-Packard (A)," in W. F. Glueck, *Business Policy and Strategic Management* (New York: McGraw-Hill, 1980), pp. 384–385.

might be expected if it continues. From there, once objectives have been specified and other analyses have been performed, determinations can be made about whether such a definition can continue successfully, or must be altered to close gaps. In other words, the strategic management process starts with the current business definition but proceeds with other questions: What business should we be in? Who are our customers? How do we serve them? That is, some conditions might call for a strategic change in products, markets, or functions, or changes in the way in which that business definition is going to be accomplished (competitive strategy and policies). For example, long after cars, interstate highways, and airplanes sent many railroad companies into bankruptcy court, some railroad companies are reemerging with new corporate identities. The Reading Company, a major regional railroad established in 1833, now owns only 16 miles of track. Like many former railroad firms, Reading is now a major real estate operator (even though the Monopoly game board earns it immortality as a railroad).

A problem many firms find themselves with is that through acquiring a series of businesses unrelated to their mission or business definition, they become conglomerates, with little to tie them together other than financial objectives. Many firms have found a need to return to basic business definitions because they cannot effectively manage the diversity. It took General Mills longer than most, but after 17 years of trying they finally sold off their toy division and nonfood lines to "get back to the kitchen," which they knew best about.

Changing the business definition is one of the basic strategy alternatives to be described in Chapter 6. But before strategy determination is made, the other major aspect of strategic gap analysis is a determination of whether desired objectives will be attained. Analysts must determine if continuation with the mission and adherence to the business definition will lead to expected outcomes close to those desired. Our next section, then, begins the examination of objectives themselves to answer the question, Why are we in business?

What Objectives Are Pursued? [11]

Objectives are the ends which the organization seeks to achieve through its existence and operations.[1] A variety of different objectives are pursued by business organizations. Some examples include continuity of profits; efficiency (for example, lowest costs); employee satisfaction and development; quality products or services for customers or clients; good corporate citizenship and social responsibility; market leadership (for example, to be first to market with innovations); maximization of dividends or share prices for stockholders; control over assets; adaptability and flexibility; service to society.

It is important that several points be made about objectives so that you understand their nature fully. These are as follows:

• The list just given contains 10 objectives, which is not to suggest that most organizations pursue 10 objectives or these exact 10. But research clearly demonstrates that firms have many objectives. *All but the simplest organizations pursue multiple objectives.*

• Many organizations pursue some objectives in the short run and others in the long run. For example, with respect to the list of 10 objectives, many firms would view efficiency and employee satisfaction as short-run objectives. They would probably view profit continuity, service to society, and good corporate citizenship as long-run objectives. Some other objectives such as adaptability or asset control may be medium-range objectives. *In sum, the objectives pursued are given a time weighting by strategists.*

One of the major dilemmas of corporate-level strategists is the short-term–long-term trade-off decision. With the logic of net present value and the importance of return on investment, combined with pressures from Wall Street and corporate raiders for good quick profits and cash flows, modern managers have been pressured toward short-term thinking. This kind of thinking also filters down to the business level, where a desire for quick returns may influence SBU managers. There appears to be less patience to invest in the future in the United States than there is in other countries (such as Japan). This lack of patience can have a severe impact on strategic decision making; and the timing of goal accomplishment needs careful analysis in this regard.

• Since there are multiple objectives in the short run at any one time, normally some of the objectives are weighted more highly than others. The strategists are responsible for establishing the priorities of the objectives. Priorities are crucial when resources and time are limited. At such times, trade-offs between profitability and

---

[1]We use the terms "objective" and "goal" synonomously.

market share, etc., must be known so that the major objective of the particular time is achieved. Thus *strategists should establish priorities for each objective among all the objectives at corporate and SBU levels.*

• There are many ways to measure and define the achievement of each objective. For example, some objectives can be measured through the use of an efficiency criterion; others may be measured in terms of effectiveness. Efficiency is the ratio of inputs to outputs. Effectiveness refers to the degree of achievement of a goal in relation to some ideal. At times, trade-offs between efficiency and effectiveness are required. For example, installing pollution-control equipment may be effective in achieving clean-air goals, but these goals may be achieved at the expense of a goal of efficient plant operation. At other times, trade-offs of efficiency goals within units of an organization are required. This is a basic factor in *suboptimization*. As each subsystem seeks efficiency, the entire system may lose effectiveness. For example, a credit manager is charged with establishing a policy to minimize credit losses; a sales manager is asked to maximize sales. If they both maximize in their own way, conflict is likely. Sales to some classes of customers will increase credit risk. Trade-offs in the goals of each unit may be called for. Here, goal priorities of the whole organization need to take precedence. In each part of the organization such goal conflicts are likely and require resolution. The guidance should come from mission definitions. *The implementation phase of strategic management involves clarifying the measurement of achievement of objectives.*

• There is a difference between official objectives and operative objectives. Operative objectives are ends *actually* sought by the organization. They can be determined by analyzing the behavior of the executives in allocating resources. Official objectives are ends which firms *say they seek* on official occasions such as public statements to general audiences. The objectives that *count* are those the strategists put their money and time behind. For instance, executives' official goals may focus on providing employees with a quality work environment; whether operative goals are the same depends on how much money is spent to improve actual working conditions.

An official goal may be to contribute to social responsibility; yet a firm may fail to spend money on pollution-control equipment or even fight regulations designed to prevent acid rain because of the costs involved. Or a firm may state that it wishes to integrate activities of SBUs to achieve synergy while its organization structure grants decentralized autonomy to divisions which prevent this from happening. Anderson, Clayton & Co. has searched for an acquisition in the food business for a decade; but analysts suggest its refusal to take on a debt to clinch a big acquisition really suggests that its operative goal is to not discourage potential buyers of the firm itself. According to one former officer, ''they are managing the company to be sold.''

• *There may be limits to the attainment of some goals.* Some firms may try to maximize shareholder wealth but find that they are constrained by the need for funds to achieve lower-cost operations to meet competition. Excessive increases in market share might come at the cost of unpleasant antitrust consequences, which, in effect, could be counterproductive from a survival perspective. Again, there are trade-offs among goals which managers must make.

• Finally, *objectives are not strategies*. Strategies are means to an end. Note that expansion was not among the objectives listed. Expansion is one type of strategy but not an end in itself. In itself, expansion of sales or assets may not improve performance. But cutting back (retrenchment) in certain areas of the operation could also be a way to increase efficiency and improve performance. So expansion and retrenchment are ways in which goals can be achieved, and both can lead to performance increases (e.g., growth in returns). Not all managers agree with this distinction, but we believe it is an important one. (This is a problem with strategic management terminology in general.)

One other issue regarding objectives which has become important to strategists is the priority attached to objectives relating to social responsibility [12]. Social responsibility is an ill-defined term, but the basic idea is that the economic functions provided by business *ought to be* performed in such a way that other social functions are, at worst, unharmed and, at best, promoted. Thus businesses are urged to be as concerned with human rights, environmental protection, equality of opportunity, and the like, as they are with providing outcomes such as economic efficiency.

Several dilemmas arise. A major problem is how to define socially responsible behavior. Value systems are so diverse that achieving consensus on this issue is difficult. Equally problematic is the fact that economic organizations automatically take resources from organizations in other sectors and often detract from performing other societal functions. Businesses weren't designed to promote public health, safety, and welfare (though some use charitable giving as a marketing ploy). A common example is detrimental health effects from pollution created by the production of goods. Do we stop producing goods? Do we increase costs to the extent that other societal goals are adversely affected? For instance, a completely safe automobile might be so expensive that possible cost increases to protect human safety become detrimental to economic well-being. Cost-benefit trade-offs are extremely difficult to make.

In some cases, external threats can be so severe as to call into question the legitimacy of the mission of the organization, as in the case of utilities which generate power with nuclear plants. Policies to deal with these concerns include ignoring the issue, using public relations campaigns to try to mitigate unfavorable publicity, and altering goal priorities and changing strategies. Some creative strategists try to turn these kinds of threats into opportunities. For instance, some coal companies have increased the value of land originally used for strip-mining by converting the strip mines into recreation complexes. But these options are not always available. In any case, decision makers are being urged to increase the priority given to these concerns by some.

On the other hand, businesses are also criticized if they stray too far from their economic function. For instance, business firms are chastised for creating political action committees as a means to influence their environment.

While research evidence is mixed, the predominant view is that social responsibility bears little (positive or negative) relationship to financial performance objectives. Clearly, then, establishing goal priorities and resource allocation requires a consideration of issues beyond simple economic efficiencies.

Why Objectives [13]

Why do firms have objectives, and why are they important to strategic management? There are four reasons.

1 *Objectives help define the organization in its environment.* Most organizations need to justify their existence, to legitimize themselves in the eyes of the government, customers, and society at large. And by stating objectives, they also attract people who identify with the objectives to work for them. Thus objectives define the enterprise.

2 *Objectives help in coordinating decisions and decision makers.* Stated objectives direct the attention of employees to desirable standards of behavior. It may reduce conflict in decision making if all employees know what the objectives are. Objectives become constraints on decisions.

3 *Objectives provide standards for assessing organizational performance.* Objectives provide the ultimate standard by which the organization judges itself. Without objectives, the organization has no clear basis for evaluating its success.

4 *Objectives are more tangible targets than mission statements.* The products of an organization or the services it performs (outputs) are probably the most familiar terms in which people tend to think of objectives or goals. (It's easier to see Hallmark as a producer of cards and gifts than to imagine the company as being in "the social-expression business.") Output goals may also be thought of in terms of quality, variety, and the types of customers or clients who are the intended target. Nonetheless, it may be deceptively easy to link output goals with mission definitions. For instance, Henry Ford's original mission of "providing transportation for the common man" was easily seen through the production of the Model A. But the private hospital offering a large range of services with the best doctors and equipment may be available to only a few rich clients; it may be profitable with these services and judged effective by some, but others will argue that it fails to satisfy a larger mission of equal health care treatment (note the social responsibility element here).

Mission and objectives ought to be considered at each stage of the strategic management process. In the assessment of environmental conditions, expected changes may force rethinking about goal priorities (e.g., changing government tax regulations may suggest a different treatment of dividend payout or retained earnings). In an analysis of internal conditions, a goal of employee welfare might alter perceptions about unionization. In choosing alternative strategies, a change in business definition could lead to decisions to get out of some businesses in favor of others. If a goal of flexibility is desired, the implementation of a strategy could lead to a new form of organization structure. So at each stage of the process, mission, business definition, and objectives should guide decision making.

To carry this a bit further and illustrate how objectives relate to the process as a whole, we consider the gap analysis as outlined in Exhibit 2.6. Point A is the current level of attainment an enterprise has reached at this time (t_1). Point B is the ideal point at which management would like to see itself at some point in the future (t_2). If, as a result of following the strategic management process, the firm sees itself

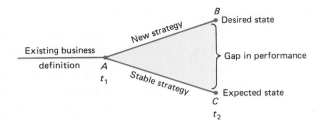

EXHIBIT 2.6   **Gap analysis for objectives.**

pursuing the *same strategy* with a given set of assumptions about its environment, management may believe it will arrive at point C at t_2. The gap of interest which could trigger either *strategic change or goal change* is that between B and C. Note that the gap between the existing state and the desired state is not as important as the gap between the *expected state* and the *desired state*.

As we discussed in Chapter 1, the perception of this gap is important in terms of significance, importance, and reducibility. With these conditions in mind, note that several basic choices are available. If the gap is significant, important, and reducible, an attempt could be made to alter strategy so that the expected state (point C) will come closer to the desired state (B). If the gap is significant and important but not reducible, point B might be altered (e.g., expectations might be lowered). If the gap is significant and reducible but not important, once again point B can be altered. The goal that is sought becomes less critical when compared with other goals. If the gap is *neither* significant, important, nor reducible, no change will occur—a stability strategy (continuing past approaches in similar ways) is likely to be followed.

This is a prescriptive way to examine the analysis of objectives as a component of the strategic management process. But other factors influence the nature of the perceptions of these gaps as objectives are formulated. These are discussed next.

How Are Mission and Objectives Formulated? [14]

We believe that missions and objectives are formulated by the corporate-level strategists. But these executives do not make choices in a vacuum. Their choices are affected by several factors: the realities of the external environment and external power relationships, the realities of the enterprise's resources and internal power relationships, the value systems and goals of the top executives, and past strategy and development of the enterprise. Let us discuss each of these influencing factors and then summarize.

The first factor affecting the formulation of mission and objectives is *forces in the environment.* As discussed in Chapter 1, the stakeholders with whom the organization has an exchange relationship will present demands or claims (expectations). These can be thought of as constraints on objectives. The stakeholders may vary, the nature of their constraints (expectations or claims) can change, and their power vis-à-vis the organization and one another may change. Taken together, they represent one set of forces within which managerial objectives must be established. The claims of the most powerful stakeholders will be met, so long as the entire set of objectives falls within the constraints imposed by the set of stakeholders.

Suppose that managers want to choose maximization of sales as an objective. They may have to modify this objective because of governmental regulations regarding excess profits, antitrust legislation, consumer labeling, and so on. Trade unions may require higher-than-market wage rates or fringe benefits which lead to higher costs (possibly reducing sales). Competitors may sell other products or services at unrealistically low prices and spend excessive amounts on advertising. Suppliers may become monopolized and charge outrageous prices. If the organization is more dependent on suppliers than on any other stakeholders, the operative objective may very well be limited by the availability and cost of supplies. As discussed in Chapter 1, then, the political-behavioral realities of the situation influence the choice of objectives.

So the prudent strategist will ask a variety of questions when establishing mission, objectives, and strategy: Who are the critical stakeholders? What are our critical assumptions about each stakeholder? How do stakeholders affect each division, business, or function at various points in time. And what changes can be expected among the stakeholder groups in the future?

The second factor affecting the formulation of mission and objectives is the *realities of the enterprise's resources and internal power relationships*. Larger and more profitable firms have more resources with which to respond to forces in the environment than do smaller or poorer firms.

In addition to this, the internal political relationships affect mission and objectives. First, how much support does management have relative to others in the organization? Does the management have the full support of the stockholders? For example, Paul Smucker has the support of the Smucker family stockholders to emphasize quality as an objective for his jam and preserves firm. If the management has developed the support of employees and key employee groups like the professional employees' lower and middle management, then it can set higher objectives that employees will help achieve.

Mission and objectives are also influenced by the power relationships among the strategists either as individuals or as representatives of units within the organization. Thus if there is a difference of opinion on which objectives to seek or the trade-offs among them, power relationships may help settle the difference.

A final internal factor is the potential power of lower-level participants to withhold information and ideas. To the extent that this occurs, the evaluation of past goal attainment and expectations about the future can be affected. For instance, consider the sales manager who tries to hide the fact that a competitor's new product is starting to hurt sales. This might be an attempt to protect the unit, but it could mislead top managers regarding future goals and strategies. Or lower-level managers might decide whether or not to forward a proposal which could lead to goal changes on the basis of what they *think* top management is (or is not) ready to accept. Thus the exercise of this type of informal power can play a role in the selection of objectives.

Mintzberg has advanced a theory about formulation of objectives that combines the stakeholder forces described earlier with the internal power relationships. He believes that power plays result from interactions of internal and external coalitions.

EXHIBIT 2.7   SIX PURE POWER CONFIGURATIONS AFFECTING
OBJECTIVES FORMULATION

External coalition	Internal coalition	Power configuration
Dominated	Bureaucratic	The Instrument
Passive	Bureaucratic	The Closed System
Passive	Personalized	The Autocracy
Passive	Ideologic	The Missionary
Passive	Professional	The Meritocracy
Divided	Politicized	The Political Arena

Source: Henry Mintzberg, *Power In and Around Organizations* (Englewood Cliffs, N. J.: Prentice-Hall, 1983), p. 307.

• The external coalition includes owners, suppliers, unions, and the public. These groups influence the firm through social norms, specific constraints, pressure campaigns, direct controls, and membership on the board of directors. Mintzberg specifies three types of external coalitions, noted in Exhibit 2.7.

• The internal coalition includes top management, middle-line managers, operators, analysts, and support staff. These groups influence the firm through the personnel control system, the bureaucratic control system, the political system, and the system of ideology. Mintzberg specifies 5 types of internal coalitions, shown in Exhibit 2.7.

Mintzberg says that there are six basic power configurations, as shown in Exhibit 2.7. In the instrument power configuration, one external influence with clear objectives, typically the owner, is able to strongly influence objectives through the top manager. In a closed-system power configuration, power to set objectives rests with the top manager, who sets the objectives. This is also true in the autocracy power configuration. In the missionary power configuration, objectives are strongly influenced by past ideology and a charismatic leader. Ideology tends to dictate the objectives. In the meritocracy power configuration, the objectives are set by a consensus of the members, most of whom are professionals.

Thus the formulation of mission and objectives can be a simple process: the top manager sets them subject to the environment. Or, more frequently, they are set by a complex interplay of past and present, internal and external role players.

The third factor affecting the formulation of mission and objectives is the *value system of the top executives*. Enterprises with strong value systems or ideologies will attract and retain managers whose values are similar. These values are essentially a set of attitudes about what is good or bad, desirable or undesirable. These in turn will influence the perception of the advantages and disadvantages of strategic action and the choice of objectives. Exhibit 2.8 lists the extremes of six selected values. Let's look at each of these to see how they might affect objectives.

EXHIBIT 2.8   VALUES TOWARD VARIOUS GROUPS IN THE
STRATEGIC SITUATION

1 Very combative	Very passive
2 Very innovative	Noninnovative
3 Risk-oriented	Risk-aversive
4 Quality	Quantity
5 Autocratic	Participative
6 Personal goals	Shareholder goals

The following list corresponds to the continuum in Exhibit 2.8. Each dimension is explained below:

1 Some executives believe that to be successful a firm must attack in the marketplace. Others believe that you "go along to get along."

2 Some executives believe that to succeed a firm must innovate. Others prefer to "let others make the mistakes first."

3 Some executives know that to "win big, you must take big risks." Others comment, "Risk runs both ways."

4 Some executives believe that one becomes successful by producing quality. Others go for volume.

5 Some executives believe that one should treat employees in a manner that makes them know who the boss is. Others believe that cooperation comes from a participative style.

6 Some executives believe that they should be primary beneficiaries of corporate success while others think the business is operated for the benefit of stockholders.

You can see that one set of executives with the set of values on the left would be inclined to emphasize a different set or different level of objectives than those who accept the set of values on the right in Exhibit 2.8. For instance, risk-oriented innovators might see significantly larger gaps between where they want to be and where they expect to be than risk averters. Managers on the left on number 6 will avoid hostile takeovers to protect their jobs, even if it comes at the expense of shareholder loss. Corporate raiders often recognize this, and receive "greenmail" for their effort.

Prescriptively, from a "maximizing" decision perspective, these and other kinds of values *ought not* be considered when goals are being established. Yet some believe that it is better to recognize the inevitability of their influence on decision makers. That is, even if they are not explicitly stated, value assumptions will be implicit in decision premises and the types and forms of data collected. Consequently, stating these values in the form of assumptions is one technique recommended to force these values explicitly into the open. If they are included, the bases upon which decisions are made can be considered "more rational" than if decision makers pretended that these factors don't exist. Exhibit 2.9 suggests that value shifts do affect the mission and goals of a business.

EXHIBIT 2.9   EXECUTIVE SUCCESSION SHIFTS VALUES, GOALS, AND STRATEGY

Control Data Corp. is in trouble. The company lost approximately $400 million in 1985 and analysts expect it to do no better than break even in 1986. Also, the company owes nearly $400 million in loans. In 1985 Control Data went into technical default on $217 million of those loans. It is up to Robert Price, the president and now chairman and CEO of the company, to lead it out of trouble. Price recently succeeded William Norris, the founder of Control Data. Norris's retirement indicates a change in direction for the company.

The idealistic Norris vowed to use computers to serve "society's unmet needs." The operation of Control Data reflected Norris's position. For example, the company had to write off $9.7 million on a business of building energy-saving earth-sheltered homes. The pragmatic Price has a different philosophy. He sees Control Data's mission as "using computer technology to solve problems." Price is currently selling off Norris's altruistic but unprofitable ventures. Also, he is trying to revitalize the company's longtime revenue sources.

Norris, as founder, probably had enough power to lead the company in the direction he wanted, even if the board did not agree with him. Does Price have that power? It could be argued that Price is a reflection of the board of directors' values, since he now becomes the vehicle by which the board hopes to lead the company toward a more profitable direction.

Note that a shift in values after succession led to a change in mission and goals for this organization and has resulted in a retrenchment strategy.

Source: Adapted from "Can a Gentleman Farmer Get Control Data Out of Its Ditch?" *Business Week*, Jan. 27, 1986, pp. 44–45.

The fourth factor affecting the formulation of mission and objectives is the *awareness by management of the past development of the firm*. Management does not begin from scratch each year. It begins with the most recent mission and objectives. These may have been set by strong leaders in the past. The leaders consider incremental changes from the present, given the current environment and current demands of the conflicting groups. The managers have developed aspiration levels of what the objectives ought to be in a future period. But by muddling through, they set the current set of objectives to satisfy as many of the demands and their wishes as they can. The momentum of the large organization and its strategies and policies are all currently designed to accomplish the existing mission and objectives. Just as it takes time to turn a large ship around, it usually takes time to make major corporate changes.

Let's summarize what has been said so far on how mission and objectives are established. The factors are shown in Exhibit 2.10. Mission and objectives are not the result of managerial power alone. These result from the managers' trying to satisfy the needs of all groups involved with the enterprise. These coalitions of interests (stockholders, employees, suppliers, customers, and others) sometimes have conflicting interests. As the strongest coalition group, managers try to reconcile the conflicts. Management cannot settle them once and for all. Management "bargains" with the various groups and tries to produce a set of objectives and a mission which can satisfy the groups at that time. The goals of these groups are considered in relation to past goals. This is a very complicated, largely consensus-building process with no precise beginning or end. And at any given time, only a few specific goals can be grasped and comprehended by any single executive. Thus there appears to be a need for some grander vision as expressed by a mission definition.

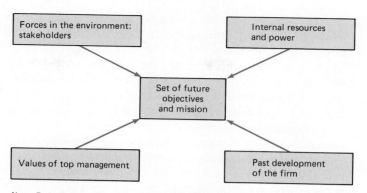

Note: Each of these factors represents a set of constraints on the establishment of the priorities among future objectives. The set of mission and objectives considered at any one time is also limited.

EXHIBIT 2.10   **Factors influencing the formulation of objectives and mission.**

Mission and objectives will become a meaningful part of the strategic management process only if corporate strategists formulate them well and communicate them and reinforce them throughout the enterprise. *The strategic management process will be successful to the extent that general managers participate in formulating the mission and objectives and to the extent that these reflect the values of management and the realities of the organization's situation.* These factors also play a role in strategic choice, as we explain in Chapter 8.

Why Do Mission and Objectives Change?

Although organizations tend toward stability, mission and objectives change over time. As discussed before, objectives could change on the basis of a rational analysis of a gap between expected and desired states. That is a normative approach. But what might lead to the determination of the states themselves? Are there some factors which would lead to different perceptions regarding the gaps between goals and how the future goal states might be arrived at?

On the basis of the foregoing discussion of how mission and objectives are formulated, we can present some descriptive reasons why mission or objectives might change.

• The aspiration levels of managers could alter goal orientations. They may begin to extrapolate past achievements and say that the enterprise can do more. Or they may look at what relevant competitors or other enterprises have achieved and decide to match or exceed these levels. The arrival of a new CEO from outside the organization is the most prevalent condition under which mission and goals are reconsidered. New managers from the outside who are not tied or committed to past strategy and ideology are more likely to alter the mission, objectives, and strategies of an organization than are new CEOs from the inside.

• *The mission can change in a crisis.* When a firm's market disappears, for example, or its reason for being ceases, a crisis exists. Some firms supplying equipment to the oil industry discovered this in 1974 and again in 1982 and 1986. Faced with an uncertain future, their objectives have begun to focus on flexibility. When the cure for polio was found, the mission of the National Foundation for Infantile Paralysis changed. So the attainment of objectives can also lead to a crisis. Or, new opportunities can create an identity crisis if a firm seeks to take advantage of them.

• *Demands from coalition groups that make up the enterprise can change.* This often occurs as the membership or leadership of groups changes or as internal power groups change. For instance, new government or labor leaders or new competitors can alter the way a business sets its goal-priorities. Similarly, if the comptroller becomes more powerful internally, the firm might begin to stress shorter-term financial goals.

• *Normal life-cycle changes may occur which alter goal orientations.* Exhibit 2.11 suggests a stage of development approach. Though the analogy with humans can be taken too far, there may be changes in objectives or strategies which "naturally" occur in the aging process. Of course, organizations may have more control over the sequencing and timing of these stages than humans. Yet it is often difficult for an organization to know what stage it is in. And we're not sure what might precipitate organizational aging or movement. We do know that commitment to the past may hinder change, and new agents in coalition groups are likely to hasten it.

These four classes of factors—aspirations, crisis, demands, and development—can be used to predict the likelihood that mission and objectives will remain similar to those of the past or be subject to redefinition. Thus in considering how mission and

EXHIBIT 2.11   ORGANIZATIONAL DEVELOPMENT AS ANALOGOUS TO HUMAN DEVELOPMENT

Human stage	Prime life thrust	Organizational objectives	Strategic focus for an organization
Birth	Trauma and survival	Survival—create new entity	Identify an entrepreneurial idea and find resources
Infancy	Adaptation and self-interest	Define mission and search environment	Define products, markets, and functions to offer
Youth	Rapid, uneven growth spurts	Quantitative growth	Increase market share; claim more territory
Young adult	Procreation and search	Achieve uniqueness and establish niche	Redefine products, markets, and functions
Adult	Establishment of self	Qualitative growth—gain reputation	Reap rewards; mine markets for benefits
Maturity	Status quo	Stabilize and contribute to society	Maintain position with stability
Old age	Survival	Survival	Procreate and retrench parts that are no longer healthy

objectives are formulated, we must examine various pressures for stability or change before a gap analysis can be effectively done.

The Specificity of Mission and Objectives [15]

Our final area of concern with these basic elements of strategic management deals with how broadly or narrowly mission and objectives should be, or are, defined. Let's separately examine mission definition and then look at objectives.

Mission

As strategists define their mission, they are usually urged to seek a *common thread* to which activities can be related. The common thread is often stated in terms of the *scope* of products, but markets or technologies in the domain of the enterprise are also used. The problem is that the firm might define the scope so broadly that strategic decisions or objectives tied to the mission become meaningless. On the other hand, an overly narrow mission definition can lead to the oversight of factors that are potentially important to the success of the enterprise. Exhibit 2.12 shows part of the dilemma.

EXHIBIT 2.12   ASPECTS OF THE PRESENT AND FUTURE DOMAIN OF TWA

Trans World Airlines is in the business of moving people from one destination to another. About half its customers (business executives) want face-to-face interaction with people at another location. They want to get there quickly and conveniently and at a relatively low cost. What are their alternatives? What business is TWA really in? What is its domain?

Most analysts see TWA as being in the commercial airline industry. Some see it as part of the transportation industry. A few suggest that its domain includes communications. Each has different implications.

If the domain is the airline industry, then some relevant key competitors are PanAm, Eastern, and United. Claims over similar territories and clients are made. But this tends to ignore the potential threats of customers using alternative modes of transportation—cars, buses, trains, private aircraft. When regularly scheduled air traffic has some advantages over these other modes, ignoring them and the factors which might lead to customers using them could result in a loss of business. This becomes clearer as you consider the communications domain.

The Wall Street Journal reports that face-to-face communication with clients and colleagues is now possible with satellite-linked TV screens. At one trial of such an approach, "participants said video conferences could substitute for a majority of face-to-face business meetings, for quicker decision-making and reduced travel time and expense." IBM and AT&T are heavily involved in these developments. Do you remember Ma Bell's response when the 1974 energy crisis hit? A series of ads promoted the use of the telephone by salespeople, encouraging salespeople to contact clients from the office instead of using the company car. Will executives soon "travel by long distance and stay awhile"? *Business Week* reports that videoconferencing is indeed an increasingly popular approach to reduce travel time and cost without loss of executive effectiveness. Exhibit 3.5 shows how this technology is gaining acceptance.

Sources: Adapted from "Dogfight in Space: The Competition Heats Up in Domestic Satellites," *The Wall Street Journal*, Sept. 8, 1978, p. 1; *Business Week*, July 7, 1980, p. 81; "Videoconferencing: No Longer Just a Sideshow," *Business Week*, Nov. 12, 1984, pp. 116–120.

If the domain of TWA is defined too narrowly, executives may miss important technological or competitive activities occurring outside the more limited domain of "other air carriers." As a result, the firm may risk the potential loss of a large part of its customer base.

Thus the domain must be sufficiently broad so that decision makers will be sensitive to important issues it may face in the future. Of course, overgeneralization, the opposite of myopia, may lead to a lack of focus on relevant issues as well. Should an airline view itself as being in the vacation business, it could lose sight of its basic mission. Paper Mate now views itself as in "office products" with the acquisition of Liquid Paper. A radio is a product, but manufacturers of radios are in the business of providing a means of delivering audio information and/or entertainment. The Boston Consulting Group statement on this issue is instructive:

> Unfortunately, there is a prevalent notion that if one merely defines one's business in increasingly general terms—such as transportation rather than railroading—the road to successful competitive strategy will be clear. Actually, that is hardly ever the case. More often, the opposite is true. For example, in the case of the railroads, passengers and freight represent very different problems, and short haul vs. longer haul are completely different strategic issues. Indeed, as the unit train demonstrates, just coal handling is a meaningful strategic issue.

Thus perhaps one of the best ways to determine a common thread is to seek out synergies which could be obtained between old and new activities. "Synergy" refers to the idea that the whole is greater than the sum of its parts ($2 + 2 = 5$). Here, if a firm can find new activities which utilize the strengths or benefits of old activities, it is likely to create more value for all activities. As noted in Exhibit 2.4 Hallmark found synergy in its markets, products, *and* technologies. Another suggestion is to give careful attention to the *utilities* provided for customers (e.g., cost, time, location, convenience) by the functions performed by the enterprise. Careful attention to categories of goods and services (rather than "products") and synergies can lead to more useful definitions of the organization's mission and domain. For instance, Sears began its move into providing financial services to complement its existing insurance business by using its broad base of retail outlets and large number of charge customers as a point of departure.[2] In essence, mission and business definition can change. It must be periodically evaluated as part of the strategic management process.

A final point before turning to the specificity of objectives is the idea that these issues of domain definition are stated in different terms at different levels of the organization, but similar questions emerge. For instance, the scope question at the corporate level implies issues concerning the overall degree of diversification in the portfolio of business operations. At the SBU levels, the breadth of the product-market scope or degree of vertical integration (technology scope) is the more common issue. At functional levels, the issues often are debated in terms of product-market segmentation or positioning.

---

[2]Sears has been one of the few which has succeeded with unrelated diversifications because of their ability to manage some synergies well.

Objectives

The differences among levels also occur in that objectives are successively narrower as one moves down into an organization. But in more general terms, firms tend to evolve through stages of more precisely defining their objectives. These are as follows:

1 *Formulation of general objectives, usually not in written form.* Once administrators are aware of the desirability of objectives, they begin to formulate them. If you ask top management what its objectives are, you might be given them in general terms. You will not find them in writing anywhere.

2 *Formulation of general, written objectives.* The next step is to get the objectives in writing, perhaps in annual reports. By the time this stage is reached, the firm is fairly large and formalized.

3 *Formulation of specific objectives.* The hurdle that appears at step 4 is to get the executives to specify the objectives. For example, an objective may be changed *from* "increase the return on investment" *to* "increase the return on investment to 6 percent in the next year." (Note the greater specificity and timing involved.)

4 *Formulation and ranking of specific objectives.* The final and most difficult step is to ask management to compute the trade-offs between objectives. This requires management to say, for example, that the return on investments (ROI) is more important than the market share and having the market share is more important than having satisfied employees. This step is found only in the most sophisticated of firms.

There are various techniques for moving the firm through these steps. One of the most popular is the management-by-objectives (MBO) technique. MBO is used to develop a company philosophy requiring top management to proceed through step 4 in formulating objectives. Then middle and lower management are expected to translate these objectives into specific targets at their level to better ensure the achievement of the objectives, as shown in Exhibit 2.13.

Finally, most management theorists suggest that objectives should not only be formal, specific, measurable, prioritized, and time-based, they should also be challenging and obtainable. There should be a reasonable opportunity for achieving goals to avoid frustration; but if they are too easily obtainable, then little satisfaction or achievement is likely. For example, in 1980 IBM declared it would match or beat the information processing industry's growth in all segments (ranging from up to 12 percent per year for mainframe computers to 40 percent for personal computers). In 1985, the company planned to double revenues by 1990, and double them again by 1994. These are lofty goals, but the company has achieved many of them; and the pace of investment has been accelerated even though economic problems and industry slowdowns created challenges to the objective.

Many firms, however, prefer to rely on more general definitions instead of publicly stated specific goals or targets. For example, one automobile industry analyst suggested that "Ford still doesn't know where it's going." But the chairman of the board, Donald Peterson, insists that Ford knows where it is headed, but he is vague on the specifics. The only goal he admits to is that of making Ford "a customer-driven company." Why do managers do this? Quinn argues that broad goal statements are preferable because specific and rigid goal pronouncements can rigidify positions,

EXHIBIT 2.13   TRANSLATION OF STRATEGIC OBJECTIVES INTO SPECIFIC TARGETS

Corporate-level strategic objectives	Corporate and/or SBU specific targets
1 Improve return on assets	1 Increase return on net assets (after taxes) from 12 to 19 percent in 3 years
2 Increase overall profit	2 Increase overall profit margin from 4 to 6 percent in 3 years
3 Increase sales by (a) Improving market penetration in existing markets	3 (a) Product A: Increase market penetration from 15 to 20 percent next year Product B: Increase market penetration from 20 to 25 percent in 2 years
(b) Opening up new markets	(b) Move product from development fo production (planned market penetration, 5 percent) in next year
4 Increase manufacturing productivity	4 Purchase new equipment: $3 million next year Establish a methods engineering department; improve rework rate by 5 percent over next year
5 Improve management-union relations	5 Establish new industrial relations department and examine management's approach to labor problems immediately; reduce turnover rate 3 percent next year

eliminate creative options, cause resistance, centralize the organization, and alert the opposition to a target for counterattack, particularly as competitors lure away top talent who have inside knowledge about specific plans. He argues for more generality so executives can keep their options open and generate identity, cohesion, and commitment around an idealized mission. Others argue that the effective manager sets general objectives to give a sense of direction but is never committed *publicly* to a specific set of objectives. In other words the manager should have objectives but should not state them publicly. Public statements of specific objectives might be avoided because it is impossible to set down specific objectives which will be relevant for any reasonable period of time since things change too fast; objectives may not be clear enough so that everyone in the organization will understand what they mean; details complicate the task of reaching objectives. If it is felt that employees will not accept the strategist's objectives, then it is useful to be vague and avoid this problem. Finally, some executives prefer to state vague and general goals because their performance evaluation is tied to accomplishment. After-the-fact explanations of goal attainment are much easier if the goals are not specific, time-based, measurable, and publicly known. Justifying that a firm has achieved ''industry leadership'' is easier on several grounds than having to show that ''we will lead our industry by attaining the highest ROI by 1990.'' Chapter 11 will refer to this again as we consider the evaluation of the performance of a firm.

SUMMARY

Chapter 2 has focused on the two strategic management elements: the mission and objectives and the strategists.

The first strategic element is that of the actors in the process. We described the general manager as an executive at the pinnacle of an enterprise or SBU. While new types of general managers are coming on the scene, these individuals have a complex task. They are organization leaders, personal leaders, and designers of mission and strategy. They play informational, interpersonal, and decision-making roles. Enormous amounts of time are spent in communicating with internal and external stakeholders while they play these roles.

Since our focus is on the strategic management role, we next described the corporate-level and business-level strategists.

• *The board*. The board of directors has the ultimate legal authority, but it primarily reviews strategies and CEOs, and it influences strategy through CEO selection and replacement.

• *Top managers*. They may be professional managers or entrepreneurs, and they are the primary decision makers.

The failure of an organization to achieve its objectives can often be traced to a breakdown at the level of the board or top management group.

Other actors influencing the development of strategy and its implementation include SBU managers, who perform roles similar to those of top managers; corporate planners, who can facilitate and do planning; consultants, who can provide advice on specific problems; and lower-level managers, who interpret policy and offer proposals up the line.

Proposition 2.1

With respect to the strategists, we propose that strategic management is most effectively performed by general managers. In larger firms, the executives may receive assistance from corporate planning staffs. In firms of various sizes, the top executives may receive assistance from consultants and guidance from the board of directors.

In all cases, we suggest that effective implementation will more likely occur if general managers and operating managers are directly involved in the strategic management process.

The second element is the starting point of the strategic management process—mission and objectives.

A mission statement defines the basic reason for the existence of an organization and helps legitimize its function in society. The business definition clarifies the nature of existing products, markets, and functions the firm presently provides.

Objectives are those ends which the organization seeks to achieve through its existence and operations. Objectives are an integral part of the strategic management process. They are the ends the firm seeks and the criteria used to determine its effectiveness.

Objectives are an integral part of the strategic management process. They are the ends the firm seeks and the criteria used to determine its effectiveness.

The chapter emphasized the following points about objectives:

• All but the simplest organizations pursue more than one objective.
• Two types of objectives can be distinguished: operational objectives are the objectives that are actually pursued; official objectives are the objectives that managers say they are seeking.
• Strategists should establish the current priorities of each objective among all the objectives, but they often don't.
• There may be limits to the attainment of some goals.
• Objectives are ends, not means.
• Social responsibility is becoming a more important consideration among the multiple objectives sought by business.

Organizations have objectives for a number of reasons: objectives help define the organization in its environment: objectives help in coordinating decisions and decision makers; objectives provide standards for assessing organizational performance; objectives are more tangible targets than mission statements.

The formulation of mission and objectives is a complex process which involves

• An analysis of the gaps between desired and expected goal attainments
• The realities of the external environment and external power relationships
• The realities of the enterprise's resources and internal power relationships
• The value systems and goals of top executives
• The past strategy and development of the enterprise

Proposition 2.2

Mission and objectives are formed for an organization when its top managers react to a complex interplay of the demands of groups in the environment and inside the firm. The managers incrementally adjust the mission and objectives, considering these demands, their own values and aspirations, and past strategy.

Changes in mission and objectives depend on several factors: the aspiration levels of managers can change; an organizational crisis may be at hand; demands from coalitions can change; normal life-cycle development may occur.

Managers are urged to define their objectives in formal, specific, time-based, prioritized, measurable terms which are challenging and attainable. But they tend to resist being specific about objectives because specificity tends to reduce flexibility. Consequently, many managers rely on more general mission statements.

If an enterprise is not achieving its objectives, it has several choices:

• Claim that the objectives being achieved will ultimately lead to long-term mission attainment.
• Change the objectives so that those being met are the objectives.
• Change the strategy in order to achieve the objectives.

• Change the strategists and keep the objectives and strategy, assuming that new strategists can achieve the objectives.

To conclude, recognize that organizations pursue multiple purposes, which are time-based. Some purposes are means to ends, while others conflict with one another and require trade-offs. An organization is usually called efficient *and* effective only if short-term and intermediate goals are attained as it moves toward its long-term mission. But even the mission and goals change over time. Finally, a complex set of factors and pressures from internal and external forces must be considered by the strategists.

As an aspiring manager you must be aware of the nature of goals and general managers and the types of conditions likely to lead to change. Middle managers interpret policy and can be held responsible for problems. To interpret wisely, you must understand the pressures faced at the top and why certain strategies or policies are being formed and pursued. More than one career has been stifled simply because the manager was on the wrong side of a power struggle. This chapter has provided some ideas about the basic dynamics involved in these processes. Finally, as you prepare ideas and proposals for consideration by your supervisors, you will find it useful to know ''where they are coming from'' and what roles they play. Your proposals will have a better chance for acceptance if you understand how they fit on ''the agenda'' of the organization.

Now that we know a little more about the strategic elements—the decision makers and their decisions about mission and objectives—we can move on to Chapter 3, which continues the discussion of the strategic management process with the analysis of the firm's environmental opportunities and threats.

REFERENCES

[1] The General Manager

Bourgeois, L. J.: ''Strategic Management and Determinism,'' *Academy of Management Review,* vol. 9 (1984), pp. 586–596.

Burck, C. G.: ''A Group Profile of the Fortune 500 Chief Executive,'' *Fortune,* May 1976, pp. 173–174 + .

Chandy, P. R. and T. Klammer: ''The Big Firm CEO,'' *Collegiate News and Views,* vol. 37 (1984), pp. 1–5.

Christensen, C. R., K. R. Andrews, J. L. Bower, R. G. Hammermesh, and M. E. Porter: *Business Policy: Text and Cases* (Homewood, Ill.: Irwin, 1982).

Hambrick, D. C., and P. A. Mason: ''Upper Echelons: The Organization as a Reflection of Its Top Managers,'' *Academy of Management Review,* vol. 9 (1984), pp. 193–206.

Kotter, J. P.: *The General Managers* (New York: Free Press, 1986).

Levinson, H., and S. Rosenthal: *CEO: Corporate Leadership in Action* (New York: Basic Books, 1983).

Mintzberg, H.: *The Nature of Managerial Work* (New York: Harper & Row, 1973).

Nussbaum, B., J. W. Wilson, D. B. Moskowitz, and A. Beam: ''The New Corporate Elite,'' *Business Week,* Jan. 21, 1985, pp. 62–81.

Sigband, N. B.: "The Changing Role of the CEO," research monograph, University of Southern California, 1984.

"Turnover at the Top," *Business Week,* Dec. 19, 1983, pp. 104–110.

[2] The Board of Directors

Baum, L., and J. A. Byrne: "The Job Nobody Wants," *Business Week,* Sept. 8, 1986, pp. 56–61.

Cochran, P. L., R. A. Wood, and T. B. Jones: "The Composition of Boards of Directors and Incidence of Golden Parachutes," *Academy of Management Journal,* vol. 28 (1985), pp. 664–671.

Jones, T. M., and L. D. Goldberg: "Governing the Large Corporation: More Arguments for Public Directors," *Academy of Management Review,* vol. 7 (1982), pp. 603–611.

"Labor's Voice on Corporate Boards: Good or Bad?" *Business Week,* May 7, 1984, pp. 151–153.

Mizruchi, M. S.: "Who Controls Whom? An Examination of the Relation Between Management and Boards of Directors in Large American Corporations," *Academy of Management Review,* vol. 8 (1983), pp. 426–423.

Zahra, S. A.: "The Composition of Board of Directors and Company Strategic Behavior and Performance," working paper 85-03, Old Dominion University, Norfolk, VA, 1985.

[3] The Board as Strategists

Boulton, W.: "The Evolving Board: A Look at the Board's Changing Roles & Information Needs," *Academy of Management Review,* vol. 3 (October 1978), pp. 827–836.

"End of the Directors' Rubber Stamp," *Business Week,* Sept. 10, 1979, pp. 72–77.

Wommack, W. W.: "The Board's Most Important Function," *Harvard Business Review,* vol. 57 (September–October 1979), pp. 48–52 +.

[4] Top Managers as Strategists

Donaldson, G., and J. W. Lorsch: *Decision Making at the Top* (New York: Basic Books, 1983).

Hambrick, D. C.: "Strategic Awareness within Top Management Teams," *Strategic Management Journal,* vol. 2 (July–September 1981), pp. 263–280.

Hickson, D. J., R. J. Butler, D. Cray, G. R. Mallory, and D. C. Wilson: *Top Decision* (San Francisco: Jossey Bass, 1986).

Hofer, C. W., and C. N. Toftog: "How CEOs Set Strategic Directions for their Organizations," paper presented at the Strategic Management Society Conference, 1984.

Mintzberg, H.: "The Manager's Job: Folklore and Fact," *Harvard Business Review* (July–August, 1975), pp. 49–61.

Shrivastava, S.: *The Executive Mind* (San Francisco: Jossey Bass, 1983).

———: *Executive Power* (San Francisco: Jossey-Bass, 1986).

Sturdivant, F. D., J. L. Ginter, and A. G. Sawyer: "Managers' Conservatism and Corporate Performance," *Strategic Management Journal,* vol. 6 (1985), pp. 17–38.

[5] Entrepreneurs

Ehrlich, E.: "America Expects Too Much from its Entrepreneurial Heroes," *Business Week,* July 28, 1986, p. 33.

"Following the Corporate Legend," *Business Week,* Feb. 11, 1980, pp. 62–66 +.

"The New Entrepreneurs," *Business Week,* Apr. 18, 1983, pp. 78–89.

Pave, I.: "A Lot of Enterprise is Staying in the Family These Days," *Business Week,* July 1, 1985, pp. 62–63.

Sykes, H. B.: "Lessons from a New Ventures Program," *Harvard Business Review* (May–June, 1986), pp. 69–74.

Van de Ven, A. H., R. Hudson, and D. M. Schroeder: "Designing New Business Startups," *Journal of Management,* vol. 10 (1984), pp. 87–107.

[6] The CEO and Failure

Bibeault, D. B.: *Corporate Turnaround* (New York: McGraw-Hill, 1982).

"Chief Executives Who Won't Let Go," *Business Week,* Oct. 8, 1984, p. 39.

Dalton, D. R., and I. F. Kesner: "Organizational Performance as an Antecedent of Inside/ Outside Chief Executive Succession," *Academy of Management Journal,* vol. 28 (1985), pp. 749–762.

Jauch, L. R., T. N. Martin, and R. N. Osborn: "Top Management Under Fire," *The Journal of Business Strategy,* vol. 1 (Spring 1981), pp. 33–41.

Pfeffer, J., and A. Davis-Blake: "Administrative Succession and Organizational Performance," *Academy of Management Journal,* vol. 29 (1986), pp. 72–83.

[7] The Corporate Planning Staff

Hunsicker, J. Q.: "The Paralysis of Analysis," *Management Review* (March 1980), pp. 9–14.

Javidan, M.: "What Does Top Management Expect from Its Corporate Planning Department?" ASAC 1982 Conference, University of Ottawa.

Lorange, P.: "Divisional Planning: Setting Effective Direction," *Sloan Management Review* (Fall 1975), pp. 77–91.

———: "Formal Planning Systems," in C. Hofer and D. Schendel, *Strategic Management: A New View of Business Policy and Planning* (Boston: Little, Brown, 1979).

"The New Breed of Strategic Planner," *Business Week,* Sept. 17, 1984, pp. 62–68.

[8] Strategic Management Consultants

"An Advisory Council to Back Up the Board," *Business Week,* Nov. 12, 1979, pp. 131 + .

"Consultants Move to the Executive Suite," *Business Week,* Nov. 7, 1977.

Robinson, R. B., Jr.: "The Importance of 'Outsiders' in Small Firm Strategic Planning," *Academy of Management Journal,* vol. 25 (1982), pp. 80–93.

[9] Lower-Level Managers' Impact on Management

Jauch, L. R., and H. K. Wilson: "A Strategic Perspective for Make or Buy Decisions," *Long Range Planning,* vol. 12 (December 1979), pp. 56–61.

Mechanic, D.: "Sources of Power of Lower Participants in Complex Organizations," in W. W. Cooper, J. J. Leavitt, and M. W. Shelly (eds.), *New Perspectives in Organizational Research* (New York: Wiley, 1964).

Wheelwright, S. C., and R. L. Banks: "Involving Operating Managers in Planning Process Evolution," *Sloan Management Review* (Summer 1979), pp. 43–59.

[10] Mission and Business Definition

Abell, D. F.: *Defining the Business: The Starting Point of Strategic Planning* (Englewood Cliffs, N.J.: Prentice Hall, 1980).

Beam, A., and J. H. Dobrzynski: "General Mills: Toys Just Aren't Us," *Business Week,* Sept. 16, 1985, pp. 105–109.

Payne, S.: "Stepping Up the Attack on Contract Abuse," *Business Week,* July 1, 1985, p. 24.

Schlumberger Annual Report, 1985.

"Some Old Railroads Never Die—They Just Stop Running Trains," *Business Week,* Nov. 19, 1984, pp. 88–89.

Whiteside, D. E.: "Roger Smith's Campaign to Change the GM Culture," *Business Week,* Apr. 7, 1986, pp. 84–85.

[11] The Objectives of Businesses

"Anderson Clayton: Shopping Around for a Food Company or Grooming to Be a Takeover Target?" *Business Week,* Jan. 23, 1984, pp. 62–67.

Richards, M.: *Setting Strategic Goals and Objectives* (St. Paul, Minn.: West, 1986).

"Will Money Managers Wreck the Economy? Their Short-Term View Derails Companies' Long Term Plans," *Business Week,* Aug. 13, 1984, pp. 86–93.

[12] Social Responsibility Objectives

"Amex Shows the Way to Benefit from Giving," *Business Week,* Oct. 18, 1982, pp. 44–45.

Aupperle, K. E., A. B. Carroll, and J. D. Hatfield: "An Empirical Examination of the Relationship Between Corporate Social Responsibility and Profitability," *Academy of Management Journal,* vol. 28 (1985), pp. 446–463.

Cochran, P. L., and R. A. Wood: "Corporate Social Responsibility and Financial Performance," *Academy of Management Journal,* vol. 27 (1984), pp. 42–56.

Preston, L. E. (ed).: *Research in Corporate Social Performance and Policy* (Greenwich, Conn.: JAI Press, 1982).

Wartick, S. L., and P. L. Cochran: "The Evolution of the Corporate Social Performance Model," *Academy of Management Review,* vol. 10 (1985), pp. 758–769.

[13] The Purpose of Objectives

Pearson, G. J.: "Setting Corporate Objectives as a Basis for Action," *Long Range Planning,* vol. 12 (August 1979), pp. 13–19.

Simon, H.: "On the Concept of Organizational Goal," *Administrative Science Quarterly,* vol. 9 (June 1964), pp. 1–22.

[14] Formulating the Mission and Objectives

Cyert, R., and J. March: *A Behavioral Theory of the Firm* (Englewood Cliffs, N.J.: Prentice-Hall, 1963).

Freeman, R. E.: *Strategic Management: A Stakeholder Approach* (Boston: Pitman, 1984).

Guth, W. D.: "Formulating Organizational Objectives and Strategy: A Systematic Approach," *Journal of Business Policy,* vol. 2 (Autumn 1971), pp. 24–31.

Mintzberg, H.: *Power In and Around Organizations* (Englewood Cliffs, N.J.: Prentice-Hall, 1983).

Samuelson, R. J.: "A Misuse of Management Power," *Newsweek,* June 25, 1984, pp. 56–57.

Zeleny, M.: *MCDM Past Decade and Future Trends: A Source Book of Multiple Criteria Decision Making* (Eastchester, N.Y.: JAI Press, 1984).

[15] Narrow vs. Broad Mission and Objectives

Edid, M., W. J. Hampton and R. A. Melcher: ''Now That It's Cruising, Can Ford Keep Its Foot on the Gas?'' *Business Week,* Feb. 11, 1985, pp. 48–52.

Harris, M. A.: ''IBM Sets Its Sights High,'' *Business Week,* Feb. 18, 1985, pp. 85–98.

Ohmae, K: *The Mind of the Strategist* (New York: McGraw-Hill, 1982).

Perspectives on Corporate Strategy (Boston: Boston Consulting Group, 1970), p. 42.

CHAPTER OUTLINE

THE GENERAL ENVIRONMENT

OBJECTIVES

- To introduce the sectors in the general environment which are crucial to the survival of a firm
- To examine the ways the environment may be analyzed
- To explore the factors affecting a diagnosis of the environment
- To indicate how the environmental analysis and diagnosis phase can be used in the strategic management process

INTRODUCTION [1]

With Chapter 3, we begin the discussion of the environment's impact on the strategic management process. The environment includes factors outside the firm which can lead to opportunities for or threats to the firm. Chapter 3 examines socioeconomic, technological, and governmental factors. Chapter 3 also introduces ways in which the factors can be *analyzed* and *diagnosed*. Chapter 4 examines the industry factors: customers, suppliers, and competition. We also explore the international environment in Chapter 4.

> *Environmental analysis is the process by which strategists monitor the environmental sectors to determine opportunities for and threats to their firms.*

Analysis is the tracing of an opportunity or threat to a source. It also involves breaking a whole into its parts to find its nature, function, and relationship. Strategic management requires searching for opportunities and threats and determining where they come from and which ones are coming.

Environmental diagnosis consists of managerial decisions made by assessing the significance of the data (opportunities and threats) of the environmental analysis.

These decisions lead to other decisions on whether to react to, ignore, try to influence, or anticipate the opportunities or threats discovered. Thus managers' *perception* of the environment may be different from its objective condition.

In effect, diagnosis is an *opinion* resulting from an analysis of the facts to determine the nature of a problem with a view to acting to take advantage of an opportunity or to effectively manage a threat.

In Chapters 1 and 2 we discussed the use of gap analysis as an aid to strategists. As we begin the analysis stage, the analyst is trying to determine whether assumptions about the environment affecting the firm in the future will permit the current strategy to be continued so that the firm can reach desired outcomes. In some cases, if the environment presents more opportunities, the strategy might be changed so that new higher objectives can be reached. If threats appear, objectives may be changed or the strategy might be adjusted so that performance gaps will not grow too large.

Specifically, Exhibit 3.1 outlines the environmental analysis and diagnosis process. As you can see, first the strategists consciously examine the relationship between the firm's strategy and their perceptions of the environment. This is necessary as a basis for comparing current strategy with potential future strategy. Then the strategists

EXHIBIT 3.1   THE ENVIRONMENTAL ANALYSIS AND DIAGNOSIS PROCESS

Environment of the firm	Strategists analyze and diagnose gaps

General (Chapter 3)
  Socioeconomic
  Technological
  Governmental
Industry (Chapter 4)
  Customers
  Suppliers
  Competition
International (Chapter 4)
	Analysis
	1 Identify the current strategy the firm uses to relate to the environment. What are the assumptions or predictions about the environment on which current strategy is based?
	2 Predict the future environmental conditions. Are the assumptions or predictions the same as in step 1? Is there a gap?
	Diagnosis
	3 Assess the significance of the gap between the current and future environments for the firm. Are changes in objectives needed? Do changes in strategy appear useful to consider? Will they reduce the gap?

attempt to assess the future environment. These are the analysis steps. If there are no gaps, then the current strategy can be fruitfully pursued. If there are gaps, then the strategists determine whether these will have a significant effect on the current strategy or objectives.

This brings us back to our model of the strategic management process. Exhibit 3.2 highlights the analysis and diagnosis phase of the strategic management process, focusing especially on the external environment. It is a concern for the achievement of objectives in the future which motivates the analysis and diagnosis phase of strategic management. Hence, an analysis of gaps could lead to the adjustment of objectives (Chapter 2) or to a consideration of the need for a new strategy. If the decision is to adjust the strategy, alternative strategies must then be generated (Chapters 6 and 7) and a new strategy chosen (Chapter 8) and implemented (Chapters 9 to 11).

WHY ENVIRONMENTAL ANALYSIS AND DIAGNOSIS? [2]

Although some of the reasons why effective strategists analyze and diagnose the environment have already been hinted at, let's summarize a number of them briefly for purposes of clarity.

Managers must systematically analyze and diagnose the environment, since environmental factors are prime influencers of strategy change. Consider a few examples of environmental changes with negative consequences. (Others will be given in the chapters.)

1 Aramco was a large firm in Saudi Arabia that produced crude oil. It was owned primarily by American firms. The Saudi government nationalized the firm.

2 Large increases in the sales of soft drinks and other beverages were influenced by the popularity of nonreturnable containers. Some governmental bodies are passing laws against these containers.

3 In 1948, some of the largest firms in the United States were Paramount, Warner Brothers, and MGM. Enter the television networks: CBS, NBC, ABC.

4 Many persons made a good living running diaper-service companies. Suddenly Procter & Gamble brought out Pampers (disposable diapers), and others joined the parade.

5 Not so long ago, copies were made by typing stencils. These were put on duplicating machines made by firms such as A. B. Dick and Company. Xerox, IBM, and others came along with a new product which captured the market from the stencils.

Environmental analysis and diagnosis gives strategists time to anticipate opportunities and to plan to take optional responses to these opportunities. It also helps strategists develop an early warning system to prevent threats or develop strategies which can turn a threat to the firm's advantage.

In the 70 years between 1918 and 1988, almost half of the 100 largest American firms went out of business or became significantly less important to our society. Often a company becomes convinced that it is almost invincible and need not examine what is happening in the marketplace. When the company ceases to adjust the environment to its strategy or does not react to the demands of the environment by changing its

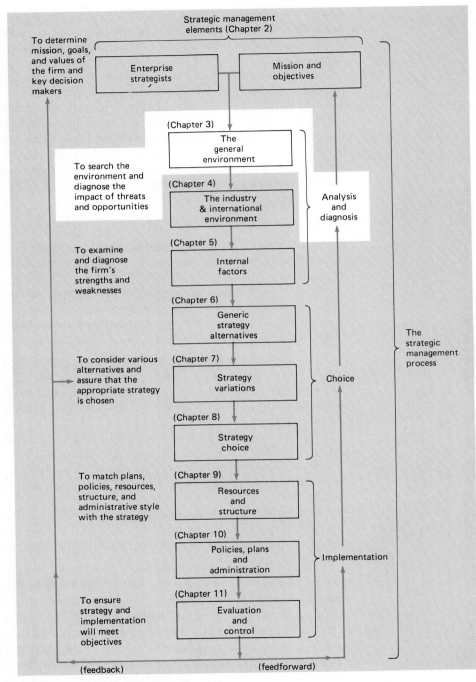

EXHIBIT 3.2 **A model of strategic management.**

strategy, the result is lessened achievement of corporate objectives. One extreme example was provided by W. T. Grant. That firm went bankrupt when it failed to meet competitive changes and the needs of its markets.

Managers need to search the environment to (1) determine what factors in the environment present threats to the company's present strategy and objectives accomplishment and (2) determine what factors in the environment present opportunities for a greater accomplishment of objectives through an adjustment in the company's strategy. Just as important, the analysis needs to recognize the inherent risks involved in trying to take advantage of opportunities. As has been observed, ''opportunism without competence is a path to fairyland.'' And there are usually threats inherent in any opportunity.

Without systematic environmental search and diagnosis, the time pressures of the managerial job can lead to inadequately thought-out responses to environmental changes. It is clear that because of the difficulty of assessing the future, not all future events can be anticipated. But some can and are. To the extent that some or most are anticipated by this analysis and diagnosis process, managerial decisions are likely to be better. And the process reduces the time pressures on the few which are not anticipated. Thus the managers can concentrate on these few instead of having to deal with all the environmental opportunities and threats in a pressure-cooker environment.

Firms which systematically analyze and diagnose the environment are more effective than are those which don't. Successful firms do more and better environmental analysis and diagnosis than do failing firms. The amount and sophistication of the analysis and diagnosis meet the demands of the environment.

The primary responsibility for environmental analysis and diagnosis rests with top management in a single-SBU firm. In multiple-SBU firms, this responsibility is shared by the SBU top executives and corporate top managements. They may use corporate planners and consultants to help them with this task. How these strategists perform the analysis and diagnosis will be discussed at the end of the chapter.

Before that, this chapter will describe the sectors in the general environment that are to be analyzed and diagnosed; the techniques used for analysis; and who is likely to do environmental analysis. The next chapter examines the industry and international environments in more detail. And we provide an overall tool, the environmental threat and opportunity profile (ETOP), to help you combine the analyses in the strategic management process.

THE GENERAL ENVIRONMENT [3]

There are a large number of factors which affect the firm in each sector of the environment. And these factors interact with one another. Exhibit 3.3 shows these relationships for a typical integrated oil company.

There are many ways to organize the sectors for analysis and diagnosis. The categories used in this chapter are socioeconomic, technological, and governmental. (Note that Exhibit 3.3 includes these and other sectors to be covered in Chapter 4.) Let's examine each sector to determine the kinds of factors that need analysis and diagnosis.

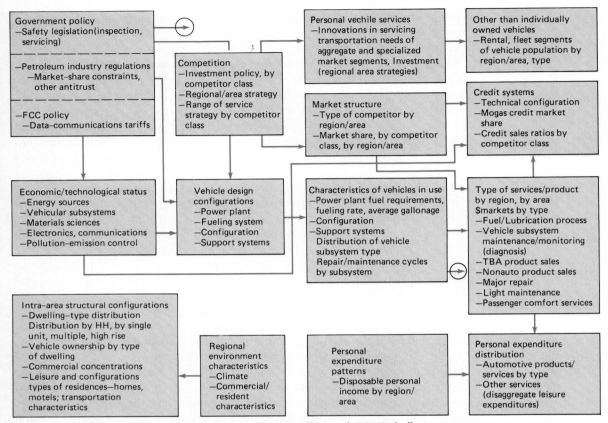

EXHIBIT 3.3   **How the environmental factors affect an integrated oil company.**
(H. Klein, "Incorporating Environmental Examination into the Corporate Strategic Planning Process,"
unpublished doctoral dissertation, Columbia University, New York, 1973.)

Socioeconomic Sector

There are a variety of factors which affect the demand for products and services and the costs of providing them. This section explores the economic, climatic, and social factors which help or hinder a firm in the attainment of objectives.

The Economy [4]

The state of the economy at present and in the future can affect the fortunes and strategy of the firm. The specific economic factors that many firms analyze and diagnose include:

• The stage of the business cycle. The economy can be classified as being in a depression, recession, recovery, or prosperity stage.

• The inflationary or deflationary trend in the prices of goods and services. If inflation is very severe, wage and price controls may be imposed.

- Monetary policies, interest rates, and devaluation or revaluation of the currency in relation to other currencies.
- Fiscal policies: tax rates for firms and individuals.
- Balance of payments, surpluses, or deficits in relation to foreign trade.

Each of these facets of the economy can help or hinder the achievement of a firm's objectives and lead to success or failure for the strategy. For example, recessions often lead to unemployment, which can lead to lower sales if the firm produces discretionary goods. If monetary policy is tightened, funds for needed plant additions may be too costly or unavailable. But other policies lead to interest-rate changes. As the interest rates rose in the late 1970s and early 1980s, less money was available for investment. As the cost of money declined in the mid-1980s, firms scrambled to refinance old debt, and more money then became available for new investment. Tax policies can reduce the attractiveness of investment in an industry or reduce the after-tax incomes of consumers, who then lower their spending levels. Changes in the balance of payments may either discourage trading partners from continuing to purchase goods from one another or encourage them to continue trading. In the early 1980s a large number of governments throughout the world were linking imports to exports, bartering goods, and protecting jobs.

Each of these facets can be an opportunity or a threat. For example, most people see inflation as a threat to corporate objectives. But for some industries, such as catalog merchandising, it has been an opportunity for better business. And disinflation is seen as a mixed blessing. High-inflation rates in the 1970s and early 1980s created the appearance that profits were good. With rates of inflation at only 3 or 4 percent in the mid-1980s, while costs were lower, firms couldn't raise prices as fast either. Hence, corporate profits, after subtracting for inflation, have been relatively flat. This has led to cost cutting, quality control, product diversification, and better debt management.

Business Week maintains that there are five separate economies in the United States.

1 *Old-line industry*. The basic manufacturing industry faces serious international competition and is in the throes of restructuring.

2 *Energy*. The United States has natural resources and good technology but can squeeze financing available to other industries.

3 *High technology*. This area can function independently of the rest of the U.S. economic scene and shows tremendous growth potential.

4 *Agriculture*. The United States has a temperate climate, and demand can grow with population, but the pace of productivity may slacken, leading to accelerating farm inflation.

5 *Services*. Employment should grow fast, and internationalization is likely; this sector should begin to show productivity gains.

Demand patterns, the availability of capital, inflation, the balance of payments, and the like affect these industries differently. So a change in economic conditions may be good for one firm but bad for another. Strategists must determine what economic factors are most important to their business and attempt to predict the changes which are likely in those conditions. That is, of course, easier said than done given the numerous explanations of why the economy operates as it does. But the best possible estimates of important economic conditions must be made as inputs for strategic decision making.

Climatic Factors [5]

Effective strategists often have climate and ecological concerns. Threats from unforeseen weather changes can be seen by firms whose products are seasonal. Ski resorts and manufacturers of snowmobiles and snowblowers were forced to change their evaluations and marketing methods when a low-snow winter occurred one year in the United States. One firm diversified into lawn mowers as a result. Large food distributors can be paralyzed by an abnormal storm that keeps their trucks off the road. Food processors may be caught with inadequate supplies because of an extended drought. However, several businesses derive opportunity by providing climate-forecasting services. One example is Oceanroutes, which employs 65 full-time meteorologists. They plot weather and sea conditions leading to the best routes for steamship lines so that time and fuel costs are minimized. Sears employs two weather forecasters for preseason and in-season decision making about inventories of merchandise such as air conditioners and snow tires. Finally, ecological issues such as the protection of endangered wildlife and the acid-rain controversy affecting the United States and Canada can affect plant location decisions and other strategic decisions. Vlasic decided to locate a pickle plant near the ocean so that the brine effluent would not foul fresh water.

Social Factors [6]

The last set of socioeconomic factors focuses on the values and attitudes of people—customers and employees—which can affect strategy. These values translate into lifestyle changes which affect the demand for products and services or the way firms relate to employees. Some examples may help you see how these factors can create threats and opportunity.

• In 1986, a government commission issued a report suggesting that pornography was creating social ills. Even though *Playboy* and some other magazines were deemed "not obscene," some retailers under consumer pressure (such as Southland's 7-11 units) no longer carry this merchandise.

• At one time, it was thought that the normal thing for a family unit to do was to have two to four children. Today not all individuals accept this, and change of attitude has had a big impact on P&G (Pampers), Gerber (baby food), builders (houses versus condominiums), Mattel (toys), and others.

• It used to be common for retired people, single people, widows, and widowers to live with relatives. Now there is a trend toward living alone, and this has had a big impact on builders, appliance manufacturers, food packers, magazine publishers, and others.

• For years most married women stayed home. Now, most work. This has caused problems for firms that sold door to door (Avon and Fuller Brush) and has increased business for a variety of firms, such as those offering nursery school service, prepared foods, restaurants (two-employee families eat out more frequently), and home security systems, to name a few.

• At one time, people lived in one place. Now there are thousands of people who are nomads—almost like the bedouins of Jordan. They live in campers and motor homes and move from place to place as jobs open up or as the spirit moves them. This provides opportunities for and threats to firms.

• Increased education has led to new attitudes on the part of employees about how many hours they wish to work, the quality of life they expect at work, and the kind of supervisory style they expect can affect how strategies are developed and implemented. New benefits programs are also needed for new lifestyles.

• Ignoring different cultural values can mean the failure of new marketing programs. Campbell Soup withdrew from markets in Brazil because housewives believed they were not fulfilling homemaker roles if they served canned soups. And many ad campaigns lose their meaning or take on negative connotations when translated into another language.

• After the Three Mile Island nuclear plant incident, more people started to question the safety of nuclear power. New-plant construction and uranium mining in Canada, the United States, and Australia have been cut drastically, while coal operators are seeing new opportunities.

So strategists must keep up with changes in educational levels and social values in order to assess the potential impact on their strategies. Typical responses of firms to these social factors, however, vary from changes in their strategy or policies to attempts to change social values and attitudes through public-relations efforts. For example, Exhibit 3.4 shows one firm that changed strategy in response to social change.

EXHIBIT 3.4   DRINKING DRIVES SEAGRAM'S

SADD and MADD (Students or Mothers Against Drunk Driving) aren't the only societal groups affecting alcoholic consumption these days. Today's health-conscious young professional orders a salad and diet soda more often than bourbon and beef for lunch. Older executives too are skipping lunch in favor of a jog or a squash match. "The change is drastic, nationwide, and here to stay." In the words of one liquor executive, the shift is nothing less than "the sobering of America."

With public sentiment against drunk driving and "happy hours" growing, Congress pushing for a national drinking age of 21, and higher excise taxes taking effect in 1985, further declines in liquor sales seem inevitable.

Joseph E. Seagram & Sons has been driven to alter its strategy since its traditional strength in "brown liquors"

has witnessed a revenue drop of 4% in just two years. Not only is America drinking less alcohol, but vodka, gin, rum, and specialty liquors attract more buyers—areas where Seagram is weakest. Only Royal Crown Canadian experienced a jump in sales while 7 Crown and V.O. lost 6 to 7% in sales over a 4-year period in the mid 1980s.

Seagram is seeking product diversification (purchased Wine Spectrum from Coca-Cola), is stressing product development into sweeter and weaker drinks, is looking toward foreign markets where alcohol consumption is still growing, and is likely to make future beverage acquisitions. Clearly, Seagram's strategy is a response to sweeping social changes in its environment. Note that this "threat" is an opportunity for other firms, such as soft drink producers.

Source: Adapted from "How Seagram is Scrambling to Survive 'The Sobering of America,' " *Business Week* (Sept. 3, 1984), pp. 94–96.

Technological Sector [7]

Besides examining socioeconomic factors for their possible impact on products, markets, or ways of doing business, effective strategists search the environment for changing technology that might affect the firm's raw materials, operations, and products and services. Changing technology can offer major opportunities for improving goal achievement or threaten the existence of the firm. Examples of product and service breakthroughs include transistors, lasers, efficient batteries for electric cars, genetic farming, computers, miniature integrated circuits, xerography, and synthetic fibers. The change in production methods in the printing industry made possible by the use of computerized typesetting is an example of how changing technology affects operating procedures. Numerical control of machines and the use of industrial robots has revolutionized the structure of some industries. An example of changes in distribution is the use of computer-controlled ''sails'' on cargo ships. Raw materials change too. Some possible changes we see involving raw materials are the use of lignite by Phillips Petroleum, shale oil for petroleum, log houses, and garbage to generate electric power.

Technical change, of course, affects the product or service life cycle. The demand for a product or service seems to pass through a life cycle. At first, the product experiences remarkable sales growth. Then it matures, and finally it declines. Sometimes the cycle can lead to growth after decline has set in. It appears, for example, that the dairy business is declining, as is gasoline retailing. The hard-liquor business appears to be mature, as do theme parks and chain food stores. The U.S. fishing industry and home canning are examples of industries and activities which have experienced growth after decline. Firms spend a great deal of energy trying to determine where they are in the cycle so that they can decide how to invest their efforts. In some cases it is necessary to invest in research and development to improve products so that their life cycle can be extended or replace products near the end of their life cycle. In other cases, environmental scanning is needed to determine what technological change will mean to existing products in terms of production processes. Technological change can also affect distribution methods, raw materials, or the skills needed by the work force.

Whether technological change comes fast or slow is a function of the creativity of people, receptiveness on the part of industry, and the availability of venture capital. For instance, 16 U.S. electronics companies want to start a joint venture to do R&D to counter the erosion in competitive ability versus the competitive ability of the Japanese. While such a venture would provide more funds than any one firm could muster, there is a concern about antitrust implications. So government incentives through tax policies, funding, and regulations also play a role in technological change. In the mid-1980s, America's scientific establishment sounded alarms because of declining and tight government budgets. Both universities and industry have become dependent on governments for almost half their funding. The concern is that further declines in R&D expenditures could erode long-term competitive advantage for U.S.-based businesses.

A willingness to innovate and take risks also seems to be a critical component. Furthermore, technological change requires a receptive socioeconomic climate, as suggested in Exhibit 3.5. Even so, investments in technology involve other risks. For

EXHIBIT 3.5   HAVE TV, WILL TRAVEL

Videoconferencing technology has been available for some time as a substitute for travel-weary corporate managers. The Picturephone was displayed at the 1964 World's Fair by AT&T. The convenience of conducting business meetings over long distances via the TV screen, however, has been offset by high prices, poor picture quality, and human aversion to substitutes for face-to-face meetings.

Now the first two problems are being tackled. Recent advances in special computers which code signals into digital computer bits have allowed costs to decline and quality of transmission to improve. Sears installed a network to link 26 cities for full-motion videoconferencing in 1985. And Exxon, Xerox, 3M, IBM, and others are expanding networks or jumping in, prompting speculation that smaller firms will follow. More conference rooms were wired in 1984 than were set up in the 3 previous years combined.

However, some firms still have trouble getting people to use the technology. Rockwell International requires workers to indicate in writing why videoconferencing cannot substitute for their proposed travel. Yet their system linking Dallas and Los Angeles is only used 30 hours a month, mainly for general business-review sessions. "It intimidates some people, and others just like to travel."

While travel savings are important, some companies believe this technology can offer a competitive edge. For example, Boeing completed a new aircraft development project ahead of schedule by linking executives, technicians, and pilots to make instant design decisions.

Still, the potential threat to the airlines will not make significant inroads until humans can be convinced that such technology satisfies their needs and can be used to accomplish their objectives.

Source: Adapted from "Videoconferencing: No Longer Just a Sideshow," *Business Week*, Nov. 12, 1984, pp. 116–120.

example, competing technologies (such as video discs vs. cassettes, or digital audio discs vs. digital tape) may require large investments without assurance that the technology will be accepted. Hence, threat and opportunity from technology also involves other factors.

Not all sectors of the economy are likely to be equally affected by technological change. Some sectors are more volatile than others. There are few good measures of likely volatility. One is the amount spent on research and development. One would expect that the more an industry spends, the more likely it is that changes will come. If this is true, the industries producing aircraft and missiles, communication equipment and electrical components, and drugs and medicine are much more volatile than the industries producing lumber, wood products, furniture, textiles, and primary ferrous metals. Strategists in industries affected by volatile technological change must be much more alert to changes than those in more stable industries. However, advanced indicators about the nature of change in technology are available; there is usually adequate time for strategists to prepare for the impact of change.

Government Sector [8]

Federal, state or provincial, and local governments increasingly affect how businesses operate. They legislate on such matters as wage and price controls, equal employment opportunity, safety and health at work, the way that consumer credit is administered, the place that the plant can be located, the chemicals that the plant can emit into the air, the amount of noise that the product can make, the way in which the firm can run advertising, and the kinds of ads that can be run. The laws and regulations change how businesses operate on a day-to-day basis.

Government philosophies about its relationships with business can change over time. This is an important aspect for strategists to examine. For instance, Exhibit 3.6 indicates some major milestones in the deregulation of three major U.S. industries. As these shifts took place, new threats and opportunities faced the firms in these industries and those connected to them. For instance, transportation costs, financial plans, and communications options have all been affected, to say nothing of the changing nature of competition in the industries directly affected.

Action by governments also affect the strategic choices of businesses. They can increase a business's opportunities or threats or sometimes both. Some examples of *opportunities* include the following:

• *Governments are large purchasers of goods and services*. It is estimated that about one-fifth of purchases are made by governments. In some industries, such as the aircraft and aerospace industries, they are the major purchasers. The U.S. General Services Administration spends over $5 billion a year on paint, pens, paper clips, desks, chairs, etc., to keep the bureaucracy going. Government policy decisions also create new industries or additional businesses. Examples include General Signal's business increase in mass transit equipment and in cleaning up water, banks' increase in business from collecting student education loans, the space shuttle program, and the manufacture of pipelines for transporting coal.

• *Governments subsidize firms and industries and thus help them survive and prosper*. For example, state and provincial governments subsidize by reducing property taxes and paying the entire cost or part of the cost of training new employees. Federal

EXHIBIT 3.6   MAJOR STEPS IN THE DEREGULATION OF FINANCE, TELECOMMUNICATIONS AND TRANSPORTATION

Finance		Telecommunications		Transportation	
1970	Federal Reserve frees interest rates on selected bank deposits	1968	Supreme Court decision permits non-AT&T equipment to be connected to AT&T's system	1978	Congress starts the process of airline deregulation
1975	SEC orders bankers to cease fixing commissions on stock sales	1969	FCC gives MCI the right to hook its long-distance system into local phone systems	1980	Congress deregulates trucking and railroads
1977	Merrill Lynch offers the Cook Management account in order to compete with banks	1974	Justice Department files antitrust suit against AT&T	1982	Congress deregulates intercity bus service
1980	Federal Reserve allows banks to pay interest on checking accounts	1979	FCC allows AT&T to sell nonregulated services	1986	Civil Aeronautics Board out of business
1981	Sears Roebuck becomes a one-stop financial supermarket	1984	AT&T divests its local phone companies		

Source: Adapted from: "Deregulating America," *Business Week*, Nov. 28, 1983, pp. 80–89.

governments subsidize directly by means of ownership or partial ownership in projects like Comsat, Amtrak, Via Rail Canada, British Leyland, and Air Canada. France and Japan seek to support industries where the government believes strength and opportunity best match. The federal government helped the U.S. shoe industry with a $56 million subsidy because of foreign competition, funneled $2.2 billion of its business to minority-owned firms, gives tax breaks to AT&T, bailed out Chrysler, subsidizes new experiments in energy with ERDA money, and provides firms with patents and royalty protections.

• *Governments protect home producers against "unfair" foreign competition.* Governments do this by imposing import restrictions, tariffs, and antidumping provisions. The steel and shoe industries are benefiting further at present. Governments also help exporters by participating in trade treaties.

• *Government policy changes can lead to increases in opportunities and new business for firms.* If firms are willing to search the government environment and respond to changes, business can increase. Banks can now pay interest on checking accounts, which can mean more business and profits for them—and more competition for the thrift institutions. The FCC has increased the number of TV stations, which means that there are more business opportunities for those wanting to start new stations and more competition for the present stations. NASA has created opportunity for numerous technological advancements, many of which have become consumer products.

Besides encouraging and helping, the government creates *threats* when it affects survival and profits negatively. Many laws and regulations can limit the strategic options of many firms. Some of these laws and regulations include the following:

• *U.S. and state antitrust laws which limit mergers.* Some mergers have been prevented by antitrust policies and lawsuits.

• *Government regulations that significantly affect the strategic options of whole industries.* States and provinces limit the ability of utilities to increase profits; thus the utilities have limited amounts for capital spending and the construction of new power plants. Indeed, Detroit Edison provides an example of the plight of several companies that started nuclear power plants in the late 1960s and early 1970s. Plans were announced in July 1968 for a new plant estimated to cost $230 million with targeted start-up in February, 1974. Because of licensing bottlenecks, new environmental rules, redesigns for new safety rules and nuclear waste storage, and the intervening inflation and interest costs due to delays, costs had risen to $3.1 billion with a start-up in 1985. The "nuclear" option doesn't even seem available to power companies at this point in time.

• *Governmental policies that change economic conditions, tax laws, etc., can create threats to individual businesses.* Exhibit 3.7 provides one example.

Aside from laws and regulations, government policy changes can lead to increases in threats to firms. As indicated above, policy changes can lead to opportunities for some firms and threats to others. But some produce mostly threats to industries. The EPA threatens the auto business. State laws controlling the weights of trucks limit where certain trucking businesses can compete. Antiredlining regulations limit where

EXHIBIT 3.7   TAXES CHANGE THE BUSINESS DEFINITION OF INTEGRATED RESOURCES

Integrated Resources faces a major business definition change as a result of shifts in governmental tax regulations.

Even though Integrated has acquired over $7 billion in real estate and has expertise in property investing, it is not a real estate company. And while it has about $6 billion of life insurance policies in force, it is not a life insurance company either. Integrated services over 125,000 clients who invested in about 500 tax-sheltered limited partnerships. Enter Congress and the IRS.

Congress has intensified its efforts to close tax loopholes and shut down tax-shelter sales companies. The Internal Revenue Service has challenged more and more tax-shelter deals, and uncertainty over future tax-code tightening further dims sales prospects.

According to one of the cofounders of Integrated, the best thing that could happen to Integrated would be for Congress to "leave the tax system alone for three to five years." But this doesn't seem to be in the cards.

Hence, Integrated is diversifying out of tax shelters, and some of its real estate programs have become less tax-oriented. The investment program dabbles in equipment leasing, energy, and cable TV. But two of the fastest growing segments of business are leveraged buy-outs of operating businesses and restaurant franchising. The company is thinking about marketing everything from variable annuities to mutual funds and money market accounts. Says one cofounder, "I would like to become a household word in managing finances."

It seems that governmental tax policy changes have moved this firm to rethink its basic mission definition.

Source: Adapted from "A Tax-Shelter Specialist That Wants to Change Its Spots," *Business Week*, Oct. 8, 1984, pp. 149–151.

a thrift institution can lend its money. And California almost passed a law that would have severely hurt the tobacco industry. Several states banned the sale of Tylenol when poison was found in one bottle.

A special case of a threat from the government is government competition with the private sector. From their beginnings, the U.S. and Canadian governments have performed certain services and produced certain products which put them in competition with firms. For example, Safeway Stores has to compete with U.S. military commissaries. A firm competing in the food industry or in some other industry likely to be involved with government competition must consider what government "firms," with no profit requirement and no tax payments, could do in the industry and must monitor the environment to see if the government is making moves toward entering the industry.

As in other sectors, threats to one firm may offer opportunities to another as a result of government actions. For instance, strict air-pollution regulation could threaten coal-burning utilities but provide opportunity for those who install smokestack scrubbers.

As you can see, government can be quite pervasive. In fact, it can influence every other environmental sector. Government strongly influences socioeconomic conditions through fiscal policy, zoning, and other regulations. It can thwart or promote innovation and technology directly or indirectly. It can affect supplies of labor and materials and especially supplies of capital. Government itself can be a direct competitor, or it can influence competition, for example through the enforcement of antitrust laws. An interesting example of how a typical firm can be affected is given in Exhibit 3.8.

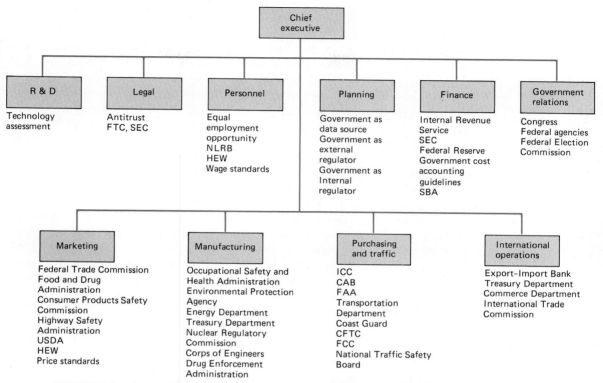

EXHIBIT 3.8   **Typical industrial corporation and federal government relations.**
(M. Weidenbaum, "Public Policy: No Longer a Spectator Sport for Business." Reprinted by permission from the Journal of Business Strategy, *vol. 1, no. 1 (Summer 1980). Copyright © 1980, Warren, Gorham and Lamont, Inc. 210 South St., Boston, Mass. All rights reserved.)*

It shows how a "shadow" organization of public officials matches the organization chart.

Corporations have finally come to the point where proactive postures are increasingly witnessed in efforts to influence government. Of course, there have always been attempts to influence legislators and regulators or public officials. But firms now are more willing to push for favorable rulings and even take regulators to court instead of negotiating. What perhaps bothers strategists most about government is uncertainty. Constant change or new interpretations or efforts make planning difficult. So political action committees and a variety of approaches are used to try to influence government actions and reduce uncertainty.

In sum, firms must search the environment, try to influence government policy, and try to seize the opportunities and mitigate the threats that government policy presents.

ANALYZING THE ENVIRONMENT

We have now discussed the sectors in the general environment typically analyzed by strategists. These are the items which strategists must monitor. By monitoring these sectors, strategists can identify conditions to determine their nature, function, and relationships. For example, social trends and values, such as concerns about smoking, may eventually find their way into government regulations. (Some states ban smoking in public facilities and the federal government has considered banning all tobacco advertising.) Hence, interrelationships among sectors must be analyzed. This leads to a determination of whether the condition is a threat to the firm's current strategy or an opportunity for the future. In addition, strategists identify the current strategy the firm uses to relate to the environment and reanalyze the assumptions about the firm's relationship to the environment, noting which ones appear to be still true and which ones may have changed.

Not all the factors are equally important to all firms. In Chapter 4 we will outline how strategists pay more attention to some than to others. Here, recall that the mission helps determine which aspects or sectors should be analyzed. For instance, TWA might look at the FCC as well as at the CAB in its governmental analysis if communication is seen as relevant to the mission of transportating people from place to place.

Before we move on to diagnosis, we want to explain how the environment can be analyzed, describe environmental analysis, and discuss who does the analysis.

Techniques for Environmental Analysis [9]

Earlier in the chapter, it was noted that the strategist assesses the future before making a diagnosis. This is done by forecasting. At this point, we will review *how* the strategist analyzes the environment. This analysis is done by means of a search of verbal and written information, spying, forecasting and formal studies, and information systems.

First of all, there is the gathering of verbal information, that is, information that we hear. This information can be gathered informally or formally (for example, at meetings and conferences).

Sources of verbal information include

- Such media as radio and television
- The firm's employees, such as peers, subordinates, and supervisors
- Others outside the firm, including (1) customers of the enterprise, (2) persons in the industry channels (for example, wholesalers and brokers), (3) suppliers doing business with the firm, (4) competitors and their employees, (5) financial executives such as bankers, stockholders, and stock analysts, (6) consultants, and (7) government and university employees.

Written or documentary information is what we learn by reading from information prepared by others for various purposes. Managers read newspapers, trade journals, industry newsletters, and general publications. In some firms top managers subscribe to clipping services, which search periodicals and papers and summarize the information for them. A number of experts point out that much can be learned from reading the annual reports and 10K's of significant competitors. The 10K is a very detailed annual report. The federal government requires that all firms listed on the stock exchange must submit a 10K to the Securities and Exchange Commission.

There are a number of sources which can tell you where to locate information on a business if you are searching the environment as a manager or analyzing a case as a student. A summary of a variety of information sources is appended to Chapter 4. The Freedom of Information Act in the United States allows competitors to acquire information about firms which do business with the government or which are in a regulated industry. However, attempts are being made to reduce the easy access to government information about competitors.

Another solution is to design a management information system (MIS) to bring the information to the strategists [10]. This approach formalizes the line and staff gathering of the information desired by the strategists on a regular basis. Many experts advocate this approach, although some feel that a formal MIS fails to work properly, since information is often limited, untimely, or unreliable. Another version of an MIS is a strategic information system (SIS), which some firms have developed. Strategic databases can be developed by relying on inputs from customers, suppliers, competitors, internal managers, the sales force, R&D units, and so on. These are often organized on the basis of answering questions which must be addressed in the strategic management process: What opportunities are available? What environmental conditions will affect us? What competitive actions will affect us? What strengths do we have? What weaknesses do we have? Strategic databases can be built from various information sources (see appendix to Chapter 4) such that the strategic management process is facilitated. Problems similar to the MIS are to get managers to accept and use the SIS adequately.

A third technique for environmental analysis, one normally used to gather information about potential or actual competitors, is spying. The top executive (or, more likely, a middle-level executive encouraged, however surreptitiously, by a top executive) employs an individual or individuals to determine trade secrets. The spy can be an employee of the competitor, one of the competitor's suppliers or customers, or a "professional" spy. Although it varies by industry and functional areas, industrial espionage appears to be increasing. This observation is based on survey data and expenditures on systems to protect trade secrets and industrial processes.

A fourth approach to analyzing the environment is formal forecasting [11]. Normally it is performed by corporate planners or other staff personnel or consultants at the request of top management. There is a group of consultants specializing in this called "futurists," and there are a number of journals dealing with this subject, such as *Technological Forecasting and Social Change, Journal of Environment and Planning, Early Warning Weekly, Futures,* and *Journal of Forecasting.*

The advent of personal computers and software to do economic forecasting has made it cheaper and easier to test many different policies or strategies with what-if scenarios. While there are problems with all models, most are a good tool to organize thinking.

All the factors in the environment have been subjected to forecasting, some more successfully than others. And a number of forecasting techniques are available. Another technique is polling. Many firms pay thousands of dollars yearly to receive reports of social attitudes about the economy, government, their products, and so on. Of course, market research departments can provide important pieces of environmental information as well.

Descriptions of Environmental Analysis [12]

In the previous section, we outlined the *prescription* for performing an analysis on all sectors of the environment. Here, we want to summarize the *descriptive* conclusions about these approaches.

First, strategists generally seem to be more concerned with the economy than with any other factors, although competition is also seen as important. Other factors become more important depending on the general state of the economy. Second, strategists do seem to spend a significant amount of time (up to 2 hours daily) analyzing the environment in some fashion, though this varies by industry. Third, the primary method is making verbal contacts inside and outside the firm, although this varies by level in the organization, with lower levels using more written sources. Fourth, formal prediction techniques such as forecasting, modeling, and using an MIS are viewed skeptically by many strategists, but the use of these techniques may be increasing. Finally, even though they are concerned, some executives may be psychologically unprepared to cope with change.

To summarize, there are several prescriptive implications of the realities of environmental analysis:

1 It is critical for strategists to develop an effective network of human sources to provide inputs for environmental analysis. These should be well-informed, knowledgeable sources inside the organization (in various functions and in all geographic areas) and outside the organization.

2 Those who favor MIS or SIS approaches must learn how to get their findings more quickly and more easily to this informal network if they are to have any impact at all. A strategic information system could help here.

This brings us to the role of managers in diagnosing the meanings of the findings of environmental analysis. They do not just react automatically to what they find—*they* must impute meaning to it and make decisions accordingly.

The Role of Strategists in Analysis and Diagnosis [13]

As discussed in Chapter 2, there are several groups of strategists involved in strategic management. How does each group relate to the environmental analysis and diagnosis phase of strategic management? Exhibit 3.9 summarizes this relationship.

As can be seen, the top managers of corporations or SBUs are involved in verbal search behavior and supplement their work with help from corporate planners and occasionally the board. Again, these people engage in verbal search and occasionally

EXHIBIT 3.9   THE ROLE OF STRATEGISTS IN THE ANALYSIS AND DIAGNOSIS OF THE ENVIRONMENT

| Strategists | Analysis | | | | Diagnosis and decision making |
	Verbal search	Documentary search	Formal forecasts and studies	MIS/ SIS	
Top managers	Regularly	Rarely	Rarely	Rarely	Performs
Corporate planners	Regularly	Occasionally	Occasionally	Rarely	Advises as requested
Board of directors	Occasionally	Rarely	Rarely	Rarely	Occasionally advises
Consultants	Rarely	Occasionally	Rarely	NA	Occasionally hired to advise

use other methods of search. Then the top managers diagnose the significance of the findings. Let's examine that issue now.

DIAGNOSIS OF THE ENVIRONMENT

After analysis is complete, the strategists must diagnose the results. They assess the significance of the opportunities and threats discovered by the analysis of environmental conditions.

In Chapter 1, we discussed the conditions under which decisions would be made. The first condition was that the strategists perceive a gap between expected accomplishment and desired accomplishment. This is the decision-recognition phase. The environmental analysis may indicate a gap due to threats or opportunities. Once this is recognized, the strategists focus on the threats and opportunities if they are motivated to improve the future and feel that the company can do something to close a gap which may exist due to environmental factors.

The diagnosis requires the strategists to decide which sets of information to believe and which data to ignore, and to evaluate some information as important and other information as less important. This is the heart of diagnosis.

In Chapter 2, we discussed the strategists and their jobs and values. Since they are doing the diagnosis, it is useful to recall that value systems, internal power, etc., are important to the strategic management process. Here, similar factors emerge to affect a diagnosis of the environment: factors about the strategists, factors about the strategist's job, factors about the group of strategists, factors in the strategist's environment.

Diagnosis and Strategists' Characteristics [14]

A large number of characteristics of the strategist determine how well and whether the strategist diagnoses opportunities in and threats from the environment. Only a few can be discussed here.

The more *relevant experience* the strategist has, the greater the tendency to do a more accurate and higher-quality diagnosis. Older executives take longer to diagnose but usually do a better job of it. Cognitive capabilities can also be developed through training and education to improve diagnostic ability (one of the reasons for this book).

The *higher the aspiration* level of the strategist—in other words, the more motivated the executive is—the better the diagnosis (assuming data are available and used). Motivation is affected by the strategist's needs (for example, the need for achievement, the need for affiliation, and the need for power) and the rewards received for performance. Diagnosis may not be effectively performed if the rewards are based on short-run actions and results. This leads to behavior which may not be conducive to good diagnosis. A junior-level marketing executive is rewarded for today's and this week's sales, not for sales forecasting. A junior-level operations executive is rewarded for getting today's work out, not for planning a plant addition for 5 years from now. The junior accountant is rewarded for getting statements out on time. If the whole career learning is based on speedy feedback and rewards for short-run results, the executives carry these behavior patterns into senior management positions.

Individuals' perceptions of the environment are based upon their predispositions for dealing with the uncertainty of information. The *perceptual mode* influences the kind of diagnosis made. Persons who are *risk-aversive* will perform environmental analysis conservatively, analyzing and diagnosing one attribute at a time. Those who are willing to take risks will focus on gambling, varying more than one attribute at a time. Risk seekers vs. risk averters also react differently to environmental conditions. Some see the glass half empty, others see it half full. Some are *reflective,* while others are *impulsive.* Some strategists take a small amount of information and seek a speedy "gestalt closure." They impulsively diagnose and quickly act. Executives who are *dogmatic,* whose "minds are made up," make rapid diagnoses on the basis of inadequate information. Some strategists are so dogmatic that they tend to ignore the environment, or they believe it to be more stable than it really is. (For example, Singer executives believed that their sewing machine business was in great shape in 1979.) Many organizations have found it useful to include in their executive group an individual who disagrees with the basic belief systems of the other executives to make sure that contrary possibilities are brought up and discussed. This is the maverick executive, or the devil's advocate. People with *abstract conceptual structures* process many dimensions of information and use a complex approach to integration. The ability to deal with abstract aspects is valuable for the diagnosis of changes in the environment.

The *psychological mood* at the time of diagnosis (or any decision) can make an executive feel optimistic or pessimistic. Problems in their private lives can make them devote less time to diagnosis or give them a pessimistic attitude toward diagnosis and analysis.

Other than the mood at the time, the psychological ability to accept change is important to environmental diagnosis (and the entire strategic management process). It is widely observed that people resist change. This is not just perversity. We spend our time and use our ego building present procedures and ways of doing things. To change these is to experience in a small way death and predeath, retirement. If the old ways must change, the "old" executives can be threatened.

All these factors and more in the strategist determine whether diagnosis takes place, how well diagnosis is performed, and some of the outcomes of the diagnosis. For instance, if the strategist is risk-oriented and optimistic, a greater search for change is likely. Opportunities are more likely to be perceived than threats from the same data. Moreover, a *proactive* rather than *reactive* posture is likely to result. That is, strategies to force change can result. This is most easily seen in the technology sector. Proactive innovators create change; others react. While changes in some sectors of the environment are beyond *control,* they are not beyond the *influence* of strategists.

Diagnosis and the Strategist's Job [15]

The second set of factors influencing diagnosis concerns the nature of the executive's job. Several factors seem important.

Time pressures and stress seem to reduce the emphasis placed on environmental analysis and diagnosis. Executives can have many things to do; for example, they meet customers, promote people, and handle ordinary tasks. And ordinary short-run tasks have a way of filling up the day. Simon called this phenomenon "Gresham's law of planning": present pressing duties drive out long-run consideration. It should be pointed out that top managers can create the conditions for more or less stress by means of effective delegation and similar management techniques.

The *significance of the decision* will influence how much time executives devote to diagnosis. More time is given if the relative impact of a "correct" diagnosis is great.

If the firm has substantial *resources,* it can take the time and use extensive resources to analyze and diagnose the environment. If the resource base is weak, this may prevent effective diagnosis.

If managers believe that they have *discretion* to make decisions, they will engage in search activities more so than if they feel they are unable to make a decision. This applies more to the activities of SBU executives than to the activities of top corporate managers.

Diagnosis and the Group of Strategists [16]

In many cases, diagnosis is performed by several strategists—the top management team. The kind and amount of diagnosis which takes place will be affected by the presence or absence of *team spirit,* the extent to which the strategists are a *cohesive group* (without serious conflict), and by the *power plays* which may be taking place within this group. If there is significant conflict, diagnosis may become a battle: if one executive diagnoses the situation one way, a rival will take the opposite position. If there is good team spirit, all can bring their talents to the diagnosis and probably improve the process. However, Janis cautions that if the group is overly cohesive, it may make an inaccurate diagnosis or ignore important information. As before, a devil's advocate may be a useful addition to a top management group.

Descriptively, you should be aware that planning groups may believe that top management is not prepared to deal with change. As a result, senior managers may be shielded from bad news or threats in the environment.

THE ENVIRONMENT-STRATEGY INTERFACE [17]

The preceding sections indicate that the process of diagnosis is affected by a number of factors. But how do firms use the diagnosis?

Managers view the impact of their environment in different ways. Some see ambiguity (uncertainty) as threatening and some see it as opportunistic. Some perceive changes as threats or opportunities which merely require adaptation of the organization or its strategy. In other words, many executives respond reactively to change. Others view their environment proactively. They seek to make choices about which parts of the environment can be manipulated and then seek to set up a strategy to start manipulating. For example, in the governmental sector, firms set up political action committees or use public relations offices to influence governmental policy and decision makers in ways favorable to them. In the technological sector, some firms scan the research and then move their labs in the direction the technology appears to be moving. Other firms seek to strike out on their own to gain acceptance for the technological direction in which they have chosen to proceed.

A very interesting descriptive study of how firms deal with technological changes in the environment serves to point out that a variety of strategic choices are actually made by firms. Cooper et al. studied how diesels replaced steam locomotives, transistors affected vacuum tubes, ball-point pens affected fountain pens, nuclear plants affected fossil-fuel boilers, and electric razors challenged safety razors. Some of the key findings follow:

- Sales of the old technology continued to expand, in some cases 40 years after the new technology was introduced.
- When sales did decline, it took from 2 to 11 years for sales of the new technology to exceed sales of the old one.
- New technologies often created new markets and invaded old markets by capturing a series of submarkets sequentially.
- The commercial introduction of new technology often was made by a firm outside the traditional industry.
- All but one of 15 firms made an effort to participate in the new technology, three by acquisition.
- An early and rapid commitment to new technology was often unsuccessful.
- The old technology reached its highest stage of development after new technology was introduced, and all companies continued to invest heavily in the old technology.

A number of implications can be drawn from this study. But a major conclusion is that strategic responses to environmental threats can vary significantly. Moreover, there is ample time to respond to environmental change, and attempts to influence the nature of the change and its impact can be made. Furthermore, environmental assessment seems to require a broader definition of the scope of the firm's mission so that the firm can detect changes occurring outside the traditional view of its industry. Finally, it may be relatively difficult to change past strategy, even in view of significant competitive threats.

Thus while environmental assessment is a critical process, you should also be aware

EXHIBIT 3.10   A LONG-TERM ECONOMIC ASSUMPTION GUIDES THIS STRATEGY

Andre Horn, chairman of Joy Manufacturing, is a believer in economic theory. In the fall of 1981, Joy used the controversial "long-wave" theory of Russian economist Nikolai Kondratieff to foresee the worst recession in decades. Months ahead of competitors, Joy dropped uncompetitive businesses and cut its work force in half. Despite a 37 percent drop in sales, Joy stayed in the black in 1983 while most rivals suffered losses.

Horn believes that the world economy is in a 10-year transition period between two 45- and 60-year growth cycles. During the transition, which Horn believes began in 1979, the United States is shedding excess capacity. A sustained growth period should begin in 1990 according to this theory. In step with these cycles, Joy has laid out a strategy to survive early in the transition and then to reposition itself for the next upturn by increasing its presence in capital goods.

Horn is once again warning that capital goods producers will face another wrenching downturn during the 1980s. This time, instead of slimming down, Joy is embarking on an acquisition plan to double its size by 1990.

In this case, long-term economic assumptions have led to a sequential strategy of retrenchment to be followed by expansion. Note that perceptions of threat and opportunity, and strategic choices, varied based on economic assumptions.

Source: Adapted from "Joy Mfg.: Out to Double Its Size as It Predicts a 1990s Boom in Capital Goods," *Business Week,* Apr. 9, 1984, pp. 61–62.

that internal conditions may vary and consequently constrain the very usefulness of this process.

Exhibit 3.10 indicates how one firm has made some long-term economic assumptions and pursues a strategy to fit these expectations. Again, there appear to be a variety of ways that firms can choose to look at the general environment. And strategic choices about how to deal with the environment allow for substantial managerial discretion.

SUMMARY

It is the crucial job of top management to create the conditions for effective analysis and diagnosis of the environment. This means that the management must determine what factors in the environment are most crucial, which in turn influences what information will be gathered and where in the enterprise it will be analyzed and diagnosed.

The general environment includes factors in several sectors outside the firm which can lead to opportunities or threats. These include the socioeconomic, technological, and governmental sectors.

Strategists try to cope with the environment through analysis and diagnosis. Environmental analysis is the process by which strategists monitor the environmental settings. Analysis is the process of identifying observed conditions (socioeconomic, technological, etc.) in order to determine whether they present a threat for existing strategy or an opportunity for a new strategy. Environmental diagnosis consists of decisions made as a result of the environmental analysis. These decisions are an assessment of the significance of the opportunities and threats discovered by the analysis. In effect, diagnosis is an opinion resulting from an analysis of the facts to determine the nature of a problem with a view toward acting to take advantage of an opportunity or to effectively manage a threat. Exhibit 3.1 outlined the analysis and diagnosis process to examine the important gaps associated with the environment.

Propositions 3.1 and 3.2 summarize why environmental analysis and diagnosis is performed.

Proposition 3.1

A firm whose strategy fits the needs of its environment will be more effective.

Proposition 3.2

The major causes of growth, decline, and other large-scale changes in firms are factors in the environment, not internal developments.

The chapter discussed in some detail the three sectors in the general environment which strategists analyze and diagnose.

- The socioeconomic sector includes economic, climatic, and social factors.
- The technological sector affects raw materials, operations, and the product or service life cycle.
- The government sector seems to be increasingly important, since its roles include tax collector, regulator, competitor, customer, researcher, and supplier. It has an impact on every other environmental sector.

Then the methods of analyzing the environment were discussed. The methods used include the gathering of verbal and written information, the use of clipping services, the use of management information systems (MIS), formal forecasting, and spying. The conclusions of this section can be summarized in Propositions 3.3. to 3.5.

Proposition 3.3

Most top managers gather information about the environment verbally. Written information, forecasting, and MIS are not significant sources of information for analyses by top managers, but their use may be increasing.

Proposition 3.4

The more information contacts the strategist seeks, the better is the environmental analysis. In larger organizations, the contacts are primarily internal. In smaller organizations, the contacts are normally external.

Proposition 3.5

The more sectors and the more factors that are analyzed, the more effective is the environmental analysis.

Next we examined the role of the strategists in environmental analysis and diagnosis. Again, the top managers are the crucial analysts and diagnosticians. They may be helped by a corporate planning staff and consultants in larger organizations.

Then we discussed the diagnosis of the data generated in analysis. How the data are diagnosed depends on

• Factors concerning the strategist, such as experience, motivation, perception, and psychological mood
• Factors related to the strategist's job, such as time pressures and stress, resource availability, and discretion
• Factors in the strategist's group, such as team spirit, cohesiveness, and power plays

Environmental analysis and diagnosis is a crucial part of the strategic management process. If the environment is ignored (or partially ignored) by strategic decision makers, the process cannot be effective. Effective strategists try to anticipate what is coming, or attempt to influence the environment in favorable directions. Usually the lead time for change is long, not overnight. This requires a long-term strategic vision and commitment to strategic management. As Cooper points out, diesel locomotives were first built in 1924 and received great publicity. But it was not until 1934 that General Motors produced its first diesel, and the Baldwin and Lima Companies remained in the steam locomotive field even after 20 years of declining sales (and increasing diesel sales).

If a firm focuses its analysis primarily internally, in all but the most stable environments its strategic management process will also be less effective. You should recognize that environmental analysis interrelates with the formation of objectives, the generation of alternative strategies, and the other aspects of strategic management.

Chapter 4 examines in more detail some other sectors of the environment managers focus on as well. Many of the approaches and factors discussed here for the general environment also apply to diagnosis of the industry and international environments. We won't repeat those ideas. But we will introduce other tools for diagnosis to help summarize conclusions from the analysis of the general, industry, and international environments. The sectors of the general environment described here must be added to those from the industry and international environments for a comprehensive picture of threats and opportunities for the firm and its strategy.

REFERENCES

[1] The Role of the Environment in Strategic Management

Aguilar, F.: *Scanning the Business Environment* (New York: Macmillan, 1967).

[2] The Importance of Environmental Analysis

Bourgeois, L. J.: "The Environmental Perceptions of Strategy Makers and Their Economic Correlates," working paper, University of Pittsburgh, 1978.

Grinyer, P. H., and D. Norburn: "Planning for Existing Markets: Perceptions of Executives and Financial Performance," *Journal of Royal Statistical Society,* vol. 138 (1975), part I, pp. 70–97.

[3] Categorizing the Environment

Lenz, R. T. and J. L. Engledow: "Alternative Models for Analyzing Organizational Environments," working paper, Graduate School of Business, Columbia University, 1983.

[4] Economic Factors

"America's Restructured Economy," *Business Week,* June 1, 1981, pp. 55–100.
Farrell, C., T. Mason, and R. Mitchell: "The Rush is On to Cut the Cost of Debt," *Business Week,* Mar. 24, 1986, pp. 33–34.
Menosh, E., K. Pennar, S. Weiss, and D. Cook: "Living with Disinflation," *Business Week,* July 15, 1985, pp. 54–60.
Pennar, K., N. Jonas, S. Bartlett, H. Gleckman, and B. Riemer: "Hooray for Cheap Money," *Business Week,* Mar. 24, 1986, pp. 30–33.
Toffler, A.: *The Third Wave* (New York: Morrow, 1980).

[5] Climatic Factors

"Perverse Weather," *Business Week,* Feb. 27, 1978, pp. 60ff.
"Struggling to Cope without Snow," *Business Week,* Feb. 18, 1980, p. 66.

[6] Social Factors

Burck, C.: "Changing Habits in American Drinking," *Fortune,* Oct. 1976, pp. 156–161, 164 ff.
"Bidding for an Elusive Market," *Business Week,* Nov. 7, 1977, p. 72.
"Campbell Soup Fails to Make It to the Table," *Business Week,* Oct. 12, 1981, p. 66.
Higgins, J. C., and D. Romano: "Social Forecasting: An Integral Part of Corporate Planning?" *Long Range Planning* (April 1980), pp. 82–86.
"New Benefits for New Lifestyles," *Business Week,* Feb. 11, 1980, pp. 111–112.
Sease, D.: "The Nomads," *The Wall Street Journal,* Aug. 21, 1978.

[7] Technological Factors

Chase, M.: "U.S. Electronics Firms Consider Joining in Research Venture to Counter Japanese," *The Wall Street Journal,* Mar. 1, 1982, p. 7.
Clark, E., and A. Hall: "America's R&D Establishment Is Not Just Crying Wolf," *Business Week,* Mar. 24, 1986, p. 38.
"The Dark Side of the Business Tax Cuts," *Business Week,* June 11, 1984, pp. 135–138.
Sahal, D.: *Patterns of Technological Innovation* (Reading, Mass.: Addison-Wesley, 1981).
"Thinner Cream for the Dairy Business," *Business Week,* July 31, 1978.
Ulman, N.: "Bon Voyage: After Years of Decline, U.S. Fishing Industry Is Beginning to Boom," *The Wall Street Journal,* July 25, 1977.
"Vanishing Innovation," *Business Week,* July 3, 1978.
Wasson, C.: *Dynamic Competitive Strategy and Product Life Cycle* (St. Charles, Ill: Challenge Books, 1974).

[8] Governmental Factors

"Behind AT&T's Change at the Top," *Business Week,* Nov. 6, 1978.

"Breaking a Bottleneck in Long Haul Trucking," *Business Week,* Mar. 6, 1978.

"Business Comes Out Swinging at Regulators," *Business Week,* Apr. 7, 1980, p. 112.

"Deregulating America," *Business Week,* Nov. 28, 1983, pp. 80–89.

"General Signal Cashes In on Federal Dollars," *Business Week,* Mar. 21, 1977.

Shipper, F. and M. M. Jennings: *Business Strategy for the Political Arena* (Westport, Conn.: Greenwood Press, 1984).

"Too Many Cereals for the FTC," *Business Week,* Mar. 20, 1978.

"Where Utilities and Antinuclear Activists Agree," *Business Week* Apr. 16, 1984, pp. 185–187.

[9] Techniques for Environmental Analysis

Bowman, E.: "Strategy, Annual Reports, and Alchemy," *California Management Review,* vol. 20 (Spring 1978), pp. 64–71.

Fahey, L., and V. K. Narayanan: *Macro Environmental Analysis for Strategic Management* (St. Paul, Minn.: West, 1986).

Montgomery, D. et al.: "The Freedom of Information Act: Strategic Opportunities and Threats," *Sloan Management Review* (Winter 1978), pp. 1–13.

Thietart, R. A., and R. Vivas: "Strategic Intelligence Activity: The Management of the Sales Force as a Source of Strategic Information," *Strategic Management Journal,* vol. 2 (1981), pp. 15–25.

[10] The MIS System for Analysis

Hershey, R.: "Competitive Intelligence for the Smaller Company," *Management Review,* vol. 66 (January 1977), pp. 18–22.

King, W. R. and D. Cleland: "The Strategic Information Subsystem," *Strategic Planning and Policy* (New York: Van Nostrand Reinhold, 1978).

Mintzberg, H.: *Impediments to the Use of Management Information* (New York: National Association of Accountants, 1975).

Radford, K. J.: "Some Initial Specifications for a Strategic Information System," *Omega,* vol. 6 (1978), pp. 139–144.

[11] Forecasting

Armstrong, J. S.: *Long Range Forecasting* (New York: Wiley, 1985).

———: "How Expert are the Experts?" *INC* (December 1981), pp. 15–16.

Holloway, C.: "Does Futures Research Have a Corporate Role?" *Long Range Planning* (October 1978), pp. 17–24.

"How Personal Computers Are Changing the Forecaster's Job," *Business Week,* Oct. 11, 1984, pp. 123–124.

LeBell, D., and O. J. Krasner: "Selecting Environmental Forecasting Techniques from Business Planning Requirements," *Academy of Management Review* (July 1977), pp. 373–383.

Rippe, R.: "The Integration of Corporate Forecasting and Planning," *Columbia Journal of World Business,* vol. 11 (Winter 1976), pp. 54–61.

Wheelwright, S., and S. Makridakis: *Forecasting Methods for Management* (New York: Wiley, 1977).

[12] What Executives Analyze

Glueck, W. F.: *Business Policy and Strategic Management,* 3d ed. (New York: McGraw-Hill, 1980).

"Japan's Business Intelligence Beehive," *Business Week,* Dec. 14, 1981, p. 52.

Lewis, M. F.: "Assessment of Environmental Issues—A Three-Industry Comparison," paper presented at the Academy of Management meeting, New York, 1982.

[13] Who Does Environmental Analysis

Engledow, J. L., and R. T. Lenz: "Whatever Happened to Environmental Analysis?" *Long Range Planning,* vol. 18 (April 1985), pp. 93–106.

———— and ————: "The Evolution of Environmental Analysis Units in Ten Leading Edge Firms," working paper #S.C. 39, Graduate School of Business, Columbia University, 1984.

Preble, J. F.: "The Selection of Delphi Panels for Strategic Planning Purposes," *Strategic Management Journal,* vol. 5 (1984), pp. 157–170.

[14] Strategists' Characteristics Affecting Diagnosis

Duncan, R. B.: "Characteristics of Organizational Environments and Perceived Environmental Uncertainty," *Administrative Science Quarterly,* vol. 17 (1972), pp. 313–327.

Miller, D., M. F. R. deVries, and J. Toulouse: "Top Executive Locus of Control and the Relationship to Strategy Making, Structure, and Environment," working paper, McGill University, Montreal, December 1980.

O'Hanlon, T.: "Behind the Snafu at Singer," *Fortune,* Nov. 5, 1979, pp. 76–80.

Taylor, R.: "Psychological Determinants of Bounded Rationality," *Decision Sciences,* vol. 6 (July 1975), pp. 409–429.

————: "Age and Experience as Determinants of Managerial Information Processing and Decision Making Performance," *Academy of Management Journal,* vol. 18 (1975).

[15] Job Characteristics Affecting Diagnosis

Anderson, C. et al.: "Managerial Response to Environmentally Induced Stress," *Academy of Management Journal,* vol. 20 (1977), pp. 260–272.

Dickson, J.: "The Relation of Individual Search Activity to Subjective Job Characteristics," *Human Relations,* vol. 29 (1976), pp. 911–928.

ElSawy, O. A.: "Understanding the Process by Which Chief Executives Identify Strategic Threats and Opportunities," *Academy of Management Proceedings,* 1984, pp. 37–40.

Simon, H.: *Administrative Behavior: A Study of Administrative Processes in Administrative Organization,* 3d ed. (New York: Free Press, 1976).

[16] Group Factors Affecting Diagnosis

Janis, I. L.: *Victims of Groupthink* (Boston: Houghton Mifflin, 1972).

[17] The Environment-Strategy Interface

Aplin, J. C., and W. H. Hegarty: "Political Influence: Strategies Employed by Organizations to Impact Legislation in Business and Economic Matters," *Academy of Management Journal,* vol. 23 (1980), pp. 438–450.

Boulton, W. R., W. M. Lindsay, S. G. Franklin, and L. W. Rue: "Strategic Planning: Determining the Impact of Environmental Characteristics and Uncertainty," *Academy of Management Journal,* vol. 25 (1982), pp. 500–509.

Cooper, A. et al.: "Strategic Responses to Technological Threats," *Proceedings of the Academy of Management* (1973).

Jauch, L. R. and K. L. Kraft: "Strategic Management of Uncertainty," *Academy of Management Review,* vol. 11 (1986), pp. 777–790.

Lenz, R. T.: "Environment, Strategy, Organization Structure and Performance: Patterns in One Industry," *Strategic Management Journal,* vol. 1 (July–September 1980), pp. 209–226.

Smircich, L., and C. Stubbart: "Strategic Management in An Enacted World," *Academy of Management Review,* vol. 10 (1985), pp. 724–736.

CHAPTER OUTLINE

CHAPTER 4

THE INDUSTRY AND INTERNATIONAL ENVIRONMENT

OBJECTIVES

- To introduce the sectors in the industry environment which should be analyzed and diagnosed
- To introduce the international environment
- To examine ways the industry environment can be analyzed
- To introduce the environmental threat and opportunity profile (ETOP) for summarizing the results of analysis and diagnosis of the environment
- To indicate how the ETOP can be used in the strategic management process

INTRODUCTION

This is the second chapter that focuses on the analysis and diagnosis of environmental factors that present threats and opportunities to the firm. Exhibit 3.1 listed the general, the industry, and the international environments as areas strategists must examine for factors which could lead to strategic gaps. The last chapter introduced the general environment and described various aspects of performing analysis and diagnosis. As Exhibit 4.1 indicates, this chapter describes the industry and international environments. It also provides additional techniques for analyzing these sectors of the environment, as well as an overall tool—the environment threat and opportunity profile—which can be used to summarize all the environmental conditions to help focus the diagnosis on the most significant factors affecting the strategy of the firm. The appendix provides some sources of information that you can use to find information on all the sectors of the environment.

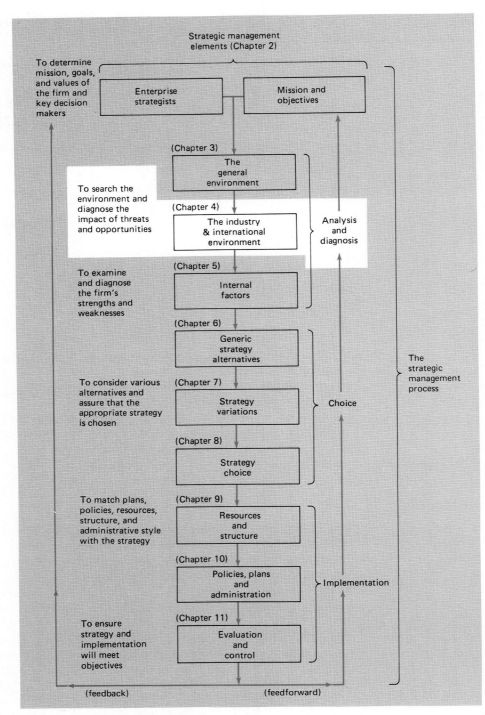

Strategic management
elements (Chapter 2)

To determine
mission, goals,
and values of
the firm and
key decision
makers

Enterprise
strategists

Mission and
objectives

(Chapter 3)

The
general
environment

To search the
environment and
diagnose the
impact of threats
and opportunities

(Chapter 4)

The industry
& international
environment

Analysis
and
diagnosis

To examine
and diagnose
the firm's
strengths and
weaknesses

(Chapter 5)

Internal
factors

(Chapter 6)

Generic
strategy
alternatives

To consider various
alternatives and
assure that the
appropriate strategy
is chosen

(Chapter 7)

Strategy
variations

Choice

(Chapter 8)

Strategy
choice

To match plans,
policies, resources,
structure, and
administrative style
with the strategy

(Chapter 9)

Resources
and
structure

(Chapter 10)

Policies, plans
and
administration

Implementation

To ensure
strategy and
implementation
will meet
objectives

(Chapter 11)

Evaluation
and
control

The
strategic
management
process

(feedback)   (feedforward)

EXHIBIT 4.1   A model of strategic management.

THE INDUSTRY ENVIRONMENT [1]

The strategies and objectives of a firm (or its SBUS) will be affected by the attractiveness of the industry in which it chooses to do business and its relative competitive position within that industry. An industry can be conceived of as a set of firms which are in competition with one another for customers of their goods and services and which rely upon others that supply critical inputs (supplies). This section of the chapter describes these three sectors of the industry environment—customers, suppliers, and competitors.

Customer Sector

Effective strategists are concerned with who their customers are and their customers' needs and desires. They are also interested in who and where potential customers might be and trends in the future which may lead to changes in customer buying patterns. In effect, opportunities come through identifying and providing for customer utilities, and threats come from failures to meet changing customer requirements. This sector explores three factors that strategists include as part of their industry analysis of the customer sector—buyer identification, demographic factors which create changes in certain customer classes, and geographic locations of markets.

Buyer Identification [2]

Different customers have various reasons for interest in a product or service. They have needs, desires, or requirements to be satisfied by the purchase. Marketers generally indicate three distinct classes of customers. Each of these groups have somewhat different factors that affect their decisions to purchase, as illustrated in Exhibit 4.2.

EXHIBIT 4.2   FACTORS INFLUENCING DIFFERENT BUYERS

Consumers		
Availability	Price	Variety
Convenience	Quality	Warranty
Credit	Reputation	

Retailers and/or Wholesalers	
Competitive product	Product turnover
Consumer recognition	Profit potential
Product availability	Promotional and merchandising support
Product line breadth	Supply dependability

Industrial and/or Institutional Buyers		
Cost vs. profitability	Price	Product performance
Financing	Product information	Source availability
Legal conformity	Product line	Technical assistance

These factors vary in importance depending on the type of product as well. For instance, industrial purchasers of durable goods may be less concerned with price and more concerned with setup or maintenance costs of equipment as a factor in their own profitability. These same purchasers may be very price-sensitive to commodities (such as pens or paper). Exhibit 4.3 indicates how consumer products firms are adapting their strategies as consumer needs have shifted and as demographic changes (discussed below) have come into play.

Strategists identify the nature of these customers and their utilities in order to avoid threats of loss of customers and to find or create opportunities for themselves to find new customers or sell more to existing ones. Again, these customers and their needs may not be static. Our next section indicates a critical factor in the consumer segment to which environmental analysts should pay close attention.

Demographic Factors [3]

There are several important conditions associated with the general population that affect the market for goods and services for different industries. Economists and marketing experts often refer to these as "primary demand factors." The most important of these are as follows:

• *Changes in population.* As the total population changes, the demand for products or services changes. If there are fewer people to buy a good or service, this affects the primary demand for products and services. The population growth rate for the United States, Canada, and the rest of the developed world is declining. The Third

---

EXHIBIT 4.3   THE NEW CONSUMER MAKEUP

The blush is off the cosmetics markets due to changes in the consumers of makeup and their needs and desires. The last big surge was fueled by baby-boom girls who started wearing makeup as teenagers and continued to be heavy users as they moved into the work force in record numbers. But recently, revenues have been flat, and long-term trends look ominous. Avon, Max Factor, and Revlon have suffered large profit declines and loss of market share.

While the number of working women is expected to continue rising, the population of teenagers is declining. With more women working, fewer are left at home to answer the door when a sales representative calls, and fewer are available to become members of the sales force. Moreover, working women have less time and are apt to buy makeup where they do the rest of their shopping—the food stores and discount outlets. Another factor is the shifting reasons believed to motivate the purchaser. Notes a vice president at Revlon, who sells both mass-market and prestige brands, "Cosmetics companies used to sell fantasies and dreams. Women now buy reality and value."

To keep pace with changing consumer lifestyles, values, and demographics, cosmetics firm are using several strategies. Shifts in distribution approaches are being made. For example, Avon now sells at the office. New customers—men—are being targeted by Estee Lauder's skin-care products. And many firms are expanding product lines, revising old products, and changing advertising practices. Clearly, changing patterns of purchase behavior by consumers have provided both threats and opportunities for the strategists of cosmetic firms.

Source: Adapted from A. Dunkin and C. Dugas, "How Cosmetics Makers Are Touching Up Their Strategies," *Business Week,* Sept. 23, 1985, pp. 66–73

World's is not. This can affect a firm's location strategy. If you are operating in a region of a country where the population is declining, you may move your business to a fast-growing area. Or if the population of a city is growing or shifting to the suburbs, this can affect where you concentrate your effort. Population movement to the sunbelt, for example, hurt some firms and helped others.

• *Age shifts in the population.* As the total population changes, the age distribution changes. If the birthrate declines and health care improves, more older people and fewer babies populate an area. Primary demand declines or increases. Because there are fewer babies, strategy changes are taking place in the bubblegum, toy, and soft-drink industries. Even enrollment patterns at colleges and universities are affected by age changes.

• *Income distribution of the population.* In some areas of the world a majority of the income is in a few hands, and most of the people have little money. Sometimes this is true of races. In other areas, there are fewer differentials between upper-, middle-, and lower-income persons and between races. If the middle-income group is smaller than it was 10 years ago, this will affect the primary demand for goods and services with regard to some autos, but not Rolls-Royces.

These kinds of changes create threats and opportunities, and affect strategies of different types of firms and different industries. For instance, in the early 1980s, demographers defined a group known as the Yuppies—young urban professionals— who were the subject of intense efforts by marketers. In the mid- to late 1980s, marketers discovered the "graying of America." The *parents* of the Yuppies in general had greater disposable income and were more inclined to purchase certain classes of products and services. Lodging chains, retailers, airlines, travel agencies, hospitals, and even the Yellow Pages have discovered new opportunities to attract senior citizens. With a growing diversity in market segments and consumer lifestyles, mass marketing is giving way to segmentation.

Geographic Factors

The effective strategist also scans the geographic environment to look for opportunities and threats as part of analyzing the customer sector. Essentially the strategist is trying to determine if conditions are better elsewhere for achieving corporate or SBU objectives. The strategist seeks new locations to add to current locations. Or the strategist can search the environment for areas in which to relocate (either in the same region or in a new region). Sometimes a change involves moving corporate headquarters to a new region. It could also mean moving the plant or operations location from the city to a suburb or from one city to another. A change can come about because of shifts in the general population, because the firm wants a population of customers with the required income for purchasing goods and services or because costs are lower or the quality of life is better in the new location. So while this factor is primarily concerned with the location of markets for customers, other factors such as operating costs could be involved too.

In the customer sector of the industry environment, then, the firm's strategy must take into account who its customers are, what they want, how they are changing, and where they are located.

Suppliers provide capital, labor, materials, and so on to a firm. Effective strategists are concerned about supplier changes in the environment. The strategist is concerned with the cost and availability of all the factors of production used in the business. The cost and availability of raw materials, subassemblies, money, energy, and, to a lesser extent, employees are affected by the power relationships between the firm and the supplier, as described by Porter, who has summarized the relative power of suppliers as follows:

1 The power the supplier has to raise prices and lower buyer profits is dependent on how far the supplier is from the free-competition model. The farther away the supplier is, the greater its power.

2 The power the supplier has to raise prices and lower buyer profits is lessened if the buying firm is a monopolist or oligopolist.

3 The power the supplier has to raise prices and lower profits is greatest when the buyer is not an important customer. The supplier has the least power when there are substitute materials available at a reasonable cost and the most power when there are no acceptable substitutes.

4 The power of the supplier is greatest when the supplier can integrate forward, that is, purchase or control the channel in front of it. For example, a shoe factory could buy the shoe store that sells its shoes.

5 The supplier threat in item 4 can be offset if the buyer can integrate backward and is in a very profitable industry or if it can purchase or control the supplier. For example, the shoe factory could purchase the leather company.

The power of the buyer also affects the cost of supplies. The buyer's power is at a maximum when the buyer's industry is concentrated, when the buyer represents a significant portion of the supplier's business, and if the buyer can virtually integrate backward. The buyer's power is at a minimum when the buyer's industry is competitive, when the cost of switching to a substitute is high, when the supplier's product is an especially important part of the production process, and when the supplier can virtually integrate forward.

Availability and Cost of Raw Materials and Subassemblies

In addition to bargaining with suppliers of raw materials over cost and availability, strategists must search the environment to examine long-run trends in the availability and cost of materials. Some materials are increasing in cost. For example, water used to be a cheap resource. In some areas (for example, Arizona) water is becoming more expensive and its availability is uncertain. Oil refiners (and others) have had to cope with dramatic changes in the supply and cost of crude oil as a basic raw material ever since OPEC became a force in 1974. Shortages and excesses have occurred, as have rapid price increases and decreases over the past 15 years. As will be discussed in Chapter 7, many firms are more and more buying subassemblies and entire products from outside sources—a distinct change in function strategy due to lower costs.

Availability and Cost of Energy

The petroleum situation is one in which key suppliers may be able to cut off the supply, and the long-run costs of petroleum are likely to rise. Strategists must decide what to do—use substitutes, withdraw from a business that relies on energy, or expect rising costs. Similar conditions exist as natural gas, nuclear power, and hydropower become more costly, thus limiting some substitution potential. While coal is a substitute, pollution control costs become a limiting factor. New technologies may help, but energy may be an important strategic factor for firms dependent on this input.

Availability and Cost of Money

Actions by central banks like the Federal Reserve and the Bank of Canada and international currency fluctuations affect the availability of money and the cost to suppliers of money: banks, thrift institutions, and other lenders. Strategists must be aware of conditions in the money market and how they will affect strategy. The cost or availability of capital can limit a firm's strategic options, as we discussed in Chapter 3.

Availability and Cost of Labor

Strategists cannot develop a strategy without determining whether skilled employees are available and at what cost. Coal companies wanted to expand faster than the availability of well-trained miners would permit in the late 1970s. Sports businesses are being affected by the explosion in player costs. And competition is fierce for engineers, technicians, and skilled labor in high technology areas.

Many firms have turned to locating facilities in foreign countries to take advantage of lower-cost labor; some have stopped domestic production entirely and get products from suppliers who have a competitive edge due to low labor costs.

Finally, in addition to availability and cost, lead time must be recognized as a potentially limiting factor for strategies. If the supply of factors of production is not available *when* needed, the strategy may not be effective, or it may be limited in terms of its timing. Exhibit 4.4 provides an example of several issues that strategists can consider in their analysis of supply factors.

Competitor Sector [5]

Besides looking at primary demand and supply factors, strategists examine the state of competition the firm must face, because this also determines whether a firm will remain in its current business and what strategies it will follow in pursuing its business. Four factors must be examined regarding competition: entry and exit of major competitors, substitutes and complements for current products and services, and major strategic changes by current competitors, as shown in Exhibit 4.5.

Entry and Exit of Major Competitors

One of the first questions a strategist asks about the competitive environment is, How has the competition changed? Are there new competitors entering our business?

EXHIBIT 4.4   THE POWER OF SUPPLY

In late 1982, IBM announced plans for a "passive investment" of $250 million for a 12 percent stake of Intel, a semiconductor maker. Intel was IBM's only outside source of supply for computer chips at the time. Observers speculated this was the opening salvo in a change in strategy for many high-tech U.S. companies who may be abandoning a strategy of backward vertical integration (self-control of raw-material inputs).

The prevalent opinion was that IBM was trying to block the Japanese before they do to computers what they did to the U.S. television industry. Japanese TV makers used low bidding to undermine the component suppliers that supported the industry. The same thing began happening with integrated circuits—the vital components of all computers. The independent semiconductor firms began facing financial problems as the Japanese offset new innovations with lower-priced competitive chips. United States chipmakers couldn't get their innovation investment back.

IBM was quite concerned about depending on foreign suppliers of chips. So the move to invest in Intel was seen as a way to make sure its supplier was adequately financed to remain a key supplier. And IBM was establishing unusually close relationships with other outside suppliers. Other computer, communications, and semiconductor firms were similarly increasing cooperation with one another through strategies of joint ventures, technology exchanges, and other ownership agreements.

In effect, supply factors of availability of money and raw materials are involved here. But the relative power of suppliers and buyers is also being altered to offset a threat of greater power by the foreign competitors and suppliers.

Source: Adapted from "IBM and Intel Link Up to Fend Off Japan," *Business Week,* Jan. 10, 1983, pp. 96–98; "Reshaping the Computer Industry," *Business Week,* July 16, 1984, pp. 84–98; and "Chip Wars: The Japanese Threat," *Business Week,* May 23, 1983, pp. 80–96.

Old rivals leaving it? If competitors leave, many times the probability of achieving corporate objectives increases. When RCA and GE left the computer business, this increased IBM's, Burrough's, and Control Data's chances of success. Indeed, Burroughs later acquired Sperry to reduce competition even more. Most of the time this is the case. But when GAF left the amateur photography business, Kodak wasn't completely happy. For this left the industry consisting of Kodak, Berkey, Inc., 3M, and Japanese firms making film and print paper. The exit of GAF left Kodak in a vulnerable position regarding charges by Berkey of assuming a monopoly position.

The opposite case involves the entry of new competitors. New competition often makes it tougher to achieve objectives unless together the current and new companies can increase the primary demand. Surely watch companies such as Bulova weren't pleased when Texas Instruments entered their business. American and Canadian businesses are often concerned when competitors from abroad enter the North American market. Examples include Japan's Sharp Corporation entering the U.S. computer business and Alumax, a joint venture of Mitsui and Amax, challenging the big three in aluminum.

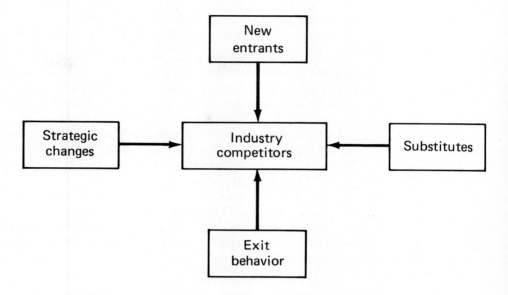

EXHIBIT 4.5   Factors to be analyzed in the competitor section.

Whether entry or exit takes place depends on the barriers to entry or exit. Porter contends that the following factors must be assessed with respect to their impact on *barriers to entry* in an industry:

• *Product differentiation.* There is strong customer loyalty to existing brands. Often the cost of getting customers to switch brands is high.

• *Economies of scale.* The costs of production, distribution, selling, advertising services, R&D, and financing decline as more units are sold. If economies of scale exist, then a firm that wishes to enter must do so at a unit-cost disadvantage, or the firm must enter the industry at the scale of the existing competitors.

• *Absolute cost advantages.* These are cost advantages deriving from patents, control of proprietary technology or especially skilled labor, control of superior raw-material sources, experience which leads to lower costs, capital at low cost, and depreciated assets which are useful, or experience or learning-curve advantages.

• *Access to marketing channels.* If the present firms own or have strong influence over the major channels, it can be very costly to enter a business.

• *Likely reaction of current firms.* If current firms will "live and let live," a proposed entry may be viable. If they "fight us on the beaches," it may be too costly.

Porter also explains *barriers to exit* from an industry. He contends that many firms do not leave an industry even though their objectives are not being met because

• *Managerial values prevent it.* Managers may be so tied to the industry psychologically that the firm doesn't exit.

• *Other products or services are related to exit candidates.* If other profitable products share marketing channels, production facilities, and other forms of joint activity, the firm may stay in the industry.

• *Costs are sunk in assets.* The costs of doing business in many industries include having large sums of money invested in assets that are useful only to the industry. Thus when the chemical business is bad, few leave it who have huge investments in plant, R&D, and other assets.

• *Direct exit costs are high.* Firms will not leave an industry whose direct exit costs (severance pay, relocation costs, etc.) are high.

• *Indirect costs may reduce exit behavior.* Some managers believe that social responsibility to the community and their employees prevent them from leaving a business or a particular location.

In effect, the combination of these barriers may serve to create new competitive conditions, and strategists should assess the impact of these barriers when they consider the likelihood of new firms entering their markets, or when considering strategies of entering or exiting themselves.

Availability of Substitutes

How profitably and successfully a firm operates depends in part on the availability of quality and less costly substitutes for the firm's products or services; and how competitive the substitute is will determine how viable the substitute is. Successful strategists also scan the environment for the loss or potential loss of business to substitutes. Thus sugar companies must be concerned about fructose and corn syrup. Marathon Oil must be concerned about the potential of solar energy as well as Peabody Coal. Can companies must pay attention to alternative packaging materials. Some substitutes may have cost advantages or other characteristics valued by buyers.

Major Strategic Changes of Current Competitors

While strategists are concerned with the previous two factors, they probably watch more carefully when major competitors change their strategies in significant ways. Xerox has had to react to much more aggressive competition from copier competitors such as IBM, Savin, SCM, and Kodak. When Pepsi offered to buy Seven-Up, Coca-Cola countered with an offer for Dr Pepper, even though both deals were later abandoned.

The amount of concern about the competition varies with the economic structure of the industry. An industry can be a monopoly (as nickel used to be) or an oligopoly (like the auto and aluminum industries), or it can be engaged in monopolistic competition (like parts of the computer industry) or competition (like the wheat production industry). Greater rivalry among firms in an industry leads to much more competition on the basis of price, quality, service, and other factors which can affect whether objectives are reached or not. Exhibit 4.6 provides an example of an industry in the throes of such change.

In essence, strategic groups tend to evolve in an industry. These groups tend to segment and compete more directly with one another. For instance, the beer business has a group of national competitors (such as Anheuser-Busch and Miller), local and regional brewers, and some who are attempting to become national. Firms can enter or exit segments. Coors is seeking to join the national brewer segment, while Falstaff became a regional brewer after it found it could not compete on a national basis. Heileman is a "national" brewery based on its strategy of acquiring and operating a series of regional breweries and brands and evolving a national brand name. Barriers

---

EXHIBIT 4.6   ON ENTRIES, EXITS, AND COMPETITIVE BEHAVIOR

In the summer of 1978, personal computers were high-tech toys selling slowly. But a few farsighted software developers saw great potential for these 30-pound paperweights. A graduate student at Harvard made a decision to go into business for himself selling an imaginative electronic spreadsheet he dreamed up at school. A year later, his program was commercially introduced as VisiCalc, and an industry was born.

Within 8 years since 1978, the personal computer software business has become a $5 billion industry with 14,000 companies and 27,000 different products. But the entry stage appears to be over. In 1985, 57 software firms were bought out, up from 23 in 1984. Many others died quietly. Changing competitive behavior can be explained by shifts in another industry environment factor—buyer behavior.

Until recently, software producers sold to individuals who used computers mostly on the job—and had discretion to buy programs they wanted. Now corporations want to tie computers into information networks. Data-processing managers have taken over the buying function, and they are a hard sell. "The package has to be from someone reputable; it's got to be bug free; the manual's got to be good; it's got to be teachable; and it's got to have some reason to displace what we already have."

These changes in buyer patterns have forced competitive behavior changes. Software makers have had to develop better quality control, special corporate sales and support forces, and high-volume pricing policies. And new-product development is important. One-product companies who can't keep the creative juices flowing to think up and produce follow-up products will not grow big enough to gain corporate acceptance and will likely exit the industry.

This is leading to speculation that three tiers (or strategic groups) will emerge in the industry structure. Several major competitors will sell all the basic software needed for word processing, spreadsheets, graphics, communications, and database management. A second tier of smaller firms will write programs for specific jobs in niche markets too small or narrow to concern larger firms. The third tier will be software makers that can't reach corporations. They will be able to survive by selling through retailers to individuals who now make up about half the market. But they also face increasing rivalry and buyer problems. Retailers are skeptical of small firms whose simple product line may generate little traffic. It is more profitable for the retailer to push fewer and fewer products, especially if service and support are necessary for the user.

It appears that in a very short time, this industry has gone from introduction to rapid growth to a shakeout stage. Consolidation in the industry and further exits are likely among those unable to switch from the entrepreneurial seat-of-the-pants management to more professional operating procedures.

Source: Adapted from A. R. Field, C. L. Harris, B. Buell, R. Brandt, and S. Ticer,: "Software: The Growing Gets Rough," *Business Week*, Mar. 24, 1986, pp. 128–139.

to entry to or exit from strategic group segments on an *intraindustry* basis (mobility) are the same as those for *interindustry* movement described earlier.

As the competition is analyzed, strategic moves are carefully watched, especially by those in one's strategic group. For example, are competitors developing cost advantages? Are they taking market share? How are they doing it (e.g., price, promotion, etc.)? Are they encroaching on market niches or developing new products? In other words, executives are examining relative competitive position and behavior, both to see what threats competitors are creating and to look for opportunities for improving their own position.

Thus competitor action can provide a significant opportunity or threat. The analyst must assess these characteristics of the competitor sector to determine their impact. On the basis of these and other factors, Porter summarizes the intensity and direction of competitive rivalry in a set of propositions.

- Rivalry increases and industry profits fall as the number of competitors in the industry increases and they become more similar in relative size and bargaining power.
- Rivalry increases as overall industry growth slows.
- Rivalry increases where fixed costs are high, efficient increments to capacity are large, or external factors lead to recurring or chronic excess capacity.
- Rivalry increases as products in the industry become less differentiated (more standardized as commodities) from the buyer's viewpoint.
- Rivalry becomes more volatile as firms in the industry become more diverse in personality, strategic approaches, and historic origins.

Industry Analysis and Diagnosis [6]

The appendix provides a variety of sources of information which can be used to gather data about customers, demographics, suppliers, and competitors along with other aspects of the general environment. Exhibit 4.7 is an intriguing commentary on how several techniques for competitor analysis have been utilized by business firms. As Chapter 3 indicated, there are a number of ways to proceed with analysis of environmental factors.

Yet it is particularly useful to get a sense of the favorability of the industry environment for the future strategy of the firm. Each factor can be subjected to an examination of threats or opportunities (e.g., do demographic trends provide opportunity or threat to our products?). But such a piecemeal approach may not result in an overall assessment useful for strategy generation. If the strategist is concerned with major strategic issues such as expansion into or retrenchment out of an industry, an overall assessment of the industry is necessary. Here, several of the factors we discussed earlier along with other criteria can be integrated, as shown in Exhibit 4.8, to begin to diagnose this segment of the environment.

By exploring these factors, strategists can determine profit potentials and begin to draw conclusions about the favorability of their current industry or new ones they may choose to consider as part of the business definition. Of course, these diagnoses

EXHIBIT 4.7   ARE THEY REALLY SPYING?

A 1982 issue of *Business Week* reported that microelectronics has supported a boom in the practice of "bugging" corporate offices. Counterbugging services are fast-growing businesses, even though it is illegal to make, sell, or possess eavesdropping devices in the United States. But this type of spying is only one of a number of techniques for competitive intelligence gathering, others of which are less "questionable" from a legal standpoint.

"The most serious and closed-mouth practitioners of competitive intelligence are often found among industry leaders." IBM has a "Commercial Analysis Department," Texas Instruments keeps "fairly formal files," and Citicorp has a manager whose title is "Manager of Competitive Intelligence." While clandestine activities are not usually disclosed, a picture of techniques for analysis does emerge. Examples include analyzing government contracts to discern technological strengths; back engineering—taking apart a competitor's product; preparing call reports—urging sales personnel to report on competitors from what they hear from customers; filing patent

mistakes to throw off competitors who review patent files; reviewing trade publications, 10K reports, annual reports, and securities analyses; debriefing engineers and scientists after professional meetings; hiring competitors' key employees; holding quarterly meetings to review competitor products with experts from marketing, manufacturing, engineering, and finance; monitoring the test marketing done by competitors; and feeling out firms involved with direct mail and catalogs, for they have lead times for publishing new offerings.

The key to the analysis is putting together bits of information in a puzzle to get an overall picture of future developments. In most companies, the process is informal. But those using formal approaches claim that they can "come up with amazingly clear pictures." As one executive put it, "The most important information to us is, 'What is his basic strategy?'" Clearly, an analysis of the competitive environment is important for strategists, and a variety of techniques are useful for obtaining "pieces of the puzzle."

Sources: Adapted from "Business Sharpens Its Spying Techniques." *Business Week,* Aug. 4, 1978, pp. 60–62; "New 'Bugs' Make Spying Easier," *Business Week,* July 12, 1982, pp. 74–75.

are not done in a vacuum. Relative firm power must be considered, which is the subject of Chapter 5.

Note that one of the factors noted in Exhibit 4.8 in two places is foreign opportunity and threat. This is the final sector of the environment that we explore.

EXHIBIT 4.8   ANALYSIS AND DIAGNOSIS OF THE INDUSTRY ENVIRONMENT

Markets and customers
  1 Size (present and potential)
  2 Growth and cyclicality (product life cycle)
  3 Customer segments and utilities
  4 Foreign opportunities
Suppliers
  1 Availability of needed inputs
  2 Costs of inputs
  3 Exits and entry of suppliers
  4 Power of suppliers

Competitors
  1 Concentration ratio (number of firms and market-share control)
  2 Capacity utilization
  3 Exits and entry barriers, especially foreign threats of entry
  4 Competitive behavior
  5 Strategic groups and mobility across strategic groups
  6 Availability and costs of substitutes from other industries

THE INTERNATIONAL ENVIRONMENT [7]

Many strategic managers now operate in what has been termed the "global village." United States business managers must consider threats and opportunities in the international business community. Nor can non-U.S. managers ignore what is going on in America or the rest of the world. Governments, economies, and business firms are increasingly intertwined in foreign trade and competition. Since World War II, the volume of goods traded between nations climbed from less than $100 billion to more than $1 trillion. In 1983, the 100 largest U.S.-based multinational companies earned an average of 37 percent of operating profits abroad. And direct foreign investment in the United States exceeds $70 billion, largely from Japanese, West German, and French firms.

With a focus on international competition, we have witnessed encroachment of international rivals into one another's market territories. International status and domestic prosperity has been linked to trade expansionism. Domestic economies of scale have financed pricing penetration into overseas markets by both U.S. and foreign firms. New competitors have forced innovations, price cutting, and quality improvements, but at a cost of competitive instability. This has further led to economic and strategic linkages among trading partners, such that mergers, joint ventures, cross licensing, and other strategies have become endemic.

Within this context, the international environment is a "special case" of the general and industry environments deserving special attention by strategists. That is, all the other factors—socioeconomic, government customer, competitor, and so on—discussed before apply here, as well as being shown in Exhibit 4.9. But the nature of the threats and opportunities take on a different focus. Compared to firms operating in a single country, the international environment is more competitive, heterogeneous,

EXHIBIT 4.9 EUROPE'S ENVIRONMENT

Strategists in multinational corporations are diagnosing threats to their business from broad changes occurring in Europe. A number of forces seem to be operating:

• *Socioeconomic:* Monetary exchange rates are increasingly uncertain; the European monetary system is expected to falter; economic growth is slowing.

• *Supply:* Labor unions seem to be increasingly hostile as unemployment increases; the availability of capital is decreasing as more capital is being used to pay for oil.

• *Technology:* Nationalistic policies are leading to government support of "home-grown" industrial development.

• *Competition:* Outmoded industries are not competitive in world markets.

• *Government:* There are increasing regulations on business and restrictions on operations; governments are seen as less stable; Europe has lost hope for unity, and this has led to greater nationalism.

While few U.S. companies are abandoning Europe, U.S. firms are reorienting their investment strategies by investing in services and improving plants rather than building new capacity. Some see joint ventures as a means for maintaining a presence with less risk. And European multinationals are investing more in the United States and in third-world countries. Note that elements of hostility, volatility, and the degree of development are involved in the assessments and strategic choices being made.

Source: Adapted from "Europe's Economic Malaise," *Business Week,* Dec. 7, 1981, pp. 74–79.

and complex because of different societies and cultures; educational practices; legal, political, and economic structures; and ideologies about appropriate business practices. Relative values of currencies vary rapidly and can quickly turn profits into losses. And government-to-government as well as firm-to-government relationships can have a bearing on attaining objectives. This is amply illustrated by comparing the differences between U.S. and multinational operations that affect strategic management noted in Exhibit 4.10.

The following sections discuss some of the threats and opportunities firms face in the international environment. The perspective is usually that of the U.S.-based multinational or international firm. That is, the multinational is a firm which operates in a number of countries, with offices or production facilities located outside the U.S. borders. However, the threats or opportunities could be reversed if the perspective were of a firm looking at U.S. companies entering their markets or seeking to enter U.S. territories. In each case, you should be aware that the sectors of the general or industry environments are interconnected with the discussion.

Opportunities for International Activities [8]

First, we should recognize that the economic world is not composed only of haves and have-nots. There are *resource-rich* countries such as in the OPEC bloc and many parts of Africa. There are *labor-rich,* rapidly developing countries, such as Hong Kong, Singapore, Korea, Mexico, Brazil, and Taiwan. These are countries which have done better than some others that have as much labor but have not grown. There are also *market-rich* countries, such as Europe, Brazil, Mexico, Phillipines, and many South American countries. These countries have some purchasing power in contrast to other countries such as India or China that although they possess large populations, they suffer from lack of purchasing power. Of course, there is business that can be done in the U.S.S.R. and Warsaw pact countries, but there are attendant difficulties because of extra legal hurdles.

In each instance, then, different opportunities prevail. For example, Northern Electric added the United States to its Canadian markets, while Dr Pepper entered European and Asian markets. The opportunities for market expansion were great in these market-rich areas. In western Europe and Japan, gross domestic product expansion (similar to GNP) was on the rise in 1986 because of lower oil prices, thus creating significant opportunity for business expansion. On the other hand, many U.S. firms have set up ''off-shore'' manufacturing operations to use lower-cost advantages available in the labor-rich areas. Raw material or energy resource requirements might be satisfied by foreign activities, such as INCO engaging in worldwide exploration, mining, and production of nickel where rich ore deposits are more readily available. The strategy sometimes involves internal investment and development. Often, as a result of governmental or political restrictions, joint ventures are set up with firms in the ''host'' countries involved. For example, United Technologies established six separate joint ventures in Britain, Belgium, China, Taiwan, Japan, and France between 1984 and

EXHIBIT 4.10   COMPARING U.S. AND INTERNATIONAL OPERATIONS

Factor	U.S. operations	International operations
Language	English used almost universally	Local language must be used in many situations
Culture	Relatively homogeneous	Quite diverse, both between countries and within a country
Politics	Stable and relatively unimportant	Often volatile and of decisive importance
Economy	Relatively uniform	Wide variations among countries and between regions within countries
Government interference	Minimal and reasonably predictable	Extensive and subject to rapid change
Labor	Skilled labor available	Skilled labor often scarce, requiring training or redesign of production methods
Financing	Well-developed financial markets	Poorly developed financial markets; capital flows subject to government control
Market research	Data easy to collect	Data difficult and expensive to collect
Advertising	Many media available; few restrictions	Media limited; many restrictions; low literacy rates rule out print media in some countries
Money	U.S. dollar used universally	Must change from one currency to another; changing exchange rates and government restrictions are problems
Transportation/ communication	Among the best in the world	Often inadequate
Control	Always a problem; centralized control will work	A worse problem; centralized control won't work; must walk a tightrope between overcentralizing and losing control through too much decentralizing
Contracts	Once signed, are binding on both parties, even if one party makes a bad deal	Can be voided and renegotiated if one party becomes dissatisfied
Labor relations	Collective bargaining; can lay off workers easily	Often cannot lay off workers; may have mandatory worker participation in management; workers may seek change through political process rather than collective bargaining
Trade barriers	Nonexistent	Extensive and very important

Source: R. G. Murdick, R. C. Moor, R. H. Eckhouse, and T. W. Zimmerer, *Business Policy: A Framework for Analysis,* 4th ed. (Columbus, Ohio: Grid, 1984).

1986, along with two independent start-ups in Spain, a merger in Italy, and co-production in Australia of aircraft, air conditioning, elevators, and other products.

Other opportunities may involve economic considerations such as more favorable tax advantages from operating in ''duty-free'' zones. Even with the communists taking over Hong Kong in the late 1990s, opportunities for businesses there are expected to be good for some firms.

Other sources of opportunity include the chance to secure sources of funding from international investors who believe conditions are good for investing in the United States. In some cases, a joint venture is set up in the United States where the domestic firm markets the foreign firms' outputs. Or, several domestic and foreign producers may set up joint operations for manufacturing and marketing, as has happened in the auto industry. Conversely, the U.S. firm may seek a foreign partner to license or market its goods. This route is taken by increasing numbers of smaller U.S. manufacturers.

Hence, opportunity exists for some firms to produce in one country, assemble in another, and market in yet others, as the ''global economy'' and the firm evolves. For example, firms may first get their feet wet by limited exporting or licensing. Then the firm might use foreign sales offices and/or joint venturing. If successful, international divisions for marketing and/or production might be established. Eventually, the firm may be engaged in multinational activities.

Companies go multinational when it appears that they can achieve objectives of high-level sales, higher profits, lower costs, and employee satisfaction. However, going multinational is a complex decision. For example, tax structures, product and service preferences, and employee skill levels can be different. Chapter 10 describes this in more detail. The firm may face expropriation of its properties. Sometimes going multinational means getting involved in local politics, as ITT found out in Chile and United Brands found out in Central America. A multinational strategy can complicate a firm's structure and top executive relationships, consideration of which brings us to the discussion of threats from the international environment.

Threats from International Activities [9]

A major threat to many U.S. firms appears to come from international competitors. Those possessing advantages of natural resources and labor have begun using them. Exhibit 4.11 indicates a list of two dozen U.S. industries which have experienced significant market-share losses in the last decade or so. And now the U.S. semiconductor industry appears threatened.

In industry after industry, manufacturers are closing up shop and becoming marketing organizations for other producers, mostly foreign. Autos, steel, machine tools, industrial robots, fiber optics, and semiconductor chips are some of the markets where the United States is losing (or has lost) dominance. This forces the U.S. economy to become more service-oriented. It is harder to achieve parity in productivity growth and personal income in service sectors compared to manufacturing, leading some to suggest that the U.S. economy is headed for serious trouble. Moreover, the advantages in service may be no less vulnerable to competition than are those in autos or steel.

EXHIBIT 4.11 THE IMPACT OF FOREIGN COMPETITION ON SOME U.S. INDUSTRIES
(Data by year reflect imports as a percent of the total U.S. market)

Industry	1972	1984	Industry	1972	1984
Blowers and fans	3.6	29.2	Precious jewelry	4.9	24.9
Converted paper	10.4	20.1	Printing machinery	8.5	22.9
Costume jewelry	10.4	28.6	Radios and TV	34.9	57.5
Dolls	21.8	54.7	Semiconductors	12.3	30.5
Electronic computers	0.0	14.2	Shoes	17.1	50.4
Lighting fixtures	4.2	17.4	Sporting goods	13.0	23.2
Luggage	20.7	52.4	Telephone equipment	2.1	12.1
Men's and boy's outerwear	8.7	26.8	Tires	7.2	15.1
Men's and boy's shirts	17.8	46.1	Women's blouses	14.9	33.0
Musical instruments	14.9	25.2	Women's suits and coats	7.3	24.5
Fertilizers	4.3	19.4	Wool yarn	6.1	17.4
Power handtools	7.5	23.2	Zinc	28.4	51.5

Source: Business Week, Oct. 7, 1985, pp. 94–95.

Some of the reasons for these inroads reflect not only competitive strength of foreign competitors but internal weaknesses on the part of U.S. firms. For instance, U.S. products are often not competitive because of poorer quality, and many firms lack technological superiority because of past failure to invest in R&D. While U.S. firms invented robots, the Japanese put them to more effective use earlier than U.S. firms. However, U.S. firms are not entirely to blame. Government assistance (reflecting U.S. ideology) is usually not competitive with foreign governments who often work closely with their own corporations to secure major contracts, obtain insurance, or provide other financial subsidies. And business behavior is sometimes not competitive with foreign firms because of U.S. restrictions such as tax laws, antibribery rules, or environmental regulations. The U.S. government can also create threats to importers if protectionism sentiments lead to further restrictions on world trade (though this could be an opportunity for selected domestic producers in protected industries). And of course, monetary policy affecting the value of the dollar helped imports in the early 1980s at the expense of U.S. manufacturers. Similarly, freight costs as well as labor rates (U.S. workers often earn two to five times foreign counterparts) put U.S. firms at a cost disadvantage.

The Japanese seem to have commanded the most attention of U.S. managers as key competitors in industry after industry. When the Japanese began showing up at U.S. trade shows and scientific meetings in the 1960s, they were an amusing sight to many Americans as they listened intently to interpreters and took hundreds of photographs. But they became less entertaining when Japanese products from automobiles to televisions flooded the market. Now the Americans are starting to look over the Japanese shoulders to find out what they are up to. With increased investment opportunity as a result of a higher rate of savings, lower cost of labor, a culture of cooperation, and unstinting efforts to improve quality and productivity to solve problems of insufficient labor availability, Japan has been able to overcome a total absence of natural resources to become a world economic powerhouse. And they are starting to lead the world in many new technological breakthroughs in selected areas where they have focused research efforts.

To dispel the rumor that the Japanese are infallible, let us hasten to add that they are experiencing their own foreign-competition problems. Strengthening of the Japanese yen has shifted price advantages to the "four tigers"—South Korea, Singapore, Taiwan, and Hong Kong. Korea competes directly with Japan in autos, steel, and videocassette recorders both in Japanese and U.S. markets. It might be noted that several of these firms, notably in Singapore, are subsidiaries of U.S. companies. Hence, the multinational U.S. firm which faces some threats from "foreign" competition can turn this into opportunity by shifting production to locations which possess certain competitive advantages (in this case labor cost).

Aside from competition, U.S. firms seeking to operate in foreign countries face a variety of threats because of restrictions placed on them by host countries such as

- Ownership. Typically, the host country or firm from the host country must own a major or controlling interest.
- Employment. Almost always, host countries demand that certain positions in management and technological areas be held by host-country nationals.
- Profits and fees. Typically, profits and fees are set at some maximum level.
- Internal debt capital. Internal debt capital is often set according to a preestablished formula.
- Training and development. Insistence on training and development for host-country nationals is common.
- Host-country markets. Most host countries demand development of their exports.
- Technological bases. Most host countries seek technologically based industry rather than extractive industry.

These factors can make the decision to operate in the host country particularly problematic. The threats may offset the opportunities or advantages originally thought available.

Finally, threats may come from a variety of sources of potential risk when operating in a foreign country. Examples of these include

1 Political risks: war, occupation by foreign powers, disorders caused by territorial claims, ideological differences, conflict of economic interests, regionalism
2 Social risks: civil wars, riots, unequal income distribution, union militancy, religious divisions, antagonism between social classes
3 Economic risks: continuous slow GNP growth, strikes, rapid rise in production costs, fall in import earnings, sudden increase in food or energy imports
4 Financial risks: fluctuating currency exchange rates, repatriation of profits and capital, changing tax policies

These risks can even exist in "friendly" countries, as an anti-U.S. backlash was seen in Britain in 1986 after several U.S. firms made attempts to buy British-government-owned businesses. In some instances, governments may expropriate your business, or you may lose substantial amounts of money as exchange rates move up or down.

Firms must decide whether the environment they are examining is subject to these risks before deciding to set up operations. Once there, policies may be needed to guide managers in maneuvering in the host country in ways different from domestic operations. Or the firm may have to decide, as some are now in South Africa, whether the risks of staying are worth the costs of abandoning a location.

While it may be noted that U.S. firms have been losing competitive ability in the world arena, stronger efforts have been made to improve productivity and quality and restore competitive strength. But many firms have done this by exploring international strategies to take advantage of the opportunities of collaboration and avoid some of the threats we have noted.

The final point we wish to make in this section is that in the special case of a multinational business, the complexity and scope of the business suggest that environmental analysis must be far-reaching indeed. A greater emphasis on the socioeconomic, government, and competitor sectors seems to be called for. While common sense suggests that overseas risk is greater in less-developed countries, greater volatility in developed countries may be more significant. Sudden changes in currency exchange rates, so-called nontariff trade restrictions, licensing laws, political embargos, etc., can be as damaging as coups, revolts, or seizures. And since the stakes may be higher in developed markets, the ultimate losses may be greater. In fact, Garreau suggests that within North America itself there are nine distinct regions with their own sociopolitical and economic configurations which create quite different markets and strategic situations.

Now that we have examined all the sectors of the environment, it should be quite clear that strategists cannot do in-depth analysis and diagnosis of all the various factors. Our next section provides suggestions for limiting this task.

FOCUSING THE DIAGNOSIS [10]

The strategist usually has a limited amount of time and limited cognitive skills for diagnosing the information gathered in the analysis phase. If they let themselves, managers can be bombarded with information from the environment. They are faced with choices on what information to continue to examine and whether they should act upon that information. They must avoid a breakdown in effective diagnosis because of information overload. To avoid this cognitive strain, the strategist has several options.

One is to delegate some diagnosis and focus on the most significant diagnosis duties. Instead of the top manager doing all the diagnosis, the management team can be involved in the diagnosis. The team in turn can delegate some of the less crucial diagnoses to the subordinates. The initial diagnosis of each factor could be delegated to the functions most affected (e.g., technology to R&D, economic to finance, customer to marketing, supplier to production). These diagnoses can be pooled and integrated by the top management team or strategists. The key is systematic linking of the diagnoses together.

A second approach is to try to train the strategists in more effective diagnosis. One technique which a few firms have experimented with is the use of scenarios. The approach that GE uses is shown in Exhibit 4.12. Royal Dutch Shell in London has adapted this technique to training. Its goal is to open the executives' minds to possible futures which they don't want to come. Shell creates two scenarios—far enough away from the present condition yet not the most visionary possibilities. Then the top managers of Shell make operating and strategic change decisions based on these two *possible* futures. It is not important whether the scenarios become the future. They are a training vehicle which stretches executives' minds so that they can deal more effectively with the future environment—whatever it is.

A third approach is called issues analysis. This is related to scenario building and

EXHIBIT 4.12 **How scenarios are constructed at General Electric Company.**
(General Electric Company.)

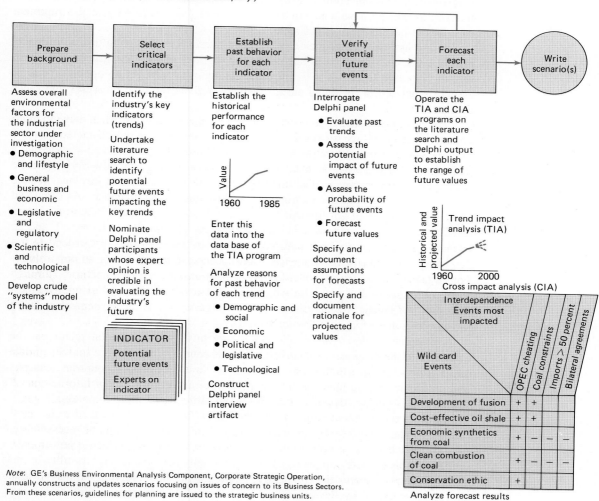

Note: GE's Business Environmental Analysis Component, Corporate Strategic Operation, annually constructs and updates scenarios focusing on issues of concern to its Business Sectors. From these scenarios, guidelines for planning are issued to the strategic business units.

contingency planning. An "issue" is a factor (internal or external such as emerging political, social, or economic trends or controversies) which if it develops, could have a significant effect on the firm in the future. Issues are identified, a probability is assessed with respect to its possible occurrence, and a weight is given to its expected effect. These issues are brought to the attention of management so proactive behavior may be taken to deal with the issue. For example, the issues staff at Atlantic Richfield was tracking 140 issues in 1985 that might be brought to the attention of top executives, planners, and government or public relations staff. However, not all issues can be diagnosed ahead of time. Surprises, or unanticipated events, are bound to arise. Nonetheless, management can prepare contingency plans to be put into effect if such events arise. For example, if a supplier suddenly becomes a competitor, the firm could be prepared ahead of time to respond appropriately. The key is to diagnose possible surprises (errors in the computing system, terrorist action in a foreign plant, takeover bids, etc.) and sketch out a plan to be put into effect. For more-probable and important surprises, a detailed plan is desirable.

The last approach for reducing information overload is satisficing instead of maximizing when maximization is beyond the capabilities of the strategist or will cause serious cognitive strain. That is, the manager doesn't try to get an optimal focus or diagnosis but settles for doing an acceptable job given the time pressures and other demands.

Certain characteristics of the environment may operate in ways which demand more or less attention by the strategist. We think that several general characteristics are important in explaining what factors can be diagnosed. [11]

Diagnosis of the environmental analysis data is influenced by how *dependent* the firm is on the environment. The more powerful the stockholders or key owners, the more their perception of the environment might influence the diagnosis. As discussed earlier, if the power of government is great vis-à-vis the organization, the firm is more dependent on the government and its actions. As discussed in Chapters 1 and 2, exchange relationships with a number of agents in the environment can lead to dependence, thus influencing strategists. Dependence can be a threat or an opportunity. For instance, firms develop interdependent relationships with competitors (through trade associations, for example) which can lead to an opportunity to improve performance. Of course, threats can occur if the organization is overly dependent (as in the case of some firms with few customers).

The degree of *development and complexity* in the environmental sector can be important to the diagnosis. A highly developed economy creates more sources of data and a greater infrastructure to support diagnosis. In less-developed countries, analysis and diagnosis may be hindered by the absence of accurate or timely information. If complexity is greater, diagnosis becomes more difficult and more important.

A *hostile* environment is one where the factors being diagnosed tend to be unfavorable for the organization. For instance, economic conditions might be recessionary, or social values may be negative toward some operations (e.g., electric power companies). Firms in more competitive industries usually perceive greater hostility in this sector. The more hostile the competitive environment, the more vital the diagnosis of that sector is, and the more quickly the firm responds to challenges. While this seems to stress the threats, you should be aware that the opposite of hostility—favorableness—can provide opportunities and also will command managerial attention. Estimates of favorable customer demand and favorable changes in governmental policies (such as deregulation) are examples of environmental changes which could create opportunities and should lead to greater attention and diagnosis. Note that *developed* environments tend to be viewed more favorably also.

Volatile environments are those in which substantial change occurs but is infrequent, irregular, and thus less predictable. (Some call this uncertainty.) Recall that earlier we noted how technological factors are particularly subject to volatility. Comprehensive and timely diagnosis is more necessary in *volatile, dynamic* environments than in stable environments. Firms which face dynamic, uncertain, and *complex* environments develop more complete diagnoses (and strategies). Those not doing so are more likely to fail.

Once again, both opportunities and threats can result from volatility, although many executives tend to perceive change negatively. Indeed, *The Wall Street Journal* reported that many executives are frustrated and spend significantly more time examining volatile currency exchanges. In fact, some multinationals buy several services which forecast exchange rates, because predictions vary widely.

Closely related to volatility is the question of how *time* affects diagnosis. If time pressures are great, diagnosis may have to be speedily done. Thus near-term or long-term environmental change is important to assess. Some suggest that a useful approach is monitoring sectors for signs which are weak or strong. For instance, weak signs of changes in the composition of the work force with regard to women began appearing in the early 1970s. The signs became stronger over time that significant changes were occurring. As a sign becomes stronger, a more extensive diagnosis of the sector is necessary. These changes over time can create "double-edged swords" of threat and opportunity. Consider the impact of the women's movement on Avon, noted in Exhibit 4.3. Exhibit 4.13 suggests another aspect of changes in an environmental factor over time. Thus possible gains from every opportunity can also present a threat of "downside" risk to a firm.

The cost of the search and luck are the final factors affecting diagnosis. If the cost of the search is excessive for the firm, this may cause the executives to do less diagnosing than they might prefer. And as with most decisions in life, luck is a factor. Sometimes a diagnosis is done on the right factor at the right time by chance or luck. This can help or hurt the diagnosis.

ENVIRONMENTAL THREAT AND OPPORTUNITY PROFILE: ETOP [12]

In Chapter 3, diagnosis was defined as an assessment of the significance of information developed in analysis. Specifically, how significant is the difference between the future environment and the present environment with regard to our strategy to achieve the objectives? Diagnosis seeks a statement of the problems and opportunities the environment is offering us.

If first-generation planning is used, this diagnosis is based on the most probable future. If second-generation planning is used, several scenarios of the future are

EXHIBIT 4.13   FROM OPPORTUNITY TO THREAT AT ENVIROTECH

The major line of business for Envirotech until 1980 was construction projects to help companies and municipalities meet pollution control regulations. From 1970 to 1980, total sales grew from $60 million to $580 million; half this total was accounted for by an agglomeration of 30 companies involved in controlling air and water pollution which Envirotech had acquired, thereby becoming the largest pollution control business in the United States.

The company's first strategic plan was put together in 1976. It noted that the pollution control business would slow down by 1983 or 1984. Thus weak signs of a slowdown were evident. In fact, the waste-water treatment market began to deteriorate in 1978. Management assumptions and perceptions concerning market growth and changes in regulations and government funding were inaccurate.

There were, of course, internal management difficulties, such as signing long-term, fixed-price construction contracts in areas where Envirotech had little expertise. But the major problem was a volatile environment.

Envirotech made a proactive effort to influence change. In late 1979, the CEO met with government policymakers to try to convince the Environmental Protection Agency to change its regulations. This had no impact, and Envirotech has sold or shrunk most of its acquisitions and reduced employment from 8900 to 5600.

In 1981, the company made plans to abandon air quality control after the completion of some 130 projects. Water pollution control equipment still represents 15 percent of Envirotech's business, but the company plans to emphasize mining and mineral processing machinery.

Clearly, what was once an opportunity became a threat for Envirotech. It anticipated this, but not soon enough. It made efforts to proact, but in the end it was forced to react by changing its strategy. Reports indicated that Envirotech was up for sale in late 1981.

Sources: Adapted from "Envirotech: Controlling the Red Ink That's Polluting Its Balance Sheet," *Business Week,* Oct. 19, 1981, pp. 140–141; "Envirotech Offer by Baker International," *The Wall Street Journal,* Nov. 18, 1981, p. 14.

drafted, with best-case, most-probable, and worst-case assumptions. Then several diagnoses are made.

To do this effectively, managers should use a systematic technique. Several available approaches are listed in the references. The one we suggest is the preparation of an environmental threat and opportunity profile (ETOP), which allows you to conveniently summarize the diagnoses of all the various sectors of the environment which you have deemed most important to the strategic gaps facing the firm.

An example of an ETOP is given in Exhibit 4.14. Note that the environmental sectors in the analysis are listed in summary fashion for simplicity's sake. In a more extensive diagnosis, the subfactors would be examined first and then the summary ETOP would be prepared, as shown in this exhibit. For example, instead of showing only the "socioeconomic" sector, a more extensive profile would list the subfactors: economic, climatic, and social. As you analyze cases and businesses, this approach should be used for each factor. For each one, a time-based prediction of the most likely events must be prepared (for first-generation plans).

The firm shown in this ETOP is Alza Corp., a small company which markets a unique type of intrauterine device called Progestasert. While the ETOP appears generally negative, Alza has been given what seems to be the possibility of increasing annual sales from the current $1 million up to $100 million. That prospect, however, is very risky and many factors will influence management's strategy, just as various factors influenced the opportunity. Unfortunately, Alza's product was introduced in 1976, just after A. H. Robins Company withdrew its IUD, the Dalkon shield, from

EXHIBIT 4.14   ENVIRONMENTAL THREAT AND OPPORTUNITY PROFILE (ETOP)
FOR ALZA CORPORATION

Environmental sectors	Impact of each sector
Socioeconomic	− Perception of public about IUDs − Influence on public of Searle's and A. H. Robins' withdrawal from the market − Possibility of increased legal problems + Planned Parenthood and doctors support IUD products + Huge market demand for pregnancy prevention
Technological	+ Product is unique; not just an IUD + Does not use estrogen with its side effects 0 Must be replaced yearly
Government	+ FDA approval continues − More legal problems may change government support
Customer	− Best used in monogamous relationships; U.S. divorce rate = 50% + Loyalty of present IUD users
Supplier	− Liability insurance agreement may change; rates may become too high to afford
Competitor	+ Searle's and A. H. Robins' withdrawal from the market − Allegations posed against IUD makers − Birth-control pills becoming safer − Condom alternative also prevents STDs; has reached a 40 percent female market − Makers of alternative forms of birth control will step up marketing efforts
International	+ Chinese government policies promote single-child families

Note: + indicates opportunity; − indicates threat; 0 indicates neutral impact.

the market, because of allegations that it caused injury and even death.[1] As of January, 1986, G. D. Searle & Co. had decided to remove its last remaining IUDs from the market. This decision was also caused by a rapidly increasing number of lawsuits. (The FDA, doctors, and Planned Parenthood all endorse Alza's product, but the risk of legal tangles is high—although they have never lost a case—and the company may not be able to afford the liability insurance necessary.) Although Alza could inherit the abandoned IUD market, there are good and bad attributes to their product, and producers of alternative birth control methods are stepping up market penetration based on their own strengths.

The environment basically created this opportunity for the company. Pressure from the public has caused competitors to abandon the market to Alza. The public's perception that Progestasert is as dangerous as the other IUDs is Alza's biggest threat. (There is the probability that the company will get hit by more lawsuits itself, even though it has support from doctors, Planned Parenthood, and the U.S. government

[1]Robins then went into Chapter XI bankruptcy.

through the FDA.) However, IUDs are recommended mostly for women in stable, exclusive relationships—a market that could be diminishing with the ever-increasing U.S. divorce rate. Also, increased legal problems could cause the government to withdraw its approval. Technologically, the product is unique; it is made of plastic and does not have the side effects of estrogen associated with contraceptive pills. The fact that Progestasert must be replaced every year is described as a threat, but in reality, many women in the U.S. normally go to a gynecologist once a year for other reasons, so this may not be a drawback after all.

The exit of competition by IUD manufacturers has created the opportunity for Alza to take over this niche but also signals their unwillingness to continue defending the product. Other potential competitive entrants with their eye on this market are the birth-control-pill manufacturers who have lowered estrogen levels and stepped up marketing (as has VLI Corp., makers of contraceptive sponges, and condom makers). The latter can also promote the fact that condoms prevent sexually transmitted diseases (STDs). Alza's supply of liability coverage is not assured in the future, so financial and/or legal risk is a large problem.

The future strategies Alza's management is considering all attempt to find a solution to the legalrisk problem considered as the most significant threat:

1 Sell Progestasert to another company to produce and market
2 Find a marketing partner to share risk with the company
3 Create a separate division and thus insulate the rest of the company

Alza has already diversified into alternative drug-delivery systems that are more lucrative. The threats posed by the current environment affecting the birth-control industry may cause Alza's management to withdraw or to simply minimize exposure and risk to the company. However, the opportunities to increase involvement exist and could be seized by Alza.

The summary ETOP can be prepared so that top management can identify the most critical sectors of the environment and focus intensively on their potential impact on the strategy of the firm as a whole and key aspects of its operations. That is, top managers could focus on some areas and delegate others. We suggest that top management should focus on the areas which are perceived to be more developed, more volatile, and more hostile (or favorable) and where greater organizational dependence exists. Prescriptively, long-term signals should be diagnosed; descriptively, near-term factors are likely to command more attention. This focus should then lead to detailed predictions about the sector in question.

A more detailed ETOP should be developed to focus the diagnosis more precisely. It should provide data and estimates for revenue and cost implications of these factors as well as estimates on the likelihood that certain events will occur and their timing. The key, then, is to identify the relevant trends expected and assess their likely impact. This diagnostic tool, ETOP, will be matched with the strategic advantage profile (SAP), described in Chapter 5. Together, these diagnostic tools provide the input for generating strategic change alternatives and determining whether gaps might exist between expected and desired outcomes and why.

SUMMARY [13]

This chapter completes our look at the environmental factors which create threats and opportunities. We continued our description of the sectors in the environment which strategists analyze and diagnose beyond the general environment discussed in Chapter 3.

First we described the industry environment as consisting of customers, suppliers, and competitors. Effective strategists must analyze who their customers are, where potential customers might be located, and what changes in customer buying patterns might occur. This involves identifying buyers and their utilities, assessing basic demographic factors which create primary demand for products or services, and scanning the geographic environment for potential markets and customers.

Strategists also must determine the availability and costs of supply conditions including raw materials, energy, money, and labor. We noted that the power of suppliers (and buyers) can influence a firm and its strategy.

Then we discussed the competition. The exit and entry of competitors, the possibility of substitute products or services, and major strategic changes by competitors are the important factors to be analyzed and diagnosed in this sector of the industry environment.

We concluded our look at the industry environment by indicating how to put together a diagnosis of these various sectors to draw conclusions about the favorability of an industry. This is an important component of the overall environmental analysis as an input to the strategic management process.

Next we pointed out that the international environment is an increasingly important source of opportunity and threat to business firms. The global village includes all other aspects of the environment but is a special case deserving special attention by strategists. Effective strategists examine opportunities and threats from areas of the nation and the world other than the ones they are presently doing business in. But we pointed out how because of heterogeneity and complexity, analysis here is more difficult but must be far-reaching.

Next we discussed how managers focus the diagnosis to limit cognitive strain and to make the process more effective. This can be done by delegating some of the diagnoses to vice presidents or by scenario building. Top managers must still narrow their focus and more closely monitor the areas which presently are likely to offer the most significant opportunities and threats. Propositions 4.1 to 4.6 provide some clues on how to focus the top manager's analysis and diagnosis.

In effect the focal zone of the strategist is narrowed by the conditions of each factor. Exhibit 4.15 illustrates this point. In this case, the competitor sector may be seen as volatile and uncertain, with new competitors entering and strategies changing. Thus there is a greater focus on this sector than on any other. Few changes may be occurring with suppliers, but technologies may be changing. Due to competitive conditions, the government in this example is viewed as relatively unimportant. There may be problems in the economy or social changes which are requiring more managerial attention. Few geographic factors are of importance, but the international environment is increasing in significance.

Proposition 4.1

The more dependent the enterprise is on a sector, the more it will focus its environmental analysis on that sector of the environment.

Proposition 4.2

The more developed the sector, the more a firm will focus on that sector of the environment.

Proposition 4.3

The more hostile the sector, the more vital the diagnosis of that sector.

Proposition 4.4

The more volatile and uncertain the sector, the more the diagnosis will focus on that sector.

Proposition 4.5

The greater the time pressure and cost of search, the less likely it is that in-depth diagnosis will result.

Proposition 4.6

The greater the complexity of the environment, the more sectors managers must focus on.

So the executive does not seriously analyze and diagnose the shaded area of Exhibit 4.15 but closely analyzes and diagnoses the white area (focal zone), where most of the current opportunities and threats are coming from. The effective executive systematically diagnoses these areas, using a mechanism like the ETOP to make sure that effective analysis and diagnosis takes place.

EXHIBIT 4.15 **How the focal zone is narrowed.**

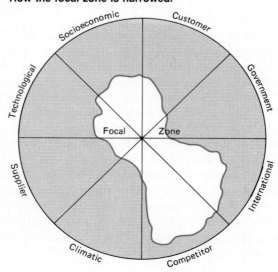

The ETOP can be used to systematically summarize all aspects of the environment. This tool when combined with the strategic advantage profile (SAP) to be described in the next chapter provides a basic input to the generation of strategic alternatives and choice of strategy in the overall strategic management process.

Appendix: Business Facts: Where to Find Them*

This appendix provides business executives, government officials, academicians, and students with a concise reference list of sources for locating published material which can be used in analyzing business operations. The list contains references to both primary data sources and bibliographical publications.

Sources of primary data and statistical information:

1 Government publications
2 Trade publication statistical issues
3 Business guides and services

General reference sources of business information and ideas:

4 Indexes
5 Periodicals and periodical directories
6 Bibliographies and special guides
7 Trade associations
8 Other basic sources
9 Specialized Sources: On-line data bases

Sources of Primary Data and Statistical Information

1 Government Publications

Probably no one collects more business information than the U.S. government does through its various agencies. The Department of Commerce maintains excellent reference libraries in field offices in many major cities, for example, and the Small Business Administration assists with business problems and maintains field offices in over 85 cities.

A Indexes   *The Federal Register* (National Archives). Published daily. Contains all regulatory matter issued by all governmental bodies.

Monthly Catalog of United States Government Publications (GPO), issued monthly. A comprehensive list by agencies of federal publications issued during each month.

Monthly Checklist of State Publications (GPO), issued monthly. A record of state documents and publications received by the Library of Congress.

B Selected Basic Sources   The following list of selected sources is representative of the types of information available through the government.

---

*This appendix was adapted by the authors from an article of the same title by C. R. Goeldner and L. M. Dirks originally published in *MSU Business Topics* in 1976. That article was based on an article by S. M. Britt and I. A. Shapiro, "Where to Find Marketing Facts," *Harvard Business Review,* September–October 1962. Updates are adapted from J. S. Mulitonovich, "Business Facts for Decision Makers" *Business Horizons,* March–April 1985, pp. 63–80.

Business Conditions Digest (U.S. Department of Commerce, Bureau of Economic Analysis), published monthly. Provides many economic time series statistics used by forecasters and planners.

Commerce Business Daily (U.S. Department of Commerce: Office of Field Operations), published daily. Lists U.S. government procurement invitations, contract awards, sales of surplus property, and foreign business opportunities.

County Business Patterns (U.S. Department of Commerce, Bureau of the Census), issued annually. A volume showing county, state, and U.S. summary statistics on employment, the number and employment size of reporting business units, and taxable payrolls for approximately 15 broad industry categories. The statistics are particularly suited to analyzing market potential, establishing sales quotas, and locating facilities.

Economic Indicators, issued monthly. A digest of current information on economic conditions of prices, wages, production, business activity, purchasing power, credit, money, and federal finance presented in charts and tables.

Employment and Training Report of the President (U.S. Manpower Administration), published annually. Reports employment, earnings, size, and demographic characteristics of the labor force. Historical data and projections included.

Federal Reserve Bulletin (Board of Governors of the Federal Reserve System), issued monthly. A source of statistics on banking, deposits, loans and investments, money market rates, securities prices, industrial production, flows of funds, and various other areas of finance.

Foreign Economic Trends and Their Implications for the United States (U.S. Bureau of International Commerce), pamphlets issued semiannually or annually for each country. Prepared by embassies; contains analysis of economic trends and possible implications in various countries.

Index of Patents Issued from the U.S. Patent Office (U.S. Patent Office), published annually. Volume 1 indexes patents by name of patentee. Volume 2 lists patents by subject of invention.

Monthly Labor Review (U.S. Department of Labor, Bureau of Labor Statistics), issued monthly. A compilation of trends and information on various current labor statistics.

Small Business Bibliographies (U.S. Small Business Administration), published irregularly. Briefly describes particular business activities.

Statistical Abstract of the United States (U.S. Department of Commerce, Bureau of the Census), issued annually. A standard summary of statistics on the social, political, and economic organization of the United States.

Statistical Yearbook (New York: United Nations), issued annually. A body of international statistics on population, agriculture, mining, manufacturing, finance, trade, education, and so forth.

Survey of Current Business (U.S. Department of Commerce, Bureau of Economic Analysis), issued monthly. The official source for gross national product, national income, and international balance of payments. A survey that brings about 2600 different statistical series up to date in each issue under these headings: General Business Indicators; Commodity Prices; Construction and Real Estate; Domestic Trade; Labor Force, Employment and Earnings; Finance; Foreign Trade of the United States; Transportation and Communications; and several headings on specific raw material industries.

C Census Data   By far the most extensive source of information on the United States and its people and businesses is census data. The list provided gives a sampling of the information available through the census surveys. Because the census surveys are conducted at regular intervals, trends can be noted and comparisons made by using similar data from several census years. The following are all from the U.S. Department of Commerce, Bureau of the Census.

Bureau of the Census Catalog of Publications, issued quarterly with monthly supplements and accumulated into an annual volume. An index of all available Census Bureau data.

Census of Agriculture. Reports data for all farms and for farms with sales of $2500 or more by county and by state.

Census of Housing, issued every 10 years. Reports data on structure, household characteristics, ownership, etc., in several volumes.

Census of Manufacturers, issued every 5 years. A presentation of geographic and industrial data on manufacturers. *Final Industry Reports* includes a series of separate reports on the value of shipments, capital expenditures, value added by manufacturing, the cost of materials, and employment for approximately 450 manufacturing industries. The data are classified by geographic region and state, employment size, class of establishment, and degree of primary products specialization.

Census of Population, issued every 10 years. There are several series, two of which are the following: *Series B: General Population Characteristics.* A description and cross-classification of the number of inhabitants of the United States, with characteristics about age, sex, race, marital status, and relationship to head of household for states, counties, Standard Metropolitan Statistical Areas, etc. *Series C: General Social and Economic Characteristics.* Describes and cross-classifies the number of inhabitants. Data include nativity and parentage, state of birth, mother tongue, school enrollment by level and type, years of school completed, families and their composition, occupation groups, and class for states, counties, Standard Metropolitan Statistical Areas, etc.

Census of Retail Trade. A compilation of data for states, Standard Metropolitan Statistical Areas, etc., by kind of business. Data include number of establishments, sales, payroll, and personnel.

Census of Selected Services. Includes data on hotels, motels, beauty parlors, barbershops, and other retail service organizations. The survey also includes information on the number of establishments, receipts, and payrolls for states, Standard Metropolitan Statistical Areas, counties, and cities.

Census of Wholesale Trade. Presents statistics for states, Standard Metropolitan Statistical Areas, and counties on the number of establishments, sales, payrolls, and personnel by kind of business.

2   Trade Publications

Publications serving specific industries often compile data annually in special articles, factbooks, or issues. Some of those available are the following:

Appliance (Elmhurst, Ill.: Data Chase Publications), monthly.

Broadcasting (Washington, D.C.: Broadcasting Publications), weekly.

Chain Store Age—Super Markets (New York: Lebhar-Friedman Publications), published monthly with an extra issue in July.

Computerworld (Newton, Mass.: Computerworld), published 51 times a year.

Drug and Cosmetic Industry (New York: Drug Markets, Inc.), monthly.

Editor & Publisher (New York: The Editor & Publisher Company), weekly.

Forest Industries (San Francisco: Miller Freeman), monthly.

Implement & Tractor (Kansas City, Mo.: Intertec Publishing Corporation), published 24 times a year.

Men's Wear (New York: Fairchild), twice a month.

Merchandising Week (Cincinnati, Ohio: Billboard Publications), weekly.

Modern Brewery Age (Stamford, Conn.: Business Journals), tabloid published weekly; magazine issued every other month.

National Petroleum News (New York: McGraw-Hill), magazine issued monthly and twice in May.

Quick Frozen Foods (New York: Harcourt Brace Jovanovich), monthly.

Sales Management (New York: Bill Communications), magazine published twice a month, but once in December.

Survey of Buying Power, published in July. A prime nongovernment authority for buying income, buying power index, cash income, households, merchandise line sales, population, and retail sales for the United States. The data are divided into national and regional summaries and market rankings, metro-market data by states and county-city data by states. Some data on Canada are now included.

VENDing Times (New York: VENDing Times), journal published monthly with one extra issue in February and in June.

3 Business Guides and Services

Directory of Corporate Affiliations (Skokie, Ill.: National Register Publishing Company), published annually; includes quarterly updates. Directory lists approximately 3000 parent companies with their 16,000 divisions, subsidiaries, and affiliates; an index of "who owns whom."

Moody's Industrial Manual (New York: Moody's Investors Service), published annually. A brief background, a description of the business and products, a history, a mergers and acquisition record, and a principal plants and properties list are given for each company. Principal officers and directors are given as well as 7 years' worth of financial statements and a 7-year statistical record for each company.

Standard & Poor's Corporation Services (New York: Standard & Poor's). Some of these services include *Industry Surveys,* an annual publication with three to four current surveys of each industry and a monthly section called "Trends and Projections"; *The Outlook,* a weekly stock market letter; *Stock Guide,* a monthly summary of investment data on common and preferred stocks; and *Trade and Securities,* a monthly listing of statistics on business and finance, stocks and bonds, employment, foreign trade, production, and so forth.

Standard & Poor's Register of Corporations, Directors and Executives (New York: Standard & Poor's), issued annually; three volumes. Volume 1 includes an alphabetical list of nationally known corporations with the titles of their important executives, the names of directors and principals, and annual sales. Volume 2 provides an alphabetical list of directors and executives in the United States and Canada. Volume 3 indexes corporations by Standard Industrial Classification, geographic area, new individuals, obituaries of individuals, and new companies.

Standard Directory of Advertisers (Skokie, Ill.: National Register Publishing Company), published annually in two editions, classified and geographical; plus *Directory of Advertising Agencies* and an updating service. A concise record of more than 17,000 companies and their agencies doing national and regional advertising. Each entry includes the company name, address, and telephone number; the names of top executives, including financial, marketing and advertising, and purchasing managers; the approximate sales; and the agency. Most listings also include advertising budget information and the method of product distribution.

Standard Rate & Data Service Publications (Skokie, Ill.: Standard Rate & Data Services). These publications provide information required by advertisers and agencies for preparing advertising and placing it in various media. In addition, a good deal of consumer market data are provided in *Newspaper Rates and Data, Spot Radio Rates and Data,* and *Spot Television Rates and Data.*

Thomas Register of American Manufacturers and Thomas Register Catalog File (New York: Thomas Publishing), issued annually; 11 volumes. A directory that classifies manufacturers by products and services and also includes an alphabetical list of 60,000 brand or trade names. This work is a source of information on companies incorporated for less than $1 million.

General Reference Sources of Business Information and Ideas

4 Indexes

Accountants' Index (New York: American Institute of Certified Public Accountants). A detailed list by author, subject, and title of publication covering the fields of accounting, auditing, data processing, financial management and investments, financial reporting, management, and taxation.

Advertising Age Editorial Index (Chicago: Crain Communications). An index which cross-references the 52 issues of *Advertising Age* articles by key words, subject category, company name, and author. Some abstracts.

Applied Science & Technology Index (New York: H. W. Wilson). A cumulative subject index to periodicals in the fields of aeronautics and space science, automation, chemistry, construction, earth sciences, electricity and electronics, engineering, industrial and mechanical arts, materials, mathematics, metallurgy, physics, telecommunications, transportation, and related subjects.

Business Periodicals Index (New York: H. W. Wilson). A cumulative subject index covering periodicals in accounting, advertising, the automotive field, banking, communications, finance, insurance, labor, management, marketing, and taxation and periodicals of specific businesses, industries, and trades.

F & S Index of Corporations and Industries (Cleveland, Ohio: Predicasts). An index which covers company, industry, and product information from more than 750 business-oriented newspapers, financial publications, special reports, and trade magazines. Information is arranged by SIC number, by company name alphabetically, and by company according to SIC groups.

Public Affairs Information Service Bulletin (New York: Public Affairs Information Service). A selective list by subject of the latest publications relating to economics and public affairs.

The Wall Street Journal Index (Princeton, N.J.: Dow Jones). An index of all articles that have appeared in *The Wall Street Journal*.

5 Periodicals and Periodical Directories

Business periodicals feature articles of use and of interest to the business manager. Frequently research studies or new developments are reported in these specialized journals. The following list illustrates some of the periodicals available: *Academy of Management Journal, Accounting Review, Business Week, Dun's, Fortune, Harvard Business Review, Industrial Marketing, Journal of Advertising Research, Journal of Business, Journal of Finance, Journal of Marketing, Journal of Marketing Research, Journal of Retailing, Management Accounting, Management Science, Nation's Business, Personnel, Personnel Management, Sales Management.* In addition to general business periodicals, there are hundreds of trade publications covering almost every field. The following directories can help you find these periodicals.

Ayer Directory of Publications (Philadelphia: Ayer Press, 1975), issued annually. A comprehensive listing of newspapers and magazines and trade publications of the United States (by state), Canada, Bermuda, the Republic of Panama, the Republic of the Philippines, and the Bahamas.

Business Publications Rates and Data (Skokie, Ill.: Standard Rate & Data Services), issued monthly. A listing of more than 3000 U.S. business, trade, and technical publications arranged according to 175 market-served classifications.

Management Contents (Skokie, Ill.: Management Contents Inc.), published biweekly. Lists the tables of contents of hundreds of periodicals in accounting, finance, management, marketing, and related disciplines.

Ulrich's International Periodicals Directory, 15th edition (New York: Bowker), two volumes. Issued every 2 years. An index of subject entries for more than 55,000 in-print periodicals published throughout the world.

6 Bibliographies and Special Guides

Bibliographies and other guides can quickly lead you to original sources of information on selected topics. Examples of bibliographies and special guides are provided in the following selections.

Bibliography of Publications of University Bureaus of Business and Economic Research (Boulder, Col.: Business Research Division, University of Colorado), issued annually. A bibliography of publications by bureaus of business and economic research and by members of the American Association of Collegiate Schools of Business.

Encyclopedia of Business Information Sources, 2d edition (Detroit: Gale Research Company), two volumes. Edited by Paul Wasserman et al. A listing of primary subjects of interest to managerial personnel, with sources of information on each topic.

Management Information Guides (Detroit: Gale Research Company). A group of bibliographical references to information sources for various business subjects. Each volume includes books, dictionaries, encyclopedias, filmstrips, government and institutional reports, periodical articles, and recordings on the featured subject.

The Marketing Information Guide (Garden City, N.Y.: Hoke Communications), cumulative indexes issued quarterly. An annotated bibliography that shows both the source and the availability for each item listed.

National Planning Association Publications (Washington, D.C.: Planning Association), published annually. An annotated bibliography for the publications of the National Planning Association.

7 Trade Associations

Don't overlook trade sources. Many trade associations maintain research departments and collect basic data on sales expenses, shipments, stock turnover rates, bad-debt losses, collection ratios, returns and allowances, and net operating profits. One of the following directories will help you locate a particular trade association.

Encyclopedia of Associations (Detroit: Gale Research Company).

National Trade and Professional Associations of the United States and Labor Unions (Washington, D.C.: Columbia Books), issued annually.

8 Other Basic Sources

In addition to the specific references listed, the following are general sources of valuable information for the researcher.

Commercial Atlas & Marketing Guide (New York: Rand McNally), published annually. A volume containing statistics and maps. It provides data on population estimates, principal cities, business centers and trading areas, county business, and sales and manufacturing units; also zip code marketing information and transportation data for the United States. General reference maps of Canada and foreign countries are included.

The Conference Board Record (New York: The Conference Board), monthly. A report to management on business affairs which provides an analysis and interpretation of current statistical tabulations.

Exporter's Encyclopedia (New York: Dun and Bradstreet), published annually. Detailed facts on shipments to every country in the world. Covers regulations, types of communication and transportation available, foreign trade organizations, general export information, and listings of ports.

National Economic Projection Series (Washington, D.C.: National Planning Association), published annually. A report providing forecasts of the gross national product and its principal components, including historical and projected 5-, 10-, and 15-year forecasts for capital investment, consumption and savings, government revenues and expenditures, output and productivity, and population and employment.

P. Wasserman, C. Georgi, and J. Woy, *Encyclopedia of Business Information Sources* (Detroit: Gale Research Co., 1983). Quick survey of basic information sources covering 1215 subjects.

9 Specialized Sources: On-Line Databases

Computer technology has revolutionized the search for business facts. By using a database, decision makers benefit from the accessibility and adaptability of massive resources now available. This tool is expensive but can be cost-effective when measured by time savings.

The actual process of a computer search is a simple one. A questionnaire is completed, specifically describing the problem and indicating important authors, journals, or key facts useful in retrieving references. Citations are printed immediately or mailed.

Three major vendors offer on-line interactive search access to hundreds of databases. Bibliographic Retrieval Services (Scotia, N.Y.) and DIALOG/Lockheed Informations Services (Palo Alto, Cal.) store general bibliographic data. SDC Search Service (System Development Corporation, Santa Monica, Cal.) emphasizes technical and statistical information.

Listing of computer based services can be found in the following directory.

Directory of Computer Based Services (Washington, D.C.: Telenet Communications Corp.), published annually. Lists data banks, commercial service bureaus, educational institutions, and companies that offer interactive computer-based services to the public through the nationwide Telenet network.

The business databases are divided into three areas: bibliographies, statistics, and directories.

Bibliographies On-line interactive search access to various bibliographic databases.

Management Contents (Skokie, Ill.: Management Contents, Inc.), monthly. Current information on a variety of business and management-related topics for use in decision making and forecasting. Articles for 200 U.S. and foreign journals, proceedings, and transactions are fully indexed and abstracted to provide information in areas of accounting, design sciences, marketing, operations research, organizational behavior, and public administration.

Monthly Catalog of U.S. Government Publications (Washington, D.C.: U.S. Government Printing Office). Published monthly with annual cumulations. Reports, studies, fact sheets, maps, handbooks, and conferences.

Predicasts Terminal System (Cleveland: Predicasts, Inc.). Bibliographic and statistical database providing instant access to many business journals and other special reports for searches of current articles, statistics, geographic location of companies.

Statistics In-depth statistics easily adapted for a wide variety of manipulations.
Economic Time Series
Business International/Data Time Series (Business International Corp.). PTS/U.S. Time Series (Predicasts, Inc.).
Marketing Statistics
BLS Consumer Price Index (Department of Labor, Bureau of Labor Statistics).
BLS Producer Price Index (Department of Labor, Bureau of Labor Statistics).
Financial Statistics
Disclosure II (Washington, D.C.: Disclosure, Inc.), 1977 to present; updated weekly. Extracts of reports filed with the U.S. Securities and Exchange Commission by publicly owned companies. 11,000 company reports provide a reliable and detailed source of public financial and administrative data. Source of information for marketing intelligence, corporate planning and development, portfolio analysis, legal and accounting research.

Directories
CATFAX
Directory of Mail Order Catalogs.
EIS Industrial Plants (Economic Information Systems, Inc.).
Foreign Traders Index (Department of Commerce).
Trade Opportunities (Department of Commerce).

REFERENCES

[1] Industry Attractiveness

Hax, A. C., and N. S. Majluf: *Strategic Management* (Englewood Cliffs, N.J.: Prentice-Hall, 1984).

[2] Identifying Buyers and Their Utilities

Boulton, W. R.: *Business Policy* (New York: MacMillan, 1984).
Kiechel, W., III: "The Food Giants Struggle to Stay in Step with Consumers," *Fortune,* Sept. 11, 1978, pp. 50–56.
"Listening to the Voice of the Marketplace," *Business Week,* Feb. 21, 1983, pp. 90–91.

[3] Demographic Factors

"Americans Change," *Business Week,* Feb. 20, 1978, pp. 64–69.
Brown, P.: "Last Year It Was Yuppies—This Year It's Their Parents," *Business Week,* Mar. 10, 1986, pp. 68–74.

[4] Supplier Factors

"A Capital Crunch That Could Change an Industry," *Business Week,* Mar. 23, 1981, pp. 82–84.
Menzies, H.: "Why Sun Is Educating Itself Out of Oil," *Fortune,* Feb. 27, 1978, pp. 42–44.
Norris, W. C.: "A Risk Avoiding, Selfish Society," *Business Week,* Jan. 28, 1980, p. 20.
Porter, M. E.: *Competitive Strategy: Techniques for Analyzing Industries and Competitors* (New York: Free Press, 1980).

"Venture Capitalists Raid Silicon Valley," *Business Week,* Aug. 24, 1981, p. 112.

"The Wave of the Future: Shipping by Sail," *Business Week,* Aug. 24, 1981, p. 112.

"Why the Next Oil Crisis Could Be a Disaster," *Business Week,* Nov. 23, 1981, pp. 132–133.

[5] Competitor Factors

Abernathy, W. J., K. B. Clark, and A. M. Kantrow: "The New Industrial Competition," *Harvard Business Review* (September–October 1981), pp. 68–81.

Grossman, R.: "Why IBM Reversed Itself on Computer Pricing," *Business Week,* Jan. 28, 1980, p. 84.

Levy, R.: "The Big Battle in Copiers," *Dun's Review* (May 1977), pp. 97–99.

Porter, M. E.: *Competitive Advantage* (New York: The Free Press, 1985).

Sammon, W. L., Kurland, M. A., and R. Spitalnic: *Business Competitor Intelligence* (New York: Wiley, 1984).

[6] Industry Analysis and Diagnosis

Galbraith, C. S., and C. H. Stiles: "Firm Profitability and Relative Firm Power," *Strategic Management Journal,* vol. 4 (1983), pp. 237–249.

Hatten, K.: "Heterogeneity within an Industry: Firm Conduct in the U.S. Brewing Industry, 1952–1971," *Journal of Industrial Economics,* vol. 26 (December 1977), pp. 97–113.

[7] The Global Village

"Drastic New Strategies to Keep U.S. Multinationals Competitive," *Business Week,* Oct. 8, 1984, pp. 168–172.

Garland, J., and R. N. Farmer: *International Dimensions of Business Policy and Strategy* (Boston: Kent, 1986).

"Global Trade Skirmish Looms as Restrictions on Services Multiply," *The Wall Street Journal,* Oct. 5, 1981, p. 1.

Lorange, P.: "A Framework for Strategic Planning in Multinational Corporations," *Long Range Planning* (June 1976), pp. 30–37.

Pearce, J. A., and R. B. Robinson: *Strategic Management* (Homewood, Ill.: Irwin, 1985).

Porter, M. E.: *Competition in Global Industries* (New York: Free Press, 1986).

[8] International Opportunities

Comes, F. J., and J. Rossant: "France Gets Set for a Capitalist Comeback," *Business Week,* Mar. 31, 1986, pp. 42–44.

"The Future of Hong Kong," *Business Week,* Mar. 5, 1984, pp. 50–64.

Glasgall, W., F. J. Comes, R. A. Melcher, S. Miller, R. Lewald, and L. Armstrong: "In Western Europe and Japan, The Party is Just Beginning," *Business Week,* Feb. 10, 1986, p. 80.

King, R. W., A. Borrus, and J. Heard: "UTC adds Westland to Its Growing Foreign Arsenal," *Business Week,* Feb. 24, 1986, pp. 88–89.

Yang, D. J., and D. Griffeths: "China: A Dream Market for Western Arms Makers," *Business Week,* Feb. 24, 1986, p. 48.

[9] International Threats

"America Starts Looking Over Japan's Shoulder," *Business Week,* Feb. 13, 1984, pp. 136–140.

Cetron, M.: *The Future of American Business* (New York: McGraw-Hill, 1985).

"The Four Tigers Are Pouncing on Japan's Markets," *Business Week*, Mar. 24, 1986, p. 48.

Haner, F. T.: "Rating Investment Risks Abroad," *Business Horizons*, vol. 22 (April 1979), pp. 18–23.

"The Import Invasion: No Industry Has Been Left Untouched," *Business Week*, Oct. 8, 1984, pp. 172–174.

Jones, N.: "The Hollow Corporation," *Business Week*, Mar. 3, 1986, pp. 57–59.

Melcher, R. A.: "Yanks, Go Home," *Business Week*, Mar. 24, 1986, p. 50.

"Why Carmakers Will Mourn if Export Quotas Die," *Business Week*, Feb. 18, 1985, pp. 46–47.

Wilson, J. W., M. Berger, P. Hann, and O. Port,: "Is It Too Late to Save the U.S. Semiconductor Industry?" *Business Week*, Aug. 18, 1986, pp. 62–67.

[10] Focusing the Diagnosis

Amara, R. C. and A. J. Lipinski: *Business Planning for An Uncertain Future: Scenarios and Strategies* (New York: Pergamon, 1982).

Gottschalk, E. C., Jr.: "Firms Hiring New Type of Manager to Study Issues, Emerging Troubles," *The Wall Street Journal*, June 10, 1982, p. 21.

Hofer, C. W.: *Instructor's Manual to Accompany Strategic Management* (St. Paul, Minn.: West, 1981).

Kalaska, P.: "Multiple Scenario Approach and Strategic Behavior in European Companies," *Strategic Management Journal*, vol. 6 (1985), pp. 339–356.

Wack, P.: "The Use of Scenarios at Shell," International Research Seminar in Strategy, Saint-Maximin, France, June 1979.

[11] Diagnosis and the Strategist's Environment

Ansoff, H. I.: "Managing Strategic Surprise by Response to Weak Signals," *California Management Review*, vol. 18 (Winter 1975), pp. 21–33.

Bourgeois, L. J.: "Strategic Goals, Perceived Uncertainty, and Economic Performance in Volatile Environments," *Academy of Management Journal*, vol. 28 (1985), pp. 548–573.

Engwall, L.: "Response Time of Organizations," *Journal of Management Studies*, vol. 13 (February 1976), pp. 1–15.

"Exchange Rates: Pick a Forecast," *Business Week*, Apr. 26, 1982, p. 108.

Osborn, R. N., J. G. Hunt, and L. R. Jauch: *Organization Theory* (New York: Wiley, 1980).

Pine, A.: "Wide Swings in Imported Currencies Vex Businessmen, Bankers, Government Aides," *The Wall Street Journal*, Dec. 29, 1981, p. 30.

Regan, D.: "Uncertainty Is Breeding Fear," *Fortune*, Oct. 19, 1981, pp. 62–67.

Smart, C., and I. Vertinsky: "Strategy and the Environment: A Study of Corporate Responses to Crises," *Strategic Management Journal*, vol. 5 (1984), pp. 199–213.

[12] Systematic Ways to Diagnose the Environment

DeSouza, G. R.: *System Methods for Socioeconomic and Environment Impact Analysis* (New York: Arthur D. Little, 1979).

"Searle's Troubles Give Alza Its Big Break," *Business Week*, Feb. 24, 1986, pp. 123–125.

[13] Summary

Paine, F., and C. Anderson: "Contingencies Affecting Strategy Formulation and Effectiveness: An Empirical Study," *Journal of Management Studies*, vol. 14 (1977), pp. 147–158.

INTERNAL ANALYSIS
AND DIAGNOSIS

CHAPTER OUTLINE

INTERNAL ANALYSIS AND DIAGNOSIS

- To describe the process of internal analysis and diagnosis
- To introduce internal strategic factors and to illustrate how they affect a firm's objectives
- To examine some techniques which have been developed and used for internal analysis
- To consider factors that affect the diagnosis of internal strengths and weaknesses

INTRODUCTION [1]

This chapter completes the three-chapter unit on analysis and diagnosis. Chapters 3 and 4 focused on analysis and diagnosis of the environment to determine which opportunities and threats could be significant to the firm in the future. Chapter 5 describes the parallel process which involves determining the strengths and weaknesses the firm has at present or might develop. These are diagnosed in order to develop competitive advantages, and to minimize weaknesses, or consider how they will limit strategy or can be corrected.

Every firm has strengths and weaknesses. The largest firms have financial strengths, in comparison with smaller firms, but they tend to move more slowly and be less able to serve small market segments effectively. No firm is equally strong in all its functions. Proctor & Gamble was known for its superb marketing, Maytag is known for its outstanding production and product design. American Telephone and Telegraph is known for its outstanding service and personnel policies. Yet each of these firms is

> *Internal analysis is the process by which the strategists examine the firm's marketing and distribution, research and development, production and operations, corporate resources and personnel, and finance and accounting factors to determine where the firm has significant strengths and weaknesses. Internal diagnosis is the process by which strategists determine how to exploit the opportunities and meet the threats the environment is presenting by using strengths and repairing weaknesses in order to build sustainable competitive advantages.*

not strong "across the board." Within a company, each division has varying strengths and weaknesses. General Electric was strong in jet engines and weak in computers a few years ago. So a firm must determine what its distinctive competencies are—what makes it unique to the competitive arena—so that it can make decisions about how to use these abilities now and in the future. And it must determine whether weaknesses will limit strategic options or identify weaknesses which can be overcome.

Exhibit 5.1 indicates how strengths and weaknesses at ITT may influence that company's strategy.

EXHIBIT 5.1   THE STRENGTHS AND WEAKNESSES AT ITT

ITT spent $105 million in 1985 to introduce to the United States its System 12, a sophisticated telephone switch which has been routing calls and data abroad since 1981. System 12 is ITT's most crucial vehicle for cracking the telecommunications market dominated by AT&T and Northern Telecom Ltd. While analysts and customers agree that the System 12 is very innovative and "quite a step forward," its complexity is producing time delays resulting in an increasing flow of lost customers. ITT spent more than $1 billion developing System 12, eliciting from some analysts the opinion that it should be dropped in the United States, a move that could add 25 cents a share to earnings. On the other hand, System 12 seems crucial to Chairman Rand Araskog's strategy. Its failure could jeopardize his own future.

ITT perceived a technological opportunity—cracking the telecommunications market with an innovative telephone switching system. In its effort to exploit this opportunity, ITT utilized its financial and marketing (distribution, promotion, sales) strengths. Yet these strengths have not successfully evolved into a strategic advantage, as less than 10 percent of the 129 million lines ordered since 1978 have been delivered; and after 3 years, only one quarter of the 10,000 lines installed in Salamanca, Spain, are working. The successful conversion of strengths into advantages was thwarted by a prevailing weakness, not in the finance or marketing areas but in the product development and organization and management areas. Three teams were set up in the United States and Europe to develop System 12. According to M. Peter Thomas (former president of ITT's Network Systems Division), "The product is so complex and the organization is so complex that without focused management it was hard to design a major system." This fault in the strategic planning stage resulted in the numerous delivery delays leading to decreased customer confidence. In addition, ITT may have expended too much of its resources in pursuit of this perceived opportunity, allowing other advantages to atrophy to the point where ITT's future could be dependent upon the success or failure of this single project.

In a stunning reversal of strategy, Araskog announced an attempt in mid-1986 to sell most of the telecommunications business to the French. If the deal is rejected, he may not find a buyer at a reasonable price, leading to more problems for ITT's troubled balance sheet.

Source: Adapted from "The Project ITT Can't Seem to Bring Home," *Business Week,* Feb. 17, 1986, pp. 52–55; "Behind the ITT Deal: Will Araskog's Radical Surgery Work?" *Business Week,* July 14, 1986, pp. 62–65.

Unless the executives are fully aware of their competitive advantages, they may not choose the one opportunity of the many available at the time that is likely to lead to the greatest success. Unless they regularly analyze their weaknesses, they will be unable to face the environmental threats effectively. In effect, these assessments must be combined with environmental analysis so that decisions can be made about how to use or add strengths and minimize weaknesses.

This chapter focuses on how to analyze the internal factors realistically and diagnose their significance. It is at this point that executives can develop a strategic advantage profile (SAP) and match it with an environmental threat and opportunity profile (ETOP) to create optimal conditions for adjusting or changing strategies or policies.

Exhibit 5.2 reminds us of how this process fits into the total strategic management process. And as before, we are interested in how the internal factors relate to the gap analysis. That is, management performs internal analysis and diagnosis to identify clearly the current strengths and weaknesses of the firm. Management also examines the most probable *future* strengths and weaknesses. On the basis of these assessments, expectations are developed about goal attainment given the internal and external conditions. If gaps exist between desired and expected objectives, new strengths must be developed or weaknesses preventing goal attainment must be overcome.

Since this chapter parallels Chapters 3 and 4, much of what was said there applies here and will not be duplicated. The similarities include the definitions of analysis and diagnosis, the purposes of analysis and diagnosis, and factors affecting diagnostic decisions.

This chapter also provides parallel information on the internal factors. This includes

* Strategic factors to be analyzed and diagnosed
* Techniques and problems of internal analysis
* The role of strategists in internal analysis and diagnosis
* Diagnosis and preparation of a summary assessment (SAP)

INTERNAL FACTORS TO BE ANALYZED

In the discussion of internal factors, it is not possible to consider in depth the material presented in courses such as marketing management and personnel and labor relations. Some of the leading books on the subject are listed in the references for each section. All that will be attempted here is a listing of the most crucial internal factors and a presentation of brief illustrations of the competitive advantages (and weaknesses) that are possible. The order of discussion does not indicate importance—it is just a convenient ordering of line and staff factors and follows a fairly typical budgeting format. But you should remember that each area interacts with the others.

Marketing and Distribution Factors [2]

Marketing and distribution means moving goods or services from the producer to the customer. It starts with finding out what customers want or need and whether the product and/or service can be sold at a profit. This requires doing market research,

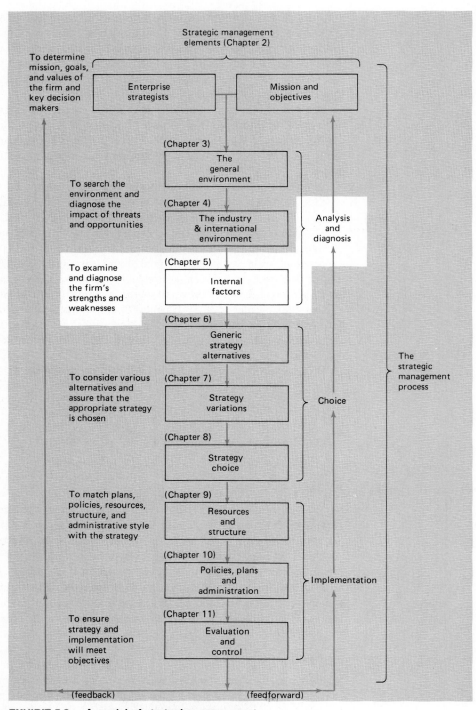

EXHIBIT 5.2 **A model of strategic management.**

EXHIBIT 5.3   INTERNAL FACTORS: MARKETING AND DISTRIBUTION

1 Competitive structure and market share: To what extent has the firm established a strong market share in the total market or its key submarkets?

2 Efficient and effective market research system.

3 The product-service mix: quality of products and services.

4 Product-service line: completeness of product-service line and product-service mix; phase of life cycle the main products and services are in.

5 Strong new-product and new-service leadership.

6 Patent protection (or equivalent legal protection for services).

7 Positive feelings about the firm and its products and services by the ultimate consumer.

8 Efficient and effective packaging of products (or the equivalent for services).

9 Effective pricing strategy for products and services.

10 Efficient and effective sales force: close ties with key customers. How vulnerable are we in terms of concentrating on sales to a few customers?

11 Effective advertising: Has it established the company's product or brand image to develop loyal customers?

12 Efficient and effective marketing promotion activities other than advertising.

13 Efficient and effective service after purchase.

14 Efficient and effective channels of distribution and geographic coverage, including internal efforts.

identifying the market, developing product, testing customer reaction, working out production and costs, determining distribution and service requirements, and deciding on advertising and promotion approaches.

As simple as this sounds, many corporations all but forgot such basics in the 1970s when inflation kept revenue high. But vast economic and social changes have made marketing strengths more important for most firms. The recession in the early 1980s and demographic and life-style shifts created problems for those who pursued mass marketing and brand loyalty as the keys to marketing success. Likewise, intense international competition, rapid technological change, and deregulation have created new weaknesses in typical marketing approaches. The changing nature of competition, then, requires a close look at marketing strengths and weaknesses in order to build competitive advantage in increasingly fragmented markets. Exhibit 5.3 is a list of the marketing and distribution factors. The strategist is looking to see if the firm is substantially stronger in marketing and distribution than its competitors.

As you look at the factors, you will see that strength can come from a variety of approaches. The operational marketing questions of segmentation, positioning, and mix (product, price, promotion, distribution) are quite important to the firm's ability to compete effectively. Of course, firms compete on any and all of these factors. Some firms prefer approaches involving low prices, lower quality, more promotion, and wide distribution; others prefer orientations toward higher prices, higher quality, and custom design.

An assessment of the weaknesses in relation to market potential also suggests areas where improvements can be made. For instance, if there appears to be a gap in the product line, new-product development or acquisition is called for to fill out the existing line or create new ones. A gap in distribution might lead to efforts to build intensity, exposure, or coverage. If usage gaps exist, price or promotion can lead to increased frequency of purchase, or new uses or users (customers) can be found for products.

Just as important as these questions are other areas which focus on how the marketing organization functions. For instance, the organization may have the ability to accumulate better knowledge about its markets than the competition has. If properly used, this can become a major advantage with respect to assessing the need for changes and determining their timing. Similarly, if the marketing organization maintains good relationships with production or new-product engineering, the translation of marketplace needs into the timely creation of goods or services can lead to a competitive edge.

Finally, the importance of marketing to the overall success of the company needs evaluation. In some firms, such as those which supply to a few customers who specify their precise needs (e.g., defense contractors), the marketing function need not be particularly strong. In other industries, the greatest share of internal resource allocation may go to marketing units (e.g., consumer products producers). As competitive needs are assessed, the relative strength of marketing and the way it is managed in relation to major competitors may lead to indications of strength or weakness. Exhibit 5.4 provides an example of how marketing has become a weakness at Proctor & Gamble due to the way it is managed in a changing environment.

EXHIBIT 5.4   MARKETING BY THE NUMBERS

Like all packaged-goods marketers, Proctor & Gamble operates in a tougher world than the past, when it had the midas touch. The firm has stumbled lately. It no longer has commanding leads on branded products such as Crest and Pampers. And its competitors are smarter.

P&G's traditional strengths—a massive commitment to product research and exhaustive test marketing—have not been as potent as in the past. Its markets are mature, and "the old mass audience delivered by mass media for the mass markets isn't working anymore," says one P&G alumnus.

P&G's earlier successes often came from a strategy of acquiring brand names (e.g., Charmin, Duncan Hines, Folger's); and using marketing expertise, it put those names on one product after another to dominate its field. But the firm has yet to turn recent acquisitions into big profit producers. Proctor has done little more than reformulate some new products while competitors have captured substantial new business by segmenting markets and products. Insiders suggest that the problems at P&G reflect a corporate culture which is stifling. Decisions are "made by the numbers." In an age when creative thinkers often get freedom to try ideas without interference from the top, P&G remains bureaucratic and centrally controlled. The president wants to "know what the facts are." He is a no-nonsense analyst who gets involved in nitty-gritty matters, with a fetish for memoranda and a burdensome system of communication. This slow-moving perfectionist style worked to P&G's advantage during less-competitive times. But now this approach is hurting some key markets.

Recently, President Smale has been showing greater flexibility. P&G is working more closely with retailers; it has cut down on its memos and livened up its ads. Forgoing its usual thoroughness, P&G rolled out half a dozen products since 1984 with no test marketing. However, unless its weaknesses resulting from insularity and adherence to centralization are reduced, Proctor's past marketing glories may not provide the strengths to accomplish its goal of doubling unit volume each decade.

As Exhibit 5.8 points out, P&G still faces problems from competitors who are beating them to the punch, but this "defensive" posture fits the style of its current management practices.

Source: Adapted from Z. Schiller and A. Dunkin: "P&G's Rusty Marketing Machine," *Business Week,* Oct. 21, 1985, pp. 111–112.

EXHIBIT 5.5   INTERNAL FACTORS: R&D AND ENGINEERING

1 Basic research capabilities within the firm
2 Development capability for product engineering
3 Excellence in product design
4 Excellence in process design and improvements
5 Superior packaging developments being created
6 Improvements in the use of old or new materials
7 Ability to meet design goals and customer requirements

8 Well-equipped laboratories and testing facilities
9 Trained and experienced technicians and scientists
10 Work environment suited to creativity and innovation
11 Managers who can explain goals to researchers and research results to higher managers
12 Ability of unit to perform effective technological forecasting

R&D and Engineering Factors [3]

The research and development (R&D) and engineering function can be a competitive advantage for two prime reasons: (1) It can lead to new or improved products for marketing, and (2) it can lead to the development of improved manufacturing or materials processes to gain cost advantages through efficiency (which could help to improve pricing policies or margins). Exhibit 5.5 presents the list of factors which might be analyzed in the R&D and engineering area.

In Chapter 3 we noted that major technological changes often occurred outside the immediate industry. Even so, research and development can provide significant strength for the ongoing business.

The R&D process is commonly viewed as proceeding through the stages of basic research, applied research, developmental research, and commercialization. Exhibit 5.6 graphically represents the time savings in producing a new product, process, or service with accelerated developmental research. One axis shows the time lapse from a basic research breakthrough to commercialization and the other shows the R&D states. The actual improvement in time will vary, but under unaccelerated conditions, the normal gap between a research breakthrough and commercialization is about 25 years. The figure was developed by looking back from commercialization to basic research. Accurate forecasts of the commercial applications of basic or developmental research are rare and difficult to produce. But for the individual firm assessing its own R&D capabilities, the key is to examine the ability to produce product or process improvements and the timing and effectiveness of its future efforts.

A firm can choose to pursue an offensive approach to R&D or pursue defensive "fast second" or "imitator" approaches. Exhibit 5.7 describes the kinds of differences you would expect in these approaches to R&D. The offensive approach would accelerate the applied and developmental research efforts (B_1 in Exhibit 5.6). The "fast second" approach would emphasize accelerated developmental research (B_2 in Exhibit 5.6). The "imitator" would wait for commercial developments and follow up with minor changes or improvements (B_3 in Exhibit 5.6). Exhibit 5.8 suggests when these various approaches might be more suitable to use.

Some firms do both offensive and defensive R&D work. For example, TDK corporation (Japan) characterizes its work as positive technology, negative technology,

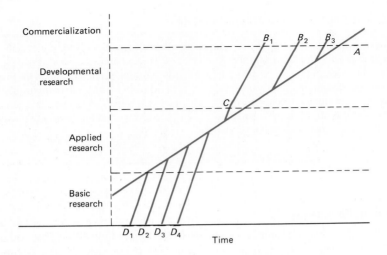

A   TYPICAL R&D PROCESS
B_{1-3} ACCELERATED DEVELOPMENTAL RESEARCH
C   ACCELERATED APPLIED RESEARCH
D_{1-4} BASIC RESEARCH FINDINGS

EXHIBIT 5.6 **Looking back from successful commercialization: transforming basic research into viable products.**
(Based on B. Gold, "Technological Diffusion in Industry: Research Needs and Shortcomings." The Journal of Industrial Economics, *vol. 39 [March 1981], pp. 247–269.)*

or nonexistent technology. Positive technology involves research for the purpose of upgrading existing technologies and improving products. Research on negative technology is done on processes, materials, or technology which could present a threat to existing technology. While this entails time, cost, and risk, it enhances the possibility of accumulation of new technology and keeps a firm abreast of potential substitutions. Nonexistent technology research focuses on new developments which could provide threat or opportunity in the future. Without this, delays in research of negative technology would be inevitable, and new products would cease to be developed.

As with marketing, the importance of R&D to success in business is much higher

EXHIBIT 5.7 A COMPARISON OF OFFENSIVE AND DEFENSIVE R&D APPROACHES

	Offensive	**Defensive**
Products or processes	Dramatically new ones	Improvement of existing ones
Production design	Flexible and responsive	Rigid, with efficiency goals
Volume	Less emphasis on cost per unit	High-volume emphasis
Implementation	New divisions or new firms	Existing structures
Timing	Longer term	Immediate impact
Environment	Proact—Use R&D to achieve change suited to your research	React—Adjust R&D to needs forecasted

EXHIBIT 5.8   AN INNOVATOR TURNED IMITATOR

In 1986, Procter & Gamble unveiled its newest product innovation, Ultra Pampers, a diaper endorsed by the National Pediatrics Nurses Association for helping to maintain healthy skin. The recent introduction signals a comeback in a market that P&G virtually created but lost ground in when it failed to realize that consumers would pay more for better-quality diapers. Last spring, Kimberly's Huggies took the number one market-share position with its contoured fitting diapers. P&G's comeback resulted from a $500 million revamp of diaper-making equipment. Kimberly is presently changing its equipment to make an equivalent product.

According to P&G, it is using a proven strategy of demonstrating consumer benefit, however slight, to take over market share. Other examples of P&G's product-differentiation strategy include the addition of tartar control to Crest and the introduction of Liquid Tide, a laundry detergent with superior cleaning power. However, competitors continue to innovate (e.g., the pump dispenser for toothpaste), leaving P&G to follow in their footsteps. Note how this relates to the management style discussed in Exhibit 5.4.

The strategy pursued by P&G adds light to our discussion of R&D with regard to offensive and defensive approaches. Although the biggest firms are thought to be fast seconds, this seems to vary with the level of technology. Reportedly, P&G lost ground to "nimbler competitors" in the market in the recent past, by lacking in offense—or innovative leads. It has assumed the imitator position in both diapers and the pump toothpaste, eventually making up lost market share. Where technologies are relatively simple, the imitator position may be quite suitable. Changes are slower but more lasting and much less modifiable, making the imitator spot more attractive. In other areas, where technology is more complex, the innovator or fast-second position is usually more desirable. Innovators, however, are usually smaller firms and often come from outside the industry.

Source: Adapted from "Procter and Gamble Banks On a New Baby: Ultra Pampers," *Business Week*, Feb. 24, 1986, pp. 36–37.

for some than for others. For instance, computer or pharmaceutical firms generally have much larger R&D budgets (5 or 6 percent of sales) than do many other industries (which are in the 1 percent range). Yet even there, some firms choose to innovate with new products, while others develop new applications or minor improvements. Of equal importance, R&D is seen as a way to improve productivity in manufacturing. Increased R&D has led to increasing factory automation after two decades of neglect in the United States. Even the service industries are recognizing the need to boost productivity. In the United States, capital investment in technology per worker averaged less than $450 per worker in the 1960s through mid-1970s. By the mid-1980s, this figure jumped to over $1000 per worker (in constant dollars).

It might be noted that while many U.S. firms have been lagging in long-term commitment to investment in risky R&D with unknown time and payoff lags, Japanese companies have surged ahead. Now many of the imitators are becoming the inventors. But even here, different firms pursue different approaches. Sony is an innovator; Matsushita is a copycat in the consumer electronics arena.

Production and Operations Management Factors [4]

Exhibit 5.9 lists the factors for analyzing production and operations management.

If we were to identify one functional area where North American firms have become less competitive in relation to overseas competitors, it would be operations. The United

EXHIBIT 5.9 INTERNAL FACTORS: PRODUCTION AND OPERATIONS MANAGEMENT

1 Lower total cost of operations compared with competitors' total costs
2 Capacity to meet market demands
3 Efficient and effective facilities
4 Raw materials and subassemblies costs
5 Adequate availability of raw materials and subassemblies
6 Efficient and effective equipment and machinery
7 Efficient and effective offices
8 Strategic location of facilities and offices
9 Efficient and effective inventory-control systems
10 Efficient and effective procedures: design, scheduling, quality control
11 Efficient and effective maintenance policies
12 Effective vertical integration or supplier relations
13 Flexibility in operations

States used to be cited as the leader in this area. Now it seems that Japanese, Taiwanese, Korean, or European firms are the leaders. In particular, the Japanese have pushed hard on factors 1, 6, and 10 through the use of robots (five times more in use than in the United States, even though they were invented by Americans) and quality-control circles in a national effort to improve productivity. If we are to be able to compete, we cannot continue to yield whole businesses such as television and radio manufacturing and clothing to overseas competition. Steel may be the next major loss. Efforts are being made now in U.S. industry to improve quality. "Doing it right the first time" may provide more benefit to the bottom line than any realistic boost in sales volume—and frequently for an investment that is returned in less than a year.

Consider the U.S. steel firms. Their facilities are out of date and they haven't been able to raise funds to modernize. They are at a serious disadvantage against the Japanese on factors 1 and 2, though they are showing signs of making a turnaround.

With regard to factors 1 and 6, Eastern Airlines used to compete with Delta. Delta's equipment was newer and less costly to operate. Delta had a cost advantage. With the newer equipment there are fewer breakdowns, too, and so Delta had an advantage on factor 11.

With regard to factor 3, consider some of the major food chains. Safeway and Kroger have larger and newer stores than A&P. A&P has had to spend large sums to try to catch up. A&P also has factor-8 problems. Many of its stores were located in older neighborhoods with no parking. And A&P is inadequately represented in the faster-growing areas.

Consider factors 4 and 5. Ashland Oil does not own its own crude oil. In the 1973–1974 oil crisis, only government policy allowed it to continue in the gasoline business. Exxon did not have these problems.

Your exposure to production and operations management provided you with tools to help you decide how a firm can improve with regard to factors 9 to 12. The development of careful production planning and control systems, productivity improvements, supplier relations, and plant capacity and location decisions can lead to important competitive advantages for a firm. If a firm can produce at a lower cost, has the capacity to handle business when others can't, or can get raw materials at favorable prices, it has a competitive advantage.

Finally, factor 13 suggests that operations flexibility could become a competitive advantage. Since the beginning of this century, efficiency through economies of scale

EXHIBIT 5.10   THE INCREDIBLE SHRINKING PLANT

The reduction of plant size to more manageable scales is well under way at Westinghouse. A new office furniture plant at Grand Rapids employs 600 people. Its general manager, Russell Nagel, used to run a 5000-worker appliance factory before Westinghouse got out of that business. Nagel sees an enormous difference between managing big and small plants.

In the large-appliance plant, Westinghouse was trying to develop and manufacture an energy-efficient low-cost refrigerator. Nagel recalls, "For six or eight months we couldn't get the key guys from marketing and manufacturing into the same room to talk about what we were trying to do." At any given time, many were out of town or working on other projects. Westinghouse introduced the product a year late.

It is easier to keep tabs on what is happening at the new furniture factory. When Nagel took over, he realized almost immediately that it was throwing away at least $100,000 a year of wood scrap. Within a few weeks, he set up a task force of managers and union workers to deal with the problem. Within a few months they reduced the scrap to $7000 a year. "The bottom-line effect of being able to identify goals and communicate them quickly in a smaller environment is dramatic," says Nagel. "Ten years ago, if you asked me whether by going to smaller plants, you gave up a lot of efficiencies, I would have said 'yes.' Now, I can't think of any."

Source: Adapted from "Small Is Beautiful Now in Manufacturing," *Business Week,* Oct. 22, 1984, pp. 152–156.

has dominated the thinking of production executives. Longer and bigger runs can cut per-unit costs. But as we noted before, technological and economic international competitive conditions are changing the ground rules. Because of nonunion and foreign competition, it is increasingly difficult to run large plants at capacity. And as technological change shortens product life cycles (e.g. consumer electronics), plants become obsolete sooner than expected. Combined with computer-aided design and manufacturing, productivity can be raised but large plant capacities become uncompetitive.

Manufacturing people are now discussing diseconomies of scale. Huge manufacturing complexes are being replaced with newer, smaller plants which are becoming more automated, as suggested in Exhibit 5.10. While some firms still use economies of scale to gain advantage, others are finding that they have more flexibility to shift production requirements in smaller plants, achieve greater productivity, and eliminate some bureaucracy, which often leads to smoother labor relations. In an era where mass marketing gives way to a focus on needs of fragmented population groups which seem to change rapidly, flexibility in operations can very well become a competitive strength. Firms can increase process flexibility and product design flexibility, as well as add flexibility to the production infrastructure (personnel, training, inventory, quality control, and planning and scheduling). This creates aggregate manufacturing flexibility.

Corporate Resources and Personnel Factors [5]

Exhibit 5.11 lists a set of corporate resources and personnel factors which can provide competitive advantages for a firm. Each of the factors can add to the ability of a firm to achieve its objectives. Some firms are well known for these factors. General Electric, for example, has advantages with regard to most of them.

EXHIBIT 5.11   INTERNAL FACTORS: CORPORATE RESOURCES AND PERSONNEL

1 Corporate image and prestige.

2 Effective organization structure, climate, and culture.

3 Company size in relation to the industry (barrier to entry).

4 Strategic management system.

5 Enterprise's record for reaching objectives: How consistent has it been? How well does it do compared with similar enterprises?

6 Influence with regulatory and governmental bodies.

7 Effective corporate-staff support systems.

8 High-quality employees.

9 Balanced functional experience and track record of top management: Are replacements trained and ready to take over? Do the top managers work well together as a team?

10 Effective relations with trade unions.

11 Efficient and effective personnel relations policies: staffing, appraisal and promotion, training and development, and compensation and benefits.

12 Lower costs of labor (as measured by compensation, turnover, and absenteeism).

13 Effective management information and computer systems.

Some firms have attracted and held high-quality, highly productive, and loyal employees and managers. IBM, Texas Instruments, and other firms are known for this. Since these people make the decisions for all functions, this can be a crucial advantage. Many firms have purchased other firms just to get their top-quality managerial, professional, and other employees. By the same token, an organization's structure, climate, and culture can be a key advantage. Disney is well known for an overriding emphasis on a few core principles which guide decisions, employee behavior, and the operations of its business.

Being unionized can be a competitive disadvantage because of the loss of flexibility or because of the higher direct costs of labor. Some firms are unionized but have had good relations with efficient and effective unions, leading to potential advantage.

Many of these factors become particularly important when managers try to determine whether a strategy can be implemented. Weaknesses in these areas could lead to a decision of not attempting a given strategy because of the inability to carry it out effectively. For example, an acquisition candidate whose organization structure is incompatible with the structure of your firm could be a poor choice. Or a strategy to close a plant could be affected by union contracts.

Thus, factors 8 to 12 deal with the so-called people issues. And managers (whether labeled personnel, industrial relations, or human resources managers) who deal with these issues are recognized at some leading companies as a source of competitive strength. More of these managers are reporting to the CEO and are involved in making strategic decisions. If companies are constantly acquiring, merging, spinning off new divisions, entering new businesses, or getting out of old ones, management must consider the human resource questions involved—matching skills with jobs, keeping key personnel after a merger, solving human problems that arise with new technology or the closing of a plant, and so on. According to one of the new breed of human resource managers, ''Chief executives have finally come to realize that people are what give you a competitive edge, and we're telling them how to get the right people.''

Finally, with the advent of management information systems development, and usage, many firms are finding that they can turn data and information power into a potent strategic weapon. Exhibit 5.12 suggests a number of ways that firms can

EXHIBIT 5.12   TEN WAYS TO USE INFORMATION TECHNOLOGY

1 Better financial management. By setting up computer links between the treasurer's office and your banks, you can obtain financial information faster—and that means better cash management.

2 Customer service. By letting customers tap into your database to track their orders and shipments, you build loyalty and smooth relations.

3 Locking in customers. By creating exclusive computer communications with customers for order entry and exchange of product and service data, you can help thwart competitors.

4 Market intelligence. By assembling and manipulating data on demographics and competitors, you can spot untapped niches, develop new products, and avoid inventory crunches.

5 New businesses. Information technologies make whole new operations possible. Federal Express, for one, could not work without computer-equipped trucks and facilities.

6 Product development. By providing a toll-free number for consumer questions and complaints, you get ideas for product improvements and new products. In-house electronic publishing can help turn out product manuals faster for speedier introductions.

7 Sales. Giving salespeople portable computers so that they can get messages faster and enter orders directly adds up to quicker deliveries, better cash flow, and less paperwork.

8 Selling extra processing power. By using off-peak processing power to develop completely new services for outsiders, you can transfer some of the high costs of building your information network.

9 Telemarketing. Testing cold leads by telephone first—using computer runs to ferret out the best prospects—helps slash sales-force expenses and boost productivity.

10 Training. Training or retraining workers using videodisks lets them learn at their own speed—and lets you cut training costs.

Source: Adapted from J. Hamilton and C. L. Harris, "Information Power," *Business Week,* Oct. 14, 1985, pp. 108–116.

develop strengths by using information technology to gain a competitive edge. Quick access to up-to-date data on which to base decisions and make plans is now available to strategists from all over the corporation. In fact, many firms have installed a chief information officer (CIO) in their organizations. These new managers often have several functions and characteristics:

- Oversee the company's technology, including data processing, office systems, and telecommunications
- Report directly to the chairman or CEO
- Concentrate on long-term strategic use of information, leaving day-to-day operations of the computer room to subordinates.

Finance and Accounting Factors [6]

Exhibit 5.13 lists some of the major factors in finance and accounting. The appendix to this chapter provides a summary of financial analyses which can be done to help you assess this area.

One objective of the analysis is to determine if the focal firm is stronger financially than its competitors (Exhibit 5.13, factor 1). Can it hold out longer or compete more effectively because it has the financial strength to do so?

Analysis of the comparative financial condition of the firms is primarily done to determine whether the firm is capable of undertaking a particular strategy, or if it is advisable to do so. For example, many entrepreneurs fail to account for their financial

EXHIBIT 5.13   INTERNAL FACTORS: FINANCE AND ACCOUNTING

1 Total financial resources and strength—liquidity, leverage, profitability, activity, cash flows	**5** Advantageous tax conditions and insurance to minimize risk exposure
2 Low cost of capital in relation to the industry and competitors because of stock price and dividend policy	**6** Efficient and effective financial planning, working capital, and capital budgeting procedures
3 Effective capital structure, allowing flexibility in raising additional capital as needed; financial leverage	**7** Efficient and effective accounting systems for cost, budget and profit planning, and auditing procedures
4 Amicable relations with owners and stockholders	**8** Inventory valuation policies

weakness in their start-up phase. Their firms go "belly-up" because of the cash-flow weakness if they have not planned for it. And many firms have planned costly plant expansions only to find that they are financially incapable of paying for them.

Another purpose of financial analysis is to help pinpoint strengths or weaknesses in other functional areas, from operational and strategic perspectives. The other factors listed add efficiency (factors 2, 5, and 6) or a strategic value (factors 3 and 4) to a firm. The accounting staff function (factor 7) is a necessary one for legal and management information purposes. Accounting policies for inventory valuation (factor 8) can have strategic value when changed in response to inflation and other external changes.

This last point suggests two other important ideas to keep in mind as the financial position of the firm is analyzed. First, the financial value of a firm must be carefully considered in terms of the basis upon which the valuation is made. Stock market prices may reflect *short-term* judgments of analysts. And these judgments may be based on changes in the accounting treatment of assets for tax purposes, which may make returns appear better than they are. The book value may be ridiculously out of date based on long-term historical costs or the method of depreciation used.[1] In either case, if a firm or subunit is being valued for acquisition (or for divestiture or liquidation), the financial valuation process itself must be assessed in addition to other factors affecting such decisions. So the assessment of strength or weakness depends on the analytical approach and the interpretation of "hard" numbers.

A second major issue is the working capital needs for strategic versus ongoing operations. Because of past strategic choices, firms may have tied up so much cash that future options are limited. This happened to Ford and Seagrams. On the other hand, cash-rich firms must determine how long existing strengths will provide a continuous flow of funds and decide how to invest this wisely. Thus timing questions are important to financial analysis.

The final issue we wish to raise concerns the process of financial management. Earlier we suggested that the way valuations are made influences the content of the financial analysis. Also, other corporate resources factors were seen to be important, including the quality of management. Factors 4, 6, and 7 in Exhibit 5.13 hint at the

---

[1] Some analysts now suggest the computation of a Q ratio to aid investment decisions. This is the ratio of the market value of physical assets to the cost of replacing those assets.

important role of the policies and procedures established for performing financial analysis. Thus the role of the financial executive in providing support for planning can lead to a strategic advantage for the firm. Too often, the chief financial manager is seen as important only at budget preparation stages or for providing "number crunching" as input for decisions. These roles are important. But frequently the financial executives are excluded from real involvement in strategic planning because it is believed that they have short-term orientations, focus on selective components rather than on comprehensive pictures, and value precision over less tangible issues. (These remarks often apply to executives in other functional areas as well.) As a result, decision processes can suffer from what has been called a "paralysis of analysis." It is suggested that the chief financial officer's tasks of forecasting capital structure, determining resource allocation and cash flows, and raising external funds are critical functions in determining the competitive advantage of the firm.

Thus a firm at a particular time can be strong (or weak) financially, and this condition allows it to make (or prevents it from making) strategic changes. Financial ratio and accounting analyses help measure this strategic advantage. But an analysis should also be made of the process of financial management, since it too can provide advantages for the firm. Of course, as suggested in the section on corporate resources, the quality of management in any of the functional areas can provide advantages for the firm.

In sum, firms can have competitive advantages on a number of the factors just discussed. Strengths usually lead to greater "slack"—a cushion of resources which allows an organization to be flexible and adapt internally or externally. Slack enhances the ability of a firm to choose from a greater number of alternative strategies. Weaknesses or disadvantages limit the strategic options of a firm. The list of resources and factors also serves as a checklist of items to analyze about a firm (or a case) with a view to improving its operations and identifying its distinctive competencies. It is not an exhaustive list. But it does provide a useful beginning.

ANALYSIS OF STRENGTHS AND WEAKNESSES

There are a variety of ways each area of potential competitive advantage (or disadvantage) might be analyzed. First we will provide some prescriptions for how analysis should be done. Then we will summarize some evidence about whether it is done that way and what is analyzed.

Techniques of Internal Analysis [7]

As suggested earlier, a number of basic references for each area of internal analysis have been provided. It is beyond the scope of this book to summarize the techniques of analysis for the areas most business school curriculums cover in detail. For instance, a partial but far from comprehensive list of tools is identified in Exhibit 5.14.

Data for analysis and diagnosis of the factors come from several sources. One source is the data gathered in the environmental analysis and diagnosis stage of strategic management. The other source is the internal data generated in doing business

EXHIBIT 5.14   A FEW TOOLS FOR INTERNAL ANALYSIS

Finance and accounting: Capital asset pricing model; pay-back; accounting return; present value; internal rate of return; financial ratios (see appendix); fixed and variable budgets

Human resources: Turnover analysis; morale surveys; training budgets; analysis of personnel needs and capabilities

Marketing: Sales forecasts; market-share analysis; price-volume relationships; sales-force analysis; product and market-lines analysis

Operations: Inventory analysis; aggregate and shop-floor simulations; break-even analysis; labor, material, and overhead-cost analysis; materials requirement planning (MRP); operations-research techniques

R&D: Patents generated; project analysis; value analysis

and available from the management information system and the functional departments (such as marketing). One writer has suggested that the annual report, with all its faults, is another valuable source of information. So as before, verbal sources, documents, formal studies, or a management information system can provide data inputs for analysis.

In addition to these sources, there are two other analytical aids you might use to guide the internal analysis. The first is the functional-area profile. This type of profile is shown in Exhibit 5.16 (pages 172–173). The idea is to present a matrix of functional areas with characteristics common to each.

Then the strategist prepares the functional-area resource-deployment matrix (Exhibit 5.15). The firm records where it is spending its dollars and currently exerting its efforts. This information should be recorded each year so that the firm can determine the relative importance of each functional area (compared with competitors' functional areas) over time. This approach allows the firm to analyze the strategic deployment of funds and its strengths and weaknesses over time as compared with those of competitors.

We also wish to make some suggestions about how you can apply some of these techniques for strategic analysis. First, each area must be considered with respect to what its policies and approaches were, are, and will be. That is, how do current conditions *relate to* the past attainment of objectives, future expectations, or internal requirements? This question is critical to the overall gap analysis, and the answer will help you determine which areas are most important for the future. As we noted before, what is viewed as a strength now may become a weakness later. Looking at each area over time allows you to see if advantages are being developed or are deteriorating. For instance, a decline in the number of patents being generated may be a sign of potential problems in R&D or new-product development. Increasing grievances may suggest labor problems. An increase in the cost of goods sold could indicate production difficulties. Increases in the rework rate may indicate quality-control problems. A host of indicators in each area can be examined over time. In finance, the ratios noted in the appendix can be examined over several years, and pro formas can be prepared for the future. Each indicator also must be analyzed in relation to goals or requirements.

For instance, are sales quotas being met? Does the trend in debt to equity suggest

EXHIBIT 5.15   A FUNCTIONAL-AREA RESOURCE-DEPLOYMENT MATRIX

Functional areas	Resource-deployment emphasis	5 years ago	4 years ago	3 years ago	2 years ago	1 year ago	This year	Next year
R&D + engineering	% of strategic development dollars							
	Focus of efforts							
Manufacturing	% of strategic development dollars							
	Focus of efforts							
Marketing	% of strategic development dollars							
	Focus of efforts							
Finance	% of strategic development dollars							
	Focus of efforts							
Management	% of strategic development dollars							
	Focus of efforts							

problems in meeting any conditions of loan agreements with bankers? Are our hiring procedures meeting the requirements of the Equal Opportunity Employment Commission so that we can continue to secure government contracts? Any of these areas could be sources of weaknesses or strengths. For example, your firm may be a favored employer if its hiring practices are "better" than those of competitors.

Second, the analysis can be done on a piecemeal basis, with each area viewed independently of the others. However, the strengths and weaknesses must be compared *in relation to* one another. Trade-offs will inevitably result, but it is better to consider the needs and desires of each area together rather than let each suboptimize. Consider Exhibit 5.17 as a case in point. Manufacturing may see strength through a policy of long, steady mass production runs of a limited product line. Finance may set policies which value a low finished-goods inventory and high turnover for cash-flow improvement. It may suggest capital budgeting and investment policies which minimize the number of factories and warehouses, freight costs, etc. So far so good; these policies

EXHIBIT 5.16   TYPICAL FUNCTIONAL-AREA PROFILE

	R&D engineering (conceive/design/develop)	Manufacturing (produce)

Focus of financial deployments	$ for basic research
	$ for new product development
	$ for product improvements
	$ for process improvements
		$ for plant
		$ for equipment
		$ for inventory
		$ for labor

Physical resources	Size, age, and location of R&D facilities Size, age, and location of development facilities	No., location, size, and age of plants Degree of automation Degree of integration Type of equipment
Human resources	Nos., types, and ages of key scientists and engineers Turnover of key personnel	Nos., types, and ages of key staff personnel and foremen Turnover of key personnel
Organizational systems	System to monitor technological developments System to control conceptual/design/ development process	Nature and sophistication of purchasing system; production scheduling and control system; quality control system
Technological capabilities	No. of patents No. of new products % of sales from new products Relative product quality	Raw materials availability Trends in total constant $ per-unit costs for raw materials and purchased parts; direct labor and equipment Productivity Capacity utilization Unionization

could be seen as ways to improve efficiency and gain a competitive advantage. But suppose marketing and sales efforts are directed toward the exclusive distribution of high-quality, high-priced, custom-designed outputs. The company has developed promotion policies to tap a market opportunity in this area. Its goal is better customer service through well-stocked warehouses and a wider product line. Suddenly, the assessment of production and finance strengths takes on a different meaning. And the

Marketing (distribute/sell/service)	Finance (finance)	Management (plan/organize/control)

$ for sales and promotion
$ for distribution
$ for service
$ for market research
	$ for short-term cash management
	$ for raising long-term funds
	$ for allocating long-term funds
	$ for management development
		$ for planning system
		$ for control system
		$ for management development

No. and location of sales offices No. and location of warehouses No. and location of service facilities	No. of lock boxes No. of major lenders Dispersion of stock ownership No. and types of computers	Location of corporate headquarters
Nos., types, and ages of key salespeople Marketing staff Turnover of key personnel	Nos., types, and ages of key financial and accounting personnel Turnover of key personnel	Nos., types, and ages of key managers and corporate staff Turnover of key personnel
Nature and sophistication of distribution system; service system; pricing and credit staff; market research staff	Type and sophistication of cash management system; financial markets forecasting system; corporate financial models; accounting system	Nature of organizational culture and values Sophistication of planning and control systems Delegation of authority Measurement of reward systems
Trends in total constant $ per-unit costs for sales and promotion; distribution and service % retail outlet coverage Key account advantages Price competitiveness Breadth of product line Brand loyalty Service effectiveness	Credit rating Credit availability Leverage Price-earnings ratio Stock price Cash flow Dividend payout	Corporate image prestige Influence of regulatory and governmental agencies Quality of corporate staff Organizational synergies

types and numbers of personnel to manufacture custom-designed products, staff warehouses, process and ship orders, etc., become quite different. Clearly this is an extreme example. But the point should be clear that what may be a strength in each area can result in overall weakness if the company is "pushing the cogs" in opposite directions.

In a similar view, weaknesses must be compared with strengths. Weaknesses may prevent us from taking advantage of an opportunity. They can prevent us from readily shifting strategies. But too many executives put on unneeded "blinders" by emphasizing weaknesses instead of strengths. Instead of taking a pessimistic view ("if anything can go wrong, it will"), successful strategists often take an optimistic view ("we didn't know it couldn't be done, so we did it"). Thus instead of allowing weaknesses to dominate, it is often more fruitful to take advantage of an opportunity by capitalizing on strengths. However, this must be done within the legitimate, *real* constraints which may exist because of the firm's weaknesses.

In addition to being compared over time in relation to goals and to one another, strengths and weaknesses are compared in relation to environmental conditions. The comparison is usually based on competitors, but it could include the firm's position relative to technological changes, suppliers, or the product life cycle.

Most strategists are concerned with how their firms are placed strategically relative to competitors in similar businesses. It is vital that the proper comparisons be made. For example, as the PIMS data have shown, companies with a high degree of investment intensity are often less profitable than those with lower investment-sales ratios. Similar differences exist if the firm being compared is substantially different on characteristics other than investment intensity. Thus a statement about the mission of the business as discussed in Chapter 2 becomes important as a basis for determining the relevant comparison groups. Furthermore, aside from the group itself, the company within the group that you compare your firm with makes a difference with regard to the interpretation of strengths and weaknesses. Consider ratio analysis, for example. Besides studying changes of your organization over time, should you compare these with industry *averages* or with the changes experienced by leaders? If low performers on ROI in the industry have high liquidity, for example, is the high liquidity of your firm a strength or a weakness? That may depend on other factors unique to your firm's own situation. In other words, many industries are composed of different strategic groups. Comparing ratios of Anheuser-Busch to Heilemann or LoneStar or with beer-industry averages may not make much sense. Hence, comparisons with leaders of strategic groups (or to upper- and lower-quartile performers) is more likely to reveal valid and meaningful conclusions than using "industry averages" as the basis for comparing financial ratios or other data such as marketing outlays, plant size, R&D expenditures, labor costs, and so on. Indeed, TWA was criticized when its former CEO urged executives to measure their company against industry averages than to shoot for the top. So caution in the interpretation of data is required.

It is also important to compare firms which are in the same or similar phases of the product-service life cycle. If our firm's main products or services are in the maturity stage of the life cycle, improper comparisons would be made with a firm whose main products are in the growth phase of the cycle. One representation of the life cycle is given in Exhibit 5.18.

Finally, it is important to compare strengths and weaknesses relative to their overall significance to the strategy of the firm. Crisis managers can get bogged down in analyzing fine details and "lose sight of the forest for the trees." Daily operational fluctuations and problems may drive attention away from areas of strength or weakness that are far more important to overall success. Of course, clinical judgment is required

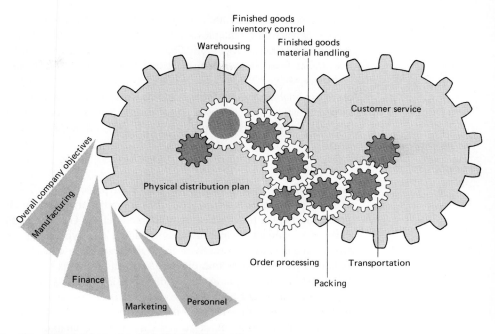

EXHIBIT 5.17   **"Cogwheels" in a physical distribution system.**
(R. Ball, "Physical Distribution: A Suitable Case for Treatment," Long Range Planning [February 1980], p. 3.)

EXHIBIT 5.18   **A common product-service life cycle.**

Phase I (Development)	Phase II (Growth)	Phase III (Maturity)	Phase IV (Shakeout)	Phase V (Decline)
Development of the product and/or service and/or process and/or market characterized by: inception; missionary work; lack of customer knowledge; much personal selling and service; continued product and/or service development; little or no competition	Growth of product and/or service and/or process and/or market characterized by: demand exceeding supply; increase in production capacity; order taking; little promotion; low sales effort; competitors enter market	Maturity of product and/or service and/or process and/or market effort; low margin mass selling; over-capacity in production; much competition	Industry consolidation; many firms exit; some focus on specific niches; others merge or take over market share from those leaving; beginning of slow decline in demand and capacity	Decline of product and/or service and/or process and/or market characterized by high substitution, decreased demand, and competitors leaving the market

for determining which areas and indicators these are. (We have more to say about this in the section on diagnosis.) The key is to identify areas and indicators which top management should focus on. Four key questions can be asked as you examine the five areas: What does this firm do particularly well? Do these competencies count, and if so, when? What does the firm do poorly? Does it matter? As companies and cases are analyzed, our advice is to not worry about head colds—if pneumonia seems to be indicated, that requires more serious analysis. (Nonetheless, if it appears that the head cold can become pneumonia, it may require treatment.)

Descriptions of Internal Analysis [8]

The discussion of analysis so far has been prescriptive. There is little descriptive research on whether and how strategists actually perform strategic advantage analysis. On the basis of a few studies two things are clear. One is that the process of internal analysis is subject to internal bias by level and type of executive. There is often disagreement among executives about the distinctive competence of their firm. Second, it does not appear that clear patterns of strengths or weaknesses emerge. Each firm seems to be unique in how it develops and uses its advantages.

But this isn't very helpful. The question is, How do you identify and use competitive advantages? You identify them on the basis of the diagnosis and analysis of strengths and weaknesses discussed earlier in the chapter. For example, distinctive competence could result from a superior delivered low-cost position or a differentiated product offering. Competitive advantages could consist of superior quality, superior service or technical assistance, a strong brand name, a unique or innovative product or service, or the status of being a full-line producer with wide distribution. Such advantages result from the strength of superior skills or resources, lower costs of manufacturing or distribution, lower cost of capital, design expertise, good trade relationships, fast and flexible response capabilities, and so on. Identification of these involves careful analysis of the various factors identified earlier.

One of the factors discussed in the operations and corporate resources sectors was whether size was a strength or weakness. The ''advantage'' of size deserves special treatment since we think that too many believe ''bigger is better.'' A larger size in relation to the competition is normally viewed positively. It can give strength by allowing greater economies of scale or providing barriers to entry. However, there are some potential weaknesses associated with a larger size. Diseconomies of scale can result from rapid increases in size as we discussed earlier. The organization becomes more difficult to manage. This is typical of young, overly aggressive companies. Furthermore, large firms often become the targets of regulators, legislators, consumer activists, and competitors; many equate size with the potential for misuse of power. Moreover, small firms or SBUs are often thought to have an advantage of flexibility that allows them to change and maneuver, while larger firms or units find it more difficult to do this.

Another dilemma associated with size is its relationship to goals. A number of studies suggest that size is not necessarily directly correlated with better performance.

For instance, expansion may entail internal diseconomies of scale. And there may be limits to continued growth in a particular business. Under certain circumstances, the size of the market share itself is related to returns in a U-shaped fashion where large *and* small shares may be related to higher ROI than medium market shares.

For example, the do-it-yourself retail business has long been dominated by small mom-and-pop hardware stores and lumberyards. Several large firms (K Mart, Home Centers of America, etc.) believed they could jump in, build mammoth stores, offer discount prices, and attract customers with advertising. Instead of killing off the little guys, the big chains are fighting each other for market share and sites needed to break even on large warehouse stores. Massive advertising, cost cutting, and loss leaders to build traffic have cut gross margins tremendously. And the little guys fought back by forming alliances for buying and advertising clout and by offering personal service to the naive new do-it-yourselfers.

These and other examples suggest that expansion strategies carry with them seeds of potential competitive disadvantage where sheer size creates new management problems. Hence each firm must determine whether it is better to be a big fish in a little pond or a little fish in the sea. There are advantages in both situations, and strength or weakness can go along with a large size. Careful thought must go into the diagnosis of whether conditions being analyzed are strengths or weaknesses.

There are also some descriptions about how businesses can strengthen their competitive position and develop distinctive competence. Ohmae suggests that managers should use their analysis of strengths and weaknesses in ways which lead to competitive advantage.

1 The first approach is to readjust resource allocation to strengthen certain areas of the business. If management allocates resources exactly the same way competitors do, there will be no change in competitive position. So this approach suggests that resources should be concentrated in areas where there are key success factors (KSF) so the firm can gain a strategic advantage. Even though a firm may have no more total resources than competitors, it can achieve distinction if it focuses those resources on one crucial point.

One typical example here is the use of market segmentation. A Japanese shipbuilder segmented customer groups into seven markets and ship types into 12 product categories. After identifying key product market groups, it focused its resources and attention on these sectors to gain competitive advantage.

2 It may be that the KSF struggle is being waged, but a firm may exploit differences between itself and a competitor. Here the strategist either (*a*) makes use of the technology, sales network, and so on, of those of its products which are not directly competing with the products of competitors or (*b*) makes use of other differences in the composition of assets. Thus relative superiority is used to avoid head-on competition.

Ohmae provides an example of a Japanese film producer who could not compete with Fuji on the basis of an image problem associated with its name. Advertising could not overcome the negative connotations. However, it had a relative advantage in its costs of production; hence, it lowered prices and started to do battle on economic issues where it possessed superiority.

3 A competitor in a well-established stagnant industry may be hard to dislodge. Here an unconventional approach may be needed to upset the key factors for success that the competitor has used to build an advantage. The starting point is to challenge accepted assumptions about the way business is done, or the nature of products or processes, and gain a novel advantage by creating new success factors.

For example, a camera manufacturer wondered why photographs have to go through the negative stage before being printed, or why a camera couldn't have a built-in flash to spare users the trouble of finding and fixing an attachment. Federal Express wondered why packages were delivered point to point instead of funneled through a centralized facility. Challenging basic assumptions with questions can lead to novel ideas.

4 Finally, a competitive advantage may be obtained by means of innovations which open new markets or lead to new products. Innovation often involves finding new ways of satisfying the customer's utility function.

Suppose that you manufacture coffee and determine that the utility function of target customers is superior taste. What determines coffee taste? Kind and quality of beans, type of roast, fineness of grind, time between grinding and brewing, water hardness and temperature, style of brewing, and so on. Some of these are beyond the manufacturer's control. But others involve degrees of freedom: Water hardness could probably be overcome by incorporating a regenerable filter in the machine. The approach here is to think creatively for innovations which expand degrees of freedom to accomplish goals and develop new strengths.

In each of these approaches the principal point is to avoid doing the same thing as the competition on the same battleground. So the analyst must decide which of these approaches might be pursued to develop a sustainable distinctive competence.

The Role of Strategists in Analysis and Diagnosis

Exhibit 5.19 shows how each of the groups of strategists is involved in internal analysis and diagnosis.

If you compare this exhibit with Exhibit 3.9 you'll note that the role performances are similar, except that from what the research tells us, firms perform internal analysis less frequently and less formally, which is why there are differences between the exhibits. Given some findings that internal analysis is time-consuming and distorted, we might understand why managers are reluctant to perform internal analysis themselves. Outside consultants are not necessarily a panacea, however. An investment firm's report, for instance, may inject a bias for emphasizing financial specifics. Prescriptively, several approaches are probably useful with top management discussion on points of disagreement.

Of course, in a single-SBU firm, advantages are analyzed and diagnosed at the corporate level. In multiple-SBU firms, they are analyzed at the SBU level and then reevaluated at the corporate level and compared across SBUs.

EXHIBIT 5.19 THE ROLE OF STRATEGISTS IN INTERNAL ANALYSIS AND DIAGNOSIS

| Strategists | Analysis | | | | Diagnosis and decision making |
	Verbal search and interviews	Docu-mentary search	Formal studies	MIS	
Top managers	Occasionally	Rarely	Rarely	Rarely	Performs
Corporate planners	Occasionally	Rarely	Occasionally	Rarely	Advises as requested
Board of directors	Occasionally	Rarely	Rarely	Rarely	Occasionally advises
Consultant	Rarely	Rarely	Rarely	NA	Occasionally hired to advise

DIAGNOSIS OF STRENGTHS AND WEAKNESSES [9]

As indicated earlier, the diagnostic process for internal factors parallels that process for environmental factors. Similar factors such as the strategist's characteristics, the strategist's job, and the strategist's environment affect the decision. Focusing on diagnosis of internal factors is similar to focusing on the environmental diagnosis as described in Chapter 4. However, we will add some other factors, since we are discussing the importance of subunits to the organization and its strategy.

Organization theorists suggest that the most critical units are those in the "technical core." Essentially, these are the units which perform the basic transformation of inputs into outputs called for by the mission definition. Note that this need *not* necessarily include mass production (though it could), because other types of missions do not call for this kind of transformation. Hence banks, wholesalers, retailers, and real estate and travel agents have a technical core that is somewhat different from the technical core of cigarette manufacturers. The core units for the organization in question are the primary areas for the initial diagnosis of strengths and weaknesses.

However, other units not in the technical core attempt to build their power and become important to the organization so that they may increase their share of resource allocation. Identifying these units is also important for narrowing the diagnosis of strengths and weaknesses. These units can be identified by determining how many other units they are interconnected with, whether they have a direct impact on the technical core units, and whether they are specialized in such a way that they can help reduce uncertainty. Let's consider an example. Suppose that a data processing unit builds a management information system which provides useful data for estimates of sales and production scheduling as well as for tracking the performance of warehouse operations. It has positioned itself to deal with important uncertainties, and its work flow is important input for decisions by several core units. We can expect that its potential power in the organization may lead it to become an important unit for the diagnosis of strengths and weaknesses. To the extent that other subunits are dependent on a given unit, it is more powerful and requires analysis by top management.

Of course, this discussion relates essentially to functions within SBUs. At the corporate level of analysis in a multiple-SBU firm, similar suggestions are made. But here one is analyzing the importance of entire strategic business units to overall corporate performance and strategy. That is, how dependent is the corporation on a given SBU? At this level, more global assessments of SBU strengths and weaknesses are often made and are based on relative competitive position and environmental opportunity. Chapter 7 examines how these factors can be combined to assist in strategic decision making.

Once the key areas for diagnosis have been analyzed, it is useful to prepare a strategic advantage profile (SAP) for the firm being analyzed. Similar to the ETOP, this is a tool for providing a picture of the more critical areas, which can have a relationship to the strategic posture of the firm in the future.

Exhibit 5.20 presents an example of an SAP for a hypothetical firm. Note that this firm has weaknesses in channels of distribution, facilities, and R&D and is experiencing union difficulties. This may preclude certain strategies, such as market expansion in the southwest. On the other hand, it may suggest to managers that a conscious choice to correct this weakness is important. The final conclusions depend on environmental factors, objectives, and the pattern of other strengths and weaknesses identified. For example, the financial strengths could lead to a decision to invest in updated facilities or build a sales force in the southwest if the environment shows opportunity there. Chapter 8 describes in more detail how the SAP is combined with other factors to lead to strategic decision making.

If first-generation planning is used, this diagnosis is based on the most probable future. If second-generation planning is used, several scenarios of the future are drafted—with best-case, most-probable, and worst-case assumptions. Then several diagnoses are made.

As in the preparation of an ETOP, several stages may be required before the final SAP is displayed. That is, each of the subfactors identified in Exhibits 5.3, 5.5, 5.9, 5.11, and 5.13 should be subjected to the comparative analysis discussed in our section

EXHIBIT 5.20   STRATEGIC ADVANTAGE PROFILE

Internal area	Competitive strength or weakness
Marketing	+ Product line is extensive, and service is excellent. − Channels of distribution are weak in the southwest.
R&D	− No R&D performed.
Operations	+ Excellent sourcing for raw materials. − Facilities are old and becoming outdated.
Corporate resources	0 Company size is about average for the industry. 0 Profits have been consistent but average. − Union employees complain frequently.
Finance	+ Balance sheet shows ability to obtain needed capital; low debt-equity ratio, high working capital position, and favorable stock price.

Note: + indicates strength; 0 indicates neutral; − indicates weakness.

on techniques for analysis. For example, a set of financial ratios (see the appendix) can be exhibited as a supplement to the SAP. Then a *diagnosis* of the most important ones for the organization is summarized in the final SAP.

This latter stage is probably the most crucial and most difficult. In effect, the comparative analyses require you to consider the environmental factors and time simultaneously. Let's clarify this statement.

Suppose that your analysis shows a high quick ratio for the firm compared with the ratio of your major competitor. One assessment could be that there is a potential cash management weakness. But suppose you also identified in the ETOP a threat of insufficient capital available to the industry for needed investment. Now your perception of the cash position of this firm may turn out to indicate strengths. Similarly, a high inventory position which might otherwise be viewed as a weakness could be considered a strength if demand conditions appear to be growing or if a strike appears likely.

By the same token, assessments of environmental opportunities and threats can be altered depending on your diagnosis of the internal factors. Let's say that your environmental analysis indicated a threat of the exit of sources of supplies of raw materials for your industry. Your internal analysis, however, shows that your purchasing agent has developed close contacts with the remaining suppliers; your firm is assured of a steady stream of needed inputs. Now the perception of the supplier threat is one of an opportunity to gain a competitive advantage due to your firm's particular strength in this area.

In these examples note that diagnosis involves the perception of threats and opportunities and strengths or weaknesses *in relation to one another*. The analysis of data and information can be done independently. But diagnosis requires that you consider integrating the relative information to draw conclusions. One further step is needed, however.

We have discussed this as a static process. You should recognize that events can change. Thus diagnosis also involves estimating scenarios of likely future conditions to reflect dynamic realities.

Consider the example where your firm's strength of supply contacts offsets a threat of the exit of suppliers. How long will that strength exist? Will the suppliers remain loyal or bend to pressure to supply your firm's competitors? Will the competitors alter their strategy? For instance, some may leave the business. Some may integrate backward to make their own raw materials. Others may try new methods or materials to reduce their dependence on the remaining suppliers. Each of these alternatives might be considered by your competitors. They, too, are looking to build a competitive advantage.

Another issue related to time is the question of how long a strength will remain if it is relied on extensively or overused. For instance, the KSF approach prescribes building a unique strength by concentrating resources in a single area or in a few areas. For instance, a football team may rely on a single superstar to carry the ball. Several conditions may result over time. First, competitors may start to "key on" the factor—they may try to attack it, steal, or copy your firm's strength. If the strength happens to be technological, it can become obsolete. If the strength lies in personnel, key people may resign, retire, or die. Finally, if one area receives the bulk of the resources, other areas where new competitive advantages might be generated will not develop their potential. Suppose, for example, that you have analyzed your firm's work force and found that it is made up of highly skilled and trained personnel. This could be a competitive advantage, but you observe that the facilities, machines, tools, and materials that they need to do their work effectively are out of date or lead to inefficiencies. Thus your firm cannot *use* its strength as a potential competitive advantage unless resources are allocated to correct the weakness. Some of the other approaches suggested earlier may be necessary.

Of course, the obverse problem should be recognized. If resources are spread too thinly across many areas, there is a danger that the firm will not develop a distinctive competence. Firms (and individuals) have been known to seize an opportunity without commensurate ability. As Christensen et al. suggest, "Opportunism without competence is a path to fairyland." This is particularly a danger when managers believe that they have superior ability and can succeed at almost anything on the basis of past success. And as we mentioned before, if the strengths of interdependent units are actually working against one another (Exhibit 5.17), the resulting suboptimization may lead to a competitive disadvantage.

The weaknesses of an organization may inhibit or preclude certain strategies from being considered as capable of implementation. For example, a firm with an abnormally high debt-equity ratio may find it is unable to pursue a merger because it has reached its debt "limits." Nonetheless, the role of perception creeps in here in terms of the diagnosis of this weakness. That is, the debt weakness might be corrected with an issuance of equity, assuming other financial factors are reasonable and the equity markets (environmental factor) are favorable. So it is with other weaknesses. More than one entrepreneur has been heard to remark that "We didn't know it couldn't be done, so we went ahead and did it."

In effect, a firm should develop a strategy over time which revolves around an area of distinctive competence. With this approach the firm can develop slack resources that can evolve into new areas of strength when old ones falter (and they inevitably do). At the same time, the weaknesses which are identified as potentially important to the future should receive management attention. This may require a strategy to acquire personnel or other strengths which are currently lacking, if the firm is incapable of developing them because of internal resource weaknesses.

Many U.S. companies are trying to be more competitive these days with the kind of strategic thinking we have identified here. Many firms are planning to invest in more efficient plants and equipment, invest in more research and development, improve quality of service to customers, adopt more aggressive marketing tactics, and try to reduce labor costs in an effort to develop sustainable competitive advantage. Exhibit 5.21 shows a firm in this process.

As you may have noticed, the discussion has begun to address the pros and cons of alternative strategies. The Boston Consulting Group suggests that the number of competitive advantages and the size of the advantages lead to different kinds of strategies. Exhibit 5.22 explains this. For example, if there are many ways to create advantages such as in the fast food business but the size of those advantages is small, then the firm should probably seek to stabilize.

EXHIBIT 5.21   DEVELOPING A STRATEGIC ADVANTAGE

Compared with AT&T, GTE, and IBM, Continental Telephone would hardly be viewed by most as a firm with the kinds of strengths needed to compete in the booming market for transmitting data communications. In the amalgam of 1800 rural telephone exchanges spread over 37 states, 30 percent of the subscribers still share party lines. The holding company has little research and development and no manufacturing capability of its own. Compared with the assets of AT&T, its $3 billion in assets is minuscule, and its 1980 revenue of $1.1 billion was just over 2 percent of the revenue of its giant competitor. The price-earnings ratio is about standard for regulated utilities but far lower than the ratios of the computer companies expected to play a major role in the market.

However, a key strength is an aggressive management team atypical of the management of regulated telephone companies. At age 70, the founder and chairman believes that the best defense is a good offense. A carefully planned series of acquisitions and joint ventures has been designed so that the company can develop the strengths it needs to become a major supplier of data and voice communication services.

A joint venture with Fairchild (Am Sat) gives Continental strength in satellite transmission. A satellite receiving station can be set up for 10 percent of the cost of what AT&T needs to lay out comparable ground lines. The purchase of Executone, a PBX marketing firm, provided a base from which to build a business in intelligent terminals and digital telephone switches, which will become the hub of the automated office. The joint-venture approach, in particular, provides Continental with a way to use its limited resources to enter areas that it could not enter on its own.

Of course, some observers are skeptical. A GTE executive sees little synergy in the recent acquisitions (but Continental executives see them as complementary). And the task of integrating the pieces into a single network is difficult to accomplish. Further, AT&T, GTE, IBM, and Xerox are not standing still. If it's a game for giants, Continental does not yet qualify.

The perception at Continental, though, is that it has a head start, and it can keep the customers it gets before its regulated competitors are allowed to enter the fray. Furthermore, Continental sees its size as an advantage. Even if it captures only 5 percent of the market, that will represent a revenue increase of almost 700 percent. It can turn its business around faster and has already started putting the pieces together.

The weaknesses it believes require long-term development are the need for aggressive marketing and the need for skilled personnel who can manage and integrate high technology. Additional acquisitions and joint ventures are planned to correct these weaknesses.

You might note that several of the points discussed in this chapter are brought together here. Perceptions of relative strength and weakness, relevant comparison groups, long-term development of resources, and the relationship between competitive advantage and environmental threats and opportunities have all helped determine the way in which this firm has chosen to orient itself strategically.

Source: Adapted from "Continental Telephone: Taking On the Giants in Telecommunications," *Business Week*, Feb. 9, 1981, pp. 50–56.

However, we think that this ignores some of the environmental factors described in our earlier chapters. And it is hoped that you can find ways to increase either the size or number of advantages to increase your options. Thus, diagnosis of combining the ETOP and the SAP should lead to examining a wider variety of strategy alternatives than is suggested here, which is the subject of Chapters 6 and 7.

SUMMARY

The chapter described the internal analysis and diagnosis process paralleling the environmental analysis process covered in Chapters 3 and 4. Internal analysis and diagnosis is the process by which the strategists examine the firm's internal factors to

Size of the competitive advantage which can be achieved

	Small	Large
Many	**Key competitive feature:** Many ways to gain an edge, but the size of the edge counts for little in the marketplace. Strategy prescriptions: ● Carve out a position and hold it. ● Emphasize profits now. ● Minimize investment. ● Be cautious about expansion.	**Key competitive feature:** A specialized approach to the many market segments is essential and so is creating and protecting the advantage in serving these segments. Strategy prescriptions: ● Seek a niche. ● Get in position to serve selected segments. Spend heavily to build and fortify the chosen advantage. ● Stay ahead of rivals who aspire to gain the same advantage. ● Watch out for change.
Few	**Key competitive feature:** Almost a pure cost–price game; on other factors, all firms are in about equal position. In the absence of price–cost differences, there is a virtual competitive stalemate. Strategy prescriptions: ● Use aggressive cost reduction strategies. ● Emphasize ways to improve efficiency. ● Manage to increase cash flow. ● Look for diversification opportunities.	**Key competitive feature:** Only those who get and keep one of the large competitive advantages will survive; usually low cost is the primary advantage that is available. Often, the name of the game is volume. Strategy prescriptions: ● Pursue economies of scale. ● Ride the experience curve downward by getting volume up. ● Go after the customers of weak firms. ● If weak, get out or look for new ways to compete.

Different ways a competitive advantage can be created

EXHIBIT 5.22   Strategies based on competitive advantages.
(Adapted from an approach suggested by Alan Zakon, Boston Consulting Group, in an address to the Academy of Management, 1982.)

determine where the firm has significant strengths and weaknesses. This is needed so the firm can exploit opportunities, meet threats, and correct weaknesses inhibiting a desired strategy or putting the firm at a competitive disadvantage.

The areas covered in the chapter include internal factors to be analyzed and diagnosed, techniques of internal analysis, the reality of internal analysis, the role of strategists in this process, and the diagnosis of the internal factors.

The internal factors that management analyzes and diagnoses are marketing and distribution, R&D and engineering, production and operations management, corporate resources and personnel, and finance and accounting. Each of these factors was broken down and each subcategory was illustrated to help you digest the internal analysis and diagnosis process. It was suggested that strengths are needed to build slack to give firms greater strategic options, and weaknesses must be overcome where possible.

Techniques of internal analysis were described. Data and indicators of various subfactors should be gathered so that *relative comparisons* can be made. Comparisons are necessary in the following areas to get a clearer picture of strengths and weaknesses: past, present, and future conditions; internal goals and external requirements; the way that each functional area relates to other functional areas; and environmental factors: competitors, technology, suppliers, and the product life cycle. Two analytical tools were suggested as useful guides for the analysis, and four key questions were suggested to help identify distinctive competencies—What does the firm do well? Do these competencies count? What does the firm do poorly? Does it matter?

Research on internal analysis indicates that this process is not scientific. But very little research has been done on this subject. The studies which exist indicate that executives perceive strengths and weaknesses differently and that firms seem to be unique in their particular pattern of competitive advantages. That uniqueness can be developed into competitive advantages in a variety of ways.

A brief section on the role of strategists in the internal analysis and diagnosis process suggests the need to formalize the process of internal analysis for better strategic management.

The chapter concludes with our suggestions for performing internal diagnosis. Focusing the diagnosis is affected by factors outlined in Chapter 4. But in addition, the analyst should determine the areas of greatest importance to strategic performance: technical core units and units which are pervasive and can reduce uncertainty. Once the diagnosis is focused, the strategic advantage profile (SAP) is defined and its development is outlined.

> *The strategic advantage profile is a tool for making a systematic evaluation of the enterprise's internal factors which are significant for the company in its environment.*

What this profile does is give a visual representation of what the company is as a result of developing from past strategic decisions and interaction with its environment. Suggestions are offered for interpreting an internal analysis.

In sum, the chapter focused on how to analyze the internal factors realistically and how to diagnose their significance. Then the executive can develop an SAP and match it with the ETOP to create conditions for adjusting or changing strategies or policies.

The process is summarized in proposition form as follows:

Proposition 5.1

A firm whose strategy fits its environment, considering its competitive advantages, will be more effective than one whose strategy does not.

Proposition 5.2

A firm which develops slack resources through distinctive competence will be more effective than one which does not.

This chapter completes the analysis and diagnosis discussion. Chapter 6 begins the three-chapter discussion of the choice phase of the strategic management process. We have now examined conditions (internal and external) which might create a gap between the ideal and expected positions of the firm in the future. Next we will examine ways in which the gap may be reduced, by examining strategy alternatives and the choice of a strategy.

Appendix: Using Financial Analysis*

One of the most important tools for assessing the strength of an organization within its industry is financial analysis. Managers, investors, and creditors all employ some form of this analysis as the beginning point for their financial decision making. Investors use financial analyses in making decisions about whether to buy or sell stock, and creditors use them in deciding whether or not to lend. They provide managers with a measurement of how the company is doing in comparison with its performance in past years and with the performance of competitors in the industry.

Although financial analysis is useful for decision making, there are some weaknesses that should be noted. Any picture that it provides of the company is based on past data. Although trends may be noteworthy, this picture should not automatically be assumed to be applicable to the future. In addition, the analysis is only as good as the accounting procedures that have provided the information. When making comparisons between companies, one should keep in mind the variability of accounting procedures from firm to firm.

There are four basic groups of financial ratios: liquidity, leverage, activity, and profitability.

Depicted in Exhibit 5.23 are the specific ratios calculated for each of the basic groups. Liquidity and leverage ratios represent an assessment of the risk of the firm. Activity and profitability ratios are measures of the return generated by the assets of the firm. The interaction between certain groups of ratios is indicated by arrows.

Typically two common financial statements are used in financial analyses: the balance sheet and the income statement. Exhibit 5.24 is a balance sheet and Exhibit 5.25 an income statement for the ABC Company. These statements will be used to illustrate the financial analyses.

Liquidity Ratios

Liquidity ratios are used as indicators of a firm's ability to meet its short-term obligations. These obligations include any current liabilities, including currently maturing long-term debt. Current assets move through a normal cash cycle of inventories—sales—accounts receivable—cash. The firm then uses cash to pay off or reduce its current liabilities. The best-known liquidity ratio is the current ratio: current assets divided by current liabilities. For the ABC Company the current ratio is calculated as follows:

$$\frac{\text{Current assets}}{\text{Current liabilities}} = \frac{\$4,125,000}{\$2,512,500} = 1.64 \ (1988)$$

$$= \frac{\$3,618,000}{\$2,242,250} = 1.61 \ (1987)$$

*Prepared by Elizabeth Gatewood, University of Georgia.

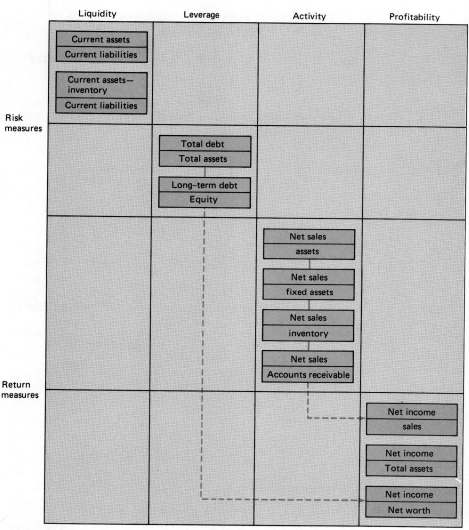

EXHIBIT 5.23   Financial ratios.

Most analysts suggest a current ratio of 2 to 3. A large current ratio is not necessarily a good sign; it may mean that an organization is not making the most efficient use of assets. The optimum current ratio will vary from industry to industry, with the more volatile industries requiring higher ratios.

Since slow-moving or obsolescent inventories could overstate a firm's ability to meet short-term demands, the quick ratio is sometimes preferred to assess a firm's liquidity. The quick ratio is current assets minus inventories, divided by current liabilities. The quick ratio for the ABC Company is calculated as follows:

$$\frac{\text{Current assets} - \text{inventories}}{\text{Current liabilities}} = \frac{\$1,950,000}{\$2,512,500} = 0.78 \ (1988)$$

$$= \frac{\$1,618,000}{\$2,242,250} = 0.72 \ (1987)$$

A quick ratio of approximately 1 would be typical for American industries. Although there is less variability in the quick ratio than in the current ratio, stable industries would be able to safely operate with a lower ratio.

EXHIBIT 5.24   ABC COMPANY BALANCE SHEET AS OF DECEMBER 31

		1988		1987
Assets				
Current assets:				
Cash		$ 140,000		$ 115,000
Accounts receivable		1,760,000		1,440,000
Inventory		2,175,000		2,000,000
Prepaid expenses		50,000		63,000
Total current assets		$4,125,000		$3,618,000
Fixed assets:				
Long-term receivables		$1,255,000		$1,090,000
Property and plant	$2,037,000		$2,015,000	
Less: Accumulated depreciation	862,000		860,000	
Net property and plant		1,175,000		1,155,000
Other fixed assets		550,000		530,000
Total fixed assets		$2,980,000		$2,775,000
Total assets		$7,105,000		$6,393,000
Liabilities and Stockholders' Equity				
Current liabilities:				
Accounts payable		$1,325,000		$1,225,000
Bank loans payable		475,000		550,000
Accrued federal taxes		675,000		425,000
Current maturities (long-term debt)		17,500		26,000
Dividends payable		20,000		16,250
Total current liabilities		$2,512,500		$2,242,250
Long-term liabilities		1,350,000		1,425,000
Total liabilities		$3,862,500		$3,667,250
Stockholders' equity:				
Common stock (104,046 shares outstanding in 1983; 101,204 shares outstanding in 1982)		$ 44,500		$ 43,300
Additional paid-in capital		568,000		372,450
Retained earnings		2,630,000		2,310,000
Total stockholders' equity		$3,242,500		$2,725,750
Total liabilities and stockholders' equity		$7,105,000		$6,393,000

EXHIBIT 5.25 ABC COMPANY INCOME STATEMENT FOR THE YEARS ENDING DECEMBER 31

		1988		1987
Net sales		$8,250,000		$8,000,000
Less: Cost of goods sold	$5,100,000		$5,000,000	
Administrative expenses	1,750,000		1,680,000	
Other expenses	420,000		390,000	
Total		7,270,000		7,070,000
Earnings before interest and taxes		$ 980,000		$ 930,000
Less: Interest expense		210,000		210,000
Earnings before taxes		$ 770,000		$ 720,000
Less: Federal income taxes		360,000		325,000
Earnings after taxes (net income)		$ 410,000		$ 395,000
Common-stock cash dividends		$ 90,000		$ 84,000
Addition to retained earnings		$ 320,000		$ 311,000
Earnings per common share		$ 3.940		$ 3.90
Dividends per common share		$ 0.865		$ 0.83

Leverage Ratios

Leverage ratios identify the source of a firm's capital—owners or outside creditors. The term "leverage" refers to the fact that using capital with a fixed interest charge will "amplify" either profits or losses in relation to the equity of holders of common stock. The most commonly used ratio is total debt divided by total assets. Total debt includes current liabilities and long-term liabilities. This ratio is a measure of the percentage of total funds provided by debt. A total debt–total assets ratio higher than 0.5 is usually considered safe only for firms in stable industries.

$$\frac{\text{Total debt}}{\text{Total assets}} = \frac{\$3,862,500}{\$7,105,000} = 0.54 \ (1988)$$

$$= \frac{\$3,667,250}{\$6,393,000} = 0.57 \ (1987)$$

The ratio of long-term debt to equity is a measure of the extent to which sources of long-term financing are provided by creditors. It is computed by dividing long-term debt by the stockholders' equity.

$$\frac{\text{Long-term debt}}{\text{Equity}} = \frac{\$1,350,000}{\$3,242,500} = 0.42 \ (1988)$$

$$= \frac{\$1,425,000}{\$2,725,750} = 0.52 \ (1987)$$

Activity Ratios

Activity ratios indicate how effectively a firm is using its resources. By comparing revenues with the resources used to generate them, it is possible to establish an efficiency of operation. The asset turnover ratio indicates how efficiently management is employing total assets. Asset turnover is calculated by dividing sales by total assets. For the ABC Company, asset turnover is calculated as follows:

$$\text{Asset turnover} = \frac{\text{Sales}}{\text{Total assets}} = \frac{\$8,250,000}{\$7,105,000} = 1.16 \ (1988)$$

$$= \frac{\$8,000,000}{\$6,393,000} = 1.25 \ (1987)$$

The ratio of sales to fixed assets is a measure of the turnover on plant and equipment. It is calculated by dividing sales by net fixed assets.

$$\text{Fixed asset turnover} = \frac{\text{Sales}}{\text{Net fixed assets}} = \frac{\$8,250,000}{\$2,980,000} = 2.77 \ (1988)$$

$$= \frac{\$8,000,000}{\$2,775,000} = 2.88 \ (1987)$$

Industry figures for asset turnover will vary with capital-intensive industries, and those requiring large inventories will have much smaller ratios.

Another activity ratio is inventory turnover, estimated by dividing sales by average inventory. The norm for American industries is 9, but whether the ratio for a particular firm is higher or lower normally depends upon the product sold. Small, inexpensive items usually turn over at a much higher rate than larger, expensive ones. Since inventories are normally carried at cost, it would be more accurate to use the cost of goods sold in place of sales in the numerator of this ratio. Established compilers of industry ratios such as Dun and Bradstreet, however, use the ratio of sales to inventory.

$$\text{Inventory turnover} = \frac{\text{Sales}}{\text{Inventory}} = \frac{\$8,250,000}{\$2,175,000} = 3.79 \ (1988)$$

$$= \frac{\$8,000,000}{\$2,000,000} = 4 \ (1987)$$

The accounts receivable turnover is a measure of the average collection period on sales. If the average number of days varies widely from the industry norm, it may be an indication of poor management. A too low ratio could indicate the loss of sales because of a too restrictive credit policy. If the ratio is too high, too much capital is being tied up in accounts receivable, and management may be increasing the chance of bad debts. Because of varying industry credit policies, a comparison for the firm over time or within an industry is the only useful analysis. Because information on credit sales for other firms is generally unavailable, total sales must be used. Since not all firms have the same percentage of credit sales, there is only approximate comparability among firms.

$$\text{Accounts receivable turnover} = \frac{\text{Sales}}{\text{Accounts receivable}} = \frac{\$8,250,000}{\$1,760,000} = 4.69 \text{ (1988)}$$

$$= \frac{\$8,000,000}{\$1,440,000} = 5.56 \text{ (1987)}$$

$$\text{Average collection period} = \frac{360}{\text{Accounts receivable turnover}}$$

$$= \frac{360}{4.69} = 77 \text{ days (1988)}$$

$$= \frac{360}{5.56} = 65 \text{ days (1987)}$$

Profitability Ratios

Profitability is the net result of a large number of policies and decisions chosen by an organization's management. Profitability ratios indicate how effectively the total firm is being managed. The profit margin for a firm is calculated by dividing net earnings by sales. There is wide variation among industries, but the average for American firms is approximately 5 percent.

$$\frac{\text{Net earnings}}{\text{Sales}} = \frac{\$410,000}{\$8,250,000} = 0.0497 \text{ (1988)}$$

$$= \frac{\$395,000}{\$8,000,000} = 0.0494 \text{ (1987)}$$

A second useful ratio for evaluating profitability is the return on investment—or ROI, as it is frequently called—found by dividing net earnings by total assets. The ABC Company's ROI is calculated as follows:

$$\frac{\text{Net earnings}}{\text{Total assets}} = \frac{\$410,000}{\$7,105,000} = 0.0577 \text{ (1988)}$$

$$= \frac{\$395,000}{\$6,393,000} = 0.0618 \text{ (1987)}$$

The ratio of net earnings to net worth is a measure of the rate of return or profitability of the stockholders' investment. It is calculated by dividing net earnings by net worth, the common-stock equity and retained-earnings account. ABC Company's return on net worth, also called ROE, is calculated as follows:

$$\frac{\text{Net earnings}}{\text{Net worth}} = \frac{\$410,000}{\$3,242,500} = 0.1264 \text{ (1988)}$$

$$= \frac{\$395,000}{\$2,725,750} = 0.1449 \text{ (1987)}$$

It is often difficult to determine causes for lack of profitability. The Du Pont system of financial analysis provides management with clues to the lack of success of a firm. This financial tool brings together activity, profitability, and leverage measures and shows how these ratios interact to determine the overall profitability of the firm. A depiction of the system is set forth in Exhibit 5.26.

The right side of the figure develops the turnover ratio. This section breaks down total assets into current assets (cash, marketable securities, accounts receivable, and inventories) and fixed assets. Sales divided by these total assets gives the turnover on assets.

The left side of the figure develops the profit margin on sales. The individual expense items plus income taxes are subtracted from sales to produce net profits after taxes. Net profits divided by sales gives the profit margin on sales. When the asset turnover ratio on the right side of Exhibit 5.26 is multiplied by the profit margin on sales developed on the left side of the figure, the product is the return on assets (ROI) for the firm. This can be shown by the following formula:

$$\frac{\text{Sales}}{\text{Total assets}} \times \frac{\text{Net earnings}}{\text{Sales}} = \frac{\text{Net earnings}}{\text{Total assets}} = \text{ROI}$$

EXHIBIT 5.26   **Du Pont's financial analysis.**

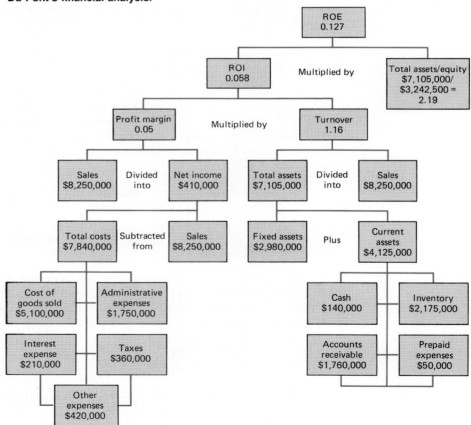

The last step in the Du Pont analysis is to multiply the rate of return on assets (ROI) by the equity multiplier, which is the ratio of assets to common equity, to obtain the rate of return on equity (ROE). This percentage rate of return could, of course, be calculated directly by dividing net income by common equity. However, the Du Pont analysis demonstrates how the return on assets and the use of debt interact to determine the return on equity.

The Du Pont system can be used to analyze and improve the performance of a firm. On the left, or profit, side of the figure, attempts to increase profits and sales could be investigated. The possibilities of raising prices to improve profits (or lowering prices to improve volume) or seeking new products or markets, for example, could be studied. Cost accountants and production engineers could investigate ways to reduce costs. On the right, or turnover, side, financial officers could analyze the effect of reducing investment in various assets as well as the effect of alternative financial structures.

There are two basic approaches to using financial ratios. One approach is to evaluate the corporation's performance over several years. Financial ratios are computed for different years, and then an assessment is made about whether there has been an improvement or deterioration over time. Financial ratios can also be computed for projected, or pro forma, statements and compared with present and past ratios.

The other approach is to evaluate a firm's financial condition and compare it with the financial conditions of similar firms or with industry data in the same period. Such a comparison gives insight into the firm's relative financial condition and performance. Financial ratios for industries are provided by Robert Morris Associates, Dun and Bradstreet, and various trade association publications. (Associations and their addresses are listed in the *Encyclopedia of Associations* or the *Directory of National Trade Associations.*) Information about individual firms is available through *Moody's Manual,* Standard and Poor's manuals and surveys, annual reports to stockholders, and the major brokerage houses.

To the extent possible, accounting data from different companies must be standardized so that companies can be compared or so that a specific company can be compared with industry data. It is important to read any footnotes of financial statements, since various accounting or management practices can have an effect on the financial picture of the company. For example, firms using sale-leaseback methods may have leverage pictures that are quite different from what is shown as debts or assets on the balance sheet.

Analysis of the Sources and Uses of Funds

The purpose of this analysis is to determine how the company is using its financial resources from year to year. By comparing balance sheets from one year to the next, one may determine how funds were obtained and the way in which these funds were employed during the year.

To prepare a statement of the sources and uses of funds it is necessary to (1) classify balance sheet changes that increase cash and changes that decrease cash, (2) classify from the income statement factors that increase or decrease cash, and (3) consolidate this information on a sources and uses of funds statement form.

Sources of funds that increase cash are as follows:

1 A net decrease in any asset other than a depreciable fixed asset
2 A gross decrease in a depreciable fixed asset
3 A net increase in any liability
4 Proceeds from the sale of stock
5 The operation of the company (net income, and depreciation if the company is profitable)

Uses of funds include

1 A net increase in any asset other than a depreciable fixed asset
2 A gross increase in depreciable fixed assets
3 A net decrease in any liability
4 A retirement or purchase of stock
5 Payment of cash dividends

We compute gross changes to depreciable fixed assets by adding depreciation from the income statement for the period to net fixed assets at the end of the period and then subtracting from the total the net fixed assets at the beginning of the period. The residual represents the change in depreciable fixed assets for the period.

For the ABC Company the following change would be calculated:

Net property and plant (1988)	$1,175,000
Depreciation for 1988	+ 80,000
	$1,255,000
Net property and plant (1987)	− 1,155,000
	$ 100,000

To avoid double counting, the change in retained earnings is not shown directly in the funds statement. When the funds statement is prepared, this account is replaced by the earnings after taxes, or net income, as a source of funds and dividends paid during the year as a use of funds. The difference between net income and the change in the retained-earnings account will equal the amount of dividends paid during the year. The accompanying sources and uses of funds statement was prepared for the ABC Company.

A funds analysis is useful for determining trends in working-capital positions and for demonstrating how the firm has acquired and employed its funds during some period.

ABC CO.'S SOURCES AND USES OF FUNDS STATEMENT
FOR 1988

Sources	
Prepaid expenses	$ 13,000
Accounts payable	100,000
Accrued federal taxes	250,000
Dividends payable	3,750
Common stock	1,200
Additional paid-in capital	195,500
Earnings after taxes (net income)	410,000
Depreciation	80,000
Total sources	$1,053,450
Uses	
Cash	$ 25,000
Accounts receivable	320,000
Inventory	175,000
Long-term receivables	165,000
Property and plant	100,000
Other fixed assets	20,000
Bank loans payable	75,000
Current maturities of long-term debt	8,500
Long-term liabilities	75,000
Dividends paid	90,000
Total uses	$1,053,450

Ratios and working capital	1984	1985	1986	1987	1988	Trend	Standard	Interpretation
Liquidity: Current								
Quick								
Leverage:								
(etc.)								
Working-capital position								

EXHIBIT 5.27   **A summary of the financial position of a firm.**

Conclusion

It is recommended that you prepare a chart such as Exhibit 5.27 so that you can develop a useful portrayal of these financial analyses. The chart allows a display of the ratios over time. The Trend column could include arrows to indicate "favorable" (↑), "neutral" (—), and "unfavorable" (↓) for the ratios over time. The Standard column could include the desired (or required) ratio. The Interpretation column can be used to describe the meaning of the ratios for this firm. The chart gives a basic display of the ratios as one aspect of the firm's financial condition.

REFERENCES

[1]   Strategic Advantage Factors

Croon, P.: "Aids in Determining Strategy: The Internal Analysis," *Long Range Planning,* vol. 12, no. 4 (August, 1979), pp. 65–73.

Porter, M. E.: *Competitive Strategy: Techniques for Analyzing Industries and Competitors* (New York: Free Press, 1980).

Steiner, G.: *Strategic Factors in Business Success* (New York: Financial Executives Research Foundation, 1965).

Wirnerfelt, B.: "A Resource-Based View of the Firm," *Strategic Management Journal,* vol. 5 (1984), pp. 171–180.

[2]   Analyzing Marketing and Distribution

Abell, D. F., and J. S. Hammond: *Strategic Market Planning* (Englewood Cliffs, N.J.: Prentice-Hall, 1979).

Kotler, P.: *Marketing Management* (Englewood Cliffs, N.J.: Prentice-Hall, 1980).

"Marketing: The New Priority," *Business Week,* Nov. 21, 1983, pp. 96–106.

[3]   Analyzing R&D and Engineering

Boseman, B., M. Crow, and A. Link (eds.): *Strategic Management of Industrial R&D* (Lexington, Mass.: Lexington Books, 1984).

Gold, B.: "Strengthening Managerial Approaches to Improving Technological Capabilities," *Strategic Management Journal,* vol. 4 (1983), pp. 209–220.

Helm, L.: "The Big Two of Consumer Electronics," *Business Week,* Dec. 30, 1985, pp. 62–64.

Joseph, J., and A. Hall: "Japan Focuses on Basic Research to Close the Creativity Gap," *Business Week,* Feb. 25, 1985, pp. 94–96.

Mitchell, R.: "High Tech to the Rescue," *Business Week,* June 16, 1986, pp. 100–104.

"A Productivity Revolution in the Service Sector," *Business Week,* Sept. 5, 1983, pp. 106–108.

"Spending for Research Still Outpaces Inflation," *Business Week,* July 6, 1981, pp. 60–75.

[4] Analyzing Production and Operations Management

Buffa, E.: "Making American Manufacturing Competitive," in G. Carroll and D. Vogel (eds.): *Strategy and Organization: A West Coast Perspective* (Boston: Pitman, 1984).

Ignatius, D.: "Aging Mills: U.S. Steel Makers Fail to Modernize Quickly, Fall Behind Japanese," *Wall Street Journal,* Aug. 3, 1977.

Kiechel, W.: "The Food Giants Struggle to Stay in Step with Consumers," *Fortune,* Sept. 11, 1978.

"Quality: The U.S. Drives to Catch Up," *Business Week,* Nov. 1, 1982, pp. 66–69.

"Small is Beautiful Now in Manufacturing," *Business Week,* Oct. 22, 1984, pp. 152–156.

"Steel's Sea of Troubles," *Business Week,* Sept. 19, 1977.

[5] Analyzing Corporate Resources and Personnel

"Business is Turning Data Into a Potent Strategic Weapon," *Business Week,* Aug. 22, 1983, pp. 92–98.

Cushman, R.: "On Becoming a Billion Dollar Company," *Business Week,* May 19, 1980, p. 14.

Dobrzynski, J. H., J. P. Tarpey, and R. Aikman: "Small Is Beautiful," *Business Week,* May 27, 1985, pp. 88–90.

Ginzberg, E., and G. Vojta: *Beyond Human Scale: The Large Corporation at Risk* (New York: Basic Books, 1985).

"Hardware Wars: The Big Boys Might Lose This One," *Business Week,* Oct. 14, 1985, pp. 84–90.

Hoerr, J.: "Human Resource Managers Aren't Corporate Nobodies Anymore," *Business Week,* Dec. 2, 1985, pp. 58–59.

"Management's Newest Star: Meet the Chief Information Officer," *Business Week,* Oct. 13, 1986, pp. 160–168.

"Sony: A Diversification Plan Tuned to the People Factor," *Business Week,* Feb. 9, 1981, pp. 88–89.

[6] Analyzing Finance and Accounting

"Asset Redeployment," *Business Week,* Aug. 24, 1981, pp. 68–74.

Naylor, T. H.: "Management Is Drowning in Numbers," *Business Week,* Apr. 6, 1981, pp. 14–15.

Peavy, J. W.: "Modern Financial Theory, Corporate Strategy, and Public Policy," *Academy of Management Review,* vol. 9 (1984), pp. 152–157.

"The Q-Ratio: Fuel for the Merger Mania," *Business Week,* Aug. 24, 1981, p. 30.

"Seagram: Its Cash Hoard Is Spent, and Its Future Is Up in the Air," *Business Week,* Dec. 21, 1981, pp. 98–102.

[7] Techniques for Analyzing Strengths and Weaknesses

Ball, R.: "Physical Distribution: A Suitable Case for Treatment," *Long Range Planning,* vol. 13 (February 1980), pp. 2–11.

Dubin, R. A., and J. R. Norman: "The Airlines," *Business Week,* July 1, 1985, p. 22.

Hofer, C., and D. Schendel: *Strategy Formulation: Analytical Concepts* (St. Paul, Minn.: West, 1978), p. 149.

Lieberman, M. B.: "The Learning Curve, Diffusion, and Competitive Strategy," research paper #766a, Graduate School of Business, Stanford University, 1985.

[8] Descriptions of Internal Analysis

Day, G. S.: *Strategic Market Planning* (St. Paul, MN: West, 1984).

Hitt, M. A., and R. D. Ireland: "Corporate Distinctive Competence, Strategy, Industry and Performance," *Strategic Management Journal,* vol. 6 (1985), pp. 273–294.

Ohmae, K.: *The Mind of the Strategist: The Art of Japanese Business* (New York: McGraw-Hill, 1982).

Stevenson, H. H.: "Defining Strengths and Weaknesses," *Sloan Management Review,* vol. 17, no. 3 (Spring 1976), pp. 51–68.

[9] Diagnosing Internal Factors Strategically

Christensen, C. R., K. R. Andrews, and J. L. Bower: *Business Policy* (Homewood, Ill.: Richard D. Irwin, 1978).

"Fighting Back: It Can Work," *Business Week,* Aug. 26, 1985, pp. 62–68.

Kiechel, W.: "Three (or Four, or More) Ways to Win," *Fortune,* Oct. 19, 1981, pp. 181–188.

Porter, M. E.: *Competitive Advantage* (New York: Free Press, 1985).

Zakon, A.: Address to Business Policy and Planning Division, Academy of Management, New York, 1982.

CHAPTER OUTLINE

GENERIC STRATEGY ALTERNATIVES

OBJECTIVES

- To understand why strategists should consider several alternative strategies prior to making a strategic choice
- To review the major strategic alternatives available to firms
- To understand the advantages and disadvantages of various alternatives

INTRODUCTION

Chapter 6 begins a three-chapter unit on the strategic choice phase of the strategic management process. Let us now assume that you as the strategist have thoroughly analyzed the environment for opportunities and threats. You have prepared the environmental threat and opportunity profile (Chapters 3 and 4). You have done a good job assessing the enterprise's strengths and weaknesses. You have prepared the strategic advantage profile (Chapter 5). You have also reexamined ideal goals in light of the expected outcomes of pursuing the existing strategy (Chapters 1 and 2). As a result, you should be in a position to consider the underlying potential for a gap between expected and ideal performance outcomes.

As indicated in Exhibit 6.1, you have completed the analysis and diagnosis phase of the strategic management process and are ready to begin the choice phase. This phase consists of two activities:

1 The generation of a reasonable number of strategic alternatives that will help fill the gaps matching the environmental threat and opportunity profile with the strategic advantage profile (Chapters 6 and 7)

2 The choice of a strategy to reduce the gaps (Chapter 8)

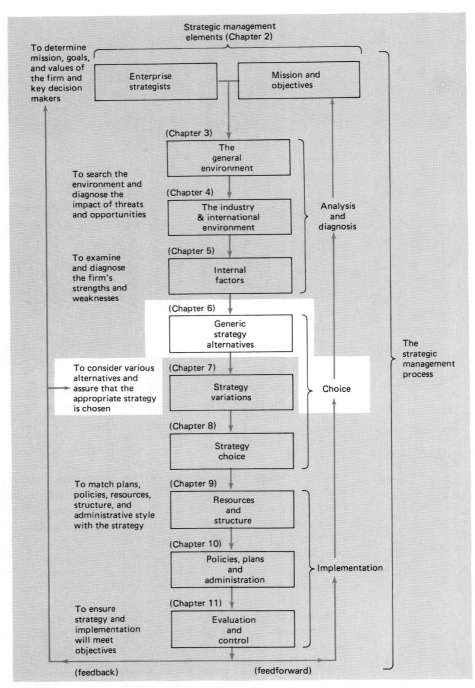

EXHIBIT 6.1 **A model of strategic management.**

This chapter and the next look at how the strategic decision makers generate alternative strategies to fill the gaps found when the results of the two profiles and the firm's goals are compared. Relative to the gap analysis, you start with the current strategy. If the gap is small or nonexistent (on the basis of analyses of goals, external factors, and internal factors), then we assume that current strategy is adequate and little or no change is required. As the gap increases (threats, opportunities, strengths, weaknesses, or goal changes create gaps), then strategy alternatives to close the gap need to be considered. By comparing the ETOP and SAP, you will acquire clues about the nature of strategic alternatives to close any gaps. For instance, if a substantial environmental opportunity exists with an internal ability to take advantage of it, expansion alternatives are most likely. If environmental threats seem most pressing, it may be that the way to improve performance is by retrenching. If no gaps are perceived (or if gaps are not significant, or if you believe they are out of your control), you are likely to pursue a stable approach. Note that at this stage, the alternatives for change are being generated with the perspective of improving performance by taking action to close performance gaps expected in the future.

As shown in Exhibit 6.2, in a corporation the primary generator of strategic alternatives is the top manager, and in a multiple-SBU firm, the primary generators are the SBU top managers and the corporate top manager. Lower-level managers are involved to the extent that they prepare proposals for consideration by top managers. For instance, an R&D unit may propose that additional resources be allocated for the development of a new product. Top managers need to analyze these proposals, taking into account strategic considerations that are broader than the merits of any single project. Functional-level managers are also involved to the extent that plans to implement strategies are considered as part of the strategy formulation process, and strengths and weaknesses coming from functional levels are evaluated by these managers as inputs to the total process.

EXHIBIT 6.2 THE ROLE OF STRATEGISTS IN CONSIDERING STRATEGY ALTERNATIVES

Strategists	Generate strategy alternatives	Analyze strategy alternatives
SBU-level managers	Regularly	Regularly
Top managers	Regularly	Regularly
Corporate planners	Occasionally	Regularly
Board of directors	Rarely	Occasionally
Consultants	Occasionally hired to advise	Rarely
Functional-level managers	Prepare proposals	Regularly

STRATEGIC ALTERNATIVES AND THE DEFINITION OF THE BUSINESS [1]

The central factor that is examined at the beginning of strategy consideration is the mission definition—the business the firm is in or wants to be in. We described this in Chapter 2. Here we start to get more specific. That is, the definition needs to clarify the products or services provided, the market niches served, and the functions performed.

The choice of products or services requires questions about the breadth and depth of the offering. Should the line be broad or narrow? This is part of the scope issue discussed in Chapter 2. How are the products or services to be differentiated? Can additional uses be found for them? Are they to be of high quality or low quality? Perhaps the fundamental question regarding products or services is, What is offered in the way of customer *utility?* Does the product or service provide time, place, form, or information utility or other utilities valued by customers? The business definition should clarify the nature of the product or service offerings initially. Alternative strategies can then be developed around the definition (or the definition can be changed).

The choice of markets basically involves territories, channels, and customer types. Do we serve local, regional, national, or international markets? Do we use wholesale or retail distributors, rely on direct sales, or consume outputs ourselves? Do we serve commercial or industrial firms, nonprofit enterprises, individual consumers, or military or governmental units? How do we segment customers into classes? Should we serve more markets or fewer? Do we go after a large share of submarkets (concentrate), seek a share of many markets (undifferentiated), or differentiate markets and customize programs for each?

The question of functions (or technologies) revolves around how the firm wishes to add value. It may create new ideas or plant seeds, locate resources or grow them, or extract or harvest, refine or process, manufacture, assemble, or pack, store, or distribute goods and services. These are usually thought of as the processes used to transform into inputs, beginning with creation and ending with delivery to the end user. Production is the stage most people usually think of. Here, of course, assembly lines are a common form. But other types of approaches are available. Craft-oriented job shops or teams of specialists can be used to produce goods. In addition, the organization can serve to link parties who desire to exchange goods, services, or money (banks, wholesalers, retailers, and employment agencies are examples). In this case, a physical transformation is not intended. At each stage from creation to delivery to the end user, choices include the processes used to add value. Further, the business definition needs to clarify which of the stages the firm will focus on, ranging from complete vertical integration at one extreme to specialization in only one stage at the other.

Once the initial choice of product, market, and function scope has been determined, strategic alternatives abound. A firm can accomplish strategic change by expanding or retrenching in any of or all these areas, or by stabilizing in some and expanding in others. It can do this simultaneously or over time, yielding a huge number of options for consideration. In effect, this is why firms can pursue so many different kinds of strategies which seem to be successful in attaining objectives.

For smaller firms, this business definition is simple enough. The product or service, market, and functions are usually limited to one category or a few categories. This is true for many medium-sized organizations as well. A majority of large firms are involved in multiple businesses. So their business definition is more complex.

Some firms are in so many businesses that it is hard if not impossible to describe the ''business'' they are in. In one study of three conglomerates (Litton, Indian Head, and Bangor Punta) it was found that their strategy making did not involve delineating specific businesses. Their definition of business involved only the specifications in detail of the corporate objectives in terms of growth rates, financial policies to guide their acquisition of funds and firms, and organizational policies.

Decisions regarding business definition and mission are made at the corporate level. Corporate-level strategies involve issues of which businesses to be in. Business-level strategies involve questions of what to do with those businesses—expand them, retrench them, or stabilize them. At the functional level within business units, alternative plans and policies are set forth to specify ways in which the strategies will be made to work. Thus corporate-level strategic alternatives revolve around the question of whether to continue or change the business(es) the enterprise is currently in. Business-level strategic alternatives involve improving the efficiency or effectiveness with which the firm achieves its corporate objectives in its chosen business sector.

The central strategic alternatives to consider are the following:

1 What is our business? What should it be? What business should we be in 5 years from now? 10 years?

2 Should we stay in the same business(es) with a similar level of effort? (stability)

3 Should we get out of this business entirely or some parts of it? (retrenchment)

4 Should we expand into new business areas by adding new functions, products, and/or markets? (expansion)

5 Should we carry out alternatives 3 and 4, 2 and 4, or 2 and 3? Simultaneously or sequentially? (combination)

These strategic alternatives will be described shortly. Note that in all instances, the major reason for pursuing the strategy is to maintain or improve performance, or reduce gaps if they exist. Thus in all cases, question 1 is a beginning point. You have to know where you are and where you want to be before you can decide how you're going to get there from here. In this sense, the existing business definition prevents you from considering certain alternatives. Only in rare instances can you abandon your past.

THE GENERIC STRATEGY ALTERNATIVES

Whether dealing with corporate- or business-level strategy, there are four generic ways in which alternatives can be considered: stability, expansion, retrenchment, and combinations. These are options for the pace or level of effort in the current business definition, or for changing the mission. Exhibit 6.3 shows a matrix of these basic options with some representative examples of approaches for carrying out the strategy. That is, the firm may decide to change its *business definition* by expanding or retrenching the scope of its products, markets, or functions. If it chooses to maintain

EXHIBIT 6.3   GENERIC STRATEGY ALTERNATIVES

	Expand		Retrench		Stabilize		Combinations*
	Business definition	Pace	Business definition	Pace	Business definition	Pace	Definition and/ or pace
Products	Add new products	Find new uses	Drop old products	Decrease product development	Maintain	Make package changes, quality improvements	Drop old while adding new products
Markets	Find new territories	Penetrate markets	Drop distribution channels	Reduce market shares	Maintain	Protect market shares, focus on market niches	Drop old customers while finding new ones
Functions	Forward vertical integration	Increase capacity	Become captive company	Decrease process R&D	Maintain	Improve production efficiency	Increase capacity and improve efficiency

*Can include activities from across two or more of these cells simultaneously or sequentially over time: for example, "maintain stability of product offerings while expanding market territories at the same time," or "improve efficiency before later expanding into new products in a planned sequence."

its definition, it still may alter its strategy by changing the *pace* of effort within the stable business definition in order to become more efficient or effective in the way it carries out its mission. Of course, combinations of options are possible at the same time or over time. The rest of this chapter will describe some features of these generic options. Our next chapter explains some variations for carrying them out. Chapter 8 describes factors affecting the choice among alternatives.

STABILITY STRATEGIES [2]

A stability strategy is a strategy that a firm pursues when:

1 It continues to serve the public in the same product or service, market, and function sectors as defined in its business definition, or in very similar sectors.

2 Its main strategic decisions focus on incremental improvement of functional performance.

Stability strategies are implemented by "steady as it goes" approaches to decisions. Few major functional changes are made in the product or service line, markets, or functions. In an effective stability strategy, a company will concentrate its resources where it presently has or can rapidly develop a meaningful competitive advantage in the narrowest possible product-market-function scope consistent with its resources and market requirements.

A stability strategy may lead to defensive moves such as taking legal action or obtaining a patent to reduce competition. Stability usually involves keeping track of new developments to make sure the strategy continues to make sense.

Note that the stability approach is *not* a "do nothing" approach; nor does it mean that goals such as profit growth are abandoned. The stability strategy can be designed to increase profits through such approaches as improving efficiency in current operations. As suggested in Exhibit 6.3, the business definition may be stable (no change in products, markets, or functions), but the *pace* of activity may be changed in combination with this stable definition. By the same token, a stable pace may be pursued, but the management may try a competitive strategy to be sure desired performance outcomes are accomplished (such as making packaging changes or making pricing changes to protect market share). Such competitive changes are characteristic of a stable pace, but do not imply that management is sitting idle.

This strategy is typical for firms in a mature stage of development, or mature product-market evolution. Frequently, firms will segment markets or pursue product differentiation and seek to use assets efficiently. For a small firm, this strategy is frequently used to maintain a comfortable market or profit position. Or it can be used to bring control to a company experiencing wide swings in past performance. Usually, however, the level of goal attainment is not set as high as might be found in firms following expansion strategies. Or stability may be used in combination with expansion to provide a base of support for other strategic moves and an element of risk reduction.

Why Do Companies Pursue a Stability Strategy?

A number of explanations can be offered to support stability.

1 The firm is doing well or perceives itself as successful. Management does not always know what combination of decisions is responsible for this. So ''we continue the way we always have around here.''

2 A stability strategy is less risky. A high percentage of changes fail, whether we are talking about new products or new ways of doing things. So conditions must be really bad (or opportunities good) if a firm decides to take the additional risk. The larger the firm and the more successful it has been, the greater is the resistance to the risk.

3 Managers prefer action to thought. A stability strategy can evolve because the executives never get around to considering any other alternatives. Many of the firms that pursue this strategy do so unconsciously. They react to forces in the environment and will change their business definition only in extraordinary times.

4 It is easier and more comfortable for all concerned to pursue a stability strategy. No disruptions in routines take place.

5 The environment is perceived to be relatively stable, with few threats to cause problems or few opportunities the firm wishes to take advantage of.

6 Too much expansion can lead to inefficiencies. In effect, many decision makers do not perceive a significant gap between the future level of goal attainment they expect to reach and their ideal objectives.

A firm's executives may also believe that resources or other environmental changes prohibit the continuation of expansion in the business definition that may have occurred in the past. Here the analysis could suggest that continued expansion could actually

EXHIBIT 6.4   A NEW BABY FORMULA

Gerber Products Company had long dominated the U.S. baby food market. But a declining birthrate in the 1970s forced the firm to begin seeking growth elsewhere. Forays into marketing adult foods failed, and day-care centers were only moderately successful. But Gerber did begin to build the only national baby-products brand name, with more than 400 items ranging from bottles and toys to humidifiers and clothes. By 1978 the birthrate had begun to climb, and the strategy was "selling more to the same mothers."

Five years later, this stability strategy was still in force. Gerber's baby food market share stood at 71%, and merchandise sales were double the amount they had been 5 years earlier. Growth prospects look good. A small but positive 1% annual growth in births is expected until 1990, per capita use of baby foods is rising, and 40% of babies are first-born, the ones who get the most new accessories.

Gerber does not expect its market share to grow much, but planners believe the market will grow 3%. President Smith says the company "has a few ideas, but none of the projects we have under way have yet resolved themselves to a direction." And none is particularly innovative. One might simply be to revive an earlier product failure.

For Gerber, the formula is still to sell a little more each year to a few more mothers. Concentrating on slow, steady growth with a stability strategy seems to make sense when a firm is doing well in a moderately stable environment.

Source: Adapted from "Gerber: Concentrating on Babies Again for Slow Steady Growth," *Business Week,* Aug. 22, 1983, p. 80.

increase the *performance gap*. Thus stability in the *pace* of activity becomes desirable. Executives may realize that the consequences of expansion could become dysfunctional. For instance, expansion (for example, by some types of acquisitions) could lead to antitrust pressure from government or attacks from competitors or pressure groups. Or the firm may need a breathing spell. It may have expanded so fast that it must stabilize for a while or else become inefficient and unmanageable. Its costs may have gotten out of hand, especially if it appears that hard times are coming. This is a particularly difficult problem for aggressive entrepreneurs of successful small firms which have been expanding rapidly.

Stability is not the kind of strategy that makes news. It is news to say that 8 million are unemployed, and it is not news to write about 110 million employed. So articles and research usually do not focus on this strategy. However, we would have to infer that since most firms pursued this strategy at some point, stability is effective when the firm is doing well and the environment is not excessively volatile. Exhibit 6.4 provides an example. This means that for many industries and many companies and SBUs, the stability strategy is effective. As one owner of a successful private firm put it, "I've got only one egg in my basket and I watch that basket very carefully."

EXPANSION STRATEGIES [3]

An expansion strategy is a strategy that a firm pursues when:

1 It serves the public in additional product or service sectors or adds markets or functions to its definition.

2 It focuses its strategic decisions on major increases in the pace of activity within its present business definition.

A firm implements this strategy by redefining the business—either adding to the scope of activity or substantially increasing the efforts of the current business.

Again, Exhibit 6.3 shows some ways in which expansion is pursued. For instance, changes in business definition could lead to new product lines or new markets being added. Or a retailer might decide to supply its own goods and make, instead of just buy, its products (backward vertical integration). Even without a change in mission, many firms seek pace expansions. The most common approach is an effort to increase market share substantially, often accompanied by plant expansion (pace increase in functions).

This is often considered an ''intrapreneurial'' strategy, where firms are found to develop and introduce new products and markets or penetrate markets to build share. Small firms are often in the emergence stage of the life cycle or in introduction and growth stages of product-market evolution. High investment is implied, often with aggressive risk taking to finance new resources (plants, personnel, etc.).

Expansion is usually thought of as ''the way'' to improve performance. An increase in assets or size is thought by many to yield growth in profits or ROI. Several studies support this proposition. But the opinions and research of others suggest that short-run inefficiencies often result. As we pointed out in Chapter 5, greater size may lead to trade-offs in profits or returns. And as noted before, rapid expansion can lead to antitrust pressures or competitor reactions. In essence, strategists need to distinguish between desirable and undesirable expansion. Expansion which fails to make resources more productive is ''excess fat.'' Volume, by itself, may represent a ''cancer'' which needs to be cut out. Nevertheless, expansion is popular in the literature.

Why Do Companies Pursue Expansion Strategies?

After reading the list of reasons for pursuing the stability strategy, it may be hard to imagine reasons for adopting an expansion strategy. Stability has a number of things going for it.

The reasons given for adopting expansion are as follows:

1 In volatile industries, a stability strategy can mean short-run success, long-run death. So expansion may be necessary for survival *if* environments are volatile.

2 Many executives equate expansion with effectiveness.

3 Some believe that society benefits from expansion.

4 Managerial motivation. It is true that there is less risk with stability. But there are also fewer financial and other rewards. There are many managers who wish to be remembered, who wish to leave a monument to themselves in the workplace. Who remembers the executive who stood at the helm for 5 years ''steady as it goes''? Strategies may result from the power needs of many executives; the recognition needs are strong in these executives too. Thus these needs or drives encourage some executives to gamble and choose a strategy of expansion. Their companies also become better known, may attract better management, and often leads to higher pay.

EXHIBIT 6.5 HOW HIGH CAN YOU FLY?

Donald Burr, chairman-founder of People Express Airlines, is the epitome of the modern entrepreneur. A missionary, he seized the opportunity of deregulation to create a new kind of airline. People Express was founded on the belief that if all workers were owners, their commitment would assure success. Burr's buzzwords are "worker participation," "responsibility sharing," and "high growth."

Indeed, high growth has occurred, with 4000 current employees from the original 250, and from 3 planes to over 70. Yet the competition is getting rougher, and the explosive growth is straining the structure of the firm, which requires people to switch jobs depending on work needs (even pilots handle ticketing or baggage on occasions).

Some pilots refer to the strong leadership of Burr as evangelistic, referring to him as "Guyana Jones"—an allusion to the Jonestown incident where Jim Jones's followers blindly heeded instructions to drink poisoned Kool-Aid. Unwillingness to delegate authority led to the resignation of the second-in-command for a high-level job at Pan Am in 1982. In 1985, the president and cofounder resigned, and another cofounder was dismissed.

In 1985, Burr acknowledged some of the problems of dramatic growth, saying, "We intend to pull back and consolidate. It's time for some fine-tuning." Yet the philosophy still appears to be "grow-grow-grow" and "Don't worry about profits, they'll come later." Indeed, in 1986 People acquired Frontier and another airline. But says another airline CEO, "There's a point where structure counts. It's great to be an entrepreneur and provide direction. But when you get big you've got to delegate." In many cases, entrepreneurs learn this lesson the hard way. Burr may learn he can only fly so high without making sure the "equipment"—his organization—can accommodate the pressures. Indeed, by mid-1986, trouble appeared and People Express was bought by Texas Air.

Source: Adapted from R. A. Dubin, "Growing Pains at People Express," *Business Week,* Jan. 28, 1985, pp. 90–91.

5 Belief in the experience curve. There is some evidence that as a firm grows in size and experience, it gets better at what it's doing and reduces costs and improves productivity.

6 Belief that growth will yield monopoly power.

7 External pressure from stockholders or securities analysts.

Perhaps the major reason for its popularity is the *belief* that rapid environmental change requires expansion. Further, there is a belief and some evidence that expansion results in performance improvements. However, some suggest that volatility is not as great as it seems, and others prescribe stability to avoid overreaction to change. Also, critics of expansion point to firms "engulfed in a growth syndrome"—expansion at any cost—which they believe leads to inefficiencies and a lower quality of life due to harm from the environment. We believe the jury is still out on these issues. Exhibit 6.5 is an interesting case in point.

RETRENCHMENT STRATEGIES [4]

A retrenchment strategy is pursued by a firm when:

1 It sees the desirability of or necessity for reducing its product or service lines, markets, or functions.

2 It focuses its strategic decisions on functional improvement through the *reduction of activities* in units with negative cash flows.

A firm can redefine its business by divesting itself of a major product line or an SBU. It could abandon some market territories. A firm could also reduce its functions. For example, a firm may choose to sell most or all of its output to a single customer (e.g., Sears). In effect, it has permitted another firm to perform its distribution function. This is known as a "captive company." Of course, the ultimate redefinition is a write-off or total liquidation.

As for retrenching in pace, a firm could use layoffs, reduce R&D or marketing or other outlays, increase the collection of receivables, etc. Note that these efforts and those in redefining the business through retrenchment *can* improve performance. In fact, selling profitable assets to gain resources to be put to use elsewhere is not uncommon in combination with expansion. Retrenchment alone is probably the least frequently used generic strategy. Yet the mid-1980s witnessed huge write-offs because of overcapacity, obsolescence, failed strategies, and long-term structural change in some basic industries.

Retrenchment is frequently used during the decline stage of a business when it is considered possible to restore profitability. Or if prospects appear bleak, controlled disinvestment can be used. Firms might abandon market shares, reduce expenses and assets, prune products, and pursue maximum positive cash flows.

Why Do Companies Pursue a Retrenchment Strategy?

This strategy is the hardest to pursue; it goes against the grain of most strategists. It implies failure. Just as most business executives hate to cut prices, they hate a retrenchment strategy. Why do they follow it, then? A few reasons are as follows:

1 The firm is not doing well or perceives itself as doing poorly.

2 The firm has not met its objectives by following one of the other generic strategies, and there is pressure from stockholders, customers, or others to improve performance.

3 The environment is seen to be so threatening that internal strengths are insufficient to meet the problems.

4 Better opportunities in the environment are perceived elsewhere, where a firm's strengths can be utilized.

Any strategy, if chosen at the right time and implemented properly, will be effective. However, the retrenchment strategy tends to be reserved for dealing with crises, even though there can be positive reasons for its use. The retrenchment strategy is the best strategy for the firm which has tried everything, has made some mistakes, and is now ready to do something about its problems. The more serious the crisis, the more serious the retrenchment strategy needs to be. For minor crises, pace retrenchment will do. For moderate crises, divestiture of some divisions or units may be necessary. For serious crises, a liquidation may be necessary. Exhibit 6.6 describes a firm which believes that its crisis is serious enough to warrant a retrenchment in pace, which could lead to liquidation.

EXHIBIT 6.6   FROM A GREYHOUND TO A DACHSHUND

The Greyhound bus station, with its sleek figure of a swift dog, has been a part of the American landscape for years. But it appears that this familiar figure may need a new mascot—the stubby little dachshund.

In 1985, only 33 million Americans rode Greyhound, down from 64 million in 1979. Bus riders are switching to cheap airlines, and employees have rejected cost-cutting proposals.

President Teets has embarked on a significant pace retrenchment which could eventually become a retrenchment in business definition if Greyhound gets out of the bus business entirely. In 1985, terminal and route cutbacks were planned until labor leaders sought a substitute package that included a 3-year wage freeze and permission for outside operators to run empty terminals. This would have forced 3000 employees to work for less pay—or lose their jobs. The pact was rejected by 59% of the union's members; and Teets accelerated his retrenchment plans.

He will close at least half of Greyhound's 98 company-owned depots, and drop all bus service in a number of states. One-third of Greyhound's 10,000 workers may lose their jobs. In cities where service will continue but costly terminals will be shut, Greyhound will make deals with other bus companies—or just drop passengers off on a downtown street. Teets was also considering dropping charter service.

In late 1986, Teets was prepared to take another crack at labor, asking for major concessions on a new 3-year pact. He remarked, "If labor balks, it would be easy to walk away from the bus business. Our assets are liquid."

Shutting down an $800 million bus business would be drastic, but such a retrenchment may be the only prudent alternative for a company faced with stiff competition from substitute transportation, and a recalcitrant labor union.

Source: Adapted from S. Toy: "Labor Can't Blunt Greyhound's Ax," *Business Week,* Feb. 10, 1986, pp. 28–29.

The retrenchment strategy is the hardest strategy for the business executive to follow. It implies that someone or something has failed, and no one wants to be labeled a failure. But retrenchment can be used to reverse the negative trends and set the stage for more positive strategic alternatives. Many U.S. business firms began withdrawing from Europe in the early 1980s due to the stubborn recession, high labor costs, high taxes, and competition from government-subsidized industries. And in the mid-1980s many conglomerates began "asset redeployments" to get out of old businesses and into new ones, or to get back to basics.

Foreign managers appear more willing to consider retrenchment than U.S. managers. The first question the Japanese, German, or French strategist asks is likely to be "What are the old things we are going to abandon?" This provides resources for innovation, new products, or new markets.

COMBINATION STRATEGY [5]

A combination strategy is a strategy that a firm pursues when:

1 Its main strategic decisions focus on the conscious use of several grand strategies (stability, expansion, retrenchment) at the same time (simultaneously) in several SBUs of the company.

2 It plans to use several grand strategies at different future times (sequentially).

With combination strategies, the decision makers consciously apply several grand strategies to different parts of the firm or to different future periods. The logical possibilities for a simultaneous approach are stability in some areas, expansion in others; stability in some areas, retrenchment in others; retrenchment in some areas, expansion in others; and all three strategies in different areas of the company.

The same logical possibilities exist for time-phased combinations, but the number of possibilities is greater, especially when the products, markets, and functions are considered and when the choice occurs through changing the pace or the business definition. For instance, the sequential expansion in the pace of the business with some business redefinition later seems to be a common approach; it may be followed because of the recognition of risks and problems in rapid expansion or redefinition. Often a firm pursuing this strategy initially concentrates on one product or service line. It expands incrementally by adding greater market penetration, adding new products or services after extensive testing, adding new markets geographically, etc. Some firms even follow a strategy that allows them to seek a low market share in their industry as a whole. Much of the literature and PIMS data make it appear that this is suicidal. Yet it has been shown that firms like Crown Cork and Seal, Union Camp, and Burroughs achieved excellent return-on-invested-capital objectives through effective market segmentation, effective use of R&D, and a lowering of production and processing costs through increased efficiency. Firms pursuing combinations need to be especially alert to competitor reactions. For example, you may want to combine stability in one area to provide cash for expansion in another area. A shrewd competitor may attack the stable area in an attempt to divert your management time and resources away from the expansions to protect your ''stable'' base of operations. Such multiple-point competition is particularly problematic for the multiple-SBU firm trying a combination strategy.

Exhibit 6.7 shows how one firm has used a combination of strategies, although perhaps it didn't plan it that way.

Why Do Companies Pursue a Combination Strategy?

A combination strategy is not an easy strategy to use. It is much easier to keep a firm in one set of values or one strategy at a time. But when a company faces many environments and these environments are changing at different rates, and the company's products are in different stages of the life cycle, it is easy to visualize conditions under which a combination strategy makes sense.

Thus it is possible that when the economy is performing well, most industries are doing well. Therefore, the generic strategy might be expansion. But at the start of a recession, some industries begin to suffer, while others are still doing well. Thus a combination strategy makes sense for a multiple-industry firm at that time.

In the case of time-phased combination strategies, several scenarios come to mind. For example, a firm realizes that some of its main product lines are beyond the optimum point in the product life cycle and that it is not worth the investment to

EXHIBIT 6.7   A PICTURE IN TIME

1986 will be a year of retrenchment for Kodak. During the past few years, Kodak has followed all three of the generic strategies of stability, expansion, and retrenchment.

At one point, Kodak had been expansion-oriented, and a product development leader in the photographic business. After 1970, when it left the 35mm camera to the Japanese, the firm seemed content with a long period of stability. Up until late 1984, except for the imitative instant camera introduction long after Polaroid, the firm sort of slumbered in contentment. Its revenues became steady at about $10.5 billion, primarily in the photographic arena. But Kodak failed to see or ignored changes in its markets, customers, and competitors while it pursued its stability strategy.

In early 1985, it seemed as if Kodak was waking up, but it also became apparent that Kodak was just about to sleep through its final exam. Expansion was the initial instinct of the recently awakened giant. Kodak reorganized its photographic division into 17 "entrepreneurial" business units with the intention of making decisions easier to make. It also launched a barrage of new products to present an image of innovation. To help speed the introduction of these new products—such as 8mm video cameras, 35mm cameras, and an electronic publishing system for corporate documents—Kodak brought these products from Japanese firms already producing them and marketed them under the Kodak name. In effect, this approach represents product expansion combined with "retrenchment" in certain functions in that Kodak does not supply its own product needs. Competition in these new areas is tough and Kodak is finding them of little help in its attempts to improve its sales and profits. So it has also expanded by offering photofinishing in retail stores through "minilab" technology.

Kodak recently lost a patent suit with Polaroid, necessitating the write-down of $400 million in assets from its instant photography division. This, along with its already poor profitability, has caused the firm to announce the layoff of 12,900 workers in a program to cut costs. Kodak will also cut back in services and marketing. In a word, the company is also retrenching. Kodak, then, is simultaneously pursuing function retrenchment with product expansions after a long period of stability.

This rapid succession of generic strategies has not been properly planned, so it can't be considered an intentional time-phased combination strategy. However, retrenching at this time may be just what Kodak needs to give it time to wake up and develop an effective long-range strategy capable of eliminating the large gaps created by its expectations.

Source: Adapted from "Kodak Just Can't Get Its Giant Feet Moving Fast Enough," *Business Week,* Mar. 4, 1986, pp. 37–38.

"prop the product up." The firm may choose to retrench in this area and follow an expansion strategy in a new product area.

Most large firms such as *Fortune*'s 500 largest industrials are probably the most frequent users of combination strategies. Even here, it is the multiple-industry firm that is most likely to use them. The medium-sized firm that is multiple-industry-based is also a likely user. An example is NCR, which sold a unit to buy back some debt and then expanded.

All strategies can be effective. The question is, When is a combination strategy most likely to be effective? What should have become clearer in this section is that combination strategies are most likely to be effective for larger, multiple-SBU firms in periods of economic transition or periods of transition in the product-service life cycle. The combination strategy is the best strategy for a firm whose divisions perform unevenly or do not have the same future potential.

ALTERNATIVES AND PERFORMANCE [6]

Before we conclude our discussion of generic alternatives, it will be useful to recapitulate and reinforce our earlier statements about the relationship of strategies to performance. First, Exhibit 6.8 graphically presents the alternatives which are possible. Each dimension represents an overlay so that they *all intersect one another*. That is, expansion, stability, or retrenchment can be applied to products, markets, or functions. And combinations of these are possible. If change occurs, it may be in the pace or the business definition. Our intent is to convey the idea that there is overlap in how these strategic approaches can be put together for any given firm. The particular configuration of alternatives considered by any firm will not be this large, however. Managers are more likely to focus on a few of these for a detailed analysis.

Second, keep in mind that any alternative or combination has the potential to improve performance. One is not necessarily superior to another in all circumstances. As shown in Exhibit 6.9, advantages and disadvantages are associated with each. Naturally, if substantial growth in size is the objective, expansion is a more likely alternative. But this may come at the expense of other objectives, at least in the short run. Growth in profits could be enhanced by a retrenchment. For instance, financial theory suggests that if the net present value of a liquidation is greater than the expected value of continued operations, selling assets to gain funds to invest elsewhere will be a good alternative for the goal of improving cash value. The breakup value of some firms may be large due to ''hidden'' assets or unrealistic book values. So retrenchment may ultimately lead to growth (in terms of cash goals). Some tax laws give companies a reason to spin off subsidiaries to shareholders or sell assets and distribute proceeds, because companies liquidated within a year of an asset sale are exempt from taxation on related capital gains. Of course, such tax laws can change, and analysis of these

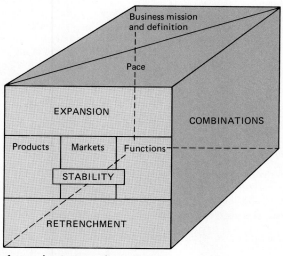

EXHIBIT 6.8   **Overlays of generic strategy alternatives.**

EXHIBIT 6.9   PROS AND CONS OF STRATEGY CHOICES AT IBM

All strategy alternatives have advantages and disadvantages. The options facing IBM are a case in point. Known as clones, company after company now produces a personal computer which is compatible with the IBM product. Frequently, these competitor products claim to be cheaper, faster, and more reliable while they offer similar hardware options and use the same software.

IBM has considered several strategy options, each of which has pros and cons, to deal with the competitive threat from clones.

Strategy option	Advantage	Disadvantage
A. Introduce a low-price replacement for the basic PC using newer, less expensive technology.	IBM would regain market share lost to clones and add a model ideal for the education market.	IBM might sacrifice gross margins, divert sales from more profitable models, and possibly hurt corporate earnings.
B. With new hardware and software, alter the PC to make cloning more difficult and to prevent clones from participating fully in IBM computer networks.	IBM would keep major corporate customers, rebuild market share as they shift to the new technology, reestablish control over prices and margins.	Consumers, especially small businesses, might stick with the current PC, for which there are thousands of software packages.
C. Bring out a steady stream of new PCs that include more features, while cutting prices on older models.	By continuously updating and improving the PC, IBM could quickly make most clones obsolete and improve prices for its products.	A rash of new models might make inventories of IBM PCs obsolete and could clog the dealer channel. With demand slackening, new models might not sell better than current ones.
D. Withdraw from the low-end, "commodity" PC market, leaving the clones to battle each other in a low-margin business.	IBM would be free to concentrate on selling more profitable versions of the PC to large corporations and, by linking those PCs into company data networks, would ultimately stimulate demand for mainframe computers to support them.	IBM would be walking away from as much as $3 billion in annual revenues. Such a move also would hinder its efforts to win big shares of the education and home markets.

Source: Business Week, July 28, 1986. In April 1987, IBM chose B.

These strategies range from product-line expansion (C), to market retrenchment (D), to stability (A and B involve product modification and improvement). The choice may come to repeating IBM's historical practice of sticking to high-margin businesses (D). In any case, important trade-off decisions usually arise when strategy alternatives are considered.

Source: Adapted from "The PC Wars: IBM vs. the Clones," *Business Week*, July 28, 1985, pp. 62–68.

EXHIBIT 6.10   STRATEGIC CHANGE IS A MEANS TO AN END

Change is frightening. It can paralyze powerful executives. It can cause entire organizations to drag their corporate feet. It's the stuff sleepness nights are made of. Not long ago, International Harvester was in the shadow of an even more frightening prospect. The reaper was already at our doorstep. We had to change. Or else.

We consolidated facilities. Eliminated five levels of bureaucracy. Doubled manufacturing productivity. Cut inventory by two-thirds. And orchestrated the largest private debt restructuring in history. An old company, set in its ways, changed. And was reborn as Navistar International Corporation.

In doing so, we learned a lession. Change is not a nemesis. It is vital to our organization. To any organization. Properly managed, change is progress. It's the road to improved quality, and to new products that will help our customers meet their changing needs. It's a competitive edge. Change helps us further strengthen our number one position. Yet we know we must never change merely for the sake of change. Change is not a goal. It's the means to a goal.

Today, we're still changing. Change, however, still keeps us awake at night. But these days it's because we're dreaming of new ways to accomplish it.

Source: Adapted from a Navistar ad, *Business Week*, July 7, 1986, p. 21.

laws should be an integral part of environmental analysis. If an entrepreneur's objective is to maintain control of a business, stability may enhance this more than expansion. If the goal is to spread risk, business definition changes may be in order. Thus it is inappropriate to necessarily equate "growth" with "expansion." And retrenchment should not be considered a sign of failure or pursued only when threats appear. Stability does not imply that goal improvements are not being accomplished. In other words, don't confuse the strategy, as a means to an end, with the objective. Exhibit 6.10 provides an example of an advertisement making just this point.

SUMMARY

We have just completed the first chapter that deals with the strategic choice part of the strategic management process. This chapter has discussed the generation of a reasonable number of generic strategy alternatives that will help fill the gaps faced by a firm.

The central factor that is examined at the beginning of the consideration of strategic alternatives is the business the firm is in. Business definitions will vary from the simple definition (for a one-product or one-service firm) to the very complex definition (for a large firm involved in multiple businesses). Products, markets, and functions need to be identified as part of corporate-level strategy. Once the business the firm is in has been defined, various questions (such as, Should we get out of this business entirely? Should we try to expand?) will help the strategist focus on the type of strategic alternative the firm should pursue.

The generic strategy alternatives are to expand, stabilize, or retrench with regard to the pace or the business definition of products, markets, or functions. Combinations of simultaneous activities or sequential options are included. All of these can be designed to improve performance, but several propositions are offered for when each is more likely to be successfully pursued.

Proposition 6.1

Stability is more likely if the firm is doing well, the environment is not excessively volatile, and the product or service has reached the stability or maturity stage of the life cycle.

Proposition 6.2

Expansion is more likely in highly competitive, volatile industries, particularly early in the product-service life cycle.

Proposition 6.3

Retrenchment is more likely if the firm is not doing well, greater returns can be gained elsewhere, or the product or service is at a later stage of the life cycle.

Proposition 6.4

Combinations are more likely for multiple-SBU firms, in periods of economic transition, and during changes in the product-service life cycle.

These are overall estimates, but a variety of reasons were suggested for why each strategy could be followed, and the advantages and disadvantages associated with each were stated.

Our next chapter elaborates on these generic strategies by providing you with variations on the themes of expansion, stability, retrenchment, and combinations. There are a number of approaches for carrying out these strategies. The approach will depend on various internal strengths and weaknesses, environmental threats and opportunities, and the value preferences of the strategists. Before concluding this segment with strategic choice, you should be aware of the many options for creatively carrying out these generic strategies.

REFERENCES

[1] The Starting Point of Strategy—Business Definition

Abell, D. F.: *Defining the Business: The Starting Point of Strategic Planning* (Englewood Cliffs, N.J.: Prentice-Hall, 1980).

Levitt, Y.: "Marketing Myopia," *Harvard Business Review,* vol. 38 (July–August 1960), pp. 45–60; and *Harvard Business Review,* vol. 53 (September–October 1975), pp. 26–28.

[2] The Stability Strategy

Clifford, D. K., Jr.: "Thriving in a Recession," *Harvard Business Review* (July–August 1977), pp. 56–65.

Fruhan, W.: "Pyrrhic Victories in Fights for Market Share," *Harvard Business Review* (September–October 1972).

Ketchum, B. W.: "Privately Held Companies in the U.S.," *INC.,* (December 1981), p. 39.

[3] The Expansion Strategy

Drucker, P.: *Management* (New York: Harper & Row, 1974), chap. 60.

Guth, W. D.: "Corporate Growth Strategies," *The Journal of Business Strategy,* vol. 1 (Fall 1980), pp. 56–62.

Thompson, A.: "Corporate Bigness—For Better or for Worse?" *Sloan Management Review* (Fall 1975), pp. 36–61.

[4] The Retrenchment Strategy

Bibeault, D. B.: *Corporate Turnaround* (New York: McGraw-Hill, 1982).

Ehrlich, E.: "Industry Cleans House," *Business Week,* Nov. 11, 1985, pp. 32–33.

Brand, D.: "U. S. Business Reduces Rate of New Investing in European Facilities," *The Wall Street Journal,* Aug. 12, 1982, p. 1.

Klein, H.: "Liquidations Are Growing More Popular," *The Wall Street Journal,* Aug. 12, 1982, p. 17.

Mingle, J. R.: *Challenges of Retrenchment* (San Francisco: Jossey-Bass, 1981).

Toy, S.: "Splitting Up: The Other Side of Merger Mania," *Business Week,* July 1, 1985, pp. 50–55.

[5] The Combination Strategy

Ansoff, H. I.: *Corporate Strategy* (New York: McGraw-Hill, 1965).

Drucker, P.: *Management* (New York: Harper & Row, 1977), chaps. 56, 57.

Karnani, A., and B. Wernerfelt: "Multiple Point Competition," *Strategic Management Journal,* vol. 6 (1985), pp. 87–96.

[6] Strategies and Performance

Buzzell, R. D., B. T. Gale, and G. M. Sultan: "Market Share–A Key to Profitability," *Harvard Business Review* (January–February 1975), pp. 97–106.

"The Latest in Tax Relief: Committing Corporate Suicide," *Business Week,* Jan. 14, 1985, pp. 116–117.

Rumelt, R. P.: *Strategy, Structure and Economic Performance* (Boston: Harvard University Press, 1974).

Weiss, S.: " 'Breakup Value' Is Wall Street's New Buzzword," *Business Week,* July 8, 1985, pp. 80–81.

Note: Also see Chapter 7 references.

CHAPTER OUTLINE

CONSIDERING STRATEGY VARIATIONS

* To understand how generic strategies can be pursued and implemented in different ways
* To illustrate conditions under which strategy variations are considered appropriate
* To consider how strategy variations apply in the international setting
* To explain the advantages and disadvantages of mergers and diversification

INTRODUCTION

Numerous variations of the generic strategy alternatives outlined in Chapter 6 are possible for a given organization. Exhibit 7.1 provides examples to be discussed in this chapter. Consideration of these depends on the particular configuration of objectives, ETOP, SAP, and the generic strategy itself. It is convenient to think of these as possible dimensions which supplement the matrix outlined in Exhibit 6.3. The dimensions are internal and external, related and unrelated, horizontal and vertical (backward and forward), and active and passive. These may apply to one or more generic strategies. In each case, the dimension refers to various approaches for carrying out a generic strategy.

Exhibit 7.2 reminds us that we are trying to identify the alternatives from which to choose to close strategic gaps.

EXHIBIT 7.1 POSSIBLE STRATEGY VARIATIONS

	Expansion	Stability	Retrenchment	Combination
Internal	Penetrate existing markets; add new products; add new markets.	Seek production and marketing efficiencies; reorganize.	Reduce costs; reduce assets; drop products; drop markets; drop functions.	Subcontracting.
External	Acquisitions; mergers.	Maintain market shares.	Divest SBUs; liquidations; bankruptcies.	Cross-licensing. Joint ventures.
Related	Seek synergy from new products, markets, or functions (concentric diversification).	Improve products.	Eliminate related products, markets, or functions.	
Unrelated	Conglomerate diversification in products, markets or functions.		Eliminate unrelated products, markets, or functions.	
Horizontal	Add complementary products or markets.		Eliminate complementary products or markets.	
Vertical	Add new functions.		Reduce functions.	
Active	Innovative, entrepreneurial moves.			Grow to sell out.
Passive	Imitator in R&D, new products.	Reactive defense of position.		

INTERNAL AND EXTERNAL ALTERNATIVES

This dimension usually applies to expansion, but it may also apply to retrenchment. The basic question is whether the organization wishes to pursue a strategy independently (internal) or in conjunction with other parties (external).

Internal Expansion [1]

This is the most common approach. In effect, the firm tries to increase the sales and market share of the current product or service line faster than it has been. It is probably the most successful strategy for firms whose products or services are not in the final stages of the product-service life cycle. But Exhibit 7.3 presents the case of a firm using this strategy even though the main line is in decline.

Most of the approaches to internal expansion deal with product-market realignments. In fact, when growth in sales and profits is mentioned, most executives think of market share first. The usual approaches to internal expansion that are considered are as shown in Exhibit 7.4. In cell 1, firms try to expand sales by increasing primary demand and encouraging new uses for present products and services in the territories served now. This is often done by changing pricing and promotion. This strategy is effective for firms with small market shares, whether the product is in the high-growth

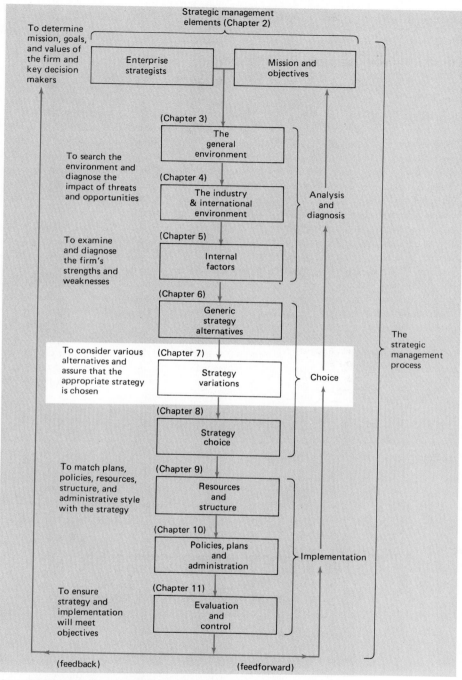

To determine
mission, goals,
and values of
the firm and
key decision
makers

Strategic management
elements (Chapter 2)

Enterprise
strategists

Mission and
objectives

(Chapter 3)

The
general
environment

To search the
environment and
diagnose the
impact of threats
and opportunities

(Chapter 4)

The industry
& international
environment

Analysis
and
diagnosis

To examine
and diagnose
the firm's
strengths and
weaknesses

(Chapter 5)

Internal
factors

(Chapter 6)

Generic
strategy
alternatives

To consider various
alternatives and
assure that the
appropriate strategy
is chosen

(Chapter 7)

Strategy
variations

Choice

The
strategic
management
process

(Chapter 8)

Strategy
choice

To match plans,
policies, resources,
structure, and
administrative style
with the strategy

(Chapter 9)

Resources
and
structure

(Chapter 10)

Policies, plans
and
administration

Implementation

To ensure
strategy and
implementation
will meet
objectives

(Chapter 11)

Evaluation
and
control

(feedback)

(feedforward)

EXHIBIT 7.2   A model of strategic management.
(Robert H. Waterman, Jr., Thomas J. Peters, and Julian R. Phillips, "Structure Is Not Organization," Business Horizons, June 1980, p. 18; Copyright © 1980 by the Foundation for the School of Business at Indiana University. Reprinted by Permission.)

EXHIBIT 7.3 LOOKING INWARD FOR EXPANSION

In the late 1970s, John M. Richman, Chairman of Kraft Foods, was convinced the company's performance could be improved by diversifying into higher-margin, nonfood items. This led to the 1980 merger with Dart Industries (Tupperware and Duracell). Hobart Corp. (Kitchen Aid) was acquired in 1981. But diversification proved to be a detour away from better profits. Newly acquired businesses had management problems and were vulnerable to the recession. When Esmark became available for purchase in 1984, analysts assumed Dart & Kraft would jump in because its product portfolio fit the collection of Dart & Kraft brands. Stated Richman, "We never intended to become a conglomerate, and we don't now."

Instead Dart & Kraft is looking for internal expansion by adding new products, extending existing lines, and spicing up slumping brand names with aggressive marketing to move the firm into the top 20% of the consumer products industry on return on capital. Says a rival, "Kraft was sleepy in the 1970s. Management was busy on the acquisition trail, and Kraft missed an opportunity to leverage its high-quality name by moving into new food categories."

Kraft commands 45% of the U.S. cheese market and strong shares of other foods with brand names like Miracle Whip, Sealtest, and Parkay. But these markets are mature, so Kraft is counting on product-line additions to boost sales. Kraft added eight new salad dressings under the Philadelphia Brand name, and is pushing hard for other new products. A new level of product manager was assigned to 20 top marketing people. Previously, R&D had concocted new concepts without close coordination with brand managers, who were mainly interested in existing products.

After the Dart merger, declines that hit several divisions have spurred new products and marketing efforts as well. Tupperware, a victim of social changes in women's working and life-styles, introduced a new line of stackable containers aimed at smaller families. And it planned to introduce a line of cookware for microwave ovens. Duracell introduced a new line of flashlights in 1983. And Hobart broadened its Kitchen Aid line of dishwashers and trash compactors.

While Richman does not rule out further acquisitions, he appears convinced that internal growth is best for his business, and food is targeted as the biggest growth sector.

Source: Adapted from "Dart & Kraft Turns Back to Its Basic Business," *Business Week,* June 11, 1984, pp. 100–105.

EXHIBIT 7.4 **Internal expansion through products and markets.**

PRODUCTS

	Current	New
Current	Penetrate existing markets with existing products (1)	Add new markets (2)
New	Add new products (3)	Add new products and new markets (4)

MARKETS

stage or maturity stage of the life cycle. The firm increases its pace of activity without changing its business definition.

This penetration approach implies that the firm specializes where it has, or believes it can obtain, a significant competitive advantage. The benefits from higher market shares are thought to come from cost savings due to the learning curve effect and economies of scale. However, short-run profit trade-offs are likely, as the expense of penetration can be high. Further, as greater shares are achieved, the firm is more likely to become a target of consumer groups, government agencies, and other competitors. Finally, the risks of specialization involve industry cycles or downturn.

Thus many firms segment markets or products to take advantage of opportunities. For instance, in cell 2, firms try to expand sales of the existing product or service by seeking additional types of customers or moving into additional geographic areas. In cell 3, firms may attempt to increase sales by introducing new products or services to the same markets served now. Other firms move to cell 4 by adding new products *and* markets or by introducing minor modifications in the product or service to new segments of the markets. Examples include new sizes or shapes and private labeling or brand labeling. These moves also entail risks, however. Moving into new areas may require new skills that the firm may be unfamiliar with. Failure rates are high. And the barriers to entry discussed in Chapter 4 can play a role here.

Internal Stability [2]

This is probably self-explanatory. However, an interesting approach is associated with the purpose for which it can be used in a multiple-SBU firm. When the main objective for an SBU is to generate more cash than it spends, the SBU is known as a "cash cow." It is "milked" while it maintains its position; if necessary, it may even sacrifice some market share. In effect, a stability business definition may be combined with an internal retrenchment in the pace of some activities. This will be discussed shortly.

Aside from the cash-cow use, a stability approach can be used by a firm trying to offset the risk of expansion in other SBUs by providing a stable base of operations. Internal stability can also be used as a "pause" between other strategies. A firm may have expanded, and now the organization needs a "break" period to catch up with itself. Or the executives may believe that conditions are unfavorable for further expansion at the present time, so they pursue stability. Thus internal stability is often a useful approach in combination with other plans.

Internal Retrenchment [3]

This is usually called an "operating turnaround" strategy. The emphasis is on improving internal efficiency, as the steel industry is attempting to do. The environmental conditions leading to turnaround strategies usually include recessions or depressions in the economy as a whole or in the industries the firm does business in.

The major approaches for turnaround strategies include:

1 *Reducing costs.* Examples include cutting the number of employees through attrition or layoffs, reducing less crucial maintenance costs, trimming the airline travel

expenses of executives, using less costly stationery, and leasing equipment instead of purchasing it.

2 *Increasing revenues.* Examples include better investment of cash and current assets, tighter inventory controls, better collection of receivables, and the use of *more effective* advertising, sales promotion, etc., to generate an increase in sales and profits without increasing expenditures.

3 *Reducing assets.* Some airlines sold 747s when the number of passengers decreased. A firm can sell land, buildings, and equipment no longer needed (obsolete) or those needed to implement expansion that now appears unrealistic. For example, Chrysler decided to build a plant in the eastern United States, but before the building was completed, Chrysler sold it to another firm.

4 *Reorganizing products and/or markets to achieve greater efficiency.* Operating turnaround involves mostly changes in pace. But internal retrenchments can also include dropping some products or markets or vertically integrating (discussed in a later section). These ''strategic turnarounds'' reverse the flow implied in Exhibit 7.4. Exhibit 7.5 provides an example of a firm attempting a strategic turnaround.

Internal retrenchment may be called for if many or most of these conditions are present:

- The unit's product is in a stable or declining market.
- The unit doesn't provide sales stability or prestige for the firm.
- The unit's market share is small, and it would be too costly to increase that share.
- The unit does not contribute a large percentage to total sales.
- The corporation has better uses for its funds.
- The decline in sales will be less rapid than the reduction in corporate support.
- The price or availability of raw materials presents problems.

EXHIBIT 7.5   A SMALLER CAT FOR ANOTHER LIFE

Caterpillar Tractor Co. is learning to think small in its quest for recovery. As the largest manufacturer of giant construction equipment, Cat historically focused on equipment for heavy mining, construction, and energy-recovery jobs. But demand began plummeting in 1982, and the firm lost over $1 billion in 3 years.

Although critics charge the crash of its markets caught Cat napping, the company began a retrenchment to bring expenses into line in 1982. Cat reached its goal of slashing costs by 22% by the end of 1985, a year ahead of schedule. It reduced its work force by one-third and increased the number of parts acquired from outside suppliers. Cat also reduced its debt by more than $1 billion, to 33% of total capitalization. And it intends to continue cutting, slashing manufacturing capacity by 25% through 1989.

Finally, Cat has turned its attention to marketing smaller equipment it already sells to large customers. Cat may be in for a dogfight here. The low end of the construction equipment market is more competitive and price-sensitive than the firm is used to, with well-entrenched competitors. And its legendary distribution system is not geared to selling to small contractors. Nor will small machines ever replace big earth-moving equipment for dollar volume. But, at least in the near term, such retrenchment appears to be a viable strategy.

Source: Adapted from K. Deveny, ''Caterpillar Is Betting Big on Pint-Size Machines,'' *Business Week,* Nov. 25, 1985, p. 41.

Various policies can be used to achieve turnarounds. Selective price increases is one. Cost reduction without price reductions is another. Essentially, firms limit the amount of support they give the SBU, and perhaps over time they will provide no support at all.

Many firms have found that turnaround strategies require different kinds of experience, managerial focus, and leadership style. Sometimes they have "turnaround specialists," managers who are put in charge of units needing turnaround or who take charge at times when a turnaround strategy is required. They often get the reputation of being "head choppers" who are hired for 2 or 3 years to shape up an organization and then move on. Some turnaround specialists buy firms that are in trouble, "turn them around," and then sell them.

External Retrenchment [4]

This includes divestiture and liquidation. In these cases, other parties are involved in the strategy (usually as buyers). This approach is the reverse of a merger, which is an *external expansion* approach. (External expansion will be discussed later.) It is another, more serious form of strategic turnaround. A divestment strategy involves a selling off or liquidation of an SBU or a major part of an SBU by the strategists. Divestment is, in fact, a substitute for a turnaround strategy. It is often used after turnaround has not solved the problems it was expected to solve or as a way to change the business definition through the elimination of products, markets, or functions. Or it can be used as a combination with an internal retrenchment program. For example, the Bank of America divested its stake in 45 foreign operations and Finance America at the same time it was selling its headquarters building, closing 187 California branches, and dropping 1000 of its 3000 North America corporate clients.

Why do divestments take place? A number of reasons can be advanced. Some are inadequate market share or sales growth, lower profits than for other SBUs and the availability of better alternatives, technological changes requiring the firm to invest more resources than it is willing or able to invest, antitrust requirements, and the poor adjustment of some SBUs after mergers. Another reason is to slim down after an earlier attempt at acquisition. Many firms that failed to divest units became takeover targets, and the raiders followed up with a divestiture themselves. A final reason is a desire to "get back to basics." Many firms (such as General Mills) discover that a diversification strategy fails to accomplish its objectives. One-half to two-thirds of all mergers don't work; one in three is later undone. In 1985, for every seven acquisitions, there were three divestitures—many of which had once been high-hope acquisitions. Firms that had pursued unrelated (conglomerate) diversification found that they did not know how to effectively manage their new businesses. Divesting units unrelated to the basic business they *did* know how to run allowed these firms to improve their performance.

The decision to divest is a very difficult decision for management to make. Porter says that there are at least three sets of factors which work against this decision.

1 Structural factors: durable and specific assets, useful primarily to one company, one industry, or one location. The more durable and more specific the assets, the more difficult the divestment.

2 Corporate strategy factors. The more interrelated or complementary the SBUs within the corporation, the more difficult the divestment.

3 Managerial factors. These are as follows:

   a There is inadequate information about an SBU—management doesn't realize that the SBU isn't doing as well as it should be.

   b The divestment hurts the manager's pride and is seen as a sign of failure.

   c The divestment severs identification with a business and hurts specialized careers.

   d The divestment conflicts with social responsibility objectives.

   e Incentive systems for managers reward large size.

Divestment can be accomplished in one of several ways:

1 If the SBU is viable, it can be spun off as an independent firm. The parent may or may not continue an ownership interest.

2 If the SBU is viable, it can be sold to its employees.

3 The SBU can be sold to an independent buyer who would find it useful.

4 The SBU can be liquidated and its assets sold.

Most managers regard liquidation as the least attractive strategy and choose it only if the alternative is bankruptcy or if the stockholders would be better off with the result of liquidation than with an attempt to keep the firm going. The decision to liquidate is a decision that few are able to make. It implies failure. It is rarely made, except in extreme circumstances. However, as Exhibit 7.6 suggests, liquidation can be a successful strategy; it was growing more popular in the early to mid-1980s, as it offered a quick return on stockholder investment.

Of course, we should mention that bankruptcy is always an alternative which can be used. It does have the advantage of leading to a restructuring of the finances of the firm, which could allow the firm to start up again as a new entity, as happened with International Harvester (Navistar). In fact, if an attractive offer of liquidation is not found, other parties such as stockholders and debt holders may prefer this approach.

While many firms have criteria for evaluating acquisitions, few have developed criteria for making divestiture choices. It would seem prudent for firms to plan this ahead of time in order to reduce some of the emotionality involved in such decisions.

Just as there are specialist managers for turnaround strategies, there are consultants who are brought in to liquidate firms. Indeed, in all these forms of retrenchment, it is likely that the old CEO will be replaced, which is another reason why retrenchment is not viewed as an attractive strategy by many CEOs.[1]

---

[1]Nonetheless a few managers and individuals have used the bankruptcy laws in a proactive strategic manner, even though they were not insolvent. Wilson Foods Corp., Manville, and others have used Chapter 11 to shelter themselves against such threats as unfavorable union contracts or legal claims in asbestos-related diseases.

EXHIBIT 7.6 IT'S WORTH MORE DEAD THAN ALIVE

It is unusual for managers to recommend that their businesses be liquidated, particularly voluntarily as opposed to forced bankruptcy. Some of the reasons, of course, involve the problems of finding buyers of assets, loss of jobs, and confusion among suppliers and distributors. But the major reason for resistance is probably that managers want to deny defeat, assuming that selling out implies failure.

Yet liquidation need not be a sign of failure. A case in point is UV Industries, formerly number 357 in the *Fortune* 500. Through acquisitions, its sales had been increasing over a 15-year period from $31 to $600 million, with profits going from $2.3 to $40 million. Before liquidation plans were announced, its stock was selling for $19 a share; the price jumped to $30 after the announcement. One analyst estimates that the sales of assets will net stockholders $33 or more.

Of course, if a firm is not doing well, a liquidation may be justified also. An example here is the case of Overseas National. After running operating losses of over $2.7 million in 5 years, the airline sold its planes. Inflation and long waits for new jets in 1978 raised the price of used planes to the point where sales of the company's assets brought in $114 million, or $23 million over book value. In this case, the firm was controlled by investors rather than "airline types," and the investors doubled their equity value through the liquidation.

While some managers choose liquidation because they are pessimistic about the future, others believe that depressed stock prices understate the true value of the firm. Not surprisingly, top officers and directors owned large amounts of stock in many of the companies which chose liquidation.

Liquidation tends to be easier for smaller, less complex firms which have a few highly salable hard assets such as land and resource reserves. Firms whose operations are neatly packaged so that a sell-off doesn't disturb the rest of the business also have an easier time liquidating. The liquidation of giant Kaiser Industries, with stakes in aluminum, steel, cement, broadcasting, engineering, and aerospace, has been much more difficult; Kaiser's plan is now in its fourth year.

Perhaps more executives ought to consider the option of examining expected future returns against present value. They, too, may find that the company is worth more dead than alive.

Sources: Adapted from "Overseas National Exits in Style," *Business Week,* Oct. 2, 1978, p. 36; "When a Company Is Better Dead," *Business Week,* Mar. 26, 1979, p. 89; and P. W. Bernstein, "A Company That's Worth More Dead than Alive," *Fortune,* Feb. 26, 1978, pp. 42–44.

As you consider internal or external retrenchment or stability, you should keep in mind a particular phenomenon known as the "declining industry" [5]. Harrigan notes a number of conditions here, the most prevalent being saturation and a decline in the product life cycle. Under these circumstances, firms might use "endgame strategies."

The strategies used by the successful endgame players are (1) dominate the market (internal expansion), (2) hold the market share (internal stability), (3) shrink selectively (internal retrenchment), (4) milk the investment (internal stability or retrenchment), and (5) divest now (external retrenchment).

Corporate and industry strengths dictate which of these to follow, as indicated in Exhibit 7.7. Industry conditions that are favorable for an endgame include low uncertainty in the environment, low exit barriers, and relatively less rivalry among competitors. Strengths and weaknesses vary as discussed in Chapter 5. So some firms have successfully profited from careful management of products when most firms felt they were obsolete and left the industry. Exhibit 7.8 contrasts firms in the tire industry to highlight this.

EXHIBIT 7.7   CONDITIONS FOR USING ENDGAME STRATEGIES

	Possess relative corporate strengths	Have relative corporate weaknesses
Favorable industry traits for endgame.	"Dominate market" or "hold market share."	"Shrink selectively" or "milk."
Unfavorable industry traits for endgame.	"Shrink selectively" or "milk."	"Get out now!"

Source: Kathryn Harrigan and Michael Porter, "A Framework for Looking at Endgame Strategies," *Proceedings of the Academy of Management* (August 1978), p. 14.

External Expansion [6]

This is the flip side of divestiture or liquidation. Thus far in this section, the emphasis has been on retrenchment or expansion from *within* a company. But companies also expand externally, acquiring other firms or parts of firms which they feel would add

EXHIBIT 7.8   ENDGAME STRATEGIES FOR TIRES?

What strategy does a firm follow if it is a big business in a mature, marginally profitable industry? Some firms will try to dominate or hold on, some will shrink, and others will get out. The tire business is a case in point. Goodyear is expanding in tires. Many competitors are diversifying to shrink their emphasis on tires, and this is leading to less rivalry and some "exit" behavior. General seems to be reducing its diversification, and it seems likely that it will try to sell its tire operations.

Goodyear is betting $374 million that it can increase its market share. It announced plans to build a new technical center in 1978, and several new plants have come on stream or are being built. This expansion is happening precisely at the time when producers are facing 5 years of poor profits and low growth. The belief is that Goodyear has the marketing muscle to succeed where others can't. For example, Goodrich introduced an all-weather tire in 1965, and it bombed. Goodyear's introduction of the same "round, black tire" turned into a success. Its economies of scale are believed to be benefits in the competition with Michelin.

General is the most diversified of the tire and rubber manufacturers. It owns RKO and operates aerospace, plastics, and other businesses in addition to the tire and rubber businesses. The board was working on a plan in 1981 to spin these off into separate companies to achieve a higher stock price in a market that refuses to place a premium on conglomerates. The tire operations earned less than $10 million on $1.5 billion in sales, while Aerojet General and RKO earned over $40 million each on sales of $700 million and $529 million, respectively. After the spin-off, the tire business may be merged with another business—in effect, the tire business will be sold off.

Goodrich and Uniroyal reduced their tire operations by seeking high-profit niches. In 1980 Uniroyal closed two plants, trimmed its product line, and went private with a leveraged buyout. In 1985, Goodrich closed two tire plants. In 1986, these two formed a 50-50 joint venture to become the nation's second largest producer. The two companies have complementary strengths: Goodrich is strong in high-performance tires for the replacement market while Uniroyal is the preeminent tire supplier to General Motors. Many of the minor players are dropping out or switching to highly specialized products or selling to a single big customer.

Clearly a number of "endgame strategies" can be pursued in this declining industry.

Sources: Adapted from "Goodyear's Solo Strategy," *Business Week,* Aug. 28, 1978, pp. 67–78; "General Tire: Pondering Spinoffs to Make the Most of Its Assets," *Business Week,* Sept. 7, 1981, pp. 98–102; and "Can Goodrich and Uniroyal Keep Each Other Off the Skids?" *Business Week,* Feb. 10, 1986, p. 28.

to their effectiveness. Mergers have become increasingly popular. There are a number of terms used for external expansion: acquisitions, mergers (one company loses its identity), and consolidations (both companies lose their identity, and a new company arises). But one term will be used for all these: mergers.

A merger is a combination of two or more businesses in which one acquires the assets and liabilities of the other in exchange for stock or cash, or both companies are dissolved and assets and liabilities are combined and new stock is issued. Mergers can take place within one country or across national borders.

There are many reasons why a firm may desire to merge. They can be grouped under buyer's motives and seller's motives.

The buyer's motives for merging include the following:

- To increase the value of the firm's stock. Mergers often lead to increases in the stock price and/or price-earnings ratio.
- To increase the growth rate of the firm.
- To make a good investment. A firm may make a better use of funds by purchasing instead of plowing the same funds into internal expansion.
- To improve the stability of the firm's earnings and sales. This is done by acquiring firms whose earnings and sales complement the firm's peaks and valleys.
- To balance or fill out the product line.
- To diversify the product line when the current products have reached their peak in the life cycle.
- To reduce competition by purchasing a competitor (possible violation of the Sherman Act).
- To acquire a needed resource quickly—for example, high-quality technology or highly innovative management.
- For tax reasons. It may be desirable to purchase a firm with prior tax losses which will offset current or future earnings.
- To increase efficiency and profitability, especially if there is synergy between the two companies. (Synergy is discussed later in the chapter.)

The seller's motives for merging include the following:

- To increase the value of the owner's stock and investment in the firm.
- To increase the firm's growth rate by receiving more resources from the acquiring company.
- To acquire the resources to stabilize operations and make them more efficient.
- For tax reasons. If the firm is owned by a family or an individual, a merger makes it easier to deal with estate tax problems.
- To help diversify the owning family's holdings beyond the present firm.
- To deal with top-management problems such as management succession for an entrepreneur or dissension among top managers.

As can be seen from examining the two lists, there are a number of "matching" reasons. When there are enough matches, mergers are more likely to take place.

Recently, however, mergers seem to not necessarily rely on a "match." Indeed,

EXHIBIT 7.9   A FEW EXAMPLES OF MERGERS IN POST-1980 U.S. INDUSTRY

Brand-name mergers

Pantry Pride pays $2.7 billion for Revlon.
Proctor & Gamble acquires Richardson Vicks for $1.24 billion.
Monsanto buys G. D. Searle for $2.8 billion.
Greyhound buys Purex for $264 million.
Coca-Cola acquires Columbia Pictures, Embassy Communications, Merv Griffin Enterprises,
   Walter Reade Organizations, and joint ventures with Tri-Star Pictures (total = $1.5 billion).

Tobacco and food

R. J. Reynolds buys Nabisco for $4.9 billion and Canada Dry for $175 million.
Phillip Morris buys General Foods for $5.75 billion (which acquired six firms from 1982 to 1984).
Beatrice, going private in leveraged buyout, buys Esmark, which had bought Norton Simon, for
   $2.7 billion.
Nestle buys Carnation for $2.9 billion.
Quaker Oats buys Stokely Van Camp for $226 million.
Ralston Purina seeks ITT's Continental Baking for $475 million.

The oil and gas patch

Texaco is involved in a court battle ($11 billion judgment on appeal) for derailing merger of
   Pennzoil and Getty.
Exxon buys $4 billion of its own stock to ward off suitors.
Dupont pays $7.3 billion for Conoco.
InterNorth buys Houston Natural Gas.
Carl Icahn threatens Phillips Petroleum.
CSX buys Texas Gas Resources for $1.1 billion.
Chevron pays $13.2 billion for Gulf.
Phillips buys some R. J. Reynolds properties for $1.7 billion.

Exhibit 7.9 provides some evidence that merger mania—the corporate game of "Let's Make a Deal"—has hit American business firms. In 1985 alone, firms acquired in whole or in part averaged 11 *per day*. Between 1969 and 1980, only 12 transactions valued at over $1 billion took place between U.S. firms. In 1985, 35 deals worth at least that amount took place. And megamergers are not just an American phenomenon. They have taken place in Britain, Japan, and a few other countries. What's going on?

For one thing, acquisitions have boosted stock prices of target firms an average of 30 percent. Corporate raiders have seen an opportunity to "get rich quick"; with access to enough borrowed cash, they have put pressure on existing managers to "get more value for the stockholder." Arbitragers, speculators who snap up stock when an acquisition play is announced, will take big risks in the hope of a rapid stock price rise. And with takeover artists on the prowl, managers may look for protection by seeking mergers instead of planning new products or considering new markets. Thus many recent mergers have been based more on issues of short-term financial gain or job protection (of top managers) than on strategic considerations.

The use, success, and implementation of mergers has been the subject of substantial research and writing. We include in the appendix for this chapter some technical

EXHIBIT 7.9   A FEW EXAMPLES OF MERGERS IN POST-1980 U.S. INDUSTRY (*Continued*)

The raiders

T. Boone Pickens goes after Gulf Oil, which finally sells out to Chevron for $13.3 billion.
Ted Turner tries to buy CBS; settles for MGM/UA Entertainment. [CBS buys back $1 billion
   (20%) of its shares to avoid takeover.]
James Goldsmith acquires Crown Zellerbach.
Carl Icahn buys TWA, then buys Ozark.

Airlines

United Airlines buys Pan Am's Pacific routes.
Southwest Air buys Muse Air.
People Express buys Frontier, then sells it.
Piedmont acquires Empire Airlines.
Northwest buys Republic.
Texas Air buys Eastern.

Others

Southern Pacific merges with Santa Fe, valued at $5.1 billion (under challenge).
GE buys RCA for $6 billion (largest non-oil merger to 1986).
Capital Cities buys American Broadcasting for $3.5 billion.
W. R. Grace buys back stock to ward off possible takeover.
GAF makes $4 billion takeover bid for Union Carbide.
GM acquires Electronic Data Systems and buys Hughes Aircraft for $5.2 billion.
CIT Financial (formerly owned by RCA) pays $1.5 billion for Manufacturers Hanover.
IBM pays $1.2 billion for Rolm.
Ameritech buys Applied Data Research.
Monsanto buys G. D. Searle for $2.7 billion.
LTV merges with Republic Steel.
Maytag merges with Magic Chef for $711 million.

Sources: Compiled from J. Greenwold, "Let's Make a Deal," *Time*, Dec. 23, 1985, pp. 42–51; "The New LTV Steel," *Business Week*, Apr. 16, 1984, pp. 129–133; C. Hawkins and A. Bernstein, "Airlines in Flux," *Business Week*, Mar. 10, 1986, pp. 107–112; "Why Nabisco and Reynolds Were Made for Each Other," *Business Week*, June 17, 1985, pp. 34–35; "Mainframe Software Makers Have Seen the Future, and It's Rugged," *Business Week*, Dec. 23, 1985, pp. 69–70; "The New Food Giants," *Business Week*, Sept. 24, 1984, pp. 132–138; P. B. Brown, "New? Improved?" *Business Week*, Oct. 21, 1985, pp. 108–110; "The Top 300 Deals," *Business Week*, Apr. 18, 1986, pp. 266–284; "Columbia Pictures: Are Things Really Better with Coke?" *Business Week*, Apr. 14, 1986, pp. 56–58.

details associated with mergers. We can sum these up here by making several observations:

1 Mergers must be carefully planned.

2 Human considerations are as important as financial ones.

3 The valuation of a merger candidate is an important process.

4 Legal factors must be carefully assessed.

5 Much of the research suggests that mergers are less successful than internal expansion.

6 Mergers which create synergy are likely to be more successful.

7 The acquiring firm's managers usually have more to gain than the stockholders of either firm or the acquired firm's managers.

Internal and External Combinations [7]

A firm may decide to cooperate with another firm (or firms) in a contractual agreement which allows each to remain independent, but which leads to gains for both. In effect, the firm pursues both an internal (independent) and external (cooperative) strategy simultaneously. There are many variations possible here. *Subcontracting* on a long-term or short-term basis may be done. *Cross-licensing* or technology sharing can lead to benefits from patents which might require substantial internal investments otherwise. Several firms in an industry may benefit from forming a *consortium* for research or development of standardization of production processes or technologies. *Franchising* allows a firm to grant exclusive rights to other firms, while still retaining the right to operate its own company-owned units. Probably the most common variant is the *joint venture* for expansion. A joint venture involves an equity arrangement between two or more independent enterprises which results in the creation of a new organizational entity. (There has been one joint venture to buy and manage an existing firm, but it is highly unique.) As noted in Exhibit 7.10, a joint venture is a combination of internal and external expansion.

There are three joint-venture strategies (sometimes called *strategic alliances*).

Spiderweb Strategy

A small firm establishes a series of joint ventures so that it can survive—and not be absorbed by its larger competitors. An example is an oil firm which jointly bids for drilling rights with five or six other firms. It may not have enough funds to bid on its own, or it may wish to spread resources to increase the chances of success or reduce the risk of a takeover.

Go Together–Split Strategy

In this strategy, the firms agree to a joint venture for a specific project or length of time. When the project is completed, they "split." Examples of this kind of strategy have been seen in many construction projects, such as the Alaska pipeline project and R&D projects. This strategy can also evolve as the two partners grow to the point where they don't need each other for economies of scale or efficiency reasons.

EXHIBIT 7.10 **Internal-external combinations.**
(S. Gullander, "Joint Ventures and Corporate Strategy," Columbia Journal of World Business, vol. 11, no. 1 [Spring 1976], p. 106.)

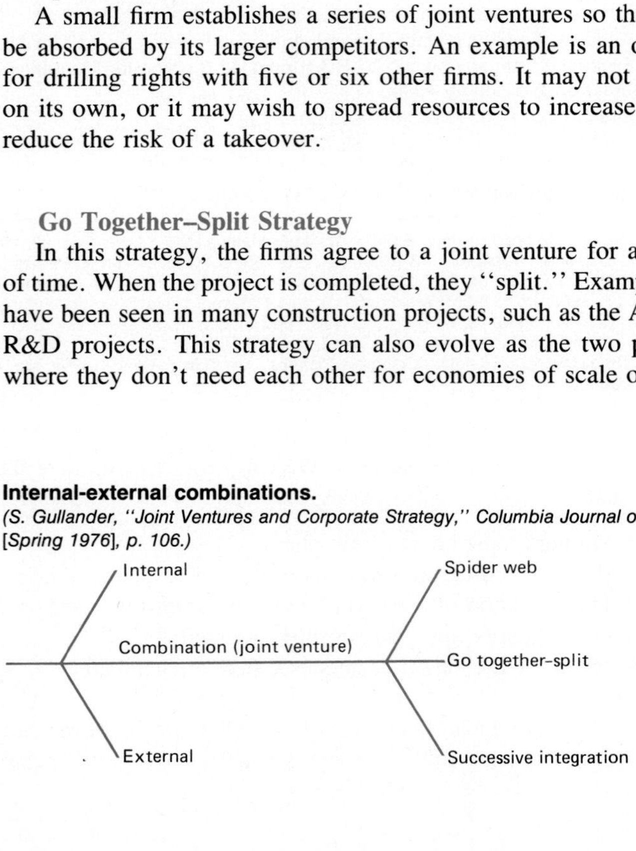

Successive Integration Strategy

A firm begins a relationship that is weak and then develops several joint ventures that can lead to a merger. In fact, joint ventures could become a laboratory setting prior to a merger, as happened with Conoco and Du Pont (see Exhibit 7.8).

The spiderweb strategy makes sense for small companies or large, undiversified firms organized into an oligopoly. Go together-split makes sense for firms that prefer independence but are financially unable to go it alone. Successive integration is chosen by firms whose management is risk-aversive regarding mergers but uses joint ventures to test the water.

Reasons advanced by advocates of joint ventures include the following: to reduce the high risk of new ventures; to help smaller companies to compete with giants; to introduce new technology or new products quickly; to save financial outlays, thus lowering costs for both parties; to increase sales, thus lowering production costs; to provide speedy channel acceptance, thus reducing marketing costs; to maintain the independence of both companies.

Joint ventures will be formed when firms cannot obtain strategic objectives on their own. If the need to cooperate comes from insufficient resources, lack of markets, or competitive timing advantages, joint ventures are highly opportunistic arrangements. For example, several highly publicized joint ventures between Japanese and American automakers have resulted in advantages for both parties. And Apple Computer set up a joint venture after it learned that Mexico was about to nationalize its manufacturing operations. Even AT&T has found joint ventures useful—for breaking into European markets which are highly protected. Nonetheless, many managers prefer to ''go it alone'' where possible. A number of studies indicate that larger firms may use joint ventures to control, influence, or reduce competition or as a means of influencing suppliers. And a joint venture may be used as a way to get into markets which would otherwise be restricted, without risking high investment. If these are true, then potential legal problems may be a possible drawback or trade-off. And many of these relationships have been too unstable to endure. For example:

• Financial troubles at McLouth Steel required its partners (Inland Steel, International Harvester, Cleveland Cliffs Iron) in a mine project to find a buyer for its share. They didn't, and $264 million of debt came due.

• Conoco was involved with a joint-venture partner in the construction of a prototype industrial boiler to cleanly burn high-sulfur coal. But due to a weak economy Conoco deferred capital investment and left its partner in a bind.

• Du Pont's purchase of Conoco created competitive problems that wrecked a joint venture between Conoco and Monsanto, which competes with Du Pont.

A number of crucial decisions must be made when setting up joint ventures, including decisions about the share of control and voting strength, the share of ownership, the share of ''rewards,'' and the choice of partners. Where the venture crosses national boundaries, these decisions can be particularly difficult because of differences in culture and economic development. As differences increase, joint-venture problems increase. However, joint ventures can provide a ''front-row seat'' in a new country.

Locals can interpret the industrial language and customs of the country, thus reducing the host government's nationalistic fear that foreigners are taking over.

RELATED AND UNRELATED ALTERNATIVES [8]

These approaches are usually found with expansion of the business definition either internally or externally. New products, markets, or functions that are added are "related" if they conform to or are very similar to the current business definition. The addition of related products, markets, or functions is termed a "concentric diversification." For instance, if a food company decided to sell kitchen equipment, the equipment could be considered either a product or a market-related addition (if sold through the same channels of distribution used for food). Major advantages of related expansion are thought to be the concentration of strength, the ability to act more quickly (than firms with unrelated expansion), exploitation of a market niche, and the development of synergy.

Synergy can be developed through internal expansion but is usually discussed in terms of external expansion (mergers). The argument is that the "whole is greater than the sum of its parts." Synergy exists when the strengths of two companies more than offset their joint weaknesses. *Sales synergy* arises from many products having the same salespeople, warehouses, distribution channels, and advertising. *Investment synergy* arises from many products having the same plant, inventories, R&D, and machinery. *Operating synergy* arises from many products making possible a higher utilization of facilities and personnel and the spreading of overhead. *Management synergy* arises from management experience in handling problems in one location or industry that helps to solve problems in another. Exhibit 7.11 indicates how an international news company wants to create operating and investment synergy in the services it provides.

Synergy can be negative too. In most mergers, at least one and possibly more of the factors can be negative. In theory, the concept of synergy is appealing. It should be pointed out that there has been little systematic proof that synergy actually exists. But the combined resources of two companies, if properly integrated, can create a stronger operation than stand-alone firms.

The "unrelated" approach is usually termed a "conglomerate diversification." There are a number of reasons why a firm might wish to diversify internally or externally. Only a few can be discussed here.

• The first is that the firm fears that its product or service line is in a business approaching market saturation or obsolescence. The firm may wish to stabilize its earnings and dividends in a cyclical industry. It does this by diversifying into an industry with complementary cycles. Or the market may be too small to allow the firm to achieve growth objectives efficiently. In sum, it feels uncomfortable being dependent on one product line.

• The current product or service is producing more cash than can be usefully reinvested. The opportunities with other products or services provide better returns.

EXHIBIT 7.11   CREATING SYNERGY

Reuters Ltd. is a London-based international news company that sells its services to publishers and broadcasters throughout the world. In 1981 its plan was to attempt to acquire United Press International from E. W. Scripps of Cincinnati. A Reuters-UPI network would form a news-gathering outfit with revenues about twice the size of those of the Associated Press.

Executives and industry observers noted that a remarkable synergy would be created by this merger. Reuters needed to fill a gap in its U.S. news bureaus. UPI's 78 overseas bureaus would augment Reuter's 81. In addition, UPI operates a new international telephoto service, and Reuters lacks this service. Further, UPI would give Reuters a base from which to invade North America with computerized data services—an area in which it has been developing expertise. About 15,700 subscribers are now linked to Reuters so that they can retrieve news and prices with regard to commodities, foreign exchange, securities, and financial instruments in global markets.

While Reuters faced possible opposition from National Public Radio (NPR), Scripps has few options if UPI is to remain intact, since it has been unprofitable for 25 years. From Reuters's point of view, the synergy obtainable in this horizontal merger would be worth the price it would have to pay to obtain UPI, despite its losses. But from Scripps's point of view, the tax deduction of a sale to NPR could have offset the annual losses. What is interesting is that a private consortium of investors bought UPI from Scripps. NPR did not have sufficient resources to compete with the consortium's offer. Clearly, buyer and seller goals in a merger are also important.

Sources: Adapted from "Why Reuters Wants UPI on Its Wires," *Business Week*, Sept. 21, 1981, p. 33, and "NPR Directors Vote to Consider Takeover of UPI Wire Service," AP news release, Jan. 16, 1982.

- Tax policy induces reinvestment in research and development at present. Diversification can arise when R&D develops a new product or service which is not in the present product or service line.
- Antitrust prohibitions appear difficult in the present industry.
- A firm may diversify, usually by means of a merger, to try to prevent a hostile takeover. For example, if the firm trying to take over is in the bread business, the target firm acquires a bread company. Such a merger may result in legal problems for the firm trying to take over, or the new combination might be too large to be acquired by the hostile firm.
- A firm may diversify, usually by means of a merger to acquire a tax loss.
- A firm may diversify, usually by means of a merger, to enter the international sector quickly.
- A firm may diversify, usually by means of a merger, to attain technical expertise quickly.
- A firm may diversify to attract more experienced executives and to hold better executives who may become bored in a single-product or single-service-line business.

Recognize, however, that unrelated diversification is not a panacea. Some old problems may not be solved through diversification. It can lead to spreading resources so thinly that no competitive advantage is obtained. And management may find it difficult to control and coordinate the increased activities which result. A section in the appendix on concentric and conglomerate diversification provides additional details and examples.

The unrelated-related dimension is most often associated with expansion, as we said earlier. But many conglomerates have not been successful due to past unrelated diversification and have pursued a strategy of divesting themselves of unrelated SBUs. Thus retrenching out of unrelated businesses is also an approach that is possible in this dimension.

HORIZONTAL AND VERTICAL ALTERNATIVES [9]

The horizontal dimension is quite similar to the "related" dimension. However, it usually applies to the addition of products, or services, and/or markets which complement the existing business definition. If this expansion occurs via a merger, the legal aspects must be carefully considered. Exhibit 7.11 is an interesting example (Reuters wished to expand horizontally).

Vertical integration is a strategy which expands or contracts the business definition primarily in terms of functions performed. As a firm takes some input and transforms it into output, it adds value in the form of utility to a buyer of its output. Exhibit 7.12 suggests that the value added varies at different stages in the chain of transformation. The vertical integration strategy question is whether to perform more or fewer functions than are now performed. There are two kinds of vertical integration. A *backward integration* is associated with strategies affecting the supply of a firm's inputs (toward the raw material stage). *Forward integration* refers to moves altering the nature of the distribution of the firm's output (toward end users). Note that expansion or retrenchment is possible. The firm can add or subtract functions. Vertical integration is the primary form of a make or buy decision.

Examples of vertical integration may help clarify these distinctions.

• Ashland Oil could integrate forward if it decided to sell its entire output of gasoline through its own service stations instead of most of it through distributors.

EXHIBIT 7.12   **The value added to a product at different stages in the production chain of raw material to consumer.**
(J. L. Bower, Simple Economic Tools for Strategic Analysis [Boston: Intercollegiate Case Clearing House, no. 9-373-094, 1972].)

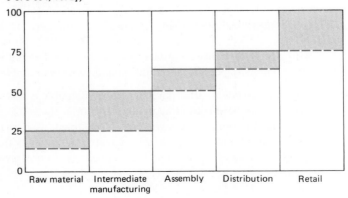

- Seven-Up vertically integrated backward when it bought its flavor supplier and the lemon groves which provided the raw materials for the flavor company and Seven-Up.
- Kellwood was formed through a backward vertical integration strategy when several suppliers of clothing were merged to produce most of their output for Sears. Instead of producing and distributing, they retrenched out of the distribution function, letting Sears market the products.
- Carter Hawley Hale has rediscovered customer service in its department stores after cutting corners by doing away with many salespeople.

Advantages of vertical integration are thought to be better control of suppliers or distributors and possible cost savings. Disadvantages may come in the form of increasing dependence on one industry or the risk of possible antitrust violations. Recognize that expanding forward or backward could result in the addition of new markets for products, and the firm may compete with former distributors or suppliers.

Perhaps these pros and cons can be seen more clearly if we examine the "captive-company" strategy—retrenching by means of vertical integration as in the Kellwood example. A captive-company strategy is followed when (1) a firm sells more than 75 percent of its products or services to a single customer and (2) the customer performs many of the functions normally performed by the independent firm.

The captive-company strategy may be chosen because of:

1 The inability or unwillingness to strengthen the marketing function or other functions.

2 The perception that this strategy is the best means for achieving financial strength. It will be rationalized as a security strategy but is in fact risky and costly to the prestige and independence needs of the manager.

In effect, when you become captive, your captor makes many decisions for you. Perhaps some of these decisions concern product design, production control, and quality control. The captor negotiates the price of the goods, usually from a position of strength, assuring for itself an adequate return much in the way a public utility and the public service commission of a state relate. It may be able to avoid cost squeezes from competitors in this fashion. But the captive becomes closely tied to the results of the actions of its major purchaser, and this can be risky. Still, the strategy is a way to assure adequate profitability, especially if the captive company competes with much bigger companies that can spend large amounts on advertising and marketing. Most captive companies are not well known, but they can be large.

This strategy requires a management that is able to develop good long-term relationships with its major customer. In a way, it is a strategy that can be as risky as doing most of your business with the military. But if the contractual relationship is a good one, the firm can prosper and hedge against the loss of business by developing its own line, as Whirlpool did very successfully. Still, many executives intuitively like to be relatively independent, and this strategy may be unrewarding to them. It may be one of the few choices a firm has at times. It is also a strategy which is easy to drift into unintentionally. A few large customers buy more and more of your output until you find yourself dependent on them for future business.

Retrenchment out of functions reaches an extreme when a firm becomes a "shell" corporation. Such firms may subcontract out manufacturing, marketing, and in some cases even collection functions. This vertical "disintegration" is seen as a way to reduce capital needs and add flexibility. However, these firms become vulnerable to their subcontractors and often have volatile earnings. Companies who use this strategy are Nike, Esprit, Emerson, and Schwinn Bicycle, among others.

ACTIVE AND PASSIVE ALTERNATIVES [10]

The last dimension refers to management's attitude and timing with regard to pursuing its strategy alternatives. Depending on the strategists, there may be a preference for active or passive strategies.

An *active,* or offensive, strategy is one in which strategists act before they are forced to react to environmental threats or opportunities. A *passive,* or defensive, strategy is one whose major characteristic is that strategists react to environmental pressures only when forced to do so by circumstances.

Active or passive approaches may occur with any of the generic strategies. Obviously, firms can develop strategies which are offensive (active) with regard to one part of the business definition and passive with regard to the other parts. In fact, a crucial characteristic determining the choice of active or passive strategies may be the relative size of the firm in its market. In general, large and dominant firms will be effective if they develop active strategic alternatives in their major market segments. Small firms will survive if they have passive strategies concerning the large firms' major market and if they have active strategies concerning market segments which are ignored by the dominant firm(s) and which they can develop.

The approach to research and the development of new products is another area where this dimension becomes important. Firms can be active or passive in this function in the following ways:

1 *Being innovative—the first to market.* This is an offensive, active approach in both research and development. In some instances, however, the firm is strong in research but weak in marketing products. It tries to make the environment accept its approach.

2 *Being a fast second.* There are firms which are active in development but passive in research. They need superior competitive intelligence and enough research to make sure that the gaps between them and innovators don't become too large.

3 *Being an imitator—a slow third.* Some firms emphasize applications engineering based on product modifications to fit particular customer segments. These firms tend to react to the needs they identify in the environment.

A typical prescription these days is that innovation is mandatory so that the firm can get "fast down the learning curve" and thus preclude competition. Other advocates argue that firms should seek to create barriers to entry in their industries by seizing the initiative and becoming the "first occupant" who can preemptively erect such barriers (see Chapter 4 for a discussion of barriers to entry). Yet some firms prefer to let others test the waters and make the mistakes which they can learn to avoid. A number of follow-up approaches such as the acquisition of inventions, securing licenses, and outright imitation are available to those who prefer passive approaches or who may have limited capital. Exhibit 7.13 presents some of the pros and cons of follow-up, or passive, approaches in the R&D area.

Interestingly, in some areas the large firms with more resources are those who are fast seconds or imitators, leaving innovation to smaller firms. And as discussed earlier in the book, as technological change occurs in the environment, strategic response patterns vary from stability in old technologies to expansion into new ones. Clearly, executives have different preferences for passive or active approaches, and these influence the alternative strategies which are likely to be considered.

A good example of an active approach to a sequential combination of expansion and retrenchment is known as a "grow to sell out" strategy. Here we find many entrepreneurs who plan from the start of their business to expand, but when it gets to the high-growth-rate apex of the product life cycle, they will sell out (usually for stock) to a larger firm. Typically, they take the proceeds in stock (for tax purposes) and stay on as consultants for 3 to 5 years. Usually they agree not to compete with the acquiring firm for a period. With this agreement they can maximize their return and retire early or build up another firm to be sold out. Many entrepreneurs have used this approach, but this combination strategy has not been studied in any depth. Note that the difference between the active approach and the passive approach here is the idea that the "retrenchment" was planned from the start, that it was not a reaction to "unfavorable" circumstances.

Of course, this dimension does *not* imply that flexibility is inappropriate. Active preplanning of "contingency" strategies does not suggest that the firm is merely

EXHIBIT 7.13 ADVANTAGES AND DISADVANTAGES OF PASSIVE RESEARCH AND DEVELOPMENT

Advantages	Disadvantages
• Involvement based upon calculable risk	• Difficulties involved with the search for suitable objects
• Quick availability of new technologies	• Payment of license fees
• Reduction of the high risk normally associated with R&D	• Reduced opportunity to train specialists for the future
• Cooperation with or financing by third parties easier to obtain	• Reduced opportunity to obtain knowledge for new ideas
• Effective way to achieve short-to-medium-range diversification	• No technological advantage over competitors
• Easy adaptation of the supply to the demand in different markets = flexible marketing strategy	• Increased risk to investments and ongoing programs from new developments not anticipated by a firm doing little exploratory research

Sources: Adapted from D. Altenpohl, "Acquisition of Technology as One Specific Way to Achieve Technology Transfer," in H. Davidson, M. Cetron, and J. Goldhar, *Technology Transfer* (Leyden, the Netherlands: Noordhoff, 1974), and D. Altenpohl, paper presented at the NATO Advanced Study Institute on Industrial Applications of Technology Transfer, Les Arcs-Bourg St. Maurice, France (June–July 1975).

passive. For example, many firms attempt to forecast product life cycles so that new-product introductions can be developed (see Exhibit 7.14). In effect, this is an *active, sequential combination* of *expansion, stability,* and *retrenchment* in *products.* It can be flexible in that the exact timing of stability and phaseout may be contingent on prespecified conditions; the firm does not have to passively await saturation or decline. In other words, it can plan for exit at the time of entry.

More typically, firms passively or unintentionally pursue different strategies as the product life cycle changes occur. During youth stages, new products and new markets are introduced. If they are successful, diversification, mergers and joint ventures, or vertical integration may be pursued during growth stages. At the maturity stage, stability or operating turnarounds may be pursued. At the stage of saturation and decline, strategic turnarounds, divestments, and other retrenchments are pursued. The prescription for active planned entry and exit is based on this idea, but it urges a greater degree of control instead of passive reaction to external conditions. Further, remember that endgame strategies need not be passive. Retrenchment is not preordained, and an active approach can be successful even in a declining industry.

Finally, whole typologies of firms' past strategies have been developed around the active-passive dimension. The best known is the Miles and Snow framework. Miles and Snow propose that, historically, firms have had four strategic postures:

Defenders. These are firms which penetrate a narrow product-market domain and guard it. They plan intensively, have centralized control, use limited environmental scanning, and are cost-efficient. This is the passive end of the strategic continuum.

Prospectors. At the active end of the continuum are the firms which use broad planning approaches, decentralized controls, and broad environmental scanning. They also have some underutilized resources. The prospectors seek new product/market segments.

Analyzers. In between the two poles are two choices, one of which is the analyzer. The analyzers have some of the characteristics of prospectors some of the time and some of the characteristics of defenders the rest of the time.

Reactors. The other in-between choice is the reactor. The firm that realizes that the environment is changing but cannot effect the necessary realignment of strategy

EXHIBIT 7.14   **A common product life cycle.**

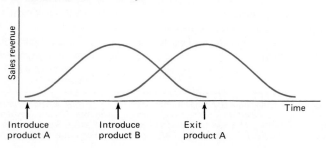

and environment fits in this category. Reactors must either become one of the other three choices or die. They have an unstable strategic posture.

Thus the active-passive dimension provides another approach to examining the pursuit of alternative grand strategies.

INTERNATIONAL STRATEGY VARIATIONS [11]

In Chapter 4 we noted threats and opportunities associated with the international environment. This leads to a special case of strategy variation. While the alternatives explained earlier apply here as well, it is useful to explore in more detail some of the strategies which firms can consider if they seek an international presence.

New Markets

Some firms seek to open up new markets in other countries when they face slower growth rates at home or a restricted domestic market. This has been a major reason for Japanese expansion, for example. Firms must identify a critical mass of GNP and population growth before exploring the international alternative further. Of course, other factors, such as competitor activity in the market, ability to produce domestically or in the foreign market, and so on, must be taken into account. For example, the firm's domestic competitors may not be located in selected foreign markets, possibly allowing the company to obtain a better price. On the other hand, competitors based in the foreign country may enjoy favored treatment by customers or the government. Whatever the circumstances, the prudent strategist must determine the firm's ability to compete effectively.

Some strategists have opened new foreign markets for diversification and risk-spreading purposes. When a domestic economy slumps, foreign economies operating in a lagged cycle may provide a way to stabilize sales and earnings. To the extent that a "global economy" begins to emerge, such a strategy could lose its appeal. Other factors, such as political considerations, may emerge as a reason to go into foreign markets. For example, some foreign firms may invest in the United States because it is seen as politically stable.

In some cases, the motivation to compete in domestic markets may be done to protect a position already secured in the multinational marketplace. A case in point was the strategy of Heinz in the 1960s and 1970s. The U.S. baby food division at Heinz was competing with Gerber for declining baby food demand in the United States. Heinz held only a 5 percent market share in the United States, yet it used low pricing as a primary weapon against Gerber. While its pricing policy led to marginal profitability in the United States, the Heinz strategy was designed to protect the high profits it reaped from control of an 80 percent share of the multinational baby food market. By keeping Gerber busy at home, Heinz sought to reduce Gerber's resource capability and direct management attention away from Gerber's interest in foreign expansion. Similarly, banks, accounting firms, market researchers, and so on have established operations in foreign locations to prevent competitors from gaining access to key customers in those locations.

New Products

Firms can sometimes introduce new products sooner into a foreign market than at home. This is especially so for U.S.-based pharmaceutical firms. FDA delays in approving new products have led some firms to develop and market drugs in foreign countries before introducing them in the United States. On the other hand, as more Americans have traveled overseas, they have returned home with a heightened awareness of the different products available. American marketers send buyers around the world to locate new products which they can import to meet the demand. Large retailers such as Sears and J. C. Penney have permanent foreign buying offices to identify products that can be successfully sold in the United States.

Functions

As we discussed in Chapter 4, firms can identify particular countries as *energy-rich, resource-rich,* or *labor-rich.* Any of these conditions can lead to the decision to produce goods in foreign locations to lower the cost of goods sold. And firms which have been exporting to a given country may find that producing in that location can yield benefits as well. For instance, a host government may prohibit imports to the country if there is a given level of ''domestic-content'' production in existence. Such protectionism serves as a trade barrier, but can benefit the firm which decides to open a production facility in such a country. In the Chilean market, General Tire was competing with a dozen or so exporters. But once General Tire began producing in Chile, it became the only supplier of tires for the entire market. Finally, some countries provide incentives (tax breaks, loans, grants, etc.) to locate there.

Protection of domestic markets may be another reason for locating production facilities abroad. If a firm faces lower-priced foreign imports, it may move part or all of its facilities to the source of its competition to take advantage of the lower costs of labor, materials, or energy. Strategists can manufacture selected components and assemble at home, or send components elsewhere for final assembly. For example, many U.S. clothing manufacturers have opened facilities in Mexico or the Far East to take advantage of lower labor costs. Some send cloth to be processed by foreign laborers, then ship finished goods back to domestic markets.

By the same token, suppliers will often locate new facilities in countries where their customers are locating. As Japanese car manufacturers moved to open U.S. plants, many Japanese suppliers began to consider opening facilities as well. Note, then, that there is both threat and opportunity for domestic suppliers when foreign manufacturers enter a market. Entry of new customers *and* competitors may go hand in hand.

Supply of raw materials or technology may also be a reason for choosing to locate production facilities in another country. Canadian firms, such as INCO, have invested in developing nations where new deposits of important ores or other resources have been found. And some foreign firms have located in the United States to gain knowledge of computers and semiconductors, areas in which the U.S. has held an edge in development.

Sequential Combinations

As we mentioned in Chapter 4, the movement toward international markets is frequently incremental. Most firms begin by exporting. This includes relatively low investment and risk. Depending on internal capabilities, firms may export directly (internal) or indirectly (external). That is, strategists may assign someone within the firm to handle this function or set up their own sales company in foreign locations. If the firm has no special expertise, export agents may be sought out. Depending on the nature of the business, franchising or licensing are other options by which a firm can begin to establish a presence in foreign locations.

The next stage for a firm may be to engage in a joint marketing venture with a foreign local who will act as its agent. In either the joint-venture or export case, issues of the need for product modification (to suit "local" tastes), different promotional tactics, control procedures, and so on will need to be considered. These are implementation issues which can affect the choice of entry.

EXHIBIT 7.15   TIME HORIZON OF SEQUENTIAL INTERNATIONAL STRATEGIES

Now	2 years	5 years
Market research—consider countries	Market research—study selected target markets	Continuing market analysis
Sell present product—no modification	Consider product modification	Consider new products
Limited penetration and promotion	Moderate penetration— special promotion	Full penetration and promotion
No servicing	Limited servicing	Full servicing
No new investment in production facilities	Add local investment of facilities to service foreign sales	Foreign investment
Use present supply sources	Contract manufacturing or possible overseas assembly in leased facility	Overseas manufacturing
Independent exporters	Overseas agents or representatives	Foreign sales branch or subsidiary
Correspondent relationships	Contractual relations or branch offices	Joint ventures or foreign subsidiary
No specialized personnel	Specialized personnel	Internationally oriented staff
No organizational changes	Minor organizational changes	Major organizational changes
Tight control	Loose control	Decentralized control

Source: Adapted from R. D. Robinson, *International Business Management: A Guide to Decision Making* (New York: Holt, 1973).

Once a foreign presence is obtained, the strategist may decide to expand the firm's activities. Specialized products may be developed, with new investments made in local manufacturing facilities. Or direct investment in the foreign economy may be made. This can be done a number of ways. A wholly owned subsidiary could be formed by building new facilities or acquiring a going concern in the foreign location. The factors affecting these choices are complicated by issues of personnel policies, legal requirements, and so on, which, as we suggested before, vary from country to country. Hence, many firms find it easier to use a successive-integration joint-venture arrangement which may eventually lead to complete ownership. Eventually a merger or buyout would occur if the joint venture became important to the company's core business.

Exhibit 7.15 indicates a number of the issues which can be involved over time as a strategist makes long-range plans for foreign involvement. Of course, the strategies given in this time line are implemented only if the firm is successful and expanding its presence, investment, and control. Retrenchment is possible if objectives are not being reached, or management finds better opportunities elsewhere.

SUMMARY

Various approaches to the generic strategies were identified. These are listed below in outline form.

1 Internal and External Dimensions
  a Internal moves suggest that the firm pursues its strategy independently.
    (1) Internal expansion can occur through the addition of products, markets, or functions to the business definition or through an increase in the pace of operations (through market penetration, for example).
    (2) Internal stability is used to maintain the pace or business definition.
    (3) Internal retrenchment in pace is an "operating turnaround" strategy that involves cutting costs, improving efficiency, reducing assets, or reorganizing. Internal retrenchment is a "strategic turnaround" strategy if it involves dropping products, markets, or functions.
  b External moves are those requiring the involvement of other entities.
    (1) External expansion involves a merger with another firm.
    (2) External retrenchment involves the divestment of SBUs or the liquidation of the entire business.
  c Internal and external combinations are usually in the form of a joint venture.
2 Related and Unrelated Dimensions
  a In related moves, changes in products, markets, or functions conform in some way to the current business definition. Related internal expansion can be used to create synergy.
  b Unrelated approaches imply a diversification into areas that do not conform to the current business definition.
3 Horizontal and Vertical Dimensions
  a Horizontal changes imply related moves which result in the addition of products or markets that complement or supplement the existing business definition.

    b Vertical changes expand or contract functions.

       (1) Backward integration is movement toward suppliers.

       (2) Forward integration is movement toward end users.

       (3) A firm which retrenches via backward vertical integration is known as a "captive company."

4 Active and Passive Dimensions

    a An active strategy is one in which strategists act before they are forced to react.

    b Passive strategies are defensive reactions to environmental pressures.

    c A "fast-second" strategy involves a simultaneous combination of active moves in one function (development) and passive moves in another (research).

    d A "grow to sell out" strategy is a sequential combination of expansion and retrenchment.

5 International Strategy Variations

    a New international markets may be sought for offensive or defensive reasons.

    b New products may be introduced in foreign markets for timing reasons or to import for domestic markets.

    c Foreign production may be done to take advantage of energy, resources, labor, or technology available elsewhere.

    d The movement to foreign activities is usually a sequential combination of a variety of strategies.

The advantages and disadvantages of these variations were described. In essence, any alternative or combination has the potential to improve performance. But we believe that the following proposition applies to many firms in moderately volatile environments.

Proposition 7.1

Firms with higher growth objectives are more effective if they expand their pace from a base of proven competitive abilities in the current business definition, organize divisions or departments to promote new opportunities in related fields, and take moderate risks.

This chapter has described various extensions of the generic strategy alternatives available to firms. The Appendix describes several expansion strategies in more detail. In Chapter 8, we will review how the manager chooses the strategy from the alternatives developed.

APPENDIX: Diversification and Mergers

Expansion through diversification and merger has received substantial attention in the literature. We chose not to bog you down in the chapter with the various technical matters associated with these strategies. Here we present some of the factors associated with these forms of expansion and review some of the research.

Diversification [12]

In and of itself, the term "diversification" can really refer to a host of different types of strategies. It can refer to changes in products, markets, or functions; it can be done internally or externally, horizontally or vertically; and it can involve related or unrelated changes. Although he uses slightly different terms, Ansoff has done the most theorizing on diversification strategies. Exhibit 7.16 presents one of his many mechanisms for analyzing diversification decisions.

This matrix can be used to plan the kind of diversification the firm should pursue insofar as nonfinancial aspects are concerned. But note that diversification is not *a* strategy; it is a number of kinds of strategies.

Drucker provides as good a list as any for why firms might pursue a diversification strategy. He lists the internal and external factors as follows:

1 Internal pressures
  a Psychologically, people get tired of doing the same things over and over again. They also believe that diversification will help them avoid the danger of overspecialization.
  b Diversification is seen as a way to balance the vulnerabilities due to one's wrong size.
  c Diversification is seen as a way to convert present internal cost centers into revenue producers.
2 External pressures (more important than internal pressures)
  a The economy (or market) the firm is operating in appears too small and confined to allow growth.
  b The firm's technology and research lead to the development of products which appear to have promise.
  c Tax legislation encourages reinvestment in research and development instead of the payment of dividends, and this leads to new products which are often a base for diversification.

Diversification is a much-used approach to strategy. Research has shown how single-product-line expansion has declined in relation to diversification for years in Europe, Japan, and the United States. Less than 1 percent of establishments are diversified (operate in more than one industry group). But this 1 percent employed 38 percent of the working people in the United States. The diversified firms are often concentrated in rapid-growth industries, with high increases in labor productivity and a high ratio of technical employees to all employees. It is

EXHIBIT 7.16   ANSOFF'S DIVERSIFICATION MATRIX

New functions	New products	
	Related technology	Unrelated technology
Firm is its own customer	Vertical integration	
Same type of product	Horizontal diversification	
Similar type of product	Marketing and technology-related concentric diversification	Marketing-related concentric diversification
New type of product	Technology-related concentric diversification	Conglomerate diversification

Source: H. I. Ansoff, *Corporate Strategy* (New York: McGraw-Hill, 1965), p. 132.

believed that firms diversify because they feel it is easier than trying to increase primary demand or market share. But diversifiers have not been found to reduce systematic risk.

Note that when we define diversified firms as those operating in more than one industry group, we are relying on a commonly used criterion of the numbers of different products produced. Thus as the number of different Standard Industrial Classification (SIC) definitions of products increases, diversification is thought to increase. Stated differently, diversity increases as *products* become *less related*. However, this definition ignores non-product-oriented aspects of diversification such as those in Exhibit 7.16.

A less precise but more strategically relevant measure of diversification has been developed by Rumelt. He established a set of categories defined largely in terms of ''relatedness'' and designed to capture important differences in the extent of diversity of a company as well as in the nature of the managerial relationships among the various businesses of a company. He examined the performance from 1949 to 1969 of 250 large U.S. firms in a very sophisticated research project. First he classified the firms into strategic categories at various points in recent years as shown in Exhibit 7.17. Then he examined the performance of these firms. Performance varied within each category (for example, single business), and subgroups performed differently. The *worst* performers were in the dominant (vertically integrated) and unrelated classes. The *highest* performers were in the related classes.

Rumelt did not separate those which diversified internally from those which diversified by means of a merger. However, several other researchers have done so, particularly in the examination of conglomerates. For instance, Berg has clarified some of the differences between diversified majors and conglomerates. He defined a conglomerate company as a firm which has at least five or six divisions which sell different products principally to markets rather than to

EXHIBIT 7.17   ESTIMATED PERCENTAGE OF FIRMS IN EACH STRATEGIC CATEGORY

Strategic category	1949	1959	1969
Major classes:			
Single business*	34.5	16.2	6.2
Dominant business†	35.4	37.3	29.2
Related business‡	26.7	40.0	45.2
Unrelated business§	3.4	6.5	19.4

*95% or more of business in one end-product business.
†70 to 94% of business in one end-product business.
‡Less than 70% in one end-product business, and diversification primarily in concentrically related products.
§Less than 70% in one end-product business, and diversification unrelated to primary product group.
Source: R. Rumelt, *Strategy, Structure, and Economic Performance* (Boston: Harvard Business School, 1974).

Acquisition type	Percentage of total	Percentage of failures
Vertical integration	3	0
Horizontal	25	11
Concentric marketing	13	26
Concentric technology	14	21
Conglomerate	45	42

each other. (If the divisions sell privately to each other, the firm is an integrated firm.) Berg says that conglomerates diversified quickly, primarily through mergers, and usually into product or service lines unrelated to their prior business. By "diversified majors," Berg means firms which developed their diversification over a long period of time primarily through internal expansion into products or services related to their prior business. Examples of diversified majors were Koppers, Borg Warner, and International Harvester.

Berg says that the conglomerate management style is different. He says that when you compare conglomerates with diversified majors, you find these differences:

• Conglomerates' central offices are much smaller than the central offices of diversified majors. Usually they have no staff officials (for example, for research and development).

• Conglomerates tend to place most major operating decisions at decentralized divisional levels. This is often because the central office has no one expert in making operating decisions in that business.

• Thus division managers are autonomous as long as the division "delivers."

• Diversified majors have better opportunities for synergy than conglomerates.

Berg and other advocates of conglomerates believe that by placing responsibility where it belongs—at the divisional level—conglomerates can evaluate the performance better and not become involved in operating decisions which prevent top management from performing the strategic planning and evaluation functions.

Conglomerates expand quickly primarily by purchasing other companies in exchange for stock when their own stock has a much higher price-earnings ratio than the target company's stock. Thus the conglomerate growth rate can remain high because of mergers and sometimes because of internal growth as well.

One other study we would like to highlight examined the performance of mergers (which we will explain in more detail later) for the purpose of diversification. Kitching studied 22 firms that merged over a number of years and examined 69 of the 181 mergers of 20 percent of the companies in the period studied (1960–1965). A number of his important findings are summarized below.

1 Nearly half of the mergers were of the conglomerate type. Horizontal acquisitions were the next most common type, followed by concentric technology, concentric marketing, and vertical integration. There is a relatively high risk of failure in concentric acquisitions and a relatively low one in horizontal mergers.

2 A "size mismatch" (where the acquired company's sales were less than 2 percent of the parent company's sales volume before the merger) occurs in 84 percent of the acquisitions considered failures.

3 In 81 percent of the failures, the organizational format (either the reporting relationships established after the merger or the extent of autonomy allowed) is disturbed at least once after the acquisition is first brought into the new "family."

4 Theoretically, synergy in mergers should be greatest where production facilities are combined because economies of scale are possible. Combinations based on technology (process know-how and R&D transfer), marketing, organization (personnel economies and productivity increases), and finance (additional and cheaper capital) should be of diminishing value, in that order. According to top managers, however, the ease with which synergy is actually realized improves in the reverse order; that is, synergy is most easily accomplished where financial resources are pooled, and it is most difficult to achieve where production facilities are combined. Furthermore, the dollar payoff is actually lowest, on the average, where production and technological resources are put together; it is highest where financial resources are combined.

5 Failure rates vary by type of merger:

Drucker agrees strongly with Kitching, especially with his fifth point. He says:

> Never was the belief in diversification (especially diversification by merger) as a panacea more widely held than in the 1950's and 1960's. Yet the success stories of these years were not the businesses that diversified (by mergers) let alone the conglomerates. They were businesses with one central product or product line, one central market, one central technology.

Our next section discusses mergers at more length. What we wish to point out is that diversification, particularly of the unrelated conglomerate forms, appears to lack some justification on a performance basis. Indeed, there is a body of research to suggest that specialized and related firms are more profitable with respect to their portfolio of business activities. Further, only limited synergy seems to be obtained in conglomerate mergers. However, there may be other considerations, especially antitrust reasons, for the development of conglomerates. If a firm can't move to related areas because of the fear that it will reduce competition, it might choose entirely unrelated areas. However, the last part of our next section summarizes other research which supports our negative view of the conglomerate merger for diversification.

Mergers

This external approach to expansion has received more attention than any other single type of strategy. In the following sections, we elaborate on why companies merge, how they merge, and the financial, legal, and human considerations involved in mergers. Finally, we review some of the research on the effectiveness of mergers.

Why Companies Merge (See [6])

In the chapter we identified a number of *objectives* which might be accomplished by means of external expansion through a merger. There are also *strategic* reasons for a merger that are related to some objectives. Exhibit 7.18 shows how our active-passive dimension might intersect with this form of external expansion.

EXHIBIT 7.18 **Motivations to merge.**
(F. T. Haner, Business Policy, Planning, and Strategy [Cambridge, Mass.: Winthrop, 1976], p. 399.)

Survival requirement	Protection against	Diversification	Gains in
• Capital structure deterioration from losses • Technological obsolescence • Loss of raw materials • Market loss to superior products	• Market infringement • Lower cost position of a competitor • Product innovations by others • An unwanted takeover	• Countercyclical • Counterseasonal • International operations • Multiple strategic plans	• Market position • Technological edge • Financial strength • Managerial talent

Merger motivations

Defensive (Passive)   Offensive (Active)

The defensive strategies are probably more often reasons why sellers might seek a merger. Offensive approaches are usually taken by the acquirers. But remember that when buyer and seller objectives are matched, a merger is more likely to occur.

How Companies Merge [13]

Before a successful merger can take place, there must be sound planning. There are various approaches to effective planning for mergers. One of the more useful summaries of this type of literature is that of Willard Rockwell. He has been personally involved in a number of mergers and gives these "10 commandments" on acquiring a company:

"Must" factors
1 Pinpoint and spell out the merger objectives, especially earnings objectives.
2 Specify substantial gains for the stockholders of both companies.
3 Be able to convince yourself that the acquired company's management is—or can be made—competent.
4 Certify the existence of important dovetailing resources—but do not expect perfection.
Other key considerations
5 Spark the merger program with the chief executive's involvement.
6 Clearly define the business you are in (for example, bicycles or transportation).
7 Take a depth sounding of strengths, weaknesses, and other key performance factors— the target company's and your own.
8 Create a climate of mutual trust by anticipating problems and discussing them early with the other company.
9 Do not let "caveman" advances jeopardize the courtship. Do not threaten the management that is to be acquired.
10 Most important of these latter six rules, make people your number 1 consideration in structuring your assimilation plan.

In effect, Rockwell is suggesting that the firm plan the merger well by profiling the two companies and comparing them. Thus you could prepare strategic advantage profiles and environmental threat and opportunity profiles for both companies and systematically compare them. He advocates good strategic management (commandments 1, 4, 6, and 7). Rockwell also believes that crucial to merger success are the human and financial considerations. We will address those next. In essence, a firm attempts to learn a great deal about a candidate so that the factors Rockwell talks about can be analyzed. In fact, some firms go to the point of hiring acquisitions specialists to manage the process.

Financial Considerations in Mergers [14]

Rockwell's number 1 and 2 "must" factors include establishing financial goals. And, of course, one of the important questions about strengths and weaknesses is the financial condition of a merger candidate. Two issues seem to be involved here: (1) How much is a company worth? (2) How does the acquirer pay for it?

The first issue—How much is it worth?—depends on your strategy and what you are looking for. Exhibit 7.19 suggests another set of strategic purposes for mergers. What you should realize is that the approach to *assessing the value* for each will emphasize different characteristics such as plant value, market opportunity, earnings potential, or stock value. However, a common procedure is to estimate the present value of discounted cash flows (DCF) and expected after-tax earnings attributable to the acquisition. Of course, establishing the required rate of return and cost of capital is important.

EXHIBIT 7.19   STRATEGIC APPROACHES TO ACQUISITION

Acquisition "play"	Strategy to achieve performance premium
1 Acquire synergistic product/market position.	Achieve scale economies of distribution, production, or technology.
2 Acquire position in key international markets.	Achieve scale economies for global production and technology investments.
3 Acquire a "beachhead" in an emerging high-growth market.	Anticipate high-leverage business growth equations by identifying market-forcing functions.
4 Acquire a portfolio of minority investments.	Apply pressure for improved short-term earnings and sell stock. Gain improved information on future potential.
5 Acquire a company with underutilized financial strength.	Use borrowing capacity or other financial strengths (e.g., underutilized tax loss carry-forwards or foreign tax credits) to achieve an immediate performance premium.
6 Acquire an underskilled company in a related industry.	Apply superior marketing, technology, or production expertise to enhance the competitive position and performance of the acquisition candidate.
7 Acquire an underexploited physical asset.	Anticipate shortages and price increases in the physical asset's value. Invest to exploit the resource, using distribution capacity.
8 Acquire an undervalued corporate portfolio.	Apply more aggressive portfolio management to restructure resource allocation and upgrade results.

Source: M. G. Allen, A. R. Oliver, and E. H. Schwaille, "The Key to Successful Acquisitions." Reprinted by permission from *The Journal of Business Strategy,* vol. 2, no. 2 (Fall 1981). Copyright © 1981 by Warren, Gorham and Lamont, Inc., 210 South St., Boston, Mass. All rights reserved.

In addition to estimating the present value of DCF, it is necessary to value existing assets, particularly if the assets are being liquidated. Capital asset pricing methods (CAPM) can be used here. But we would like to add a caution, because valuation can be tricky, depending on how you account for inflation and other factors. Inflation can greatly affect the true value of existing assets or outlays in five areas: (1) the proportion of assets in cash inventories, or fixed assets, (2) the inventory valuation methods used and the turnover rate, (3) the age of assets and the depreciation method used, (4) the composition of expenditures—such as for construction or energy, and (5) the capital structure—debt is more favorable assuming that the firm is facing inflation. In other words, it is highly unlikely that the book value is the same as the market value for either a liquidation or an ongoing firm, given that inflation affects the present value of assets. Even political factors can have an impact on value, as in the case of Exxon selling its oil and natural gas assets to the Libyan state oil company for "slightly less than book value."

The second major issue, once value has been determined, is the method by which the merger will be financed. Exchange of shares is one approach. In this case, the acquiring firms should also be valued. Of course, cash tender offers are possible. If the purchase price cannot be met with existing resources or direct borrowing, creative financing options are available. Firms can and do borrow on the target company's assets and cash, using techniques such as "leveraged buyouts" or "bootstrap acquisitions."

It is beyond our purpose to discuss the details of techniques such as DCF, CAPM, or leveraged buyouts. Entire volumes are available on ways to assess financial value. And many firms will call in consultants who specialize in acquisitions. But according to one finance specialist quoted in *The Wall Street Journal,* "about the best any investment banker can do in a price fairness opinion is to come up with a figure within 10 or 15 percent above or below true value. Negotiations or takeover strategy decide the rest."

Thus remember that sellers are involved also. Their approach to valuing their business might be different from the buyer's. And their interest in the type of offer can vary. For instance, reluctant merger participants might be tempted by preferred stock or subordinated, convertible debentures. Selling a company is an investment decision whose objective should be to increase the value of the owner's equity in the future. Frequently, the decision to divest is hasty, ill thought out, and dependent on the first buyer who offers or whoever the top executive feels will treat the company "right." Once the decision to divest is made, the company should decide what it is worth on the basis of its tangible assets, its management, its products, and all intangible assets. Skillful companies wishing to sell will select buyers as carefully as merger-bound companies seek acquisitions. They will evaluate offers in the same way they would consider a merger: they will discount the future flow of funds to the present value. Effective managers-owners choose to sell out or terminate business under three conditions: (1) when they perceive their firm is unable to compete, (2) when they wish to leave the business for personal reasons such as retirement, and (3) when they perceive that there are better opportunities for them in another business.

To conclude this section, we can state that the final negotiations between the buyer and the seller are what ultimately set the true financing value.

Legal Considerations in Mergers [15]

Another question to consider is, Will the relevant government body approve the merger? In the United States, the Antitrust Division of the Justice Department might get involved. And many states also try to prevent mergers. In the United Kingdom and the Common Market, there are monopolies commissions. Canada also has a "watchdog" to examine multinational mergers. However, in the United States the political climate is such that mergers are less likely to be challenged by the Justice Department. New guidelines include the Herfindahl index, which is used to determine market concentration—the percentage of the market held by each seller is squared, and the totals are added. If the index is less than 1000 after a proposed merger, the merger is not likely to be challenged. But antitrust laws are still used by competitors, as happened when some Big Eight accounting firms challenged the merger attempt between Price Waterhouse and Deloitte Haskins.

Many firms try to protect themselves from a takeover by increasing the percentage of shareholders who must agree to a merger. Some firms change corporate bylaws to prohibit partial tender offers; others use "poison pills" that raise the costs of a takeover to a buyer, or use "shark repellents," "white knights," or proxy fights to fend off unwanted suitors.[1] This can lead to lengthy legal battles.

---

[1]A "poison pill" is a tactic designed to make a company very expensive to take over. For example, shareholders (other than a hostile bidder) might be given certain rights or warrants to trade stock which, if exercised, would cost a takeover bidder substantial sums. "Shark repellents" include such things as requirements that a raider pay an equivalent price for all shares, or "supermajority" rules requiring control of substantial shares. A "white knight" is a friendly bidder who will buy a firm under more favorable conditions (to the existing managers) than are being offered by a hostile bidder, hence "rescuing" the firm from a takeover.

Tax laws are also relevant to the financial aspects of mergers. Some observers claim that changes in tax laws have given firms more reasons to use acquisitions than to expand internally.

Finally, legal considerations may prompt takeover attempts. For example, a flurry of moves by tobacco companies to acquire other firms in the mid-1980s (Philip Morris–General Foods; Reynolds–Nabisco; American Brands holding company) was seen as an attempt to use diversification as a way to protect corporate earnings against potential liability from smoking-related lawsuits.

Human Considerations in Mergers [16]

Although some of the literature might give you the impression that merging is primarily a financial question, more evidence is arising that the human factors are crucial to a merger's success.

For example, Ebeid examined one form of mergers: the cash tender offer. He studied 117 cash tender offers over a 17-year period. He really was interested in seeing whether there were more successful ways of bidding, better stock market times, and more advantages with regard to certain similar factors. One of his major conclusions was that a merger offer was most likely to fail when the management of the target firm opposed the merger offer. This made the merger more costly if it was consummated. But more important, a merger was less likely to be consummated. Mergers were more likely to be opposed because the executives involved didn't like each other than for financial reasons. Similar findings arose from other research.

The psychologist Levinson has studied merger failures. His major conclusion was as follows:

There are many reasons for merger, including psychological reasons. Many mergers have been disappointing in their results and painful to their participants. These failures have been attributed largely to rational financial, economic, and managerial problems.

I contend that some psychological reasons not only constitute a major, if unrecognized, force toward merger, but that they also constitute the basis for many, if not most, disappointments and failures. At least those that have turned sour, or have the most dangerous potential for turning sour, are those that arise out of some neurotic wish to become big by voraciously gobbling up others, or out of obsolescence. Such mergers flounder because of the hidden assumptions the senior partner makes, and the condescending attitudes toward the junior organization which then follow. These result in efforts at manipulation and control which, in turn, produce (*a*) disillusionment and the feeling of desertion on the part of the junior organization, and (*b*) disappointment, loss of personnel, and declining profitability for the dominant organization.

Many of the human problems develop when the executives of the acquiring company seem threatening to the target company, and the executives of the target company fear that they will have to leave the firm. In sum, human relationships may be a much more significant factor in a successful merger than most analysts realize. Indeed, the takeover battle involving Allied Corp., United Technologies, Martin Marietta, and Bendix in 1982 was characterized in *The Wall Street Journal* as follows:

This epic struggle involving four big companies and more than four bankers and hordes of lawyers is not about economics, is not about using assets wisely, is not about economic growth. It's a struggle between a few ambitious men using public companies, in which they own a fractional share, for their own gain.

Aside from the premerger problems noted here, postmerger human difficulties often arise. Corporate cultures and policies can clash, as happened at IBM and Rolm. Top managers who are being counted on may leave the firm, as happened at Kodak after a recent acquisition. And the structure of relationships between the partners can create problems. Such implementation problems should be considered before a merger but often are not. Thus, after a merger is consummated, such pitfalls as low executive involvement in the postmerger integration process, breakdowns in reporting and control relationships between parent and acquired firm, changes in responsibility within the parent for overseeing the acquired firm's activities, and the attitudes of personnel in both firms can significantly affect the degree of success of the venture.

Effectiveness of Mergers [17]

Earlier we cited some research about the performance of firms that merged, particularly conglomerate or unrelated mergers. At this point, let us reflect on whether a merger or acquisition is an effective strategy. There are four perspectives to consider: namely, those of the stockholders, the executives, the employees, and society.

Exhibit 7.20 summarizes the findings of the research. In general, society and the noted stockholders lose because the earnings growth rate tends to decline as compared to when the two separate firms' growth rates existed. Stockholders of the acquired firm can gain in the short run if their stock is bid up and they sell it at high prices.

The acquiring company's executives tend to gain, since salaries tend to be correlated with corporate size. The acquired company's executives usually suffer a disadvantage in that they lose status, authority, and often their jobs. Sometimes the acquired company executive gains when the acquirer seeks specific executives for their experience or if a quid pro quo exists—that is, in exchange for "friendliness" in the takeover, certain executives of the acquired company are "taken care of." But employees of the acquired firms usually lose out, even in "friendly" takeovers. The results for the unrelated acquired firm (friendly or unfriendly) vary for this reason and depend on how the acquiring firm structures the acquisition. If it remains autonomous, the acquired firm can be better off if its performance was lagging and it receives an inflow of capital.

If the new management reorganizes or brings in new management, employees can lose. Society usually loses, since with a lower earnings rate, fewer job opportunities are created. Antitrust legislation also exists to prevent too much concentration of economic and political power, which can lead to higher prices or less variety in the products and services offered.

Can mergers ever be a benefit? Yes. As indicated, not all mergers lead to dire conditions. If the acquired firm is worth saving (is effective but may be failing for lack of financial support), a merger may save it. For instance, a firm might have a great product or service, but it lacks

EXHIBIT 7.20   EFFECTIVENESS OF MERGERS (EXTERNAL EXPANSION STRATEGIES)

	Related		Unrelated	
	Acquiring firm	Acquired firm	Acquiring firm	Acquired firm
Stockholders	Usually negative	Can be positive	More negative than toward a related merger	Varies
Executives	Positive	Negative	Less positive than toward a related merger	Varies
Employees	Neutral to negative	Usually negative	Neutral	Varies
Society	Negative	Varies	Negative	Varies

financial expertise or some other skill, and a bank can't or won't provide it. An acquiring company could provide needed resources. And some mergers may create specialized firms which are stronger and more productive. Some research concludes that firms that were taken over should have been taken over because their rates of return were low at the time, and therefore the stockholders stood to benefit from the takeovers. Low rates of return may be due to incompetent management and stockholders may gain from takeovers. This is the argument used by corporate raiders. Still, many firms deserve to fail. Banks and venture-capital firms can usually help out if a firm is viable.

Hermann offers an explanation for why conglomerate and nonconglomerate postmerger profitability may vary. He examined acquisitions criteria used in 96 companies. While both types of firms sought good returns, the major distinctions were that conglomerate acquirers wanted existing managers to continue, and they were more interested in the reduction of earnings risk than in increases in earnings per se. However, a large body of research suggests that diversifications have not reduced systematic risk and that risk spreading can be done better by individual stockholders than by corporations.

In sum, we believe that there are substantial disadvantages to mergers as compared with internal approaches for expansion or related diversification. We will cite two other studies to support this conclusion.

Gutman studied 150 firms in the period 1954–1958. The 53 firms whose growth rate was twice the rate of growth in gross national product in that time acted thus:

1 They chose industries whose sales increased more rapidly than the growth of the economy as a whole.

2 They chose the subsectors and submarkets within each industry which grew more rapidly than the industry and *concentrated* on these sectors, not on the whole industry.

3 They entered the subsectors earlier than competing firms.

4 More than 80 percent of the growth firms introduced new products for current customers.

5 About 40 percent introduced new products for new consumers. Only about 7 percent tried to sell existing products to new customers.

6 Two-thirds of the high-growth firms sold their products outside the United States.

7 Those whose growth included mergers did not outperform those that grew entirely by means of internal methods.

Recognizing that these firms operated in a favorable economic climate, let's look at Clifford's study. Clifford examined over 1800 companies between 1970 and 1975 in 32 different industries. During the 1974–1975 recession, he distinguished top performers as companies whose earnings per share grew by 33 percent on the average, while the earnings per share of the other firms declined by 23 percent annually. What were the main characteristics of these firms?

1 They focused unremittingly on limiting financial risk by maintaining price discipline, which they accomplished by
   a Pricing ahead of inflation.
   b Reducing response time to price changes.
   c Pricing to value.
2 They emphasized cost discipline to maintain margins.
3 They emphasized financial control over balance sheet items.
4 They emphasized product discipline by
   a Exploiting winners and getting rid of losers.
   b Redesigning products.
   c Raising the hurdle required for margins on new-product entry.

5 They stayed close to their market niche by
  a Building on the strength of their core product lines.
  b Avoiding excessive diversification.
  c Finding specialized niches for opportunity.

The main characteristic of the losers in this period was that they aggressively diversified, paying little heed to the markets or to the complex structures being developed. Many mergers fail because of the following ''seven sins,'' which seem to be committed too often by those making acquisitions:

1 Paying too much
2 Assuming a boom market won't crash
3 Leaping before looking
4 Straying too far afield
5 Swallowing something too big
6 Marrying disparate corporate cultures
7 Counting on key managers staying

The findings of these studies and others provide the basic support for many of our propositions in Chapters 6 and 7.

REFERENCES

[1] Internal Expansion Strategies

Buaron, R.: ''How to Win the Market Share Game? Try Changing the Rules,'' *Management Review* (January 1981), pp. 8–17.

Buzzell, R. D., and F. D. Wiersema: ''Successful Share-Building Strategies,'' *Harvard Business Review* (January–February 1981), pp. 135–144.

Chakravarthy, B. S.: ''Strategic Self-Renewal,'' *Academy of Management Review,* vol. 9 (1984), pp. 536–547.

Kotler, P.: *Marketing Management* (Englewood Cliffs, N.J.: Prentice-Hall, 1976).

Kuhn, R. L.: *Mid-Sized Firms: Success Strategies and Methodologies* (New York: Praeger, 1982).

[2] Internal Stability Strategies

Hambrick, D. C., and I. MacMillan: ''Efficiency of Product R&D in Business Units,'' working paper SC #41, Graduate School of Business, Columbia University, New York, 1985.

Tavel, C.: *The Third Industrial Age: Strategy for Business Survival* (Homewood, Ill.: Dow Jones–Irwin, 1975).

[3] Internal Retrenchment Strategies

Hambrick, D. C.: ''Turnaround Strategies,'' in W. O. Guth (ed.), *Handbook of Strategic Management* (New York: Warren, Gorham and Lamont, 1986).

O'Neil, H. M.: ''Turnaround and Recovery: What Strategy Do You Need?'' *Long Range Planning,* forthcoming.

————: ''An Analysis of the Turnaround Strategy in Commercial Banking,'' *Journal of Management Studies* (March 1986), pp. 165–188.

''Steel Jacks Up Its Productivity,'' *Business Week,* Oct. 12, 1981, pp. 84–86.

[4] External Retrenchment Strategies

"B of A is Becoming the Incredible Shrinking Bank," *Business Week,* Jan. 27, 1986, pp. 78–84.

Dobrzynski, J. H.: "Inside a School for Dealmakers," *Business Week,* July 7, 1986, pp. 82–85.

Norman, J. R.: "What the Raiders Did to Phillips Petroleum," *Business Week,* Mar. 17, 1986, pp. 102–103.

Porter, M.: "Please Note Location of Nearest Exit," *California Management Review,* vol. 19 (Winter 1976), pp. 21–33.

[5] Endgame Strategies

Glaberson, W. B.: "The Bankruptcy Laws May Be Stretching too Far," *Business Week,* May 9, 1983, p. 33.

Harrigan, K. R.: "Strategic Planning for Endgame," *Long Range Planning* (December 1982), pp. 45–48.

———: "The Effect of Exit Barriers upon Strategic Flexibility," *Strategic Management Journal,* vol. 1 (1980), pp. 165–176.

———: *Strategies for Declining Businesses* (Lexington, Mass.: Heath, 1980).

———: "Exit Decisions in Mature Industries," *Academy of Management Journal,* vol. 25 (1982), pp. 707–732.

[6] External Expansion Strategies

Davidson, K. M.: *Megamergers* (Cambridge, Mass.: Ballinger, 1985).

———: "Looking at the Strategic Impact of Mergers," *The Journal of Business Strategy,* vol. 2 (1981), pp. 13–22.

"The Great Takeover Binge," *Business Week,* Nov. 14, 1977, pp. 176–184.

Greenwald, J.: "Let's Make a Deal," *Time,* Dec. 23, 1985.

Steiner, P. O.: *Mergers, Motives, Effects, Policies* (Ann Arbor: University of Michigan Press, 1975).

Note: Also see [12] to [17] below.

[7] Internal and External Combination Strategies

Bresser, R. K., and J. E. Harl: "Collective Strategy: Vice or Virtue?" *Academy of Management Review,* vol. 11 (1986), pp. 408–427.

"GM Moves into a New Era," *Business Week,* July 16, 1984, pp. 48–54.

Gullander, S.: "Joint Ventures and Corporate Strategy," *Columbia Journal of World Business,* vol. 11 (Spring 1976), pp. 104–114.

Harrigan, K. R.: "Integrating Parent and Child: Successful Joint Ventures," working paper SC #44, Graduate School of Business, Columbia University, New York, 1985.

———: "Coalition Strategies: A Framework for Joint Ventures," *Academy of Management Proceedings* (1985), pp. 16–19.

Helm, L.: "AT&T's European Invasion Finally Gains the High Ground," *Business Week,* Mar. 10, 1986, pp. 44–46.

"How Supron's Buyers Would Slice the Pie," *Business Week,* Mar. 1, 1982, pp. 23–24.

"What Made Apple Seek Safety in Numbers," *Business Week,* Mar. 12, 1984, p. 42.

"When Joint Ventures Come Unglued," *Business Week,* Apr. 26, 1982, p. 100.

[8] Related and Unrelated Strategies

Biggadike, R.: "The Risky Business of Diversification," *Harvard Business Review* (May–June 1979), pp. 103–111.

Harris, P. R.: "The Seven Uses of Synergy," *The Journal of Business Strategy,* vol. 2 (Fall 1981), pp. 59–66.

Leontiades, M.: *Strategies for Diversification and Change* (Boston: Little, Brown, 1980).

Steiner, G. A.: *Strategic Planning: What Every Manager Must Know* (New York: Free Press, 1979).

Note: Also see [12] below.

[9] Horizontal and Vertical Strategies

Bower, J. L.: "Simple Economic Tools for Strategic Analysis" (Boston: Intercollegiate Case Clearing House, No. 9-373-094, 1972).

"A Duel of Giants in the Dishwasher Market," *Business Week,* Oct. 9, 1978.

Dunkin, A.: "How Department Stores Plan to Get the Registers Ringing Again," *Business Week,* Nov. 18, 1985, pp. 66–67.

Harrigan, K. R.: "Vertical Integration and Corporate Strategy," *Academy of Management Journal,* vol. 28 (1985), pp. 397–425.

Jauch, L. R., and H. Wilson: "A Strategic Perspective for Make or Buy Decisions," *Long Range Planning* (December 1979), pp. 56–61.

Williamson, O.: "The Vertical Integration of Production: Market Failure Considerations," *American Economic Review* (May 1971), pp. 112–123.

[10] Active and Passive Strategies

Ansoff, W. I., and J. M. Stewart: "Strategies for Technology Based Business," *Harvard Business Review,* vol. 45 (November–December 1967), pp. 71–83.

Hambrick, D. C.: "Some Tests of the Effectiveness and Functional Attributes of Miles and Snow's Strategic Types," *Academy of Management Journal,* vol. 26 (1983), pp. 5–26.

Harrigan, K. R.: *Strategic Flexibility* (Lexington, Mass.: Lexington, 1984).

MacMillan, I.: "Preemptive Strategies," *Journal of Business Strategy,* vol. 4 (Fall 1983), pp. 16–26.

———, M. L. McCaffery, and G. V. Wijk: "Competitors' Responses to Easily Imitated New Products," *Strategic Management Journal,* vol. 6 (1985), pp. 75–86.

Miles, R. E., and C. C. Snow: *Organizational Strategy: Structure and Process* (New York: McGraw-Hill, 1978).

Windsor, D., and F. D. Tuggle: "The Role of Technological Innovation in a Firm's Strategy," *Human Systems Management,* vol. 2 (1981), pp. 306–315.

[11] International Strategy Alternatives

Ball, D. A., and W. H. McCullock, Jr.: *International Business* (Plano, Tex.: Business Publications, 1985).

Davidson, W. H.: *Global Strategic Management* (New York: Wiley, 1982).

[12] Diversification Strategies

Berg, N.: "What's Different about Conglomerate Management," *Harvard Business Review* (November–December 1969), pp. 112–120.

Bettis, R. A., and W. K. Hall: "Diversification Strategy, Accounting Determined Risks, and Accounting Determined Return," *Academy of Management Journal,* vol. 25 (1982), pp. 254–264.

Carter, J. R.: "In Search of Synergy: A Structure-Performance Test," *Review of Economics and Statistics,* vol. 59 (August 1977), pp. 279–289.

Drucker, P.: *Management* (New York: Harper & Row, 1974), chaps. 56, 57.

Kitching, J.: "Why Do Mergers Miscarry?" *Harvard Business Review,* vol. 45 (November–December 1967), pp. 84–101.

Pitts, R. A., and H. D. Hopkins: "Firm Diversity: Conceptualization and Measurement," *Academy of Management Review,* vol. 7 (1982), pp. 620–629.

Rumelt, R.: *Strategy, Structure, and Economic Performance* (Boston: Harvard Business School, 1974).

Steiner, G.: "How and Why to Diversify," *California Management Review,* vol. 6 (Summer 1964), pp. 11–18.

Note: Also see [17] below.

[13] How and Why Companies Merge

Ansoff, H. I., et al.: *Acquisition of U.S. Manufacturing Firms 1946–1965* (Nashville, Tenn.: Vanderbilt University Press, 1971).

Birley, S.: "Acquisition Strategy or Acquisition Anarchy?" *Journal of General Management,* vol. 3 (Spring 1976), pp. 67–73.

Kusewitt, J. B.: "An Exploratory Study of Strategic Acquisition Factors Relating to Performance," *Strategic Management Journal,* vol. 6 (1985), pp. 151–170.

"Poppa Tests His Golden Touch," *Business Week,* Jan. 18, 1982, p. 102.

Rockwell, W., Jr.: "How to Acquire a Company," *Harvard Business Review,* vol. 46 (September–October 1968).

[14] Financial Factors in Mergers

Aplin, R. D., et al.: *Capital Investment Analysis: Using Discounted Cash Flows* (Columbus, Oh.: Grid, 1977).

Cameron, D.: "Appraising Companies for Acquisition," *Long Range Planning,* vol. 10 (August 1977), pp. 21–28.

"Deciding How Much a Company Is Worth," *The Wall Street Journal,* Mar. 19, 1981, p. 29.

"Exxon Agrees to Sell Oil and Gas Assets in Libya to Government for Net Book Value," *The Wall Street Journal,* Jan. 6, 1982, p. 4.

[15] Legal Factors in Mergers

"A Bid to Stop Big Eight Firms from Getting Bigger," *Business Week,* Nov. 19, 1984, p. 49.

Blustein, P., and D. Rotbart: "Court Rulings on U.S. Steel and Mobil May Change Merger Game," *The Wall Street Journal* (Jan. 7, 1982), p. 19.

Clark, L. H., Jr.: "Are the Corporate Raiders Really White Knights?" *The Wall Street Journal,* July 16, 1986, p. 33.

Ehrlich, E., and J. R. Norman: "Getting Rough with the Raiders," *Business Week,* May 27, 1985, pp. 34–36.

Hertzberg, D.: "Poison Pill Defense No Longer Is Seen as a Sure Way to Repel Hostile Suitors," *The Wall Street Journal,* Oct. 31, 1985, p. 3.

"Justice Overhauls Its Rules on Mergers," *Business Week,* June 8, 1981, p. 55.

"A Loosening of Merger Rules," *Business Week,* May 17, 1982, p. 120.

"Specialist Says Mergers Zooming under Reagan," Associated Press release, July 15, 1981.

Taylor, R. E.: "U. S. Eases Merger Guidelines, Allowing Somewhat More Concentrated Markets," *The Wall Street Journal,* June 15, 1982, p. 3.

[16] Human Factors in Mergers

"Atex: An Editing System That Isn't Printing Out for Kodak," *Business Week,* Sept. 3, 1984, pp. 70–72.

Ebeid, F. J.: "Tender Offers: Characteristics Affecting Their Success," *Mergers and Acquisitions* (1976), pp. 21–30.

"IBM and Rolm Cope with Prenuptial Jitters," *Business Week,* Nov. 19, 1984, pp. 166–170.

Levinson, H.: "A Psychologist Diagnoses Merger Failures," *Harvard Business Review* (March–April 1970).

"The 4 Horsemen," *The Wall Street Journal,* Sept. 24, 1982, p. 1.

[17] Effectiveness of Mergers

Clifford, D. K.: "Thriving in a Recession," *Harvard Business Review* (July–August 1977), pp. 56–65.

Gutmann, P. M.: "Strategies for Growth," *California Management Review,* vol. 6 (1964), pp. 81–86.

Herrmann, A. L.: "Corporate Acquisition Criteria: A Study," *Mergers and Acquisitions,* vol. 8 (Summer 1973), pp. 4–11.

"How the New Merger Boom Will Benefit the Economy," *Business Week,* Feb. 6, 1984, pp. 42–54.

Ingrassia, L.: "Employees at Acquired Firms Find White Knights Often Unfriendly," *The Wall Street Journal,* July 7, 1982, p. 21.

O'Hanlon, T.: "Swinging Cats among the Conglomerate Dogs," *Fortune* (June 1975), pp. 114–119ff.

Prokesch, S. E., and W. J. Powell: "Do Mergers Really Work?" *Business Week,* June 3, 1985, pp. 88–91.

Samuels, J. M.: "The Success or Failure of Mergers and Takeovers," in J. M. Samuels (ed.), *Readings on Mergers and Takeovers* (New York: St. Martin's, 1972).

Note: Also see [12] above.

STRATEGIC CHOICE

CHAPTER OUTLINE

STRATEGIC CHOICE

OBJECTIVES

- To review the importance of strategic choice
- To learn how to focus on a few of the many alternatives
- To learn how managers make a choice among alternatives
- To learn some tools and prescriptions to aid in making the choice

INTRODUCTION [1]

Chapter 8 completes the three-chapter unit on choice of strategy, as Exhibit 8.1 indicates. That is, when the analyses of environmental and internal conditions (ETOP and SAP) are completed, potential strategies are considered. These include stability, expansion, retrenchment, a combination, and some strategic variation of these generic strategies. All the while, the strategists are asking themselves the crucial questions: What are our objectives? Are these being met by our strategy? By the business definition we've chosen? Will they be met in the future? In other words, the gap between expected and ideal outcomes is examined vis-à-vis the alternatives being considered. If the gap is negligible, a stability strategy is likely, and the process shifts to better implementation. If the gap is large and important, a new strategy is necessary.

Strategic choice is the decision to select from among the alternatives the strategy which will best meet the enterprise's objectives. The decision involves focusing on a few alternatives, considering the selection factors, evaluating the alternatives against these criteria, and making the actual choice.

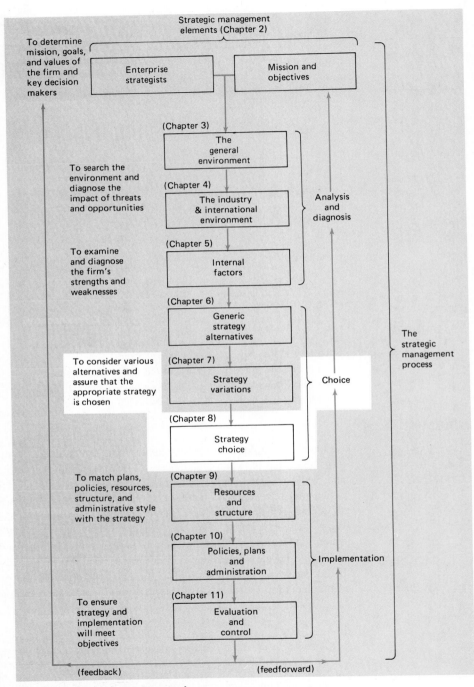

Strategic management
elements (Chapter 2)

To determine
mission, goals,
and values of
the firm and
key decision
makers

| Enterprise strategists | Mission and objectives |

(Chapter 3)
The
general
environment

To search the
environment and
diagnose the
impact of threats
and opportunities

(Chapter 4)
The industry
& international
environment

Analysis
and
diagnosis

To examine
and diagnose
the firm's
strengths and
weaknesses

(Chapter 5)
Internal
factors

(Chapter 6)
Generic
strategy
alternatives

To consider various
alternatives and
assure that the
appropriate strategy
is chosen

(Chapter 7)
Strategy
variations

Choice

(Chapter 8)
Strategy
choice

The
strategic
management
process

To match plans,
policies, resources,
structure, and
administrative style
with the strategy

(Chapter 9)
Resources
and
structure

(Chapter 10)
Policies, plans
and
administration

Implementation

To ensure
strategy and
implementation
will meet
objectives

(Chapter 11)
Evaluation
and
control

(feedback)   (feedforward)

EXHIBIT 8.1 **A model of strategic management.**

Since strategic choice is a decision, all the things which were said in Chapters 1 and 2 about decision making apply to this decision. Remember that *descriptively*, managerial intuition and politics play a role. These pressures will constrain the choice process. *Prescriptively*, rational analytical models should aid the process of decision making.

We begin this chapter with a blending of these views. We suggest that the set of alternatives to choose from can be narrowed to a more manageable list. Then we discuss some prescriptive approaches to choosing from these alternatives. Next we discuss some of the managerial factors which constrain these "rational" models. Finally, we suggest an approach which attempts to integrate these perspectives to aid strategic decision making, and we conclude with a discussion of the need for contingency strategies in the choice process.

FOCUSING THE ALTERNATIVES FOR SELECTION [2]

If you reconsider Exhibit 7.1, you are immediately faced with a huge number of possible alternatives from which strategists can choose. Normative decision theorists will tell you to "consider all the alternatives." This is impossible because:

1 You do not know all of them and cannot know all of them. You are not omniscient. Using our simple classification system with only two sides to each dimension yields over 23,000 different possible strategies, to say nothing of various ways they can be implemented.

2 It would take too much time and energy. And so, if the situation appears to need moderate changes, you will probably consider a few strategies that make minor adjustments to your present strategy. If the situation appears to be serious or quite different from situations you have faced before, you will consider creative, brainstorming alternatives.

3 The managerial perception of risk, dependence, past strategy, and power will limit the number of alternatives considered. This will be discussed later in the chapter.

Why consider strategic alternatives at all? Why not just accept that first strategy that pops into the decision maker's mind? This is the opposite of the normative statement: Consider *all* alternatives. Our answer is that few decision makers are so bright or intuitive that they wouldn't be better off considering a few alternatives. Trying to generate several reasonable alternatives allows a systematic comparison of their trade-offs, strengths, and weaknesses. Thus the choice is likely to be a much better choice.

STRATEGIC CHOICE PROCESSES

Where do "reasonable" strategic alternatives come from? You do not consider alternatives out in the wild blue yonder. You begin to consider alternatives which you know about or which are proposed by subordinates, which you think will work, and which do not involve major breaks with the past (unless you have clearly diagnosed the situation as desperate).

So the alternatives you consider are incremental steps, usually small incremental steps, from your present pace and business. This is why a clear business definition is useful. You can choose alternatives by trying to work forward from the present to the future state and see how you can get there from where you are now.

This approach is implied by the use of the gap analysis described in Chapter 2. The purpose of strategic choice is to accomplish objectives. A strategy can be chosen to close the gaps in objectives. We think that the size of the gap, the nature of the gap, and whether or not management believes that it can be reduced will strongly influence the choice of some alternatives over others. For example, if the gap is narrow (small, not very important, or hard to reduce), certain dimensions are more likely to be considered than others, as shown in Exhibit 8.2. Thus, if the gap is perceived to be narrow, a stability choice is more likely; some pace changes may occur internally, but they are likely to be passive responses to minor external changes. For example, Mr. Coffee might offer a $5 rebate to maintain its market share.

Of course, the nature of the gap is also relevant. If the gap is large due to past or expected poor performance, retrenchment is more likely. If it is large due to expected environmental opportunity, expansion is more likely. If the gap is due to internal weakness, retrenchment is more likely. In Chapter 7, Exhibit 7.6 gives an example of a ''negative'' gap leading to retrenchment. Other case studies have illustrated ''positive'' gaps or opportunities leading to expansion.

We have no evidence to support these prescriptions. They are ways that we think managers can narrow and focus their choice of alternatives. The gap analysis in Exhibit 8.2 also reflects our ideas about the influences of managerial perceptions, which we will discuss later in this chapter and which we discussed earlier in Chapter 2. You can combine this analysis with our propositions in the summaries for Chapters 6 and 7 to construct a matrix showing which strategies to pursue under which circumstances.

We would like to carry you one step further in a prescription of how this sort of analysis can be combined with the diagnoses of internal and external conditions to narrow the list of alternatives. The gaps, of course, are coming from perceptions of desired and expected goal attainment along with the diagnoses. So the factors associated with your assessments of the decision makers, their values, their perceptions, and so on, play a role here, as discussed in Chapter 2. But as discussed in Chapters

EXHIBIT 8.2 **Perceived gaps, strategic conditions, and alternative dimensions.**

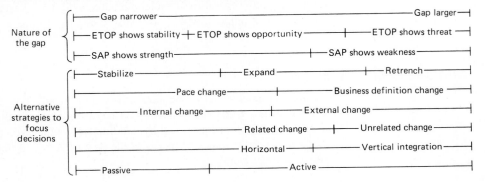

EXHIBIT 8.3 STRATEGIC SITUATION 1: IMPLEMENT STABILITY

ETOP		SAP	
Socioeconomic	0	Marketing and distribution	+
Technological	0	R&D and engineering	0
Competitor	0	Production and operations management	−
Supplier	0	Corporate resources and personnel	0
Government	0	Finance and accounting	0

3 to 5, the generation of reasonable alternatives can also be accomplished through a systematic comparison of the ETOP and SAP in relation to the gap. Exhibits 8.3 to 8.5 give several examples of this. There are a large number of possible combinations, but these three lead to suggestions of several strategies.

Exhibit 8.3 is for a firm that is likely to be considering a grand strategy of stability. It has its pluses and minuses, but the ETOP shows no significant threats or opportunities. The performance gap is likely to be small. This firm would probably focus on improving productivity in manufacturing. It would emphasize passive internal modifications. (See Proposition 6.1.)

In the case of Exhibit 8.4, however, the conditions may be right for expansion. Economic factors are positive, and perhaps the government is expected to deregulate the industry. This may open up the threat of new-competitor entry. However, the firm's marketing strengths may allow it to meet this threat or move into new markets which were closed to it before. To do this, however, the firm may be required to use its financial strength to improve the weaknesses in operations that exist, since it had not served these markets previously. Thus the timing of the firm's expansion may not allow the firm to fully take advantage of all the potential available immediately. The alternatives will focus on market and function dimensions; active approaches may be taken here, with perhaps external alternatives considered to improve production (e.g., a joint venture, subcontracting, or a merger with a manufacturer) if timing is important. If timing is less critical, internal development of operations may be considered more appropriate.

Suppose that the same ETOP is matched with another firm whose performance gap is negative, and the SAP indicates serious weaknesses as a result of deregulation. The firm represented by Exhibit 8.5 faces a situation in which a retrenchment may be useful for improving its performance (or increasing its chances for survival). For instance, this firm may be unable to compete effectively against new arrivals in many

EXHIBIT 8.4 STRATEGIC SITUATION 2: IMPLEMENT EXPANSION

ETOP		SAP	
Socioeconomic	+	Marketing and distribution	+
Technological	0	R&D and engineering	0
Competitor	−	Production and operations management	−
Supplier	0	Corporate resources and personnel	0
Government	+	Finance and accounting	+

EXHIBIT 8.5   STRATEGIC SITUATION 3: IMPLEMENT RETRENCHMENT

ETOP		SAP	
Socioeconomic	+	Marketing and distribution	−
Technological	0	R&D and engineering	0
Competitor	−	Production and operations management	0
Supplier	0	Corporate resources and personnel	+
Government	+	Finance and accounting	−

of its markets. One alternative is to abandon some territories so that resources can be focused where strength exists. The firm may be passive in some market areas, active in others. Good personnel in certain areas may be pooled to use advantages there and become more efficient.

Note that these comparisons are subject to substantial interpretation by the strategists doing the analysis. For instance, in view of the marketing strengths in strategic situation 1, more venturesome strategists may consider attempts to expand the market share as opposed to stability. In situation 2, less risk-oriented managers may believe that the operations weaknesses are severe enough to limit expansion; external possibilities are not considered. They may be satisfied to get whatever improvements come from their environment without making any changes in the pace or business definition. In effect, the gap in performance outcomes is not perceived to be so great as to require change. Optimistic or risk-oriented managers may look at situation 3 and believe that their strong personnel will be able to overcome marketing problems and take advantage of opportunities which will ultimately improve the firm's financial condition. They may not change the business definition, but they may try to increase employee output and effort to expand the pace of operations.

Thus perceptions of the environment and the internal need for change vary from case to case. This is clearly seen in the watch industry, where Japanese firms are pursuing rapid expansion while the Swiss and some American firms are trying turnarounds or retrenchments.

Of course, in situations where environmental factors are decidedly threats and where executives perceive weakness, a total liquidation may yield the greatest performance outcome possible. For example, Bayuk Cigars decided to liquidate for $28 million after declining a takeover offer of $15 million. It assumed that the industry was in a steady decline and that it "would have to become increasingly competitive to maintain its position."

Thus the search methods and diagnostic approaches described in Chapters 3 to 5 can be used by the strategists to search for strategic alternatives. Once a problem is perceived as a gap, the decision maker begins to generate alternative solutions. The decision maker can choose routine methods to generate alternatives (for example, looking at what the organization did before in such cases) or creative approaches. The latter can include such techniques as brainstorming. The alternatives may also be proposed from below. In this case, we would suggest that several others be generated for comparison and discussion on the basis of the gaps, ETOP, and SAP. But the ETOP and SAP are likely to show more than one threat or opportunity and weakness or strength within each sector or factor. This would suggest that a number of options are usually available to a firm. But the approach suggested here can reduce the alternatives to a relatively limited number of reasonable possibilities.

Once a reasonable number of alternatives are generated, managers will have to decide which one should be used to close the gap. A number of "rational" approaches have been developed to guide the manager in this decision situation. Our next section outlines some prescriptions for the choice.

PRESCRIPTIONS FOR THE STRATEGIC CHOICE [3]

Aside from our prescriptions to guide the strategic choice in Exhibit 8.2, a number of techniques have been developed to help managers make strategic choices. The Boston Consulting Group product portfolio matrix shown in Exhibit 8.6 is one of the best-known examples.

Stars are products or SBUs which are growing rapidly, need large amounts of cash to maintain their position, and are leaders in their business and generate large amounts of cash. Cash flows will be roughly in balance (in and out) and represent the best opportunities for expansion.

Cash cows are low-growth, high-market-share products or divisions. Because of their market share, they have low costs and generate cash. Since growth is slow, reinvestment costs are low. Cash cows provide funds for overhead, dividends, and investment for the rest of the firm. They are the foundation of the firm, and stability is prescribed.

Dogs are products or divisions with low growth and a low market share and there-

EXHIBIT 8.6   **The business portfolio or growth-share matrix.**
(B. Hedley, "Strategy and the Business Portfolio," Long Range Planning [February 1977], p. 10.)

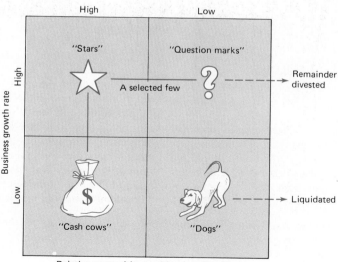

fore poor profits. They may need cash to survive. The dogs should be minimized by means of divestment or liquidation.

Question marks are high-growth, low-market-share products or divisions. Their conditions are the worst, for their cash needs are high, but cash generation is low. These, if left in this cell, become "cash traps." Since growth is high, market share should be easier to get for them than for dogs. So question marks should be converted into stars, then later into cash cows. This strategy will lead to a cash drain in the short run but positive flow in the long run. The other option is divestment.

The basic assumption of BCG analysis is that a high market share for faster-growing products or services normally leads to high profitability and stable competitive situations. On the other hand, if a firm has products in slowly growing markets, increasing the market share is normally costly. So the BCG recommends taking cash out of these businesses, even at the expense of market share. A firm will choose a strategy of expansion in market share if it has competitive strength, the funds to shift, and the estimated costs of gaining the share. The goal of all this is to have a balanced portfolio of products or divisions. This technique, then, usually applies to multiple-SBU firms making decisions about what SBUs should be expanded, maintained, or retrenched.

As Exhibit 8.7 suggests, firms can't always follow these prescriptions and might do better pursuing some other strategy. Further, some of the BCG prescriptions could ultimately lead to a lack of innovative product introductions, since, by definition, new products start as dogs or question marks.

EXHIBIT 8.7   ONE WAY TO CURE A DOG

General Host was a diversified firm with a problem. Its Cudahy Foods subsidiary represented 61 percent of sales but just 18 percent of its 24.2-million-dollar operating profit in 1979. The prescription for this SBU clearly called for selling off this operation and replacing it with high-margin expanding businesses to close the large performance gap. Clearly, Cudahy was a "dog," with a low market share in a mature market. The only dilemma in applying this formula was that the old-line meat-packing firm, faced with price and efficiency problems, couldn't find buyers for its business. How many firms want dog businesses?

General Host decided on a different tack—a forward vertical integration. It purchased Hickory Farms, the largest specialty food store in the United States. In addition to selling other products such as cheese, Hickory Farms sells processed meats from fresh cuts, which provide higher margins. Hickory Farms will be expected to switch purchases from archrival Armour & Co. and be supplied by Cudahy.

The purchase fit Host's strategy to reduce past diversification and reshape the business around specialty retailing and food processing. Over the last 6 years Host divested itself of a number of properties and added canned hams, frozen Italian foods, the Hot Sam pretzel shops, and Lil General convenience stores. Now Hickory Farms is seen as a centerpiece for internal expansion by Host.

Still, by getting rid of Cudahy, Host could put itself into a substantially higher return-on-equity position. But the president has set lower goals for returns because he does not expect to be able to sell Cudahy. Thus while some strategic prescriptions may be beneficial, barriers to implementation may be in the way. In this case, one way around the barriers was via vertical integration and a change in the size of the perceived gap due to the belief that nothing else could be done about it.

Source: Adapted from "General Host: Vertical Integration to Save a Subsidiary It Couldn't Sell," *Business Week,* Jan. 19, 1981, pp. 103–104.

Hofer criticizes the BCG approach because it inadequately represents new businesses in new industries that are just starting to grow and he offers an extension of BCG analysis that remedies that inadequacy. Hofer analyzed businesses in terms of their competitive position and stage of product-market evolution. Exhibit 8.8 outlines his suggestions. Circles represent the sizes of the industries involved. The pie wedges within the circles represent the market shares of the firms. He suggests that these be plotted for present and future businesses. Strategic choices based upon such a scheme might follow the logic below:

1 Business A appears to be an emerging star, and thus a target for excess resource allocation—especially to strengthen its competitive position in light of its strong market share.

2 Business B might follow much the same scenario as business A, but corporate resource allocation would probably be contingent on determining why B has been unable to obtain a higher market share, given its strong competitive position, and on the presentation of sound plans to rectify that deficiency.

3 Businesses C and D are question marks, though C is a strong candidate for retrenchment.

4 Business F and, to a lesser extent, business E represent cash cows within the corporate portfolio and would be key targets for corporate resource generation.

5 Business G appears to be an emerging dog, managed to generate short-term cash flow and targeted for eventual divestiture or liquidation.

EXHIBIT 8.8 **Product-market evolution portfolio matrix.**
(Adapted from C. Hofer, Conceptual Constructs for Formulating Corporate and Business Strategies [Boston: Intercollegiate Case Clearing House, no. 9-378-754, 1977], p. 3.)

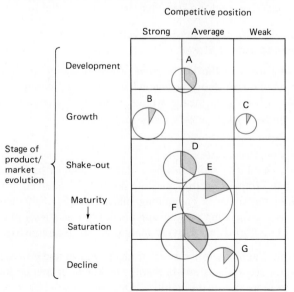

Hofer's approach can be a useful tool to aid the thinking of strategists in multiple-SBU firms who are considering alternative strategies for their various SBUs. Even within a single SBU with multiple products and/or markets, the approach can aid the thinking about the desired portfolio.

Another approach is to apply financial analysis to various alternatives. For example, what is the value added to the firm by pursuing a given alternative? Discounted cash flow methods could be applied to the expected financial outcomes of an alternative to assess the viability of a given strategic action or to determine whether an SBU is a dog or a star.

Finally, a new tool seems to be on the horizon. Spreadsheets, data bases, and various computerized management science techniques have been around for a while. But there is a new breed of decision-making programs designed to help executives use their personal computers in developing strategies and making qualitative decisions. Such programs allow the user to organize and evaluate a vast array of data and information. But they are, of course, only as good as the assumptions and criteria plugged in.

These programs have had an impact on the way business executives approach decision making. Many have in common the idea of setting up a matrix with internal factors (SAP) and external factors (ETOP) on the axes. Analyzing the matrix according to a prescribed formula leads to a recommendation of a particular strategic choice or choices. We suggest, however, that "choice by formula" should not and cannot replace strategic thinking. Computer programs can aid your thinking, but they should not replace the decision maker, especially since there is evidence that growth rates (the usually desired objective) do not always correlate with profitability. In effect, we agree with Seeger, who argues against oversimplification by suggesting: "We must remember that the dogs may be friendly, the cows may need a bull now and then to remain productive, and the stars may have burned themselves out."

Prescriptions for Choice of Business-Level Strategy

Most of the tools in the last section primarily apply to corporate or multiple-SBU activities as opposed to business-level strategies. Although some of those models are applicable to individual business units, there are other ways in which business-level strategic choices can be approached.

Expansion Prescriptions [4]

A large amount of work has been done to suggest how managers can accomplish growth goals. Expansion strategies are normally conceived as the best way to do this, and usually the focus is on gaining market shares. But there are other interesting suggestions for choosing various approaches to this strategy. One set of prescriptions (based on U.S. firms in relatively mature and stable industries) is as follows:

1 The first guide is to focus on products whose markets are growing. Never focus on slow-growth products unless there is technical or market know-how you can learn to apply to more promising markets. Or enter these markets only if you can produce a much simpler, much cheaper product when the dominant firms are not innovating.

2 It is better to be a big fish in a small pond if the pond (market segment) is growing. Get out of small nongrowth markets. Don't be a follower.

3 Choose feasible markets to compete in. Don't try to compete against larger firms with strong brand loyalty (in consumer goods) or large firms with strong financial capacity (in industrial goods).

4 In growing markets, it is easier to expand by combining a push for primary demand with a secondary demand push. Small firms with limited cash resources and a small market share should ignore primary demand. A major emphasis on secondary demand is optional when the objective is a limited market share in a very competitive market.

The strongest proponents of the value of market share come from the Profit Impact of Market Strategies (PIMS) studies. Essentially, PIMS is a cross-sectional study of the strategic experience of over 100 firms operating with over 1000 SBUs. The information has been gathered from the businesses in the form of about 100 pieces of data supplied by them in a standardized format. From this data models are generated using regression equations for ROI and cash flows.

Early results indicated that market share, investment intensity (ratio of total investment to sales), and product quality were the most important determinants of pretax return on investment. The PIMS studies also provided some interesting insights into the reasons for the link between market share and profitability. The results point to economies of scale and opportunities for vertical integration. High-share businesses (those with a share greater than 40 percent) tended to make rather than buy and tended to own their own distribution facilities.

The importance of economies of scale is also supported by the learning curve concept. The Boston Consulting Group (BCG) studied 24 products in seven industries longitudinally. Its focus was on the cost-to-price relationship which results from the experience curve (unit cost decreases as volume doubles). Its results suggest the following:

1 Get the biggest market share you can as early as you can.

2 Initially, the products will be sold below cost, but then as volume builds, the cost must be lowered. With the largest market share, this should be easy to do.

3 Hold costs and prices down. This will reduce the attractiveness of entrance to the market.

The prescriptions from these studies would seem to suggest that increasing the market share is almost a goal unto itself rather than one strategy to attain other objectives. Yet a variety of studies question whether this is so.

A study of the internal expansion of firms in the maturity or saturation stage of the product life cycle is that of Fruhan. He studied the relationship between market share and profitability and found that it was *not* economically worthwhile to increase the market share *if* (1) extremely heavy financial resources were required, (2) the expansion might have to be stopped before the firm reached its market share target, or (3) regulatory agencies might restrict the firm's activities. Other studies suggest that cash flow benefits may come at the expense of profits. As a result, some low-share SBUs may contribute cash to the overall firm even if, by themselves, they are not making high profit contributions.

Woo and Cooper, using the PIMS data, challenge the basic conclusion that a high market share is mandatory for a favorable ROI. Of particular importance is their finding that some successful low-share firms operate in very stable environments, characterized by high purchase frequency, high value added, and large numbers of competitors. What is interesting is that most of these firms sold *standardized industrial components and supplies*.

This key finding calls into question the validity of the product life cycle (PLC) concept as commonly understood, and on which much of the ''market share imperative'' is grounded. Indeed, Rink and Swan have reviewed the product life cycle research and concluded that ''investigators have focused almost exclusively . . . on nondurable consumer goods. Industrial items, as well as major product changes, have been nearly ignored.'' Moreover, they have identified *eleven* other PLC patterns which various researchers have uncovered for different kinds of products.

What do we conclude from these studies and their critics? Basically, we think that increasing the market share is not the only strategy alternative worth exploring. Even the supporters of the market share imperative point out that the explanation for the market/share-profitability relationship may reflect an underlying factor called ''quality of management''; that is, those who control costs get productivity from employees, and so on. So the implementation of a strategy may be just as important as the strategy itself.

A different matrix of alternatives, shown as Exhibit 8.9, suggests another way in which other factors can be brought into the choice process, particularly for the single-SBU situation. Here the idea is to consider a selected set of alternatives (changing the pace or business definition in products and/or markets) in relation to the ETOP, the SAP, and managerial values such as risk.

Position ①, expansion in the pace of present product and market development, would be prescribed if the SAP shows strength in the present products, the ETOP shows continued market opportunity, and management has relative low risk orientations. This penetration strategy also implies that there is a relatively small gap between desired and expected performance.

EXHIBIT 8.9   **A matrix of typical expansion alternatives.**

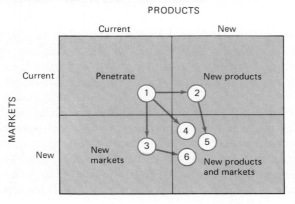

If the ETOP suggests that the market is saturated or that stronger competition or other threats to the market exist and the SAP shows weakness in distribution or strength in product development, position ② might be prescribed. This could be related or unrelated product development depending on the size of the gap or risk preferences. Other dimensions (such as internal or external expansion) might depend on financial strengths or timing; for instance, if speed is desired, a joint venture or merger could be used depending on financial ability.

Position ③ is similar to ②, but the SAP might suggest adding markets for existing products due to greater distribution strengths but production or product development weaknesses.

Position ④ is the combination alternative of simultaneously adding new products and new markets. The ETOP should indicate greater opportunity, the SAP should show greater strength, the gap should be larger, and the managers will probably have a higher risk propensity.

Positions ⑤ and ⑥ suggest that the long-range plan is to ultimately add new products and markets. But this is arrived at by a sequential combination of adding products (or markets) first, followed by markets (or products). In this case, strengths and opportunities are assumed to be as before, but new ones will be developed in the process. As opposed to their attitude in 4, then, managers are willing to accept a longer time horizon and are less risk-seeking. Exhibit 8.10 describes a firm which chose this approach.

EXHIBIT 8.10   STEADY AS SHE GOES

One way to reduce a performance gap is to set modest goals and work to achieve them slowly but surely. In the 1970s, President Duval of Hammermill Paper sought "average paper-company profitability," which itself was achieved with a struggle. Internal weaknesses at Hammermill included poor economies of scale, high costs of transportation between pulp and paper mills, antiquated equipment, and the inability to finance expensive new machinery.

Duval began in 1971 to make a gradual change in Hammermill's products and businesses to exploit its strengths and minimize its weaknesses. He decided to stick to specialized niches in papermaking with sustained expansion through acquisitions, primarily in paper distribution. He grabbed an early lead in making paper for photocopying and dropped products such as commodity-grade papers which Hammermill could not make efficiently. Duval also moved into the distribution of hardwood lumber. Paper distribution and lumber distribution are fragmented businesses where Hammermill can be a major competitor.

Hammermill's slow but steady progress has resulted in an improvement of financial position such that more aggressive expansion is about to start. Rebuilding of old equipment began a few years ago, and plans are to double the output of an Alabama pulp mill to help growth in its paper niches and to add the ability to export pulp as well. This will add risk, but opportunities are seen to be large. Duval's new goal is to raise Hammermill to the top quarter of the industry.

Hammermill has made steady progress, given its willingness to accept a moderate goal. It progressed by sequencing its moves over a period of time so that eventually it added new products and markets without taking large risks, given its internal weaknesses. Having accomplished this, it is changing its goal and risk orientations, largely due to moving from a position of greater strength.

Source: Adapted from "Hammermill Paper: A Slow but Sure Shift of Products and Businesses," *Business Week,* Jan. 11, 1982, pp. 119–120.

At any position, of course, retrenchment is possible if a firm moves in the opposite direction from the one that is suggested. Again, this would be prescribed depending on the gaps, the ETOP, the SAP, and risk orientation.

Retrenchment Prescriptions [5]

While less popular than expansions, there are some suggestions for when and how to choose retrenchment. A few of these suggestions follow. Break-even analysis can guide the turnaround approach, as shown in Exhibit 8.11.

Hofer's recommendations are to liquidate or sell assets if sales are less than a third of the break-even point. If sales are 30 to 60 percent of the break-even point, it is suggested that the firm increase revenues by focusing on existing products with price cutting, more advertising, or a more direct sales effort. In the 60 to 80 percent range, combinations of asset reduction, revenue increasing, and cost cutting are suggested. If the firm is below but close to break-even point and has high direct labor or fixed expenses, short-term decreases in costs are probably most effective.

Before a turnaround is attempted, the magnitude of the problem should be assessed. For instance, if the probability of bankruptcy is high or too much time is needed, the effort may be futile. (Beaver, Altman, and Wilcox have proposed several techniques which they claim can be used to predict failures well in advance.) In addition, for the turnaround strategies to be effective, existing managers will most likely have to be

EXHIBIT 8.11   **Deciding on the type of turnaround strategy to follow.**
(C. W. Hofer, "Turnaround Strategies," Reprinted by permission from The Journal of Business Strategy, vol. 1, no. 1 [Summer 1980]. Copyright © 1980 by Warren, Gorham and Lamont, Inc., 210 South St., Boston, Mass. All rights reserved.)

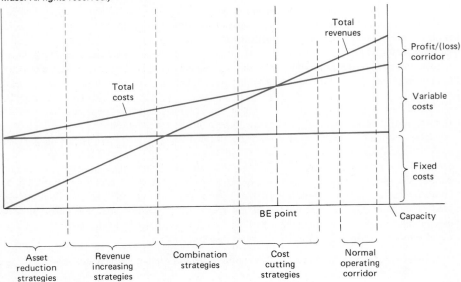

replaced, since they will be committed to existing strategy or will perhaps be seen as having to admit "defeat," leading to a belief that they are ineffective managers.

Empirical tests of these recommendations on turnaround with the PIMS data suggest that asset reductions occur with low levels of capacity utilization. Selective product-market pruning was pursued by businesses with high-capacity usage. In effect, this supports Hofer's prescriptions.

Bibeault studied the turnaround of 81 firms. He found that 88 percent of the firms used divestment of some sort during the course of the turnaround. And 37 percent shut down entire facilities. Sixty-six percent of these firms decreased staffing levels in selected functional departments, and 92 percent pursued a strategy of eliminating losers from the product line. An interesting sidelight is that the average turnaround cycle took 7½ years from the recognition of a problem to the resumption of healthy expansion. He also listed the following reasons for why a turnaround became necessary: bad luck (1 percent), external factors (23 percent), combination of internal and external factors (24 percent), internal problems (52 percent). In other words, sins of commission on the part of managers seems to be what gets most firms into trouble.

Retrenchments combined with other strategies have been prescribed for many old-line basic industries in the United States and elsewhere (mining, steel, etc.). Plants are outmoded and hobbled by low productivity, interest costs and low returns have precluded investment in new equipment, overcapacity has contributed to high overhead costs, labor rates are high, and markets must be fought for against new foreign competitors who aren't bothered by many of the domestic ills. To solve these problems, many firms will retrench by selling out or merging with cash-rich partners in an attempt to modernize factories. Others will abandon some traditional product lines to concentrate on specific market niches. A few will seek diversification to support a declining business; this strategy is riskier than others due to high expenditures and diversion of assets and attention from basic problems. Many firms pursue a strategy of stability, which has the effect of milking the business. Under these circumstances, prescriptions often heard include:

1 Reduce vertical integration; this reduces capital requirements, increases flexibility, and focuses effort. Disintegration means abandoning some functions. For example, many automakers now buy parts or even whole vehicles for sale in domestic markets.

2 Increase effective use of capital equipment. Add shifts or justify deviations from full use of capacity. Restructure labor contracts to add flexibility. (The steel industry has tried this with moderate success.)

3 Simplify product lines to become the low-cost producer in a specific niche to build competitive advantage. The trade-off here must be carefully considered vis-à-vis the risk of reducing volume, resulting in less effective use of capacity.

The dilemma is that managers are too often committed to past strategy, or signals of problems go unrecognized, and retrenchments are perceived as "failures." It took over 8 years, for example, for Mobil to finally admit that its acquisition of Montgomery Ward was a mistake. In 1985, a $500 million write-down was taken and Ward was retrenched in size, most likely to prepare it for a potential sale if Mobil could find a buyer.

Stability Prescriptions [6]

Business executives hear more and more people telling them to "stick to your knitting" and "do what you do best." This is sound advice, as long as it is done intentionally, with awareness of the alternatives. In an era of megamergers, firms see the allure of diversification, and too frequently follow the "ready, fire, aim" sequence. Yet more firms are following the recommendations of getting back to basics.

In some cases, the strategy is defensive—protection against loss. In others, gains are expected from an offensive strategy—using basic existing skills in new ways. While the business definition is stability, the prescription is pace expansion. Exhibit 8.12 provides an example of this.

Combination Prescriptions [7]

Our final section on prescriptions for business-level strategic choice deals with various combinations of alternatives for different settings. One set of prescriptions for SBU strategies comes from the Japanese director of McKinsey & Co.—Kenichi Ohmae. His argument is that you can classify businesses into four categories on the basis of the demand patterns of products, and he has prescribed strategies for each type.

• *Replacement demand.* This category includes industries where demand fluctuates in direct response to current economic conditions. Consumer durables (e.g., refrig-

---

EXHIBIT 8.12   A CHANGE OF PACE FOR AIRLINES

While airlines have diversified for some time, many into the hotel business, recent moves have been made to achieve greater productivity out of existing assets by sticking to what they know best. The "diversifications" now being considered involve developing revenues by finding new uses for the people, skills, and equipment basic to the central business of airline operations.

United Airlines takes in about $15 million a year training flight crews for other airlines. They formed a new subsidiary to go after a 5-year $250 million contract to train crews for the Air Force's C-5 transport program.

Computerized reservations systems in use by American, United, TWA, and Delta are currently leased to travel agents. In time, these systems are expected to be leased to cable companies for home computer users.

Firms which have grounded some fleets will lease those out and try to get more business servicing aircraft. Contract maintenance and ground-handling work are expected to allow some airlines to increase their pace of activities.

In effect, firms are being creative about the use of huge asset bases to develop new revenues where low costs are possible and the synergistic links are already in place. Such stable business definition together with expanded pace of functions allows for improved performance.

Source: Adapted from "New Airlines are Diversifying by Sticking to What They Know Best," *Business Week,* May 7, 1984, pp. 70–72.

erators) is one example. In this situation, Ohmae prescribes lowering the break-even point by increasing the ratio of variable costs to fixed costs.

* *International displacement*. Markets in this category have not experienced any major fluctuations, and there is no fear that demand will disappear. But costs have increased rapidly in the businesses. Examples are petrochemicals, textiles, and shoes. Top management here must seriously consider vertical integration, backward or forward, to gain some control over costs.

* *New economic order*. A heavy drop in demand for this set of businesses resulted from the price of oil. Producers of oil tankers and the electric power industry are in this category. In this situation diversification or retrenchment is mandatory.

* *Accelerated life cycle*. Industries here include those where product life cycles are progressively shorter. The microelectronics industry has required businesses which use its components to rapidly introduce new products to keep up with demand. To cope with this environment, firms need active and aggressive strategies with some restructuring of operations. For instance, R&D needs redirection into applied research, and some companies are shifting control over R&D to production or marketing. Others are using computer-aided design and manufacturing (CAD and CAM) to slash the turnaround time of product development. Markets must be treated as if they were part of the fashion industry.

Yet another strategy, one which gained favor in the mid 1980s, is private ownership through a leveraged buyout (LBO). This is prescribed for those who may wish to avoid a takeover, or for those who want control to manage for the long-term rather than the short-term expectations of Wall Street. Private ownership, however, when done with the LBO, is often a temporary resting place in a sequential combination strategy involving eventual sale of the firm. Otherwise, the new owners, usually the managers themselves and institutional investors, may not cash in. In effect, the business is being run to support finance, rather than finance being used to support the business. Hence, plans or decisions at functional levels may lead to strategic directions unintended by top-level executives.

In conclusion, different combinations of strategies are appropriate for differing circumstances. Thus decision makers must rely on the strategic processes of analysis and diagnosis, and then, with the appropriate prescriptions and tools in hand, ask several key questions when considering whether to accept each given alternative:

* Is the strategy responsive to the external environment?
* Does it involve a sustainable competitive advantage?
* How does it relate to other firm strategies?
* Does it provide adequate flexibility for the business and the firm?
* Is it consistent with the business mission and long term objectives?
* Is it feasible to implement?

The set of questions listed above is discussed in more detail in Chapter 11, since the final choice of a strategy should also take into account its plan for implementation. But, while we support the various analyses which can aid strategic thinking, we want you to be aware of another set of factors which influences and constrains managers as they make strategic choices. Our next section describes those factors.

DESCRIPTIONS OF MANAGERIAL CHOICE FACTORS [8]

While a planning staff or line executives often do provide analyses of various alternatives, there is some question as to whether executives pay much attention to them. And it is often difficult to pinpoint when the choice among alternatives is actually made. Many executives do not appear to use sophisticated decision-making techniques. They frequently rely on assumptions and the collective wisdom of the group. As a consensus begins to emerge, the CEO seems to ratify the emerging position. After an apparent pause, the consensus position with some modifications becomes policy. Thus policies or positions evolve from a process of creeping commitment.

You may ask, Why isn't a more rational process used? Is this any way to run a business? Why don't executives use the models and support data for ''better'' decision making?

Some argue that top management has little confidence in the data to support alternatives. Some techniques are unfamiliar, or the models are not trusted. Realistic assumptions may be violated in an attempt to find ''optimal'' solutions to problems. Besides, anyone can manipulate numbers to support a position. Others explain that power politics are involved, and model builders are weak power holders or naive politicians. But the creeping commitment approach to strategic decision making can also be traced to certain other managerial factors which limit the choice of alternatives. Remember our discussion in Chapter 1 about how several forces are at work in decision situations.

As a result of these forces a limited number of alternatives and consequences are considered. Positions are likely to be similar to or extensions of existing strategy. Executives will select targets of opportunity. Where events such as retirement, a scheduled review, or a major external threat or opportunity force a change, executives may take the opportunity to install modified programs, policies, and procedures. So let's examine the managerial factors that are crucial to an understanding of strategic choice.

Strategic choices are influenced by four managerial selection factors: (1) perceptions of external dependence, (2) attitudes toward risk, (3) awareness of past enterprise strategies, and (4) power relationships.

Managerial Perceptions of External Dependence [9]

Firms do not exist in isolation from the external environment. They depend on other units for their survival and prosperity. These units include the owners, competitors, customers, government, and community, as was made clear in Chapters 3 and 4. The more dependent a firm is on these other units, the less flexible its strategic choices can be. Thus the range of strategic choices is limited. Strategic choices result from interactions of the firm with its environment. Thus strategic choices are outcomes that are negotiated as various parties maneuver to reach their objectives. Propositions in the summary specify how.

These dependencies can be objectively measured. A stockholder who controls 51 percent of the voting stock clearly has more power, and the firm is more dependent on the wishes of the majority owner. But in addition to the objective phenomena there are the *subjective* views of the decision makers. Facts do not speak for themselves. Executives interpret these facts. Two firms of equal power (objectively measured in the environment) can be headed by executives who see the firms differently, as discussed in Chapter 2. One firm's executives can see their firm as weak and dependent, the other as strong (relatively). Thus the weights they put on the strategic alternatives can vary. For instance, a strategy requiring lower prices to gain market share may be rejected if managers believe that their union has the power to gain greater wages and benefits than their competitors offer.

Exhibit 8.13 suggests that diversification strategies are often used to reduce dependence. Of course, captive-company strategies have the opposite effect—they increase one firm's dependence on another.

Dependence does not necessarily always restrict alternatives, however. For instance, a firm can pursue active strategies to reduce dependence rather than allow it to dominate the choice process. For example, consider dependence on a supplier. If the gap in performance is unsatisfactory due to this factor, several approaches can be followed—new suppliers can be found, the firm can vertically integrate to make the input, or the firm can enter into a joint venture or merger with a supplier to reduce the dependence. Thus dependence (as well as the other factors to be discussed) is, in reality, only a constraint to the extent that it is *perceived* to be a limiting factor; i.e., managers believe that these variables are beyond their influence or control. In some cases they will be. But many managers sometimes limit themselves and their strategies unnecessarily.

EXHIBIT 8.13   WHAT'S BAD FOR GM IS GOOD FOR LOF?

For 50 years, the top priority at Libbey-Owens-Ford was to manufacture glass for General Motors. But in 1980, the first manufacturing executive in the history of LOF was appointed to head the glass operations, and the firm has restructured to make the automotive original-equipment group only one of three distinct business units. These changes and others revolve around a goal of "ending the days when General Motors drove what we built, where we built it, and what kinds of plants we built it in."

The nature of glass making leads to highly volume-sensitive production runs. So the relationship with GM made good sense when LOF could gear to GM's relatively predictable needs. However, GM's troubles and shifts in supply practices (giving more business to competitor PPG) has made the LOF dependence on GM's business a problem. Glass operations lost $6 million in 1980 due to huge plant operating costs and the lack of a diversified customer base to pick up the slack left by GM's decreased purchases.

The overdependence on GM in the past has also created problems for LOF in the sense that it must now catch up in the potentially lucrative architectural glass area. The irony is that the company invented insulating glass in the 1930s, but it tended to downplay the market for this product while it leaned on GM. Now the company is forced to diversify in markets due to its past dependence. Even diversification away from glass is not out of the question. While diversification is usually justified on the basis of spreading risk, it may also be a strategy of choice to reduce dependence. The dependence itself at LOF was a factor which influenced its choices in the past and now affects its future strategy.

Source: Adapted from "Turning Around Libbey-Owens," *Business Week,* Aug. 10, 1981, pp. 94–96.

Managerial Attitudes toward Risk [10]

As we suggested in our discussion of Exhibit 8.12, another factor influencing strategic choice is how much risk the firm, its stockholders, and management can tolerate. Managerial attitudes toward risk vary from comfort if not exhilaration with high risk to strong risk aversion. The risk averters probably view the firm as very weak and will accept only defensive strategies with very low risks. Three polar conditions with regard to risk can be conceived (Exhibit 8.14).

Risk attitudes can change, and vary by industry volatility and environmental uncertainty. In very volatile industries, executives must be capable of absorbing greater amounts of risk; otherwise, they cannot function. Exhibit 8.15 provides an interesting example of how risk attitudes can change and are important to strategic thinking in volatile conditions. You should also be aware that there is need to assess the "downside" risk of failure against the "upside" gains of opportunity from the environment. If executives' perception of an opportunity is overly optimistic, the risk of the opportunity may be overlooked.

Risk attitudes can also vary on the basis of the internal conditions discussed in Chapter 5. How much are you "gambling" on any given project? If you are betting the whole company, your risk assessment may be different than if you have little to lose. Similarly, how much can you afford to lose? And is it your money? Are you financially strong or weak? Past success also has an influence on the perception of risk. If you've won recently, you may see less risk in the future. (Also see Exhibit 8.10.)

Thus assessing the manager's perception of risk will help you understand the potential acceptability of a given strategic option. Insofar as they influence managerial attitudes, the risk attitudes of the managers and stockholders will eliminate some strategic alternatives and highlight others. For instance, if risk is being balanced, managers are likely to pursue stability in major parts of the business with expansion in one or a few SBUs. Note that this balanced risk position is assumed by the BCG product portfolio prescriptions. But if risk is seen as necessary, firms are likely to eliminate stability as a viable option.

EXHIBIT 8.14 RISK ATTITUDES AND STRATEGIC CHOICE

Managerial attitudes toward risk	Probable choice filters	Probable strategies
1 Risk is necessary for success. Optimistic; high risk leads to reward.	1 High-risk projects are acceptable or desirable.	1 Expansion
2 Risk is a fact of life, and some risk is acceptable.	2 Balance high-risk choices with low-risk choices (bet hedging).	2 Combination
3 High risk is what destroys enterprises; it needs to be minimized.	3 Risk aversion: risky projects are rejected.	3 Stability

EXHIBIT 8.15   THE RISKS AT GOULD

William T. Ylvisaker, chairman of Gould Inc., was initially successful in his first decade of running the company. Under his direction Gould went from being a battery maker with $100 million in sales to being a $2 billion conglomerate. The strategy responsible for this success was that of acquiring "old-line manufacturing companies and jolting their performance with stringent financial controls."

But later this strategy seemed to no longer be working for Gould Inc. Its profit margin had been slipping since it peaked in 1977. This caused Ylvisaker to take a look at the direction in which he was leading the company. Before the strategic change, Gould was into four businesses—electrical, battery, industrial, and electronics. Because Ylvisaker believes that electronics has by far the greatest growth opportunities in the 1980s and 1990s, that is where he decided to concentrate Gould's investment. This "strategic about-face" was also influenced by the high multiples that investors usually give high-technology stocks.

Gould has been divesting itself of many of its divisions and subsidiaries engaged in the electrical, battery, and industrial fields while at the same time investing more in the electronics field. It has also been emphasizing more internal growth in the future, and its acquisition targets will be smaller companies. (Gould acquired more than a few large companies in the past.) Eventually, Gould hopes to be the prime supplier for the systems that would provide not only computers and controllers but also electronic sensors, imaging equipment, and other products.

The move to electronics involves enormous risks. Gould is a newcomer to the fast-changing, highly competitive environment of high-tech products. This type of climate usually requires aggressive risk taking with less top-management control. Ylvisaker was known as a heavy-handed executive whose authoritarian manner led to high management turnover. But the setbacks Gould experienced apparently forced him to reconsider the direction and management style. It appears as though Ylvisaker does not intend to let his past management practices get in the way of his new strategy. He has completely reshaped the Gould hierarchy and has promised to take a less forceful role in managing the day-to-day affairs of operating units. Evidence already shows that top managers are listening more to middle managers than they did in the past.

Clearly, the risk implications and approaches to managing this business have changed along with the strategy.

Source: Adapted from "Bill Ylvisaker Bets His Company on Electronics," *Business Week,* Nov. 2, 1981, pp. 86–92.

Managerial Awareness of Past Strategies [11]

This factor's influence can be summarized very simply: Past strategies are the beginning point of strategic choice and may eliminate some strategic choices as a result. Recall that in the gap analysis it is assumed that the beginning point of the process is the present position of the firm. From there, the initial question is, Will the continuation of our strategy lead to the expected attainment of desired objectives? To the extent that the gap is small, past strategy will be continued. And to the extent that managers are committed to continuing the strategy, other alternatives will be ignored.

The corporate cultures built up to implement the past strategy also get in the way of choosing a new strategy. A corporate culture is the "personality" of an organization. As our chapters on implementation will suggest, changing a corporate culture represents new patterns of resource allocation, norms, communication, leadership, rewards, and so on. Such changes will be needed if a new strategy diverges very far from the past one. It is often difficult and time-consuming to change corporate culture, as GM found out when it acquired EDS. The cultures clashed, leading to some problems for both. Even the past image of the firm may make a new strategy harder to implement. For example, in attempts to avoid costly errors, conservative executives at Owens-Illinois moved cautiously into new product lines extending beyond their basic glass-container operation. But customers and analysts still believe that ''the company's heart belongs to glass.'' So the values of management and perceptions of the firm from *outside* as a result of long commitments to past strategy are preventing the firm from moving rapidly into new growth areas. The same problem affected Dow Chemicals. In the era of the Vietnamese war, Dow was attacked as a supplier of napalm and Agent Orange. In 1985, Dow began a $50 million 5-year ad campaign featuring idealistic students and recent graduates working for Dow to make the world a better place. Executives believed this new image was needed to support a strategy aimed at reducing dependence upon commodity chemicals and a stronger move into consumer product lines.

On the basis of research into the longitudinal choice process in 10 separate businesses, Mintzberg and several colleagues have concluded that past strategic choices strongly influenced later strategic choices. Specifically, they found that:

1 The present strategy evolves from a past strategy developed by a powerful leader. This unique and tightly integrated strategy (a gestalt strategy) is a major influence on later strategic choices.

2 Then the strategy becomes programmed. And the bureaucratic momentum keeps it going. Mintzberg calls this the ''push-pull phenomenon'': the original decision maker pushes the strategy, and then lower management pulls it along.

3 When this strategy begins to fail because of changing conditions, the enterprise grafts new substrategies onto the old and only later gropes for a new strategy.

4 As the environment changes even more, the enterprise begins to consider seriously the retrenchment, combination, or expansion strategies previously suggested by a few executives who were ignored at the time.

In many cases strategic change is more likely to come about when new managers are brought in from outside the firm. Strategic change is less likely if new executives are promoted from within, and it is least likely if the existing management group remains in power. An interesting example of this was given in Exhibit 2.7. Thus the selection of a new CEO is one area where the board of directors has a particularly strong influence if strategic change is necessary or desirable. And policies of promotion from within need to be carefully considered. If insiders are committed to past strategy, policies, and people, and changes are needed, a new strategy may require an outsider.

Finally, expectations about the product life cycle can influence strategic change. In this sense, past strategic decisions regarding product introductions may influence future decisions. Where the firm's major products or services are in the product-service life cycle determines how critical it is if the firm is too heavily tied to past strategies. In the earlier stages, it is less critical if the firm is tied to historical strategies than in the maturity or decline stages.

Managerial Power Relationships [12]

Those with experience know that power relationships are a key reality in organizational life. In many enterprises, if the top manager begins to advocate one alternative, the decision to choose it is soon unanimous. In others, cliques develop, and if one clique begins to support an alternative, the other opposes it.

Sometimes personalities get involved in the strategic choice: whom the boss likes and respects has a lot to do with which strategic choice is made. And sometimes if "mistakes" are made, the powerful can shift the blame to lower-level executives. The power of the CEO plays a role, too. The manager's personal goals, ambitions, values, and motivation can affect the choice of strategy. If the CEO is very powerful, the organization's goals become intertwined with personal goals in the choice process.

No one doubts that power and politics influence decisions, including strategic decisions. The question is, How often is power a crucial factor in these decisions? We concluded in Chapter 1 that the significance of the decision, the degree of time pressure, the degree of uncertainty, and the style of the decision maker influence the relative roles of analytical, political, and intuitive approaches to decision making. Also, recall that external political pressures are involved in determining the trade-offs among objectives, as discussed in Chapters 1 and 2.

From all that we've said up to now, we would conclude that politics always plays a role, even to the extent of influencing objectives (criteria for choice) and the way the analytical approaches are used and interpreted. And politics seems to be an *over-riding* factor in the strategic choice process about 30 percent of the time according to Mintzberg. Thus it is important to analyze the values and goals of the key managers, as we indicated in Chapter 2, if you are to understand the probability of acceptance of a given strategic recommendation.

Analytical purists no doubt abhor such a recommendation. Should the descriptions about *what is done* lead to a prescription that this is the way it *ought to be done?* Perhaps not. Yet from a pragmatic perspective, the strategy chosen has little chance of success unless it will be implemented effectively; it is unlikely that a politically unacceptable strategy will be carried out successfully.

Remember that the power of lower-level participants also plays a role in strategic decision making. We discussed this in Chapter 2 also. Of course, top managers make the strategic choices. But earlier strategic choices made by their subordinates limit the strategic choices usually considered. Recall that subordinates can choose to hold or submit proposals for strategic change. They can also influence the choice by providing analytical data which support their proposal (as opposed to "unbiased" pros and cons). Moreover, strategies must be implemented, and lower-level managers have the power to make or break a strategy.

Decision makers also have opportunities to select the type of environment within which they will operate. In large organizations, they have the power to influence conditions prevailing in the environments in which they are operating. According to Child, threats and opportunities perceived in the environment, which affect strategic choice, "are functions of the power exercised by decision makers in the light of ideological values." Hence, power constrains choices on the one hand, and expands choice opportunities on the other. The key is the *perception* of power and its use.

Finally, in Europe and elsewhere, sometimes workers' councils have an influence on strategic choices. This is true in Sweden, for example. Volvo's decision to open a plant in the United States was influenced by the demand of the workers' council not to close any operations in Sweden. German workers' councils have had an effect on Volkswagen's strategic choices in shifting its resources. Even in the United States, union leaders are sometimes "elected" to the board of directors. Thus, like the "dependence" variable discussed earlier, the power of "insiders" and "outsiders" can be a strong political influence on the strategic decision. Coalitions develop to influence the formation of objectives *and* strategies.

THE TIME DIMENSION AND STRATEGIC CHOICE [13]

The timing of decisions and time pressures were included among other decision factors we discussed in Chapter 1. We wish to expand on how this factor affects the strategic decision process and the quality of the decision.

The deadlines for making a strategic choice are often set not by the manager but by others. Consider the following strategic choice situation: Firm A (the Raider) offers a merger with a less than ideal set of conditions and a short response date, and it has another potential merger partner waiting if you do not accept now. Firm B (the White Knight) has not decided whether it will give you a merger offer or what conditions it will require. As you can see from this example, sometimes the strategist must make decisions in time frames set by others. In other cases, the strategist has more time to seek alternatives and choose among them.

When time pressures are significant, strategists may be unable to gather enough information or consider an adequate number of alternatives. Time pressures also affect the strategic choice process itself. For example, managers under time pressure put more weight on negative evidence than on positive evidence and consider fewer factors in making decisions.

Of course, these results could differ, depending on the alternatives being considered. For example, several studies indicate the following:

1 In making difficult decisions, managers take longer to select from two good alternatives and two poor ones than from four good alternatives.

2 In making easy decisions, managers take longer to select from four good alternatives than from two good ones and two poor ones.

Perhaps in the first case the job looks difficult when there are four good alternatives, and the managers impulsively pick one, whereas with two bad alternatives they feel competent in rejecting two and take their time choosing one of the remaining two. In the second case they feel capable of deciding that it takes longer to compare four alternatives than two.

Finally, the desire to accomplish certain objectives within a specific time frame will more naturally lead to the choice of some alternative strategies. For instance, expansion through active external approaches (e.g., mergers) may be chosen if the objective is to increase size rapidly. So time pressures and the time dimension influence some strategic choices.

SUMMARY OF THE CHOICE PROCESS [14]

The choice of a strategy is not a routine or easy decision. Strategic choice, like all decisions, is made in the context of the decision maker and the decision situation.

The manager's attitude toward risk and feelings about where the enterprise fits blocks out certain choices from view. Unable to follow the "rational model" of strategic choice because of a lack of ability, the lack of costly information, or fast-changing conditions, the strategist focuses on choices from alternatives which change the status quo by increments.

Exhibit 8.16 is one attempt to explain how the strategist focuses on less than all the possible strategic choices: Imagine that the whole rectangle represents all possible strategies. But the factors discussed earlier eliminate some possible choices. For example, time or resource limitations force us to ignore some possibilities. External dependencies won't allow certain strategies because they are not feasible. Risk aversion is such that other choices are viewed as too risky. Political problems within the firm screen out other choices, and the past strategy is the beginning point of the strategic choice. So these factors screen out many choices. And the strategist looks at and ranks only the new incremental choices within what we call the "choice zone" in Exhibit 8.16. This figure shows the small choice zone that is left after the risky, unfeasible, and unacceptable choices are eliminated. Well, how does the strategist decide within this choice zone?

Integrating Description and Prescription

We started this chapter by suggesting that some dimensions of strategy alternatives were more likely to be considered than others, depending on the size of the gap. Then we suggested that some prescriptive techniques could be used to aid in the choice. But we just finished saying that managerial factors will limit the size of the choice

EXHIBIT 8.16 **Strategic choice given factor overlays.**

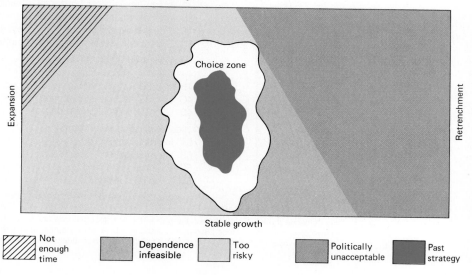

zone. In effect, these factors are what led us to hypothesize that some alternatives are more likely than others.

Now the decision maker is left with a narrower range of alternatives to choose from. But prescription suggests that we apply analytical tools to help us look at more alternatives. We think that the following procedure takes the prescription and description into account and can be used to guide the choice process.

First we begin with the past strategy, as noted in Exhibit 8.17. Note that as you move down the table, the strategies move further away from the past strategy, increase risk, alter dependencies, and probably become more unacceptable politically. So the arrangement of alternatives to be considered, in order, is based on the managerial factors and the size of the gap.

The procedure for making a choice is as follows:

1 First, analytically compare the present strategy with the next incremental change (e.g., 1 versus 2). Use the ETOP and SAP for analysis.

2 If the gap between expected objectives and desired objectives will be met by the present strategy, your choice is made; stay with the former strategy.

3 If the gap is not closed or the next strategy is expected to lead to the attainment of additional important objectives, proceed to compare the next two alternatives.

EXHIBIT 8.17   INCREMENTAL STRATEGIC CHOICE MODEL

Step	Choice*	Strategy
	1	Stable pace
1	2	Stable business definition: active pace expansion
2	3	Combination: passive, stable pace with active product or market change 3A Internal expansion: horizontal, related 3B Internal expansion: horizontal, unrelated 3C External expansion: horizontal, related 3D External expansion: horizontal, unrelated
3	4	Expansion of business definition 4A Like 3A, without stable pace 4B Like 3B, without stable pace 4C Like 3C, without stable pace 4D Like 3D, without stable pace
4	5	Vertical expansion in functions 5A Internal, backward 5B Internal, forward 5C External, backward 5D External, forward
5	6	Repeat of 2 through 5, but retrench rather than expand

*Choose the lowest numbered alternative that will close the gap unless analysis shows that the next alternative down the list will close the gap *and* result in substantially greater performance. If such a higher numbered alternative meets that criterion, proceed with pairwise analysis until gap is closed.

For example, you would start by comparing the stable pace strategy with pace expansion (e.g., increase market share in existing product-market segments). If the objectives (gap) will be achieved by a stable pace, your choice [of (1)] is made, unless expected outcomes will lead to attainment of new objectives which emerge in the analysis. If the latter is true, or if the gap is not closed, then compare the pace expansion with the first approach in step 2. That is, will a related, horizontal, internal expansion in part of the business (such as adding a related new product) combined with stability in the major parts of the business be superior to a pace expansion in terms of closing the gap in objectives? If so, you can then go on to compare 3A with 3B.

This process continues until the perceived gap is no longer significant or the strategist believes that nothing more can be done to close it. Remember that the gap can be created by internal and/or external conditions. In this sense, the SAP and ETOP provide the basic data for comparing pairs of alternatives. Also, remember that multiple objectives will probably require trade-offs due to external pressures. Thus a prescriptive analytical approach is implied but is limited to very few alternatives unless the gap is large. The matrix techniques discussed earlier could also be applied when paired alternatives are considered.

If you consider this procedure carefully, note that *if* the gap is large and due to an environmental opportunity, the comparisons will allow you to continue considering more alternatives, but they increase risk and require greater political acceptability for successful implementation. If the gap is large and due to a threat, you will probably begin considering retrenchments, although threats can be met by expansion. The retrenchment is placed where it is not because it is inferior but because it is considered less politically acceptable.

Also recognize that there is built-in efficiency of analysis. Each alternative step is usually only slightly different from the previous strategy. So the analysis in the previous stage is not wasted and can be used as the basis for considering additional factors if another pairwise comparison is necessary. Thus the time factor in the process is also incorporated in this procedure.

Finally, recognize that not all the possible combinations are considered here. These are our estimates of the more common alternatives. Further, timing (such as with sequential or simultaneous combinations) should be recognized as another factor to be incorporated. In this sense, more developed strategic plans will incorporate contingency strategies. This becomes more complex and deserves a bit more comment.

CONTINGENCY STRATEGIES [15]

The type of planning process used by a firm will influence the generation of alternatives. Strategists will choose to look at one set of strategic alternatives in first-generation planning and multiple sets of alternatives in second-generation or contingency approaches to strategic management. In more developed strategic management, managers also prepare alternative strategies that they can consider if conditions should change. When conditions change sufficiently, consideration of the contingency strategies is triggered. *Business Week* reported the following:

> Instead of relying on a single corporate plan with perhaps one or two variations, top management at more and more companies is now getting a whole battery of contingency plans and alternate scenarios. "We shoot for alternative plans that can deal with either/or eventualities," says the manager in charge of planning at du Pont.
>
> Companies are reviewing and revising plans more frequently in line with changing conditions. Instead of the old 5-year plan that might have been updated annually, plans are often updated quarterly, monthly, or even weekly. Arizona Public Service Company adopted a "dynamic" budget; changes in the price of a prime commodity can kick off a change in the company's cost models and the whole corporate plan may change accordingly. In the end, of course, that puts more pressure on top management, which must operate with an eye to numerous plans instead of being able to follow a single scenario. At Exxon Corporation, for instance, most-probable-case forecasts have been replaced by less definitive "envelopes" that include a range of possibilities. Says one corporate planning manager: "Today you still have to have a game plan. How do you get to that? Top management judgment and intuition. We don't really pin some things down anymore. There's a lot more thrown at the management."

Thus we can add one more dimension to our list of alternative approaches to strategic choice—a programmed or contingency strategy. A *programmed strategy* is a strategy which is planned in such a detailed and integrated way that it is difficult to change it once it has begun to be implemented. A *contingency strategy* requires the planner to choose the preferred strategy given the best estimate of conditions and other strategic choices. But it is flexible enough to allow for shifts in the thrust of the plan when conditions warrant it. In effect, programmed strategies emanate from first-generation planning. Second-generation planning leads to contingency strategy formation.

Programmed planning is suitable for stable environments with people who prefer well-defined roles. The contingency strategy is suitable for unstable environments with people who prefer variety and stimulation. Conditions change rapidly. Since 1972 large firms have chosen their strategies and have also developed plans B, C, and D on a "what if" basis. If the "what if" comes to be, plan C (or B or D) becomes the strategy. This requires that plan A include enough flexibility to allow the firm to recognize the need and then shift if necessary. In effect, the firm must provide for "anticipatory flexibility" with careful environmental monitoring and more frequent evaluation so that it can respond to signals as they become stronger.

Exhibit 8.18 describes a firm which practices contingency planning due to the mere complexity of its situation. Other firms have "disaster" contingency plans for continuing business if a disaster (such as a fire, a flood, a power outage, or the loss of computer records) strikes.

Most writers argue that moderately flexible strategies are the most effective. But those strategies are easier to advocate than pull off. In the period 1973–1974, the environment gave special problems to the auto industry. The energy crisis appeared to dictate a shift to compact cars. General Motors and others began to convert their factories to this strategy about the time that the crisis disappeared from motorists' minds and consumers began buying regular-sized cars again. Consumer preferences

EXHIBIT 8.18   CONTINGENCY PLANNING AT AMF

Attention to detail is a requirement at AMF due to its internal complexity. President York, who has a financial background, is in charge of an executive group that receives 1500 financial statements monthly. Then there are the 74 plants in distant nonurban locations using a variety of manufacturing technologies and distribution systems. After weeks of research, AMF concluded that it had either 41 or 54 SBUs in 1979, depending on how they were counted, organized within two industrial and five leisure-oriented divisions. Add to this the diverse environmental factors affecting these areas, and you have what is called "a killer" of a job managing the company.

In addition to an elaborate financial control system and bimonthly meetings with the seven groups, detailed strategic plans are required for each SBU. By themselves, these add complexity because of products which, at the time, ranged from sportswear (with short product life cycles) to motorcycles (with a long lead time for development calling for 10-year plans).

In 1978, the business units began providing contingency plans to "examine critical risks in achieving proposed profit objectives." The plans also required that steps be implemented if a specified event occurred. Many of the 1979 plans dealt with a possible recession and identified "trigger points" that would signal a need for certain steps. The proposed steps become more serious as successive trigger points are hit.

What is interesting is that many AMF executives don't believe that the contingency plans add much. "Many share the opinion 'Every good manager is thinking contingencies all the time.' " It is speculated, though, that the indifference has much to do with the vigor of their business in the late 1970s. Thus few of the plans faced a need to take the steps called for because the trigger points had not been reached by 1979. Further, the plans seemed to be defensive—the trigger points emphasized threats and defensive steps, not opportunities and offensive moves.

Just 2 years later, though, several contingency plans had been put into effect. The economic recession and inflationary gasoline prices cut heavily into recreational sales. Apparently these triggers were severe enough to lead to rather significant changes in the business definition, and the contingency plans provided some guidance for its direction. In 1981 AMF sold the Head Sports Wear Division and Harley Davidson and discontinued a number of product lines. After these moves, there was almost a 50-50 balance between leisure products and industrial products. Since then, the firm has expanded into electronic and energy-related areas, and it purchased a biotech subsidiary. York claims that the restructuring is designed to allow AMF to "grow some in bad times and a lot in good times."

Sources: Adapted from C. J. Loomis, "AMF Vrooms into Who Knows What," *Fortune,* Apr. 9, 1979, pp. 76–88, and *The New York Times,* Apr. 8, 1981, p. D1.

have changed again, of course. But once the equipment is purchased and plans are drawn to shift to compact cars, it is hard for a capital-intensive firm like General Motors to be flexible. Contingency strategies would have required several fallback strategies when conditions worsened. Moreover, if flexibility turns into vacillation, confusion in the marketplace and within the firm can lead to problems from a lack of consistency over time. So a balance needs to be struck between providing maneuverability and maintaining a thrust toward consistent objectives over time. This is why some firms are pursuing joint ventures, subcontracting, and "network" organizations—they add flexibility.

CHOOSING INTERNATIONAL STRATEGIES [16]

The decision to engage in international markets (or retrench from them) is similar to other strategic choices. However, because this is a more complex decision, it is useful to examine how strategists consider the various options we noted in Chapter 7. Both prescriptive and descriptive approaches exist.

As we discussed in Chapter 4, risk assessments are usually made for various countries in which the strategist considers doing business. In other words, an environmental analysis, considering threats and opportunities, is a requisite first step. But the usual internal assessment must incorporate the additional dimension of existing capabilities (personnel, production, management, and so on) from an international perspective. For example, what strengths and weaknesses exist in the firm for operating in foreign locations, and what are the abilities of the firm vis-à-vis domestic *and* foreign competition?

Once these factors are analyzed, tools similar to those described earlier can be applied. For example, Exhibit 8.19 shows a matrix used by Ford Tractor International to help it decide where to invest, divest, engage in joint venture, and so on. Such a matrix, which is a country portfolio, is similar to a product-portfolio matrix. Ford defined its country attractiveness scale as:

Market size [+] (2 [x] market growth) [+] (0.5 [x] price control/regulation [+] 0.25 [x] nontariff barriers [+] 0.25 [x] local content compensatory export requirements) [+] (0.35 [x] inflation [+] 0.35 [x] trade balance [+] 0.3 [x] political factors)

EXHIBIT 8.19 **Key country matrix.**
(G. D. Harrell and R. O. Kiefer, "Multinational Strategic Market Portfolio," MSU Business Topics [Winter 1981], pp. 5–15. Reprinted by permission.)

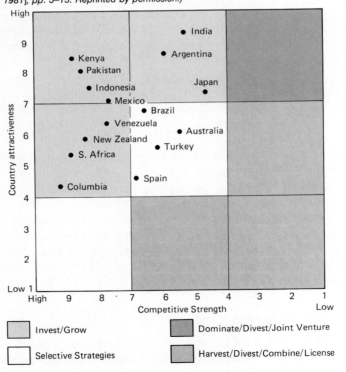

Ford defined its competitive strength as:

2 [x] (0.5 [x] absolute market share [+] 0.5 [x] industry position) [+] product fit [+] (0.5 [x] profit per unit [+] 0.5 [x] profit percentage of net dealer cost) [+] market support

Other techniques exist, of course, and vary with strategic requirements. As before, any tool is only as good as the assumptions which underlie it.

Recall from Chapter 7 that firms will often use a sequential strategy to enter foreign markets, and may seek foreign ''partners'' at some stage. In this case, the choice problem is compounded by the strategic desires of the foreign party. Davidson provides a way to help evaluate possible strategies when such negotiations become necessary. Exhibit 8.20 indicates that approaches will depend on whether the interests of the host country party are similar to or different from those of the focal firm. For example, if the focal firm has a declining product in domestic markets, but chooses to seek foreign markets, it is not likely to seek a joint venture or ultimately invest overseas. In such a case, it may want to license a foreign partner. But the nature of the license sought by the host country partner will vary according to whether it sees the business opportunity as one presently related to its core, or as one expected to become a related business in the future. The focal firm can usually expect nothing better than minority participation if its future business resides in the core businesses of the host partner. Empty cells for the focal firm in its core business mean that the firm would risk developing a wholly owned subsidiary (direct independent foreign investment or acquisition). While the tool illustrated in Exhibit 8.20 can be helpful, factors such as marketing expertise, technological emphasis, and relative financial strength between the parties are not considered, even though these can be important in determining which international strategic alternative is chosen. In effect, the com-

EXHIBIT 8.20 **Negotiating selected international strategic options.**
(William H. Davidson, Global Strategic Management [New York: Wiley, 1982], p. 58. Copyright © 1982 by Wiley. Adapted with permission from John Wiley & Sons, Inc.)

Host country partner

Focal Firm	Core	Related	Future	Unrelated
Unrelated declining businesses	Exclusive current and future license (4)	Standard license (5)	Agent contrast (9)	
Future businesses	Minority joint venture (3)	Co-owned joint venture (6)	Majority joint venture (8)	
Related businesses	Co-owned joint venture (2)	Majority joint venture (7)		
Core businesses	Majority joint venture (1)			

plexity of strategic choice increases as firms consider international options, because other parties often become involved. This is a major reason why many strategists prefer to pursue internal (independent) as opposed to external international strategies when the host governments allow it. Host governments, then, can also affect the choice of which foreign locations to enter (those allowing independent action being favored *ceteris paribus*).

You should not forget that the various managerial factors we described earlier in the chapter are also involved in international strategic choice. An interesting expansion of those concepts is illustrated in Exhibit 8.21. Note that this decision model incorporates many of the factors we described in earlier chapters which play a role in strategic decision making. Here external stakeholders are expanded to include *foreign* business groups and customers, foreign governments, and so on. Note that past foreign experience and strategy, and the involvement and interest of strategists, are key factors in the process. As with all strategic choices, managerial commitment plays an important role in international decisions.

SUMMARY

This chapter completed the three-chapter unit on choice of strategy. It is focused on the height of the drama of the strategic management process: the actual choice of the strategy. *Strategic choice is the decision to select, from among the alternatives, the strategy which will best meet the enterprise's objectives.* The decision involves focusing on a few alternatives, considering the selection factors, evaluating the alternatives against these criteria, and making the actual choice.

There are a number of useful tools to aid the decision maker's thinking about which alternatives are best. Many of these are matrices based on assessments of internal and external conditions, which, depending on circumstances analyzed, lead to prescriptions for choosing one strategy or another. Yet these techniques often fail to recognize the complexity involved, and sometimes ignore realities affecting managerial decision processes. And many techniques have been developed with only the multiple-SBU unit in mind.

Strategists will choose to look at one set of strategic alternatives in first-generation planning and at multiple sets of alternatives in second-generation or contingency approaches. Where will these strategic alternatives come from? Strategists begin with alternatives which they know about or which are proposed by subordinates and which they think will work and do not involve major breaks with the past (unless the situation is dire). Thus the size of the perceived gap in performance is likely to lead to a consideration of some strategies rather than others. Two propositions are offered here:

EXHIBIT 8.21   **Process by which a firm reaches a decision to commit resources to overseas projects.**
(R. D. Robinson, International Business Management: A Guide to Decision Making [New York: Holt, 1973].)

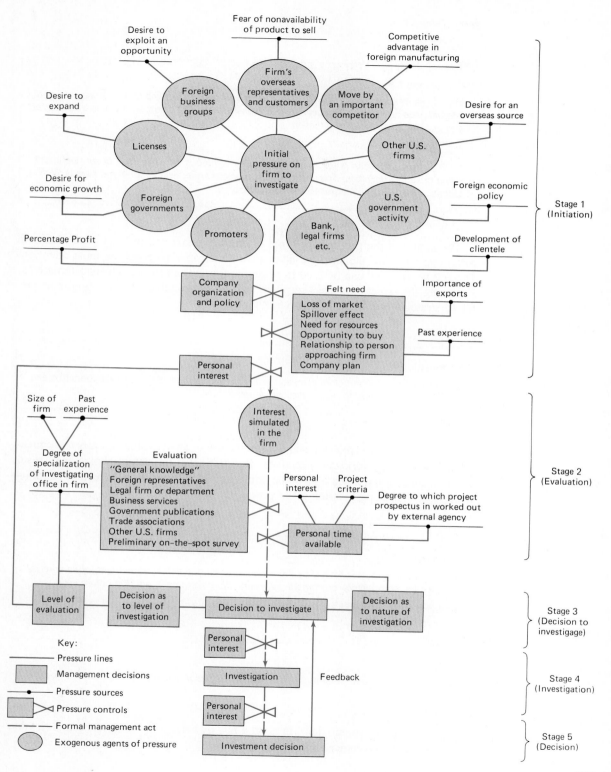

295

Proposition 8.1

If the performance gap is narrow, the alternatives considered will focus on stability and internal pace changes. If the business definition is altered, the change is likely to be passive and in a horizontal, related direction.

Proposition 8.2

If the performance gap is large, the alternatives will focus on expansion or retrenchment in the business definition. Active change in unrelated areas with external partners is likely. Occasionally, vertical integration will be considered.

The nature of the gap and the types of environmental and internal conditions will determine which of the strategic alternative dimensions receives the most attention. The ETOP and SAP can be used to guide the focusing in the search for alternatives.

During the selection phase, corporate and SBU executives decide upon their preferred strategic choice. Proposition 8.3 applies here.

Proposition 8.3

Effective companies hold formal meetings involving all or most of the top managers to make strategic choices and to record the criteria used.

This is a prescriptive approach and implies the use of analytical techniques to compare alternatives with prioritized objectives. Descriptively, the actual choice may result from creeping commitment due to the influence of four managerial selection factors—dependence, risk, past strategy, and power.

Proposition 8.4

The strategic choice is limited by the extent to which the firm is dependent for its survival on owners, competitors, customers, suppliers, the government, and the community.

Proposition 8.5

The more dependent the firm, the less flexibility it has in strategic choice except in crisis conditions.

1 The more dependent the firm is on a few owners (or a family), the less flexible it is in its strategic choice.

2 The more dependent the firm is on its competitors, the less able it will be to choose an aggressive strategy. ("Dependent" is defined as relatively weak in the competitive struggle.)

3 The more dependent the firm is for its success and survival on a few customers and suppliers, the more responsive the effective firm will be to their wishes.

4 The more dependent the firm is on the government and community, the less responsive it will be to market conditions and owner's desires.

Three polar conditions with regard to risk can be conceived: (1) risk is necessary for success; (2) risk is a fact of life, and some risk is acceptable; (3) high risk is what destroys enterprises—it needs to be minimized. Where the firm's managers fall along these attitudes about risk determines how innovative or risky the strategic choice will be. The manager's attitudes eliminate some strategic alternatives and highlight others. The volatility of the industry and the internal conditions of the firm affect the risk factor also.

Proposition 8.6

The strategic choice is affected by the relative volatility of the market sector the firm chooses to operate in. The more volatile the sector, the more flexible the strategic response needs to be in effective organizations.

Past strategies are the beginning point of strategic choice and therefore may eliminate some strategic choices.

In the next dimension of the strategic choice process, power relationships are a key reality in determining which choice is made. Personalities get involved—whom the boss likes and respects has a lot to do with which strategic choice is made. And lower level managers and workers' representatives can exert power within the firm to influence the choice process. Combined with the power aspects of dependence, then, internal and external coalitions serve to constrain choices and managerial discretion in decision making.

Finally, the timing of desired outcomes and the amount of time the decision maker has in which to make the strategic decision influence the final choice too.

Since the actual choice process is so complex, the model given in Exhibit 8.16 attempts to explain how the strategist focuses on less than all the possible choices. This model is used to suggest a procedure which attempts to integrate the managerial factors with the prescriptions for the use of analytical devices (Exhibit 8.17). In effect, the decision maker considers choices closest to the present strategy and incrementally moves from the most preferred strategies to the least preferred (riskier, less politically acceptable, and involving greater dependence). The decision maker stops when it appears that the gap has been closed.

Since conditions affecting the above process may change at any given moment, instead of relying on a single corporate plan with perhaps one or two variations, more and more top managers are getting a whole battery of contingency plans and alternate scenarios prepared. Anticipatory flexibility is urged as a response to the need for some consistency over time.

As with other strategies, the choice to engage in international activities is a difficult one. But added complexity is involved, since a wider range of external and internal characteristics need analysis, and since multiple parties are often involved. Various prescriptive tools can assist the strategist considering international options. But the managerial factors affecting commitment to this strategy must be carefully considered.

Now that the strategic choice has been made, what comes next? Chapters 9 through 11 describe the implementation of strategy. But our discussion of the role of past strategy and internal power relationships should make you realize that implementation may itself be a factor limiting the strategic choice. For convenience, it comes next sequentially. But the past strategy being implemented now affects the strengths and weaknesses of the firm, which in turn influence the new strategy. So remember that the model of the strategic management process requires a consideration of implementation as a component in strategic choice and the analysis stage. A strategy which can't be implemented would be a poor choice indeed.

REFERENCES

[1] Strategic Decision Making

Bateman, T. S., and C. P. Zeithaml: "The Context of Strategic Decision," *Academy of Management Proceedings* (1985), pp. 2–6.

Mintzberg, H., et al.: "The Structure of Unstructured Decision Process," *Administrative Science Quarterly,* vol. 21 (June 1976), pp. 246–275.

Shrivastava, P., and J. H. Grant: "Empirically Derived Models of Strategic Decision Making Processes," *Strategic Management Journal,* vol. 6 (1985), pp. 97–114.

[2] Focusing Alternatives

"Bayuk Cigars Inc. Holders Approve Liquidation Plan," *The Wall Street Journal,* Dec. 14, 1981, p. 11.

"Japanese Heat on the Watch Industry," *Business Week,* May 5, 1980, pp. 92–106.

Proctor, T.: "Theory of Search," *Journal of Management Studies* (February 1978), pp. 56–67.

[3] Techniques for Corporate-Level Strategy Choices

Allen, G.: "A Note on the Boston Consulting Group Concept of Competitive Analysis and Corporate Strategy" (Boston: Intercollegiate Case Clearing House, no. 9-175-175, 1976).

Emshoff, J. R., and A. Finnel: "Defining Corporate Strategy: A Case Study Using Strategic Assumptions Analysis," *Sloan Management Review,* vol. 20 (Spring 1979), pp. 41–52.

Field, A. R.: "Programs That Make Managers Face the Facts," *Business Week,* Apr. 8, 1985, p. 74.

Reimann, Bernard C.: "Strategy Valuation in Portfolio Planning: Combining Q and ROI Ratios," *Planning Review* (January 1986), pp. 18–45.

Staw, B. M.: "Knee-Deep in the Big Muddy: A Study of Escalating Commitment to a Chosen Course of Action," *Organizational Behavior and Human Performance,* vol. 16 (June 1976), pp. 27–44.

Wedley, W. C.: "New Uses of Delphi in Strategy," *Long Range Planning,* vol. 10 (December 1977), pp. 70–78.

[4] Prescriptions for Expansion—Market Share Imperatives

Anderson, C., and F. I. Paine: "PIMS: A Reexamination," *Academy of Management Review,* no. 3 (July 1978), pp. 602–612.

Cooper, A. C., G. Willard, and C. Woo: "Strategies of High-Performing New and Successful Firms," paper presented at the Strategic Management Society Conference, Philadelphia, 1984.

Fruhan, W., Jr.: *The Fight for Competitive Advantage: A Study of U.S. Domestic Trunk Airlines* (Cambridge, Mass.: Harvard University Press, 1972).

Hambrick, D. C., and D. Lei: "Toward an Empirical Prioritization of Contingency Variables for Business Strategy," *Academy of Management Journal,* vol. 28 (1985), pp. 763–788.

Perspectives on Experience (Boston: Boston Consulting Group, 1970).

Ramanujam, V., and N. Venkatraman: "An Inventory and Critique of Strategy Research Using the PIMS Database," *Academy of Management Review,* vol. 9 (1984), pp. 138–151.

Rink, D. R., and J. E. Swan: "Product Life Cycle Research: A Literature Review," *Journal of Business Research,* vol. 7 (September 1979), pp. 219–242.

Schoeffler, S., et al.: "Impact of Strategic Planning on Profit Performance," *Harvard Business Review* (March–April 1974), pp. 137–145.

Wensley, R.: "PIMS and BCG: New Horizons or False Dawn?" *Strategic Management Journal,* vol. 3 (1982), pp. 147–158.

Woo, C., and A. C. Cooper: "Strategies of Effective Low Share Businesses," *Strategic Management Journal,* vol. 2 (1981), pp. 301–318.

[5] Prescriptions for Retrenching

Bibeault, D. B.: *Corporate Turnaround* (New York: McGraw-Hill, 1982).

Ellis, J. E., W. Glasgall and A. Dunkin: "Mobil Tries to Make the Best of a Bad Buy," *Business Week,* May 20, 1985, p. 61.

Hamermesh, R. G., and S. B. Silk: "How To Compete in Stagnant Industries," *Harvard Business Review,* vol. 57 (September–October 1979), pp. 161–168.

Harrigan, K. R.: *Strategies for Declining Businesses* (Lexington, Mass.: Heath, 1980).

Hofer, C. W.: "Turnaround Strategies," *The Journal of Business Strategy,* vol. 1 (Summer 1980), pp. 19–31.

Platt, H. D.: *Why Companies Fail* (Lexington, Mass.: Lexington, 1984).

"Survival in the Basic Industries," *Business Week,* Apr. 26, 1982, pp. 74–84.

Willard, G. E., and A. C. Cooper: "Survivors of Industry Shake-Outs," *Strategic Management Journal,* vol. 6 (1985), pp. 299–318.

[6] Prescriptions for Stability

Peters, T. J., and R. H. Waterman, Jr.: *In Search of Excellence* (New York: Harper & Row, 1983).

[7] Combination Strategy Choice

Ohmae, K.: *The Mind of the Strategist: The Art of Japanese Business* (New York: McGraw-Hill, 1982).

Pauly, D., and T. Namuth: "The Pleasures of Privacy," *Business Week,* Mar. 19, 1984, p. 73.

[8] Managerial Choice Factors

Katz, D., and R. Kahn: *The Social Psychology of Organizations* (New York: Wiley, 1978).
Quinn, J. B.: *Strategies for Change: Logical Incrementalism* (Homewood, Ill.: Irwin, 1980).
Zeleny, M.: "Managers without Management Science?" *Interfaces,* vol. 5 (1975), pp. 35–40.
Note: Also see Chapter 1 references on Decision Making.

[9] Perceptions of Dependence Affect Choices

Murray, E., Jr.: "Strategic Choice as a Negotiated Outcome," *Management Science,* vol. 24 (May 1978), pp. 960–972.
Pfeffer, J., and G. Salancik: *The External Control of Organizations: A Resource Dependence Perspective* (New York: Harper & Row, 1978).

[10] Risk Attitudes and Strategic Choices

Anderson, C. R., and F. T. Paine: "Managerial Perceptions and Strategic Behavior," *Academy of Management Journal,* vol. 18 (December 1975), pp. 811–822.
Baird, I. S., and H. Thomas: "Toward a Contingency Model of Strategic Risk Taking," *Academy of Management Review,* vol. 10 (1985), pp. 230–243.

[11] The Influence of Past Strategy on Choices

Byrne, J. A.: "Should Companies Groom New Leaders or Buy Them?" *Business Week,* Sept. 22, 1986, pp. 94–96.
Jauch, L. R., T. N. Martin, and R. N. Osborn: "Top Management under Fire," *Journal of Business Strategy,* vol. 1 (Spring 1981), pp. 33–41.
Miles, R. E., and C. C. Snow: *Organizational Strategy: Structure and Process* (New York: McGraw-Hill, 1978).
Miller, D., and P. H. Friesen: "Archetypes of Strategy Formulation," *Management Science,* vol. 24 (May 1978), pp. 921–933.
——— and ———: "Strategy-Making in Context: Ten Empirical Archetypes," *Journal of Management Studies,* vol. 14 (October 1977), pp. 253–280.
Mintzberg, H., et al.: "The Structure of Unstructured Decisions," working paper, Faculty of Management, McGill University, Montreal, 1974. Mimeographed.
Mitchell, R.: "Dow Chemical's Drive to Change Its Market—And Its Image," *Business Week* (June 9, 1986), pp. 92–96.
"Owens-Illinois: A Cautious Venture beyond Glass," *Business Week,* July 4, 1983, pp. 84–85.
Schwenk, C. R.: "Information, Cognitive Biases, and Commitment to a Course of Action," *Academy of Management Review,* vol. 11 (1986), pp. 298–310.
Whyte, G.: "Escalating Commitment to a Course of Action: A Reinterpretation," *Academy of Management Review,* vol. 11 (1986), pp. 311–321.

[12] Power Relationships Impact Choices

Bower, J.: *Managing the Resource Allocation Process* (Boston: Harvard Business School, 1970).
Carter, E. E.: "The Behavioral Theory of the Firm and Top Level Corporate Decisions," *Administrative Science Quarterly,* vol. 16 (1971), pp. 413–428.
Child, J.: "Organizational Structure, Environment and Performance: The Role of Strategic Choice," *Sociology,* vol. 6 (1972), pp. 1–22.

MacMillan, I., and P. E. Jones: *Strategy Formulation: Power and Politics* (St. Paul, Minn.: West, 1986).

Mintzberg, H., and J. A. Waters: "Tracking Strategy in an Entrepreneurial Firm," working paper, Faculty of Management, McGill University, Montreal, 1980.

[13] The Impact of Timing on Choices

Jamieson, D., and W. Petrusic: "Preference and the Time to Choose," *Organizational Behavior and Human Performance,* vol. 19 (June 1977), pp. 56–67.

Toy, S., E. Ehrlich, A. Bernstein, and S. Crock: "The Raiders," *Business Week,* Mar. 4, 1985, pp. 80–90.

Wernerfelt, B., and A. Karnani: "Competitive Strategy under Uncertainty," *Academy of Management Proceedings* (1984), pp. 42–46.

[14] The Overall Strategic Choice Process

Berlin, V. N.: "Administrative Experimentation: A Methodology for More Rigorous 'Muddling Through,' " *Management Science,* vol. 24 (April 1978), pp. 789–799.

Braybrooke, D., and C. Lindblom: *A Strategy of Decision* (New York: Free Press, 1963).

Fredrickson, J. W.: "Effects of Decision Motive and Organizational Performance Level on Strategic Decision Processes," *Academy of Management Journal,* vol. 28 (1985), pp. 821–843.

McCall, M. W., and R. E. Kaplan: *Whatever It Takes: Decision Makers at Work* (Englewood Cliffs, N.J.: Prentice-Hall, 1985).

[15] Contingency Strategies

Ansoff, H. I.: "Managing Strategic Surprise by Response to Weak Signals," *California Management Review,* vol. 18 (Winter 1975), pp. 21–33.

Harrigan, K. R.: *Strategic Flexibility* (New York: Lexington, 1984).

"Piercing Future Fog in the Executive Suite," *Business Week,* Apr. 28, 1975, p. 56.

"When Computer Disaster Strikes," *Business Week,* Sept. 6, 1982, p. 68.

[16] International Strategic Decisions

Davidson, W. H.: *Global Strategic Management* (New York: Wiley, 1982).

Robinson, R. D.: *International Business Management: A Guide to Decision Making* (New York: Holt, 1973).

CHAPTER OUTLINE

CHAPTER 9

IMPLEMENTATION: RESOURCE ALLOCATION, ORGANIZATION, AND THE PLANNING SYSTEM

OBJECTIVES

* To understand why firms and SBUs must implement the chosen strategy
* To learn how implementation is related to strategy
* To understand the processes of resource allocation and budgeting as they affect strategy
* To learn how the organization structure evolves with strategy
* To understand the role of a planning system in linking strategies and plans

INTRODUCTION [1]

Some of you may think that the strategic management process ended with Chapter 8. The top manager(s) made the strategic choice. Now the enterprise knows how it is going to achieve its objectives. Exhibit 9.1 reminds us that we are not through yet. The choice does not mean that the enterprise will follow the decision.

Implementation is necessary to spell out more precisely how the strategic choice will come to be. Structural and administrative mechanisms which are compatible and workable need to be established to reinforce the strategic direction chosen and provide guides for action. A good strategy without effective implementation is not likely to succeed. Closing the gap between ideal and expected outcomes requires more than making a strategic choice.

Exhibit 9.2 is one consulting group's representation of the fact that strategy formation is but one component of a network of organization activities which must be integrated to accomplish objectives. The McKinsey framework suggests that the following components must fit together to make a strategy work effectively:

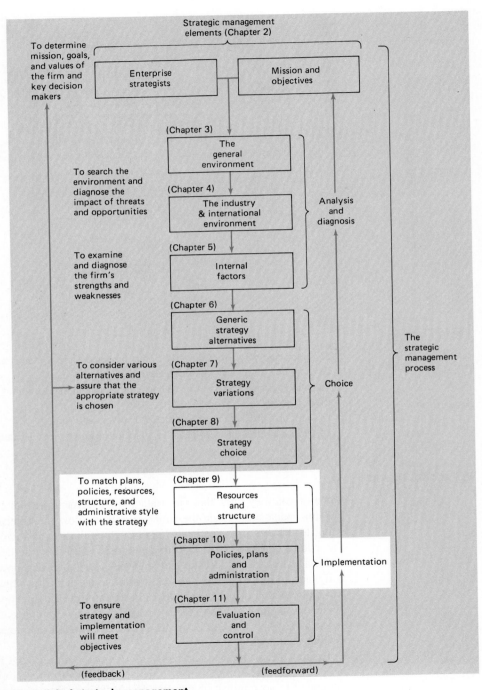

EXHIBIT 9.1 A model of strategic management.

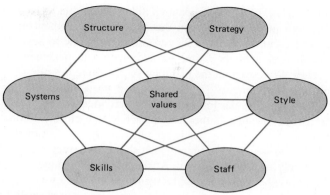

EXHIBIT 9.2 **McKinsey 7-S framework.**
(Robert H. Waterman, Jr., Thomas J. Peters, and Julien R. Phillips, "Structure Is Not Organization," Business Horizons [June 1980], pp. 14–26.)

1 *Strategy*. A coherent set of actions aimed at gaining a sustainable advantage over competition, improving position vis-à-vis customers, or allocating resources.

2 *Structure*. The organization chart and accompanying baggage that show who reports to whom and how tasks are both divided up and integrated.

3 *Systems*. The processes and flows that show how an organization gets things done from day to day (information systems, capital budgeting systems, manufacturing processes, quality control systems, and performance measurement systems all would be good examples).

4 *Style*. Tangible evidence of what management considers important by the way it collectively spends time and attention and uses symbolic behavior. It is not what management says is important; it is the way management behaves.

5 *Staff*. The people in an organization. Here it is very useful to think not about individual personalities but about corporate demographics.

6 *Shared values* (or superordinate goals). The values that go beyond, but might well include, simple goal statements in determining corporate destiny. To fit the concept, these values must be shared by most people in an organization.

7 *Skills*. A derivative of the rest. Skills are those capabilities that are possessed by an organization as a whole as opposed to the people in it.

Implementation involves a number of interrelated choices and activities. The resources of the enterprise must be allocated to reinforce the strategic choice, and the organization of the SBUs and corporation must reflect the strategy and objectives. The right strategists must be in charge of the SBUs and in key leadership positions to see that the strategy will work. The functional strategies and short- and medium-range policies must be developed such that they are consistent with the strategic choice. And some system is needed to link strategies with plans for implementation. Otherwise, the strategy that has been chosen will never see the light of day.

For example, joint ventures became an extremely popular strategy in the 1980s.

Yet 7 out of 10 of those ventures didn't meet objectives or were disbanded. One of the major problems has been that executive investment in implementation has been weak. Executives devoted 23 percent of their time to developing a joint venture, but only 8 percent of their time to setting up a management system to implement the strategy. Moreover, in the planning stages, there has often been inattention to making sure that the "parents" agree about how the "child" is to be operated.

We have split the implementation activities into the next three chapters. As with the rest of the model, they are in fact related closely to one another, and decisions about each are usually made simultaneously, as Exhibit 9.2 suggests. That is, resources are allocated to units which should be structured in such a way that they can effectively use the resources. At the same time, policies about the use of those resources are being established by managers in such a way, it is hoped, that the intended strategy will be accomplished. This chapter focuses on the resource allocation and organizational and planning system aspects of implementation, while Chapter 10 emphasizes the development of policies and administrative processes. Chapter 11 describes the control and evaluation system for integrating and following through on plans. As each topic is examined, however, remember that all the activities must be consistent if the firm is to operate effectively.

THE IMPLEMENTATION PROCESS [2]

In the conclusion for Chapter 8 we noted that there is a link between implementation and choice of strategy. That is, the chosen strategy must be put into action. Thus choice of strategy itself is constrained by the ability to alter past resource commitments, organizational structures, policies, and administrative systems. If the strategy calls for major alterations in these areas, strategists must be willing and able to change and make plans to do so. If the strategy choice process is to be effective, the implementation process must go hand in hand.

Exhibit 9.3 shows another way the process of implementation can be viewed. In the next three chapters we will discuss each of the topics identified in the flowchart. The "flow" itself is somewhat arbitrary in that there is not necessarily a *sequence* of activities. As with strategy formation, these aspects of implementation are interdependent. Also, note that implementation flows *from and into* the determination of strategy. Strategy formation and implementation are interdependent. Remember that in most cases, policies, structures, reward systems, and so on, are already in place. As such, this affects strategy formation.

Exhibit 9.4 indicates the roles various strategists usually play in the process of strategy implementation. For instance, the board would act if major organizational changes were needed, such as replacing a CEO or establishing different structures. The board would also be involved in approving major resource allocation decisions such as a merger or new-plant construction. Top managers are setting goals and strategies and negotiating with SBU managers, who will be pushing for the acceptance of their objectives and strategies and resource needs. However, SBU and corporate top managers have primary responsibility for deciding where to allocate resources,

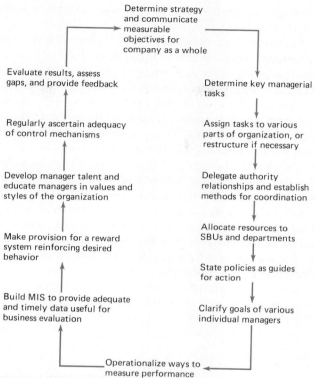

EXHIBIT 9.3   **Strategic implementation process.**

EXHIBIT 9.4   THE ROLE OF STRATEGISTS IN STRATEGY IMPLEMENTATION

Strategists	Resource allocation and organizing	Setting policies and administrative systems
Corporate top managers	Decide	Decide
SBU top managers	Decide for their units	Decide for their units
Corporate planners	Advise	Advise, and help manage planning system
Board of directors	Approves major changes	Rarely involved
Consultants	Occasionally hired to advise	Often hired to advise.

how to organize, what policies to establish, and how to coordinate and control the system.

Once basic decisions are made, of course, implementation takes place in a cascade fashion through the basic structural hierarchy of the organization. Choices are made at corporate headquarters and communicated to the SBUs. The SBUs then choose their specific strategies and implement them into their departments. For instance, major policy decisions are made by the top manager or SBU manager. These executives may ask the corporate planning staff to work out detailed policy changes in conjunction with affected line executives. If there is a small corporate planning staff or no corporate planning staff, consultants may be hired to help out. At that point, tasks are assigned to the organization, budgets are provided, and communications through the administrative system are designed to inform people of their responsibilities. Any personnel or organization changes which might be needed must also be made.

If the firm is a single-SBU firm, one step is removed. In more decentralized firms, the primary implementation takes place at the SBU level and lower. This process requires effective communication and negotiations among all the strategists concerned.

Our last section in this chapter focuses more on designing a planning system to facilitate the interrelationships we just described. The role of a planning staff takes on particular significance here. And the design of these systems helps other implementation processes such as resource allocation and is related to the way the firm is organized. So let's examine those topics first.

RESOURCE ALLOCATION [3]

Strategists have the power to decide which divisions, departments, or SBUs are to receive how much money, which facilities, and which executives. This is what we mean by resource allocation.

Recall that in Chapter 2 we suggested that there was a difference between official and operative objectives. The resource allocation decisions are very similar in that they set the *operative* strategy for the firm. Assume, for example, that resources are allocated to existing units on some formula basis (e.g., 10 percent above last year's budget). The implicit operative strategy is pace expansion. If the official strategy is expansion in some lines of business with stability in others, then greater resource flows to areas targeted for expansion are necessary to give force to the strategy. The formula approach (such as 10 percent above last year's budget for all lines of business) would *not* reinforce such a strategy. What is important to understand is that once the strategic choice is made, resources must follow the strategy, or we haven't put our "money where our mouth is." SBU and lower managers are smart. If a firm's strategists describe a strategy in words but do not shift money and executive talent and other resources to support it, the strategy will be considered a paper strategy. As with objectives, there can be a difference between "official" and "actual" strategy. So resource allocation decisions about how much to invest in which areas of the business reinforce strategy and commit the organization to its chosen strategy. Exhibit 9.5 shows an example of this.

EXHIBIT 9.5   REALLOCATING CAT'S RESOURCES

Caterpillar Tractor Company isn't used to bad news. But after a 48-year streak in continuous profits, worldwide demand for its giant yellow machines dropped like the rocks it was used to moving. Cat is faced with excess industry capacity, eroding overseas earnings due to the dollar's value, less construction in oil-rich countries suffering from lower prices and debt-ridden third world countries, and a Japanese competitor coming on strong.

To hold its market share, Cat is changing. And with the change, Cat is altering traditional resource allocation patterns. Cat slashed its dividend 2 years in a row, to a fifth of what it was in 1982. It is shrinking costs by lowering capital investment and allocating some production responsibilities to joint-venture partners overseas. Cat closed six plants and reduced its labor force by 19% from its 1982 level. Cat's make-or-buy decisions have been changed to alter its resource allocations among procurement and manufacturing functions. From hardly any at all, Cat now purchases over 16% of its components from overseas firms, including some who are competitors. And it has moved the sales force out of Peoria into dealer districts to convert them from order takers to sales generators—a personnel resource reallocation. Further, Cat has allocated money to a new finance subsidiary to prop up its dealers and provide customer financing.

Clearly, Cat's strategy and resource allocation patterns among stockholders, labor, operations, and personnel have been dramatically reoriented to meet the requirements of a new environment.

Source: Adapted from ''A Shaken Caterpillar Retools to Take On a More Competitive World,'' *Business Week,* Nov. 5, 1984, pp. 91–94; and ''Even American Know-How Is Headed Abroad,'' *Business Week,* Mar. 3, 1986, pp. 60–74.

Let's consider how resource allocation is important to several strategic options. If new-product development is seen as the key to an active offensive strategy, more funds and personnel will be needed in research and development, with the possibility of longer-term capital expenditures for a new plant or new equipment. If the strategy calls for expansion in new markets, greater flows of funds for advertising, sales personnel, and/or market research will be required. If retrenchment is under way, resource allocation is of particular significance. Care must be taken to protect units which provide long-term competitive advantages. Unfortunately, the ''easy way out'' is often used—everyone is cut back equally, or resource flows are reduced for units which have a longer-term payout but are short-term users of resources without commensurate revenue generation. The usual example is to cut R&D or maintenance—the very places where long-term developments may be most critical for future competitive advantage. Thus shortsighted resource allocation decisions may come at the expense of the ability to pursue a long-term strategy. Exhibit 9.6 provides an example of this problem. It is instructive that in 1986, with collapsing export markets and falling profits, Japan's industrialists slashed capital spending budgets, but fattened their R&D budgets in the face of competition from the four tigers in Asia.

Of course, resource allocation decisions are linked to objectives through the strategies being implemented. Decisions about dividend policies, for instance, are important in relation to objectives and the long-term ability to attract sources of capital. Thus how to share expected profits among investors, management, and labor and whether to reinvest in the business are important resource allocation choices with long-term strategy implications. As we suggested in Chapters 2 and 3, many influences are at work during the formulation of objectives and strategies. External parties play a major

EXHIBIT 9.6   DID CUTBACKS CUT THEIR THROATS?

In October of 1979, it looked like Archie McCardell's turnaround plan for International Harvester was taking hold. A cost-cutting campaign had saved the firm $460 million in 2 years, helping the firm reach a 15-year high: an after-tax margin of 4.4% on earnings of $370 million. On November 1, 1979, the bubble burst when 36% of the work force went out on strike. McCardell chose to hold firm against the UAW and demanded work-rule concessions to further hold the line on costs. Union officials perceived this as "an outgrowth of McCardell's overzealousness in slashing costs." McCardell eliminated 11,000 jobs of the 15,000 he wanted to cut when he joined the company.

What is interesting is that the image of McCardell in the investment community caused problems in raising needed capital. He was "roundly criticized for cutting costs at Xerox at the expense of product innovation." His plan, despite the strike, was to forge ahead with increased R&D spending and a newly centralized team for new-product development. But reports of Harvester's troubles in late 1981 indicated that capital markets remained skeptical.

After a long strike, "McCardell may find his challenge not in cost reduction, research, or modernization, but in winning back customers taken by competitors." Indeed, the cost-cutting campaign in the interest of short-term gains did not result in the kind of turnaround required—one yielding longer-term benefits. McCardell lost his job in 1982. By 1985, IH had declared bankruptcy and Navistar emerged from the ashes as a very different firm from the old IH.

Source: Adapted from "International Harvester: When Cost-Cutting Threatens the Future," *Business Week*, Feb. 11, 1980, pp. 98–100.

role. For instance, government regulations may require a firm to invest large amounts of capital in "nonproductive" assets such as pollution-control equipment. Influential stockholders may force the firm to make greater dividend payouts. Thus the strategic agenda is partially set by the factors influencing the setting of objectives, since they will limit the resources available for implementing strategy as expressed in the allocation decisions. Finally, resource allocation is linked to the development of competitive advantage. In Chapter 5 we discussed some approaches to developing distinctive competence. It is presumed that those approaches were considered during strategy formulation. The key here is to make sure that preferential distribution of capital goes to the most critical units—the units where the strategy is directed at creating competitive advantages.

Tools for Allocating Resources [4]

In Chapter 8 we discussed the BCG product portfolio matrix. This is one tool that strategists can use to link resource allocation decisions to choices of strategy. If you recall, several prescriptions for investment and cash flow decisions were made depending on the type of SBU identified in the matrix. Thus "cash cows" are SBUs from which resources can be obtained for allocation to "question marks" or "stars." Of course, we suggested that there are several problems with this approach for strategic choice, and they apply here as well. For instance, resource allocation for new SBUs with initially low market shares might be overlooked. But for multiple-SBU firms this is one tool to aid thinking about how to allocate resources.

The primary approach to resource allocation in the implementation process is through the budgeting system. One system for budgeting resources within one firm is the product life cycle budgeting system used by Lear Siegler. This firm believes that the product life cycle of the product lines should influence its budgeting of resources. It believes that cash flow, departmental expenses, revenues, and capital expenditures should vary during the cycle. Therefore the balance sheets and income statements should look different at different stages of the cycle. The firm suggests adjusting resources accordingly. Thus to the extent that the product life cycle influences strategy, budgets tied to such a cycle will affect the product strategy. Others agree with this approach and suggest that zero-based budgeting is particularly useful when retrenchment strategies are being used.

From a long-term perspective, the capital budget is very critical. Here, plans for securing and distributing capital for large-scale investments are needed to accomplish strategy. Mergers, introductions of major new product lines, an increase in plant capacity, and vertical integrations are key mission changes which will require long-term capital investment decisions.

The more routine year-to-year allocation decisions are made within this context. But they are also important for making sure that the strategic direction of the firm is being followed, and they serve as a guide to future strategy. So let's look at this budget process in more detail.

Remember that resource allocation as expressed in the budget needs to be carefully linked to strategy. Exhibit 9.7 shows one explanation of how these can be linked in a multiple-SBU firm. Note that the process will involve planning at various levels in a back-and-forth fashion over time. In a series of negotiations among managers at the SBU and corporate levels, the strategy and plans to implement it are worked out. The final output is a set of budgets which give force to the overall plan. Let's look at these stages of the budgeting process in a bit more detail.

EXHIBIT 9.7   **A framework for the strategic budgeting process.**

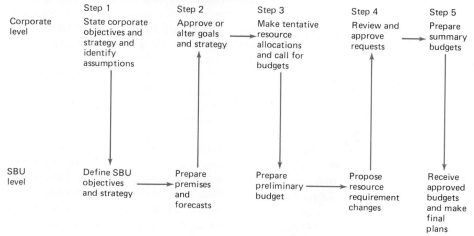

Step 1

Top management initiates the budgeting process. It does this by communicating the objectives of the firm for the period. It also announces the assumptions it uses—the predicted economic and competitive conditions, for instance—to set these objectives.

Of the various internal planning premises and assumptions which must be formulated, the sales forecast is clearly the most fundamental. Indeed, since anticipated product demand must be determined before budgets and plans for resource inputs are made, the sales forecast is typically cited as the basis or "key" for all internal planning. Among other things, the sales forecast is the basis for production planning, materials planning, capital planning, cash-flow analysis, personnel planning, and advertising and sales promotion planning. Moreover, projected sales, in whatever form—tax revenues for a city, dollar output for a company, or donations for a charity—constitute the revenue side of an organization's income statement. Thus on the basis of forecasted sales, an organization is able to project production requirements, establish what materials need to be purchased, determine the number of personnel to be recruited, estimate the level and timing of required financial resources, and decide what it can afford in the way of operating expenses (such as those for advertising and sales promotion) for the purpose of exacting a certain profit level.

Step 2

The budget department (in large firms) or administrator communicates information and offers advice to the units preparing the budgets. This unit prepares the forms and procedures for developing a budget. It helps those preparing budgets with technical problems and in the actual preparation. If there are budget specialists at the division level, it trains these persons and coordinates their work.

Step 3

Each unit prepares a preliminary budget for the next period. Normally the unit begins with the previous period's budget and performance against this budget. Next the unit states how the next period will differ from the current period. So the next year's budget that the unit proposes is based on the past budget plus or minus expected changes. This shows how the unit's management expects to achieve its objectives. This is a critical stage if strategic change is taking place. The unit must specify what resources it will need to accomplish the strategy.

Step 4

The preliminary budgets developed in step 3 are reviewed and approved. The budget department analyzes and reviews each unit's past performance and determines whether its projections are realistic given likely future conditions. After comparing the budgets of the various units, the budget department submits them to top management along with recommendations for approval or adjustment. Top management examines the budgets and approves them if they are consistent with past performance, anticipated revenues, and the firm's strategy.

This is the stage at which the resource allocation choice will be made. Who gets the money to hire more people, buy new furniture or machinery, or build a new building? In most enterprises resources are scarce, and not every unit can be given what it wants (and says it needs). The allocation of funds can be crucial to the success of a unit (and to the career of its manager). Loss of marketing funds for TV spots at a strategic time, for example, can wreck a unit's results. Because the decisions involved are so difficult, they are often made by a budget committee or a number of managers.

Step 5

At this stage summary budgets are usually prepared. Projected receipts and expenses are put together, and subsidiary budgets are developed—for example, the operating budget, financial budgets, the capital budget, and expense budgets. The operating budget specifies materials, labor, overhead, and other costs. Financial budgets project cash receipts and disbursements; the capital budget projects major additions or new construction. The expense budgets project expenses not covered in other budgets, such as marketing costs. Finally, in the summary budget (profit and loss or income statement), the total obtained by combining the subsidiary budgets is subtracted from the projected receipts. The remainder is a profit or loss. If the budgets meet objectives, approvals are made, and the budgets are enacted. If changes are needed, negotiations will take place.

The mechanics of preparing capital and operating budgets are beyond our purview. But this process is important, as it relates to the formation and implementation of strategy. Through the entire process, a variety of real problems of relevance to strategists often emerge. Estimating both revenues and costs is very difficult. In the case of an automaker, for example, how many new cars will the company sell? This depends on a number of factors, such as the economy, competitors' products, and how consumers evaluate its product in comparison with competing products. The company's pricing policy and marketing image affect this estimate, as do product quality, engineering, and the aggressiveness and reliability of dealers. Managers often handle this problem by making their best guesses—"ball-park" estimates. Sometimes they miss. The point is, the issues we addressed earlier affect budget preparation.

Moreover, the question of who gets the most money from the budget has a major effect on the work environment as well as on the careers of managers. If, as a manager, you "lose the budget battle," your employees will have to do more work with fewer helpers and less desirable equipment. They will feel that you have failed them, and they will treat you accordingly. This is one of the problems with using the product portfolio approach. Few managers want to have their units known as dogs or cash cows. It is also a problem affecting retrenchment strategies. Negotiations to protect a unit in the budget battle may come at the expense of pursuing a strategy in the best interests of the overall organization. Indeed, gamesmanship, overstatement of real budget needs, and even secrecy can lead to highly political budget battles across departments.

Another problem is that the usual budget process tends to be designed for allocating resources to existing departments or various investment proposals. These may or may not be tied to strategic changes desired by the organization; if they are not, then the budget process reinforces existing resource allocation patterns.

The budget process itself can lead to problems if it is not tied to the strategic direction of the firm. In fact, the process sets the operative strategy as we suggested earlier. So if lower levels are unaware of shifts in strategic direction, and if top managers fail to communicate strategic change or are weak negotiators, any intended strategy change is unlikely to take place.

Finally, you should note that the budget process is tied to the way units and divisions are arranged organizationally. New SBUs can be at a disadvantage if they are unaware of the "ins and outs" of the budget procedures used in their organization. And if truly major strategic shifts are occurring, the structure is likely to change along with the way resources are allocated. So let's turn to the second aspect of implementation—structuring for strategy implementation.

ORGANIZATIONAL IMPLEMENTATION [5]

Strategic management posits that the strategy and the organization structure used by the firm must match. In essence, the top manager looks at the organization now and asks, Do we have the right organization for our strategy? As Exhibit 9.8 suggests, structural change may be needed when organizations experience problems or are faced with strategic shifts.

Organization involves dividing up the work among groups and individuals (division of labor) and making sure that the parts are linked together in such a way that they will work together effectively (coordination).

EXHIBIT 9.8   THE GM OVERHAUL

General Motors has had a long presence in Europe. Vauxhall (Britain) was acquired in 1925, and Opel (Germany) was bought in 1929. GM operates in 17 European countries. Yet, recently, GM has had trouble wringing profits from those countries. Many blame its difficulties on its organization structure.

Prior to 1986, Opel executives were responsible for design and engineering functions throughout Europe, including Vauxhall. But there have been squabbles over investment and marketing decisions. General Motors poured $6 billion into automating its plants and bringing out new models. And it has increased its market share in Europe. Yet it still lags Ford in profits, and is fending off Japanese imports.

In effect, with the split between Vauxhall and Opel,

European operations suffered from the lack of "a coherent strategy and strong management." In 1986 GM determined it would end its European losses. It has created a European headquarters (GM-Europe) in Zurich. It has moved 100 executives from Opel Germany and about 100 from Vauxhall Britain and other European operations to its new headquarters. GM executives in Detroit believe this new approach will improve coordination and planning, and eliminate the country-by-country decision making on pricing, marketing, and cost cutting.

While critics suggest that merely moving key players to one location may not solve its woes, apparently GM is trying to foster a link between strategy and structure to accomplish its goal of improving profits.

Source: Adapted from "General Motors' Big European Overhaul," *Business Week,* Feb. 10, 1986, pp. 42–43.

Thus several basic questions are being addressed by the managers:

1 What tasks are needed to accomplish the strategy?
2 To whom should these tasks be assigned?
3 To what extent are these tasks interdependent?
4 How can we be sure that the tasks assigned will be performed?

The first two questions deal with dividing up labor. The latter two address issues of coordination and control. In this chapter we emphasize division of labor through resouce allocation and departmentation. Chapters 9 and 10 examine administrative systems for coordination and control. Again, our separation of these is "artificial" in that the structure and style must work together to be effective.

Basic Structures for Strategy [6]

The effective organizer tries to group duties into meaningful subunits while avoiding duplication of efforts or excessive specialization, which can lead to boredom or tunnel vision in the enterprise's executives. Cannon, a long-time consultant with McKinsey & Company, put it this way:

> The experience of McKinsey supports the view that neither strategy nor structure can be determined independently of the other. . . . Strategy can rarely succeed without an appropriate structure. In almost every kind of large-scale enterprise, examples can be found where well-conceived strategic plans were thwarted by an organization structure that delayed the execution of the plans or gave priority to the wrong set of considerations. . . . Good structure is inseparably linked to strategy.

There is a great deal of research which indicates that when the strategy is properly implemented with the right organization structure, the firm is more effective. For example, Chandler found that when firms shifted their strategies to diversification, they had to change their organization to a divisional form. In studying Swedish firms, Rhenman found that problems result from an inability or unwillingness to adapt the organization after strategic changes. Many other studies have found this linkage.

But the basic question has been raised: Which structure for which strategy? First let's review the kinds of structures which evolve. The emphasis here is on the horizontal division of labor, or forms of departmentation.

Department Evolution [7]

Organization structures evolve with changes in strategy. In the smallest enterprises, it is hard to determine much of an organization other than the boss and employees. As the enterprise develops and more and more employees are added, the first type of organization which arises is the functional type, as shown in Exhibit 9.9. In a firm organized by functional departments, the boss groups employees by the type of work the enterprise does: production and operations (goods and services), accounting and finance (money), personnel (people), research and development (ideas, new ways of doing things), and environmental relations (marketing, public relations, etc.). This

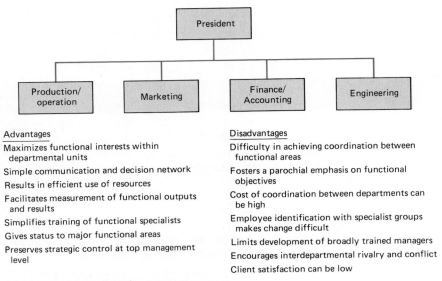

Advantages

Maximizes functional interests within
  departmental units

Simple communication and decision network

Results in efficient use of resources

Facilitates measurement of functional outputs
  and results

Simplifies training of functional specialists

Gives status to major functional areas

Preserves strategic control at top management
  level

Disadvantages

Difficulty in achieving coordination between
  functional areas

Fosters a parochial emphasis on functional
  objectives

Cost of coordination between departments can
  be high

Employee identification with specialist groups
  makes change difficult

Limits development of broadly trained managers

Encourages interdepartmental rivalry and conflict

Client satisfaction can be low

EXHIBIT 9.9   Firm organized by functional departments.

structure is believed to maximize economies of scale and specialization. However, the coordination and integration of units are often problems. Firms pursuing stability or pace expansions are quite likely to use the functional form.

If the enterprise grows by expanding the *variety* of operations it performs, then another level of management is inserted above the functional level, and thus the divisional (or multidivisional) structure is developed (Exhibit 9.10). It is thought that this structure maximizes the coordination of the subunits and increases the speed of response to changes in the environment. A basic problem, though, is that there tends to be less concern for efficiency and greater goal emphasis at the divisional level than in the overall system, as suggested by Exhibit 9.11.

Note that the divisional structure in Exhibit 9.10 is based on a product-oriented strategy. But the strategy could call for emphasis on markets, and thus divisions would be arranged by client type or territories. For instance, a firm might divide its operations into industrial, governmental, and retail sales divisions, as in Exhibit 9.12. Here, the strategy may be to rely on the internal ability to service specific customer needs.

Most large organizations which are geographically dispersed also specialize by territory. Exhibit 9.13 might represent a firm pursuing a multinational expansion strategy. In very large firms, especially multinationals, combinations of these forms are quite likely.[8]

Some very complex organizations can take one or both of two more steps. The first concerns the matrix organization. In firms whose products change frequently and are short-lived (especially defense firms), functional and divisional managers may form project groups. The purpose of project development and project implementation managers is to achieve speedier responses and better coordination. The project groups

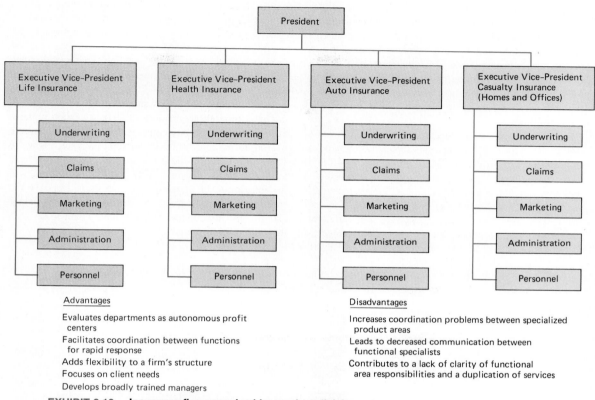

Advantages

Evaluates departments as autonomous profit
  centers
Facilitates coordination between functions
  for rapid response
Adds flexibility to a firm's structure
Focuses on client needs
Develops broadly trained managers

Disadvantages

Increases coordination problems between specialized
  product areas
Leads to decreased communication between
  functional specialists
Contributes to a lack of clarity of functional
  area responsibilities and a duplication of services

EXHIBIT 9.10   Insurance firm organized by product divisions.

are temporary and are scrapped when the project is completed. Exhibit 9.14 shows a firm whose strategy may involve several new venture projects.

In the most advanced organization, an innovative structure is used.[9] Fast-changing enterprises divide themselves into current business groups and innovation groups. The innovators invent and pretest products and services. Once the products and services are ready for the marketplace, they are transferred to the current business units. This amounts to creating a current business division and innovation divisions parallel to the current business division. With this form, an effort is made to combine the best features of the functional, divisional, and matrix forms of organization.

So, as the strategy changes from a single product or product line to a dominant product to related diversification to conglomerate unrelated diversification, the structure in effective organizations changes from primitive to functional to divisional or matrix. Note, then, that there seems to be a change in the forms of departmentation with the size and complexity which result from expansion strategies. But the exact way in which departments are put together needs to match the strategic direction of the firm. In this regard, many firms have begun to organize around their strategic business units, opting for a more product-oriented form of departmentation.

EXHIBIT 9.11   A PROBLEM OF INTEGRATION

In 1975 it appeared that 3M had positioned itself as a major competitor in the emerging office automation market. Acquisitions of a small word processing company with a leading edge in technology and a firm leading in facsimile devices added to 3M's already formidable base in the copier business. But 3M squandered its lead, and observers doubt that it can grasp much of a share of the $100 billion office equipment and supplies market. Fast-moving word processing firms overtook 3M, and in 1979 3M bowed out.

Some observers point to the structure and climate at 3M as the culprit. The company's reputation for innovation emanates from the autonomy granted to its 40 divisions. Each division has responsibility for its own research and development, manufacturing, and, for the most part, marketing. "But what works for Scotch tape does not necessarily work in the office." Sales to the "office-of-the-future" market seem to require a concerted, integrated "systems effort." The divisional lines giving 3M its en-

trepreneurial flair inhibit communication between product groups that would lead to the evolution of more complex office systems. The company did try to establish an office systems task force to coordinate divisional activities. But according to a former 3M executive, "the problem is 3M doesn't believe in strategic planning, so the task force really had no way to implement a plan across divisional lines."

It seems that 3M still wants to make some effort in this area through acquisitions. But the question remains as to whether it can buy companies that fit into its culture without losing its edge. Says one top executive, "If we're going to succeed in the office market, we may just have to do things like the rest of the world." If it does, will the integration of divisions come at the expense of the strengths established by its autonomous operations? Clearly, the structure at 3M will have much to do with its strategy in the future.

Source: Adapted from "3M's Problems in the Office of the Future," *Business Week,* Oct. 13, 1980, pp. 123–126.

EXHIBIT 9.12   **Firm organized by customer departments.**

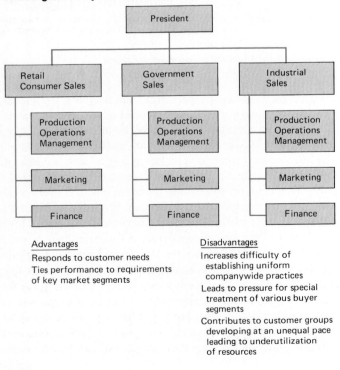

Advantages

Responds to customer needs
Ties performance to requirements of key market segments

Disadvantages

Increases difficulty of establishing uniform companywide practices
Leads to pressure for special treatment of various buyer segments
Contributes to customer groups developing at an unequal pace leading to underutilization of resources

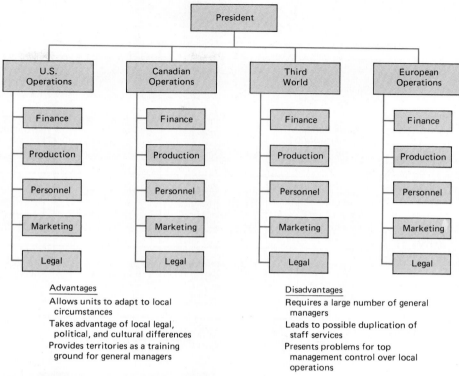

Advantages

Allows units to adapt to local
circumstances

Takes advantage of local legal,
political, and cultural differences

Provides territories as a training
ground for general managers

Disadvantages

Requires a large number of general
managers

Leads to possible duplication of
staff services

Presents problems for top
management control over local
operations

EXHIBIT 9.13   **Firm organized by territorial departments.**

A few academics are promoting the idea that organization structures for the future will need to be very adaptive and open to the environment. Such structures would be more complex, with departments existing in many forms (some product-market, some limited-term-project, etc.). Decisions would need to be decentralized, and organizational structures more transitory. In effect, there is a call for structures to follow the strategic philosophy of anticipatory flexibility along several dimensions:

1 Operational flexibility—the ability to react efficiently to a change in production volume, as in the case of temporary decreases in demand

2 Strategic flexibility—the ability to change the product-market composition by means of product renewal, switching markets, acquisition, or divestment

3 Structural flexibility—the ability to change the existing structure in an easy way

Perhaps the innovative structure described before will be the next form to receive the plaudits of consultants as "the best way" to organize. Or perhaps the "network" companies now emerging will provide a new way to increase flexibility. Exhibit 9.15 indicates that some firms are becoming "shell corporations," which contract out to other agents functions such as manufacturing, distribution, marketing, or even financial activities. In effect, such firms are retrenching by "vertical disaggregation" out

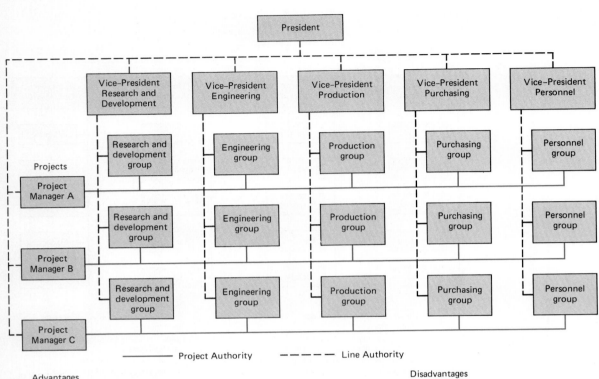

Advantages

Adapts to fluctuating work loads

Establishes one person as focal point for all
 matters pertaining to an individual project

Permits maximum use of limited pool of
 functional specialists

Provides a home base for functional specialists
 between projects

Makes it possible to respond to several
 environmental sectors simultaneously

Disadvantages

Places a premium on teamwork

Leads to possible conflict with existance
 of two separate operating systems

Creates possible power struggle between
 project managers and functional area heads

Slows decision making and increases costs
 in certain instances

Promotes narrow management viewpoint

EXHIBIT 9.14   Matrix organization.

of traditional functions, and the structures of the firms reflect this strategy. The structure comprises agents in various geographic locations linked by computer. This allows the firms to take advantage of lower-cost foreign labor and to pounce more quickly on new markets or new technologies, and offers a way to exploit some of the advantages foreign companies have. We believe the dictates of environmental and internal factors affecting strategy should be the determining factors in structural choice. Our next section explains this.

Which Organization Form Is Best? [10]

A lot of energy, blood, sweat, and tears has been spent in attempts to find the "best" organization form for all businesses. The results of all the research can be summarized

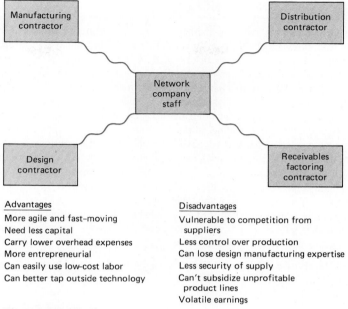

Advantages

More agile and fast-moving
Need less capital
Carry lower overhead expenses
More entrepreneurial
Can easily use low-cost labor
Can better tap outside technology

Disadvantages

Vulnerable to competition from
  suppliers
Less control over production
Can lose design manufacturing expertise
Less security of supply
Can't subsidize unprofitable
  product lines
Volatile earnings

EXHIBIT 9.15   Network organization.

as follows: An organization whose strategy has been implemented with an organization structure that fits its characteristics will be more effective than an organization whose structure does not fit its characteristics. There is no one "right" way to organize. Our previous descriptions of structures suggested that the "best" structure is related to the form of strategic advantages desired by management.

All organization forms work somewhere. So the analyses given here only represent general tendencies. In general, functional organizations work best in stable environments, with less need for cross-department coordination and communication and less need for innovation. The narrower the product line and markets, the better the functional structure works. Strategic choices determine whether products or markets are narrow or broad.

Divisional organizations work best in changing environments, which require faster adaptation, more coordination and communication, and innovation. Usually, the more complex the product line and markets, the better divisional (or even matrix) forms work. Always, strategic choices regarding complexity must be made. Exhibit 9.16 provides an example.

These guidelines should give you clues as to when a structural change is needed. For instance, if the strategy is rapid expansion through a merger, increased size may require new structures. If the strategy is to serve new markets or add unrelated products, the added complexity and diversity call for a changed structure. If the performance gap due to competition is such that retrenchment is needed, some SBUs may be dropped from the structure, or units may be recombined to gain greater

EXHIBIT 9.16   BANK OF AMERICA'S NEW STRUCTURE

Deregulation has affected the banking business dramatically. Those who could react fastest to changing customer needs and new competitors had the best chance to survive.

Bank of America has restructured in recognition that faster adaptation and better coordination and innovation are needed to face its environment. The Bank has created a new division to focus on more efficient handling of transactions. But the retail operations, including worldwide lending, deposit gathering, and other services, have not performed well enough as operating expenses have increased and some loans have gone sour.

Hence, Bank of America began reorganizing the retail bank operations in 1985. Under the new structure, the 220-person product development and marketing staff was split to focus on three market segments: individual customer accounts, personalized service for customers with sophisticated needs, and small business customers. And four newly independent sales and service units, including B of A's California branch network, national and international units, and an electronic delivery unit, will support each market group.

Under the old system, new product decisions were strictly made by senior management. And profit and loss controls were the responsibility of branch managers, who in fact had little control of overhead. The new approach attempts to spread decision-making responsibility to lower levels of the bank, and each market segment unit is responsible for profit or loss in its market. The new structure is expected to help make B of A more responsive to changes in its environment, and fits its strategic needs to reduce its image as a stodgy competitor.

Source: Adapted from "Bank America Hustles to Make Up for Lost Time—And Money," *Business Week,* Mar. 11, 1985, p. 38.

efficiency (a decrease in divisional structure). For example, General Mills divested its toy and fashion divisions, creating two new separate companies. This strategy was a function of the inability of the existing bureaucracy at General Mills to allow those divisions to quickly respond to the volatility of their markets. But many strategies can be accomplished through the existing anatomy with only fine-tuning or alterations in the administrative system which operates within the structure. Our next chapter will explore these aspects of implementation in more detail.

The final point we wish to make concerns the relationship between strategic choice and structural implementation. There is some debate about which comes first—strategy or structural change. As we indicated at the beginning of the chapter, we think that the process is circular. Structure constrains strategy to some extent. But if truly major strategic changes are made, structural change will be necessary. Exhibit 9.17 provides an example of how "misfits" between strategy and structure can create strategic problems. So the critical question is how the entire package of strategy and implementation is integrated to accomplish objectives.

Vertical Division of Labor [11]

Recognize that the emphasis here has been on forms of departmentation which tend to evolve as a strategy of expansion is put into place. Of course, the vertical structure is important also. That is, the number of levels in the hierarchy, the spans of control for managers, and the location of staff units can vary substantially. These can have an impact on strategy and vice versa. For instance, as the number of levels increases,

EXHIBIT 9.17   STRUCTURAL WOES AT DEC

Digital Equipment Corporation has more than Big Blue to contend with these days. A management reorganization has created other strategic problems for DEC.

Through 1982, DEC's structure was built around 18 separate groups that concentrated on selling to specific industries (e.g., education, engineering). This structure was originally a strength since it enabled the firm to respond quickly to customer needs. Even though most groups used the same products and components, each had discretionary funds for product development, and each handled its own market strategies, pricing, order processing, and inventories. Each group contracted with a central department for jobs needed done in manufacturing, field service, or engineering.

Eventually, these groups became fiefdoms that grew more and more protective of their own interests and lost sight of the company's long-range goals. They began fighting among themselves for limited central engineering and manufacturing resources. The process of new product development became so complex that it became difficult for DEC to move decisively.

In 1983, founder and president Kenneth Olsen per-formed radical surgery to cut out the bureaucracy. He created 4 regional management centers to do the fore-casting and sales support once done by the 18 headquar-ters-based groups. But the reorganization created a new set of headaches. "The corporate overhaul destroyed a delicate web of alliances that allowed people to get their jobs done in DEC's confusing matrix organization." As jobs were eliminated and reshuffled from headquarters to new jobs in regional centers, battles broke out over who was going to shoulder new responsibilities. Fifty man-agers from the old groups and six vice presidents left the company. Says one former manager, "The strategic di-rection at the top was not translated into job charters or communicated to us. It still is not clear."

As a result, forecasting, order processing, and pro-duction scheduling broke down. Manufacturing was put-ting out the wrong mix of products and too few disk drives rolled off the floor. Shipments to customers stalled, and inventories rose. Many customers received the wrong shipment, partial shipment, or none at all. Sales went flat.

Clearly, new strategic problems resulting from struc-tural adaptation now face DEC.

Source: Adapted from "The Dark Side of DEC's Rebound," *Business Week,* Jan. 30, 1984, pp. 51–53.

communications become more difficult. Information needed about changes in the marketplace may take longer to reach the top. As spans of control become larger, decision making takes longer, since there is a tendency to involve more people. And as staff specialists (such as personnel, information systems, or legal specialists) or line units are centralized or decentralized, there is an impact on costs, the quality of decisions made, and the strategy itself.

The structure by itself doesn't tell you everything about how the organization functions. Mechanisms for control and coordination of units can vary within a given structure. And the power of a given subsystem manager to influence strategy or receive disproportional shares of resources may not be reflected by the organization structure, although centralizing units near the top usually gives them more clout. We will discuss some of these issues in more detail in Chapter 10. For now, it should still be clear that the structure itself can help or hinder the implementation of strategy. For instance, if departments are arranged so as to serve customer groups which are no longer significant to the future strategy of the firm, a mismatch is present, and the intended strategy is not likely to be accomplished without a reorganization. However, beware the "organization quick fix." Structural alterations are not always necessary or de-sirable. Our next section indicates when some changes might be needed, but don't assume that every strategy change requires an organizational accommodation.

PLANNING SYSTEMS TO IMPLEMENT STRATEGIC MANAGEMENT [12]

Exhibit 9.7 outlined one way to establish a planning system for linking the process of formulating a strategy with plans for its implementation. Of course, the assumption there was that a multidivision organization structure was in place. But mechanisms for planning differ from firm to firm. And the roles played by corporate strategists in the development of strategies, plans, and systems for integrating them also vary. In this section we will explore how planning systems have evolved and the role of planning departments in these processes.

Wrapp describes four ways in which companies organized for the planning function in the years when the use of strategic planning was gaining impetus:

1 There was a planning committee composed of top management which had responsibilities for both planning and operations; subcommittees undertook studies, while existing corporate staff groups were made available on request.

2 There was a central planning committee with subcommittees to plan specific projects; however, top-management members assigned to the committee became full-time planners with no operating responsibilities.

3 Planning was decentralized to a general manager in each division; home office staff personnel were available for assistance, but planning was primarily a divisional activity.

4 A special planning staff was charged with responsibility for developing long-range plans; this approach created the classic split between planners and doers, and the evidence indicated that line management seldom implemented completed plans.

This latter concern has prompted many firms to reduce the size of their planning staff and refocus their efforts. For example, GE slashed the corporate planning group from 58 to 33 in 1984, and purged scores of planners in various operating sectors, groups and divisions. Eaton reacted to a "rebellion against the 'planocrats' " and cut its staff from 35 to 16. The CEOs of the new generation coming to power believe they are "strategic thinkers," and think their key line operating people should be as well. Higgins puts it this way:

> To remove the planning function from the mainstream of organizational life, i.e., setting up separate staff groups, increases the probability that the planning effort will be attended to but also increases the likelihood that plans generated by such a process will be ill-suited for decision-making purposes.

Exhibit 9.18 indicates that planners can emphasize two kinds of tasks. One task is to contribute to substantive decisions about strategies and plans (*content*). The other is to perform an instrumental role in the design and implementation of a planning system (setting up the *process* in which substantive decisions are generated). Note that depending on the relative emphasis and tasks performed, planners might be viewed as catalysts (mostly involved with process), analysts, or strategists (mostly involved with content). Thus strategist roles of a planning staff could include making acquisition studies, identifying strategic options, narrowing down alternatives, and providing information about choices; or the planning staff could give advice on the relative merits of various planning documents submitted by SBU executives. The catalyst roles could

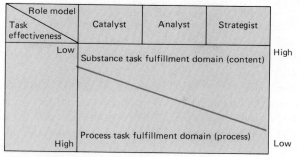

EXHIBIT 9.18   **Tasks and roles of planners.**
(P. Lorange, Corporate Planning: An Executive Viewpoint, p. 273. Copyright ©1980, Reprinted by permission of Prentice-Hall, Inc., Englewood Cliffs, N.J.)

include such activities as developing a conceptual framework for planning tailored to the needs of the organization, discussing the system with line executives, and assisting them in the use of the system (e.g., preparing planning manuals, disseminating planning calendars, distributing common planning assumptions, or arranging meetings to review interdepartmental plans).

We expect that recent changes and concerns about the ''formula planning'' approaches used by planning staffs, and the inability to gain commitment of the line to plans ''dreamed up'' by the staff, will lead to a greater focus on planning staff as catalyst for the line. This staff may perform analyses at headquarters, but the strategic decisions will be restored to those charged with implementing the plans.

SUMMARY

This is the first chapter on the implementation segment of strategic management. The implementation process involves an integrated set of choices and activities that are used to allocate resources, organize, assign key managers, set policies, and establish an administrative system to reinforce, control, and evaluate a strategy.

Proposition 9.1

A good strategy without effective implementation has a lower probability of success than if implementation decisions match strategic choices.

Strategists have the power to decide which divisions, departments, or SBUs receive what amount of money, which facilities, and which executives. These resource allocation decisions set the operative strategy of the firm.

The primary tool for making resource allocations is the budget process. A series of negotiations across organizational levels will result in final decisions about the operating budgets for SBUs or other units. Capital budgets, financial budgets, and summary budgets prepared at corporate levels are established to give force to objectives and strategies intended to be accomplished. Several problems in budgeting were noted, indicating that this process can lead to unintended strategic directions if managers are not sensitive to the need to link resource deployment to activities needed to accomplish a strategy.

The second aspect of implementation discussed in this chapter is organizational implementation. Organization involves dividing up the work among groups and individuals (division of labor) and making sure that the parts are linked together to ensure that they will work together effectively (coordination).

Several propositions are useful in understanding organizational implementation, although not all would agree with these conclusions.

Proposition 9.2

As firms move from a single product to related products to unrelated diversification, effective firms move from a functional organization structure to a divisional organization structure.

Proposition 9.3

Organizations that operate in a stable environment, are small, and have a single product/ market scope will be more effective with a functional organization structure.

Proposition 9.4

Organizations which operate in a moderately dynamic environment, are large, and have diversified from a single product/market will be more effective with a divisional organization structure.

Proposition 9.5

Organizations which operate in a dynamic environment, are large, have technologically intense businesses where the economies of scale are not important, and have short-lived projects or products will be most effective with a matrix organization structure.

Proposition 9.6

Organizations which operate in a dynamic environment, are large, have intensive technologies and marketing where economies of scale are important, and assign a large percentage of the budget to innovation will be more effective with an innovative organization structure.

Which organization form is best? The best organization structure is one which fits the organization's environment and internal characteristics giving rise to a strategy. Effective strategic management suggests that the organization structure should change if strategy changes or if the organization experiences problems. We suggested some guidelines in this regard.

The last section of the chapter indicated the need to match the strategic planning system with the needs of the organization's structure and strategy. Planners tend to emphasize different roles depending on the evolution of the use of a formal planning system and the type of strategy and structure. As structure and strategy become more diverse and complex, corporate-level planners focus on catalyst roles. The line is expected to play a more significant role in the content of strategic planning in the future. The key to an effective planning system, though, is to make sure it is designed so that the strategy and implementation plans are closely integrated.

Our next chapter explores some outputs of the planning process—the policies and plans for implementing strategic choices—as well as some other administrative aspects of the strategic management system.

REFERENCES

[1] Integrating Strategy and Implementation

Bourgeois, L. J., and D. R. Brodwin: "Strategic Implementation: Five Approaches to an Elusive Phenomenon," *Strategic Management Journal,* vol. 5 (1984), pp. 241–264.

Bradford, D. L., and A. R. Cohen: *Managing for Excellence* (New York: Wiley, 1984).

Hrebiniak, L. G., and W. F. Joyce: *Implementing Strategy* (New York: Macmillan, 1984).

Levine, J. B., and J. A. Byrne: "Corporate Odd Couples," *Business Week,* July 21, 1986, pp. 100–105.

"The New Planning," *Business Week,* Dec. 18, 1978.

Note: Also see Chapter 10 references on Implementing Strategies [1]

[2] The Implementation Process

Lorange, P.: *Implementation of Strategic Planning* (Englewood Cliffs, N.J.: Prentice-Hall, 1982).

Vancil, R. F., and P. Lorange: "Strategic Planning in Diversified Companies," *Harvard Business Review* (January–February 1975), pp. 81–90.

[3] Allocating Resources

Bower, J. L.: *Managing the Resource Allocation Process: A Study of Corporate Planning and Investment* (Cambridge, Mass.: Harvard University Press, 1970).

Gluck, F.: "The Dilemmas of Resource Allocation," *The Journal of Business Strategy,* vol. 2 (Fall 1981), pp. 67–71.

Northcraft, G. B., and G. Wolf: "Dollars, Sense, and Sunk Costs: A Life Cycle Model of Resource Allocation Decisions," *Academy of Management Review,* vol. 9 (1984), pp. 225–234.

Treece, J. B.: "Companies Cut the Budget but Spare the R&D," *Business Week,* Apr. 14, 1986, p. 50.

[4] Budgeting and Other Tools for Resource Allocation

Camillus, J. C., and Grant J.H.: "Operational Planning: The Integration of Programming and Budgeting," *Academy of Management Review,* vol. 5 (1980), pp. 369–379.

Lorange, P., and R. F. Vancil: *Strategic Planning Systems* (Englewood Cliffs, N.J.: Prentice-Hall, 1977).

Savich, R. S., and J. A. Thompson: "Resource Allocation within the Product Life Cycle," *MSU Business Topics,* vol. 26 (Autumn 1978), pp. 35–44.

[5] Structuring for Strategy

Ansoff, H. I.: "The Changing Shape of the Strategic Problem," in D. E. Schendel and C. W. Hofer (eds.), *Strategic Management: A New View of Business Policy and Planning* (Boston: Little, Brown, 1979).

Chandler, A., Jr.: *Strategy and Structure: Chapters in the History of the American Industrial Enterprise* (Cambridge, Mass.: Harvard University Press, 1962).

Child, J.: "Organizational Structure, Environment and Performance: The Role of Strategic Choice," *Sociology* (January 1972), pp. 1–22.

Frederickson, J. W.: "The Effect of Structure on the Strategic Decision Process," *Academy of Management Proceedings* (1984), pp. 12–18.

Hall, D. J., and Saias M. A.: "Strategy Follows Structure!" *Strategic Management Journal,* vol. 1 (1980), pp. 149–163.

Kay, N. M.: *The Evolving Firm: Strategy and Structure in Industrial Organization* (New York: St. Martin's, 1982).

[6] Basic Structures for Strategy

Cannon, J. T.: *Business Strategy and Policy* (New York: Harcourt, Brace, 1968).

Child, J.: *Organization* (New York: Harper & Row, 1977).

Galbraith, J., and R. K. Kazanjian: *Strategy Implementation: Structure, Systems and Process* (St. Paul, Minn.: West, 1986).

Rhenman, E.: *Organization Theory for Long Range Planning* (New York: Wiley Interscience, 1973).

[7] Forms of Departmentation

Lawrence, P. R., and Lorsch J. W.: *Organization and Environment: Managing Differentiation and Integration* (Homewood, Ill.: Irwin, 1967).

Miles, R. E. and C. C. Snow: *Organizational Strategy, Structure and Process* (New York: McGraw Hill, 1978).

Sayles, L.: "Matrix Management: The Structure with a Future," *Organizational Dynamics,* vol. 5 (1976), pp. 2–17.

Thain, D. H.: "Stages of Corporate Development," *Business Quarterly* (Winter 1969), pp. 33–45.

"A U.S. Concept Revives Oki: Reorganizing into Strategic Business Units," *Business Week,* Mar. 1, 1982, pp. 112–113.

[8] Multinational Organization Structures

Brooke, M. Z.: "Multinational Corporate Structures: The Next Stage," *Futures,* vol. 11 (April 1979), pp. 111–121.

Daniels, J. D., R. A. Pitts, and M. J. Tretter: "Strategy and Structure of U.S. Multinationals: An Exploratory Study," *Academy of Management Journal,* vol. 27 (1984), pp. 292–307.

Harrigan, K. R.: "Managing Innovation within Overseas Subsidiaries," *Journal of Business Strategy,* vol. 4 (1984), pp. 4–19.

Rumelt, R. P.: *Strategy, Structure and Economic Performance* (Cambridge, Mass.: Harvard University Press, 1974).

[9] Innovative Forms of Structure

Burgelman, R. A.: "Managing the New Venture Division: Research Findings and Implications for Strategic Management," *Strategic Management Journal,* vol. 6 (1985), pp. 39–54.

Krijnen, H. G.: "The Flexible Firm," *Long Range Planning,* vol. 12 (April 1979), pp. 63–75.

Nord, W., and S. Tucker: *Implementing Routine and Radical Innovations* (Lexington, Mass.: Lexington, 1984).

Wilson, J. W., and J. H. Dobrzynski: "And Now, the Post-Industrial Corporation," *Business Week,* Mar. 3, 1986, pp. 64–71.

[10] Factors Affecting Structural Choice

Dewar, R., and J. Hage: "Size, Technology, Complexity and Structural Differentiation: Towards a Theoretical Synthesis," *Administrative Science Quarterly,* vol 23 (1978), pp. 111–136.

Horovitz, J. H., and R. A. Thietart: "Strategy, Management Design and Firm Performance," *Strategic Management Journal,* vol. 3 (1982), pp. 67–76.

[11] Vertical Division of Labor

Frederickson, J. W.: "The Strategic Decision Process and Organizational Structure," *Academy of Management Review,* vol. 11 (1986), pp. 280–297.

Osborn, R. N., J. G. Hunt, and L. R. Jauch: *Organization Theory: An Integrated Perspective* (New York: Wiley, 1980).

[12] Planning Systems

Camillus, J. C.: "Strategic Planning Systems in the Eighties: Challenging the Conventional Wisdom," paper presented at the Strategic Management Society conference, Philadelphia, 1984.

Dyson, R. G., and M. J. Foster: "The Relationship of Participation and Effectiveness in Strategic Planning," *Strategic Management Journal,* vol. 3 (1982), pp. 77–88.

Gottschalk, E. C., Jr.: "Firms Hiring New Types of Manager to Study Issues, Emerging Troubles," *The Wall Street Journal,* June 10, 1982, pp. 23, 28.

Lorange, P., and R. F. Vancil: *Strategic Planning Systems* (Englewood Cliffs, N.J.: Prentice-Hall, 1977).

"The New Breed of Strategic Planner," *Business Week,* Sept. 17, 1984, pp. 62–71.

"Sending the Staff Out to Solve Other Companies' Problems," *Business Week,* Jan. 16, 1984, pp. 54–56.

Wheelwright, S. C., and R. L. Banks: "Involving Operating Managers in Planning Process Evolution," *Sloan Management Review* (Summer 1979), pp. 43–59.

Wrapp, E.: "Organization for Long Range Planning," *Harvard Business Review,* vol. 35, no. 1 (January–February 1957).

CHAPTER OUTLINE

IMPLEMENTATION: PLANS, POLICIES, LEADERSHIP, AND INTERNATIONAL STRATEGY

OBJECTIVES

- To illustrate the major types of plans required to implement strategy
- To understand the process of policy implementation
- To indicate how executives handle leadership implementation
- To describe implementation aspects of international strategy

INTRODUCTION [1]

In Chapter 9 you learned how planning systems can be used as aids in the tasks of developing and implementing strategy. We also outlined what some of those tasks were—specifically, allocating resources and organizing jobs.

But there are other interrelated concerns that strategists must deal with if a strategy is to be effectively implemented. The organization requires some mechanisms to ensure that the activities are integrated and coordinated. Further, it is important that the plans developed be coupled with the strategies; otherwise, the plans may move the firm in an unintended direction. The importance of these efforts cannot be ignored, since field studies indicate that obstacles encountered by companies in implementing strategy are leading to executive disenchantment with strategic planning because ''nothing happens, or what happens is not a consequence of planning.'' To close gaps created by internal conditions, plans must be made to accomplish the tasks assigned to functional areas.

The major way in which these aspects of implementation are accomplished is through the development of plans, policies, and administrative processes. Each functional area of the business needs a plan to give direction and timing to its activities and personnel in the use of resources consistent with the demands of the strategy. Policies are guides to action. They indicate how the tasks assigned to the organization might be accomplished and provide a basis for lower-level managers on which to make decisions about the use of the resources which have been allocated. The other major administrative process discussed in this chapter is leadership implementation. Managers need to be selected, developed, and motivated to accomplish the jobs assigned and interpret plans and policies which give force to the strategy.

We will defer a discussion of several other aspects of administrative processes to our last chapter. That is, a follow-through on implementation requires an effective control and information system to provide accurate, complete, and timely feedback for evaluating progress toward objectives. Exhibit 10.1 reminds you, then, that these aspects of the strategic management process are interrelated with one another.

PLAN AND POLICY IMPLEMENTATION [2]

Changes in strategic direction do not occur automatically. Operational plans and tactics must be established to make a strategy work. While middle managers in functional areas usually make such decisions, they need to be guided by the strategy so that the plans and tactics are geared to the accomplishment of desired objectives. Thus plans and policies for the functional areas of the business are established to assist in this process.

Our last chapter described the strategic planning function. We suggested that line managers need to be involved because they implement the strategy. In effect, functional managers make plans to use the resources allocated to them in specific ways. While some refer to these as functional "strategies," we prefer to regard them as *plans,* or *tactics,* for carrying out the business strategy. Such plans are drawn up within guidelines set at higher levels—policies.

An enterprise could develop hundreds of policies to cover the important areas of the business. But a policy does not tell the manager how to handle a specific promotion or add a specific product. It serves as a guide to middle and supervisory managers in making certain choices.

Plans and policies are developed to ensure that (1) the strategic decision is implemented, (2) there is a basis for control, (3) the amount of time executives spend making decisions is reduced, (4) similar situations are handled consistently, and (5) coordination across units will occur where necessary.

Development of Plans and Policies [3]

Creating plans and policies leads to conditions where subordinate managers will know what they are supposed to do and willingly implement the decision.

Managers create plans and policies to make the strategies work. Policies provide the means for carrying out plans and strategic decisions. The critical element is the ability to factor the grand strategy into plans and policies that are compatible, workable, and not just "theoretically sound." It is not enough for managers to decide to change the strategy. What comes next is at least as important: How do we get there?

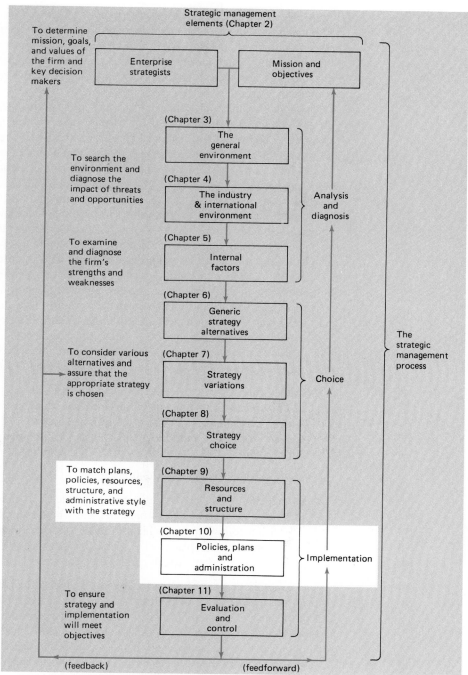

EXHIBIT 10.1   **A model of strategic management.**

When? and How efficiently? A manager answers these questions by preparing plans and policies to implement the grand strategy. For example, let us say that the strategic choice was to diversify. Now the executive must decide what to diversify into, where to diversify, how much money will be needed, where the money will come from, and what changes are needed in marketing, production, and other functions to make diversification work.

The amount of planning and policymaking in the formal sense will vary with the size and complexity of the firm. If the firm is small, or if it is a simple business, a few policies and plans will suffice. The plans and policies are generally understood and verbal. Larger and more complex firms find that policies and plans on every major aspect of the firm—marketing, finance, production and operations, personnel, and so forth—are necessary, for the competitive advantage of the large firm is its power, not its speed. That is where the smaller firm or decentralized division excels.

The processes involved in establishing plans and policies are quite similar to those influencing strategy formation and choice. That is, environmental factors can influence the choices; internal policies and the power of subunits jockeying for position play a role; etc. After all, these are going hand in hand with resource allocation decisions (see Chapter 9). Hence, resistance to change, conflict resolution techniques, and coalition building will all be at play in the development of plans and policies.

Without good plans and policies managers would make the same decisions over and over again. And different managers might choose different directions, and this could create problems. On the other hand, plans and policies should never be so inflexible as to prevent exceptions for good reasons. So criteria for judging the adequacy of plans and policies developed would include the following:

- Do they reflect present or desired company practices and behavior?
- Are they practical, given existing or expected situations?
- Do they exist in areas critical to the firm's success?
- Are they consistent with one another, and do they reflect the timing needed to accomplish goals?

As a result, policies and plans will:

1 Specify more precisely how the strategic choice will come to be—what is to be done, who is to do it, how it is to be done, and when it should be finished.

2 Establish a follow-up mechanism to make sure the strategic choice, plans, and policy decisions will take place.

3 Lead to new strengths which can be used for strategy in the future.

One example of a set of plans for several strategies is given in Exhibit 10.2. For each of these plans, a set of policies will have to be established for the appropriate area of the business. The policies will ensure that the plans are carried out as intended and that the different areas are working toward the same ends. Companies have plans and policies that cover nearly every major aspect of the firm. The example in Exhibit 10.2 illustrates only a few areas. The minimal plans and policies which must be developed are the key functional decisions for each area of the business. We will highlight some of the more important issues for each area in the rest of this section.

EXHIBIT 10.2   ALTERNATIVE BUSINESS STRATEGIES AND PLANS

Strategy	Marketing–product line plans	Manufacturing plans	Human resources plans	Financial plans	Timing
Retrenchment	Identify product lines for divestment—those with low sales or margins.	Identify plants to close on the basis of capacity utilization.	Reduce personnel on the basis of skills needed in the future and seniority.	Eliminate or reduce dividends, and manage cash flows.	Sell plants and reduce personnel in 1 year; cut dividends now.
Stability	Push the high-margin products in the line.	Defer plant and equipment investments over $200,000.	Invest in training programs to improve management skills.	Develop good bank relations, maintain steady dividends, and strengthen the balance sheet.	Continue for three years unless trends show high opportunity.
Expansion	Extend and improve product lines; volume is more critical than margins.	Expand plant capacity to support new products as necessary.	Hire additional sales, R&D, and production workers and managers.	Increase the debt-equity ratio by one-third. Consider the impact of dividend policy on cash-flow needs.	Evaluate market share position and financial condition after 2 years.

Then we will return to some questions about how these are to be integrated, since our criteria suggest that plans and policies need to be consistent, provide for coordination, and deal with timing issues.

As we discuss each area, recognize that we are not presenting an exhaustive list of issues. Specialists in each area develop plans and policies in much more breadth and depth than we can cover here. But the list indicates the types of major questions which need to be addressed if strategy is to be implemented effectively.

Financial and Accounting Policies and Plans [4]

Financial and accounting plans and policies are closely related to the resource allocation process discussed in Chapter 9. But financial policies may be set to provide guidelines in advance for where capital will come from, how capital may or may not be used, and how recurring needs will be met. Accounting policies will be established to deal with such questions as how to handle inventories, which accounts to capitalize, which tax approaches to use, and how to treat expenses and costs. These policies can make a huge difference in the firm's appearance of success or failure.

Capital

Long-term versus short-term plans are needed in relation to how to finance activities of the business. For instance, a policy is usually established with respect to the desired proportion of short-term debt, long-term debt, and preferred and common equity. Of course, philosophies regarding borrowing, the use of leverage, and control of the business, as well as such economic factors as the availability and cost of capital and tax implications, play a role in these decisions. For instance, in the 1980s many U.S. firms began replacing costly debt (due to high interest rates) with low-yielding stock. Policies regarding dividend payouts (e.g., regularity and rate) and reinvestment of profits in retained earnings are also related here and further reflect the impact of such factors as tax laws and owner influence and objectives. For example, tax benefits have enhanced the use of employee stock options (ESOPs) as a tool to raise capital or a means to become private in a leveraged buyout.

Lease or Buy

Sources of capital are related to uses of capital. A prime example is leasing versus buying fixed assets. A policy to lease classes of assets will change the nature of the need for funds over time and the nature of the balance sheet. Thus owning a building (say, the Pan Am building in Manhattan) versus leasing such space has an impact on working capital needs and the ability to finance other types of activities. Hence a strategy of rapid expansion, if funds are limited in the short term, might be accomplished through leasing rather than buying. Sale-and-leaseback arrangements became quite popular in the early 1980s because of the favorable tax benefits associated with such policies.

Risk

Other financial policies concern the evaluation of proposals for investing in certain projects. For instance, a "hurdle rate of return" may be specified as a policy guide before some strategic options will be considered. Hurdle rates may differ, depending on how risk is assessed. Another method for assessing potential investment alternatives includes a risk-adjusted discount rate in the net present value approach. A policy of a mix of investment risks is as useful as marketing-mix policies or planning a mix of basic and applied research. The investment-risk mix is related to strategic choice, of course. If expansion is the desired strategy, greater risks are acceptable. A mix of low-risk projects only may be an indication that retrenchment is on the horizon. In the mid-1980s, corporate treasurers made increasing use of "swap transactions" which allowed firms to trade interest rate payments and limit some exposure to risk of interest rate fluctuation. In addition, more and more firms sought to hedge foreign currencies as part of their financial plans.

The other area in which risk plans are needed is in the area of insurance. Corporate liability insurance in the mid-1980s was becoming very expensive, and in some instances difficult to get at all. Some firms were forced out of business because they did not believe they could expose themselves to the risk of doing business without insurance. Other firms chose a plan of in-house protection, but such plans require a large resource base. Still others joined consortia to pool resources as an alternative to traditional insurers. Another possibility is to change the nature of coverage for catastrophic risks and at the same time reduce or eliminate coverage for more common risks. Choices here can affect the strategy in terms of costs of doing business, or even lead to ultimate retrenchment (liquidation or sale).

Use of Assets

Specific targets for current assets and cash flows are also needed for items such as inventories (finished goods and raw materials) and accounts receivable and payable. Policies for the desired proportion of funds tied up in these accounts and the accounting treatment (e.g., LIFO or FIFO, or book or market value) are relevant here, as are rules for financial disclosure based on historical or "inflation-related" reporting. Some of these policies are mandated by the SEC or other government bodies, but managers should decide which approach provides them with the most useful information for decision making (as opposed to which treatment makes the books "look better"). Alternative treatments of accounting data can lead to significant differences in the data upon which managers base their decisions.

Policies governing asset use have a direct impact on other components of strategy and cannot be made in isolation. For example, a policy with respect to maintaining a particular monetary value of safety stock of finished goods relates to marketing policy regarding customer relations and the ability to deliver outputs, as well as to production policy regarding lead times and the size of production runs. Or if an airline is trying to enhance relations with travel agents in a new territory, then extending the time for accounts receivable on the payment for tickets may be an important decision affecting marketing and finance.

Financial plans also become important in particular strategic actions such as mergers or liquidations or bankruptcies. In some cases, legal factors restrain choices. But there are usually several options which require a financial decision as to how to best implement the strategy. For example, the appendix for Chapter 7 suggested that a leveraged buyout was one option for financing a merger. Such an option would require a policy decision or would be made in relation to other plans associated with the desired financial structure of the business.

Exhibit 10.3 provides an interesting example of how some financial policies relate to the strategy of a firm. If a firm is divesting or liquidating, financial policies as well as other plans will need to be specified. For instance: How urgent is it? What will the cash flow look like? What will creditors get? Who are the potential buyers? What will the price be? How will we lay off people? In the early 1980s, many firms began to alter their plans to focus on debt reduction and increasing the cash flow due to stability strategies taken in response to disinflation.

Finally, some financial policies can have an indirect effect on strategy through the executive compensation system. For instance, firms which use stock options as a form of compensation may ultimately change the nature of control of the business or influence risk choices made by the executives involved. The implications could be positive or negative, and so such outcomes should be considered as these plans and policies are established.

EXHIBIT 10.3 TCI IS A MAMMOTH TAX SHELTER

Tele-Communications Inc. is the third largest cable company in the United States. Its strategy has been to buy existing small systems in small markets as opposed to competing for franchise rights in large cities. But it has steadfastly refused to invest in upgrading its systems, preferring to accumulate a large subscriber list by acquisition.

It uses some interesting financial policies. In fact, "it has so many subsidiaries and off-balance-sheet assets that it is hard to get a clear picture of what TCI owns." What is most interesting is that TCI seems to care little about earnings growth. The scheme is to go contrary to earning money, paying taxes, and issuing dividends. Says John Malone, president, "If TCI does not have earnings, it won't pay taxes, and that means more cash to buy systems." He expects that after-tax earnings will not be strong for the foreseeable future and prefers to keep TCI as "a mammoth tax shelter." Thus many of its acquisitions are based on sheltering income with expenses, and the firm has been aggressive in its use of accelerated depreciation.

TCI extends borrowing capabilities by creating nonconsolidated operations that hold assets and can borrow for acquisitions and buy company stock. Another move to raise equity and avoid takeovers was to create a new class of common stock with 10 votes per share which management then took in exchange for old shares with one vote.

However, these financial approaches to implement expansion may also be a signal that the company is growing to sell out. While investing in existing systems offers economic stability for relatively long periods, franchise licenses may no longer offer a risk-free cash cow. Competition and demands from city councils may require heavy investment to upgrade systems. If that becomes a greater issue, TCI may be in a position where its large subscriber list makes it an attractive takeover target. So the financial policies to implement strategy may lead to a new strategy as well.

Source: Adapted from "How TCI Builds a Cable Empire," *Business Week,* Nov. 23, 1981, pp. 74–76.

Hence, some of the crucial financial questions needing implementation include:

- Where will we get additional funds to expand, either internally or externally?
- If external expansion is desired, how and where will it be accomplished?
- What will the strategy do to our cash flow?
- What accounting systems and policies do we use (for example, LIFO or FIFO)?
- What capital structure policy do we pursue? No debt or a heavily leveraged structure?
- How much should we pay out in dividends?
- How much cash and how many other assets do we keep on hand?
- Should we hedge our foreign currency exchange risk?

It is crucial that financial plans and policies are such that the funds needed are available at the right time and at the lowest cost.

Marketing Policies and Plans [5]

Some of the crucial marketing plans and policy questions include:

- Specifically, which products or services will be focused on, present ones or new ones?
- Which channels will be used to market these products or services? Will we use exclusive dealerships? Multiple channels?

• How will we promote these products or services? Is it our policy to use large amounts of TV advertising or no advertising? Heavy personal selling expenses or none? Price competition or nonprice competition?

• Do we have an adequate sales force?

In other words, marketing plans include the competitive tactics to use in the marketing mix. Specifically, how will we price, promote, and distribute, and what specific lines of products will we develop with what kind of quality?

Products and Markets

Assume, for example, that we have chosen a strategy of expansion in related products. Do we want a complete line? How many sizes or shapes? How many new products will we add, and when? How do we define quality (appearance, purity, durability, dependability)? Will we build in obsolescence? When will we introduce new products, or modifications?

Or assume that the strategy is to expand to new markets. Which specific customer groups are we going after? Do we want to limit the share of business we do with any given customer or class of customers? Which specific geographic territories will we enter? If we have chosen international markets, are we geared to meet different cultural needs and demands? These kinds of questions require decisions which should be guided by strategic intent. By the same token, product elimination as a retrenchment strategy is often neglected, but it is a viable plan for goals of long-term growth or survival.

Distribution and Promotion

Are there preferred channels of distribution for efficient and effective delivery? If there is a trade-off, what guideline should we use for choosing distributors? As we examine our customers, what is the preferred form of promotion? What sales approaches and media do we use? How much money will we allocate for advertising? Should we guarantee delivery? If we market in foreign countries, do our promotion policies account for cultural differences? More than one firm has failed to successfully enter foreign markets because advertisements, when translated, sent unintended messages.

Price and Packaging

Pricing and other marketing policies become particularly critical at various stages of product development and the firm's strategy. Price has become a primary weapon in tactical battles to secure a market share. For example, if rapid expansion is desired early in the development of a product, pricing may be below cost. (Of course, a desire to attract customers through loss leaders may be another reason for selling below cost.) Being a price leader or follower is a policy which managers need to address.

Here in particular you can see how the development of plans can be affected by managerial values. Offensive versus defensive strategists will view a particular pricing question differently. During periods of stable demand we would expect prices to remain relatively fixed (perhaps adjusted for inflation). If the strategy is retrenchment, price increases and a reduction in promotion and distribution costs would be expected if not outright abandonment. If the firm is retrenching out of certain areas as opposed to liquidating, an orderly withdrawal through various "demarketing" mechanisms would be necessary.

Packaging can be an alternative competitive weapon in the strategy of the firm. If product stability is the strategy, packaging changes (e.g., toothpaste in a pump, or shaving cream in a brush) can help expand the pace of market penetration.

Policies and plans must be made which interrelate several aspects of the strategy. For instance, a policy of different prices for different customers (or a one-price policy) is one which can have an impact on the product and market strategy. As you will see later, plans and policies must also be set in relation to other aspects of the business—for instance, price is particularly critical in relation to volume-cost-profit conditions, which affect production and the financial condition.

In Chapter 7 we indicated that firms can pursue active or passive strategies. If a firm pursues an active strategy, marketing "warfare" such as frontal attacks, flanking attacks, encirclement, a bypass attack, or guerilla warfare conjure up tactics for identifying competitors' weaknesses and for maneuvering using internal strengths. Conversely, passive alternatives can lead to marketing plans such as position defense, mobile defense, preemptive defense, counteroffensives, flank-position defense, or strategic withdrawal. Indeed, move and countermove can occur with the strategy as when Pepsi announced the purchase of 7-Up and Coke countered with a buyout of Dr. Pepper in a head-on battle for soft-drink market-share dominance. Exhibit 10.4 presents a picture of pricing warfare in the pharmaceutical business.

EXHIBIT 10.4   AT WAR WITH PRICES

What does a pharmaceutical company do if it is losing market share on an identical drug to a cheaper competitor, new over-the-counter drugs promise more competition, and cheaper generic versions are about to enter the battle when the patent runs out? Upjohn chose to cut the price by 30% of Motrin, its biggest seller arthritis pain killer. Upjohn hoped to preserve market share and give new product extensions a good start. They were willing to sacrifice present profits for future ones.

But Boots Pharmaceuticals, a British firm, cut the prices of its Motrin equivalent by 30% also, to preserve its advantage. Boots had licensed Upjohn to make and sell ibuprofen in the United States 10 years earlier. But it also retained its rights to sell the product in the U.S. market. Upjohn did not think they would be a serious competitor. At first, Boots' entry in 1977 had little im-

pact, so Upjohn raised the price of Motrin on two occasions. But the battle took another step. Boots licensed American Home Products to make an over-the-counter version of ibuprofen, and Upjohn agreed to let Bristol-Myers sell one that Upjohn makes. Both hit the market in 1983 and the battle was on. Many arthritic patients decided to treat themselves by taking more of the cheaper version.

The price war is likely to expand to a new front. Both Upjohn and Boots applied to the FDA for approval of a more powerful second-generation version of the drug. But Upjohn will continue to pay a license fee to Boots, giving the British firm a 15 to 20% cost advantage. Hence, the strategy at Upjohn on product extensions will be affected by past strategic choices and its pricing policies used to carry out strategy.

Source: Adapted from "Price Cuts That Backfired on Upjohn," *Business Week,* Aug. 6, 1984, pp. 23–24.

Again, if the marketing plans and policies don't mesh with the corporate strategy, and if marketing plans don't fit carefully with other functional policies, the objectives will not be met.

Production-Operations Management (POM) Policies and Plans [6]

POM is another area needing implementation plans and policies. Critical questions in this area include:

* Can we handle the business with our present facilities and number of shifts? Must we add equipment, facilities, and shifts? Where? Are layoffs needed? Should we subcontract?
* What is the firm's inventory safety level? How many suppliers do we need for purchases of major supplies?
* What level of productivity and costs should the firm seek?
* How much emphasis should there be on quality control and maintenance?
* How far ahead should we schedule production?
* How is the management of production and operations integrated with our strategy?
* Should we locate facilities in foreign countries, or exit countries where facilities are at risk?

Capacity and Utilization

Plans must be made for the levels of production or operations desired to fit the strategy. If rapid expansion is desired through internal means, does the firm have sufficient capacity to accommodate such expansion? Is the plant being used on overtime, double, or triple shifts? If retrenchment is under way, do we want to cut back production volume or keep the plant going and build inventories?

These questions may call for a plan for long-term production vis-à-vis marketing plans. Generally, three options exist for scheduling capacity usage: demand matching, operations smoothing, and subcontracting. If demand is seasonal, for example, demand matching calls for producing output with the season. Operations smoothing calls for continuous production to meet average demand levels. Subcontracting allows a firm to maintain steady minimal levels of output while meeting peak periods with output from subcontractors. Each of these approaches, of course, implies some trade-offs with respect to the costs of equipment, overtime, inventories, labor, maintenance, and subcontracting. When demand downturns occur, a plan to build inventory instead of retrenching becomes a major strategic decision.

As the plan is determined, there may remain a need or desire for longer-term capacity buildup. Here the options may include adding capacity, merging with another producer, or joint ventures. In any case, questions concerning the types of equipment, the amount of capacity, and the interface with existing units need to be addressed. Naturally, the overall size of a plant is of importance here and involves questions of economies of scale. This is partly determined by the technology employed but is also influenced by production scheduling and the basic marketing strategy. A large, "efficient'' plant may not be *effective* if it is not producing the kinds of outputs called for by the strategy. Capacity planning is also related to the policy question regarding scheduling. If demand matching is used, then plant size is geared to the production of peak output; otherwise, capacity can be smaller. Exhibit 10.5 indicates how production scheduling relates to decisions on plant capacity and broader strategic issues.

Location of Facilities

Assuming that a strategy of expansion is under way, another question of importance is where to locate plants or operations facilities. For instance, a major component in airline operations is the location of facilities for aircraft maintenance.

Of course, the critical elements of the firm's marketing and financial plans are relevant to the location decision. For instance, if new distribution approaches are a part of the strategy, locating plants near potential markets may outweigh factors such

---

EXHIBIT 10.5   A RADICAL PRODUCTION SCHEDULE?

True or False? The best way to maximize a plant's profitability is not to maximize its output. The ''True'' answer to this is anathema to traditional thinking; yet the optimized production technology (OPT) system argues for just such a policy in manufacturing.

Traditional cost accounting methods suggest that it is always better to run a batch of 1000 parts through a machine than it is to run 100 parts. Yet if 900 of those 1000 are going to sit in inventory, the OPT system suggests that such an approach is less cost-effective.

OPT is a two-part package: a simulated manufacturing program and radical shop-floor production rules. OPT enables companies to increase plant output while simultaneously lowering inventory and operating expenses. It forces managers and workers to coordinate their work and the flow of parts through a factory with one principle in mind: bottlenecks (lack of skilled labor, old machinery, etc.) ultimately constrain manufacturing output. By identifying bottlenecks in advance, and scheduling work flow with this in mind, manufacturing productivity can be increased dramatically. In fact, this is the basis of the ''just in time'' approach to inventory management popularized in Japan. By running bottlenecked operations at 100% of capacity while controlling the flow of materials into the bottleneck so they do not build up, inventories can be kept to the bare bones. In a just-in-time plant, managers tend to adjust production rates only after inventory build-

ups occur. But OPT simulations allow identification of bottlenecks in advance. Then managers schedule labor and machine hours so parts move continually through the system. Companies like Caterpillar, Bendix, and Westinghouse have used OPT to reduce work-in-process inventory, thus slicing weeks off lead times on customer orders.

Strategically, many companies investing in new factory automation systems may end up only boosting production costs. Hownet Turbine Components' plant used the OPT system instead of closing the plant during a downturn. Production in several operations was halted, and workers were transferred to shipping, where the bottleneck was identified. The firm managed to stabilize employment during a severe slump and cut delivery times. Hownet held its sales decline to 10% while the rest of the industry saw 50% drops in sales.

Consciously choosing not to run expensive machines flat out, or allowing workers to do nothing or transferring them, is an extraordinary leap of faith for manufacturing managers. It can be tough to sell the boss on the idea that lots of idle time is acceptable. Yet if such a system of scheduling production is effective, strategic choices on such things as plant expansion or new machinery for ''productivity improvement'' may result in money wasted.

Source: Adapted from B. Powell, ''Boosting Shop-Floor Productivity by Breaking All the Rules,'' *Business Week*, Nov. 26, 1984, pp. 100–104.

as the availability or cost of raw material inputs. The financial trade-offs of locating facilities near sources of labor or energy versus customers also need to be examined. Naturally, the type of product and logistics costs of inputs versus outputs become relevant considerations.

Another factor of some importance is the degree of certainty associated with a new strategy. For instance, in the selection of a site for a new plant, the availability of land for further expansion later may be important if the decision is to plan for anticipated sales increases in the long run. And if the decision involves a move to foreign countries, social stability and tax conditions may play a role.

Finally, plants may be located near existing facilities to take advantage of economies of organization, purchasing, and the like. In some cases, the decision is to replace existing facilities (or equipment) with new ones to take advantage of new technologies that are replacing obsolete ones. In other cases, the decision is to add on to an existing plant or build nearby. In still others, the firm seeks to take advantage of lower-cost foreign labor by locating plants outside its home country. Again, factors such as labor, transportation, market location, and technologies play key roles in these determinations.

Processes

The types of processes to use are largely determined by the technology needed to produce given outputs. Still, some discretion or options may exist, particularly with respect to issues like the quality of the processing equipment and allowable tolerances. Many Japanese firms have gained significant competitive advantages by pursuing a policy of high-quality statistical control for their processing systems.

Equipment and Maintenance

Policies regarding investment to maintain or replace a plant and equipment can be important to the long-term ability of a firm to compete successfully and achieve objectives such as profits. Of course, the need for the maintenance of facilities varies from firm to firm. Maintenance at nuclear power plants or of aircraft is an absolute necessity. But there are often choices about whether to follow routine schedules (e.g., preventive maintenance) or whether to defer maintenance until there is a breakdown or replacement becomes necessary. Of course, keeping up-to-date, cost-effective equipment is a question of importance in creating a competitive advantage.

The overall quality component of a firm's strategy may determine the type of policy established for maintenance. But the criticality of prompt delivery of outputs may also play a role, and once again trade-offs with regard to inventory policies, the use of overtime, production schedules, and the like, become relevant.

Sourcing

Another key area in the operations of the firm involves sources of inputs or services important to the strategy. Choices about whom to purchase from involve more than a simple question of cost or availability. For instance, options may exist for shipping outputs by various forms of transportation (e.g., rail, airplane, ship). The speed of delivery versus costs may be important in the selection of the mode as well as the vendor. Further, whether to use one or more vendors or several sources for inputs and services is a question of some significance. Increasing dependence on one or a few sources may increase favorable treatment and cost savings but could come at the expense of flexibility.

Perhaps the key strategic issue involving sourcing is the make or buy question. In many instances, the decision is made by purchasing departments largely on the basis of the price to buy versus the cost to make. Yet such a policy is, in effect, a strategic decision regarding the development of competitive advantages. For instance, different financial needs are involved in making versus buying, and these can affect the capital structure. If quick delivery is important to the strategy, consideration must be given to the varying reliability of suppliers versus the control over components or supplies made in-house. If expansion strategies for new products are desired, a firm may opt for buying specialty products to round out a line or making these itself. Of course, plant capacity, personnel skills, and the financial condition all play a role in such a decision. Similarly, if retrenchment is the strategic choice, cost trade-offs of making versus buying can play a role here. In Chapter 9 we described the "network" organization. Network firms have gone to extreme vertical *dis*integration by choosing to eliminate control over internal production. Many use foreign suppliers as sources. In essence, the question of vertical integration as a strategy is implicit in make-or-buy decisions. Hence, internal and external factors as well as objectives involved in strategy formulation should guide the establishment of policies in this area; strategic choice should not be left to the purchasing department by default.

In Chapter 5 we discussed how flexibility might become an important strategic advantage in manufacturing. Here, policies such as relying on suppliers within 60 miles of a plant, or shipping finished goods immediately (instead of producing for inventory) can implement a just-in-time approach to accomplishing aggregate manufacturing flexibility. Similarly, personnel policies allowing the hiring of temporary or part-time workers for operations as necessary increase flexibility and can reduce costs. Allen-Bradley Company found that its highly automated assembly line increased flexibility, albeit at a cost of lower output. Yet the flexibility was seen as a higher-order priority than output, one that was essential to Allen-Bradley's future competitive ability.

POM is a crucial functional area in implementing strategies. Traditionally, marketing and POM have been rivals. But they must coexist and work together, and their tasks must be coordinated through appropriate policies and plans, if any strategy is to work.

Research and Development Policies and Plans [7]

Research and development is a function which straddles both POM and marketing. Crucial implementation questions for R&D include:

- Will we emphasize product or process improvements?
- Should we encourage basic research or focus on commercial development?

* Are we going to be leaders or followers?
* How much will we spend on R&D?
* Which technology should we pursue, and when should we pursue it?
* How can we manage the transition from one technology to another?
* How do we prepare the firm for technological change?

Products and Processes

Guidelines are needed to encourage the types of R&D efforts required for the strategy. For example, if new-product development is the basic strategic direction of the firm, then the research effort will be geared to focus on this activity. Of course, stability strategies which may call for product improvements would require a greater emphasis on modifications to the existing line. If a turnaround strategy is desirable, R&D efforts may be focused on improving production processes to reduce costs. Unfortunately, retrenchment strategies often are implemented by cutting R&D activities which may be needed for long-term improvements in the business. Such short-sighted policies provide an example of how the implementation of the current strategy may limit long-term strategy development.

The strategy of vertical integration (e.g., backward or forward expansion in functions) is another area where R&D policy becomes particularly relevant. The technologies involved in providing inputs or subsequent processing of outputs associated with changing functions would normally require policies to provide for resources and expertise in the new areas of activity.

Basic and Applied Research

Another area would include the relative focus of effort on performing basic or applied research. Few companies will authorize the research department to study anything its scientists may be interested in. But the extent of concern with short-term commercialization versus theoretical knowledge which may lead to major break-throughs is an issue of some importance.

If a firm is going to undertake basic research, it must be prepared to accept certain financial outcomes and commitments: longer-term risk with potentially no payout or long payback periods, and enough capital to exploit discoveries if and when they are made. Of course, the firm may need to engage in some basic research if the nature of its business requires it (e.g., most pharmaceutical firms depend on basic research).

Offensive or Defensive Strategies

Some R&D options are available which reflect whether the strategy is offensive or defensive. That is, as with policies such as pricing, strategists can choose to be leaders or followers. If leadership is endorsed, greater emphasis will be placed on R&D in order to be "first to market." Of course, the costs and risk can be high. Others prefer to be fast seconds or followers who take basic research done by others and pursue product modifications. In the follower approach, another option is to buy the R&D efforts of others (such as university, government, or independent research labs). Buying patents or paying license or royalty fees may be another option for firms which do not have strengths in the R&D area or for firms which do not wish to make a commitment to or take the risks of building technological leadership. Another option is the joint-venture strategy, which combines internal and external approaches. Such strategies require policies for negotiating contracts and agreements, using outputs from research efforts, and deciding how the firm's own R&D departments will be involved in the joint efforts.

Allocating R&D Resources

Policies as to the amount of financial commitment in R&D can be based on the following guidelines:

- Maximum range—5 to 20 percent of gross profit, depending on the industry
- Minimum range—competitor actions

However, these figures provide a potentially wide range of discretion within which managers must subjectively determine how the R&D activity fits as a component of overall strategy. Perhaps more importantly, questions of how these funds will be used need to be addressed. Exhibit 10.6 suggests that changing policies on how R&D personnel use their resources can impact a firm's strategy.

EXHIBIT 10.6   POLISHING UP ITS R&D

Chesebrough-Ponds needs an innovation. Recent troubles included a costly stock repurchase and a $95 million bill for a firm it didn't want to buy. Both involved deals with Carl Icahn, and the moves boosted its ratio of debt to equity to 47%. At the same time, sales of its diverse product line (such as Prince tennis rackets, Ragu sauces, Bass shoes, and Vaseline) have plateaued. But recent moves to spur innovation may be just what the doctor ordered.

In late 1983, Chesebrough executives began allowing employees at its main lab to quit working on their assigned projects every Friday at noon to do experimental work of theirs—as long as it related to a business Chesebrough was in. As the director of R&D put it, "research efforts, especially in cosmetics, were often subservient to marketing." Marketers would identify a niche, and direct R&D to modify an existing product to fit it. As a result, breakthroughs were seldom achieved.

But the latest policy shift has resulted in a rare innovation in a business where "me-too" products are the rule. A "Polishing Pen" has been created whereby nail polish can be applied with a marking-pen-type applicator. Early users say the polish sometimes smudges and the tip eventually loses shape. But the ease with which the polish goes on and the speed at which it dries are expected to appeal to working women who will not sit still for lengthy manicures.

The researcher who made this breakthrough took Fridays at noon off to work on his idea, and soon weekends were devoted to the project. In 4 months, a prototype was developed. Chesebrough marketers ran the product by consumers and soon called for commercialization. A team of manufacturing, development, packaging, and marketing people planned to ready the pen for introduction in one year.

Chesebrough executives hope this will be just the beginning of a new product strategy resulting from the R&D policy changes they have made to spur innovation. Although they have actually cut back R&D with staff reductions, including firing 31 high-level managers, they have sharply focused efforts toward new product development.

Source: Adapted from "How Chesebrough-Ponds Put Nail Polish in a Pen," *Business Week,* Oct. 8, 1984, pp. 196–200.

Personnel, Legal, and Public Relations Policies and Plans [8]

Besides the four major line functions, major staff functions need functional policy implementation too. The crucial implementation questions for personnel include:

- Will we have an adequate work force?
- How much hiring and retraining are necessary?
- What types of individuals do we need to recruit? College graduates? Members of minority groups?
- How should we recruit—through advertising or personal contact? What methods of selection should we use—informal interviews or very sophisticated testing?
- What standards and methods are used for promotion? (For example, do we promote from within, or on the basis of seniority?)
- What will our payment policies, incentive plans, benefits, labor relations policies, etc., be?
- Is executive compensation tied to strategic objectives?

The basic questions for the *legal* staff include:

- Are the policies and plans in other areas legal?
- What are the implications of testing the law?

Finally, public relations policies deal with the presentation of the corporate image and involvement in community activities.

Personnel

As the strategy is developed, plans and policies for human resources need to be developed as well. Human resources must be recruited, allocated, developed, and maintained. Of course, questions about recruitment are similar to the "sourcing" issues. For example: Will the necessary work force be available? Where do the workers come from? Can we afford the cost? Personnel development is correlated with the "make versus buy" issue in the sense that policies of internal promotion and training may be preferred to recruiting from outside the organization. The allocation issue involves making sure that the tasks and resources distributed to various parts of the organization include the right people—those with appropriate skills and abilities to carry out the tasks effectively. Limitations on recruitment and allocation decisions may occur if there are legal restrictions or if the firm is unionized. Industrial relations policies need to be established which deal with such questions as affirmative action, work rules, etc.

With respect to maintaining the work force, policies regarding levels of pay, supplemental benefits, and systems for performance appraisal need to be established. Such policies can be critical, particularly in labor-intensive businesses, to the ability to carry out a strategy and compete effectively.

Perhaps one of the most difficult decisions regarding personnel occurs when a firm is pursuing a retrenchment strategy. At these times, questions usually include whether or not to lay off or terminate employees, how many, and who. Again, union contracts may establish some kind of policy here (resulting from earlier negotiations where a previous policy was laid down). But a firm may also attempt to protect labor and seek a shortened workweek or maintain the level of production for a time. Such policies relate to those in production and finance. A related matter is the relative proportion of managers and workers in line and staff functions. Several writers have suggested that the policies of many U.S. firms have stressed placing the brightest and best people in staff functions at the expense of the line, which does the basic work. This has been blamed for declining productivity, inadequate plant investment, marginal quality standards, and the like. As a result, many firms have begun a streamlining program by cutting the corporate level and other staff levels. Their goal is to pare overhead costs and gain some control over unwieldy, top-heavy structures. Of course, such trade-offs must be made with other objectives and considerations in mind.

Some firms incorporate a long-term human resource plan as an integral component of the strategic plan. Human resources managers have become an integral component in the strategic management activity, particularly as firms engage in mergers or major retrenchments requiring significant changes in the work force. This requires forecasts of human resource needs (labor and management) in conjunction with other changes going on in the planning effort.

Because policies and plans dealing with management personnel are such an important aspect of implementing strategy, the leadership implementation section of this chapter explores this area in greater detail.

Legal Issues

Policies and plans with respect to all the functions of a firm normally involve some questions of legality. For instance, a merger strategy to be implemented through the purchase of a competitor involves legal questions. A marketing policy to give exclusive territories to distributors may involve legal issues. Securing favorable price breaks on large purchases of materials or hiring certain classes of employees for the executive ranks also involves legal issues, and so on. Some firms may pursue a policy for the purpose of testing a legal issue, as Sears did when it challenged the Equal Employment Opportunity Commission. Other executives may delay implementing plans until "advice of counsel" is sought as to the legal ramifications of pursuing a given strategy in a certain way. Of course, implementing a strategy by moving into international territories compounds the difficulties and introduces the question of whether policies need to be established that are common to all SBUs or whether autonomy is to be granted to suit local conditions. The legal ramifications may have a great deal to do with a firm's policy on organizing such units. More firms appear to be increasing the size of in-house legal departments as problems connected with product liability, employee health and safety, employment practices, pollution problems, and so on have grown.

Once the legal issues are explored, there are still policy issues involved. In essence, a firm may have a policy of "let's follow the letter of the law," "let's follow the spirit of the law," or "let's test the law (if we're willing to pay the possible consequences)." Depending on the importance of the issue, the risks involved, and the values of management, these options are more or less likely for a given situation. The role of the legal staff is to lay out the implications so that managers can make a decision. Unfortunately, some managers let their lawyers determine policies themselves, and this can lead to the "tail wagging the dog."

Public Relations [9]

Somewhat related to policies concerning legal issues is the whole area of social responsibility. Policies in this area remain quite nebulous. A whole variety of issues can be involved, including advertising ethics, bribing government officials (foreign or domestic), and corporate philanthropy. Like legal policies, public relations policies can cut across all the functional areas. There may be ethical questions in developing certain areas of research (such as research on DNA) or in selling products that are unsafe to certain types of consumers (such as infant formula in Africa). Of course, some production processes may be designed to use state-of-the-art technology to prevent pollution, or there may be an option to continue the legal dumping of dangerous chemical wastes. The list of issues seems to be endless. As a result, the public affairs–government relations function has grown increasingly important, more staff members and resources are being allocated to this office, and more authority to make policies has been granted.

Policies here have an impact on the image the organization wishes to present. But some can also be seen as necessary to protect long-term economic interests. For example, many firms operating in South Africa under conditions of apartheid face critical policy questions. Thus some firms may choose to encourage employee participation in community activities, involve themselves in political action committees (PACs), or provide financial support for community development projects. In many instances, these policies may be a way to "manage the environment." Remember, strategies can be active or passive. More firms these days appear to exercise active approaches to influencing their environment to create opportunity or avert threat. In addition to involvement with PACs the public relations staff or high-level executives will monitor the progress of pieces of legislation in federal or state capitals. This involves watching committee assignments for bills, noting hearing schedules for bills of interest, and determining the action to be taken on each bill (testimony at hearings, speaking with committee members, attending the hearing, briefing key legislators regarding the issues, etc.).

Of course, the degree to which a firm attempts to exercise "influence" requires a policy on how far legal limits are to be stretched (e.g., should bribery be overlooked). This is a particularly difficult problem for the international firm. Should it behave as a change agent, or adapt to local customs? Should it follow the adage "When in Rome do like the Home Office"? The usual prescription is to strike a balance of constructive interaction, but this is often easier said than done.

Integrating Policies and Plans [10]

When all line and staff functions have developed plans and policies to aid implementation of the strategic choice, implementation is not necessarily complete. There is a need to be sure that there is internal consistency in the policies and plans developed for the line and staff. And these need to be related to the assessment of the role of strengths and weaknesses as they relate to the development of competitive advantage, as we suggested in Chapter 5. Let's consider an example to illustrate this key point.

Suppose that a furniture manufacturer pursues marketing plans calling for a narrow product line, a low price, and broad distribution. Various policies would probably include decentralized storage of finished goods, large-lot-size production, a low- or medium-skilled work force, and a limited number of large-scale plants.

On the other hand, a manufacturer of high-priced, high-style furniture sold through exclusive distributors might call for production to order, many model and style changes, well-trained and highly paid workers and supervisors, etc. While the operations and labor costs and policies in the second case might be seen as less efficient and a relative weakness, nonetheless they are consistent with and effective for the chosen strategy. If the manufacturer attempted to follow the usual prescriptions for "efficient" production (large-scale mass production of items), it probably would not be *effective* in carrying out its strategy.

As we discussed each area earlier, you may have noted that effective decisions cannot be made without regard to their impact on other areas of the business. Otherwise, suboptimization is likely to result. Trade-offs are generally required in this process. A policy of minimizing the inventory may come at the expense of satisfying customers. Exhibit 10.7 shows some of the common trade-offs which can result within certain areas. But this suggests where trade-offs occur across areas as well.

Hence, top executives must be involved with negotiations and policy formulation to assure that the plans that are developed are working together to accomplish the key tasks needed to carry out a given strategy. The extent of involvement needed relates to the strategy itself. That is, in some cases stronger linkages across units become more important. Consider, for instance, the need to link R&D, production, and marketing departments. If the strategy is to develop and produce products for specific customer needs, there will be a greater need to coordinate the activities of the three departments than if a "push" strategy in marketing is in use (selling whatever products are developed and produced). An example of this is Ford's "Team Taurus." Normally, the 5-year process of creating a new automobile is sequential—product planners define a concept, the design team takes over, and then engineering develops specifications that are passed on to manufacturing and suppliers. Such an approach was creating problems at Ford. The Team Taurus approach put together a group from planning, design, engineering, and manufacturing at the beginning of the process. The group asked assembly-line workers and suppliers for their ideas, at the same time doing extensive market research and back engineering on competitors' products to identify customer-desired features. Such integration was seen as necessary if Ford was to compete with foreign automakers.

If the business is highly capital-intensive with high manufacturing costs, then a stronger linkage between R&D and manufacturing is likely to be helpful for developing cost-saving process improvements. The idea is that policies can be developed to encourage the organization to maintain a desired liaison across units to effect the communication and coordination needed. In some instances, specialized formal units (e.g., expediters) may be set up in the organization to facilitate this coordination. The management information system may be used here for coordination and control. Chapter 11 discusses these topics.

EXHIBIT 10.7 SOME IMPORTANT TRADE-OFF DECISIONS IN VARIOUS POLICY AREAS

Policy area	Decision	Alternatives
Plant and equipment	Span of process	Make or buy
	Plant size	One big plant or several smaller ones
	Plant location	Locate near markets or locate near materials
	Investment decisions	Invest mainly in buildings or equipment or inventories or research
	Choice of equipment	General-purpose or special-purpose equipment
	Kind of tooling	Temporary, minimum tooling or "production tooling"
Production planning and control	Frequency of inventory taking	Few or many breaks in production for buffer stocks
	Inventory size	High inventory or a lower inventory
	Degree of inventory control	Control in great detail or in lesser detail
	What to control	Controls designed to minimize machine downtime or labor cost or time in process, or to maximize output of particular products or material usage
	Quality control	High reliability and quality or low costs
	Use of standards	Formal or informal or none at all
Labor and staffing	Job specialization	Highly specialized or not highly specialized
	Supervision	Technically trained first-line supervisors or nontechnically trained supervisors
	Wage system	Many job grades or few job grades; incentive wages or hourly wages
	Supervision style	Close supervision or loose supervision
	Industrial engineers	Many or few
Product design/ engineering	Size of product line	Many customer specials or few specials or none at all
	Design stability	Frozen design or many engineering change orders
	Technological risk	Use of new processes unproved by competitors or follow-the-leader policy
	Engineering	Complete packaged design or design-as-you-go approach
	Use of manufacturing engineering	Few or many manufacturing engineers
Organization and management	Kind of organization	Functional or product focus or geographical or other
	Executive use of time	High involvement in investment or production planning or cost control or quality control or other activities
	Degree of risk assumed	Decision based on much or little information
	Use of staff	Large or small staff group
	Executive style	Much or little involvement in detail; authoritarian or nondirective style, much or little contact with organization

The timing of these plans and policies must be designed so that they mesh correctly. For instance, a number of computer companies attempted to rush into new products with marketing programs promising more than could be delivered. Customers were anxiously awaiting the arrival of their new machines before production was capable of providing the necessary output. So lead times within each area of the business need to be considered in relation to one another before plans are implemented. Further, some policy decisions can be made and implemented immediately (e.g., change from LIFO to FIFO, hire unskilled workers). Others take long lead times to come to fruition (e.g., research and development, building new plants). For example, Genentech had a plan whereby it would hire sales force personnel contingent on approval of a new drug by the FDA, which takes some time.

Thus, in effect, firms create a cascade of plans and policies, with the long-range choices affecting medium- and short-range decisions.

	Strategic choice
	↓
Longer than 3 years	Long-range policies, plans, programs
	↓
1 to 3 years	Medium-range policies, plans, programs
	↓
Less than 1 year	Short-range policies, plans, programs

Policies also vary over time, shifting with strategic needs. One interesting perspective sheds some light on what may be one way to determine how plans need to change with certain strategies. Fox has shown how implementation will vary depending on where the firm's main product or service is in the product-service life cycle. Exhibit 10.8 presents his framework. Of course, a multiple-SBU firm may have a number of products, each of which is in a different stage of development. Hence specific guidelines are subject to some question as to their overall usefulness. Nonetheless, the exhibit does illustrate how policies can be meshed with different demands imposed by a strategy change.

Finally, it should be remembered that if contingency planning or second-generation planning is being used, alternative functional policies for each contingency plan must be developed.

These and many other functional plans and policies are needed to implement the grand strategy. Your ability to formulate these will be a good indication of your practical ability to make the strategy work. Research suggests that the success of a firm's strategy is dependent on proper implementation and balancing of resources, plans, and policies.

LEADERSHIP IMPLEMENTATION

As we mentioned, personnel plans and policies dealing with executive personnel are of crucial significance to the firm and its ability to implement (as well as formulate) strategy. The real test of a strategic decision is whether you put the right people in the job you've just identified as crucial. Here we focus on some of the key issues associated with providing for appropriate leadership skills as a critical component of the administrative system to implement strategy. These are important because leaders can help organizations cope with change, and people will not necessarily cooperate according to the policies or plans. Effective leaders are the major component in assuring that a follow-through of the policies occurs as planned.

 Firms accomplish leadership implementation in several ways: (1) through changes in current leadership at appropriate levels, (2) by developing appropriate leadership styles and climates, (3) by getting involved in career development for future strategists, and (4) by using organization development techniques to effect changes.

Leader Choice and Assignment [11]

The first dimension of leadership implementation is to make sure that the right strategists are in the right positions for the strategy chosen for that SBU or firm. The questions pertaining to leadership implementation are as follows:

1 Who holds the current leadership positions?
2 Do they have the right characteristics to assure that the strategy will work well?
3 Who should be assigned which types of tasks?

Essential to examining leadership implementation is this question: Does the strategist have the right education, abilities, experience, and personality to implement the new strategy? For example, assume that a firm which has been handling a single product line in a stable industry has shifted to a strategy of expansion in a diversified set of product and service lines. Perhaps this firm's executive, with narrow experience in the marketing of the old product line alone, is not as qualified to head the firm as a strategist with wider experience. Or if a firm is heavily influenced by certain technologies, then education, ability, and experience relating to these would be highly useful for a strategist to have. Many CEOs have been replaced when it was discovered that they could not effectively deal with the demands of a changed environment or a new strategy. Of course, others are replaced because they are ineffective leaders or because their political skills are poor. Often, to implement a new strategy, executives tied to the past must be given the ''golden handshake'' of early retirement to allow the new strategy to work.

The firm must examine the match between the new strategy and the CEO. For instance, in a merger or acquisition, who will manage the new unit? Will the unit remain autonomous or be integrated into the existing structure? If it is integrated, do the skills and styles fit the current business? If a match between strategy and managers does not exist, serious problems of implementation could result. Indeed, Charles Brown succeeded John DeButts at AT&T, since he was in a better position to bargain

EXHIBIT 10.8 RELATIONSHIP OF IMPLEMENTATION TO THE PRODUCT LIFE CYCLE

	Functional focus	R&D	Production	Marketing	Physical distribution
Precommer-cialization	Coordination of R&D and other functions	Reliability tests Release blueprints	Production design Process planning Purchasing department lines up vendors and subcontractors	Test marketing Detailed marketing plan	Plan shipping schedules, mixed carloads Rent warehouse space, trucks
Introduction	Engineering: debugging in R&D production, and field	Technical corrections (engineering changes)	Subcontracting Centralize pilot plants; test various processes; develop standards	Induce trial; fill pipelines; sales agents or commissioned salespeople; publicity	Plan a logistics system
Growth	Production	Start successor product	Centralize production Phase out subcontractors Expedite vendors' output; long runs	Channel commitment Brand emphasis Salaried sales force Reduce price if necessary	Expedite deliveries Shift to owned facilities
Maturity	Marketing and logistics	Develop minor variants Reduce costs through value analysis Originate major adaptations to start new cycle	Many short runs Decentralize Import parts, low-priced models Routinization Cost reduction	Short-term promotions Salaried salespeople Cooperative advertising Forward integration Routine marketing research: panels, audits	Reduce costs and raise customer service level Control finished-goods inventory
Decline	Finance	Withdraw all R&D from initial version	Revert to subcontracting; simplify production line Careful inventory control; buy foreign or competitive goods; stock spare parts	Revert to commission basis; withdraw most promotional support Raise price Selective distribution Careful phaseout, considering entire channel	

Source: Reprinted by permission from *Atlanta Economic Review* (now *Business Magazine*). "A Framework for Functional Coordination," by Harold W. Fox, November–December 1973. Copyright © 1973 by the College of Business Administration, Georgia State University, Atlanta.

with the government to effect the company's new strategy. DeButts had made some enemies in Washington, D.C., and Brown was less rigid in his thinking about how to cooperate with the regulatory reformers.

As for determining areas of managerial responsibility, it has been suggested that

EXHIBIT 10.8   RELATIONSHIP OF IMPLEMENTATION TO THE PRODUCT LIFE CYCLE *(Continued)*

Personnel	Finance	Management accounting	Other	Customers	Competition
Recruit for new activities Negotiate operational changes with unions	Life-cycle plan for cash flows, profits, investments, subsidiaries	Payout planning: full costs/ revenues Determine optimum lengths of life-cycle stages through present-value method	Final legal clearances (regulatory hurdles, patents) Appoint life-cycle coordinator	Panels and other test respondents	Neglects opportunity or is working on similar idea
Staff and train middle management Stock options for executives	Accounting deficit; high net cash outflow Authorize large production facilities	Help develop production and distribution standards Prepare sales aids, sales management portfolio		Innovators and some early adopters	(Monopoly) Disparagement of innovation Legal and extra-legal interference
Add suitable personnel for plants Many grievances Heavy overtime	Very high profits, net cash outflow still rising Sell equities	Short-term analyses based on return per scarce resource		Early adopters and early majority	(Oligopoly) A few imitate, improve, or cut prices
Transfers, advancements; incentives for efficiency, safety, and so on Suggestion system	Declining profit rate but increasing net cash inflow	Analyze differential costs/revenue Spearhead cost reduction, value analysis, and efficiency drives	Pressure for resale price maintenance Price cuts bring price wars; possible price collusion	Early adopters, early and late majority, some laggards; first discontinued by late majority	(Monopoly competition) First shakeout, yet many rivals
Find new slots Encourage early retirement	Administer system; retrenchment Sell unneeded equipment Export the machinery	Analyze escapable costs Pinpoint remaining outlays	Accurate sales forecast very important	Mainly laggards	(Oligopoly) After second shakeout, only few rivals

the types of tasks and decisions should be assigned on the basis of criticality and urgency. Criticality refers to the strategic importance of decisions, while urgency refers to the timing needed for decisions. As decisions become more critical and urgent, they should be pushed to the highest levels (CEO). Division or functional managers would be held responsible for decisions that are urgent but less critical. The senior-level staff might deal with critical issues of less urgency. Typically, as issues move from analytical stages to implementation, they tend to become more urgent, but criticality may increase or decrease.

Style and Climate [12]

Leadership style is a crucial aspect of leadership implementation also. Essentially this aspect of leadership implementation relates to these questions:

1 Can the strategist lead the division effectively and relate well to peers, superiors, and subordinates with his or her present style?

2 Can the strategist change the leadership style if that is necessary to make the new strategy work?

3 Can the strategist develop the right climate and culture for the strategy?

The strategy needs to be reinforced with the right climate of managerial values and leadership style. This affects how willing the strategist is to delegate authority and develop the appropriate types and levels of controls.

As Exhibit 10.9 suggests, different management skills appear to be relevant depending on the job requirements for a given strategy or SBU. Thus an SBU that is a

EXHIBIT 10.9 A suggested framework for strategy—manager matching.

Strategy	Job Requirements		Matching Criteria		Managerial Skills and Behaviors	Person Attributes
Growth	1. Environmental scanning 2. Functional focus—source of job demands 3. Number and complexity of job related demands	Priorities	Knowledge	Priorities	1. Specific industry knowledge 2. Knowledge of organizational functions 3. Knowledge of overall company 4. Past performance	Education
Defend						Family background
Maintain			Integrative			
Divest	1. Unit and interunit cooperation and collaboration 2. Number and importance of external contacts 3. Number and importance of internal contacts		Administrative		1. Number and quality of internal networks 2. Number and quality of external networks 3. Quality of interpersonal and communication skills	Personality Needs
Etc.						Intelligence
	1. Performance goals, standards and priorities 2. Need for control 3. Need for innovative behavior 4. Types of incentives and reward systems				1. Quality of conceptual skills 2. Tendency toward innovative behavior 3. Type of control orientation 4. Flexibility in assignments 5. Preferred rewards and incentives	

Decision

Matching Contingencies

Power

Structure

Culture

cash cow will require leadership styles and characteristics different from those appropriate for an SBU pursuing significant expansion in new product-market areas. Strategists will have to determine whether existing managers can adapt to new roles or whether they will need to be replaced.

The leader is responsible for developing a "climate" conducive to the mission of the business. There are a number of ways in which climate can be viewed. Here we mean the nature of leadership, motivation, decision, communication, and control processes and the development of a corporate "culture." Let's briefly review these aspects of the administrative system.

Leadership processes as a component of climate refer to the following types of questions:

1 To what extent do superiors have confidence in and trust subordinates? (No confidence to complete trust.)

2 To what extent do superiors behave in a manner that encourages subordinates to feel free to discuss important matters about their jobs? (No discussion to full discussion.)

3 To what extent do superiors try to get ideas and opinions from subordinates and use them constructively? (Never or seldom to always.)

Motivational processes as a component of climate can be represented by the following:

1 What types of motives are used? (Fear, threats, punishment, economic rewards, noneconomic rewards.)

2 How much responsibility do various managerial levels assume for goal achievement? (Attempts to sabotage at some levels to high responsibility at all levels.)

3 What types of interactions occur? (Little interaction and distrust to extensive friendly interaction with confidence and trust.)

4 To what extent is there a feeling of teamwork? (None or damaging competitiveness to substantial cooperation and cohesiveness.)

Decision processes as a dimension of climate can be characterized as follows:

1 At what level are decisions formally made? (Bulk at the top and centralized to decentralized spread of decision authority and delegation.)

2 To what extent are decision makers aware of lower-level problems? (Unaware to fully aware.)

3 To what extent is technical and professional knowledge used in making decisions? (No extent to great extent.)

4 To what extent do subordinates get involved in decisions related to their work? (No participation to high participation.)

The communication-process component of climate includes these questions:

1 In what manner are orders issued or goals set? (Orders issued from above to goals established by means of group participation.)

2 How does communication primarily occur? (Formal written memos to informal verbal exchanges.)

3 How does communication flow? (Primarily downward to laterally to primarily upward.)

The control-process dimension of climate is characterized as follows:

1 The extent to which review and control is concentrated. (Highly concentrated at the top to widespread responsibility for control.)

2 The extent of controls and standards. (Loose to tight.)

3 The extent to which control data are used for self-guidance. (Data used for policing to coordinated problem solving.)

Finally, the elusive aspect of corporate "culture" is a dimension of climate that leaders help develop. Here we are concerned with how the other aspects of climate interrelate to develop an informal organization which supports or opposes formal goals. A corporate culture might be defined as the overriding ideology and established patterns of behavior and norms which influence actions and decisions. There are forces which covertly or overtly resist the organization or fully support and accept the ways in which it operates. Also, the underlying values of the organization (its overall personality as distinct from the personalities of its members) constitute a dimension of some significance. It is important to be perfectly clear about your culture, so that new employees, customers, and shareholders know who you are and what you stand for. But it may also be necessary to change the culture, as is happening at Proctor & Gamble, whose past marketing prowess has become rusty. Such changes require revolutionary shifts and wholesale personnel replacements. The question of combining cultures when firms consider merger strategies is a factor that must be considered when choosing the strategy or determining the structure. Exhibit 10.10 illustrates these issues.

All in all, these aspects of leadership implementation are essential components of the administrative system which can make or break a strategy. They can be used to engender commitment and loyalty to the organization and its strategies. We should hasten to add that the character of these dimensions is *not* designed to suggest that one end of the continuum is necessarily better than the other end. As with other aspects of leadership implementation, the characteristics need to fit the needs of a given strategy.

Unfortunately, there is not much evidence suggesting which of these aspects is more appropriate for given strategies. However, the business press suggests that certain key aspects of excellence in management style and approach are appropriate regardless of the strategy: a bias toward action, a simple form and a lean staff, continued contact with customers, productivity improvement via people, operational autonomy to encourage entrepreneurship, stress on one key business value, emphasis on doing what one knows best, and the simultaneous use of loose and tight controls.

There is some evidence that suggests that chief planning officers recognize that problems in these areas can lead to frustration in translating strategy into operational terms. Some of the basic problems include difficulty in achieving goal consensus, communication breakdowns, ambiguity with regard to the roles of subunits, difficulty in obtaining commitment to a plan, lack of strategic thinking, and line-staff conflicts. Many of these problems are attributed to planners' lack of cognitive ability and the

EXHIBIT 10.10   MERGING TWO CULTURES

In late 1984, marketing giant IBM paid $1.3 billion for little engineering genius Rolm, its first acquisition in 20 years. Predictions were that the marriage wouldn't work due to cultural clashes. "It looked like a corporate Odd Couple." Rolm, a leading maker of computerized phone switchboards (PBX), was the epitome of Silicon Valley's freewheeling corporate culture. IBM, on the other hand, insisted on "buttoned-down decorum" from its huge work force. A year later, the pundits were still wondering when the marriage would go on the rocks.

Yet the informal atmosphere at Rolm—workaholic frenzy occasionally relieved by a dip in the company pool or a lunchtime barbecue—has not changed. "It's not the 'blueing' of Rolm that everyone expected."

The PBX is crucial to IBM in its effort to battle AT&T for the telecommunications markets. IBM does not want to botch its chance by alienating the engineering elite at Rolm. Top executives at Rolm have remained, and morale remains high. Rolm's management has avoided bureaucratic inroads. "The general manager of one sales unit who cut out free coffee in an effort to trim costs reversed the decision when employees blamed IBM."

IBM has maintained Rolm's unusual policy of granting employees a three-month paid sabbatical after 3 years, even though that has angered some IBM employees who don't receive the benefit. And stock options are more widely distributed at Rolm than at IBM. Combined sales efforts of IBM and Rolm sales forces have been effective, largely because IBM pays double commissions on many products.

Still, the merging of the cultures will likely lead to greater similarities if the long-term strategy is to be achieved. For example, Rolm is reorganizing its 5000-strong sales and service groups from 14 independent operating groups to 4 national units with centralized decision making. This smacks of IBM's style and portends a marriage of the two firms' sales forces that may alienate many in Rolm's entrepreneurial ranks. Some top performers left when a new compensation structure placed greater emphasis on base salary than commissions, and levied a cap on earnings.

So far, joint technical development consists of making existing products work together. Creating new ones from scratch could lead to friction. Further, since stock options at Rolm are vested after 2 years instead of 5, as they were under the old plan, many options leading to employee turnover may be exercised.

Thus, it remains to be seen whether the culture clash between two very different styles can lead to the accomplishment of IBM's strategic goals without some significant short-term pain.

Source: Adapted from J. B. Levine, "How IBM Is Getting the Most Out of Rolm," *Business Week,* Nov. 18, 1985, pp. 110–111.

quality of top-level administrators. Hence another aspect of leadership implementation is preparing managers to perform the appropriate tasks. This is the subject of the next section.

Career Development [13]

Because of the significance of leadership to the implementation of strategy in general, more attention is being devoted to the career development of strategists. Several elements are necessary to effectively plan for executive development: (1) the types and numbers of executives needed for the future strategy must be anticipated; (2) the current talent available must be reviewed; (3) promotion and recruitment schedules should be prepared; (4) plans for the development of individuals for promotion should be made; and (5) reward systems to attract and hold key managers must be established.

These are, of course, common human resource approaches. But to be a successful *strategist,* the executive must understand business function decisions, especially those concerning production-operations management, marketing, and financial management. It is also desirable to understand the impact of personnel, accounting, and legal staff functions on effective decisions. So some firms rotate potential strategists through experiences in as many of these functions as possible to develop multiple-ability strategists. Or, if international activities are important to the business, careers often include at least one foreign assignment. If there are significant differences in the characteristics of different SBUs, it is useful for the experiences to take place in the different SBUs. Thus the future strategists will realize that the functions and SBUs are mutually dependent upon corporate effectiveness. More firms are planning the careers of future strategists with these guidelines in mind, though the CEO may hinder these efforts. Many suggest that selection and placement of managers should be done in accordance with the needs of the strategy to which they are best suited. For example, one study found that greater willingness to take risk, higher tolerance for ambiguity, and stronger marketing experience by an SBU manager contributed to the effectiveness of expansion strategy but hampered the effectiveness of retrenchment strategy. However, there has been a lack of thorough analysis of how strategy implementation and managerial selection should work together.

Generally it is useful for a firm to reinforce the motivation to achieve strategic objectives by tying the strategist's compensation to strategic achievements. The nature of the incentive compensation used, the timing of incentive payments, and other dimensions can accomplish this mission. The key to such a system is to tie rewards to the type of performance required by the strategy and objectives. Hence if innovation is a key to performance in the future, then time horizons for judging performance will tend to be longer, and greater rewards for risk taking might outweigh short-term profitability in the incentive scheme. The reward system for executives is discussed in greater detail in Chapter 11.

Organization Development [14]

The final aspect of leadership implementation deals with change processes. That is, if new strategies or policies are being implemented, former policies and plans, people, and the climate are likely to undergo some sort of change. Typical reactions include denying, ignoring, accepting, adapting to, and embracing change. It is up to leaders to see that readiness for change and commitment to new activities will come about. This is easier said than done, as Exhibit 10.11 suggests.

To implement change, consultants and managers use a variety of activities and techniques. These include survey feedbacks, confrontation meetings, team building, transactional analysis, and various packaged approaches (e.g., Blake and Mouton's Grid or Lippitt's ITORP—implementing the organizational renewal process). Though studies vary as to the effectiveness of various approaches, most are designed to accomplish several things:

- Unfreezing—unlearning old behavior patterns or policies
- Learning—effecting the change desired
- Refreezing—institutionalizing new patterns and policies

EXHIBIT 10.11   CAN J&J CHANGE FROM BAND-AIDS TO HIGH TECH?

Johnson & Johnson's (J&J) new modernistic headquarters stands in stark contrast to the old brick building that was its home from the late 1890s until 1983. The new architectural facade is symbolic of the changes under way at this consistently successful company. Best known for such brands as Band-Aids and Baby Shampoo, J&J has accelerated its strategic moves toward more sophisticated medical technology. Success will depend on managing very different businesses from the past. And Chairman Burke is trying to change the management style and corporate culture that have been central to J&J's success. But he is having trouble.

For years, consumer products, prescription drugs, and hospital-supply lines have flourished under the marketing-dominated, decentralized management structure at J&J. People running its "170 companies" enjoyed substantial autonomy, with most divisions having their own boards. Corporate headquarters staff was small, and only one management layer separated division presidents from a 14-member executive committee.

However, the long-time dominance of marketing and sales executives and the insularity of the autonomous units could impede J&J's ability to push into new business and react swiftly to changing competition in health care. Yet attempts to gain greater coordination across units (such as centralized ordering and distribution to maintain a lead in hospital supplies) have been met with resistance and management turnover.

"General" Johnson, CEO from 1938 to 1963, established the structure and style J&J used so successfully for so long. He wrote the corporate credo, which states that J&J's first responsibility is not to shareholders or employees, but to "doctors, nurses, patients, mothers, and all others" who use its products. This tradition helps explain why all 14 of the executive committee members have consumer-marketing or pharmaceutical backgrounds. That in itself portends problems of commitment to unfamiliar product lines and operating practices.

This tradition gets in the way of strategies to acquire and manage new medical equipment thrusts. Because of its financial and control system J&J has had trouble keeping entrepreneurs who built the acquired companies. And typical operating policies and practices have not been adapted to new needs. For example, soon after J&J acquired a dialysis business, prices for dialyzers (filters to clean blood) dropped as the government limited medicare funds. Cost-conscious customers began reusing dialyzers; but J&J was accustomed to selling products used once in a sterile environment: "It was appalling to us to think that those things would become reusable." Hence, because J&J's culture prevented change, its competitors' products, which could be prepared for reuse more easily, gained a distinct advantage.

The cooperation and communication needed for the new strategy are also alien to the old culture. For instance, one J&J unit, so used to independence, refused to take managers from other J&J companies. And mixed signals from the top have confused managers about how committed their leaders are to cooperation. For instance, three separate units proposed that three of their products be packaged in a customized surgical kit. Headquarters failed to give approval. And, instead of creating formal structures to combine efforts in hospital services, units involved with this business will maintain separate sales forces.

Perhaps the two Tylenol capsule poisoning incidents in 1982 and 1986 are the least of J&J's worries. It may need some of its own medicine to cure the headaches of changing a corporate culture to meet the requirements of its new strategy.

Source: Adapted from "Changing Corporate Culture," *Business Week,* May 14, 1984, pp. 130–138.

Specifically, with respect to implementing strategic change, Hobbs and Heany recommend six steps:

1 Before changing the strategy, make sure that serious functional overload does not exist; i.e., slack and balance are needed so that those involved in changes do not feel isolated or overburdened.

2 Contain strategic shock waves. Strategy change will upset the organization. So if you can, insulate the part of the business involved. (This is one reason why stability with expansion in one SBU is a favored strategy.)

3 Give personal top-management attention to changes.

4 If a strategic planning team is used, don't disband it until it identifies follow-through actions needed at the next operational level.

5 Communicate down about the reasons for the new strategy and the various roles needed to accomplish it.

6 Follow up 30 days after the new strategy change; ask a dozen managers at lower levels to write down the three most critical tasks needed which will determine the success or failure of the plan. Evaluation of the responses will give you an idea as to whether needed changes have been institutionalized.

For effectively accomplishing unfreezing, learning, and refreezing, the *nature of the change* may be as important as the techniques used. Here we are referring to the changes which are easiest to introduce and which generate less conflict and resistance (are more acceptable). A change is more likely to occur if it does not involve changing social roles or power configurations (if there are few organizational changes) and if people have sufficient ability to execute these roles. It is also easier to implement change if the change involved is not rapid—it usually takes time to introduce change. Thus workable targets or substrategies which don't affect the whole organization are easier to introduce. Finally, the nature of the change should include enough flexibility to accommodate later extensions. This means that attempts should be made to build in slack at the start and to provide for organizational learning over time.

Thus, as we suggested in Chapter 8, strategic choice must involve a consideration of implementation processes, among which change itself is included. These ideas argue that small incremental adjustments with anticipatory flexibility introduced over time have a higher probability of success. Again, the implementation factors discussed in Chapters 9 and 10 are the things we had in mind when we discussed limitations on strategic choice and which underlie the assumptions behind the incremental choice model we proposed. Hence you should see that the relationship suggested in Exhibit 10.1 between strategic choice and implementation involves a two-way flow.

IMPLEMENTING STRATEGY IN INTERNATIONAL SETTINGS [15]

As we have explored various aspects of implementation in this and the last chapter, we have identified selected issues of concern to strategists who operate in international arenas. Here we highlight some of the typical concerns affecting implementation due to the increased complexity for the firm pursuing an international strategy. We will follow the preceding scheme by exploring issues associated with the special case of international resource allocation, organization, plans, policies, and leadership.

Resource Allocation

International companies (IC) must find sources of capital and allocate them to domestic and foreign operations to support their strategies. This used to be a simple process of transmitting funds from the parent company to establish operations abroad. However, with greater availability of other sources in host countries and international capital markets (e.g., Eurodollars), and with the greater use of licensing and joint ventures, the corporatewide process of resource allocation is more complex. For example, global marketing systems can become a strength, providing sources of internal capital. Yet the firm engaged in foreign and domestic production must determine what funds should be allocated for maintaining older facilities (often in the home country where business was first started) and what should be allocated for investing in new capacity.

Organization

The resource allocation process will be affected by how the firm is organized. That is, resources will be allocated differently according to whether the firm establishes a global financial system or treats each foreign operation as a separate entity. In a unified system, excess cash from varied units can be allocated by central management for units that need it or to capital markets offering better returns. And new capital can generally be acquired from the lowest-cost sources. Because of differences between countries in tax rates, freedom to remit profits, risks, and so on, it is often beneficial to take a larger share of profit from business in one place than in another. A unified system has such a capability, as well as the ability to manage currency exchange rates more readily. This in itself can be a motivation for strategists to engage in foreign operations. For example, many U.S. filmmakers were shooting a third or more of their products in Canada in the early 1980s because favorable exchange rates (and more flexible unions) dramatically lowered production costs.

The international corporation can organize activities other than finance on a global basis. On the other hand, there are strong forces (e.g., economic and cultural differences as well as varying national interests) which operate against a unified organization system. For example, decision-making power held at corporate headquarters may be resented by the nation seeking to control the affairs of firms operating within its borders. Hence, the form of foreign involvement (wholly owned subsidiary versus joint venture versus licensing strategies, for example) will depend both on issues of organizational implementation and on the discretion of managers to choose the form they prefer.

Plans and Policies

As just indicated, a unified organization system can have an impact on plans and policies for implementing a strategy involving international activities. This section explores various planning and policy areas associated with an international strategy.

In the finance area, fluctuating exchange rates, currency controls, quotas, tariffs, and so on are problems the strategist must deal with if the firm operates internationally. Inflation, taxation, and fiscal and monetary policies will be affected by the domestic *and* (at least one) foreign government if the firm chooses an international strategy. Accounting principles vary from country to country. International debt crises and trade imbalances can impact the ability to move goods or services across boundaries. A unified financial system eases some of these problems. For example, the options for dealing with foreign exchange are greater because the capacity to shift funds among affiliates is easier and quicker. And centralized decision making to set exchange policy (and other financial policies) leads to greater consistency and responsiveness. As before, the disadvantages of centralization need to be considered in the context of the need to recognize different national needs and requirements.

In the marketing arena, one of the key issues is standardization of the product line across domestic and foreign markets. We noted in Chapters 7 and 8 that, at least initially, a firm usually enters foreign markets with identical products. Later, modifications or new products can be introduced. Yet, because of variations in local tastes, standards of living, climate, and so on, diversity is often desired. Incentives to move this way are strong, but the costs involve loss of the advantages of economies of scale for production and distribution on a "global" basis. Similarly, new promotion efforts designed to respond to differences in consumer attitudes and competitive conditions must be considered. Channels of distribution different from those traditionally used by the firm (before considering the international thrust) may also be required. For example, in less developed countries, wholesalers and retailers are generally more numerous, more specialized, and smaller. If the firm has traditionally distributed product through mass retailers, new marketing methods may discourage a strategist from entering certain territories. If new territories are entered, plans to establish new distribution methods will need to be made.

The area of research and development is a difficult one for some firms entering foreign markets. In some instances, the market is seen as a "dumping ground" for transfer of "obsolete" technology (in the domestic market). This may or may not be appreciated by the host country. Some governments will accept, or seek, such *intermediate* or *appropriate* technology if local skills and abilities are not developed enough to use more advanced technology. Yet some host nations seek economic progress through building technical capability, and these governments may require local R&D investment. For the IC, decentralization of R&D may duplicate effort, reduce communication, and make it more difficult to coordinate with global sales and manage production. In comparison with R&D of national companies, a unified global R&D effort allows costs to be spread over a larger base. On the other hand, responsiveness to local market conditions can lead some firms to develop multiple R&D units. As with all factors, the choice here involves an integration with other plans and policies.

Production, like marketing, is concerned with standardization to reduce costs and ease management. An ideal strategy would be a unified system in which a limited number of factories of optimum economic scale were located in sites with the lowest cost of labor and materials supplying markets all over the world. Nonetheless, volume or weight of products or breadth of product line may reduce the ability of the firm to set up such a system. And, while some processes can be transferred intact to foreign locations, others may have to be modified or replaced if new manufacturing facilities are to be set up. Furthermore, domestic legislation, the desire of labor unions to protect jobs, and so on may restrict the location of facilities to particular sites. Quite commonly, production is centralized on a regional basis, where transportation, labor, or governmental deterrents are minor compared to economics of scale. For example, the European Economic Community and other "fair trade" areas have been established to promote concentration of industrial activity in given regions. Company plans to locate facilities must recognize these conditions. Some international companies control raw materials which are used by themselves and other end-product producers in other countries. There may be internal pressures by some divisions to sell to competitors. Policies on inter- and intracompany transfer prices need to be established if such a strategy is to be pursued.

As mentioned above, labor unions may present a hurdle to a retrenchment strategy for a firm wishing to relocate in a foreign site. But labor is also a factor in plans for new sites. Asian firms opening facilities in the United States Midwest in the mid-1980s opted for locations where labor unions were weak or nonexistent. In any case, a plan for the use of labor needs to be established when an international strategy is chosen. Strategists need to determine the desired proportion of local and foreign workers and managers. When an economy slows, local citizens want jobs held by foreigners. Even in prosperity, ethnic conflicts between foreign employees and natives can occur. Benefit plans, pay scales, promotion policies, and so on will vary substantially from area to area, making a corporatewide standardized personnel system unlikely.

Leadership

Finally, managerial style is an issue which must be considered as the option of international strategy is considered. What managerial skills and techniques are appropriate given the development and culture of the host nation? For example, sophisticated consumer-behavior marketing skills may be appropriate in Europe, but may not work in Nigeria. Intensive superior-subordinate conferences using an MBO approach may work in Australia, but run counter to cultural patterns in Indonesia. The Japanese quality circle works well in some U.S. sites, but is not very effective where labor traditionally views managers as adversaries. The climate and culture of the "home office" may not fit the new setting.

The IC must also determine the importance of a foreign assignment to the career development of its managers. In making decisions on whether or not to transfer managers to a foreign location there is more to consider than the desire of host countries to have their people employed. Strategists transferring managers for an overseas assignment must also consider local living costs and expenses. Given the value of the yen, the cost of keeping an executive in Tokyo in 1986 was base salary plus at least $170,000 per year ($70,000 to rent a house, $12,000 for private schools per child, $9000 for a trip home, plus bonuses and cost-of-living allowance). Many Japanese firms have opened private schools for children of Japanese managers assigned to the United States.

It has not been our intent in this section to exhaustively cover all the various issues involved in implementing the strategies one can consider if "going international" is an option. Rather, we hope you begin to see that, as with the domestic firm, a multitude of implementation issues should be addressed before a final commitment is made to pursue an international strategy. Too many firms attempt an international strategy only to find that problems of implementation crop up which reduce chances of success. These implementation issues should influence the choice of strategies and how they are carried out. And we trust you now agree with our earlier statement that increased complexity is involved with the international set of strategies.

SUMMARY

Chapter 10 continues the discussion of the segment of the strategic management process concerned with implementing strategy. In addition to allocating resources and establishing an organizational structure, it is necessary to develop policies and plans and assign or reassign leaders to support the strategy and help achieve objectives.

Plan and policy implementation is designed to specify how the strategic choice will come to be. The firm creates plans and policies which are decisional guides to action, and these help make the strategies chosen work. The critical element is the ability to factor the grand strategy into plans and policies that are compatible, workable, and not just "theoretically sound."

The minimal plans and policies which must be developed are the key functional decisions necessary in the following areas:

1 Financial mix: (*a*) capital, (*b*) leasing versus buying, (*c*) investment risk, (*d*) use of assets, (*e*) accounting and tax treatment
2 Marketing mix: (*a*) products and markets, (*b*) distribution and promotion, (*c*) price and packaging
3 Production-operations mix: (*a*) capacity and utilization, (*b*) location of facilities, (*c*) maintenance and replacement, (*d*) sourcing
4 R&D mix: (*a*) products and processes, (*b*) basic and applied research, (*c*) offensive and defensive research
5 Personnel: (*a*) recruiting, (*b*) allocating, (*c*) developing, (*d*) maintaining
6 Legal issues
7 Public relations

Policies and plans developed for the operating and staff departments need to be consistent with one another and fit the strategic choice and timing needs of the strategy.

> **Proposition 10.1**
> *Enterprises which prepare implementation policies and plans for strategic choices will be more effective than those which do not.*

Leadership implementation is accomplished in several ways:

- Changes in current leadership at appropriate levels
- Development of appropriate leadership styles and climates

- Involvement in the career development of future strategists
- Use of organization development techniques to effect changes

Effective leadership implementation involves making sure the person has the right education, abilities, experience, motivation, and personality to enact the strategic choice. In proposition form:

Proposition 10.2

Enterprises whose strategists' abilities, experiences, and personalities match the strategy will be more effective.

The nature of the leadership style and the motivation, decision, communication, and control processes will determine how effective the leader is in developing a climate and culture conducive to making policies work. Propositions 10.3 and 10.4 summarize the last two aspects of leadership implementation.

Proposition 10.3

Enterprises which plan for executive career development will be more effective than those which do not.

Proposition 10.4

Leaders who apply organization development concepts will more effectively implement strategic change.

The processes of implementation described in Chapters 9 and 10 apply to firms following an international strategy. But an added level of complexity is involved. Essentially, strategists must decide whether to operate a unified system or try to keep foreign activities distinct and separate from domestic operations. Resource allocation, organization, plans, policies, and leadership will vary depending on the stage of development of the firm's involvement in foreign countries. As the strategy changes from exporting to direct investment in several countries, the implementation is likely to become more unified and integrated.

While detailed plans for each functional area need to be developed, top executives are interested in a summary of the strategic plan. Exhibit 10.12 provides an example. Note that the overall objectives are broken down into specific time-based targets, actions needed are specified, resource allocations are identified, and organizational responsibility is assigned. Such a summary is a useful way to portray the essence of a strategic recommendation which has been carefully thought through in terms of its requirements for successful implementation.

EXHIBIT 10.12 PLANNING SUMMARY FORM—A PAPER MANUFACTURER

STRATEGIC PLAN SUMMARY

PLAN TITLE: *Earnings improvement of the Y—Supplies Business*
PLAN PURPOSE: *Strengthen the profitability and defensibility of our position in the Y—Supplies market*

Objectives	Strategies	Tactical goals	Tactical actions	Resources required	Target dates Begin	Target dates End	Responsibility
Profitably commercialize new product YZ and achieve an annual sales rate of 1.5 million units by the end of 1990.	Introduce product YZ with a concentrated promotion campaign into the southeastern region at a premium price.	Annual sales rate of 400,000 units in southeastern region at a minimum price of $5 each by end of 1987.	Launch a 4-month direct-mail campaign at city engineers of all cities with population of 5000 or more.	$25,000 and 2 labor-months	June 1, 1987	September 30, 1987	Marketing manager of southeastern region
			Launch personal sales contact campaign at city engineers of all cities with 50,000 or more population.	$40,000 and 8 labor-months	August 1, 1987	November 1, 1987	Same
			Develop indirect sales channel by adding one distributor in Alabama and Georgia and two in South Carolina.	$100,000 cash investment for capital and 2 labor-months	April 1987	August 1987	Same
	Build a small initial plant in Birmingham with 1-million-unit capacity which can be doubled in capacity to 2 million units in 1989 if the market sustains a growth rate of 10% or more through 1989.	Construct original 1 million-unit plant within total cost budget of $1.3 million.	Use turnkey contract for speedy design and construction of the plant. Specify the X-11 vacuum-molding process in the design of equipment.	$1,300,000 and 20 labor-months	January 1, 1987	August 15, 1987	Project manager

Objective	Action	Action	Resources	Start date	Completion date	Responsibility
Upgrade quality of products Y9 through Y15 and their acceptance in the market while increasing our average Y-gross margin to 35% by the end of 1989.	Reorganize the purchasing department, and so forth.	Start up initial new plant and achieve a direct unit cost under continuous operation of $1.50 per unit by the end of September, 1987.	$50,000 and 15 labor-months	May 1, 1987	August 1, 1987	Plant manager
	Reduce spoilage in raw material, and so forth.	Complete training program of key personnel prior to completion of construction. Other tactical actions, etc. Use national account purchasing as leverage for, and so forth.				

Source: Adapted from R. O'Connor, *Corporate Guides to Long-Range Planning*, Report No. 687 (New York: Conference Board, 1976), p. 81.

Chapter 11 discusses the last phase of the strategic management and implementation process: evaluation and control.

REFERENCES

[1] Implementing Strategies

Schleh, E. C.: ''Strategic Planning—No Sure Cure for Corporate Surprises,'' *Management Review* (March 1979), pp. 54–57.
Note: Also see Chapter 9 references on Integrating Strategy and Implementation [1]

[2] The Policy Implementation Process

VanMeter, D. S., and C. E. Van Horn: ''The Policy Implementation Process,'' *Administration and Society,* vol. 6, (February 1975), pp. 445–488.

[3] Developing Policies and Plans

Friend, J. K.: ''The Dynamics of Policy Change,'' *Long Range Planning,* vol. 10 (February 1977), pp. 40–47.
Lindblom, C. E.: *The Policy-Making Process* (Englewood Cliffs, N.J.: Prentice-Hall, 1980).

[4] Policies and Plans for Finance and Accounting

Anders, G.: ''Corporations Find Help for Balance Sheets: Swap Costly Debt for Low-Yielding Stock,'' *The Wall Street Journal* (June 30, 1982), p. 23.
''Companies Make Survival Their Strategy,'' *Business Week,* July 26, 1982, pp. 46–48.
Farrell, C., R. Welch, P. Houston, J. Hamilton, and V. Cahan: ''The Insurance Crisis: Now Everyone's in a Risky Business,'' *Business Week,* Mar. 10, 1986, pp. 88–92.
''It Can Pay Off Big to Turn Common into Preferred,'' *Business Week,* July 2, 1984, p. 76.
''Matchmakers Heat Up the 'Swap' Market,'' *Business Week,* Nov. 5, 1984, p. 56.
''The Perilous Hunt for Financing,'' *Business Week,* Mar. 1, 1981, pp. 44–45.
''A Real-World Test for the New Inflation Rules,'' *Business Week,* Apr. 4, 1980, pp. 116–118.
''The Tax Magic That's Making Employee Stock Plans Multiply,'' *Business Week,* Oct. 15, 1984, pp. 158–160.

[5] Policies and Plans for Marketing and Distribution

Dunkin, A.: ''Want to Wake Up a Tired Old Product? Repackage It,'' *Business Week,* July 15, 1985, pp. 130–134.
''Flexible Pricing: Industry's New Strategy to Hold Market Share Changes the Rules for Economic Decision Making,'' *Business Week,* Dec. 12, 1977, pp. 78–85.
Hise, R. T., A. Parasuraman, and R. Viswanathan: ''Product Elimination: The Neglected Management Responsibility,'' *The Journal of Business Strategy,* vol. 2 (1982), pp. 56–63.
MacMillan, I., M. L. McCaffery, and G. Van Wijk: ''Competitors' Responses to Easily Imitated New Products,'' *Strategic Management Journal,* vol. 6 (1985), pp. 75–86.
Ries, A., and J. Trout: *Marketing Warfare* (New York: McGraw-Hill, 1985).

[6] Policies and Plans for Production and Operations

''Alumax: Winning Big by Building Inventories during the Downturn,'' *Business Week,* Oct. 17, 1983, pp. 129–130.

"The Fully Automated Factory Rewards an Early Dreamer," *Business Week,* Mar. 17, 1986, p. 91.

Miller, J. G.: "Fit Production Systems to the Task," *Harvard Business Review* (January–February 1981), pp. 145–154.

Wheelwright, S. C.: "Manufacturing Strategy: Defining the Missing Link," *Strategic Management Journal,* vol. 5 (1984), pp. 77–91.

———and R. H. Hayes: "Competing through Manufacturing," *Harvard Business Review,* vol. 63 (January–February 1985), pp. 99–109.

[7] Policies and Plans for Research and Development

"A Call for Vision in Managing Technology," *Business Week,* May 24, 1982, pp. 24–33.

Ford, D., and C. Ryan: "Taking Technology to Market," *Harvard Business Review* (January–February 1981), pp. 117–126.

"TRW Leads a Revolution in Managing Technology," *Business Week,* Nov. 15, 1982, pp. 124–130.

[8] Policies and Plans for Personnel and Legal Activities

Baird, L., and I. Meshoulam: "Implementing Human Resource Strategic Management," working paper, School of Management, Boston University, 1983.

"Managing Company Lawsuits to Stay Out of Court," *Business Week,* Aug. 23, 1982, pp. 54–55.

"A New Corporate Powerhouse: The Legal Department," *Business Week,* Apr. 9, 1984, pp. 66–71.

"A New Target: Reducing Staff and Levels," *Business Week,* Dec. 21, 1981, pp. 69–73.

Patton, A.: "Industry's Misguided Shift to Staff Jobs," *Business Week,* Apr. 5, 1982, pp. 12–15.

Slocum, J. W., W. L. Cron, R. W. Hansen, and S. Rawlings: "Business Strategy and the Management of Plateaued Employees," *Academy of Management Journal,* vol. 28 (1985), pp. 133–154.

[9] Public Relations and Politics

Baysinger, B. D.: "Domain Maintenance as an Objective of Business Political Activity," *Academy of Management Review,* vol. 9 (1984), pp. 248–258.

——— and R. W. Woodman: "Dimensions of the Public Affairs/Government Relations Function in Major American Corporations," *Strategic Management Journal,* vol. 3 (1982), pp. 27–41.

Dickie, R. B.: "Influence of Public Affairs Offices on Corporate Planning and of Corporations on Government Policy," *Strategic Management Journal,* vol. 5 (1984), pp. 15–34.

[10] Integrating Policies and Plans

Andersen, T. A.: "Coordinating Strategic and Operational Planning," *Business Horizons* (Summer 1965), pp. 49–55.

Fox, H.: "A Framework for Functional Coordination," *Atlantic Economic Review* (November–December 1973), pp. 10–11.

Hamilton, J. O.: "Genentech Gets a Shot at the Big Time," *Business Week,* Oct. 28, 1985, p. 108.

Mitchell, R.: "How Ford Hit the Bull's Eye with Taurus," *Business Week,* June 30, 1986, pp. 69–70.

[11] Leadership Issues for Strategy Implementation

"Behind AT&T's Change at the Top," *Business Week,* Nov. 6, 1978, pp. 114–139.

Gerstein, R., and R. Reisman: "Strategic Selection: Matching Executives to Business Conditions," *Sloan Management Review* (Winter 1983), pp. 33–49.

Grant, J. H., and W. R. King: *The Logic of Strategic Planning* (Boston: Little, Brown, 1982).

Gupta, A. K.: "Contingency Linkages between Strategy and General Manager Characteristics," *Academy of Management Review,* vol. 9 (1984), pp. 399–412.

————and V. Govindarajan: "Business Unit Strategy, Managerial Characteristics, and Business Unit Effectiveness at Strategy Implementation," *Academy of Management Journal,* vol. 27 (1984), pp. 25–41.

Kerr, J.: "Assigning Managers on the Basis of the Life Cycle," *Journal of Business Strategy,* vol. 2, no. 4 (1982), pp. 58–65.

Smith, N. R., and J. B. Miner: "Type of Entrepreneur, Type of Firm, and Management Motivation," *Strategic Management Journal,* vol. 4 (1983), pp. 325–340.

Smith, K. G., and J. K. Harrison: "Hands on Leadership: A Key to Strategy Implementation and Organizational Excellence," paper presented at the Strategic Management Society Conference, Philadelphia, 1984.

Szilagyi, A. D., and D. M. Schweiger: "Matching Managers to Strategies," *Academy of Management Review,* vol. 9 (1984), pp. 626–637.

"Wanted: A Manager to Fit Each Strategy," *Business Week,* Feb. 25, 1980, pp. 166–173.

[12] Management Style and Climate

Byrne, J. A.: "Up, Up and Away?" *Business Week,* Nov. 25, 1985, pp. 80–94.

"Corporate Culture: The Hard-to-Change Values that Spell Success or Failure," *Business Week,* Oct. 27, 1980, pp. 148–154.

Kilmann, R. A., M. J. Saxton, and R. Serpa (eds.): *Gaining Control of the Corporate Culture* (San Francisco: Jossey, Bass, 1985).

"Life at IBM," *The Wall Street Journal,* Apr. 8, 1982, p. 1.

"Putting Excellence into Management," *Business Week,* July 21, 1980, pp. 196–205.

Schiller, Z., and A. Dunkin: "P & G's Rusty Marketing Machine," *Business Week,* Oct. 21, 1985, pp. 111–112.

[13] Managerial Career Development

Bartee, E.: "On the Personal Development of the Strategic Manager," in H. I. Ansoff et al. (eds.), *From Strategic Planning to Strategic Management* (New York: Wiley Interscience, 1976).

Murthy, K. R., and M. S. Salter: "Should CEO Pay Be Linked to Results?" *Harvard Business Review* (June 1975), pp. 66–73.

[14] Organizational Development

Argyris, C.: *Strategy, Change, and Defensive Routines.* (Marshfield, Mass.: Pitman, 1985).

Blake, R., and J. Mouton: *Building a Dynamic Organization through Grid Organization Development.* (Reading, Mass.: Addison-Wesley, 1969).

Hobbs, J. M., and D. F. Heany: "Coupling Strategy to Operating Plans," *Harvard Business Review,* vol. 55, no. 3 (May–June 1977), pp. 119–126.

Lippitt, G.: *Organization Renewal* (New York: Appleton-Century-Crofts, 1969).

Tushman, M. L., and E. Romanelli: "Organizational Evolution," in L. Cummings and B. Staw (eds.), *Research in Organizational Behavior* (Greenwich, Conn.: JAI Press, 1985).

[15] International Strategy Implementation

Ball, D. A., and W. H. McCullock, Jr.: *International Business* (Plano, Tex.: Business Publications, 1985).

Buell, B.: "Now It's the Land of Rising Rent," *Business Week,* July 7, 1986, p. 43.

Fayweather, J., and A. Kapoor: *Strategy and Negotiation for the International Corporation* (Cambridge, Mass.: Ballinger, 1985).

"Filmmakers Discover The Canadian Solution," *Business Week,* July 15, 1986, pp. 74–75.

CHAPTER OUTLINE

IMPLEMENTATION: EVALUATION AND CONTROL OF STRATEGY

OBJECTIVES

- To understand why firms evaluate and control strategy
- To understand how firms evaluate and control strategy
- To understand how evaluation and control fit into the strategic management process

INTRODUCTION [1]

We have come to the evaluation and control phase of the strategic management process as emphasized in Exhibit 11.1. Remember that this is an integral part of implementing strategy.

Evaluation of strategy is that phase of the strategic management process in which managers try to assure that the strategic choice is properly implemented and is meeting the objectives of the enterprise.

We now assume that the infrastructure is in place. A plan to carry out the chosen strategy has been specified, and activities have been assigned to the organization; resources have been provided for doing these tasks; policies have been developed and communicated; and the leadership system and style have been formed so that the climate is geared to the strategy and plans. There are also several other crucial com-

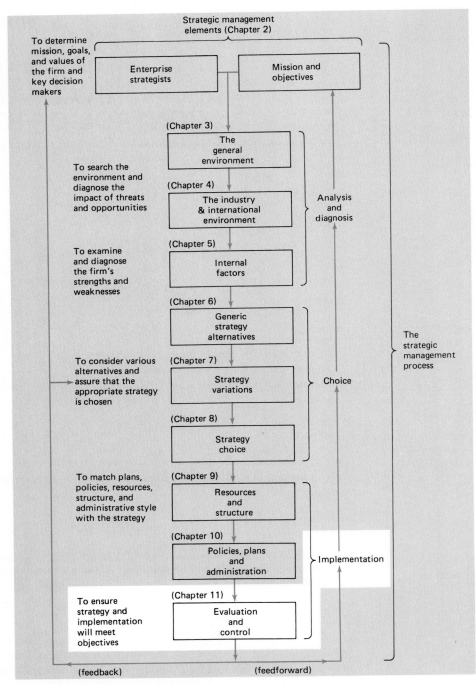

Strategic management
elements (Chapter 2)

To determine
mission, goals,
and values of
the firm and
key decision
makers

| Enterprise strategists | Mission and objectives |

(Chapter 3)
The general environment

To search the
environment and
diagnose the
impact of threats
and opportunities

(Chapter 4)
The industry & international environment

Analysis
and
diagnosis

To examine
and diagnose
the firm's
strengths and
weaknesses

(Chapter 5)
Internal factors

(Chapter 6)
Generic strategy alternatives

To consider various
alternatives and
assure that the
appropriate strategy
is chosen

(Chapter 7)
Strategy variations

Choice

The
strategic
management
process

(Chapter 8)
Strategy choice

To match plans,
policies, resources,
structure, and
administrative style
with the strategy

(Chapter 9)
Resources and structure

(Chapter 10)
Policies, plans and administration

Implementation

To ensure
strategy and
implementation
will meet
objectives

(Chapter 11)
Evaluation and control

(feedback)   (feedforward)

EXHIBIT 11.1   **A model of strategic management.**

ponents of an effective administrative system. These are needed to make sure that the other elements all work properly. A *follow-through* on strategy and its implementation requires a control system, an appropriate reward system, and an effective information system which provides managers with accurate, complete feedback in time so that they can act on the data. These are all integral elements of implementation and evaluation to be sure the plans *will work* and *are working*. The evaluation system is also needed as a way to recycle feedback as an input for new strategic planning and as a means for double-checking that the strategic choice is consistent, appropriate, and workable given internal and external analyses and the plan to implement it.

The *ways* in which subsystems perform their tasks, use resources, and interpret policy give meaning to the intended strategy. SBU and functional managers quite often have a fairly large range of discretion in interpreting policy and using resources. They may in fact work against an intended strategy. We might call this behavior a "sin of commission." Further, to the extent that these managers are protecting "their subsystem," new strategies or policies might never be considered. This could be tagged a "sin of omission." For instance, if a manager fails to forward information that is potentially damaging to the unit (e.g., if a sales manager hides the fact that a competitor's new product is hurting sales), a failing strategy might continue to be pursued. New alternatives would not be considered. Similarly, a manager may decide not to forward a proposal which is thought to run counter to the desires of top management, even though the idea may be a potentially useful alternative. (This type of manager is like students who write term papers based on what they *think* the instructor wants to see rather than on what is believed about a topic.) So the omissions and commissions of managers directly and indirectly affect the strategy of the organization as reflected in its action. In some cases, decisions are quite different from the intended strategy. Occasionally, there is feedback from clients that indicates that something is wrong. Or internal "whistle blowers" may come forth to challenge what is going on. Sins of omission and commission are two reasons why organizations establish control and evaluation mechanisms. Indeed a yawning gap in internal controls contributed to the cash management debacle at E. F. Hutton in 1985. Hutton is still trying to recover from strategic losses as a result of its guilty plea to fraud resulting from lack of control.

Control and evaluation processes help strategists monitor the progress of a plan. They seek to answer a number of questions, such as:

- Are the decisions being made consistent with policy?
- Are there sufficient resources to get the job done? Are the resources being used wisely?
- Are events in the environment occurring as anticipated? (For example, how are competitors reacting to our activities?)
- Are goals and targets being met, both short-term and long-term ones?
- Should we proceed with the plan as we have formulated it?

In effect, evaluation and control processes are set up to be sure the gap between expected and desired objectives will be closed according to the strategy.

In terms of our gap analysis approach, we want to determine whether the gaps between expected results and ideal outcomes *are being* (or will be) closed; and we want to know if any internal or external changes from the plan might alter our expectations regarding these gaps. The evaluation process should alert us to these conditions so that corrective action can be taken—getting back on track, changing the track, or changing our beliefs about the gaps and objectives. In other words, unless evaluation and control are integrated with a plan, strategic planning may be little more than pious hope rather than a means of achieving the desired future. So let's look at the components of a system which should lead to good control and follow-through.

THE CONTROL AND EVALUATION PROCESS [2]

The organization's administrative structure and style constitute the basic mechanism by which a firm attempts to control its activities. We discussed the basic elements of this in Chapters 9 and 10. Exhibit 11.2 shows how these factors are brought together for a follow-through on strategy.

The evaluation process is normally thought of as four interrelated activities:

A Establish performance targets, standards, and tolerance limits for the objectives, strategy, and implementation plans.

B Measure the actual position in relation to the targets at a given time. If outcomes are outside the limits, inform managers with discretion to take action.

EXHIBIT 11.2   COST CONTROL WITH A VENGEANCE

The systems of control at White Consolidated are essential to its strategy of competing successfully in the brutal major-appliances industry, where price competition is fierce. The doctrine of cost control has become a corporate religion, and the climate and structure are designed to control operations and achieve efficiency of plants, people, and equipment which the company acquires from larger firms that have given up.

After each acquisition, White makes massive cuts in the labor force (up to 40 percent) and takes a hard line with unions. It is willing to take strikes to get its way on other cost-cutting measures. Every product line and model is reviewed carefully, and many low-volume products are eliminated. Then the company streamlines operations; frequently it moves a given line to one plant for economies of scale in production.

There is also a decentralized management system for its 15 appliance plants. While the plant "presidents" can be overruled at headquarters, each has control over design, engineering, and product pricing as well as the man-

ufacturing process. Managers can't blame success or failure on something else. But a tight financial reporting system is imposed by headquarters. Expense, manufacturing, and profit statements are collected *each day* from every department. And each month the plant "president" *and* the plant's controller send *independent* detailed operating statements.

The emphasis on penny-pinching at all levels of management is likely to lead to short-term gains, so White is concerned about productivity improvement. But the R&D staff favors production efficiency, not marketing innovation, and the research teams are clustered at the various plants whose operations they are trying to improve.

Given the nature of the appliance business, such a control system seems necessary, and White has turned around previously unsuccessful product lines. It took the company just 3 months to break even on a Westinghouse line of appliances which had been losing $2 million per month. But White's operating profit is about average for the industry.

Source: Adapted from "White Consolidated's New Appliance Bunch," *Business Week,* May 7, 1979, pp. 94–98.

C Analyze deviations from acceptable tolerance limits.

D Execute modifications if any are necessary and/or feasible.

This process can encompass a variety of dimensions of importance to strategic management. That is, a number of aspects of control need to be achieved, according to Rowe and Carlson.

1 Management control, which is based on past performance and historic data

2 Real-time control, which is concerned primarily with technical aspects of control so that information that is as current as possible is provided

3 Performance management, which is concerned with goal congruence and organizational effectiveness

4 Adaptive control, which has to do with determining the quickest and most effective way in which to respond to changes

5 Strategic control, which involves anticipating or developing ways to minimize potential deviations from desired outcomes

Our discussion of the reward system a bit later in the chapter touches on a number of these aspects, most particularly management control and performance management. We will discuss real-time control later when we discuss feedback systems. The first two aspects are mostly concerned with internal implementation questions, while the third involves questions of objectives. The last two are of more significance to questions of evaluating strategic validity and change. To effectively accomplish these types of control, it is necessary to modify the process so that it includes environmental as well as internal assessments.

1 Establish environmental assumptions basic to the strategy and plans.

2 Monitor these environmental factors to detect any significant deviation.

3 If extraordinary deviations occur, reassess goals, the strategy, and plans.

4 Execute new strategy formulation and implementation processes as needed.

Thus the strategic control and evaluation process also requires the monitoring and feedback of environmental conditions so that strategists can be sure that the assumptions on which the strategy and plans are based remain valid.

Exhibit 11.3 shows this modified process. Stages C and D are where strategists are required to actually perform evaluations. Standards or tolerance limits may not be met because they were too high or low, or the assumptions were possibly in error or had a great deal of uncertainty attached to them. In some cases, assumptions may have been pessimistic, and so the goals and objectives need to recognize new opportunities. Of course, the objectives may not be met because the choice was not properly implemented. Or it may be because the strategy chosen was not appropriate. Last but not least, the objectives may have been unrealistic or too high. The strategist must determine which of these cause-effect relationships might be operating.

Successful strategists are like physicians when they are treating illnesses. They look at symptoms and make the most probable diagnosis. Then they prescribe the best procedure or medicine. The diagnosis results from the analysis-diagnosis and choice stages of the strategic management process. The prescription is the implementation.

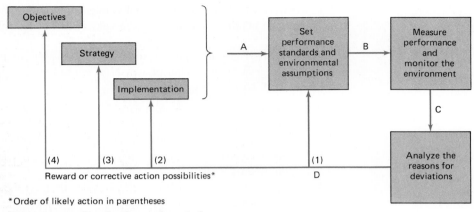

EXHIBIT 11.3   **The process of evaluation and control.**

If the prescription does not work, the physicians may believe that they made the wrong diagnosis (strategic choice), and then they may make another diagnosis. Just as physicians do not give up if the first choice does not work, so the strategists make another choice. The feedback system that they had developed showed that their strategy had failed. But they were ready, no doubt, with an alternative choice—a contingency plan. Exhibit 11.4 shows how General Mills has changed to address some of these issues.

The Role of the Strategist

The idealized evaluation process just described may not always work as effectively as you might think. Different organization levels and people are involved. The evaluation *should* take place at both the corporate level and the SBU level. If the SBUs do not take adequate steps soon enough, the corporate level may have to step in. The corporate-level executive evaluates the overall corporate strategy and also monitors the SBU-level evaluations. But here, too, problems can result.

As we mentioned in Chapter 9, the budget may often become a tool for control, since it interconnects the elements of a plan along common financial terms. This may not reflect some of the nonfinancial standards and key assumptions important to strategic control and evaluation. The *controller* at the corporate level may be in charge of the information system and budget control process as it relates to the preparation of various financial reports which are important inputs for executive decisions. This staff position, often located near the top of the structure with access to key executives, can thus lead to decision making without the assumption of responsibility. Therefore, it is important for top managers to recognize the informational role of the controller while they maintain authority over the control system as a major tool in the administrative system.

Of course, audit and executive committees of the board also play a role in evalu-

EXHIBIT 11.4   EVALUATING AND CONTROLLING DIFFERENT SBUs

For years General Mills maintained loose reins over a diverse group of entrepreneurial companies which it had acquired. Through its acquisitions the corporation got dynamic new businesses growing more rapidly than its core along with entrepreneurs to act as role models for existing managers. The entrepreneurs usually got fat contracts and access to staff support and seemingly limitless cash.

But within a few years relationships begin to chafe; the entrepreneurs deal with superiors who have little knowledge of their business; they may feel saddled with formidable reporting chores; and they may begin to compete with other SBUs for funds on the basis of standards alien to the particular business. The entrepreneur, often accustomed to an autocratic approach, may be reluctant to shift to a style stressing delegation, personnel development, and teamwork.

General Mills experienced these problems as it began to impose stringent financial controls on its nearly autonomous SBU chiefs. Says CEO Atwater, "We were so hands-off that we had little discussion of strategy and no discussion of people development." But he is concerned that he will cross the fine line between too much and too little control.

In 1980, sales at General Mills exceeded $1.1 billion. With such large numbers, stricter attention to financial control becomes necessary. Many of the new controls attempt to drive responsibility for managing capital deeper into the SBUs. "General Mills is imposing a hefty financial penalty on any subsidiary that exceeds existing working-capital guidelines unless the SBU head can prove that increased sales justify extra inventory building. It has increased internal working capital charges to 13% from 7%. And it has launched a study of the feasibility of taking

a 'balance sheet' approach that would look at the cost of financing fixed assets, and would force each subsidiary to simulate intracompany dividends. It is even toying with the idea of assigning each company a debt-equity ratio based on an 'industry average.' " Subsidiary managers will also be asked to get strategic and budgetary goals approved by corporate headquarters. And General Mills has set up new positions, insisting that each SBU hire a controller trained by the corporation.

Reaction is mixed at SBU levels. Those used to autonomy are concerned, even though some heads suggest that headquarters is more forgiving than the general financial community would be if an SBU made mistakes. But others believe that common goals and targets are inappropriate, particularly the rules about tight, daily control of working capital. Says one, "I don't know if they realize that ours is a different industry. There is an absolute tradeoff in this business between holding down inventories and continuing growth."

General Mills's change in evaluating and controlling SBUs may result in the centralization of strategic planning and a reduction of the entrepreneurial spirit. To SBU heads, the answer depends on whether the corporate parent will be willing to accept variations in financial goals and performance. General Mills is sending its SBU managers through financial management courses "that it hopes will help them make better decisions on their own." And bonuses up to 50 percent of the base salary are still based on meeting SBU goals. But who sets those goals and standards may change the picture entirely. As one SBU manager put it, "When you're by yourself, you set the standards. Here the standards are set—and they're largely General Mills's standards."

Source: Adapted from "How to Manage Entrepreneurs," *Business Week,* Sept. 7, 1981, pp. 66–69.

ating and controlling top management, and external auditors can be used to evaluate the veracity of the financial system. Just as important, if the control system is to work effectively, managers must be motivated to use it, and rewards must be based on the standards established by the control system. These are the topics in our next section.

THE MOTIVATION TO EVALUATE [3]

If a control and evaluation system is to be used effectively, the top managers must want to evaluate the performance. This motivation develops if senior managers realize that the strategy can fail and if they are rewarded for their performance in relation to objectives.

Most senior managers have had failure experiences. Too many failures can stunt a career and may make the manager so cautious that few creative decisions are made. But experiencing no failures can be equally dangerous. Human beings can believe that they are omniscient when their history includes no failures and when they are surrounded by admiring assistants. A few failures remind us that we need to determine whether our strategies are working. One can think of many examples in political history of failures that resulted from an unwillingness to evaluate the strategy—for example, Great Britain's experiences in the Crimean and Boer Wars and in India, and the United States' experiences in Vietnam. Businesses can fail for lack of evaluation too. Perhaps the key is to allow for some failure if it is associated with appropriate levels of risk.

The Reward System

The second half of the motivation to evaluate is whether managers are rewarded directly for performance. If high performance in relation to meeting objectives was rewarded, the managers would be motivated to evaluate their strategies. There is little evidence that except in emergency times, this direct tie exists in most firms. Some evidence shows that rewards such as raises and promotions continue even when performance is lacking. Too often this is because the executives themselves make recommendations about salaries and promotions to the board for themselves and each other. To the extent that the chief operating officer and associates are held to performance before reward, they will be more motivated to evaluate the strategy. Exhibit 11.5 suggests that some better-managed firms have recognized this.

If the intent of the control process is to ensure that policies and plans are being followed and that the decisions which are made are consistent with the strategy, then rewards for the kind of performance or behavior intended will assist in this process. The demands of the strategy and plans should be what guides the reward system. If an SBU is in an early expansion stage where entrepreneurial moves are needed to develop new products and markets, the manager in charge might be motivated by rewards tied more closely to the performance of the SBU in finding new niches. If, on the other hand, a stability strategy is appropriate for a given SBU, the factors such as cost efficiency, the smoothness of production and distribution, or the degree of inventory control may be more relevant in an assessment of the manager's performance. While most managers don't like to think about it, retrenchment strategies for some parts of the business are a normal occurrence (assuming that the product life cycle concept is operating). Here, too, a plan for exit may be in place, and key warning signals that indicate the need to evaluate and abandon products or markets should be established *ahead of time*. Performance measures established at the time of entry may help a firm overcome problems such as the inability to admit mistakes or covering up problems to keep things going when they should stop. Unless managers are rewarded for alerting strategists about the possible value of retrenchment, it is unlikely that they will pass on data relevant to top decision makers.

EXHIBIT 11.5   REWARDING THE PERFORMERS

During the last two decades, compensation committees measured executive performance on the basis of earnings per share. Executive pay climbed at an unbroken pace during the 1970s. In 1960, only half of all CEOs received annual raises. By 1981, 90% received raises or bonuses. Boards used bonuses to reward performance and help managers with the rising cost of living.

More recently, the earnings per share measure has come under unfavorable scrutiny, because earnings can be manipulated (by selling assets, liquidating inventory, cutting out research and development, etc.). Yet such manipulations have long-term impact on the firm and its strategy. More and more corporate boardrooms are looking for other measures to reflect growth in stockholder value, and encourage strategic instead of short-term decision making.

Scores of companies, including Sears, Roebuck, Dow Chemical, and Dayton Hudson, are now measuring the performance of their business units on total operations and awarding incentive pay based on outperforming the competition. The intent is to force corporate leaders to rethink strategies focused on maximizing short-term earnings and revenues. Steel companies, for instance, have been notorious for justifying investments on the basis of immediate payback, without considering the viability of the entire business.

To close the connection between performance and reward, many firms have restructured to make managers identifiable and responsible for performance. But a compensation system geared to the performance of the organizational unit is an important motivational tool. And the system needs to be tied to different strategies of the organizational units. For example, GE and Westinghouse have both mature and young SBUs, with different missions. At GE's mature units, short-term incentives dominate the compensation packages of managers, who are charged with maximizing cash flow, achieving high margins, and retaining market share. In the younger businesses, where developing products and marketing strategies are most important, nonfinancial measures geared to the execution of longer-term performance dictate the major portion of a manager's remuneration. With 3- to 5-year plans, companies require managers to set priorities, such as attaining a market-share figure or establishing a sales network. Performance can be measured by success in achieving a portion of the goals each year.

Pay for performance is most difficult where a culture of teamwork is critical. Says Peter Cusack, vice president at ABC, "One of our challenges is to introduce greater sophistication into performance measurement without destroying the family concept. It's very hard to introduce dramatic change into a culture."

Yet the biggest challenge is to convince the CEO that compensation should be tied to long-term results, which are riskier and take longer to evaluate. Given the CEO's ties to board members on compensation committees, self-interest may yet take precedence over rewarding strategic thinking. But evidence suggests that raising the value of the company's stock is a reflection of changes in bonuses and compensation plans for executives.

Source: Adapted from "Executive Compensation: Looking to the Long Term Again," *Business Week,* May 9, 1983, pp. 80–83; and G. S. Becker, "Why Managers Have the Stockholder at Heart," *Business Week,* July 8, 1985, p. 14.

Care must be taken in developing a compensation system to be sure that the performance rewarded lies within the range of discretion of the manager. That is, some environmental or internal factors may exist over which the manager has little or no influence. If these play a large part in the performance of the unit, then penalizing the manager for poor performance due to events out of his or her control will only encourage the manager to attempt to lay the blame at the doorstep of these events. In such a situation, the proportion of incentives tied to overall unit performance should be smaller.

The reward system is also related to career development, which we discussed in Chapter 10. That is, job rotations and promotions to develop managers must be planned with the idea in mind that the time is sufficient to assess the performance of the manager in a given position. Holding a manager accountable for a situation in-herited from another is not likely to be useful as a control or evaluation mechanism. And moving managers before the results of their activities can be properly assessed is only likely to encourage short-term decision making to show quick positive results, which may have negative long-term impacts.

Recognize that we have been *prescriptive* in laying out various aspects of ideal evaluation systems, though we did point out earlier that rewards often are not tied to performance. Part of the *descriptive* reason for this may be that it is very difficult to assess cause-effect relationships for unit performance. Further, managers will seek to protect their own interests in explaining performance. Experience suggests that if outcomes are positive, the wisdom and judgment of top management will be con-firmed. But if plans fail, subordinates or external events may be blamed. In such cases, criteria for evaluation may be adjusted, positions may be reinterpreted, or top management may say that it was just sending up a "trial balloon." Even accounting changes may be used to provide the appearance of success. In other words, managers will try to rewrite history. As we noted in Chapter 2, objectives are often stated as vague generalities. Here's another reason—that makes it easier to rewrite history or claim success. Recognize also that the time horizon for performance evaluation is frequently short term. This pressures managers to consider short-term outcomes at the expense of long-term strategy.

There are many other potentially dysfunctional consequences of performance eval-uation. Therefore, it is generally suggested that the use of a single criterion leads to undesirable or suboptimal results. For example, short-term profitability is not by itself an adequate measure of managerial performance. Return on investment is another potentially problematic criterion in that it can lead to the postponement of needed research or investment for upgrading facilities or equipment. As Christensen et al. point out,

> The management evaluation system which plays so great a part in influencing management performance must employ a number of criteria, some of which are subjective and thus difficult to quantify. It is easy to argue that subjective judgments are unfair. But use of a harmful or irrelevant criterion just because it lends itself to quantification is a poor exchange for alleged objectivity. [p. 644]

The remainder of the chapter explores the major issues in establishing the *content* of the control and evaluation system. The three major content areas in which strategic managers make decisions are (1) the criteria for evaluation, (2) the feedback system and tools to use in the control system, and (3) the outcomes of the strategic evaluation.

CRITERIA FOR EVALUATION [4]

The field of organizational effectiveness—defining and measuring evaluation factors—is very complex. It is not easy to choose the factors upon which to focus the evaluation. Evaluations can be based on objective and subjective factors. As suggested in our last section, different criteria may be appropriate depending on the purpose for the eval-uation.

Further, we think that evaluation of the *content and process* of strategy and plans should play a role in the system. That is, evaluation is typically assumed to be an *after-the-fact* or real-time method of detecting whether the *content* of strategy *is working* or *has worked*. Quantitative measurement is quite appropriate here along with subjective judgments. But qualitative assessment can also be done to address the question *Will it work?* A qualitative check of the strategic management *process* can be done *before the fact* of activating plans for change. Let's examine these two approaches separately.

Quantitative Criteria [5]

In attempting to evaluate the effectiveness of corporate strategy quantitatively, you can see how the firm has done compared with its own history, or compared with its competitors on such factors as net profit, stock price, dividend rates, earnings per share, return on capital, return on equity, market share, growth in sales, days lost per employee as a result of strikes, production costs and efficiency, distribution costs and efficiency, and employee turnover, absenteeism, and satisfaction indexes.

The list is long, and many other factors could be included. Which factors should be used? Establishing the standards and tolerance limits is not as easy as you might expect. You need to first define the critical success factors—the factors which are most important to the strategy and to being successful in the business. Many of these were discussed in Chapter 5. Then the factors and plans developed need to be stated in terms of specific measures by which you can judge whether a success factor is being attained. An example for a contractor helps to illustrate some of the indicators which might be used to translate success factors into measurable performance criteria (see Exhibit 11.6).

EXHIBIT 11.6 SUCCESS FACTORS AND MEASURES FOR A CONTRACTOR

Critical success factors	Prime measures
Image in financial markets	Price-earnings ratio Orders-bid ratio
Technological reputation with customers	Customer "perception" interviews
Market success	Change in market share Growth rates of markets served
Risk recognition in major bids and contracts	Years of experience with similar products
Profit margin on jobs	Bid profit margin as ratio of similar jobs in this product line
Company morale	Turnover, absenteeism, grievances, etc. Informational feedback
Performance to budget on major jobs	Job cost, ratio of budgeted amount to actual amount

Source: Adapted from J. F. Rockart, "Chief Executives Define Their Own Data Needs," *Harvard Business Review,* (March–April 1979), p. 89.

Of course, success factors and measures may be quite different for other firms depending on objectives and strategies. For example, the typical way executives seek to monitor manufacturing often relies on a measure of inventory turnover. This is acceptable if the strategy relies on measuring output of long production runs. But quality of output may become important to the strategy. Here, control measures such as reject or rework rates redirect the emphasis in manufacturing to a concern with quality rather than output control.

Most of these measures are internal. The comparisons of achievement are made in relation to the standards established ahead of time. But objective assessments can also be made by comparing the firm's results with the results of similar firms. As suggested in Chapter 5 this is an important aspect of the assessment of strengths and weaknesses as an input for future strategy formulation to develop competitive advantages. Four sources of ''objective'' measures are as follows:

1 *Compustat* tapes provide data on *financial* results over the past 10 years (or sometimes longer) for large companies.

2 *Dun's* publishes (usually in November) its ratios of business. This is a quantitative guide to how a firm is doing financially in wholesaling, retailing, or the manufacturing sectors.

3 *Fortune* (in May and June) publishes the *Fortune* 1000 largest manufacturers and the *Fortune* 50s: the 50 largest retailers, transportation companies, utilities, banks, insurance companies, and diversified financial corporations. At that time, it also ranks the best and worst performers on financial aspects of the business such as return to investors, sales, profits, and sales per dollar of stockholder's equity.

4 Probably the best unbiased overall evaluation of the largest corporations is in the January 1 issue of *Forbes*. The issue is called *The Annual Report on American Industry*. *Forbes* ranks the firms all together and by industry on financial factors such as earnings growth, value, and profitability (e.g., growth in return on equity and return on investment). It also ranks the firms on sales growth, stock market performance, and performance compared with that of comparable companies and industries. Finally, it provides yardsticks of managerial performance. In these, *Forbes* combines all the indexes, and it rates the firms for the year, longitudinally, and assigns overall ratings to them.

There are no magic numbers to assign evaluation factors to. But outside assessments can help executives evaluate their performance and thus their strategic performance in an other than qualitative manner. Techniques such as sensitivity tests, risk analysis, the use of outcome matrixes, the use of models, and simulation can help managers evaluate results and the strategies.

Another approach is to ask ''experts'' which firms are the most successful. This is a subjective approach: *Dun's* description of the 5 or 10 best-run American companies is an example of this method.

Measurement comparisons become more difficult when more than one criterion is used to measure success. For example, efficiency and effectiveness can be measured on a number of dimensions. Efficiency isn't too hard to judge. However, a number of problems are involved in the measurement of effectiveness:

* *Stability of criteria:* A criterion emphasized at one point may not be valid later on.
* *Time:* Do we evaluate short-run or long-run effectiveness?
* *Precision and variety of measurement:* Not all measures are easy to compute, and there are different ways of computing measures.

It is a lot easier to measure success when a company shows consistent results on most of the measures in most years. In fact, research indicates that there is a high intercorrelation among organizational variables. If a firm is a "winner" on three measures, chances are it is a winner on all measures. To us the most critical problem is the trade-off among measures. Suppose, for example, that you are measuring effectiveness as shown in Exhibit 11.7. Admittedly, success is hard to measure, especially when you have eight performance measures and at the end of 1988 you see three up, three down, and two even. In such a case, success is declared if the three measures that are "up" are the critical success factors. Organizations feel that they are successful if the most important indicators are positive. It is easy to recognize success when most indicators are positive or negative but very hard when there are results like the ones in Exhibit 11.7.

Qualitative Criteria [6]

We have already suggested that "subjective" assessments can be included with after-the-fact evaluation. Some qualitative criteria can also be used for that purpose. Moreover, as we indicated before, subjective assessments of key environmental assumptions should be included with the quantitative measures of performance to be sure the strategy is resting on safe ground. But the criteria here tend to be more appropriate for examining a *plan in its entirety* before the organization is asked to change direction or put a strategy into effect. A series of qualitative questions can be developed for

EXHIBIT 11.7   AN EVALUATION OF RESULTS IN 1987 AND 1988

	Percentage of objectives achieved	
Criterion	1987	1988
Production effectiveness:		
Production output	110	105
Market share	12	13
Efficiency:		
Return on capital	6	7
Efficiency in utilization of equipment	95	90
Adaptiveness (rate of production innovation)	50	65
Satisfaction:		
Clients	80	75
Employees	75	75
Development (training investments)	90	90

each of three criteria. The basic questions are whether the integrated and comprehensive objectives, strategy, and plans are *consistent, appropriate,* and *workable.*

Consistency

Is the comprehensive, integrated plan consistent with objectives, environmental assumptions, and internal conditions?

1 *Objectives.* Will the plan probably close the gaps of importance to us? Are the standards of performance linked to critical success factors? Are there mutually inconsistent objectives where we have made trade-off decisions? Are the goal trade-offs consistent with our real priorities? Are the goals consistent with social responsibility needs to sustain our legitimacy?

2 *Environmental assumptions.* Are we making an adaptive response to critical changes that we might anticipate? Will the plan fully exploit domestic and international opportunities? Does it mitigate threats? Are marketing policies consistent with changes in the marketplace and financial policies consistent with changes in capital markets? Are R&D and production consistent with technological or supplier developments? Have staffing policies taken into consideration governmental changes? Are contingency plans in place so that we can respond flexibly to unanticipated change (anticipatory flexibility)?

3 *Internal conditions.* Are the policies, resource allocations, organizational structure, and administrative system coordinated with one another? Is there an integrated pattern of implementation which fits the strategy and develops needed competitive advantages? Does the strategy rely on weaknesses or do anything to reduce them? Have we clarified the inevitable policy trade-offs so that suboptimization is minimized? Are performance evaluation criteria and rewards tied to the policies we want to reinforce?

Exhibit 11.8 shows what can happen when strategy changes lead to inconsistencies over time.

Appropriateness

Is the comprehensive, integrated plan appropriate given our resource capabilities, risk preference, and time horizon?

4 *Resource capabilities.* Are critical resources in place? If not, does the plan provide for obtaining them when needed? Are the total resources available appropriate for what we want to accomplish? Are the policies providing for the development of raw materials, energy, workers, executives, facilities, equipment, competence, and expertise?

5 *Risk preference.* Does the strategy entail unnecessary risk? Is the degree of risk acceptable to top management? Is it too high or too low? Are we "betting the whole company"? Is that necessary? Does the plan depend on internal resources whose continued existence is not assured? Does it depend on environmental assumptions about which we are very uncertain?

EXHIBIT 11.8   THE INCONSISTENCIES AT RCA

A retrospective evaluation of the RCA Corporation leads us to a better understanding of why it merged with GE in late 1985.

In 1973, RCA earned $183.7 million on $4.2 billion in sales. Ten years later it earned $171.5 million on $9 billion in sales. On a total sales of $67.1 billion for the 10-year period, RCA posted profits of only $1.7 billion, or about a 2% long-term profit margin. The prime cause of such dismal performance can be summarized in a single word—inconsistency.

In the space of 10 years, RCA was led by four different CEOs, each of whom pursued a different strategy. The company has been diversified, divested, directed toward long-term goals, and redirected toward short-term goals; it was nearly done in by a massive acquisition, and diddled away dollars through huge employment and disemployment contracts.

Management problems began with the legendary General Sarnoff, whose passion was technological supremacy. Critics claim this diverted attention from management of the business. When Sarnoff's son took over, the labs were doing pioneering work, but management couldn't move ideas to the market. In the absence of new products, the younger Sarnoff made acquisitions ranging from car rental and book publishing to carpet-making and frozen foods.

Eased out in 1975, he was succeeded by a CEO whose 10-month tenure ended when it was learned that he had failed to file personal income tax reports. Next came Edgar Griffiths. His 6 years were marked by continual strife with the board, and hiring and firing of top aides, compensating them handsomely both on the way in and on the way out. Because he couldn't get quarter-by-quarter improvements, he began selling earlier acquisitions to "keep earnings up." With the board vocal in its disapproval, Griffiths went for an acquisition of CIT financial services in 1980. By the time interest rates had increased and other businesses began to sour with the recession, a board activist was given a $250,000 "consulting contract" to supervise operations and find a new CEO. Thornton Bradshaw replaced Griffiths in 1981. He put up Hertz and CIT for sale. CIT sold in 1984. As of April, 1984, analysts suggested that with its cash assets, NBC television, defense business, and Hertz, RCA was a sitting duck for raiders. Indeed, the company merged with GE a year later.

In effect, RCA failed the test of consistency over time. No well-defined mission or consistent strategy served to guide decisions and management, resulting in constant change in direction and policy making, personnel turnover, and poor results. No wonder RCA merged with GE.

Source: "RCA: Will It Ever Be a Top Performer?" *Business Week,* Apr. 2, 1984, pp. 52–56.

---

6 *Time horizon.* Are the objectives stated in terms of an appropriate time for achievement? Is rapid expansion appropriate given our capabilities? Have we committed resources for a sufficient period so that the strategy will have a chance to work? Are we making changes at frequent intervals or taking drastic leaps, or are we making steady, sustained progress? Which approach is appropriate for objectives? Are criteria for evaluation being measured in time so that appropriate adjustments can be made? Is now the right time to proceed with this plan, or will economic or other conditions change?

Workability

Is the comprehensive, integrated plan feasible and stimulating?

7 *Feasibility.* Does the plan overtax our resources and management capabilities? Does it create unsolvable subproblems? Is the strategy identifiable and clear? Is the strategy reasonable? Will there be unintended consequences that we can avoid?

8 *Stimulation.* Will managers be committed to making the strategy work? Is there a consensus among executives that the plan will work? Are reward systems designed to encourage effort in the desired directions? Are the personal aspirations of key strategists taken into consideration so that they are involved in decisions about the strategy?

Again, these are qualitative criteria to be addressed *before* a new strategy is activated. If "red flags" are raised by any of these issues, then the strategist is encouraged to reassess the strategy and plans to determine if other alternatives might be preferable or if adjustments and fine tuning are possible to resolve a possible problem area.

These criteria are useful for a mental double check to see that various aspects of the strategic management process have been comprehensively integrated. For instance, questions of internal consistency deal with whether the strategy, plans, and policies (Chapters 8, 9, and 10) reflect the internal assessments (Chapter 5) in relation to goals (Chapter 2). External consistency has to do with whether the strategy choice and policies (Chapters 8 and 10) relate to the environmental assessments (Chapters 3 and 4). Risk preferences and workability are concerned with how evaluation and other policies (Chapters 10 and 11) relate to assessments of the strategists (Chapter 2). And so on.

As we said in Chapter 1 and have stressed throughout, the various aspects of the strategic management process are ongoing, interrelated components. The evaluation system is a means for integrating these components into a unified whole. The criteria could be applied when a strategic choice is made (hence the feedback arrow pointing to "Choice" in Exhibit 11.1). In effect, this reinforces the idea that strategy implementation and formation need to be considered as a whole. The use of the evaluation criteria—consistency, appropriateness, workability—forces the strategist to make a strategic choice in light of the analysis *and* implementation phases of the strategic management process.

Recognize that managers may still proceed with their plan, even if the criteria raise significant questions about its validity. Exhibit 11.9 shows you how this happens. But if managers use these criteria before activating plans, the criteria can alert them to areas where closer control and tighter evaluation may be useful as progress is monitored.

MEASURING AND FEEDBACK

The previous section outlined what the standards might be. The next phase of control and evaluation is to measure performance and provide feedback for the managers involved. Here the questions are, When do we measure? and What do we report to whom?

Timing [7]

Assume that the qualitative evaluation has been made and that the decision is to "go" as planned. A crucial issue still remains: *When* should *results* be evaluated?

From a long-term strategy perspective, the problem of timing is particularly crucial.

EXHIBIT 11.9   CONFIDENCE AT A&P?

Outside evaluators of once mighty A&P believe that the firm is on its last legs. A strategy that was inappropriately timed given the economic recession of 1980–1981 has forced further store closings and changes in plans to renew and remodel old stores. Poorly sited stores, inefficient distribution, and stodgy management are other indications of internal conditions that are inappropriate for competing in the environment. Says one observer, "With their infrastructure, there is no way in the world that they will be able to compete in this industry."

Nonetheless, management *believes* that the plans for recovery are workable. CEO Wood is committed and confident that he can turn the company around, and he predicts profitability by 1983. The feasibility may depend on the resources and patience of E. K. Haub, the head of Germany's successful Tengelmann retail group, which owns over 50% of A&P. Says Haub, "If we had to do it over again, we wouldn't do it. We reckoned it would take five years to return A&P to profitability when we bought it. But we're no longer so sure we'll make it by then. We believe, and I stress 'believe,' that we will still be able to make something out of A&P, but I still wouldn't call the outlook rosy."

It is important to note that Haub invested more than $100 million in A&P, and there would probably be few buyers. Also, liquidation and the elimination of 60,000 U.S. jobs would probably bring unwanted protests to the German firm. "Equally important, Haub is proud of his success as a food retailer in Germany, and he is not yet ready to admit defeat in the huge U.S. market."

So a variety of plans to bail out A&P are in the works, largely because of the belief that the plans are workable, regardless of the red flags raised by other evaluators.

Source: Adapted from "A&P Looks like Tengelmann's Vietnam," *Business Week,* Feb. 1, 1982, pp. 42–44.

Implementation may require some time before results can be expected. If standards are set to be achieved in, say, 5 years and measurement does not take place until the end of the fifth year, it will probably be too late to take action to correct deviations. On the other hand, if an evaluation is made too early, knee-jerk reactions could be made which will prevent the plan from having a chance to work. Many argue that if decision makers procrastinate, opportunities may pass them by. Still, it is often difficult to change direction quickly, particularly for large organizations.

As a result, in the establishment of the standards for measurement, the timing of expected or desired results must be specified. Benchmarks of progress are needed. Timing is not easy either. There are times when managers just do not know what events will lead to certain outcomes. But they must proceed with assumptions about the cause-effect relationships in the means-end chain. In effect, managers can establish the critical success factors as events along a critical-path network. Long-term targets can be broken down into intermediate steps for accomplishment. Periodically, then, measurements can be taken to compare intermediate progress. This can be done quarterly or annually, depending on the variable.

Ideally, top management should be alerted when there is significant deviation (positive or negative) from critical planned outcomes or assumptions. Two questions are important here: What is "significant deviation"? and What is meant by "critical"? Each management group must define these for itself and its strategy. Our earlier discussion suggested what some of the critical success factors might be. And in Chapter 1 we noted that the factors associated with the nature of the gaps are relevant to deviations. Further, as our earlier sections suggested, the qualitative criteria can indicate key areas where problems in a plan might exist.

Once criteria have been specified, we think that continuous versus periodic monitoring can be decided upon through the use of an analogy with the ABC system of inventory control. "A" factors are the few but most important critical success factors or environmental assumptions. These should have relatively narrow allowable variances and should receive constant monitoring and tight control (as in a perpetual inventory system). "C" items are the majority of variables. They provide advance warnings of environmental change or the firm's progress, but they are not on the critical path, so to speak. These can have wider tolerance limits for deviation and are measured periodically as suggested. They receive loose control. The "B" items are the factors which are important but take longer to become meaningfully evaluated. These should be measured as frequently as possible when the data make sense. For example, market share may be a critical success factor, but daily sales figures on a new-product introduction are probably not meaningful to most strategists for some time. This system is, of course, based on the concept of management by exception.

Feedback [8]

The foregoing implies that lower-level managers may receive some information that top strategists do not. Indeed, feedback needs for various types of information vary by manager. As far as strategic evaluation is concerned, information that is usable and timely is needed for the managers who have discretionary authority to make decisions about the critical success factors. That is, an effective management information system (MIS) is required, as well as honest and complete reporting of the results of the strategy. Of course, at many enterprises, the top managers do not want to hear bad news. So they hear what they want to hear until it is too late. The enterprise must encourage complete and accurate reporting so that top managers can react to reversals and reinforce progress. The MIS tool can assist in this.

Many early MISs were developed by staff specialists who knew how to use computer hardware. The reports that were printed out were in forms that few managers wanted or were able to use. Today, effective firms have a better system. MIS managers determine information needs and timeliness deadlines from all levels of managers. They then design the system so that it develops the required data and sends reports when the user can use them and in the form the user needs. Managers request and get reports measuring the current status in relation to each objective to be achieved. For example, reports on profitability, sales, market share, or efficiency can be delivered in time so that action can be taken. Some firms have advanced to the point where personal computers are appearing on the desks of many managers. Such a proliferation brings a greater need to manage information more closely. Thus the MIS can be used to help control the enterprise's outputs. A model of an integrated information system is illustrated in Exhibit 11.10.

However, managers can absorb only so much information, and they have only a certain amount of time for control. A manager who is not selective will be inundated with reports. Key strategic control items may be buried when this happens. Effective managers delegate the control of less significant items and objectives to subordinates. They receive MIS reports and use a strategic approach to control, concentrating only

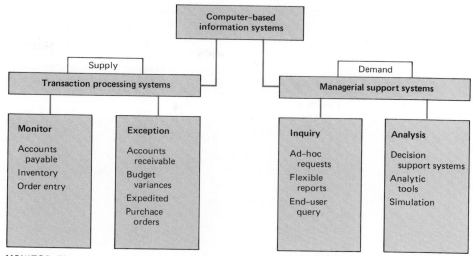

MONITOR The system monitors daily detail activity producing *standard* reports on a *fixed* schedule (daily, weekly, or monthly).

EXCEPTION The system processes detail activity reports where the *definition* of exception conditions is *fixed*.

INQUIRY The system provides a data base with flexible inquiry capability, enabling *managers* to design and change their own monitoring and exception reports.

ANALYSIS The system provides powerful *data analysis* capabilities (modelling, simulation, optimization or statistical routines) and the appropriate data base to support *managerial* decision-making.

EXHIBIT 11.10   A management information system model.

on those items necessary for meeting the most important objectives. Thus the MIS must be set up to provide the right information to the right people at the right time. It is a major tool for feedback and evaluation, and it can be a critical part of strategy implementation.

EVALUATION AND CORRECTIVE ACTION [9]

The final phase of evaluation and control is to use the timely information to determine the causes of deviations and take actions to correct these, or reward performance which remains ''in control.''

Let's assume that the MIS prepared a report for management such as the one in Exhibit 11.11. The critical success factors and measures are as indicated on the left. The report may represent progress 2 years into a 4-year plan of expansion into new product areas. At this stage managers will want to compare *progress to date* with *expectations to date*. Of primary interest are those factors where an existing deviation might lead to a *projected deviation* of some importance requiring corrective action. In this instance, competition appears to be making more progress in new-product development than was anticipated. The firm has not analyzed as many new-product ideas as it had planned, and it appears that the R&D effort is not leading to desired results. It is quite probable that this is due to the lag in recruiting senior engineers.

EXHIBIT 11.11   BENCHMARKS FOR EVALUATION

Key success factors	Overall objectives or assumptions	Expected performance at this time	Current performance	Existing deviations	Projected deviations
Financial:					
Reduce overhead cost	5%	2%	3%	+1%	+1%
Profit on sales	12%	5%	9%	+4%	+2%
Marketing:					
Analyze new-product proposals	10	4	2	−2	−3
Sales per employee	$7000	$6800	$6900	+$100	+$100
Personnel:					
Number of key managers needed	6	2	3	+1	+1
Ratio of indirect cost to direct cost	12%	14%	13%	−1%	0%
R&D:					
Recruitment of senior engineers	20	16	10	−6	−6
Increase R&D-sales ratio	5%	4%	3%	−1%	−1%
Operations:					
Increase production capacity	50%	40%	40%	0%	0%
Competitor reactions:					
Increased R&D	4%	3%	4%	+1%	+1%
Product changes	4	2	3	+1	+1

As a result of this information, managers are faced with several options. An assessment of the gaps may lead to the conclusion that internal factors account for discrepancies. Plans can be scaled up or down. For instance, greater efforts might be undertaken to place a higher priority on recruiting engineers to get new-product development back on track. On the other hand, the firm could decide to continue as planned, even though this may result in excess capacity, since plant expansion is on target. Of course, new plans to meet changed competitive circumstances might also be drawn up given projected deviations. In the example, another option is to change tactics; given the favorable profit deviation, a policy to lower prices may be feasible and could divert competitor attention on new-product development toward marketing, where the firm may have an edge.

Evaluations such as this can become much more detailed and can be done at SBU levels and at departmental budget levels in even more compressed time frames. For instance, the budget performances of units can be evaluated during the year. The budget department and line managers can review how well each unit has done in sticking to its budget. If a unit's performance in this regard is poor, then action can be taken to remedy the situation. After review and evaluation, if it is believed that the unit had a reasonable budget, the unit can be encouraged to meet the budget. In the unusual event that a unit's budget turns out to be unreasonable in practice—usually because of unforeseen difficulties—then the budget department can recommend a revised budget. Top management will approve or reject this revision just as it did for the entire current budget.

In any of these situations, care must be taken to make sure that short-term adjustments resulting from budgetary control procedures do not alter long-term plans. That is the reason for prescribing top-management approval. If adjustments will alter the plans, the strategic implications need to be assessed.

In more general terms, then, the "after-the-fact" evaluation and corrective action process should proceed as we outlined earlier in Exhibit 11.3.

Stage 1. Are the performance standards too low or too high, or are the environmental assumptions legitimate? If yes, alter by scaling up or down. If no, go to stage 2.

Stage 2. Is the implementation inadequate? Are policies, resources, or organization changes needed? If yes, alter accordingly. If no, go to stage 3.

Stage 3. Is the strategy inadequate? Has the environment changed unexpectedly? (Original assumptions are quite uncertain or faulty.) Is the contingency plan needed? If yes, use the contingency plan or begin to formulate a new strategy. If no, go to stage 4.

Stage 4. How can we alter our objectives or convince others that the gaps in performance will remain and are acceptable?

This order is established on the basis of the most likely (and easiest to change) prognosis of the conditions underlying performance gaps.

This brings us full circle to questions about the objectives of the organization. In Chapters 1 and 2 we discussed the establishment of objectives. Strategy formation and planning develops means to accomplish these and also contributes to their establishment. As we analyze gaps and set new strategies and plans, we begin to establish targets to accomplish long-term objectives. As we set up standards for measuring performance, we are getting to the real or operative objectives. As these are used as criteria for rewarding individuals, they give rise to behavior to accomplish them. If we discover that certain standards cannot be met as a result of our strategic planning process, then a reassessment of goals and objectives will result. As we suggested in our discussion about Exhibit 11.3 then, several options are available as managers analyze causes of gaps in performance.

Thus there is a feedback loop from evaluation to objectives in Exhibit 11.1. This means that through the reward and control system, management information system, and strategic planning evaluation, if managers become aware that the objectives are

- Too easily achieved, they should be raised.
- Impossible to meet, they should be lowered.

The ideal relationship is when objectives are attainable yet challenging. But remember that "success" is an elusive concept. Failure to achieve challenging goals should be considered in the light of evidence suggesting that even competent managers may have only about a ".300" batting average when it comes to innovative strategy.

Finally, through evaluation, feedback leads to the repetition of the ongoing strategic management process.

MANAGEMENT BY OBJECTIVES [10]

To sum up, we would like to suggest that the management by objectives (MBO) system in its *idealized* form is a management tool which can help managers accomplish the prescriptions we have been outlining. MBO can combine objective setting, planning, control, and reward systems, all of which are so crucial to the effective conduct of strategy formation and implementation.

An MBO system is designed to take the objectives determined during the strategic planning process. It then interprets these objectives (ends) in terms of the strategic choice (the means to these ends). Then for each subunit of the enterprise it leads to the development of a set of objectives. Implicit in the process is the involvement of those accountable for achieving objectives. Then a control and reward system is established so that progress is monitored and the achievement of objectives leads to positive outcomes for the individuals and the organization.

MBO systems found in practice tend to vary considerably from the prescriptive, idealized system. While some evidence suggests that such a system can be effective, other evidence suggests that so many things can go wrong that it is an idea whose time has gone. There has also been some criticism that MBO systems inappropriately encourage analytical decision strategies in settings which call for an ''inspirational'' strategy.

Like strategic management itself, the system is conceptually simple but difficult to use well. We can only hope that you will be able to apply the concepts while avoiding the inherent pitfalls. That is why we have tried to provide a blending of description and prescription throughout the book. With these ideas in mind, we hope you will be better prepared to manage in a superior fashion.

SUMMARY

The last phase of the strategic management process is evaluation. Evaluation of strategy is that phase of the strategic management process in which the top managers try to assure that their strategic choice is implemented properly and is meeting the objectives of the enterprise. This is necessary to assure that a follow-through on plans occurs, to provide information or needed corrective action, and to ensure the repetition of the strategic management process.

The control process requires multiple criteria, timely measurement and feedback, and an evaluation of performance deviations so that corrective action can be taken. Control and evaluation takes place at both the SBU level and the corporate level and may involve controllers, other top managers, and committees of the board.

Before evaluation will take place, the top managers must want to evaluate the performance. This motivation develops if they realize that the strategy can fail and if they are rewarded for their performance in relation to objectives. It is particularly critical to establish multiple standards of performance so that the reward system will encourage relevant strategic behaviors and decisions.

Evaluation of the content and process of strategy can be done by means of quantitative and subjective assessments for after-the-fact evaluations and qualitative criteria for assessing the comprehensiveness of a plan before it is activated.

Quantitative criteria are normally used for evaluating how the firm has done compared with its own history or with competitors' performance. Defining the critical success factors and the measures appropriate for these requires that managers consider the stability of criteria and the timing, precision, and variety of measurement.

Qualitative criteria can be used for examining the process of strategy. A variety of questions requiring subjective judgment can be asked to determine whether the integrated and comprehensive plan, strategy, and objectives developed are consistent, appropriate, and workable. These serve as a check on the nature of objectives, environmental assumptions, internal conditions, resource capabilities, risk preferences, timing, feasibility, and commitment.

Information in a usable form is necessary for evaluating the strategy. That is, an effective management information system is required, as well as honest and complete reporting of the results of the strategy. Also, information about the significant factors of environmental or internal change must be provided in time for managers to use the data to make decisions. An ABC system was suggested to guide the timing of the monitoring of success factors.

Corrective actions are needed if the evaluation shows actual and/or projected deviations from the plan as time goes on. In the order of priority, managers are more likely to consider changes in standards, then implementation, then strategy, and finally objectives themselves if performance gaps are found to exist. Thus the evaluation system provides feedback to the strategic management process in its entirety.

Since a follow-through of this type requires good objectives and standards, effective rewards, and accurate and complete feedback, a good MIS and a good MBO system can be useful tools for managers. But as with any system, effective application requires hard work.

As a way of illustrating the importance of effective evaluation to the strategic management process, the following proposition will suffice.

Proposition 9.1

Firms which systematically evaluate the results of strategic choice and control its implementation will be more effective than those which do not.

This summary is followed by a brief statement on the strategic management process in retrospect to help you focus on the overall process covered in Chapters 2 through 11.

STRATEGIC MANAGEMENT IN RETROSPECT [11]

We have discussed all the phases of the strategic management process. We have treated the phases in separate and distinct chapters. It is necessary to examine them one at a time. But we have stressed that the phases overlap and blend together in the world of work. They cannot be separated in actual strategic management. If you study the section on qualitative criteria in Chapter 11, you will quickly see why that is so.

We have tried to give you the reasons why strategic management makes good sense if managers really are interested in effectiveness. But the *irony*, the *supreme irony*, is that to perform other than superficially, the managers must do what they have never been rewarded for doing before: they must take time out from daily pressures and rewards, step back, and look at where the enterprise is now and what it is in for tomorrow. Then, they must anticipate future events and take steps to do something about them.

Strategic management requires the strategists to formalize objectives and formally assess events in the environment. It requires them to figure out formally where their firm's strengths and weaknesses are. Next, they are asked not to jump at the first solution that comes to mind but to compare several alternatives systematically. Then they must choose the best one, implement it, and take time to evaluate and make changes, if necessary, in the choice. This is hard work and requires executives with strong motivation.

These steps can be taken in many different ways. What has been presented here is a formal, normative way of going about strategic management. But we have also tried to present you with the evidence of how most executives undertake strategic management. So our formal, normative model has been tempered by descriptions of real problems in applying "rational" frameworks.

In the long run, we would still contend that our enterprises and societies would be better off if strategic management were comprehensive and formalized. We cited some of the evidence to support that belief in Chapter 1. And some other recent research hints that this is so. However, there is also nonempirical but subjective evidence about many of the ideas we have stressed. Throughout we have given examples of business firms which have succeeded and failed in efforts to apply strategic management concepts. Most of these have been from *Business Week*. The editors of that magazine summarized their impressions of enterprises in the United States. Among their conclusions are these:

> American managers have tried to maximize near term profits at the expense of long term objectives; they have catered to Wall Street resulting in shortsighted strategies; managers seem to refuse to take risks and overemphasize quantitative measures of success which reinforce short-term goals; they have resisted the winds of change, and have increased conflict with labor as they implemented their strategies.

Among their recommendations to resolve these problems are the following:

1 Reward long-range risk taking.
2 Promote young tigers who will take risks.
3 Keep research funds flowing.
4 Encourage employee differences.
5 Overhaul the business schools which stress analytical decisions at the expense of entrepreneurial strategies.

This predated the Peters and Waterman bestseller, *In Search of Excellence*. Both, however, stressed basic themes that U.S. enterprises suffer from paralysis of analysis, too much bureaucracy, too little innovation, and insufficient attention paid to customers and employees. Regaining a competitive edge is possible, however, if strategic thinking is followed and if managers stick to the skills and values they know best.

We hope our presentation of strategic management has alerted you to the need to consider many of the issues of importance to the future of organizations and societies. And we hope that further study of the ideas presented in our references will contribute to an understanding of the need for strategic management, how it is accomplished, and how it can improve organizational effectiveness.

Even as many firms are reducing the size of the planning staff, executives expect line managers to "think strategically." The process outlined here should prove helpful for performing this strategic thinking. We encourage you to apply it to your future endeavors.

REFERENCES

[1] Integrating Planning and Control through Evaluation

Bianco, A., S. Crock, and A. Beam: "Wall Street's Back Office Blues: Big Trouble Lies Ahead if Brokers' Controls Can't Cope with Growth," *Business Week,* Nov. 4, 1985, pp. 24–25.

Leonard, J. W.: "Strategic Control: Need for a New Definition," paper presented at the Strategic Management Society Conference, Philadelphia, 1984.

Merchant, K. A.: *Control in Business Organizations* (Marshfield, Mass.: Pitman, 1985).

[2] Strategic Control Processes

Daft, R. L., and N. B. Macintosh: "The Nature and Use of Formal Control Systems for Management Control and Strategy Implementation," *Journal of Management,* vol. 10 (1984), pp. 43–66.

Rowe, A. J., and J. Carlson: "Adaptive Control Systems for Operating Management," *Logistics Spectrum Journal* (September 1974).

Todd, J.: "Management Control Systems: A Key Link between Strategy, Structure and Employee Performance," *Organizational Dynamics,* vol. 5 (Spring 1977), pp. 65–78.

[3] Rewards in Evaluation

Berry, S. J.: "Performance Review: Key to Effective Planning," *Long Range Planning,* vol. 12 (December 1979), pp. 17–21.

Christensen, C. R., K. R. Andrews, and J. L. Bower: *Business Policy: Text and Cases* (Homewood, Ill.: Irwin, 1978).

"Executive Compensation: Looking to the Long Term Again," *Business Week,* May 9, 1983, pp. 80–83.

Matthews, W. E., and W. I. Boucher: "Planned Entry–Planned Exit," *California Management Review,* vol. 20 (Winter 1977), pp. 36–44.

"No Sign of Recession in Pay at the Top," *Business Week,* May 10, 1982, pp. 76–77.

Prasad, S. B.: "Top Management Compensation and Corporate Performance," *Academy of Management Journal,* vol. 17 (September 1974), pp. 554–558.

[4] Organizational Effectiveness

Steers, R.: *Organizational Effectiveness: A Behavioral View* (Pacific Palisades, Calif.: Goodyear, 1977).

Zammuto, R. F.: *Assessing Organizational Effectiveness: Systems Change, Adaptation, and Strategy* (Albany: State University of New York Press, 1981).

[5] Quantitative Evaluation Criteria

Argenti, J.: *Systematic Corporate Planning* (New York: Wiley, 1974), chap. 14.

Hofer, C.: "ROVA: A New Measure for Assessing Organizational Effectiveness," Graduate School of Business, New York University, 1979. Mimeographed.

[6] Qualitative Evaluation Criteria

Ferguson, C.: *Measuring Corporate Strategy* (Homewood, Ill.: Dow Jones–Irwin, 1974), especially chap. 6.

Rumelt, R.: "The Evaluation of Business Strategy," in W. F. Glueck, *Business Policy and Strategic Management* (New York: McGraw-Hill, 1980), pp. 359–367.

Steiner, G.: *Strategic Factors in Business Success* (New York: Financial Executives Research Foundation, 1969).

Tilles, S.: "How to Evaluate Corporate Strategy," *Harvard Business Review,* vol. 41 (1963), pp. 111–121.

[7] Timing in Evaluation

Ansoff, H. I.: "Managing Strategic Surprise by Response to Weak Signals," *California Management Review* (Winter 1976), pp. 21–33.

Slaybaugh, C. J.: "Pareto's Law and Modern Management," *Price Waterhouse Review* (Winter 1966), p. 27.

[8] MIS for Evaluation

Edstrom, A.: "User Influence and the Success of MIS Projects: A Contingency Approach," *Human Relations,* vol. 30 (1977), pp. 589–607.

"How Personal Computers Can Backfire," *Business Week,* July 12, 1982, pp. 56–59.

Wedley, W. C., and R. H. G. Field: "A Predecision Support System," *Academy of Management Review,* vol. 9 (1984), pp. 696–703.

" 'What If' Help for Management," *Business Week,* Jan. 21, 1980, pp. 73–74.

[9] Feedback for Control

Lawler, E., and J. Rhode: *Information and Control in Organizations* (Santa Monica, Calif.: Goodyear, 1977).

Nadler, D., P. Mirvis, and C. Cammann: "The Ongoing Feedback System," *Organizational Dynamics,* vol. 4 (Spring 1976), pp. 63–80.

Newman, W. H.: *Constructive Control: Design and Use of Control Systems* (Englewood Cliffs, N.J.: Prentice-Hall, 1975).

Rowe, A. J., R. D. Mason, and K. Dickel: *Strategic Management and Business Policy: A Methodological Approach* (Reading, Mass.: Addison-Wesley, 1982).

[10] Management by Objectives

Carroll, S. J., Jr., and H. L. Tosi, Jr.: *Management By Objectives: Applications and Research* (New York: Macmillan, 1973).

Dirsmuth, M. W., S. F. Jablonsky, and A. D. Luzi: "Planning and Control in the U.S. Federal Government: A Critical Analysis of PPB, MBO and ZBB," *Strategic Management Journal,* vol. 1 (1980), pp. 303–329.

Ford, C. H.: "MBO: An Idea Whose Time Has Gone?" *Business Horizons* (December 1979).

Migliore, R. H.: *An MBO Approach to Long Range Planning* (Englewood Cliffs, N.J.: Prentice-Hall, 1984).

[11] Strategic Management in Retrospect

Karatsu, H.: "The Deindustrialization of America: A Tragedy for the World," Report No. 31, Japan Institute for Social and Economic Affairs, October 1985.

Peters, T. J.: "On Political Books," *The Washington Monthly* (October 1983), pp. 56–58.

"Who's Excellent Now?" *Business Week,* Nov. 5, 1984, pp. 76–78.

Zucker, S., et al.: *The Reindustrialization of America* (New York: McGraw-Hill, 1982).

CHAPTER OUTLINE

CHAPTER 12

APPLYING THE STRATEGIC MANAGEMENT PROCESS

OBJECTIVES

- To learn about the case method
- To learn how to prepare a case analysis
- To learn how to present the findings of a case analysis

INTRODUCTION

The purpose of our final chapter is to help you apply the material you have learned. Case analysis is the most widely used method to help you understand the complexity of integrating strategic decisions from a top-management perspective. First we will briefly describe the case method. Then we will give you our suggestions for applying to cases the material in our first 11 chapters. Finally, we offer some ideas about how you might prepare reports and present analyses. Since you will eventually prepare analyses and make presentations to your peers and supervisors in organizations, it is useful to obtain some practical experience in doing this.

THE CASE METHOD [1]

A *case* is a written description of an enterprise (such as a business, an industry, a hospital, or an arts organization). A case usually contains information about numerous facets of the enterprise: its history, external environment, and internal operations. The cases used in *Business Policy and Strategic Management* are multifaceted, containing material on many aspects of the operations. Thus your analysis is expected to be comprehensive.

Cases are based on material gathered about real organizations. Most cases are undisguised; that is, the real names of the organizations are used. There are some disguised cases. The companies which are the subjects of these cases wish to remain anonymous, and so their names and locations are changed. This does not change the reality of their challenges and problems, and it serves no useful purpose for you to try to guess their identity.

Are Cases Complete?

There is no such thing as a *complete* case study. The amount of information required would make the case too long to read and too detailed to analyze. One reaction that frequently is heard is, "I don't have enough information." In reality, the manager *never* has enough information because some information is not available, some is not available at this time, or acquiring some kinds of information is too costly.

What does the manager do then? The manager makes the necessary decisions on the basis of the information at hand and after making reasonable assumptions about the unknowns. So with cases you must work with the information you have and make reasonable assumptions. A case contains enough information for the analyst to examine. Then the analyst can determine what the crucial factors are that confront management at the time. Acting on incomplete knowledge is the essence of the general manager's task. Since most cases are relatively complete, executives prefer that you do not call or write them for additional information on their companies.

Is All the Case Information Important?

When you get your mail, you may find that some of it is important, some is useless, and some is of minor interest. At work, managers are bombarded with information. It, too, is a mix of the relevant, the partially relevant, and the useless. So it is with cases. Indeed, instead of not having enough information, cases may have *too much* information, or some information which is not relevant. When the case writer gathers information, some of it will become crucial to analysis. Other pieces of information are not especially useful. Since you are training to be a manager, it is your job to do the manager's job: separate the wheat from the chaff. You also have to sort through sometimes conflicting evidence or opinions; hence, learn to deal with uncertainty.

Why Are Cases Used in Management Education?

Case studies allow a different kind of learning to take place. The approach that is used is close to a learn-by-doing approach. Cases are intended to simulate the reality of the manager's job. The material in a case provides the data for analysis and decision making. The cases become the laboratory materials that you use in applying what you have learned about how to be an effective strategist. Each case is a framework for a learning experience that goes far beyond the case facts. The discussion of the case partially simulates the emotional atmosphere in which managers must operate.

Cases require you to analyze situations, make decisions about the situations presented, and defend those decisions to your peers. In real decision making, you will need to persuade your peers and superiors that your analysis and solution are the best, and so communication and human relations skills are vital to success in management. Cases provide you with the opportunity to improve these skills too.

What Roles Do Students and Instructors Play in the Case Method?

Typically, the instructor encourages the students to analyze problems and recommend solutions. The instructor questions and criticizes and encourages the students' peers to do the same. At the end of class the instructor may summarize or simply walk away, refusing to answer questions such as, What would you do? or What did they do? That's because the relevant answer is the one which is proposed and logically defended by the analysts in class.

The student can play several roles. Some of the standard roles are the board chairperson, the president, and a consultant. We prefer the consultant's role. Thus the student can analyze a situation and recommend a solution, given the nature of the problem and the nature of the top executives. If the student feels that the suggestion is likely to be unacceptable to the president, he or she should discuss more than one solution or present a particularly convincing argument to make the recommendation acceptable and overcome objections. However, unlike consultants, internal executives cannot simply walk away from a situation. Therefore, some students are asked to play roles of executives at times.

The case method is interactive. Responsibility is placed squarely on the student to be prepared and to learn from the case experience. Just as managers must do, you will have to observe, listen, diagnose, decide, and intervene in group discussions. This will also involve competition, collaboration, compromise, and persuasion.

THE CASE PREPARATION PROCESS [2]

There are a large number of possible approaches to case preparation. This is one that has worked for some of our students.

1 Read the case. Underline and comment on parts that you think are important. Then you might try to determine what the major and minor problems are. You can jot down ideas about how you might analyze them. Then do some preliminary analysis to see if your impressions were correct. Identify the mission and strategy, and list the objectives of the firm. Put the case aside for a while.

2 Read the case again. This time prepare the environmental threat and opportunity profile and the strategic advantage profile. This will require an analysis of data (Chapters 3 to 5). At about this point, if you find it comfortable (and if your instructor allows it), you might sit down and discuss the case with several friends who have different interests or majors. You and your friends can help each other with the problem, and you can learn to understand your friends' points of view too. (We hope the instructor allows it, for in real life, if managers have a problem that has ramifications for other areas, they probably visit friends in those areas and get their points of view.)

You are then ready for real analysis. Examine your statements for implicit assumptions. Fill in areas where no ''hard'' data were presented with reasonable assumptions, and state them carefully.

3 Prepare a list of the major opportunities and problems. These should be rank-ordered in terms of importance. Prepare a list of alternative strategies (Chapters 6 and 7). Consider the advantages and disadvantages of the viable alternatives for this enterprise, using your previous analyses. Make recommendations which you have carefully thought through by asking such questions as, If I recommend that they do X in marketing, how will it affect finance, or Z company, or the sales manager?

4 Analyze the alternatives in terms of the problems and opportunities, and make a choice (Chapter 8) which seems to meet the objectives of the enterprise and reflects both the values of strategists and internal and external factors.

5 Clarify how the organization can implement your suggested strategy. Prepare a plan which specifies major resource needs, functional policies, organization design, and administrative systems supporting the strategy (Chapters 9 and 10).

6 Reevaluate your proposal in terms of the qualitative criteria in Chapter 11. Point out any possible problem areas, and state how and when they should be evaluated as the plan is put into effect.

7 Prepare notes for an oral presentation (and practice it), or prepare a final written report. Our last section of the chapter discusses these topics at more length.

It is equally easy to spend too much or too little time on case analysis. Plan to spend anywhere from 10 to 15 hours over a 4- or 5-day period in the analysis phases. Another 5 to 10 hours may be needed to prepare a report. You may spend more time if the case represents a real challenge to you. However, there is a danger that you may begin to lose perspective if you find yourself unnecessarily bogged down in detail.

Stages of Analysis

Our students seem to go through stages in handling cases. The amount of time spent in each stage varies with the student, but they all seem to go through these stages:

Stage 1: Factual Level
The first stage is characterized by the development of the ability to choose the pertinent facts from all the data in the case. In real life, managers are bombarded by cues and facts and information. In this stage of development, the students learn to separate the important facts from the unimportant ones and to see where the problem(s) is (are).

Stage 2: Preanalytical Level
This stage is characterized by rudimentary use of the tools of the trade. Thus, if in stage 1 the student perceived a problem in the financial area, they now say so and present a page of ratios, as well as various financial statements, cash budgets, etc.

Stage 3: Analytical Stage

Realizing that facts do not speak for themselves, the students enter a new stage. They now interpret the facts. They not only compute the ratios but also explain them meaningfully. They say, "The current ratio is 1:1. This is less desirable than the normal 2:1 ratio found in this industry [or risk class, etc.] and means that this firm . . ."

The students are now on the threshold of asking the right questions and establishing relationships (perhaps even cause-and-effect relationships) and can begin to apply their knowledge, experience, and judgment.

Stage 4: Problem-Solving Stage

The students have now reached the stage of "knowing" what the problem(s) is (are). What is to be done about it (them)? Usually, the students attempt to dream up potential ways of accomplishing what they want to do. They develop several potential solutions. They tell us about them, attempt to show what implications there are for each one, and weigh them as better or worse.

Stage 5: Decision-Making Stage

The students now must choose a solution to the problem. To do this, they need a weighing device. Normally, the students attempt to consider maximum goal achievement with the least effort. But there are many objectives for a firm, and sometimes, in fact oftentimes, these conflict with each other.

This final stage in the process is in many ways the least rational. In many of the earlier stages, the analysis can be fairly objective. Facts have been weighed as rationally as is possible through the use of tools that are as sophisticated as is appropriate. But at this stage, it is difficult to determine which alternative is best. Many of the alternatives have been based on estimates. Even with the use of decision trees, etc., there still exists the problem of setting probabilities of occurrence. The final stage, then, involves judgment. More emotional, more intuitive factors are used than in other stages. One value we have in our business society is rationality. We like to "stick to the facts." But these decisions have fewer hard facts to rely on. So the choice is based upon values and judgment and the experience of the executive, and we may as well face this openly. The executive also shows that his or her solution, strategy, or plan will solve the problem seen in the case.

Stage 6: Implementation Stage

After making a choice, the students now realize that they must implement the decision by adjusting the organization and setting up a control and evaluation system.

We hope that you will progress through all six stages, for they represent the kinds of processes we described in Chapter 1.

GUIDELINES FOR ANALYZING CASES

So far we have discussed the reason for and process of case analysis. Now let's look at the content of a good case analysis. Exhibit 12.1 repeats the model of strategic

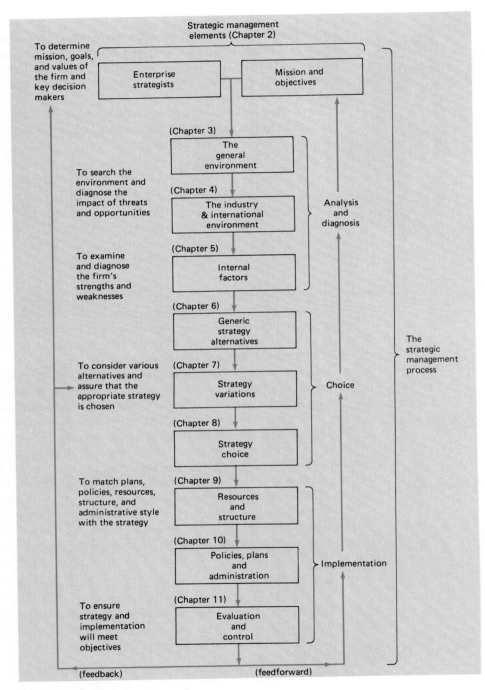

EXHIBIT 12.1 **A model of strategic management.**

management covered in the first 11 chapters. The purposes expressed in the exhibit for each aspect of the model should serve as a guide for the content of your analysis. That is, you should begin by identifying the past strategy and mission of the organization, as well as the key managers and their goals and values. Then you should analyze and diagnose the environment and the competitive advantages of the firm. From these stages, a determination of strategic gaps and alternatives to close them should be made. Next a strategy must be selected, and appropriate plans should be made for its implementation. Finally, you can apply some evaluative criteria to double-check your process and proposals.

At this point, you might want to review the summaries of the first 11 chapters, to refresh your memory of the high points of the process. In the rest of this section we will highlight a series of key questions and suggestions that you will want to address as you do your case analysis and apply the material in each of those chapters. For some cases, not all these questions may be directly applicable. In others, you may have to make some assumptions or do library research. The more of these questions you address, the more likely it is that you will do a good analysis.

The Strategic Problem

Our first chapter introduced you to the overall process of strategic management. In this regard, at all times in your analysis you need to keep in the back of your mind the ideas that you are ultimately trying to integrate. What is the current mission, and what are the objectives? What is the enterprise's business definition? What are its products and markets, and what functions does it perform? What is its environmental situation? What is its distinctive competence? Will the current strategy allow the firm to reach its objectives and meet the values and goals of its managers, or are there expected gaps with regard to accomplishing its mission in the future? Can the firm invent a creative solution to close those gaps? How can it organize and manage itself to the full advantage of its resources and implement its innovative solution? The whole thrust of your analysis should generally focus on those issues.

We also indicated in the first chapter some differences between single- and multiple-SBU firms. You will need to determine whether the case you are analyzing deals with the situation of a single SBU or whether several SBUs are involved. If the case involves a multiple-SBU firm, in your analysis you will have to examine more factors which influence different SBUs as well as the firm as a whole. And your recommendations may be different for various parts of the organization. You will probably need to recommend a corporate-level strategy and a strategy for each SBU. Similarly, if an international strategy is involved, the analysis may be more complex.

The Strategic Elements

Our second chapter described the roles of the mission and objectives and the strategists involved. Your analysis should include assessments of these elements.

Of course, one of the forces for change involves the values and goals of top management. Who are the key people with decision power in this case? What do they want? How do they make decisions? How much risk would they be willing to assume? Does the board support the CEO? If you are going to ultimately make realistic recommendations which have some probability of acceptance, you must have an understanding of who has the power (in the case) to implement your proposals. If you are playing the consultant role, you must convince the manager(s) with power that your recommendation will fit the managerial goals and values and be best for the organization. Otherwise, recommendations for changes in top-management personnel and/or implementation of planned cultural changes may be necessary.

What is the mission of the business? What is its business definition and past strategy? Prepare a statement which summarizes these elements. Exhibit 2.2 provided an example. The case itself may not state these clearly, but you need to attempt to determine this for yourself. In particular, look for synergies and utilities in the business definition (see pages 73 to 74). Also, try to make a list of objectives (the operative ones, not the official ones). Then ask if these objectives help define the organization, provide standards, and help to coordinate decisions, or if there is conflict. Since there are usually multiple objectives, how are they currently ranked? Are they long- or short-term? Are they specific or broad? Do they need to be more specific? Are they being achieved? What pressures are there to change them? Refer to Exhibit 2.10, and identify any forces which may be leading to changes in objectives. At this point, you may be able to do a gap analysis for objectives (see Exhibit 2.6).

Analysis and Diagnosis

The gaps between desired goals and expected attainment are caused by either external or internal changes. Thus the next stage of case analysis focuses on these factors.

The Environment

Chapters 3 and 4 indicated the importance of examining threats and opportunities coming from the environment. For the firm (and key SBUs if necessary), you need to analyze and diagnose the sectors of the general, industry, and international environments of importance. It is worthwhile to reexamine Exhibit 3.1, since that provides the key overall questions. What are the assumptions about the environment on which the current strategy is based? What predictions do you make for the future? Are there any gaps in those assumptions and predictions? If so, will they lead to changes in objectives or strategy?

Should this firm do more in the way of environmental analysis? What techniques do you recommend? More important for the case you are analyzing, which of your key predictions are creating threats and opportunities? You should focus your diagnosis on the critical areas—the sectors on which the firm is most dependent and where there is greater development, complexity, and volatility. In these areas, a much greater in-depth analysis should be done (see Exhibit 4.15). If the case data are insufficient, use the appendix for Chapter 4 to guide you in a search for information.

If you want to do a more sophisticated analysis, you can prepare several scenarios. These may ultimately lead to the preparation of contingency proposals. In any case, you should prepare an ETOP (see Exhibit 4.14) with a commentary based on your summary. That is, you should elaborate on data and estimates of revenue or cost implications and estimates of the likelihood of events and their timing. In the end, go back to the key questions: Where are the opportunities? Where are the threats? What strategic impact do they have? Reconsider the gap analysis for objectives if this is appropriate.

Internal Factors

Chapter 5 identified the areas within which you need to search for the firm's strengths and weaknesses. Like environmental factors, the internal factors may alter the gap between desired and expected outcomes.

You should reexamine Exhibits 5.3, 5.5, 5.9, 5.11, and 5.13. Which of these areas are in the "technical core" for the firm in the case? Those should receive your greatest attention. You need to identify distinctive competencies in these areas by asking key questions: What does the firm do well? Do these count? What does the firm do poorly? Does it matter? Remember that your analysis should focus on the data and indicators based on relative comparisons: How do current conditions relate to the past and future needs? How do the areas relate to one another? How do they relate to relevant competitors?

Prepare the SAP (see Exhibit 5.20). Also prepare any supporting documents and a commentary about distinctive competencies. At the very least you should prepare a summary of the firm's financial position (see Exhibit 5.27). The basic financial data need interpretation and point to other areas of the firm which may need to be examined. You might also prepare a resource-deployment matrix (Exhibit 5.16) and do a break-even analysis if the data are available. Your commentary should attempt to determine how the strengths and weaknesses have been used to develop competitive advantages and how they might be used later on (see Exhibit 5.22).

In the process of doing this, don't forget your ETOP. Begin to ask yourself whether the competitive advantages (the ones that exist or that could be developed) relate to the new opportunities that you identified earlier. Also, decide whether increased resources might be needed to offset any threats, and determine where those resources are now and where they need to be. In other words, how can the firm most effectively exploit the opportunities and meet the threats which the environment is presenting?

Strategy Alternatives and Choice

Before proceeding, reexamine your analyses and diagnosis in relation to the gap in the objectives of decision makers. Do the key strategists see a gap between where they want to be and where they will be if they continue with the existing strategy? Are there gaps that they should be made aware of which will result from the changes you expect in the environment or from changes in the internal condition of the firm?

Now review Exhibit 8.2 and our discussion there. Focus on the gap and the reasons for it. Focus on the generic strategy which is most relevant for the situation in the case. Also, compare this analysis with our four propositions in the summary for Chapter 6.

Next, prepare a summary of the advantages and disadvantages of following the generic strategy you are analyzing. Will it close gaps? Will it do a better job than the next alternative, which is more dissimilar than the current strategy? In other words, apply the strategic choice model (Exhibit 8.17).

If you have settled on a generic strategy, consider the various approaches for accomplishing this strategy. The summary in Chapter 7 presents the options in outline form. At this point you will want to consider the pros and cons of using one or more of these. For instance, will a particular option close gaps better than other alternatives? Does it use competitive advantages? Will it build new ones and allow the firm to develop a sustained, distinctive competence? Does it meet the challenges and opportunities in the environment? Does it change the pace or the business definition? Will that be acceptable to the power holders?

For a multiple-SBU firm, you will need to consider the portfolio of strategies of the firm as a whole. Then you will want to determine whether it is appropriate to apply a decision matrix to your case, such as Exhibit 8.6 or 8.8. Exhibits 8.19 or 8.20 might be used if international strategy options are involved.

Before recommending a choice, you should present two or three viable alternatives. Then consider managerial perceptions of dependence and risk, awareness of past strategy, and managerial power relations. Next, settle on a tentative choice for which you will develop a plan of implementation. Following that, the evaluation stage will be applied to confirm a final choice.

If you were doing a sophisticated analysis, you would compare several contingency strategies to go along with the scenarios that we suggested you prepare earlier. Hence you might have a worst case–best case–most likely set of strategies.

Implementation

Exhibit 9.3 outlines the major areas you need to consider for a plan to implement the strategy. For any given case, it is unlikely that you will be able to get to some of the details that are needed. However, several elements of a plan should minimally be included to "flesh out" your strategy recommendation.

What major changes in resource allocation are implied by your strategy? If a multiple-SBU firm is involved, will the firm need to shift resources from one SBU to another? Where will resources come from? Do you have a plan to secure needed funding? Will some functional areas need more resources? Where will they come from? If your strategy is to sell some assets, how much do you expect to get from the sale? If your strategy is expansion, will the firm use internal funds, debt, or equity, and what will the impact be on the balance sheet? If your strategy involves a joint venture, what kind of equity agreement do you recommend? A sophisticated analysis would present proforma balance sheet and income statement exhibits based on realistic assumptions of the plan based on the strategy.

A plan for implementation would also address key major changes needed in the organization structure. Usually in a case analysis, these would only occur if major redefinitions of the business resulted from your proposed strategy. However, some cases may focus on organizational issues. Here you would probably be provided with data on which to base more detailed recommendations. Depending on the recommendations, you may need to include a revised organization chart in your report. You should consider the strategic reason why any changes you propose would be necessary. For example, is the firm moving from related to unrelated product or market areas? If so, a change to the divisional form would probably be useful. Other characteristics of the firm and its environment which are related to the strategy should be considered as well (see Chapter 9, section [10]). In a few cases you may want to address the role of a planning staff as it relates to the future of the organization.

Of course, plans and policies for the functional areas need to be considered. Exhibit 10.2 suggests the kinds of issues you need to consider. Greater detail and more specifics for the case in question would be needed, but these are illustrations. The list in the summary for Chapter 10 suggests key functional decisions that you should make. Before drawing up your final proposal, look back over the decisions and ask yourself these questions: Are they consistent with one another? Are they consistent with the strategic choice?

Your plan should also consider leadership. Are changes needed in the current leadership? If yes, in what position? What kinds of changes are to be made? Is it feasible to recommend firing the president if it is the president who holds the power? Would a career development plan make sense? Can reward systems be set up to motivate managers to enact the strategic choice? How much effort will be needed to carry out your plan? If your strategy involves international moves, all these issues and others need to be considered. At the very least, issues raised by Exhibit 7.15 should be explained in the report.

Evaluation

After you have finished your analysis and prepared a plan to implement the tentative strategy, reevaluate the entire process—look at it as a whole. Is your plan comprehensive, unified, and integrated? Are the strategy and plans you developed consistent, appropriate, and workable? Will the plan close the gaps to a degree acceptable to the key strategists? If not, then you should rethink the plan for implementation. If there is no problem there but gaps are still not closed, you should consider another strategy. But if the strategy you developed is the best one available given your analyses and diagnoses, then you will have to convince the managers that their expectations about goal attainment will have to be modified (the only way left to close the gap).

If you are convinced that your proposals are the best you can come up with, complete your analysis by explaining how management can evaluate the performance of your plan over time. Set up benchmarks for evaluation (see Exhibit 11.11), and indicate when and how information should be delivered to the right managers at the right time.

Finally, if you are doing the more sophisticated second-generation planning, show how your plan is flexible enough to provide for contingencies. Indicate under what conditions and when a contingency strategy should be put into effect.

Problems in Analysis

We have taken you through our suggestions for a comprehensive basic case analysis. Remember that we have just summarized the highlights of more specific recommendations and prescriptions in the text chapters. If you really want to do a top-notch job, you will need to go beyond these basics. Some instructors may want you to supplement the case information with outside material, or expect you to relate your analyses to specific theoretical material.

In any event, we should also point out that not all questions we just raised for you to analyze will be directly addressed by most cases. In some cases, financial data are not available, or competitor data or other environmental data are lacking. In others, the focus may be on a more limited set of issues or problems. In these instances, you have several options:

- Do some library work to get additional data.
- Make assumptions and then proceed.
- Recognize that the case focus is limited, and apply the elements of the material you have learned which are most directly relevant.

Just as managers must do, you will often need to be creative; that is, you will often have to put together your own data and read between the lines to answer some questions and deal with significant strategic issues. We hope you will invest the time it takes to do that.

REPORTING YOUR RECOMMENDATIONS [3]

Each of us has our own style for presenting the results of an analysis. Now and in the future you will be asked to present, discuss, justify, and defend your recommendations. This is done in oral form and in writing. So we conclude by offering some suggestions for how you might make more effective presentations, assuming that those are backed up by the type of analysis we just outlined.

Written Presentations

Most written reports of case analyses tend to be relatively short (8 to 12 pages plus exhibits). Occasionally even shorter ''management summaries'' might be called for. In either case, a key guideline is to attempt to apply one principle: Keep it simple. Unfortunately, after hours of analysis and note taking, you will want to share your entire analysis to show what you have done. If you try that, it is likely that your report won't be kept simple. Keeping it simple and straightforward does not necessarily imply that you have done a sloppy job or that it lacks comprehensiveness. If the report is well put together, it will be apparent that it is based on good analysis.

In particular, if (as we suggested) you prepare and include supporting exhibits (such as an ETOP, an SAP, ratio summaries, break-even analyses, pro-forma financial statements, benchmarks for evaluation, and so on), you will be providing powerful evidence to justify your major arguments and recommendations and evidence that you have thought through the issues involved.

So do not be a "slave" to the particular format used in your analysis, such as a page on past strategy, another on the environment, and so on. Rather, when you begin to write, start writing from the *end* of your analysis. Sum up your major recommendations in one or two sentences or a paragraph. Then build a topical outline for the paper around these conclusions. What are the key messages from your analysis which support and build up to the recommendations? The commentary should be tightly integrated and have a logical flow from beginning to end so that the reader is led to agree with you. Remember, you are trying to convince your reader that your proposal should be adopted and that it will accomplish objectives of interest. The proper presentation of those exhibits will help. (Each exhibit should have a clear title, and there should be a source note so that the reader does not have to refer to the text.)

With regard to style, we prefer concise cases written in specifics. Generalities without a clear, precise meaning are not particularly helpful. For example, do not say that the firm's past performance has been poor and leave it at that. Indicate that specific objectives (such as an increase in sales growth or in profits as a percentage of sales) have not been reached or that the firm has missed the mark by a certain amount. Don't say "This firm needs more formal planning." If it does, indicate the types of planning it needs.

Finally, good writers do not turn in their first draft. Ask someone else to read it, or read it out loud to yourself. When you hear what you say and how you say it, you are likely to find rough areas to clean up, or you may find that you are not saying what you mean or that you failed to say something you need to say.

Oral Presentations and Discussions

You may have a chance to present your recommendations to a group that will question and challenge you. We hope that you do get such a chance, since it is good experience to stand up and justify a position and think on your feet.

Obviously, oral presentations are different from written ones. You should not just get up and read your written report. You will have to be even more precise, more specific, and more convincing. In a well-prepared written report, many of the facts you present speak for themselves. In an oral presentation, that can't happen, and the listeners do not have the time to digest exhibits which a reader might have. You should still use exhibits (handouts or material magnified by an overhead projector). But they will have to be less detailed and more to the point of summarizing key aspects of your presentation. As with the written presentation, you need to organize well in advance and prepare notes to yourself on the high points.

Guides for Oral Presentations and Discussion

Some suggestions for making more effective oral presentations are included below:

1 *Define your audience.* You need to gain audience attention and interest; consider the level of sophistication and preparation of your audience as you prepare your report. For example, if you assume the audience will follow a detailed technical explanation of a financial analysis, you would proceed differently than if you assume the audience could not understand such an analysis. By the way, the attention span of most audiences is little more than 20 minutes or so; so plan accordingly.

2 *Prepare a complete outline.* Members of an audience may not understand the sequence or relationship of topics being discussed. The outline should help give an overview of the presentation so the audience does not get lost. Generally, oral presentations start with "telling the audience what you are going to tell them"; then you tell them the message; you conclude by "telling them what you told them." The outline helps your audience understand where you are going and how various topics are interrelated. In essence, the content of main sections and subheadings should say to the audience, "This is why this material is important, so keep listening; these are the topics we are going to discuss, in this order."

3 *Provide supportive detail.* To provide justification for a position, the audience must sense you know what you are talking about. Exhibits of supportive analysis help, but you cannot provide orally the detail contained in a written presentation. Thus describe supportive detail selectively. The two or three most important analytical conclusions should be presented with a brief description of the data and the assumptions and approach used to make calculations. Don't bore or irritate the audience with long, drawn-out descriptions of endless tables of numbers.

4 *Prepare clear visual aids.* Blackboards, flip charts, scale models, or overheads and slides should be prepared in advance. Wording should be brief; letters and figures should be legible when projected; numbers should be rounded; graphics and charts should be clear. The discussion about an exhibit should discuss the concepts; do not just read the statements, but explain their significance.

5 *Introduce your topic.* Explain the purpose of the presentation, present the agenda or outline, briefly describe the methodology (how you went about your analysis), and briefly summarize the major recommendations.

6 *Present material clearly and confidently.* Stand for the presentation; maintain eye contact with the audience; start without delay; maintain a steady pace; rehearse your presentation with note cards.

7 *Come to a natural conclusion.* Don't just end your presentation with, "Well, that's it." Restate the outline of the report, briefly. And restate the recommendations of the report and major rationale for the position.

8 *Respond to questions positively.* Expect aggressive or hostile attacks and be prepared for them. Don't hurry your response, but carefully consider the intent of the question. Don't ramble in your response; address the question directly without diverting to side issues. Don't try to bluff; if you don't know the answer, admit it. On the other hand, don't avoid direct confrontation—you may be able to answer the question with another question, asking the audience to respond or the questioners to present their point of view.

9 *Listen.* As a presenter, listen carefully to the question before answering. Furthermore, many times you will be asked to listen to someone else's presentation or participate in a group discussion of a case. Once again, full and complete analyses need to be done. But here, instead of a formal presentation, you are being asked to challenge the position of others and defend your own. Do this with facts, figures, assumptions, and logic. Do not attack a position unless you have a counterposition with reasons to back it up. But do not be afraid to express your viewpoint if it differs. On the other hand, don't waste group time by repeating the same points and reasoning over and over.

10 *Avoid repetition.* In a case presentation or discussion, refrain from reviewing or rehashing the entire case background. Everyone (presumably) is familiar with that. What is of interest is your analysis of the material and your interpretations. Also, clearly distinguish between facts and assumptions.

11 *Go for it.* Take a defensible position and support it. Obviously there is some risk that you will be attacked, but don't be afraid to be criticized. You may as well learn what such criticism is like, and learn to deal with it. Different positions can always be taken based on the same facts. Since there is no one "right" answer to a case, discussion and criticism will help you hone your skills in justifying a position.

SUMMARY

The approach we have suggested is really a general approach to problem solving. Some might argue that it involves little more than common sense. That is not quite true. Hard analysis as we have suggested here may end up appearing to be "common sense" when it is all done. But the method is a specialized application of the scientific approach. And sometimes that method leads us to conclusions which are contrary to common sense but later appear to be quite natural. For example, our common sense tells us that the sun revolves around the earth. Our earthbound perspective and senses tell us that the sun "rises" in the east and "sets" in the west. And until science proved otherwise, people believed that the earth was stationary. So it is with elegant recommendations for strategy. The creative proposal is the proposal which in the end *appears* to be simple and *seems* to be based on nothing more than common sense. Yet it is likely to be the unique one which no one else ever dreamed of.

REFERENCES

[1] The Case Method

McNair, M. P. (ed.): *The Case Method at the Harvard Business School* (New York: McGraw-Hill, 1954).

Postman, N., and C. Weingarten: *Teaching as a Subversive Activity* (New York: Delacorte Press, 1969).

[2] Preparing Cases

Edge, A. G., and D. R. Coleman: *The Guide to Case Analysis and Reporting* (Honolulu: System Logistics, 1978).

Kepner, C. H., and B. B. Tregoe: *The Rational Manager* (New York: McGraw-Hill, 1976).

Raymond, R.: *Problems in Business Administration* (New York: McGraw-Hill, 1964).

Schnelle, K. E.: *Case Analysis and Business Problem Solving* (New York: McGraw-Hill, 1967).

[3] Preparing Recommendations

Hodgetts, R. M., and M. S. Wortman, Jr.: *Administrative Policy: Text and Cases in Strategic Management* (New York: Wiley, 1980).

Hosmer, L. T.: *Strategic Management* (Englewood Cliffs, N.J.: Prentice-Hall, 1982), especially chap. 14.

Ronstadt, R.: *The Art of Case Analysis: A Guide to the Diagnosis of Business Situations* (Needham, Mass.: Lord Publishing, 1984).

Turner, A. N.: ''The Case Discussion Method Revisited'' *Exchange,* vol. 6 (1981), pp. 33–38.

Index

Page numbers in *italic* indicate exhibits.